170301

Human Aging

Paul W. Foos

University of North Carolina at Charlotte

M. Cherie Clark

Queens University of Charlotte

Boston ▪ New York ▪ San Francisco ▪ Mexico City
Montreal ▪ Toronto ▪ London ▪ Madrid ▪ Munich ▪ Paris
Hong Kong ▪ Singapore ▪ Tokyo ▪ Cape Town ▪ Sydney

Executive Editor: *Carolyn Merrill*
Series Editorial Assistant: *Kate Edwards*
Marketing Manager: *Wendy Gordon*
Production Administrator: *Annette Pagliaro*
Editorial Production: *Modern Graphics, Inc.*
Composition Buyer: *Linda Cox*
Manufacturing Buyer: *JoAnne Sweeney*
Cover Administrator: *Kristina Mose-Libon*
Text Design and Composition: *Modern Graphics, Inc.*

For related titles and support materials, visit our online catalog at www.ablongman.com.

Between the time Website information is gathered and then published, it is not unusual for some sites to have closed. Also, the transcription of URLs can result in unintended typographical errors. The publisher would appreciate notification where these errors occur so that they may be corrected in subsequent editions.

Library of Congress Cataloging-in-Publication Data

Foos, Paul W.
  Human aging / Paul W. Foos, M. Cherie Clark—1st ed.
    p. cm.
  Includes bibliographical references.
  ISBN 0-205-28626-7
   1. Aging.   I. Clark, M. Cherie.   II. Title.
  QP86 .F67 2003
  612.6.'7'00973—dc21

                                                                    2002018622

Printed in the United States of America

10   9   8   7   6   5   4   3   2   1   RRD   08   07   06   04   03   02

CONTENTS

PREFACE

We began this book after searching for a textbook for our own undergraduate classes in adult development and aging that better fit our model of gerontology education. We searched for a book that balanced science and application; was complex enough to challenge students to think critically about issues; was interesting, friendly, and readable without being demeaning or shallow; and one that reflected the diversity and multidisciplinary nature of gerontology. Unable to find a textbook that fulfilled all our needs, we set out to produce one that would. We hope we have succeeded in all our aims.

Organization

Human Aging is organized like many other adult development and aging books in that it begins with an overview of gerontology and research methods in **Chapter 1.** The next twelve chapters are divided into four major sections.

- **Aging and Our Bodies** (Chapters 2, 3, and 4) looks closely at physical changes, proposed explanations for why those changes occur with advanced age, and what can be done to prolong health and longevity. We believe it is important to cover these physical changes first since much of what comes later depends on these changes.
- **Aging and Our Minds** (Chapters 5, 6, and 7) progresses from changes in our senses, how these affect perceptions, and the slowing that occurs with advanced age. These changes underlie many of the changes in memory and higher cognitive processes, which are covered in the latter two chapters. Later sections depend on students knowing the mental and physical changes that can occur in adulthood.
- **Aging and Our Selves** (Chapters 8, 9, and 10). The focus in this section is on our social selves. We examine personality, social support, and social relationships, and end with work and retirement. You will find our chapters on personality and social relationships quite different from those in other texts.
- **Aging and Our Survival** (Chapters 11, 12, and 13) looks at those conditions that threaten or facilitate our survival. From the psychopathologies of Chapter 11, through the environmental design and caregiving of Chapter 12, to death and bereavement in Chapter 13, we try to clarify complex issues and tie them back to the material presented earlier.

Chapter 14, the last chapter, presents an overview of life satisfaction for older adults and then makes predictions about the changes likely to occur in gerontology and for older adults over the next several decades. We couldn't end the text with death and bereavement and much prefer to look to the future when our readers will be the older adults.

Features

Our approach has several main features. First, we present the social science of the study of aging. The questions in aging are difficult to answer and we want to make it clear (1) why they are difficult, (2) how social scientists attempt to handle such difficulties, and (3) the successes (and failures) they have had so far. Real age differences and age/cohort differences are explained first and then highlighted throughout the discussion of research findings in various content areas. We present both sides of all issues as fairly as we can and the evidence as it exists currently. We do not hesitate to offer our own speculations but we identify these clearly and emphasize the scientific data.

Second, we tried to write the text to be friendly, active, and fun. It contains projects that you can try out (at home), a fair amount of humor, and is, hopefully, relatively easy to read. We attempt to relate the research findings to real life experiences and to use familiar examples. We have tried to clarify rather than simplify. We believe that learning should be an enjoyable and active experience; therefore, we attempt to engage the reader with thought-provoking questions.

Third, the text has applied foci throughout. We try to show how current research findings are now being applied in the real world and/or how they might be applied in the near (or not so near) future. Some applications are general and some are specific. Some applications are ones that you can use to help yourself and/or aging relatives and/or friends.

Fourth, the text is realistic and positive. Using the results of research, we present things as they are. Too often texts in aging become either negative or overly jolly. Our approach is positive because we believe there are many more genuine pluses to aging than there are minuses. We are conscious, however, of the "glossing" of aging that often occurs in some publications and we try to avoid excesses in this direction.

Fifth, we have tried to weave the evolution of the field throughout our presentation. The study of older adults is continually changing and, as cohorts also change, some findings may be only temporary. What we know now may be very different than what we know by the time our readers are old—just as what we thought we knew in decades past may no longer be true today.

Sixth, we use selected findings from other social and life sciences in addition to psychology. We draw on the most relevant sources and add to the breadth of information presented. The study of aging is interdisciplinary and you must have some exposure to the breadth of gerontology.

Seventh, we have tried to include crosscultural comparisons and ethnic group comparisons whenever possible. Diversity is an important part of the study of aging and where available we have discussed group and cultural differences both for the aging population in the United States and across the world.

Learning Aids

Each chapter also contains a number of specific learning aids to assist the reader. Each chapter opens with a **quote** from some well-known person that sets the tone and expresses the main theme of the chapter. We want to focus the reader on the important point(s) right at the start.

Each chapter also presents a **Senior View**. Senior Views are interviews that were conducted with a number of different adults together with a photograph of each senior that helps introduce the main topics in each chapter. We believe that information should be presented in a number of different ways if it is to be assimilated successfully—these interviews are one way of presenting important information. When the theory, research, and a real older adult all agree on some finding, that finding is likely to be remembered. When they disagree, that disagreement is also likely to be remembered. We were very impressed with the knowledge displayed by these older adults. Senior Views make the presentation more varied and show the operation of chapter content in real life with real people. Many students miss the opportunity to discuss class material with an older adult; this is an attempt to give you that source of information. *This is a unique aspect of our text.*

Each chapter has a **Making Choices** section at the end of the chapter where readers will be able to think about choices that they can make that might prolong life, preserve vigor, help memory, and relieve stress as they grow older. We want readers to realize that there are important choices that can be made to make middle and older adulthood more (or less) satisfactory. In addition, readers may help parents or grandparents learn about some of these choices. *This also is a unique aspect of our text.*

Each chapter includes a **Project** that you can do. The emphasis is on attempting to address some question raised in the text and providing a project that can either be done relatively simply or turned into a more elaborate project for possible independent study at a later date. Active learning is important; this is an attempt to provide such opportunities. Our projects have been tested successfully in the classroom and have been found to be helpful and enjoyable.

Each chapter contains a number of **Boxes** that add information to the text presentation. Generally the information added is outside the main focus but clearly of related interest. Some of these are in-depth looks at particular pieces of research, others are vignettes that describe real people experiencing the situations covered in the text, some are applications of the research that has been discussed, and some just provide interesting information.

Each chapter contains numerous **tables and figures** to present relevant procedures, methods, and results. We have received permission to reproduce some of these from other authors whereas we have created others ourselves. This graphic presentation helps students assimilate written text.

Each chapter contains many photographs to help the reader see the presented information. Again, we believe that information is more likely to be understood and remembered when it is presented in a number of different formats.

We have provided **Internet Resources** for the topics presented in each chapter. These are websites containing relevant information. We know that most students (most people) use the Internet today and we hope that our listed sites will encourage an active search for additional and related information.

Each chapter contains a table with **Chapter Highlights**. These summarize the main points for you and help you see the relationships among the various chapter topics.

Study questions are found at the end of each chapter to help you assess whether you have understood the main points made in the chapter. These questions range from simple definitions to more challenging applications of learned material.

We list and briefly describe **Suggested Readings** at the end of each chapter. These are, of course, standard in most texts although our suggested readings often include works of fiction in addition to articles and chapters in the handbooks of aging.

Supplementary Materials

An *Instructor's Manual and Test Bank* is available. The manual portion contains suggestions for lecture presentations and classroom discussions. We have included extra information for the instructor on various topics discussed in the text. Many of these suggestions will assist the instructor who wants a lively class discussion; others are simply extra background material for the instructor's use. We list videos and where they can be obtained. The test bank includes both multiple-choice and essay questions for each chapter.

Acknowledgments

We want to thank a great many people who helped us in preparing this book. From Allyn and Bacon, we owe special thanks to Carolyn Merrill who claimed she would nag us to finish but never did and always seemed like a true friend. Her gentle touch got us through many a difficult time. We thank Staci Wittek who visited and consistently encouraged us and smiled even when things were moving slowly. We're not sure that Staci knows how to frown. We thank Tom Pauken who probably dealt with many more questions than he wanted. We appreciate his great patience and encouragement (and the answers to all those questions). We and our book owe much to the work of Marty Tenney at Modern Graphics who found a way to make all problems disappear. We thank her very much.

We wish to thank our colleagues, friends, and family who said encouraging words, smiled, and always gave us thumbs up. We thank UNC Charlotte and Queens University of Charlotte for providing us with some release time to work on the text. Without this we would still be busy reading and writing.

We wish to thank the reviewers, hired by Allyn and Bacon, who gave us much encouragement along with constructive criticism and helpful suggestions.

Harriett Amster, University of Texas at Arlington
Paul Amrhein, University of New Mexico
Denise Arehart, University of Colorado-Denver
Renee Babcock, Central Michigan University
Janet Bitzan, University of Wisconsin-Milwaukee
James Blackburn, University of Wisconsin-Milwaukee
Bradley Caskey, University of Wisconsin-River Falls
Rita Curl, Minot State University

Laurie Dickson, Northern Arizona University
Nancy McCambridge Driskill, Colorado State University
Oney Fitzpatrick, Lamar University
Dale Lund, University of Utah
Sara Deborah Majerovitz, York College
Gary Montgomery, University of Texas-Pan American
Robin Kamienny Montrilo, Rhode Island College
Catherine Murray, St. Joseph's University
Stuart Offenbach, Purdue University
Douglas Pearson, Normandale Community College
Marian Perlmutter, University of Michigan
Jane Rysberg, University of California-Chico

We thank our students who assisted in gathering data for many parts of the book including the Senior Views in each chapter. We especially thank Arlo Clark-Foos who critically reviewed chapter projects and verified Internet resources for each chapter. Arlo is currently a junior in college and has taught us how to appreciate our field through new eyes. He has been quick (perhaps too quick) to offer suggestions on how to appeal to college students in writing, pictures, graphs, and other aspects of the text. As parents we know that we learn much from our children. As children we know that we learn much from our parents and grandparents. A final thanks goes to our parents and grandparents, who instilled in us the spark that became our love for aging.

Paul W. Foos
M. Cherie Clark

1

An Introduction to Human Aging

Old age is like everything else. To make a success of it you have to start young.

—Fred Astaire

One way to start making your old age a success, regardless of how old or young you might be, is to learn about old age and aging in general. The more you know about aging, the better equipped you will be to succeed. As you can see from our first Senior View, Dr. Hadley agrees that the more you learn the better equipped you are to deal with life. He believes strongly in learning at all ages and includes his former undergraduate students in active learning experiences.

He has spent many years helping students learn about other people and their customs and language. He believes that learning about others helps us understand everyone, and ourselves, a little better. Learning about aging has only one difference. Those "others" will, hopefully, someday be ourselves.

Why Study Human Aging?

Why study human aging? Why study older people? One might also ask why study children, history, poetry, or why study at all? A simple answer is that we study things so that we can know more about them. We want to know more about them because we as humans value knowledge and because knowledge can help us improve our lives. We study things that are of interest to us, although many students can testify that we also study many things that are not of much interest to us. But then, how do we know if something really interests us until we learn about it? One reason for studying human aging is that we value knowledge and want to learn more.

We also study aging because it is something that we all are doing everyday, and hope to continue doing for many more decades. The alternative could be quite unpleasant. The study of human aging has direct relevance to the way we live. Everyday that you live, you are aging, as are your family and friends. The things you learn from this book, and any other reading that you do, can influence the choices you make for yourself and your loved ones for the rest of your life. Another major reason for studying human aging is because you are human and you are aging. The things you learn may help you to age successfully.

Senior View

We talked to Dr. Charles Hadley, consummate educator who has won several teaching awards during his 43-year career as a professor of English at Queens University at Charlotte, North Carolina. At age 74, he enjoys teaching more now than he ever has. Dr. Hadley believes that education is the most important thing we have in life and that it has the power to transform anyone.

We asked Dr. Hadley about how he sees himself now compared to when he was young. He said he is both different and the same. He doesn't feel old because he surrounds himself with youth. "Teaching young people keeps you tuned into youth," he said. When we asked if the negative stereotypes of older persons bothered him, he said no, because he doesn't relate to them. "I have always felt different from others, and I guess I still feel that way," he said. He notices that difference

when he gets together with his same age peers. He loves their company and as he says, "We have a common language and can share memories that younger folks just wouldn't understand." But, he sees his peers looking and acting "old" and he feels that he has maintained a much younger physical and psychological image of himself. He has been known to use stereotypes of the elderly to his advantage in the classroom. Because old men are supposed to be grouchy and outspoken, he can get away with saying things in the classroom that provoke chuckles rather than indignation from students. For example, one day when a student came to class in a very revealing top, Dr. Hadley asked her, "Oh dear, my young lady, did you realize that you forgot to put your blouse on over your underwear?"

Another aspect of his life that has kept him feeling youthful, is his ongoing consulting for the film industry. Since he was 21 years old, Dr. Hadley has been coaching actors in southern dialect and culture. Some of his most famous students include Vivien Leigh, Robert Duvall, Laura Dern, Johnny Depp, and Brad Pitt. Andy Griffith has been a very good lifelong friend from the time they worked together in the outdoor theater in Manteo, North Carolina. When asked why this work helps him feel young, he said, "Actors demand a lot of energy from one another and all who work with them." He loves that energy and believes that it keeps him feeling and acting young.

Dr. Hadley and his wife, who he credits with keeping him from slowing down, regularly indulge their love of culture and teaching by leading alumni on educational trips to Europe every summer. These trips feed his soul as he is forced to study new cultures in order to provide the best experience for his lifelong learners. Many of his former students have been going on his trips for 30 or more years. He believes in fostering the love of learning and of other people in all of his students.

It is clear that Dr. Hadley believes very strongly in education of all kinds for all people. We asked him why students should study aging. After chuckling and saying, "so they can fix all my problems," he said that it was a very important area and one that is rapidly changing in terms of what we know. He thinks that with the growing number of older people in society, knowledge of aging can be very helpful to any career. While culture and language are his main interests, and the sparks that ignite his mental fire, he recognizes that everyone has something different that serves this purpose. "How in the world do you know what sparks you if you don't study as much about as many things as you can?" His advice to young people is that they study everything that they possibly can so that they can see what areas serve as sparks for their mental fire. They should then nurture that spark for the rest of their lives. He wishes everyone could say what he does at this point in his life, "Despite many setbacks throughout my life, I continually look at myself and say, my God, you are a lucky person."

Finally, we study human aging because that area of study is becoming more important with each passing year. A major reason for the importance of this area of study, and the increasing interest in aging, is because changes are occurring in the world population, particularly in countries such as the United States. The number and proportion of older adults in our population is likely to increase for quite some time. The growing number of older adults will impact everything in our lives. Here are just a few examples. Transportation will change as older drivers demand better public transportation. Older people vote in greater numbers than other age groups so policies and legislation will reflect their interests. More leisure and recreation opportunities will be developed in response to this large age cohort. Family dynamics may change as more grandparents and great-grandparents are available to give advice and help to younger people. Finally, this growing segment of the population will create job and career opportunities in fields that serve older consumers, as we will see later. Our population is changing and the more we learn about it, the better equipped we will be to succeed.

Changes in Population

The number and proportion of older adults among the world population will continue to increase for the foreseeable future. Older adults will make up one quarter of the U.S. population by the year 2020. Based on data from the U.S. Bureau of the Census (2000), approximately 35 million, or 13 percent, of the population was 65 years of age or over. This is more than 10 times the number of people who were over 65 years old in 1900, which was 3 million, or 4 percent, of the population. In 1996 there were 43 million Americans who were 60 and older. That number will nearly double, to 85 million, by 2030. Another way to think about what has been called the graying of the population is to look at the ratio of individuals over 65 to those under 65. In 1900, 1 out of every 25 people was over 65. In 1990 it was 1 out of every 10 people. It is expected that 1 out of every 4 or 5 people will be over 65 by the year 2030. We are seeing a global change with the number of people over the age of 65 growing in all industrial countries. Can you see the change in your lifetime; can you imagine how different things will be?

There are a number of factors that are responsible for the drastic change in population including the unprecedented number of people in the baby boom generation, lower birth rate, and changes in life expectancy.

Soon there will be many more older adults.

Baby Boom Generation.   The baby boom generation refers to those individuals born between 1946 and 1964. Following the end of World War II, there was a huge increase in the number of births as soldiers returned home to their families or to marry and begin a family. There were feelings of victory, security, and prosperity and couples felt good about bringing children into these happy times. They were very successful at having babies and averaged close to 3 births per fertile woman (U.S. Bureau of the Census, 1989). This was the highest birth rate since right after the Civil War (1865–1900). The impact of the baby boom generation on society can be seen throughout history by looking at the growth of products and programs to serve the needs of the "boomers" and their families. The first wave of the baby boom generation will reach age 65 in the year 2011. The proportion of older adults in the population will continue to increase from 2011 until at least 2030.

Birth Rate.   Following the great increase in birth rate after World War II, birth rate has declined. The average number of births per fertile woman is now less than 2 and some experts expect the number to go as low as 1.7. At the same time, we have a bulge in total number of births as the baby boomers have babies. They will not, however, have as many babies as there are boomers. The total proportion, as well as number, of older adults will be greater over the next several decades than it has ever been. This is where developing countries differ from developed nations. In developing countries, populations of older persons are not yet on the rise. While their birth rates are still quite high, their life expectancy remains low.

Lifespan and Life Expectancy. Lifespan refers to the maximum number of years that an organism in a species can live. Clearly, the lifespan for different species is very different and not many species live longer than humans do. Table 1-1 provides some examples of lifespans for several different common, and not so common, species. The numbers come from reports from naturalists, scientists, zookeepers, and everyday people about the lives of animals that they have observed. They are not absolute values since it is possible that a member of that species might break the current record and live a little longer. At the same time, the numbers can be considered pretty good "ballpark" figures since these current records have, in many instances, stood for quite some time.

The estimated lifespan for humans was 120 years but since Jeanne Calment, shown here, had her 122nd birthday on February 21, 1997, and died in August 1997, 122 years is the current lifespan. Who is the oldest person alive today, and how old is he or she? While that may seem like a simple question, it is not. How do you determine a person's age? What documentation do you use? A registered birth certificate is the most accepted record of age. But many people born in the late 1800s either never had a birth certificate or no longer have that documentation, especially in countries where record keeping is not advanced. A good example is a woman who died in October 2001. She claimed to be 119 years old, making her the oldest person alive in 2001. However, her birth certificate was destroyed in a fire in her small southern town courthouse. Even though family records indicated that she was indeed 119, there was no concrete proof. What do you think should be required as proof?

TABLE 1-1   Estimated Lifespans for Some Friends and Acquaintances

Queen honey bee	6 years
Rabbit	13 years
Cat	28 years
Cow	30 years
Dog	34 years
Tape worm	35 years
Gorilla	39 years
Alligator	56 years
Horse	60 years
Eagle	65 years
Elephant	70 years
Blue whale	80 years
HUMAN	122 years
Tortoise	170 years
Italian cypress	2000 years
Bristle cone pine	5000 years

Source: Most of these estimated lifespans were taken from Comfort (1964) and Kimmel (1990).

Jeanne Calment, the current record holder for oldest person, age 122.

Many scientists would argue that lifespan, once we figure out what it is, cannot be changed. (See Chapter 4 on longevity.) Life expectancy can, however, be changed and has changed since humans began recording such statistics. Life expectancy refers to the age at which half of a given birth group is expected to be living and half is expected to have died. Thus, we expect that for people born in 1993, half will live to be 75.4 years of age and half will die before reaching that age. This number is life expectancy at birth (LEAB) and, thus, takes into account all the deaths for that 1993 group that will likely occur during the first few years of life, adolescence, and young adulthood. An important factor underlying the improvement in LEAB over the past century is the significant improvement in sanitation and health care for infants and children. Since 1900, we have seen a dramatic drop in the number of young people dying from what were once common and terminal childhood diseases. Since LEAB counts all these early deaths in calculating life expectancy, one might expect that individuals who make it past those early challenges will live longer than the average 75.4 years. After all, their average will not include those early deaths that go into calculation of LEAB.

Life expectancy at a specified age (LEASA) estimates the age at which people are expected to die, given that they have made it to a certain age. In this case we can estimate how many more years people who are a certain age can, on average, expect to live. The number refers to the number of years past which, half of the group should still be living and half will have died. LEASA must be longer than LEAB since it does not include any of those early deaths in its calculation.

Another major reason for the increases in numbers and proportions of older adults is that life expectancy at birth and life expectancy at a specified age have both increased over the last several decades. That is, birth groups can expect to live longer than they could at the turn of the century as we continue to improve our ability to live through early life illness and disease; and adults who make it to an older age can expect many more years ahead of them than could adults who made it to that same specified age several decades ago. Figure 1-1, on page 8, shows differences in life expectancy at birth for people who lived in the distant past, not so distant past, and today. Some very well-known individuals did not live very long although some others lived well past the life expectancy for people living in their times. Generally, people can expect to live much longer today than they could in the past.

Clearly, there will be many more older people over the next several decades and those older people can also expect to live longer. Table 1-2, on page 9, shows life expectancy at the specified age of 65 for people making it to that age at the beginning and end of the twentieth century. Older people can expect to live longer than older people could just a few decades ago. In fact, the biggest increases over the next several decades will be for the oldest-old, people 80 years of age and over.

In short, there will be a greater number, and a greater proportion, of older adults over the next several decades as a result of the great number of births which followed World War II (baby boom), the lower birth rate in more recent decades, and the continued increases in life expectancy. These numbers carry important implications for careers and employment opportunities in the twenty-first century.

Career Implications

It is important that we know as much as we can about aging so that we can be prepared for these millions of people. This might mean the creation of new direct service jobs in fields such as elder law, geriatric health care, gerontological social work, or advocacy for elders. Box 1-1 on pages 9–10, contains a list compiled by the Association for Gerontology in Higher Education (AGHE) of jobs in the field of gerontology. While this is an impressive list, and we would like to encourage you to consider a career in gerontology, knowledge of aging and older people can serve you well in any career you choose simply because there will be more older customers/clients, supervisors, and employees as you travel through your work life. Some existing jobs may expand to take into consideration the needs and desires of the elder population, such as counseling, education and training, human resources, research, nursing, or marketing and advertising. In all cases jobs that are geared toward serving the public will need to take into consideration the growing number of older consumers. A major portion of the consuming public will be over age 65 and you can be sure that corporations will want to sell to them. After all, there will be many more of them in the not-too-distant future and many of them have substantial discretionary income. New jobs will emerge to serve the older population. Entrepreneurs in this area can make a substantial impact.

The Study of Aging

The study of aging and older adults is known as **gerontology**. This word comes from "ology" meaning "the study of," and the Greek word "gero" referring to elders. A related

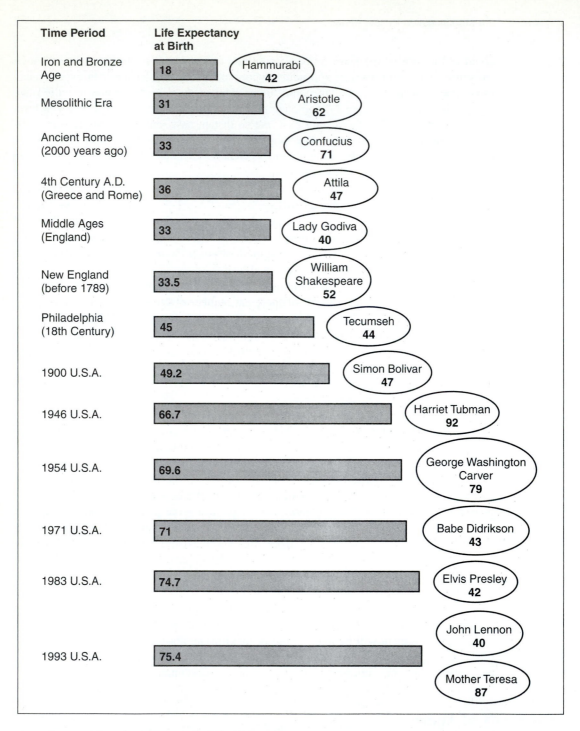

FIGURE 1-1   Historical Changes in Life Expectancy

Sources: Adapted from Katchadourian, 1987; Laslett, 1985; Lincoln Library of Essential Information, 1954; and Worldwatch Institute, 1994.

TABLE 1-2   Twentieth Century Changes in Life Expectancy at the Specified Age of 65

If you reached age 65 in this year	You could expect to live this many more years	For a grand total of this many years
1900	11.65	76.65
1920	12.30	77.30
1940	12.65	77.65
1960	14.40	79.40
1980	16.20	81.20
2000	18.01	83.01

Source: Adapted from Hooyman & Kiyak, 1996; Kimmel, 1990; U.S Bureau of the Census, 1993; and the author's own estimations.

term is **geriatrics,** which refers to the specialty within such health care fields as medicine, social work, nursing, and dentistry; it is concerned with health, disease, care, and treatment of older adults. Gerontology is a field of study unlike many others with which you may already be familiar. It is multidisciplinary, which means it includes the perspectives of many traditional disciplines like anthropology, biology, business administration, economics,

BOX **1-1**

Careers in Gerontology

Gerontological specialists work in a variety of different settings that can be listed in the following broad categories:

- Direct Service Provision—Provide care for elders in homes, hospitals, clinics, or through adult service programs; these can include health care provision, counseling, advising elders, and developing programs and activities for elders in a wide variety of settings.
- Program Planning and Evaluation—Design, implement, and evaluate programs designed to meet the needs of older persons.
- Management and Administration—Oversee operation, staffing, and evaluation of organizations and institutions serving elders.
- Marketing and Product Development—Develop and market new services and products for older persons; a wide variety of organizations, institutions, corporations, and small businesses serve as employers.
- Advocacy—Work with or on behalf of older persons before legislative bodies, politicians, or institutions; often advocating for specific programs, services, or policies.
- Education and Training—Educate and train older people and their families, health care and other service providers, and future gerontological professionals in a variety of educational settings.

(continued)

BOX **1-1**   **Continued**

■ Research—Design and conduct a wide variety of research projects dealing with aging issues.

   Newer jobs for gerontological professionals are emerging including:

■ Entrepreneurs—Self-employment, often as consultants on a variety of aging issues to businesses, individuals, organizations, and corporations.
■ Geriatric Care Managers—Assist with planning services for elders, often acting as a liaison with service providers; care managers are often hired by family members to help arrange care for an elderly relative.

nursing, psychology, and sociology; and it assumes multiple influences on development. In this book we examine gerontology primarily from the perspective of the sciences (anthropology, biology, psychology, sociology, social work) but, by definition, there will be topics that we will discuss that draw on or emanate from many of these other disciplines. Working individually or together, these researchers advance our understanding of aging. Most of this research is published in professional journals; you can get a taste of this research by browsing these journals in your library. Some of the better known journals that publish work in gerontology are listed in Table 1-3 on page 11.

All sciences use very similar methods to study aging and older adults and, although this is not a book on methods, some basic understanding of the methods used and the major problems confronted by these researchers will help you to understand the findings, theories, and conclusions drawn throughout the rest of this book.

Research on Aging

Theory

As you have undoubtedly learned, the purpose of research is to describe, understand, explain, and predict behavior. Many people outside of research criticize some research results saying, "well, duh, my grandmother could have told you that!" While she certainly could have, her sister may have had a very different explanation for the same behavior. For example, how many times have you heard someone say that giving kids sugar will make them hyperactive? And how many times have you heard others say, no that is only a myth. How do you choose which one to believe? Research provides us with an objective way to answer questions about behavior.

Research does not operate in a vacuum. Researchers draw on theories to bring together data from many different studies to draw a consistent, coherent picture of behavior. Theories drive the way we do research, including the types of topics or methods that we use and even the way we think about the behavior we study. Theories also provide us with

TABLE 1-3   Some of the Major Journals Concerned with Aging and Older Adults

Journal Name

Aging & Cognition
Aging & Society
Aging Issues
Educational Gerontology
Experimental Aging Research
Generations
Geriatrics
The Gerontologist
Gerontology & Geriatrics Education
International Journal of Aging & Human Development
Journal of Adult Development
Journal of Applied Gerontology
Journal of the American Geriatrics Society
Journal of Clinical Geropsychology
Journal of Geriatric Nursing
Journal of Geriatric Psychiatry
Journal of Gerontological Nursing
Journal of Gerontological Social Work
Journals of Gerontology: Biological Sciences, Medical Sciences, Psychological Sciences, & Social Sciences
Psychology & Aging
Research on Aging
Religion & Aging
Social Policy
Women & Aging

a unifying guide to explain our research findings. Depending on what discipline you come from, your research will be guided by one or more of the major theories in the field. For example, in the field of psychology, researchers may identify more with cognitive theory, learning theory, or psychoanalytic theory. Each discipline has its own theories to help explain data. Throughout this book, we will discuss several theories as they pertain to specific topics of interest to gerontologists. If you would like to know more about the major theories and how they explain behavior and guide research, pick up an introductory text in any field. You will find a wealth of easy-to-understand information in these texts. Of course, if you want more in-depth coverage of theories, there are several advanced texts available. An excellent discussion of several general and specific theories applied to aging can be found in Bengston and Schaie (1999).

Researchers in gerontology are always interested in age. Whether an investigator is looking at how children start using strategies to remember things, or how adolescents change strategies for remembering test information, or what strategies middle-age adults use to remember a grocery list, or how strategies may break down for elders having difficulty remembering to take their medication, the common question is how behavior remains the same and how it changes with age.

Developmental researchers frame their research questions not just with theories but with broader views about how development occurs. These views have been framed as controversies and major issues including nature–nurture, mechanistic–organismic development, continuity–discontinuity, and stability–change. While there are others, these issues pervade the majority of developmental research and will come up several times as we confront various topics in this book. We briefly describe these issues so that you can better understand the origins of much of the research discussed in this book. If you would like to learn more, a good source is Lerner (1986).

Nature–nurture refers to the relative contributions of genetics, biology, and the environment on development. For example, does the occurrence of high cholesterol levels in some people over the age of 65 result from genetic predisposition or environmental influences, such as lifestyle factors or even prenatal environmental influences? The more frequently asked question emanating from this issue is how do nature and nurture interact to produce a given outcome?

The mechanistic–organismic issue is related but a bit different. This issue asks the bigger question about what guides development. Is a person passive in his or her development with the environment exerting its influence without you having to do anything, or are you an active shaper of how you develop? An example here might be the area of social skills. Is an older person with few friends, and at high risk for loneliness, like that because they continually experienced negative social events leading to isolation? Or, has that person actively discouraged friends at various points throughout development, perhaps due to innate shyness or some other temperament characteristic, and thus ended up alone in old age?

The continuity–discontinuity issue can take several forms. One way to look at this issue is to ask the question, are the changes seen with age, smooth and gradual or sudden and abrupt. Do we have quantitative or step-like incremental changes or do we change in a qualitative or whole different way? An example of how we might use this to guide our thinking on aging is to look at memory changes with age. If people recall fewer items on standard recall tasks as they get older, does this change reflect a slow decline in the number of items they are able to store in memory over several years? Or does poorer performance in old age reflect a sudden inability to store as many items or even a completely different way of learning or storing information? Depending on which side of this issue you accept, you will look at changes with an eye toward identifying small changes or big dramatic changes.

The last issue, stability–change, may be the easiest to understand. This issue addresses what aspects of development remain primarily stable and unchanging, and which change. Furthermore, we might ask, when in development do changes occur, if they occur. This may seem like another "my grandmother could have told you . . ." point but it is really an important issue in development. For a long time, development was viewed as a series of big and small changes. If you didn't see change, it was because you weren't looking hard enough. Now we have clearly identified aspects of development that do not change, at least for a long period of time. Accepting that development is characterized by stability and change at all ages is a relatively new way of looking at development in old age.

It is important to remember that not many scientists take a strict side on these issues. Most work today is being done in the middle ground area. For example, rarely do you see a scientist take a hard-line nature or genetic approach to behavior. Rather, an attempt might be made to explain, when in development or on what aspects of development, does genetics have its strongest influences. From a developmental perspective, taking a position on these issues helps an investigator think more broadly about age-related changes seen in behavior. Thinking more broadly demands that researchers look at multiple influences on behavior. This should make sense to you. Think about who you are and why you do the things you do. You cannot point to any one thing that has helped to make you the way you are. Even if you try to look at one aspect of your behavior, you cannot point to one single cause. For example, think about your study habits. Your habits have undoubtedly been influenced by your parents, teachers, prior experiences studying, ability to sit still and concentrate, health and nutrition, social environment, and how well you learned basic concepts earlier in your education, for example. Multiple influences clearly guide our behavior. In aging, we have years of influences to add to the picture, so gerontologists are very concerned with looking broadly at behavior.

The notion of multiple influences on behavior is probably best exemplified by the lifespan developmental model that has become a major force in guiding research in gerontology. The lifespan developmental perspective views development in the context of life. In other words, we are who we are because of all that we have experienced, all that makes up who we are now, and what we think may happen in the future. Life is complex and the way we think about development should be equally complex. Paul Baltes has proposed one of the best models of the lifespan perspective (1987). He has combined the major issues and important principles in most developmental theories and has identified several key features of development and the study of development necessary to cover the complexity of who we are. These features are summarized in Table 1-4 (p.14) and guide much of the current research and thinking in gerontology. As you look at the features of the lifespan model, can you see those issues discussed earlier? Think about these features and how they contribute to who you are now.

Research Methods

The two methods used most frequently by researchers in gerontology to examine age and aging are **correlational** and **quasi-experimental**. When researches in gerontology want to know whether there is a relationship between an individual's age and some other variable, a correlational method is used. When gerontological researchers want to know whether some variable affects people of different ages the same or differently, a quasi-experimental method is used. Several examples can help clarify these differences.

Is age related to the number of close friends that a person reports having? This is a question that can be answered with the correlational method. If we wanted to know whether a person's age is related to the number of close friends they have, we might gather data from a group of people of varying ages and ask them to tell us how many close friends they have. We cannot change anyone's age or their number of close friends but we can determine whether these two variables are related. If we found that the correlation statistic allowed us to conclude that these variables were significantly related in a positive way, that

TABLE 1-4   Important Features of the Lifespan Development Perspective

Feature	Description	Example: Math Ability in Old Age
Development as a lifelong process	Development takes place over the entire lifespan and all age periods are equally important to development and so must be considered in research.	The development and maintenance of math ability at all previous ages should be considered important to present ability.
Development as multidisciplinary	Development in any area is intricately tied with development in other areas (e.g., social relies on cognitive) and so research must consider all disciplines to understand the totality of development.	How can the fields of biology, anthropology, sociology, computer science, etc., contribute to the research question regarding the development of math ability?
Development as gains and losses	At all ages development is made up of both gains and losses and so research must examine both types of change.	Consider the gains in math ability in old-age along with the losses; for example, does wisdom result in more efficient ways to complete math tasks?
Development shows plasticity	Any individual's development shows considerable modifiability; at any point a person's experiences could change the course of development and so developmental research must identify the degree of plasticity and its constraints.	How has math ability been affected by education or other experiences? Can current math ability be modified with training?
Development as embedded in history	Development occurs with a given historical-cultural context and so research must examine development as it occurs within specific sociocultural conditions and how these change over time.	What historical and cultural factors have influenced math ability; for example, did growing up in the Great Depression result in poor nutrition and less formal schooling, which in turn affected math ability?
Development occurs within a context	Individual development is influenced by an interaction among many influences: some of which are biologic and some environmental, some experienced uniquely by an individual, and some experienced similarly by many individuals, and so research must consider the multitude of influences on development.	How was math ability learned and how was it maintained? Did parents or teachers provide basic instruction? How much practice, formal and informal, with math tasks was maintained in young and middle adulthood?

Source: Adapted from Baltes (1987).

would tell us that the older a person was, the more close friends they had. (If the relationship were negative, that would mean that older adults had fewer friends.) However, we could not say why that relationship existed or what caused what. It could be that the longer you live, the more friends you make. Or, it could be that the more friends you have, the longer you tend to live. It could be that some types of people, perhaps those who are socially active, tend to live longer and have more friends. This is, of course, an imaginary result; in Chapter 9 we will talk about friendships. Correlation involves measuring two or more variables in a group of people to see if those variables are related. Correlation tells us whether or not variables are related and how strongly, but not why.

In typical quasi-experimental research, more than age differences are investigated. Most of the research you will learn about examines age and one or two other variables. For example, do the number of other people in a room influence the comfort of older and young adults differently? In this quasi-experimental study, two variables are being investigated, age and number of people. We might invite two groups of different age participants to wait in a room. In some cases, we will have them wait alone but in other cases they will wait with ten other individuals. After a period of waiting we measure their comfort level on some rating scale. If we found that the appropriate statistic allowed us to conclude that the number of people in a waiting room influenced the comfort level of the two groups differently then that would tell us that the influence was different for old and young. In this case, we could have found an age difference that could be of some importance. Maybe older adults prefer waiting with others while young adults prefer waiting by themselves; this also is an imaginary result. Quasi-experimental methods tell us whether or not group differences exist.

In the research examples described above, we tested adults of different ages. In the first example, we asked people of different ages how many close friends they had and in the second we had people of different ages wait in a room alone or with ten other individuals. When the research we conduct uses different people of different ages it is referred to as **cross-sectional** research. Most of the research conducted in gerontology is cross-sectional since it can usually be done fairly quickly, relatively inexpensively, and efficiently. It does, however, have a major problem and that is the problem of **age cohort**.

A cohort is a group of people who are companions or similar in some way. An **age cohort** is a generational group; individuals all born about the same time and, thus, who have grown up through the same world events comprise an age cohort. When a researcher conducts cross-sectional research, whether correlational or quasi-experimental, any obtained results could be age differences, cohort differences, or both. For example, it may be that people born in the early years of this century, the old adults in our quasi-experiment, feel more comfortable waiting with other people because of experiences they have had. Had they been tested when they were young, they might still have felt more comfortable waiting with others. At the same time, the young adults who felt more comfortable waiting by themselves might continue to feel this way even when they are old. Thus, our finding would not be an age difference at all; it would be a difference between different cohorts.

Cross-sectional research always has this problem. One method of dealing with the problem is to repeat the study over the course of many years. If the same findings occur, then one may feel confident that the obtained differences really are age differences rather than cohort differences since each repetition of the experiment used the same age groups but different cohorts.

Another way to deal with the cohort problem is to abandon the cross-sectional approach and use a longitudinal approach. When research uses the same people at different ages in their lives, it is referred to as **longitudinal** research. For example, a researcher might have tested young adults in waiting rooms with different numbers of other people and then retested the same adults when they were middle-age and then again when they were older. If a difference was found, then that difference could not be due to cohort since the very same cohort was used at all three age levels. Longitudinal research is a much better way to determine whether there are changes within individual people as they grow older.

Longitudinal research, however, has problems of its own. Only one cohort has been tested and, thus, any obtained result(s) could be peculiar to that cohort. However, the primary problem with longitudinal studies is the effect of time-related events, or anything that is associated with testing the same people at different times. In some cases, something could happen in between testing periods to make people perform differently on the later tests. For example, if you were interested in whether anxiety changes with age and World War III broke out sometime after the first testing, all of the respondents may show higher anxiety at the next testing. You could not, in this case, conclude that anxiety changed with age.

It is also the case that as the length of time between testing increases, many individuals become unavailable for further tests. Some move away or are hard to find, some no longer are interested or willing to participate, and some die. The group of people at the end of a longitudinal study may be very different from those at the beginning. The cost in time for longitudinal research can be horrendous. If we had to wait more than 40 to 50 years to find out if our young adults would still want to wait by themselves when they were 70, it may not be worth the wait, not to mention that you, as the researcher, would also be aging and may be more interested in retiring at 70 than retesting participants.

Researchers must choose carefully when planning to test hypotheses. The cross-sectional approach is typically chosen because it is quick and efficient and, in many instances, researchers assume that cohort differences are fairly unlikely or that replications will test for those differences. They are not always right. The longitudinal approach is a more effective way to examine change within individuals and, for that reason, may be well worth the extra time and effort. Better and more complex designs are now used in large-scale research. The most frequently used of these complex designs are sequential designs.

Sequential Research Designs

Sequential research designs are meant to control the problems inherent in any research that attempts to separate age and cohort to see where the differences truly are. Sequential designs grew out of the work of K. Warner Schaie (1965, 1977, 1990) and we will use his terminology.

Recall that in our discussion of longitudinal and cross-sectional designs we identified three problems: age, cohort, and time-related problems. Age, cohort, and time of measurement are linked. Statisticians would say that there are only two degrees of freedom (df) among these three factors. That means that once you decide the values of any two, the third is determined. For example, if I want to test 80-year-old people (1 df) who were a part of the 1925 cohort (2nd df), then I must test them in 2005. If I wait until 2008 to test them they will no longer be 80; they will be 83. Time of measurement is determined by the values selected for age and cohort.

Sequential designs are ways of pulling apart the influence of these three factors to see if any or all of them are associated with the differences that we obtain. For gerontologists, the **cohort sequential design** is the one most frequently used, although in major research projects a combination of all designs can be found. In a cohort sequential design, researchers choose the values of age and cohort that they are interested in and assume, hope, and believe that time of measurement is not an important factor in their research. Figure 1-2 shows an example of a cohort sequential design.

In this example, researchers are interested in people's concerns regarding income after retirement. Two age groups have been selected: people who are 52 years old and people who are 72 years old. This is 10 years before and 10 years after the median age of retirement, which is now 62. These researchers also are interested in possible differences between the 1930 and 1950 cohorts. Those born before World War II and who lived through it may have very different views than those born in the optimism of post-World War II. In a cohort sequential design one would measure the 1930 cohort when they turned 52 (in 1982) and again when they turned 72 (in 2002). The 1950 cohort would also be measured when they turned 52 (in 2002) and when they turned 72 (in 2022). The study would take 40 years to collect the desired data but the answers obtained would reveal both age and cohort differences, if there truly are any. Let's make up some imaginary results.

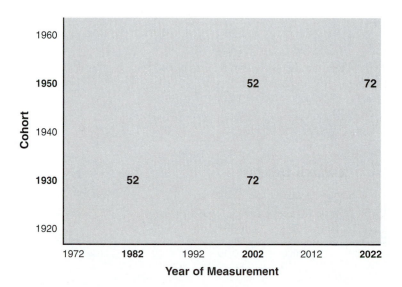

FIGURE 1-2   A Cohort Sequential Design

If researchers found that 72-year-olds were less concerned about retirement income than 52-year-olds, that difference could not be due to cohort. The 72-year-olds that we tested came from both the 1930 and the 1950 cohorts as did our 52-year-olds. If researchers found that members of the 1930 cohort were more concerned about retirement income than were members of the 1950 cohort, that difference could not be due to age. Both cohorts are composed of 52- and 72-year-olds. Age and cohort differences have been separated. The researcher can determine whether one, both, or neither are related to retirement income concerns.

When the study does take a while, like this one, it will be costly and time consuming, as longitudinal designs often are. Nevertheless, the cohort sequential design is a vast improvement over those simple cross-sectional or longitudinal designs that we examined earlier because it separates two of the three factors and allows one to examine them independently.

The very best approach is to follow a large group of people from different cohorts over a long period of time and to add new people from new cohorts at every testing. This design is shown in Figure 1-3. Here we examine whether friendships change as one grows older. Perhaps older adults have fewer friends but are much closer than younger adults. We are also interested in cohort effects. Maybe people who grew up during different generations have different numbers or types of friends. Finally, it is even possible that the information we gather about friendships depends, to some extent, on when the measurements are made. Friendships may become closer as people depend more on each other during hard economic times, for example.

Looking at this figure, imagine that it is 1990. During that year we tested people from the 1930 through 1970 cohorts. They ranged in age from 20 (the 1970 cohort) to 60 (the

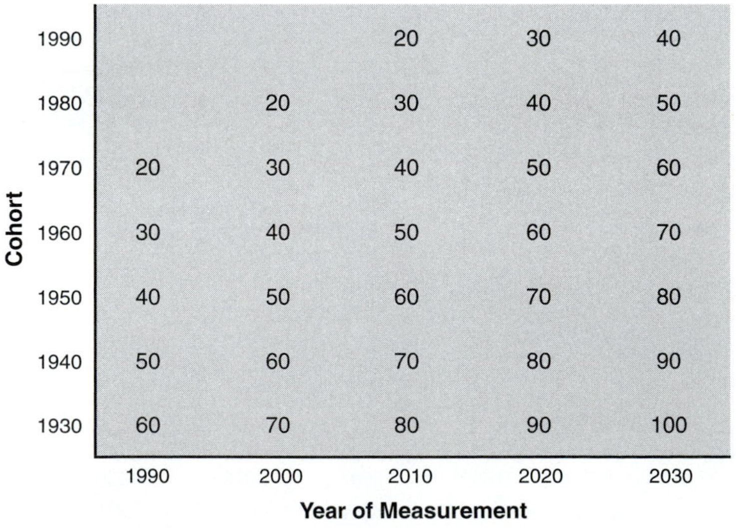

Cohort	1990	2000	2010	2020	2030
1990			20	30	40
1980		20	30	40	50
1970	20	30	40	50	60
1960	30	40	50	60	70
1950	40	50	60	70	80
1940	50	60	70	80	90
1930	60	70	80	90	100

Year of Measurement

FIGURE 1-3   The Ultimate Sequential Design

1930 cohort). In the year 2000 we tested all of these people again (or as many of them as we could find) and they were all ten years older. We also add a new group of 20-year-olds from the 1980 cohort. In 2010 we tested all of these people again; they were ten more years older; and we added a new group of 20-year-olds from the 1990 cohort. And so on every ten years. With data obtained from these people we can look at the effects of age, cohort, and time of measurement separately to see where any differences truly are.

Such an elaborate design is not often used because of the enormous expense involved. It should also be obvious that one would not take on such a major research project to answer a single question. One would attempt to gather as much information as possible each time that measurements are made. You will find examples of such designs in the text. One excellent example, presented in Chapter 7, comes from Schaie's work on investigating age, cohort, and time of measurement differences in intelligence.

Some variables can only be examined with correlational research while others can be examined using a quasi-experimental method. Table 1-5 illustrates the two methods and two approaches in summary form. These two methods, and sequential designs are the ones gerontologists use to study aging and older adults. But we must first ask the question, what is aging and who counts as an older adult?

What Is Aging/Who Is Old

Aging refers to an individual passing through time and all that occurs during the passing of time. We are aging from birth onward. Changes that occur during aging can be quick or slow, positive or negative. For example, we may hear a proud parent of a 7-year-old say,

TABLE 1-5 Two Methods and Two Approaches Used in Gerontology Research

	Research Method	
Research Approach	*Correlational*	*Quasi-experimental*
	Examines relationships between variables.	Examines differences between ages.
Cross-Sectional ☺ Data collection is fairly quick and efficient.	☺ Any obtained relationship could be due to cohort rather than or in addition to age.	☺ Any obtained differences could be due to cohort rather than or in addition to age.
Longitudinal ☺ Best way to examine change within individual.	☺ Any obtained relationship could exist just for the cohort tested.	☺ Any obtained differences could exist just for the cohort tested.
	☺ Obtained relationship cannot be due to cohort.	☺ Obtained differences cannot be cohort differences.

"He's such a big boy now; he acts so much older." Clearly, the notion of aging and getting older in this situation is a positive experience. You may also have heard people say about a grandparent, "he seems so much older than when we saw him last." Here the connotation is somewhat negative suggesting that some major decline connected to getting older has occurred. As the lifespan developmental perspective suggests, aging at every age is made up of both gains and losses. You can think of things that you are better at now than you were ten years ago and also things you do not do as well anymore.

Undoubtedly you know many older adults. Your parents are certainly older than you are, although we might still count them as middle-aged. Your grandparents are older adults and, if all are still living, you probably know them fairly well. Many of your teachers are older adults; at least the ones that you had years ago in elementary school. Look to the front of the room in all of your classes; are any of your current teachers older adults? You may have neighbors and friends who are older adults. You certainly see senior citizens whenever you go out. Of course, looking at these people may have alerted you to the fact that you may not be sure what counts as old. Where is that line between middle and old age? Or between middle and young age? Is there such a line at all?

One of the most commonly used markers to identify the boundary between old and middle-age is chronological, the age of 65. Otto von Bismarck, in late nineteenth-century Germany, chose this age as the retirement age for German workers. At that time, not many lived that long and, thus, not many workers retired and needed to receive support from the government. Age 65 remains with us today as a common retirement age.

Many researchers also divide older adults into two groups called the young-old and old-old. The former might be 65 to 80 and the latter might be people who are over age 80. The U.S. Bureau of the Census (1993) provides three subcategories of the older population: (1) the young-old (65 to 74 years); (2) the middle-old (75 to 84 years); and (3) the old-old (85 and over). While some research, particularly marketing studies, has tried to provide support for differences among these three groups, other research has failed to find significant differences. Recently, some authors have suggested adding a fourth category, the very-old who are 95 and over, since they tend to be more frail than others and because there are enough folks that age to study. Regardless of how many groups are used or how the elderly population is divided, it is important to remember that much of this division is done for convenience and to identify gross differences that might apply to many, but certainly not all, members of a group. You can probably think of someone who is quite old but who looks and acts much younger. You have probably also seen someone who is fairly young but who looks and acts quite old. Gerontologists agree that the elderly, as a group, are more heterogeneous or different from one another than any other age group. Individual differences only get stronger as you get older, and as your biology and the environment continue to interact to make you unique.

Despite what researchers say, many lay people have similar ideas about when they think old age begins. The American Association of Retired Persons (AARP) compiled information from three different surveys with thousands of respondents who were asked what they thought about a number of aging issues. One question asked was, "At what age do you think a person is old?" The majority of respondents said old age started between 60 to 69. Researchers found that the older the person answering the question was, the older age they assigned to being old. Our work that examined images of aging (Foos and Clark, 1994) found a slightly higher age, that of 70. This is the average age given by males and females, blacks and whites, young and old as the age that they "considered old." What age would you say begins old age? You might try the exercise in Box 1-2 and learn how your answers compare to others older and younger than you are.

What can we conclude from this research about when old age starts? There seems to be some agreement on the part of researchers and lay people for using chronological age, specifically 60 to 70, as the beginning of old age. But it is clear that there is no real point at which old age begins and, therefore, no one right way to identify old age. Keep this in mind as we discuss the literature on aging. Gerontology attempts to provide accurate and reliable information and hopes that such information can counteract the stereotypes about aging that are prevalent in our society.

Stereotypes

Many sources provide us with stereotypes of older adults and the aging experience. We see older adults portrayed on television, in movies, and in advertisements. We meet older

BOX 1-2
Who Is Old?

The authors (Foos & Clark, 1994) did a follow-up study on what people think about aging and older people. We collected information from a regional sample in order to compare it to a national sample reported by AARP, which is discussed in the text. Answer each of the following questions before reading the results described below, in order to compare your answers to the answers we found:

1. At what age do you consider someone to be old?
2. Describe your image of a typical old person.
3. How do you feel about your own aging?

These questions were asked of 301 men and women ranging in age from 14 to 97 (mean age of 35). There was strong agreement that the age at which someone is considered to be old is about 70. Remember that the national survey found 60 to 69 as the average age of an old person. How close was your answer to this number?

For Question 2, the most frequent characteristics listed by the adults we surveyed were the following: retired, grandparent, wise, slow, handicapped/weak, wrinkled, gray hair, cheerful/happy, inactive, isolated, fearful, and confused. Some of these images seem positive and some negative. While all of them are true of certain individuals, none are true of all individuals. There is enormous diversity among older adults and we will explore this diversity throughout this book. Although some of these characteristics fit the typical stereotype of an older adult, you will soon learn that stereotypes are not very accurate and that they can be quite damaging.

For Question 3, the vast majority of people (67 percent) said that they looked forward to aging. Another 21 percent said that they were scared and 12 percent said that they couldn't imagine growing old. Which group do you find yourself in? Why?

characters in books, hear about them in jokes, and read how aging is depicted in most birthday cards. Much of what the average person knows, or thinks they know about aging comes from these sources, and these sources are never entirely right.

Stereotypes often lead naive people to believe that exaggerations and half-truths (in many cases outright falsehoods) are not only true but are also true for every member of that group. Some anthropologists say that stereotypes influence people to believe that older adults are typically confused, disoriented, maladjusted, and incoherent. These believers then seem surprised when meeting an older adult who does not show such characteristics and may believe that the individual is just having an unusually good day. Evidence that older adults are not confused, disoriented, maladjusted, and incoherent is often considered suspect because everyone knows they are (Hazan, 1996).

Maggie Kuhn, who founded the Gray Panthers, has been very active in trying to change stereotypes about older adults, and aging, in general. In an interview in 1989, she said, "The first myth is that old age is a disease, a terrible disease that you never admit that you've got, so you lie about your age. Well, it's not a disease. It's a triumph, because you've survived. Failure, disappointment, sickness, loss, you're still here."

Not your stereotypic older adult.

Such positive views of aging are all too rare in the television shows, movies, advertisements, books, jokes, and birthday cards that continue to portray aging in a negative light. In what follows we describe some of these stereotypes and their presentation in the media. Generally, researchers have looked at the portrayal of older adults in two ways, quantitatively and qualitatively. A quantitative analysis is done to assess whether the proportion of older adults in a media presentation is equivalent to the proportion of older adults in the general population. If older adults comprise about 20 percent of the total population but older characters comprise only 2 percent of the population in a novel, then older adults are underrepresented in the novel. Of course, in some novels such an underrepresentation might be expected. A novel about an adolescent youth camp will, of course, underrepresent older and probably middle-age adults. A qualitative analysis is done to assess whether the older adults who are presented are portrayed in positive, neutral, or negative terms. If older adults are portrayed as wise, then that would be considered positive; if they are portrayed as confused, then that might be considered negative. We will examine portrayals in electronic and print media separately.

Electronic Media

Electronic media refers to television, movies, radio, and Internet portrayals of older adults, although only television has received extensive assessment. In a quantitative analysis of 22,315 television characters, most studies found an underrepresentation of older adults. This underrepresentation was particularly low during prime-time shows. Females were underrepresented to a greater extent than males. On the other hand, television commercials and daytime soap operas represented older adults at about the same proportion as in the population (Vasil & Wass, 1993). A study (Robinson & Skill, 1995) compared roles held by older persons in 1995 to those reported in previous studies from the 1970s. Older people were actually more underrepresented, than in the 1970s. So, despite the fact that the number of older people in the population has grown, and that public opinion about the elderly seems to have improved (Ferraro, 1992), their portrayals in prime-time have not improved. Swayne and Greco (1986) found the same underrepresentation of older people in television commercials. Women, again, were even more underrepresented.

Qualitative analyses show that older adults are more often portrayed negatively than positively and that this is especially true of older females. Older adults are most frequently portrayed as foolish and eccentric (Bishop & Krause, 1984). Older women are often shown as silly, lacking common sense, and unsuccessful (Gerbner, Gross, Signorielli, & Morgan, 1980) while older men are sometimes portrayed as problem solvers (Dail, 1988). Thus, even though all older adults suffer from negative portrayals on television, older females seem to suffer more. As in the quantitative analyses, the least negative portrayals are found in daytime soap operas.

Print Media

Print media refers to newspaper, book, and greeting card portrayals of older adults. As with electronic media, older adults are underrepresented in print and this is particularly true for older women (Vasil & Wass, 1993). Qualitative analyses of print media, like electronic media, shows that older adults are more likely to be portrayed in a negative way than are other age groups and the most frequent negative themes are of extreme conservatism and sexual dysfunction (Smith, 1979).

One might expect that advertisements would provide positive portrayals of aging and older adults since such advertisers are often attempting to attract older consumers. In fact, this does seem to be the case. One major study of 30 years of advertisements in *Modern Maturity* magazine (published by AARP) found that persons 50 and older were shown as healthy, important, capable, and socially active (Roberts & Zhou, 1997). They also found that 96.4 percent of the older persons in these advertisements were white. What about mainstream magazines? Miller, Miller, McKibbin, and Pettys (1999) examined advertisements in several popular U.S. magazines (e.g., *Better Homes and Gardens, Popular Mechanics*) for evidence of elderly stereotypes. They were particularly interested in examining change over time so they analyzed magazines from 1956 to 1996. Similar to the findings with electronic media, the elderly were greatly underrepresented in these ads with the percentage decreasing over the years. Overall they found little stereotyping of elders but for those few stereotypes, there was an increase in negative stereotyping and a decrease in positive stereotyping.

Birthday cards and jokes provide other examples of negative stereotyping of older adults and aging. Of course, these jokes and cards are meant to be humorous and many are quite funny. Nevertheless, one must distinguish between a good joke and a damaging stereotype. An analysis of birthday cards found that 88 percent portrayed aging in a negative way (Demos & Jache, 1982). Look at birthday cards the next time you are in a card store and you will probably see that very few portray aging in a positive way. If you want to try this in a slightly more systematic way, you might try Project 1.

Stereotyping can be found in a content analysis of jokes. We have all heard jokes about a number of different groups and they are generally not very flattering for the groups

PROJECT 1

Although the text claims that most portrayals of older adults and aging are quite negative, perhaps you are wondering if this is true. To some extent, the amount of negativity depends on the source of the stereotype. Birthday cards about aging are almost always negative, whereas advertisements are far more positive.

Go to a major source of birthday cards, such as a large department store, card store, or drug store, and read 20 cards for children, 20 for older adults, and 20 for people of unspecified age. Rate each card as being positive, neutral, or negative about that birthday age. What did you find?

The 20 cards for children are likely to be positive, the 20 for older adults are likely to be negative. You may notice, however, a sudden shift in cards designed for the very old. These cards turn sweet and gentle. Why do you think this is? How positive or negative were cards for individuals of unspecified age?

What stereotypes about aging are portrayed in these cards? Was Maggie Kuhn right?

portrayed in the joke. An analysis of jokes about old people shows that 59 percent portray old age and old adults negatively while only 23 percent portray them positively (the remaining 18 percent were considered neutral). The most negative portrayals were in jokes about death, age concealment, mental and physical ability, and appearance (Palmore, 1986). The next time you hear a joke about an older person, substitute a minority for the older person and see if it still sounds funny. We no longer consider racist and sexist jokes funny but we often don't think twice about laughing at or telling an ageist joke. Would your grandmother think that joke you are hearing or reading is funny?

A major problem with these stereotypes is that they often lead to prejudice and discrimination against older people. **Ageism**, a term coined and first described in detail by Butler (1969), is very prevalent in our society. If you think older people are forgetful, then you may not trust directions or instructions given to you by an older relative. If you think older people are confused, then you may interpret a pause at the snack counter in a theater as a reason to start offering alternatives or to skip over that person. You may not hire an older person if you think that they will have physical or mental problems on the job. Ageism is supported by, and to some extent grows out of, negative stereotypes and can result in negative attitudes toward aging and older adults.

Attitudes toward Aging

Negative portrayals of older people often result in negative attitudes toward aging. What do most people think about older people? While we have no research showing a direct link between negative portrayals and negative attitudes, we do have plenty of both and can assume they contribute to one another. The large-scale research reported by AARP (1995) concluded that there are a lot of negative feelings about older people in our society. Specifically, they found that most Americans tend to see older persons with many more serious problems than they really have, especially regarding health, loneliness, and financial worries. Interestingly, those people with less knowledge about aging, and who have had less positive experiences with life themselves, tended to view older persons in a very negative light. Many other research studies have found similar negative views of the elderly, even from children as young as 8-years-old. (Aday, Evans, & Sims, 1991).

The research studies just discussed focus on attitudes toward older persons in general. Is this view the same for all cultural groups? Are negative attitudes a universal experience? We will see in later chapters that the role of minority elders in the United States is somewhat different from that of White Americans. Holmes and Holmes (1995) suggested that social class and socioeconomic differences make it very difficult to draw conclusions about aging in different race and ethnic groups. They do offer some generalities for a few ethnic groups in United States, based on a review of the literature. Studies suggest that African Americans tend to remain very close to their families, are more respected, and are better treated than their White counterparts. It is difficult to draw many conclusions regarding Native Americans since there is great variety among the 307 officially recorded political entities (tribes, clans, nations). There is a range of attitudes toward the elderly from that of respected elder to worthless and someone who should be abandoned by the young. Across all groups, however, for those American Indians who hold to traditional culture, respect for family leads to positive attitudes toward elders. Mexican Americans have a very strong filial (family) obligation and thus tend to view their older family members positively. Old age in Mexican American families comes with increased status. Finally, Holmes and Holmes suggest that Asian Americans hold tightly to traditional respect for family and hold their elders in high esteem. What is your family background? Can you identify traditions in your family that give guidance to the treatment of elder members?

Are elders viewed differently in other cultures around the world? Sokolovsky (1997) summarizes the results of several anthropological cross-cultural studies by saying that attitudes toward elderly persons varies tremendously both within and across cultures. This fact makes it very difficult to draw generalizations or discuss the variety in a short space. Furthermore, as fast as a culture is studied, changes in the society and around the world make the data obsolete. Given those caveats, what can we say about images of aging in other places? In many cultures, aging carries high status and prestige and is associated with great respect. This seems to be the case in Japan, China, and many Eastern countries, as well as in Africa, as seen in the !Kung of Botswana and Hausa of Nigeria. Leaf (1975) reports that older Russians hold a central privileged position in society. In several Russian rural states the government is made up strictly of a council of elders. In Samoa, according to Holmes and Holmes (1995) old age is a prerequisite for family and political leadership. Elders in other countries do not fare as well. For example, elderly in Hong Kong experience very low status (Keith, Fry, Glascock, Ikels, Dickerson-Putnam, Harpending, & Draper, 1994), and frail elders in Polynesia are considered decrepit and ghost-like and, therefore, are neglected and left to die (Barker, 1997). Sokolovsky reports that the Siriono people in East Bolivia and the Chippewyan Indians in northern Canada view the elderly in very low favor.

As you can see, attitudes toward the elderly, worldwide, are mixed, at best. Although there seem to be groups in which increased status, respect, and prestige are the norm for older members, there are still others for which aging has a negative connotation, much as we see here in the United States. Can we hope for better days ahead in the view of older people? Even today, not all views are negative. Our own data (Foos and Clark, 1994), briefly described in Box 1-2, mirrored some others in finding positive images of aging. These include characterizing older people as wise, kind, nurturing, and caring. Older people tend to see themselves much more positively and often report old age as being as happy as any other stage in their life (AARP, 1995). The report concludes that personal knowledge and experience with aging are the most important predictors of how we view old age. Haught, Walls, Laney, Leavell, and Stuzen (1999) conducted a series of studies with elementary, middle, and high school students looking at knowledge and stereotypes about older adults. They concluded that both positive and negative stereotypes were held by all but that more positive stereotypes were seen in adolescents and more negative bias in younger children. Why would young children have more negative views? Perhaps the negative images of aging that abound are taken in and transformed into negative attitudes and, without the benefit of education about the reality of aging, children form less positive views of older persons. If this is so, then the remedy is easy to see. We need to reduce the negative images of aging in society and examine ways to improve attitudes. The AARP report suggests that more contact with the elderly improves attitudes while others say education about aging is important. There is empirical evidence that both are important. For example, Schwartz and Simmons (2001) found that the type of contact was even more important than the frequency of contact. People who had positive interactions with older persons had significantly better views of aging than did those whose contact was only with very sick or cognitively impaired elders. Think about your contact with older people and how it has influenced your views of aging. The questions in Box 1-2 can help you think through this issue.

Education is another route to improving attitudes, particularly for those with no or little regular contact with older persons or for those with lower quality contact. Studies have shown that education is the key to reducing all types of bias and to improving factual knowledge about a topic. As the population ages, and more students enroll in classes on human aging, more accurate knowledge of aging should translate into better images of aging, in general, and more positive anticipation of our own aging. Accurate knowledge comes from research in gerontology.

Making Choices

Each chapter in this text ends with a section on Making Choices. We present options that you could choose that could make a difference in your old age. We cannot, of course, guarantee that if you make these choices you will live longer, healthier, or happier. We strongly believe that you do increase the probability of a longer, healthier, and happier life by making such choices but there are no guarantees.

The first choice is to continue in this course and with this book. You could head for the Registrar's Office right now and drop this course and add a course in Nuclear Physics with Calculus or one in Basket Weaving. We hope you will stay with us and we believe that if you do you will gain considerable knowledge about human aging and that the knowledge you gain will be of some importance to you as you work with aging parents and grandparents, with aging clients and customers, and as you yourself become older. It's your choice.

CHAPTER HIGHLIGHTS

- There are three reasons to study human aging:
  - We value knowledge and want to learn more.
  - The things you learn may help you to age successfully.
  - The area of aging is becoming more important with each passing year.
- The number and proportion of older adults in the population is and will continue to increase in the future. By 2030, there will be approximately 85 million older adults, or 1 out of every 4 people will be over the age of 65. This has been called the graying of the population.
- A number of factors underlie the growth in the older population including: the graying of the baby boom generation, lower birth rates, and increases in life expectancy.
- Lifespan is the maximum number of years that an organism in a species can live. There are great differences in lifespan among species. Lifespan has changed very little over time. The lifespan of humans is currently believed to be 122 years of age.
- Life expectancy at birth (LEAB) is how long an individual is expected to live, on the average. It is calculated as the point at which 50 percent of the people born in any given year are dead. Life expectancy has increased dramatically over the years of human existence and continues to increase. Currently, life expectancy is about 75.4 years of age for someone born in 1993.
- Life expectancy at a specific age (LEASA) is how much longer a person is expected to live once they have reached a certain age. It is calculated like LEAB except that only those who have made it to the specific age are included.

- Increases in LEAB and LEASA contribute to more people reaching old age than ever before, and to more people reaching advanced old age; people age 85 years and over make up the fastest growing segment of the population.
- The study of aging is called gerontology; the health care field focusing on older people is called geriatrics.
- Research in aging is driven by a number of developmental issues and theories; issues are often framed as controversies and those most frequently discussed include: nature–nurture, mechanistic–organismic development, continuity–discontinuity, and stability–change.
- The lifespan model of development is a guiding perspective in gerontology and considers multiple contexts, multiple disciplines, historical and cultural contexts, plasticity, and gain and losses in life-long development.
- The two methods most frequently used in gerontological research are correlational and quasi-experimental including: cross-sectional, longitudinal, and sequential designs.
- The cross-sectional method tests age differences in people of different ages; a major drawback is that results from these studies confound age differences with differences due to age cohort, or the effects of being born at different times.
- The longitudinal method tests age differences by examining the same people at two or more different times in their lives; a major drawback is that results from studies using this design confound age differences with differences due to time of measurement.
- Sequential research designs are ways of combining cross-sectional and longitudinal approaches so that the effects of age, time of measurement, and age cohort can be separated.
- Aging refers to an individual passing through time and all that occurs during that passing of time; old age is considered by most scientists to begin at 60 or 65, however, this is just a convenient reference point; there is no one point at which old age starts.
- Researchers often divide the older segment of the population into three or four subcategories: 65 to 74 years are the young-old, 75 to 84 years are the middle-old, 85 and over have been considered the old-old, and, recently, 95 years and over are the very-old.
- Society holds many stereotypical views of older persons, some positive, some neutral, and many negative.
- Quantitative analyses of electronic and print media have found that elderly people, especially older women, are greatly underrepresented relative to their numbers in the population.
- Qualitative analyses have found that older adults are often portrayed negatively, for example, foolish, eccentric, and mentally impaired.
- Negative stereotypes can lead to ageism, prejudice, and discrimination against older people.
- Negative portrayals of the elderly often results in negative attitudes toward aging and the aged; research supports the existence of significant negative attitudes.
- Not all cultures, within the United States or across the world, hold negative views of aging; in some cultures, increased age is a sign of status and prestige, in other cultures, negative views abound.
- Research suggests that improving portrayals of older people, increasing positive experiences younger people have with older people, and education about aging can all reduce negative attitudes toward aging and the elderly.

STUDY QUESTIONS

1. What change(s) in population can we expect over the next several decades?

2. What three reasons were given for the population changes that are occurring now and will continue to occur for the next several decades?

3. Name several areas of society that have been impacted by the baby boom generation. Name several areas that will be impacted by an aging baby boom generation.

4. To what do the terms lifespan and life expectancy refer?

5. What is the difference between life expectancy at birth and life expectancy at a specified age? Which is longer? Why?

6. Define and describe the major theoretical issues that pervade research in developmental psychology. Think of examples to describe each issue and how it might be approached in research.

7. What are the advantages and disadvantages of cross-sectional and longitudinal designs in revealing age differences?

8. What are age cohort differences and why are they important in aging research?

9. Explain the advantages and disadvantages of sequential designs. Give an example of a question that might be best addressed with a sequential design.

10. What are some common stereotypes about the elderly? How do print and electronic media contribute to our stereotypes about aging?

11. Explain the cultural differences in attitudes toward aging.

RECOMMENDED READINGS

King, S. (1994). *Insomnia.* New York: Viking Press. In this book, the hero and heroine are a pair of older adults. This is a positive view of older adults who are the heroes in this major work of fiction.

Martz, S. (1987). *When I Am an Old Woman I Shall Wear Purple.* Watsonville, CA: Papier-Mache Press. This book and two other books edited by the same author, *If I Had My Life to Live Over I Would Pick More Daisies* (1992) and *Grow Old Along With Me the Best is Yet to Be* (1996), are compilations of wonderful short stories and poems written by and about older adults.

Palmore, E. B. (1999). *Ageism: Negative and Positive* (2nd Ed.). New York: Springer Publishing. An excellent resource on the topic of ageism and attitudes toward aging. The book includes a review of findings in this area and addresses ways that people have attempted to reduce ageism. The book includes the Facts on Aging Quizzes, examples of ageist humor, and an annotated bibliography on ageism.

INTERNET RESOURCES

The American Society on Aging focuses on practical applications in gerontology and has excellent information for service providers, researchers, and educators. The address is <*http://www.asaging.edu*>.

A number of sections on aging are available through individual professional organizations such as the American Sociological Society and the American Anthropological Society. Division 20 of the American Psychological Association deals with adult development and aging and also maintains a web site with useful information and links to other sites, at *http://www.iog.wayne.edu/APADIV20.*

http://www.msstate.edu/org/gerontology/index.html Facts on Aging Quizzes (1999). See how much you know about aging.

http://www.geron.org The Gerontological Society of America. This site has information on the study of aging, the society, news releases about aging, fact sheets, interest groups in gerontology, and links to other sites.

http://www.asaging.edu American Society on Aging. This site has information for service providers, researchers, and educators.

http://aging.ufl.edu/apadiv20/apadiv20.htm This site has information on the adult development of aging.

Aging and Our Bodies

2

Physical Aspects of Aging: Changes in Our Bodies

Youth is the gift of nature, but age is a work of art.

—*Garson Kanin*

In this chapter we examine the changes that can occur in our bodies with advanced age. Changes are what contribute to the work of art that is the older person. We look at older adults as one might look at an ancient cathedral, a painting completed long ago, or a sculpture carved in times gone by. Such works of art have weathered many storms and so have most older adults. The passage of time, called aging, leaves its mark on our bodies and that mark varies from person to person. We all know of people who are said to be "old before their time" and others who are "young for their age." The former comment is usually spoken with some negative connotation as if getting old was a bad thing that happened to that person far too soon. The latter comment is usually spoken with some positive connotation as if being young (especially for someone who is old) is always a good thing. In this chapter we try to avoid such connotations as we examine the physical changes that typically, but not always, occur with advanced age.

Individual Differences

Many people who are past the age of 65 look as if they're still in their 40s or 50s while many others look much older. Part of this difference is due to our inability to judge a person's age by how they look. We are simply not very good at making such judgments. People of any age, except, perhaps, very young babies, can look very different from other people who are the same chronological age. Take a look at the photographs shown here and see if you can judge the age of each person. Who do you think is the oldest? Who is the youngest? How old are these people? To find out how accurate you were, look for the answers at the end of this chapter.

One reason why it can be difficult to judge another's age, and that people of the same age can look so different, is because the storms that people weather over the course of their lives can be quite different. An individual who has had a relatively easy, stress-free life with very little hard physical labor, the best doctors, excellent nutrition, and good exercise is bound to look different than an individual who has had trying times, worked hard in the fields most of their lives, experienced lots of stress and danger, has poor health, and poor

Senior View

We spoke with Clifford and Lucia Pauling about the physical changes that have occurred in their bodies as they've grown older. Clifford was 75 years old and a retired custodian and Lucia was 69 years old and retired from the nursing center when we spoke. When Clifford retired he was awarded a plaque for outstanding service with the school board. Clifford and Lucia have been married for 35 years and have seven children.

Lucia told us that when she was in her late 40s, she experienced kidney failure and has been on dialysis for over 20 years. Clifford found out about Lucia's illness from her mother because Lucia is the "type of person who won't ever complain" about things. Clifford learned how to help Lucia do the dialysis at home. It hasn't restricted her ability to travel and that is important for her. Kidney failure is not a typical physical change that occurs in old age.

We asked Lucia if she had experienced any other physical changes and she told us that she gained a little weight, had high blood pressure, and had her thyroid gland removed. She told us that "things change slow, even physical things." The only other times she has been in the hospital was to have children.

Clifford said that he had no physical problems until he was 70, when he was told that he had "a touch of colon cancer, but it wasn't bad." Doctors performed surgery and seem to have removed the cancer. He goes for regular checkups.

We also spoke with Lori Fincher about physical changes. Lori was 76 years old when we spoke with her. She is a retired nurse who is a widow. She said that her health was pretty fair except for three chronic problems, asthma, chronic kidney disease, and osteoporosis. She also said, "I've lost four inches; that's the important one." We were surprised to find another adult who had experienced kidney failure because it is not a typical physical change for older adults.

Lori said that she has to be careful not to overexert herself, watch her diet, and not lift heavy objects. However, she said, "I frequently forget how old I am and get a little carried away in my activities." Over the last five years, she has not noticed any new physical changes.

We asked Lori if she would like to tell younger adults anything about the effects of the chronic conditions that she lives with every day. "Physical changes make you more determined to maintain your independence; physical changes are a threat to independence and once you lose your independence, you feel old," she said.

Does she feel old? "I'm just going to keep going until I can't go anymore and I don't want

someone overtreating or overmedicating me," she said.

We liked the spirit of the Paulings and Lori Fincher. Physical changes depend a lot on mental attitude and social support. The mental attitude of these seniors and the support they offer each other are major factors in their success at dealing with the physical changes they have experienced.

---

nutrition. It is not the passing of time per se that causes these changes, it is the events and experiences that occur over time and how they are dealt with, that are responsible. Furthermore, the influence of some of these environmental factors can depend on when they occur and whether they occur with other factors or by themselves. Loss of parents can be far more devastating for a young person than for an older person. Loss of parents along with loss of home can be even more devastating. Some people cope with stressful events and experiences much better than other people and are in a sense, "weatherproof." Others do not deal with stress as easily and are more likely to be battered by each stormy event. People look different in part because of the things that they have been through, when those things occurred, and their constitutional ability to deal with their experiences. The results of life's storms depend to some extent upon the psychology of the individual who experiences them and the social support that assists them.

Another reason why it is difficult to judge age is because the very same individual can show a lot of change in some ways and hardly any in other ways. One's heart and lungs may be as strong as those of a much younger person while one's digestive system has declined to a very low level and can handle only very bland foods. One's muscles may be weak and one's bones fragile while one's mind is sharp and quick. Different organs, tissues, systems, and bodily functions seem to age at very different rates. Many researchers refer to these differences by using the term **biological age(ing)**. Biological aging refers to the physical, chemical, and biological changes that occur in vital organ systems, tissues, and physical appearance over time. Systems that are biologically old have changed quite a lot as the person has gotten older. Systems that are young are those that have changed very little. It is the type of change, rather than the passage of time, which defines biological aging. Some systems within the same individual will be biologically older or younger than others.

Biological aging may increase the vulnerability of those bodily systems making them more prone to accidents, disease, and longer recovery times. The decline in bodily systems and the resulting increased vulnerability is referred to as **senescence**. Most organisms show senescence when in captivity but rarely in the wild. In the wild, organisms with advanced biological aging in some bodily system(s) are more vulnerable and are, thus, likely to fall prey to some predator. They do not live long enough to show senescence. Only among human populations and captive animals do we find (nearly) universal senescence.

It is very important to keep in mind that different physical components of our bodies change at different rates. While one's chronological age is the same for all bodily organs, since they were all formed at the same time, one's biological age may be different for different physical components. Some components show more change than others and are, as a result, biologically older. These biologically older components are likely to show

Who is oldest? Who is youngest?

more senescence, or vulnerability, than components that are biologically younger. An individual is also unlikely to show the same vulnerability for all biological components. On the other hand, an individual is quite likely to show varying amounts of senescence for different biological components. All components have grown older and are, thus, subject to biological aging and the influence of numerous external factors (Miller, 1999). We now examine these components and the biologic aging and senescence that frequently occurs.

Changes in Physical Appearance

Skin

As one ages, wrinkles appear in the skin. In fact, wrinkles appear fairly early in life and by age 30 most adults show lines in the forehead. Between 30 to 50 years of age, additional lines on the face appear. For example, "crow's feet" may appear around the eyes and the lines linking the nostrils to the side of the mouth may become more prominent. One may develop a furrowed brow as wrinkles on the forehead become more pronounced. Beyond age 50, wrinkling continues and becomes more extensive with each passing decade.

Mark Twain said, "Wrinkles should merely indicate where smiles have been." This is a nice thought but in fact, wrinkling occurs because of stiffening and a decrease in the underlying connective tissue whether you smile or frown. The connective tissues, composed of a protein called collagen, underlie the skin, surround all bodily organs, and cover the walls of blood vessels. Connective tissue and elastin fibers, which maintain normal tension in the skin, become less flexible, more rigid, and also decrease in amount after age 30. The sweat glands are also likely to show diminished function leading to less moisture in and under the skin. Wrinkles in the skin are less likely to disappear when the skin is less flexible because of the more rigid underlying elastin fibers and less moisture. Thus, wrinkles increase with advanced age (DiGiovanna, 1994).

Skin also shows the effects of a lifetime of exposure to the sun as one grows older. Skin exposed to the sun becomes stiffer and loses elasticity like leather. Skin cancers increase in frequency with age and much of this is due to extended exposure to the sun. Individuals who experience severe sunburns when they are young are far more likely to experience skin cancer as they grow older. Take this seriously and protect your skin. The outside layer of the skin, the epidermis, becomes flattened and new cells are less organized than old cells. One can see this loss of organization in the changes in geometric furrows visible on the skin's surface. Compare your skin with that of your parents and grandparents and see if you can notice the differences in epidermal organization. Subcutaneous fat, which provides the smooth padding and curves of youth, decreases on limbs in old age and collects in deposits at the waist and hips (Whitbourne, 1996).

The production of sweat glands and of skin oil, called sebum, declines after menopause for women, and females are strongly encouraged to use lotions and protective creams at that point in their lives. For males, the production of sebum remains relatively stable although moisturizing lotions are still recommended.

The coloring of light-skinned people alters due to changes in melanocyte, the pigment containing cells in epidermis. The total number of such cells declines and the ones remaining contain fewer pigment granules. Irregular dark spots, called age or liver spots, appear on the skin as do dark moles and angiomas. Angiomas are small blood vessels elevated to the surface of the skin. Capillaries and small arteries often dilate and look like small, irregular colored lines on the skin. In other cases, capillaries may be lost causing individuals to look pale.

The result of all these varied changes in the skin may be a negative effect on protective functions. With advanced age there may be a limit in temperature adaptation with less perspiration in the heat and less conservation of heat in the cold. The recovery from surface wounds may be impaired and cuts and burns may take longer to heal (Whitbourne, 1996). Biological aging of the skin can result in senescence.

Hair

As one grows older, hair turns gray due to the loss of pigment. Most adults experience the beginning of graying in their early 40s. The loss of pigment appears to have a strong genetic component, and men and women whose parents or grandparents turned gray are likely to do the same (DiGiovanna, 1994).

Pattern baldness or hair loss is also very likely. For men, baldness typically begins at the temples and proceeds to a circle in the top and back of the head. Hair loss then proceeds until the entire top of the head is bald. Baldness is largely hereditary and, like graying, can be predicted with a reasonably high level of accuracy by looking at the father, uncles, and grandfathers of a given individual. A study conducted on 1553 men with thinning hair has shown that baldness may be prevented by taking a drug called finasteride, which has been approved by the Food and Drug Administration. The drug prevents further hair loss in most men. Baldness also affects about 75 percent of women but to a much lesser extent. In women, hair tends to thin all over the scalp rather than proceeding from one starting point (Kligman, Grove, & Balin, 1985). Finasteride is not recommended for women of childbearing age because it can cause birth defects.

For males, hair loss on the top of the head is only half the picture. Males are very likely to find hair growing in and around their ears, out of their nostrils, and all over their backs. Also, the eyebrows become courser and longer. Some women, particularly those of Mediterranean or Middle Eastern origin, may grow long, dark, and thick hair over their lips and on their chins. Some also develop hair around the nipples and in the middle of the chest or abdomen (Lorber & Lagana, 1997).

Height and Weight

Height and weight also change with age, although there is some debate about the latter. Of course, there are enormous individual differences in height and weight as you can tell simply by looking around. Nevertheless, older adults typically lose height and weight, occurring at a greater rate after the 50s, and this is truer for women than for men.

On average, males lose about 1.25 inches in height between the ages of 30 and 70 while females lose about 2 inches. The greater loss for females is, in part, due to the greater incidence of bone loss in females. Functional height, which measures how high one can reach, also decreases with advanced age. You can estimate your own functional height by standing and reaching high on the wall with a marker. Make a mark at your reach level and then measure the difference between that level and your height. That difference is your functional height. The lower the number the lower your functional height. For older adults, functional height can be as low as seven inches due to changes in muscles and bones.

The typical pattern of weight change is one of gain followed by loss. From young adulthood to middle-age, weight typically increases due to changes in metabolic rate and lifestyle. Basal metabolism slows down 3 percent every ten years. At the same time, middle-age adults may continue to eat the same amount of food that they did when they were younger. With the slow down in metabolism, less food is converted to energy and is, instead, accumulated resulting in weight gain. Also, many middle-age adults are not as physically active as when they were younger. Together these factors typically result in weight gain for middle-age adults. For most individuals, weight levels off and then declines from middle-adulthood to old age. Older adults typically eat less than middle-age adults and the senescence in tissues and muscles results in weight loss, as muscle tissue is more dense and, thus, weighs more than fat (DiGiovanna, 1994).

Although this weight gain/loss pattern is thought to be typical, most evidence comes from cross-sectional comparisons and any differences could be cohort differences rather than real age differences. High fat and carbohydrate diets used to be much more the norm than they are now, so older cohorts may have eaten very differently than more recent cohorts. Recent cohorts have developed different, healthier, eating habits. At the same time, there are more overweight Americans now than at any other time. If changes in weight are a cohort, rather than age difference, what do you expect to find when people in your cohort become old? What do you expect if it really is an age difference? At present it is not clear whether the obtained patterns of weight change are due to age or cohort or both effects (Whitbourne, 1996).

Voice

Voice lowers in pitch with age. Pitch can decrease by two or three notes on the musical scale. Loss of muscle control over the vocal cords may also produce a quaver in the voice.

Facial Appearance

Changes in facial appearance are the easiest to see. After all, the face is the most exposed area of skin. There are exceptions in certain cultures. Muslim women, for example, cover much of the face. Facial muscles are always being used for eating, talking, and facial expressions. Skin on the face is, thus, more likely to show biological aging than skin on any other body part.

The accumulation of cartilage also shows on the face and head. This accumulation makes the nose grow ½-inch wider and ½-inch longer, on average, by age 70. Earlobes become fatter and the ears grow ¼-inch longer.

The head increases in circumference and has been increasing since birth. The circumference of the skull increases by ¼ inch every ten years as the skull thickens. At 20 years old, the skull is about ½-inch bigger in circumference than it was at birth. By 80, it will be about 1½-inches bigger than it is now or 2 inches bigger than it was at birth.

Changes in skin, hair, and cartilage can be easy to hide and many adults attempt to do just that by using make-up, hair color, and even plastic surgery.

Do you think that these external changes make people look old? Do you think that old people are not attractive? Do you think the Mona Lisa looked better on the day it was painted than it does now? Do you think our perceptions of what is and is not attractive change as we grow older? Taken together, changes in external appearance can create some very impressive/beautiful works of art. Think of the appearances of Bill Cosby, Sophia Loren, Paul Newman, Robert Redford, or Jessica Tandy. Like younger adults, older adults can be quite beautiful.

Internal Changes

Muscles

Muscles decline in strength, tone, and flexibility as one grows older. Muscle fiber is often replaced by connective tissue, which tends to become stiff. As a result, injured muscles are slower to heal for older adults.

Overall muscle strength begins to decline between the ages of 40 and 50 and can decline by as much as 10 to 20 percent by age 70. More severe loss occurs as one grows older. Muscle decline is most pronounced in the lower extremities (McArdle, Katch, & Katch, 1991). Grip strength and muscle flexibility also decline (Kozma, Stones, & Hannah, 1991). Figure 2-1 shows the average changes for grip strength across different adult ages. The

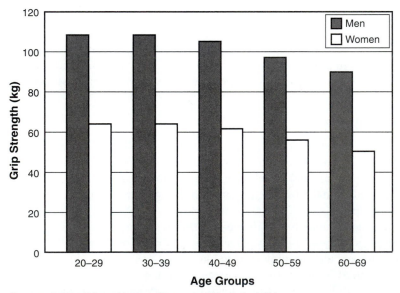

Source: Adapted from Kozma, Stone, and Hannah, 1991.

FIGURE 2-1   Average Grip Strength as a Function of Age.

muscle groups used for grip are referred to as "fast twitch" muscle fibers and are associated with rapidly accelerating, powerful contractions. These fibers atrophy and are first replaced by connective tissue and later by fat. Although nothing, at present, can be done to stop the loss of muscle fiber, the remaining fibers can be strengthened and made more efficient for individuals at any age through techniques such as resistance training. This is a case where biological aging need not lead to senescence. Whether it does depends to some extent on the individual.

Eccentric strength, involving the muscles used in lowering arm weights, slowing down while walking, or going down a flight of stairs remains stable until age 70 to 80 (Hortobágyi, Zheng, Weidner, Lambert, Westbrook, & Houmard, 1995). These muscle groups are referred to as "slow twitch" muscle fibers and are associated with maintaining posture and muscle contractions over long periods of time. These fibers remain relatively constant with age.

A recent study examined the relationship between grip strength, weight, and mortality in a sample of 6000 healthy men over a 30-year period. Men with the lowest grip strength in middle-age had the highest probability of dying earlier, independent of how much they weighed, while those with the highest grip strength had the lowest probability of dying. The researchers strongly recommend increasing muscle strength by exercising because such increased strength "may provide greater physiologic and functional reserve that protects against mortality" (Rantanen, Harris, Leveille, Visser, Foley, Masaki, & Guralnik, 2000, p. M168).

Skeletal System

The skeletal system is composed of the bones and cartilage of the body. As you learned previously, cartilage continues to increase with age and, as a result, the nose and ears grow with each passing year. The circumference of the skull also increases but the rest of the bones in the body tend to show the opposite effect.

Bone represents the deposit of calcium phosphate and calcium carbonate by cells called **osteoblasts** (think of builders, osteoblasts are bone builders). These cells take calcium from the nutrients in the blood and build bone. Thus, strong bones depend on a diet with sufficient calcium. To keep bone growth and replacement in balance, another set of cells, called **osteoclasts**, resorb bone. Resorption refers to the process of dissolving and assimilating bone tissue. When we are young and growing, the action of osteoblasts is greater and bones get bigger. During adulthood, osteoblasts and osteoclasts work in balance to maintain a strong, healthy skeletal system. As we grow older, however, the action of osteoclasts is greater, as a result the resorption of bone increases and we lose bone. Bone density decreases. This is one reason for the loss of height that we discussed earlier. Old bones become weaker and withstand pressure less well. Since more bone is being resorbed by osteoclasts than is built up by osteoblasts, older adults are frequently advised to increase their intake of calcium to 1200 to 1500 mg from the recommended daily allowance of 800 mg (Hermann, 1998).

The loss of bone has been attributed to three main factors: genetic, hormonal, and lifestyle. Together, genetic and hormonal factors account for close to 40 percent of bone loss. Individuals whose parents experienced significant bone loss are likely to have the same experience when they grow old. The hormonal changes that occur following menopause result in significant bone loss in many females. The third factor, lifestyle, accounts for close to 60 percent of bone loss. Lifestyle refers to a number of variables such as one's diet, physical activity, the amount of alcohol consumed, and whether or not one smokes. These are major determiners of bone loss during old age. The consumption of meat in greater abundance than vegetable proteins contributes to bone loss and the consumption of more vegetable products may help protect bone density as we grow older (Frasetto, Todd, Morris, & Sebastian, 2000). The lack of physical activity and stress on bones result in the loss of large amounts of bone material. Astronauts lose bone mass during weightlessness, when there is no physical stress placed on the bones. Prolonged bed rest also results in bone loss. Physical activity, such as resistance training, is an excellent way of maintaining bone mass (Whitbourne, 1996). Consuming large amounts of alcohol and/or smoking also contribute to the loss of bone density.

Hip fractures due to falls are one outcome of the loss of bone density, in addition to changes in muscles and sensory losses. A quarter of a million people are hospitalized each year with fractured hips and 30 to 40 percent of these individuals are older, independent-living adults. Individuals who experience a hip fracture are more likely to suffer long-term disability and dependency. Some loss of bone mass in the hips can be prevented by regular exercise. One recent study found that women who exercised with weighted vests, jumping three times a week for 32 weeks out of a year for five years, gained bone density compared to women who did not exercise (Snow, Shaw, Winters, & Witzke, 2000).

In extreme cases, the resorption of bone by osteoclasts is so great that bones thin and become fragile and brittle resulting in a disorder known as **osteoporosis**. Osteoporosis is particularly prevalent in postmenopausal, White and Asian American women. About 90 percent of older adults with osteoporosis are women and most of them are White (Gambrell, 1987). This difference between men and women is largely due to the relatively rapid lowering of estrogen levels in postmenopausal women (DiGiovanna, 1994). The treatments for osteoporosis have been calcium (in the form of calcitonin) and estrogen but both have had some problems. Calcinate, for example, is most effective when given as an injection however, this has prevented the easy dissemination of the drug. Estrogen has been associated with increased rates of uterine and breast cancer and, for that reason, has been avoided by many women who might otherwise benefit from such treatment. Recent work, however, suggests that estriol, a form of estrogen, may be effective in increasing bone density without the dangers associated with traditional estrogen replacement therapy. In a study, 24 women who were over the age of 75 showed a 3.5 percent increase in bone density after 30 weeks of treatment (Hayashi, Ito, Kano, Endo, & Iguchi, 2000). Further work is needed to be sure that estriol reliably produces these effects. A new drug, **alendronate**, is also available and has been approved by the FDA. Alendronate inhibits bone resorption and, thus, helps restore the balance between osteoblasts and osteoclasts. In two large studies, that included over 900 women, the alendronate increased bone density by 8.16 percent over a three-year period (*Laboratory Medicine*, 1996).

Ligaments and tendons, which are composed of collagen, hold bone but may become stiff and rigid, and even painful, after age 50. Ligaments and tendons enable smooth functioning of the body's joints.

Cardiovascular System

The cardiovascular system can be broken down into a number of different components, some of which show senescence and some of which do not. Since heart disease is the number one cause of death in the United States we will examine the system in detail.

Blood Pressure.   Blood pressure signifies the structural health and functioning of the entire cardiovascular system. Blood pressure is signified by two numbers called systolic and diastolic pressure. Thus, a blood pressure of 120 over 80 means that the systolic pressure is 120 and the diastolic is 80. Systolic pressure occurs when the heart contracts pushing blood into the arteries and diastolic pressure is when the ventricle refills with blood from the veins. Elevations in blood pressure are clear warning signals and should be dealt with by a physician.

As one ages, systolic pressure typically shows moderate increases while diastolic pressure tends to remain stable. As you can see from Table 2-1, these changes are about the same for men and women. There is some disagreement about the reported changes in systolic pressure, with many researchers finding no change (Ordway & Wekstein, 1979) or no change when physiological status and fitness are controlled (Gardner & Poehlman, 1995). Perhaps the obtained differences are due to an inclusion of individuals with hypertension and/or cardiovascular disorder in larger numbers in older samples. At present, it is not clear why systolic differences are frequently found but it is possible that these too are cohort differences. Older cohorts may have ingested more fatty foods than more recent cohorts.

The Heart.   The heart, like other muscles, shows some deterioration with advanced age and pumps less blood. One reason less blood is being pumped is the changes that can occur in veins and arteries. As one grows older, the heart gets bigger, literally. Some think that this is a built-in compensation for the muscle loss that occurs with aging but the increase in size is mostly in the left ventricle due to a thickening of the walls.

TABLE 2-1   Changes in Blood Pressure with Age

Age Range	Females		Males	
	Systolic	Diastolic	Systolic	Diastolic
25–34	117	75	126	81
35–44	124	80	128	85
45–54	133	84	135	88
55–64	144	87	140	87
65–74	153	86	147	85

Source: National Center for Health Statistics, U.S. Public Health Service, Washington, DC, 1976.

Blood Vessels.   Blood vessels can show a lot of senescence. Both veins and arteries are prone to calcification and the accumulation of fatty materials and cholesterol. These changes result in slower and less efficient contraction of the heart and reduced and delayed filling. Less blood is sent to the body. Calcification is particularly common at the aortic valve leading from the heart, and the diameter of the aorta increases with advanced age becoming less flexible and less able to push blood into the arteries. Cardiac output decreases linearly throughout adulthood dropping to 30 to 40 percent by age 65.

The clogging of blood vessels with fat and cholesterol, a condition called **atherosclerosis**, means the heart must work harder to pump the same amount of blood. Atherosclerosis is a type of arteriosclerosis, which is the name for a thickening and hardening of arterial walls. In atherosclerosis this thickening is the result of accumulated fat and cholesterol. Oxygen consumption at rest and during exercise is diminished when the vessels are clogged and this clogging begins as early as age 20. The clogging of blood vessels is one of the most harmful physical changes that occur with aging.

Blood.   Blood is composed of plasma, red and white blood cells, and platelets. Plasma is the fluid that carries cells and platelets. Red blood cells or hemoglobin carry oxygen from the lungs to all the tissues in the body. The amount of hemoglobin does not decline with age for nonsmokers. White blood cells, which are part of the immune system, show no change in number with aging. Platelets are the clotting agents in blood and, like the cells, show no change with age. Blood clotting times are not influenced by an individual's age. Blood remains healthy while the path it travels may deteriorate and become blocked.

Exercise is the primary means of enhancing the cardiovascular system. Aerobic exercise increases heart muscle strength, lowers average heart rate, and helps to counteract the negative effects of cholesterol. We discuss exercise in Chapter 4.

Respiratory System

Several changes which affect the intake of oxygen through the lungs take place with aging. The muscles that operate the lungs, like other muscles in the body, weaken and some muscle tissue may be replaced by stiffening connective tissue. The connective tissue that surrounds the lungs also stiffens reducing the ability of the lungs to fully expand. Maximum lung capacity is typically reached between the ages of 20 and 25 and then shows progressive decline. Table 2-2 shows average maximum intake of quarts of air for different age groups. Beginning at age 40, the average decrease in input is close to 1 percent per year (Lakatta, 1990).

Within the lungs, other changes occur. At birth, the lungs contain about 24 million alveoli or air sacs. This number increases to about 300 million by age eight and then remains constant throughout young adulthood. By age 40, however, the ducts which carry oxygen from the sacs to the blood vessels, and which have also been increasing since birth, begin to crowd out the air sacs which they serve. These changes decrease the surface area in the lungs that is available for the exchange of gases. At age 50, the air sacs, like connective tissue, lose elasticity and become more rigid and flatter. Gravitational pull on the lower, larger part of the lungs, where more blood flows, also results in less oxygenated blood. The air brought in is not sufficient to fill the lungs and, thus, the lower blood-rich

TABLE 2-2   Approximate Average Intake of Air for Adults of Different Ages

Age	Quarts of Air Inhaled
20	🝰🝰🝰🝰🝰🝰🝰
30	🝰🝰🝰🝰🝰🝰
40	🝰🝰🝰🝰🝰
50	🝰🝰🝰🝰
60	🝰🝰🝰
70	🝰🝰🝰
80	🝰🝰🝰

lungs receive less air. Respiration becomes progressively more difficult beginning at about the age of 40 (DiGiovanna, 1994).

The changes that are typical in the muscles, cardiovascular, skeletal, and respiratory systems frequently produce a shortage of **stamina** in the older adult. It may take longer to catch one's breath and for a racing heart to slow down after some strenuous physical activity, or even after climbing a flight of stairs. The muscles are stiffer, the lungs cannot take in as much oxygen, bones may be fragile, and the heart may have to work extra hard to push blood through partially clogged arteries. Much of this, of course, depends on how frequently an individual exercises. Remember, however, that not all changes happen to all people at the same time. For some real-life examples of older adults with very little loss of stamina read about Dorothy Cheney, Jim Eriotes, Norman Vaughan, Carol Johnston, and George Ezzard in Box 2-1 on page 44. Clearly, one can maintain very healthy muscular, cardiovascular, skeletal, and respiratory systems. One can maintain stamina.

Digestive System

Like the cardiovascular system, the digestive and elimination systems are composed of several components each of which may show senescence to a different degree. Overall, the capacity to digest and absorb food does not diminish with age.

The surface epithelium, or membrane of the **mouth**, shows some atrophy with advanced age and the underlying connective tissue may degenerate. The loss of bone, may result in the loss of teeth because the roots are no longer held in place. Teeth may become loose and move easily creating pockets for bacterial infection in the gums. Many older adults lose teeth and use dentures.

As one grows older, the lining of the **stomach** may atrophy. While this has very little effect on the overall digestion of most food, two important nutrients, which are absorbed in the stomach, may be affected. Vitamin B_{12} and iron are absorbed in the stomach and, if the stomach lining has deteriorated, less of these two important nutrients are obtained. Vitamin B_{12} is very important for normal cognitive functioning. Older

BOX **2-1**

Short on Stamina? I Don't Think So.

At age 80 Dorothy Cheney has won 279 National Tennis Championships and in 1997 won the Southern California Tennis Association Lifetime Achievement Award. She began playing when she was a child. Her mother, May Sutton Bundy, was her primary teacher. May won Wimbledon in 1905 and 1907, and Dorothy won the Australian Championship in 1938 and ranked among the top U.S. tennis players for ten years. She currently plays in the senior national championships four times a year. Opponents say she will win if they make the slightest misstep. Dorothy remembers female tennis champion Billy Jean King and played her when Billy Jean was ten or eleven. "After the match I gave her a little advice," she said. Billy Jean won many major tennis tournaments and the advice she got from Dorothy played some role in her success. Dorothy Cheney said she is not finished winning yet and expects to continue playing for a long time. Dorothy Cheney has a lot of stamina.

Jim Eriotes, at age 74, is the champion of the batting cages in Elmhurst, Illinois. In his younger years, Jim was a minor league outfielder. He decided in the late 1980s to begin batting again. In spite of glaucoma and being nearsighted, Jim hits balls thrown at Nolan Ryan speeds and once hit 20 of 30 pitches thrown at 110 mph. Running 100 yard sprints and weight-lifting keep him in shape. Also, he swings at 140 to 300 pitches a day. It doesn't matter whether the pitch is a fast ball, curve, slider, or change-up; he hits all of them. Jim said he told his wife that, "I plan to be hitting baseballs when I'm 80 or 90." Jim Eriotes has a lot of stamina.

Norman Vaughan was the chief dog sledder for Admiral Bryd's expedition to the Antarctic in 1928. He was the first American to drive a dog team in Antarctica. Byrd named a peak in the Queen Maud mountains for him and Vaughan has wanted to return and climb 10,302-foot Mount Vaughan ever since. In 1995 he reached the summit on December 16, 1995, just three days shy of his 89th birthday. Norman, with a fused ankle and a reconstructed knee, hauled 75 pounds of equipment, including a portable computer, up that slope. "I couldn't believe it was happening," he said. Norman Vaughan has a lot of stamina.

Carol Johnston of Walnut, California, is a champion pole vaulter. Carol is 85 years old, still vaulting, and the holder of the world record for his age group. That vault was 7 feet 6 inches. Carol Johnston has a lot of stamina.

George Ezzard of Salisbury, North Carolina, was named Mega Man of the Year by General Nutrition Centers. George swims 16 laps underwater everyday, plays ping pong, pool, and basketball. He hit 99 out of 100 free throws to celebrate his 84th birthday in 1997. George is interested in trying a few new sports. "I've got to find out something about golf," he said. George Ezzard has a lot of stamina.

Source: Modern Maturity magazine, Front Lines, 1997, *The Charlotte Observer*, Jan. 7, 1995.

adults with deterioration of the stomach lining are often advised to increase their intake of these nutrients because, even if they are taking the minimum daily requirement, they may not be absorbing that minimum.

The intestines particularly the **colon**, have decreased motor function and muscle tone, as do other muscles in the body. Peristalsis or contractive movement slows down.

Changes in the intestine also result in increased loss of water from the intestine. The loss of muscle tone and water results in frequent constipation for older adults.

Many older adults were brought up with the notion of the importance of "regularity," or at least one bowel movement per day. Any deviation was considered in need of correction. Most constipation, however, results from lack of fiber, recent stress, or sedentary periods. The natural frequency for defecation ranges from three times per day to once every three days. Someone who experiences a bowel movement once every third day is within the normal range and is probably not constipated. In fact, overuse of laxatives is a major cause of constipation (Minaker & Rowe, 1982).

The **liver**, which is responsible for the metabolism of drugs, hormones, and alcohol in the body, is not functionally impaired in older adults who are free from alcohol-related disease. There is a lot of redundancy in the liver so that even with major structural change function remains unaffected. The liver also has good regenerative capacity. Up to 80 percent of the liver can be removed without significantly affecting function (Schmucker, 1998; Whitbourne, 1996).

Gallbladder problems are more prevalent in older adults and are probably a result of life-long dietary patterns of fat intake rather than structural changes with age.

The **kidneys** decrease in weight and volume by 20 to 30 percent, mainly, in outer filtration units by the early 70s. The filtration rate declines by about 1 percent every year past the age of 40. The kidneys of older persons are, however, still able to meet the body's needs as long as they are not placed under extreme physiological stress. There are three conditions with which we should be concerned. First, renal blood flow is reduced during aerobic exercise as the blood is diverted to the skeletal muscles. Second, under conditions of intense heat, as well as during exercise, sodium and water can become depleted. Older adults must be careful when exercising and/or under conditions of hot temperatures. It is especially important for older adults who have not exercised, and who now are beginning to do so, to seek the guidance of a physician. Finally, the kidneys of an older adult are less efficient at transporting chemicals. When an older adult takes the same dosage of medicine as a younger adult, more of the drug remains behind in the bloodstream. Harmful levels can, thus, build up over time with repeated dosages. Drug dosage must be carefully monitored by and for older adults. (Whitbourne, 1996).

The **bladder** loses 50 percent of its capacity by age 65 and, like many other tissues in the body, becomes stiffer and less flexible. As a result of these changes, the bladder can no longer hold the volume of urine that it could in the past and can no longer completely empty itself. There is a higher volume of residual urine following each urination. These changes increase the frequency of urination. Older adults tend to urinate more often but less each time (DiGiovanna, 1994).

Reproductive System

Male and female differences in biological aging are most evident in the reproductive system since females experience a major change during **menopause**. Menopause refers to the cessation of menstruation and the accompanying changes in hormone levels. Throughout the 40s, there is a gradual decline in female reproductive ability ending with menopause, which is when menstruation ceases completely, around age 50 to 55. The process usually takes two to three years with irregular menses until complete cessation. Most women report little discomfort although some experience "hot flashes," characterized by feeling overheated, sweaty, and flushed. Estrogen levels drop dramatically and this relatively sudden drop is a factor in the development of osteoporosis. The physical changes that accompany menopause include a loss of skin elasticity, replacement of mammary tissue with fat leading to sagging breasts, and the appearance of facial hair. None of the changes directly affect sexual function but can affect the way a woman feels about her appearance. Some women may experience serious adjustment problems as a result of these changes (see Chapter 9).

Males do not experience any such dramatic change in such a short period of time. Sperm-producing tubules decline in function over a much longer period of time and the number of sperm gradually decline. Nevertheless, very old men can still father children. The oldest documented case is of a 94-year-old man fathering a child (Rockstein & Sussman, 1979). For most older men, sexual functioning is not affected by these changes, as they gradually adapt to and often enjoy the slower pace that accompanies these changes. Many older men do, of course, experience some sexual dysfunction but it is not due to declining levels of testosterone.

Many men experience a very noticeable change in the size and weight of the prostate gland as they grow older. The weight of the prostate can double by the time a man reaches his late 70s. Many men also contract prostate cancer as they age. Regular checkups after 50 are recommended.

Immune System

The body's defense against harmful invaders in the form of bacteria, germs, viruses, and toxins is called the immune system and consists of three major components. These components, when functioning correctly, recognize cells of the host body and do not attack them, are usually specific in attacking only one type of invader, and can develop memory cells in case an invader attacks again at a later date. These defensive cells are produced in bone marrow and then converted to specific types of defenders.

The first defense, consists of **T cells** which are converted in the thymus gland residing above the heart and behind the sternum. Each type of T cell is built to recognize the host body and one type of invader. It is estimated that there are as many as 100 million different types of T cells; one for each type of danger from cancer, bacteria, germs, and viruses. T cells are thought to be the primary defense against virus infection and cancer. The efficiency of T cells is influenced by a chemical called thyroxin produced by the thyroid glands on either side of the throat.

The second defense, consists of **B cells** which are converted at an unknown site. B cells manufacture and secrete antibodies and those antibodies attack the invader. B cells can attack at a distance since the antibodies they produce are carried through the blood stream. The action of B cells is influenced by T cells. B cells are thought to be the primary defense against bacterial infection and poisons.

The third type of defense cells are called **natural killer cells**. Unlike T and B cells, they are not specific to certain forms of intrusion but are stimulated by T cells. These cells function as hunters when danger is present.

Several changes in the immune system accompany aging. The thymus begins to shrink soon after puberty until close to age 50. At that point it may be only 5 percent of its original size. The hormones produced by the thymus cease by age 60. The production of new T cells does, however, continue and the migration of those new T cells to the body is proportional to the relative size (e.g., 5 percent) of the still functioning thymus (Rodewald, 1998). Research also suggests that the changes that occur in T cells are due to the increases in chronic disorders and inflammations that so often accompany aging rather than to some innate aging process (Boucher, Dufeu-Duchesne, Vicaut, Farge, Effros, & Schächter, 1998). Thyroxin, produced by the thyroid glands, also declines with advanced age. As a result of the changes in the thymus and the production of thyroxin, T cell production and efficiency typically decline with advanced age and about 75 percent of older adults show moderate or severe declines in T cell response to invasion. Since T cells are a primary defense against viral infection and cancer, these problems do increase with advanced age. Cancer, in particular, is far more common in older than in younger adults.

B cells are not directly affected by age but since their action is influenced by T cells, and since T cells usually do decline with age, some changes in B cells occur. For older adults, antibody production is slower, ends sooner, and the level reached declines faster. Older adults who encounter an invader that they encountered when young are usually very successful at fighting off the invasion. It is the production of new antibodies for new invaders that function less efficiently. One implication of these findings is that vaccinations are more effective when given to young adults, and are maintained by booster shots, then are vaccinations given for the first time to older adults. Why then do you think individuals, especially older individuals, are encouraged to get a flu vaccine every autumn?

Autoimmune diseases occur when T and/or B cells no longer recognize a set of host cells and attack the host organism. Antibodies are produced to attack the host. Arthritis is one such disease and occurs in two forms. **Osteoarthritis** is the most frequent form and breaks down cartilage between the bones at weight-bearing joints, such as the knees, hips, and fingers. **Rheumatoid arthritis** is less frequent and tends to attack freely moving joints, such as the wrists, elbows, and ankles. Both forms of arthritis are more common in women then in men, and arthritis is the most frequent chronic condition of older adults. A **chronic** condition is one which persists over a long period of time. Most researchers believe that such diseases do not suddenly appear in old age but have been causing progressive damage over most, if not all, of the individual's lifespan. Deterioration is most likely to be noticed when it has progressed over a long period of time, which is why it is reported more frequently by older adults.

Nervous System

Studies have found changes in the nervous system with advanced age. Most of the changes are in the number of nerve cells or **neurons**. Sensory neurons decline in number with age so it may become more difficult to detect a touch on the skin, a scent in the air, or the taste of salt in food. Changes in senses influence changes in perception and cognition (see also Chapter 5).

Motor neurons also decline in number reducing the number of cells that can be stimulated in a muscle. Muscle cells that are no longer stimulated degenerate and may be replaced by stiffening connective tissue (DiGiovanna, 1994). Loss of muscle fiber is usually the result of loss of motor neurons. Loss of motor neurons is typically the result of clogged blood vessels, which can no longer nourish the neurons. Clogged blood vessels are one of the most harmful physical changes that occur with aging.

The **brain** decreases in size and weight with advanced age by nearly 5 percent. Weight loss seems to accelerate after age 60 (Cunningham & Brookbank, 1988) but is not equally distributed across the entire brain. Some areas of the brain lose many neurons while others seem to show little or no loss. Loss typically occurs in visual, hearing, smell, and voluntary movement areas of the brain. Individual neurons also show structural change with advanced age. Figure 2-2 shows a neuron from a young person and one from an old person. The number of connective spikes, called dendrites, is far fewer on the old neuron. This loss of density, as well as loss of whole cells, accounts for the observed changes in size and weight with advanced age.

There is some debate as to whether the loss of dendrites and whole cells influence behavior. Much of the brain is redundant and it may be that some back-up systems have

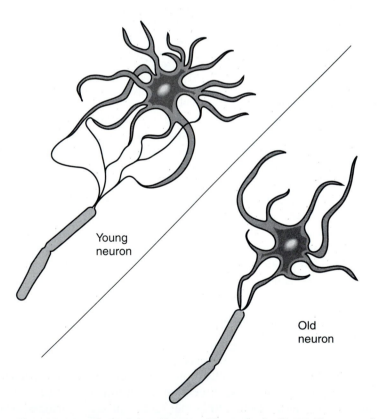

Young
neuron

Old
neuron

FIGURE 2-2   Comparison Between Neurons of a Young Person and an Older Person.

been lost but that no real effect on performance can be detected under normal conditions. At the same time, differences in performance are found on a number of tasks and, perhaps, some of those differences are due to the loss of dendrites and cells in the brain.

Nerve cells communicate with one another and with sensory and muscles cells by way of chemicals called **neurotransmitters**. The nervous system has a number of different neurotransmitters, and several pathologies of the brain are particular to a single class of neurotransmitters (see also Chapter 11). In general, the function of major brain pathways is unaffected by normal healthy aging.

But Not All

It is important to repeat that not all of these changes in the body occur for all older adults. Try Project 2 to get a feel for the variability in changes in older adults. One can easily get

PROJECT 2

One of the major points we make in this chapter is that physical change, biological aging, is highly variable both between and within individuals. It has been said that when you look at the physical changes within an individual it's a little like walking into a clock shop where all the clocks tell a different time. Some are fast, some are slow, and some show the true time. For the first part of this project, record the physical changes that you notice while observing older people in a public place, such as a mall. What changes are easiest to notice? What changes are not noticeable at all?

For the second part of this project, look at the following list of possible physical changes:

Your hair turns gray and you lose half of it.

Your bone density declines and you are in danger of developing osteoporosis; this loss of bone has loosened most of the teeth in your mouth.

Your blood pressure is now 145 over 95 and you have atherosclerosis.

Colon cancer is a danger for people in your family and your doctor wants to perform an examination every two years.

Your immune system is functioning at a very low level. You are prone to getting infections and diseases whenever you are exposed to them.

You have lost almost all feeling in your feet and hands.

Based on this list of physical changes, create an older adult by randomly selecting any three changes. Now create three more older adults by selecting randomly (with replacement) any three of these changes. Describe the adults you have created. Who is the healthiest and why? Who is least healthy and why?

Is this the way that real aging operates? Do you think that physical changes are randomly selected for older adults or do you think that some changes tend to occur together and that they depend on the choices we make when we are young?

the impression that old age is an awful time. It may seem as if every system is senescent but that is simply not true. Some systems are biologically older and more senescent than others. Remember that for older adults, change has been gradual. Gradual adaptation to change makes it almost unnoticeable for most older adults.

Chronic Conditions

With the clear possibility of senescence in a number of body components, one might expect that older adults are subject to a number of chronic conditions and that, although the differences among individuals can be quite large, some chronic conditions are fairly common. Chronic conditions refer to physical ailments characterized by slow onset and a long duration. Some chronic conditions are far more common among older adults then among younger adults and account for most of the disabilities of advanced age. Most of these conditions do not cause death, although some may.

Table 2-3 shows the ten most frequent chronic conditions for people age 65 and older. Many of these conditions have been discussed and some (changes in vision and hearing) will be discussed in Chapter 5.

Hypertension refers to abnormally high blood pressure. It is the second most frequent chronic condition and affects 38.1 percent of adults 65 and older. Hypertension is more frequent in older men than in older women. In hypertension, systolic pressure is 140 or higher and diastolic pressure is 90 or higher. High blood pressure is a clear warning signal of blockage in the arteries and an increased risk of blood clots. Blood clots can produce stroke and major loss of nerve cells in the brain. Blood clots can produce fatal heart attacks. It is important to monitor blood pressure and seek immediate consultation with a physician for any signs of elevation (Kannel, 1996).

Heart disease is the number one killer of Americans and affects 27.9 percent of people 65 and older. A major cause of heart disease is blockage of blood vessels caused by the accumulation of fat and cholesterol. Recent studies show that women are 14 percent

TABLE 2-3   The Ten Most Frequent Chronic Conditions for People Age 65 and over

Arthritis	48.3%
Hypertension	38.1%
Hearing impairment	28.6%
Heart disease	27.9%
Cataracts	15.7%
Orthopedic deformity	15.5%
Chronic sinusitis	15.3%
Diabetes	8.8%
Visual impairment	8.2%
Varicose veins	7.8%

Source: National Center for Health Statistics (1990).

more likely than men to die after a heart attack, and that the likelihood of death after aheart attack is also greater for older individuals (Malacrida, Genoni, Maggioni, Spataro, Parish, Phil, Palmer, Collins, & Moccetti, 1998).

Chronic sinusitis refers to inflammation of the sinus cavities. Such inflammation can be quite painful producing sinus headaches and burning sensation.

Diabetes refers to a reduction in or cessation of the production of insulin by the pancreas. Without insulin, the body cannot process sugars and, as a result sugar accumulates in the blood causing damage to some organs and tissues, while other organs and tissues in need of sugar starve without it. Adult onset diabetes occurs more frequently in older adults but it can usually be controlled by careful diet and medication.

Varicose veins refers to veins that have a larger than normal diameter due to the accumulation of blood in the vein. The vein may become permanently stretched. Stretched veins are more common in the legs and abdomen. This disorder is thought to be caused by the reduction of circulation due to congestive heart failure, wearing very tight clothing, or standing still or sitting for long periods of time with little movement. Besides being unattractive, varicose veins can be painful, result in clots and blockage of blood flow, and can result in tissue damage and even death. It is important to keep moving or elevate your legs if you find yourself standing still for long periods of time.

Sleep Disorders

Although not listed among the ten most frequent chronic conditions of older adults, complaints about sleep are fairly common. Many older adults say that they cannot get to sleep at night and that they suffer from **insomnia**. Insomnia refers to an inability to sleep. They may wake up frequently during the night and have trouble going back to sleep. They may wake in the morning feeling tired and then nap during the day. About one third of older White Americans complain about insomnia. Although few researchers have examined ethnic differences in complaints about sleep, some have found a lower rate of complaints among African Americans but about the same rate among Japanese Americans (Blazer, Hays, & Foley, 1995; Babar, Enright, Boyle, Foley, Sharp, Petrovich, Quan, 2000). Some research has also found, lower levels of daytime functioning for people who experience insomnia (Lichstein, Durrence, Riedel, & Bayen, 2001). Several factors play a role in complaints about insomnia. In fact, there are some common changes in sleep patterns that occur with aging.

Some complaints about not getting enough sleep are groundless. It is not the quantity that has changed but the quality. Researchers visited the homes of adults, age 65 to 95, who complained about not getting enough sleep at night. After monitoring the sleep of these individuals, researchers found that they were sleeping an average of 8-¼ hours (Ancoli-Israel, Kripke, Mason, & Kaplan, 1985). The length of the sleep cycles for these older adults was the same as younger adults. There are, however, several common changes that seem to produce very brief or longer awakenings that may affect the quality, rather than quantity, of sleep.

First, changes in the capacity and flexibility of the bladder often result in awakening to urinate. Depending on the extent of bladder senescence and amount of fluid consumed, older adults may awaken to urinate several times during the night. Such awakenings are likely to affect the overall quality of the sleep experience.

Second, **sleep apnea** is fairly common among older adults. Apnea is a sleep disorder in which respiration stops for at least ten seconds, carbon dioxide levels rise, and the individual automatically awakens and starts breathing again. Such quick awakenings are not remembered by the individual even though they may occur four or five times an hour. Apnea occurs at a slightly higher rate among men than women (DiGiovanna, 1994), and among all older adults at a rate of about 35 percent (Ancoli-Israel, Kripke, Mason, & Messin, 1981; Stone, 1993). Apnea is also related to weight; overweight people are more likely to have apnea. Sleeping pills actually increase the incidence of apnea, and lengthen these episodes as well. (Davies, Lacks, Storandt, & Bertelson, 1986; Woodruff, 1985).

Third, **nocturnal myoclonus** is also fairly common among older adults (Ancoli-Israel, Kripke, Mason, & Messin, 1981; Stone, 1993; Youngstedt, Kripke, Klauber, Sepulveda, & Mason, 1998). Nocturnal myoclonus is a disorder in which the sleeper's leg muscles twitch or jerk every 20 to 40 seconds over long periods of time. These twitches and jerks, like apnea, may produce brief awakenings, which may disrupt the overall quality of the sleep experience for the individual and his/her bed partner.

Even for an older adult not experiencing brief awakenings during the night, the amount of deep sleep is likely to be diminished. Deep sleep is characterized by a large proportion of very slow brain waves called delta waves, and it occurs during the first half of the night. Many older adults experience very little or no deep sleep during the night (Dement, Richardson, Prinz, Carskadon, Kripke, & Czeisler, 1985).

Adults of any age who are having sleep difficulties can try some simple remedies (Nakra, Grossberg, & Peck, 1991). For example, get out of bed if you can't fall asleep. Only lie in bed when you are ready to go to sleep. Check the temperature of the bedroom. A too cold or too warm bedroom can interfere with sleep. Do not engage in heavy, or strenuous activity before bedtime. Wind down with some relaxing activity such as reading or a warm bath. Avoid caffinated beverages or chocolate and avoid eating a lot before trying to go to sleep. A glass of warm milk or tea, on the other hand, often help. Avoid taking naps during the day. Finally, do not drink a lot of fluids before going to bed. This will help reduce or eliminate the need to urinate.

A number of treatments provide relief for people who suffer from insomnia (Lichstein, Riedel, & Means, 1998). Sleep deprivation, for example, seems to improve the overall quality of the sleep experience for young and old adults, increases the amount of deep sleep, and reduces the incidence of apnea episodes. (Carskadon, 1982). Going without sleep for one night may improve the quality of sleep for several subsequent nights. Researchers compared 21 adults who were 70 and older who received education about sleep or received education and reduced the time spent in bed by 30 minutes with 21 control subjects who received neither of these interventions. Education about sleep included information concerning exercise, room temperature, eating before going to bed, etc. Those who reduced their sleep went to bed 30 minutes later than they usually did but got up at the same time as always. This was a one-year study, and during the year all participants were assessed four times. At each assessment participants slept in the lab for three consecutive nights so that depth of sleep could be measured. Results showed that sleep education led to feelings of well-being when getting up in the morning and sleep reduction produced more deep sleep and fewer awakenings during the night (Hoch, Reynolds, Buysse, Monk, Nowell, Begley, Hall, & Dew, 2001).

If there are age differences in the sleep experience, are there age differences in the dream experience? The answer appears to be yes and there are a number of gender differences as well. Before looking at them in Box 2-2, you might try to guess what sort of differences exist.

Work of Art

We have looked at all the things that can decline with advanced age. It is extremely rare for all of these changes to occur in a single individual. It is also extremely unlikely that an individual will show none of these deficits. Each individual is a different work of art.

B O X **2-2**

Dreams and Aging

It is hard for most people to remember their dreams even though research suggests that everyone dreams several times per night. Thus, analyses of dream content are based only on the small proportion of dreams that are remembered by people. Such analyses do, however, suggest some interesting age and gender differences.

In comparisons of the dreams of young and older adults, no differences in the length of the dream narrative are reported, thus, we might assume that dream length is essentially the same for all adults. Older adults, however, have far less visual imagery (Fein, Feinberg, Insel, Antrobus, Price, Floyd, & Nelson, 1985) and report fewer dream themes (Soper, Rosenthal, Milford, & Akers, 1992). Young, middle-age, and older adults also differ on the emotional content in their dreams. Some researchers have found that young adults report higher levels of and more emotion than older adults, as well as different emotions. For the young, emotions like anger and fear occurred more often while for older adults emotions like enjoyment and joy were more frequent (Blick & Howe, 1984). Recent research found that only apprehension differed across age groups and that both young and old had higher levels of apprehension than did middle-age adults (Clark, Foos, Boone, Haught, Hicks, Murphey, & Vagnone, 2001). Perhaps differences in apprehension reflect the uncertainties of young- and old-age compared to middle-age.

The dreams of men and women differ also but not in terms of the emotions reported. Anxiety, joy, anger, sadness, shame, and affection are the most frequent emotions reported for both men and women (Merritt, Stickgold, Pace-Schott, & Williams, 1994). Males dream more often of other males than do females (Hall, 1984). Men also have more single characters, strangers, auditory activity, and black/white/gray colors in their dreams while women have more vivid colors, cognitive activity, and stronger intensity in their dreams (Kramer, Kinney, & Scharf, 1983).

Other work shows that dream content is influenced by the life situations in which young and old men and women find themselves. Students have more dreams with familiar characters and friendly interactions while wage-earning mothers have more dreams with families, physical aggression, and achievement striving (Rinfret, Lortie-Lussier, & de Konick, 1991). Wage-earning mothers and fathers dream more about their professional commitments while at-home parents dream more about their family (Lortie-Lussier, Simond, Rinfret, & de Konick, 1992).

Some people believe that physical appearance is very important and that older adults are less satisfied with their physical appearance than are younger adults. Research support this hypothesis. In a survey of 2000 men and women, ranging in age from 24 to 85, researchers found that women, at all ages, regarded physical appearance as more important than men, and that women were more concerned about changes in appearance as they grew older. However, when asked whether they were satisfied with their physical appearance, men were fairly satisfied at all ages while women increased in satisfaction the older they were. The oldest women were the most satisfied with their bodies (Öberg & Tornstam, 1999).

Look at the photos shown at the beginning of this chapter. The order from oldest to youngest is bottom left, middle, bottom right, top left, and top right. Look at your own grandparents. Are they not beautiful? Older adults are among the finest art ever produced.

Making Choices

Choices that you make now, and over the course of early adulthood, influence how many changes you will experience and how much they will affect you as you age. For a more successful older adulthood, it is important to have **frequent check-ups**. Many physical changes and diseases can be handled relatively easily if they are spotted early. You learned that vaccinations are more powerful when they are received by young adults and somewhat less effective when given to older adults. You might choose to **be vaccinated while still young**. You know that fat and cholesterol builds up in your arteries and veins while you are in your 20s. You could choose to **be careful in what you eat**. You know that **lifestyle factors** are the main reasons for changes in bone mass. Good nutrition and exercise are very helpful while smoking and excessive alcohol are quite harmful. Finally, accept the things you cannot change or prevent and appreciate the beauty of humans at all ages.

CHAPTER HIGHLIGHTS

- There is great variability in the physical changes that occur across the older adult population and within each individual.
- Skin shows changes in color, accumulation of dark spots, wrinkling, and decreased moisture. Changes in the skin can have a negative effect on protective functions.
- Hair usually turns gray and is lost in varying amounts; these changes seem to be largely genetic.
- Older adults lose height. Weight change, which may be a cohort effect, increases during middle-age and decreases during old age.
- Voice lowers in pitch.
- The skull, ears, and nose grow as we age.
- Fast twitch muscle fibers are lost between age 40 and 70 while slow twitch fibers remain intact until 70.
- The increased action of osteoclasts lessens bone density in older adults, particularly White and Asian American women. This loss is due to genetics, hormones, and lifestyle factors and can become osteoporosis, which is severe loss of bone.

- The cardiovascular system shows higher systolic pressure for older adults but intact heart and blood. Blood vessels, however, clog as one ages and can result in atherosclerosis. Be careful what you eat and exercise regularly.
- The lungs take in less air as we grow older due to changes in muscles, increases in ducts, and the effects of gravity.
- In spite of changes in muscles, cardiovasular system, and respiration, many older adults are able to maintain a high level of stamina.
- The overall functioning of the digestive system shows very little decline although the lining of the mouth and stomach may deteriorate, the colon loses moisture and muscle, the kidneys slow down under stress, and the bladder becomes smaller and more rigid.
- Women experience a relatively sudden change in their reproductive system and levels of the hormone estrogen when they go through menopause. This change in estrogen plays a role in bone loss. Men experience no such sudden change but often experience an enlargement of the prostate gland.
- T cell production and efficiency decline with age due to a shrinking of the thymus gland and increases in chronic disease and inflammation. The efficiency of B cells and natural killer cells is influenced by the decline in T cells, and vulnerability to a number of disorders, especially cancers and viral infections, increases with age.
- Nerve cells in the periphery and in the brain decline with age in part because of clogged blood vessels. Cell loss in the brain tends to occur in specific areas.
- Older adults frequently experience a number of chronic conditions such as arthritis, hypertension, cardiovascular disease, osteoporosis, chronic sinusitis, diabetes, and varicose veins.
- Complaints about insomnia are frequent among older adults and research suggests several reasons for lower quality sleep among older adults: loss of deep sleep, apnea, myoclonus, and smaller bladder. Education about healthy sleep and sleep deprivation are reasonable effective treatments.

STUDY QUESTIONS

1. Distinguish among chronological age, biological age, and senescence. Give an example of biological aging without significant senescence.

2. What major systems are involved in maintaining stamina and how can senescence in these systems affect one's stamina?

3. What are the major changes in physical appearance? How do these affect function?

4. What changes typically occur in the cardiovascular system? The digestive system? The nervous system? The immune system?

5. What aspects of the nervous system change and which do not? Is behavior affected by these changes? Why or why not?

6. Describe the influence of clogged blood vessels on muscles, nerves, and chronic conditions.

7. What advice would you give to an older friend who claims to be having difficulty sleeping or complains about poor quality sleep?

RECOMMENDED READINGS

DiGiovanna, A. G. (1994). *Human Aging: Biological Perspectives.* New York: McGraw Hill. A good, readable description of the major biological changes that accompany aging.

Seuss, Dr. (1986). *You're Only Old Once.* New York: Random House. A humorous view of an old man's encounter with the medical establishment.

INTERNET RESOURCES

http://www.nof.org/   For information on osteoporosis.
http://www.americanheart.org/   For information on heart disease.
http://www.arthritis.org/   For information about arthritis.

3 Theories of Senescence and Aging

Everyone desires to live long, but none would be old.

—Jonathan Swift

Most people, if not all, would like to live a long time if they could remain healthy. Not many look forward to growing helpless and frail. Yet, chronological aging is accompanied by varying rates of biological aging and senescence. Systems become more vulnerable to disease and injury and may take longer to heal as they age. In this chapter we examine theories which attempt to explain how and why senescence occurs. If we can understand what causes aging and senescence, we may be able to slow it down or stop it. At the very least, we will be better informed and may be able to minimize senescence so that old age can be a healthy, active time.

An Overview

We learned that virtually all organisms show senescence if they live long enough. Most animals in the wild do not show senescence because they fall prey to predators at the first signs of weakness. Animals held in captivity or pets show senescence because they are protected from predation. Humans show senescence because they grow old with a fair amount of protection from predators too. There are instances of wild animals that seem to live for long periods of time but do not show significant senescence. These animals may offer clues as to what causes senescence. Look at a photo of one of these amazing creatures.

Turtles, and their large relatives tortoises, live for long periods of time and also show little senescence. Careful examination of turtle tissues shows that older tissues are not much different from younger tissues. Turtles and tortoises do not seem to die because of the increased vulnerability to injury and disease that is characteristic of senescence. They die because of predators, usually humans. Some contend that turtles do not age because they are born old.

Senior View

Not many adults are familiar with the material we present in this chapter. People may know some-things about psychological theories that have to do with aging, but usually not much about theories that focus on the reasons underlying physical decline. However, we found one woman who had some knowledge and fairly strong opinions on theories that attempt to explain senescence.

Martha Russell, a widow living alone, was 78 years old when we spoke with her. She and her husband used to own a rug company. She told us that her health was quite good and that she was willing to offer her opinion on any theory of aging and senescence.

Martha was not particulary fond of evolution theories that claim that after the survival of the species is taken care of by protecting us through our child bearing and rearing years we are "programmed" to deteriorate and die. Martha said that the evidence simply does not support this view and noted "I had my child many, many years ago and I feel fine today."

She also had mixed feelings about theories that claim that our cells are programmed to deteriorate and then die. She had no evidence to disconfirm the theory but none to support it either.

Finally, Martha had also read about theories that claim that the accumulation of garbage and pollutants from the food we eat, air we breathe, and water we drink are responsible for our senescence. She said that this theory "is quite possibly true,"

because "pollutants are in lots of things and are very bad for you."

Martha was not familiar with the other theories we examine in this chapter but we are certain that if she were she would express an opinion. As we were leaving, Martha said, "We are supposed to get old and that's what happens." We are not so sure that's true. Where's the evidence? Martha just smiled.

An animal's size is related to its longevity and when senescence begins. Generally, smaller animals live shorter lives than larger animals and, consequently, show senescence at a much earlier chronological age. Turtles are an exception to the general rule, as they are relatively small animals but live a long time.

Animals who live a long time with no apparent senescence and the relationship between size and longevity, suggests a biological, perhaps genetic, explanation for senescence. Other animals live in the same environments as turtles but do not show longevity and lack of senescence. Large and small animals live in the same apparent environments but differ in longevity. Since different species have different genetic blueprints,

A turtle.

perhaps those genetic blueprints are what underlie the species' differences in aging and senescence. Of course, one could also argue that the differences are not genetic but that aging and senescence are caused by environmental factors. Different genes may only govern how influential those environmental factors are for different species and, perhaps, for different individual members of a species. We examine different theories of aging and senescence ranging from some that claim the whole process is in the genetics of the cell (biological clock) to others that claim the whole process is due to interactions with the environment (garbage accumulation).

Some theorists argue that biological and genetic theories are supported by a group of rare disorders that occur in humans. **Progeria** is a class of genetic disorders with symptoms that resemble very rapid aging. In one of these disorders, **Hutchinson-Guilford syndrome**, the individual may appear quite normal at birth but within the first year of life, the disorder becomes evident. The victim does not grow normally, loses hair, and the layer of fat under the skin is also lost. Over the next decade, atherosclerosis, osteoporosis, blocked arteries, and strokes become highly probable. The skin appears wrinkled like that of an old person. Such individuals do not, however, have other signs of aging such as arthritis, increased risk of cancer, cataracts, or dementia. Most progeria patients die by age 12, usually from heart disease. The disorder is very rare, affecting one in eight million births. It is thought to be due to a recessive or very rare dominant autosomal gene. The photo shows an individual with progeria.

Werner's syndrome is another type of progeria. It does not, however, become evident until the individual is in their 20s or 30s, and the specific symptoms of aging are also different. These patients tend to show cataracts, connective tissue cancers, diabetes, age spots on the skin but also the hair loss, wrinkles, and osteoporosis of Hutchinson-Guilford syndrome. Werner's is thought to be due to a recessive, autosomal gene. The tested intelligence of persons with either type of progeria is typically normal or above average (Cunningham & Brookbank, 1988; Schneider & Bynum, 1983).

Since these two disorders produce many of the changes that accompany normal aging, and since both of these disorders are genetic, one might wish to conclude that normal

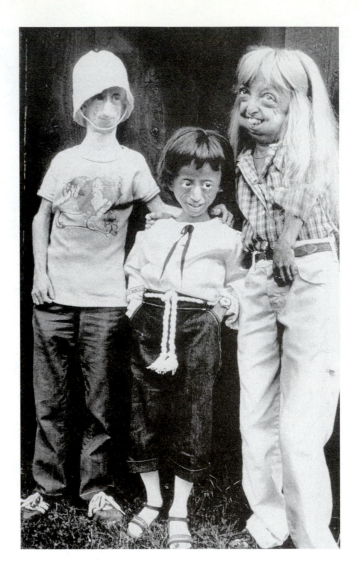

Young people with progeria.

aging and senescence are also biologic and genetic. One must, however, be cautious because there are many possible causes of senescence and it may be the case that the symptoms of progeria only resemble aging. Patients with these disorders are not really old. Scientists warn that it is misleading to draw conclusions about normal processes based on abnormal conditions.

Recent research suggests that genes may account for less of the variability in longevity than environmental factors. Examinations of human identical twins, and of different strains of mice, suggest that between 15 and 35 percent of the variability in length of life is due to genetic factors (Finch & Tanzi, 1997; McGue, Vaupel, Holm, & Harvald,

1993). As with most debates over the relative influence of nature and nurture, the answer is that both are important contributors and that it is very difficult to determine exact contributions. Nevertheless, one can still make intelligent choices to live longer and healthier regardless of genetic endowment (Rowe & Kahn, 1998).

In sum, theories of senescence must deal with the fact that most, but not all, organisms show senescence and that different body organs and systems deteriorate at different rates. Such theories are difficult to test and the evidence, when there is any, is indirect, as with the claim that since the types of progeria are genetic so must all aging be genetic. Theories of aging and senescence are divided into two categories: programmed and unprogrammed. **Programmed** theories claim that senescence follows a predetermined plan while **unprogrammed** theories claim that senescence is unplanned. Programmed theories expect the senescence of various body parts and systems to occur in the same order in nearly all members of a species while unprogrammed theories have no such expectation. There is, after all, no program. It is not always clear into which of these categories some theories fall.

Programmed Theories

Programmed theories suggest that senescence is inevitable because it is predetermined by some plan. That plan may be in our genes. We discuss three examples of programmed theories.

Biological Clock

Our genes carry the instructions for body activities and changes for each stage of life. The genes are like a ticking clock and when a certain time is reached, the clock stops. Biological clock theory is clearly an example of a programmed theory. The program is in our genes. As with all theories of aging and senescence there is no proof of these claims but there are several pieces of evidence that support the general notion of some form of biological clock and one strong nomination for what that clock could be.

Cells are not immortal. They divide and reproduce a limited number of times and that number is known as the **Hayflick number**, named for its discoverer Leonard Hayflick (Hayflick, 1965; 1996). Cells from different species have different limits on cell division. The Hayflick number for human cells is about 50. Cell cultures taken from human embryos become old and die after 40 to 60 cell divisions. The Hayflick number for a giant tortoise, which can live to 175 years, is about 110. A species' longevity is related to the upper limit on cell division, the Hayflick number. To produce a human adult from a fertilized egg takes about 40 divisions. When cells can no longer divide they deteriorate and die, although such cells living in a culture may survive for quite some time. The limit on cell division seems very much like a biological clock.

The limit on cell division seems to reside on the DNA-carrying chromosomes that carry the cell's genetic code. During cell division, the DNA molecules on chromosomes split and rebuild themselves as each adenine base acquires a new thymine partner (and vice versa), and as each cytosine base acquires a new guanine partner (and vice versa) from the nutrients in the cell. The two new cells are identical to the old cell from which they came. At the ends of DNA chromosomes are a series of repeating units called **telomeres**. Telomeres carry no genetic information and are shortened with each succeeding cell division. Figure 3-1 shows what this might look like. Cell division stops when the telomere sequence has been sufficiently shortened. This might occur because further cell division would damage genetic material, and so the telomere protects the genetic information while division occurs. When the telomere strand is too short to protect genetic information during cell division, the cell stops dividing. At that point, the cell is assumed to grow old and experience senescence (Hayflick, 1996). This theory has strong appeal because it seems very logical and relatively simple but there is some evidence that is problematic. Research has found deteriorating cells that still have long telomere sequences. Perhaps the deterioration in such cells is not due to senescence but some other cause. Other research with cloned mice has found evidence for no loss and perhaps an increase in telomeres (Wakayama, Shinkai, Tamashiro, Niida, Blanchard, Blanchard, Ogura, Tanemura, Tachibana, Perry, Colgan, Mombaerts, & Yanagimachi, 2000). These findings are not easily explained if telomeres are programmed to shorten and lead to senescence.

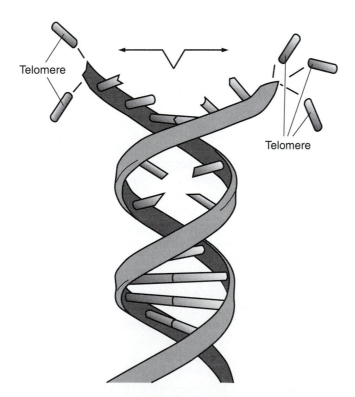

FIGURE 3-1   **Chromosome/DNA Dividing with Telomeres Breaking Away.**

One line of indirect but interesting evidence for a telomere clock comes from the study of cancer cells. Cancer cells seem to be immortal. They do not ordinarily stop dividing; they have no known upper limit. Cancer cells also have telomere sequences at the ends of their chromosomes and those telomeres are lost during cell division just as in normal cells. Cancer cells, however, have an enzyme called **telomerase** that rebuilds the telomere sequence following each cell division. In this way, one can think of cancer cells as being able to reset their biological clock so that it never runs down (Landman, Kotkin, Shu, Droller, & Liu, 1997).

Much research is now underway on telomeres as a potential biological clock (Egorov, 1997; Weng, Palmer, Levine, Lane, June, & Hodes, 1997); on the possibility of providing telomerase or some derivative to normal cells to increase their longevity (Biesmann & Mason, 1997; Weng, Granger, & Hodes, 1997); on using the detection of telomerase as a diagnostic tool for cancer (Brousset, Saati, Chaouche, Zenou, Mazerolles, & Delsol, 1997; Ohta, Kanamaru, Morita, Hayashi, Ito, & Yamamoto, 1997); and on finding drugs to inhibit telomerase in cancer cells to stop their division (Fujimoto & Takahashi, 1997; Landman, Kotkin, Shu, Droller, & Liu, 1997; Raymond, Faivre, Dieras, & Hoff, 1997).

Evolution

Another set of theories argue that senescence is programmed to occur once we reach a certain age. That age is when we can no longer reproduce and the raising of offspring is complete. According to this point of view, all animals, not just humans, have evolved to live long enough to reproduce and rear their offspring and there is no useful purpose for life beyond that point (Olshansky, Carnes, & Grahn, 1998). Life beyond that point is, therefore, not supported or protected and senescence and death occur.

One important assumption of evolution theories is that genes are meant to ensure the survival of the species rather than the survival of the individual. To do this, individuals are protected through their reproductive period so that they might reproduce and extend the species into another generation. The reproductive period can be quite long and includes the time for production of offspring and raising offspring to an age when they can survive on their own and then reproduce to further extend the survival of the species. The protected period must then include parenthood and, perhaps, the early years of grandparenthood as well. If one examines death rates for different age groups and excludes deaths that might be considered unnatural, such as accidents and homicides, one finds that infants, small children, and older adults have higher death rates while adolescents, young, and middle-age adults have lower death rates (Olshansky, Carnes, & Grahn, 1998). Some researchers have examined the same data for dogs and mice and found the same relationship (Carnes, Olshansky, & Grahn, 1996). Before and after the reproductive years, the death rate is higher than during the reproductive years. Unhealthy organisms die before reaching their reproductive years. Healthy organisms are "protected" until they reproduce and then fall prey to predators or senescence.

Senescence may be a side effect of the extension of life beyond the reproductive period and a consequence of our evolution. Most animals die before or soon after their reproductive periods end. Humans, however, live although nature never intended them to live that long. We have succeeded at putting off death through advances in medical science. As a result, humans exhibit genetic disorders that would not have appeared in a natural, wild population.

Hormones

Hormones are chemical messengers that provide instructions to different types of cells throughout our bodies. They are produced by endocrine glands such as the thyroid, the parathyroid, the adrenal cortex, the pancreas, and the ovaries and testes, all of which are controlled by the "master" gland, the pituitary at the base of the brain. The pituitary is, in turn, largely controlled by the hypothalamus, a brain structure responsible for body functions such as eating, temperature regulation, and sexual desire. Because hormones control the actions of cells in many different systems, it seems possible that they might also control the aging of cells in those different systems. Glands follow a schedule and decrease the production of certain hormones as we grow older. Those lowered levels of hormones may produce increased vulnerability (senescence) in other parts of the body.

The hypothalamus, through the pituitary gland, signals menopause in women and might be regarded as a very powerful contoller of major changes in our bodies. Menopause results in major hormonal changes in women, especially the loss of the hormone estrogen. Many other hormones decline with advanced age in both men and women. Table 3-1 lists glands of the endocrine system, some of the major hormones, and some implications for human aging and senescence. As you know from the last chapter, the immune system functions less efficiently as one ages because of the decline in T cell efficiency. As suggested in Table 3-1, this immune system decline may be the result of changes in the thyroid and thymus glands. You also know that bones weaken with advanced age due to increased resorption of bone by osteoclasts. As shown in Table 3-1, bone resorption is to some extent controlled by the parathyroid gland and the loss of estrogen following menopause.

Much of the decline that occurs with advanced age seems related to hormonal changes but there is no direct evidence that hormone changes result in senescence. Research has been conducted to determine whether restoration of higher levels of hormones will reverse observed declines. Such evidence would serve as indirect evidence for a hormone theory of senescence. Claims for such aging reversal effects with hormones appear in the popular press fairly frequently (Downes, 1995).

In an early 1990s study, medical researchers injected 12 volunteers, older men age 61 to 81, with doses of **human growth hormone**, three times a week. Human growth hormone is produced in the pituitary gland and is known to decline with age. It was hypothesized that the decline of human growth hormone might be partly responsible for observed senescence so restoring higher levels through injections might reverse any decline. The dozen men who received the injections showed significant change: decreased fat, increased muscle mass, and increases in skin thickness. They appeared to look younger. Very soon, however, some men developed diabetes-like symptoms, carpal tunnel syndrome, and the growth of breasts. When they stopped taking the hormones their bodies returned to their prior states. Follow-up work by other researchers found some of the same positive effects of increased muscle mass and fat loss but also some negative effects such as swollen

TABLE 3-1   Endocrine Glands, Hormones, and Implications for Aging

Gland	Hormones and Function	Implications for Aging
Pituitary	Human growth hormone that promotes tissue development and carbohydrate metabolism.	Growth hormone and tissue development decline with age.
Pineal	Melatonin hormone regulates biological rhythms.	Some claim that melatonin reverses aging; it does not.
Adrenal	DHEA that is converted to estrogen and testosterone and may serve other functions as well.	Research has found positive and negative effects for DHEA intake in older humans.
Thyroid	Thyroxin that affects T cell efficiency and with triiodothyronine increases oxygen consumption and regulates growth and maturation of tissues.	T cell efficiency and, thus, the immune system, declines with age.
	Calcitonin that lowers calcium in blood by inhibiting bone resorption.	Bone resorption increases with age.
Parathyroid	Parathormone that increases calcium in blood by increasing bone resorption.	Bone resorption increases with age.
Thymus	Responsible for development of immune system.	Is replaced by fat in adults; immune system declines.
Ovaries	Estrogen that is necessary for development of sex organs and secondary characteristics.	Menopause results in loss of estrogen.
Testes	Testosterone that aids development of seconary sexual characteristics and helps blood clot.	Testosterone levels decline as one grows older; blood clots may increase.

ankles, stiffened joints, and stiff hands. Generally, the results have been disappointing (Cohn, Feller, Draper, Rudman, & Rudman, 1993; Dinsmoor, 1996; Rudman, Feller, Nagraj, Gergans, Lalitha, Goldberg, Schlenker, Cohn, Rudman, & Mattson, 1990; Weiss & Kasmauski, 1997).

Melatonin is a hormone produced in the pineal gland located near the center of the brain. Melatonin regulates our biological rhythms and has been used to help people sleep better (Garfinkel & Zisapel, 1998; Sack, Hughes, Edgar, & Lewy, 1997). Melatonin has been referred to as an anti-aging drug and a protection against cancer. While there is some evidence of such benefits with animals, it is possible that the obtained results may be due to lower caloric intake (Hayflick, 1996). Work with humans suggests no anti-aging effects or protection against cancer (Dickey, 1996; Panzer, Lottering, Bianchi, Glencross, Stark, & Seegers, 1998).

The hormone **DHEA** (dehydroepiandrosterone), which also declines with advanced age, is also being investigated. In humans, this hormone is produced in the adrenal glands and its production declines about 2 percent every year following puberty. Preliminary work with rats has found that DHEA inhibits lung, breast, and skin cancers (Hayflick, 1996; Ogin, Hard, Schwartz, & Magee, 1990; Porter & Svec, 1996). Work with aging humans also seems to indicate benefits in terms of increased muscle strength, leaner body mass, and activation of immune functions (Yen, Morales, & Khorram, 1996). At the same time, no careful longitudinal trials have been completed and the long-term effects of DHEA supplements are not known. In the short-term, large doses of DHEA have resulted in hair loss, acne, and deepening of the voice in female users and may increase the risk of ovarian cancer (Helzlsouer, 1995; Mack, 1997).

In sum, hormone theories of aging have appeal because of the great influence of hormones on all bodily systems and organs. Such theories do not, however, have any evidence to support their claims that hormones are responsible for senescence or are able to reverse biological aging.

While biological clock, evolution, and hormone theories are programmed theories, there are theories that are not as easy to categorize. We have placed the following theory in a middle category.

A Middle Category

Immune System

Like hormones from the endocrine system, the immune system exerts influence in all other systems as it functions to protect the body. A decline in the immune system is hypothesized to produce senescence in two different ways that we refer to as the leaky defense and the autoimmune hypotheses.

The leaky defense hypothesis claims that senescence is a result of invasion by environmental toxins and organisms that damage cells, tissues, and organs throughout the body. This damage is a direct result of the less efficient functioning of our immune system as we age. Our defense is leaky and allows more invasion and, thus, more damage. Some have suggested that the thymus gland, which produces T cells and slowly disappears as we grow older (see Table 3-1), may function as a biological clock; when it is gone, we die. (Walford, 1969). The leaky defense theory is usually considered a programmed version of immune system theory. The immune system is programmed to deteriorate according to a predetermined schedule and that deterioration results in less efficient functioning.

The autoimmune hypothesis says that senescence and damage increase with age because our immune system begins attacking portions of the body it is meant to protect. Body tissues and organs show senescence because the body's own immune system is destroying parts of itself. It may be that the immune system is correct in attacking these body parts because they have been radically altered over time due to interactions with the environment. The alterations have made these body parts appear to be invaders. This is an unprogrammed version of immune system theory. Attacks depend on nonscheduled and damaging interactions with the environment in which one lives.

Immune theories of senescence have some problems. We already know that the immune system declines with age or shows senescence. Can the immune system be causing its own senescence and then go on to damage the rest of the body or is there another cause that results in senescence in all systems? A problem for immune theories is one of determining what causes senescence in the immune system in the first place. Another problem is that the immune system may be responding correctly when it attacks its own body. The attack may be on molecular tissue that has been altered by mutation, free radicals, error, or unrepaired damage. In such a case, it would be those errors, rather than the immune system itself, that led to any observed senescence.

Unprogrammed Theories

Unprogrammed theories refer to those theories in which there is no clear plan or schedule of senescence. Senescence may occur rapidly or slowly depending on interactions with the environment and/or interactions between environmental and genetic factors. We examine four unprogrammed theories.

Wear and Tear

Wear and tear theory claims that senescence is the result of a lifetime of random illnesses, injuries, and damage to our bodies. Environmental toxins, radiation, and other factors eventually produce failures in various bodily components and we die of weakened hearts, lungs, kidneys, and so on. We just plain wear out.

Wear and tear theories have no real support and several problems. First, senescence seems to be too regular to be the result of random wear and tear. The senescence observed in aging humans seems, in fact, to be quite regular. Certain organs and systems are most likely to show senescence before others and the pattern of decline in many systems is not random. Second, one might think about the wear and tear that could be produced by certain behaviors such as eating fiber and roughage. It seems like these should produce considerable wear and tear on our bodies. They should tear the lining of the stomach and intestines and leave them more vulnerable, but such foods contribute to health rather than senescence. Third, think about the wear and tear on our muscles, lungs, and heart as we exercise, particularly if we exercise strenuously and on a regular basis. Wear and tear theories seem to suggest that we would be better off sitting comfortably on the couch. Wear and tear is a popular notion with lay people but not with most researchers (DiGiovanna, 1994).

Free Radicals

Free radical theory states that senescence is the result of damage produced by free radicals. Free radicals are atoms or molecules with an odd number of electrons and, as a result, they are very reactive and unstable. Free radicals attempt to take on an electron or contribute an electron to other molecular structures in the body and react with almost anything nearby, such as the nucleic acids of DNA and RNA, the lipids that make up the cell's membrane, or proteins that govern the functions of cells. Molecules that interact with free radicals may then cease to function or may function incorrectly (Balin, 1982; Hayflick, 1996).

Free radicals are produced during normal metabolism. The metabolic furnace that roars in our bodies to provide us with the energy needed to function may also damage our bodies with the waste products that result. Free radicals are one such waste product. Free radicals also result from actions of the immune system on invaders, and from exposure to sunlight and radiation. After a lifetime of metabolism, immune responses, and sunlight, the damage from free radicals may eventually result in observable senescence. The effects may accumulate the longer we live (Sohal & Allen, 1985; Weiss & Kasmauski, 1997). This theory is an unprogrammed theory, because there is no plan for senescence; it occurs as more free radicals are produced and interact with cell tissues and chemicals and result in damage. Damage is more probable as one experiences more interactions with free radicals, but damage is not certain.

Our bodies have some defense against the action of free radicals in an enzyme known as sodium oxide dismutase (SOD). SOD sweeps up free radicals and neutralizes their action. Also, there is a relationship between the longevity of a species and the level of SOD; higher levels of SOD are generally found in long-lived species (Cunningham & Brookbank, 1988). Free radical theorists argue that the presence of SOD in our bodies is evidence for the harm that free radicals can produce. It would be senseless to provide a protection against some agent that could cause no harm. Some recent work has, however, shown that an abundance of SOD does not increase length of life for mice (Huang, Carlson, Gillespie, Shi, & Epstein, 2000).

Free radicals are neutralized by antioxidants, which are chemicals that inhibit oxygen from combining with susceptible molecules to produce free radicals. A normal, healthy diet contains a number of antioxidants, such as beta-carotene and vitamins C and E. Studies of animals given higher levels of antioxidants in their diet have found that the animals live longer than control animals not given the extra antioxidants. Mice, for example, can live 30 percent longer. Such studies are difficult to evaluate because the higher levels of antioxidants often detract from the taste of the food and, many of the animals eat less. It may be less eating, rather than or in addition to the higher level of antioxidants, that is responsible for longer life (Hayflick, 1996; Mahlhorn & Cole, 1985). Some work with humans has examined the relationship between certain antioxidants in the blood of older individuals and their level of independence; individuals with higher levels of the antioxidant lycopene seem to be more independent than those with lower levels (Snowdon, Gross, & Butler, 1996).

The evidence for free radical theory is circumstantial at best. Free radicals do exist in our bodies, they can combine with other crucial molecules, and such combinations could result in damage. Our bodies have built-in protection against free radicals. There is evidence that the levels of free radicals are higher in older animals but it is possible that rather than being the cause of senescence, the accumulation of free radicals is a result. (Balin, 1982; Hayflick, 1996).

Errors

Everybody makes mistakes. Error theories say that our bodies make errors all the time and that over long periods of time one is more likely to make a serious error. Some errors have relatively little effect while other errors might cascade into major senescence.

All cell components are regularly degraded and replaced. There is constant turnover in living cells. Errors may occur randomly in the replacement process as RNA misreads DNA and proteins are incorrectly formed. Incorrect proteins that are foreign to a body could lead to autoimmune responses.

Error theory need not predict the same random deterioration that wear and tear theory does. Error theory makes the claim that although errors occur randomly, we only notice the ones that produce real damage. Although the occurrence of those errors is random, the damage they produce is not. An example of how errors can result in variations in senescence within and between individuals is illustrated in the game described in Project 3.

The problem with error theories has been in demonstrating that senescence-producing errors do occur. One example of such an error has been molecular cross-linkage. A cross-linkage occurs when a molecule incorrectly links with another molecule of

PROJECT 3

This project is designed to illustrate how random events such as metabolic errors and/or free radical damage and/or damage from accumulated garbage could result in fairly regular patterns of senescence. This project is best done with a group of individuals.

Prepare the materials. Write the names of ten errors on ten different pieces of paper. Five of them are meaningless errors, and you should just write something like "oops." These are errors resulting from a metabolic mistake, free radicals interacting with some body protein, or a "bump" from accumulated garbage but one from which no damage occurs. On the other five pieces of paper, write the following errors that result in senescence: senescence to the arteries, senescence to the lungs, senescence to the skin, senescence to the bones, and senescence to the muscles. Put all ten pieces of paper in a box, hat, or bag so that they can't be seen.

Have several individuals draw papers from the hat, write down the errors as their own, and return them to the hat before the next person draws. Each draw can count as a two-year period. People are 60 years old when they start, and after five draws are 70. Thus, everyone will draw five papers to get from 60 to 70 years of age. This random assignment of errors will result in some individuals who have very little senescence, others with quite a lot, and most with a moderate amount. Although the draws from the hat are random, the obtained patterns of senescence are quite regular. Why? How did you fare?

A variation of this game is played by allowing individuals to draw the same error more than once or by making them draw a different piece of paper if they already drew one in a previous draw. Allowing them to draw the same senescence result more than once can be described as "three strikes and you are out." If they draw "senescence to the arteries" once, then they are said to have experienced a heart attack and must take it easy. If twice, then they have had major heart surgery. If three times, then they are no longer with us. The same rule applies to the other senescence events for lungs, skin, bones, and muscles.

the same or a different substance. The resulting cross-linked molecule is thought to inhibit movement of normal molecules and interfere with cell functioning. Collagen molecules cross-link more frequently with advanced age and it is thought that free radicals, glucose, and light contribute to the formation of these abnormal connections (Bjorkstein, 1974; DiGiovanna, 1994). There has not, however, been much success at finding examples of widespread cross-linking in older organisms or in demonstrating the damaging effects of such cross-links.

Garbage Accumulation

Garbage accumulation theories suggest that over time, more garbage from the environment accumulates in the cells and tissues and eventually results in senescence. It is not that the materials accumulated are necessarily toxic but that their mere presence interferes with normal cellular processes. At some point, after decades of such accumulation, cells and tissues break down under the load of accumulated garbage. If the theory is correct, then we ought to be able to find much higher levels of waste in older cells, tissues, and organs. In some cases we do.

We know that **lipofuscin** accumulates. Lipofuscin is composed of a number of metabolic waste products and accumulates in various cells throughout the body. Cells cannot eliminate it and lipofuscin appears as a dark pigment in older cells on the skin, the heart, and the brain. Such spots on the skin are referred to as liver spots. While it is true that this particular garbage does accumulate with age, it is not clear whether it results in any damage. At present, the answer seems to be that it does not.

Amyloid protein is a byproduct of normal metabolism and is found throughout the body. Its function is unknown but with age it accumulates between the cells in the brain, heart, and other organs. Amyloid is usually eliminated but in some disorders, such as Alzheimer's, it produces large areas of amyloid plaque in the brain. These plaques seem to be a major factor in Alzheimer's disease, which we examine more closely in Chapter 11. The type of amyloid that accumulates in Alzheimer's disease is different than normal everyday amyloid garbage.

In short, garbage accumulation theories point to a number of harmful substances that are thought to accumulate with age and suggest that such accumulation is the cause of senescence. Strong supporting evidence for these interesting theories has not been found. There does not seem to be enough garbage accumulation to produce the senescence that occurs and the garbage accumulation that does occur doesn't seem greater in tissues showing senescence than in those not showing it.

All (Many) of the Above

Clearly, no theory, at present, has much support. It is probably unwise to assume that senescence in all of our different cells, tissues, and organs has a single cause. Some instances of senescence may result from multiple causes, or causes may be linked to one another resulting in certain types of senescence. It seems likely that other theories will emerge and that, in the long run, we will find that several of the new theories combined with existing ones will explain senescence. Researchers are beginning to look at the interactions among several of these different factors (Torre, Silipigni, Orlando, Torre, & Aragonia, 1997).

We have thought about the connections among these different theories. In Figure 3-2, seven of the theories are included (we have not included wear and tear) and arrows connecting them suggest possible causal links. The theories at the top are all programmed theories and we think they may share a connecting link through evolution theory. If one believes that we are programmed to live long enough to produce offspring and that when those years are over we are set to deteriorate and die, then connections between evolution theory and biological clock, hormone, and immune system theories all seem possible. These other theories may specify the deterioration predicted by evolution theory.

At the middle and bottom are unprogrammed theories and we think a connecting link could be provided by free radical theory. Damage from free radicals may build up over a long life and lead to frequent errors, the accumulation of certain types of garbage, a breakdown in immune system protection, and a decline in the production of certain hormones. Free radical damage can be hypothesized to underlie all sorts of senescence in the body. Of course, some of these unprogrammed theories could be directly connected to each other without help from free radicals. Errors may, for example, increase the accumulation of garbage and the accumulation of garbage could result in increased errors.

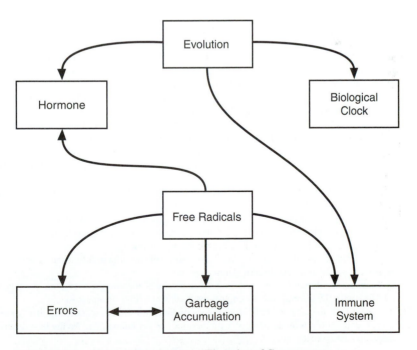

FIGURE 3-2   Connections between Theories of Senescence.

As you think about these theories and the possible connections among them, keep in mind that the research evidence is not very strong. More needs to be done.

Making Choices

There are a number of possible causes of senescence and no strong evidence in favor of any one theory. If we knew for certain what causes senescence, we might be able to offset those factors found to be responsible for cell, tissue, and organ deterioration. What choices do we have? We can choose to stay informed. We hope you will choose this path and continue to be interested all of your life. So far you have been doing an excellent job.

CHAPTER HIGHLIGHTS

- There are a number of theories that attempt to explain senescence but none have strong supporting evidence.
- All theories must deal with great variability in length of life and degree of senescence among different species some of which seem to show very little senescence (e.g., turtles); variability within a species, and variability across different environments.
- The genetically induced rapid aging of progeria is regarded by some as support for a genetic theory of aging. Other work suggests, however, that most of the variability in aging is due to environmental factors.
- Programmed theories suggest that senescence is predetermined by a plan and occurs on a relatively fixed schedule. The following three theories are programmed theories.
- Biological clock theory says that senescence is determined in our genes. The latest version of this theory says that senescence begins when cells stop dividing which occurs when telomere sequences at the end of DNA strands become sufficiently shortened.
- Evolution theory says that we are programmed to deteriorate and die after we reproduce and raise our offspring. Certain genes that result in productivity may also lead to lower levels of protection against senescence causing environmental factors.
- Hormone theories say that our glands are programmed to end production of certain hormones and that the lower levels of these hormones produce senescence.
- Immune system theories claim that decline in the immune system produces senescence. Depending on what system decline is attributed to, theories may be programmed or unprogrammed.
- Unprogrammed theories say that there is no plan for senescence, and that it occurs as a result of interactions with the environment and/or between environmental and genetic factors. The following four theories are unprogrammed.
- Wear and tear theory claims that the body wears out from a lifetime of random illnesses, injuries, and damage.
- Free radical theory says that reactive molecules produced during metabolism, exposure to radiation, and actions of our immune systems produce senescence by damaging the molecules that make up important chemicals, tissues, cells, and proteins in our bodies.
- Error theories contend that our bodies make errors all the time and that the effects of these errors accumulate over time resulting in senescence.
- Garbage accumulation theories say that waste products accumulate over time, damage tissues, and interfere with the normal functioning of our bodies resulting in senescence.
- It is most probable that no individual theory explains all of senescence and, it is more likely that some combination of them, perhaps with theories not yet known, will be the best description of the causes of senescence.

STUDY QUESTIONS

1. Do the lives of turtles or humans with progeria offer strong support for a biological/genetic theory of senescence? Why?

2. Describe the theory (theories) that claims that senescence is entirely genetic? Entirely environmental?

3. What evidence is there for the notion that senescence is due to both genetic and environmental factors?

4. Is the length of a young organism's dependence on parental care related to the life expectancy of that species?

5. How can random errors in metabolism, DNA replication, or free radical damage result in regular patterns of senescence?

6. Distinguish between programmed and unprogrammed theories of senescence. Describe several theories of each type explaining why they are regarded as programmed or unprogrammed theories.

7. Is evolution theory a programmed or unprogrammed theory? Why?

8. Can you find and describe connecting links among all seven theories?

RECOMMENDED READINGS

Hayflick, L. (1996). *How and Why We Age*. New York: Ballantine Books. Hayflick provides a very readable view of the factors that may produce senescence and a broader discussion of the points made in this chapter.

Ferrini, A. F. & Ferrini, R. L. (1993). *Health in the Later Years* (2nd ed.). Madison, WI: Brown & Benchmark. The Ferrinis present a condensed version of many of the theories described in this chapter.

Kirkwood, T. (1999). *Time of Our Lives*. New York: Oxford University Press. Tom Kirkwood presents a stimulating discussion of aging and attempts to combine many of the theories presented in this chapter. We think some such combination is inevitable.

INTERNET RESOURCES

http://www.3.hmc.edu/~clewis/aging/theories.html

http://www.albany.net/~joedono/theories.htm   Provides information on theories of aging and links to other sites.

4

Health and Longevity

With a little luck, there's no reason why you can't live to be one hundred. Once you've done that, you've got it made, because very few people die over one hundred.

—George Burns

George Burns is right that very few people die over one hundred but there may be many reasons why most people don't live that long. In this chapter we explore the factors that influence health and longevity. Longevity depends on remaining healthy. Many of the factors that we discuss are beyond the control of individuals. Genetic inheritance and gender are two such factors. Other factors such as diet, exercise and smoking are yours to manipulate to your advantage, although not many people do so. Finally, some factors beyond our control are associated with factors that are potentially within our control. Factors like race and socioeconomic status (SES) may influence health and longevity because of differences in behavior, nutrition, and access to health services. We briefly examine the quality of life for very old adults to see if living long is worthwhile. There is no magic formula for living a long, healthy life but there are a number of things you can do to increase the odds in your favor, to live to be a hundred, and then "you've got it made."

Overview

The desire to live a long and healthy life is an old one. A myth from ancient Greece relates that there was a place in the world where people, favored by the gods, lived long healthy lives. Although there is no spot on earth where people do not age, there are huge differences in longevity around the globe. Japan is the world leader in terms of life expectancy. The life expectancy for men in Japan is 76.6 and for women 83. The life expectancies for men and women in the United States are 71.8 and 78.8, respectively. Within the United States, residents of Hawaii live the longest while residents of Louisiana and Mississippi have the shortest average lives. Hawaiian life expectancies for men and women are 75.4 and 81.3, respectively (Glatzer, 1999). The life expectancy for men and women in Louisiana are 69.1 and 76.9, respectively. In Mississippi male and female life expectancies are 68.9 and 77.1, respectively (Kranczer, 1998).

Senior View

Dr. Walter Donham was in very good health and 70 years old when we spoke with him about longevity. Dr. Donham received his Ph.D. in chemical engineering in 1953 from Ohio State University and then worked for Ethel Corporation in Baton Rouge, Louisiana, for 37 years. Walter and his wife are now retired. When we arrived at his home for the interview, he was repairing the roof.

One important factor in living long is thought to be the genes you inherit from your parents. Walter agreed that genes are important and told us that most of his older relatives have lived quite long. His maternal grandfather lived to be 98 and both paternal grandparents lived to their late 80s. His mother died at 93 and his father died at age 54 from a heart attack. He said he knows several people who are 94 or 95 and are doing fine and that he would like to live to be 100.

Exercise is also thought to be an important factor for maintaining health and living longer. Walter and his wife walk one mile a day, four or five times a week. On two days he works for Habitat for Humanity doing general carpentry. He says he doesn't do much lifting, however, because his shoulder has been sore. His physician told him to start lifting 3 to 5 pound weights, 30 to 40 times a day but he admitted that he hasn't been very diligent about taking this advice. Walking is an excellent exercise for adults of all ages.

Diet is another factor that seems to be important for health and longevity. Walter eats a wide variety of foods, especially fiber, fruits, and vegetables. "Most afternoons I eat an apple for a snack," he said. As for supplements, such as vitamins and herbs, he told us that he didn't believe in the benefits of herbs but that he recently started taking a multivitamin. He thought it couldn't hurt.

The benefits and dangers of alcohol consumption have also been of interest to researchers. Walter said that he and his wife don't drink very much. "I have a bottle of wine in there and it's likely to last a year," he told us. He said it's just not one of their habits but that he saw no harm in having a glass of wine each day. He told us that most people who get in trouble with alcohol start early in life (and we will see that he is right when we get to Chapter 11). Alcohol, Walter believes, is beneficial in small amounts because it "apparently thins the blood slightly." This would help prevent clotting, heart attacks, and strokes. Aspirin is thought to do the same but Walter won't use that either. He said, "If I take aspirin very often, and scratch myself, I bleed very easily, so I don't take aspirin on a regular basis."

We asked Walter what he thought was the most important thing for maintaining good health and living to 100. "Exercise, diet, and having good genes; that's really what it gets down to," he answered. Before we could thank him he added one final thought. "Mental stimulation is a very important thing in maintaining good health; being physically and mentally active is a necessity to a long life," he said. We wholeheartedly agree.

We left and Walter climbed back up on the roof to finish his repairs.

Ponce de Leon at the Fountain of Youth.

There are also great differences in the percentages of adults 65 years of age and over in different countries. In Sweden 17 percent of the population is 65 and older while in the United States 13 percent of the population is that old. In Japan 16 percent are 65 and older (Atchley 2000). Within the United States, Florida (18.5%), Pennsylvania (15.9%), and Rhode Island (15.8%) have the highest percentages of older adults while Georgia (9.9%), Utah (8.8%), and Alaska (5.2%) have the lowest (Atchley, 2000). These proportions are expected to increase over the next 20 to 30 years.

Clearly, different people living in different places live to different ages. As we age, the death rate also declines so that the largest population increases are among the oldest-old (Vaupel, 1998). With the anticipated increases in percentages of older adults world-wide, more attention has been focused on the factors that contribute to a long and healthy life. We know that the increase in percentages is largely due to the baby boom following World War II, the lower birth rate, and increases in life expectancy (see Chapter 1).

Factors beyond Our Control

If you were born with a congenital heart condition would that affect your longevity? Probably yes. You would probably die sooner than a person born without such a condition. Genes play a role in longevity and, at present, they are largely beyond our control.

Genes influence life expectancy indirectly and it is likely that many genes are involved (Carnes, Olshansky, Gavrilov, Gavrilova, & Grahn, 1999). Genes influence susceptibility to a number of diseases, influence behavioral and biochemical responses to stress, and may influence personality characteristics, such as risk-taking behavior, for example. It is estimated that about 25 to 35 percent of the variability in human longevity is directly attributable to genetic factors (Vaupel, Carey, Christensen, Johnson, Yashin, Holm, Lachine, Kannisto, Khazaeli, Liedo, Longo, Zeng, Manton, & Curtsinger, 1998; Finch & Tanzi, 1997).

A typical method for assessing the relative influence of genetic factors has been to examine the longevity of a large sample of individuals and then correlate the lengths of those lives with the lives of their parents and grandparents. For example, almost one quarter of the immediate ancestors of Jeanne Calment, lived more than 80-years-old. In a comparison group of shorter-lived individuals, only 2 percent of immediate ancestors lived that long (Robine & Allard, 1998). Long-lived people tend to have long-lived ancestors. An investigation examined the longevity of 8409 men and 3741 women of European royal and noble families (because such families kept extensive records). Results showed that 18 to 34 percent of male longevity and 20 to 58 percent of female longevity was accounted for by the longevity of their fathers. The influence of genetic factors was highest when fathers lived past the age of 70 (Gavrilova, Gavrilov, Evdokushkina, Semyonova, Gavrilova, Evdokushkina, Kushnareva, Kroutko, & Andreyev, 1998).

Other work suggests that the maternal influence on longevity is great when deaths from cardiovascular diseases are examined, and that the longevity of grandmothers on both sides of the family is predictive of the longevity of grandchildren (Brand, Kiely, Kannel, & Myers, 1992; Vandenbroucke, 1998). The influence of the mother and grandmother on the longevity of offspring had been assumed for a long time (Pearls, 1931), but the genetic influence on longevity comes from both sides of the family and may be slightly higher for the paternal side (Gavrilov, Gavrilova, Semenova, Evdokushkina, Krut'ko, Gavrilova, Evdokushkina, & Kushnareva, 1998). Regardless of which side of the family exerts the most influence, longevity clearly runs in families.

Genes exert their influence on longevity in several ways. Illnesses that shorten life such as Downs Syndrome or Huntingtons Disease are inherited. In other cases the influence is less direct. For example, one specific gene codes for three different forms of a protein that plays a role in the metabolism of fat. These proteins are the apolipoproteins referred to as ApoE2, ApoE3, and ApoE4. Individuals inherit one form from their father and one from their mother. Individuals who live long are less likely to have two ApoE4-producing genes than any other combination. Other work suggests that such long-lived individuals are far more likely to have two ApoE2 producing genes (Schacter, Faure-Delanef, Guenot, Rouger, Froguel, Lesueur-Ginot, & Cohen, 1994; Jian-Gang, Yong-Xing, Chuan-Fu, Pei-Fang, Song-Bai, Nui-Fan, Guo-Yin, & Lin, 1998). Other researchers have not had success in finding a strong relationship between ApoE4 and longevity (Bader, Zuliani, Kostner, & Fellin, 1998).

Other researchers have compared DNA samples from centenarians to younger adults of the same gender, health, and sometimes geographic origin. Comparisons were made between DNA samples. This work has produced mixed results. The genes that are most strongly related to heart disease do not differ between centenarians and younger comparison groups (Bladbjerg, Andersen-Ranberg, de Maat, Kristensen, Jeune, Gram, & Jespersen, 1999). On the other hand, one type of protein found in the blood has been

Four generations of a Cakchiquel Mayan family in Guatemala.

found to be more frequent in centenarians than in a comparison group (Thillet, Doucet, Chapman, Herbeth, Cohen, & Faure-Delanef, 1998). Another group of researchers compared 212 centenarians with 275 younger adults and found differences in mitochondrial DNA (de Benedictis, Rose, Carrieri, de Luca, Falcone, Passarino, Bonafé, Monti, Baggio, Bertolini, Mari, Mattace, & Franceschi, 1999). Mitochondria are microscopic bodies found in the cells of living organisms that convert food to usable energy. Animal studies of mitochondria suggest that they are more likely than other structures to be damaged by free radicals due to "the nakedness of the mitochondrial genome" and its easy exposure to free radicals. Damaged mitochondria are more likely to be stimulated than undamaged mitochondria, which leads to overproduction and an increased production of free radicals (Schacter, 1998, p. 1101).

Besides genetics, other factors such as gender and race are also beyond our control but their influence on longevity may be potentially controllable.

Factors within Our Control

If you were born in Japan and moved to India would your life expectancy change? Would it depend on how old you were when you moved? If you answered yes to these questions than you must believe that the environment in which we live contributes to our longevity, and it does. Many researchers argue that genes play an important role but place no firm limit on how long a person might live (Finch, 1998). Given a perfect environment (whatever that might be) humans might live for a very long time.

The relative impact of genes and environment can be assessed by studying twins as well as by looking at the longevity of immediate ancestors. A major study of identical twins reared together or apart and fraternal twins reared together or apart looked at mortality rates. The influence of genes on longevity is assessed by comparing individuals with the same genetic inheritance (identical twins) to individuals without identical genetic inheritance (fraternal twins) to see whether the twins died closely together. If those with the same genes died closely together while those with different genes did not, then that would support a genetic influence. The influence of environment is assessed by comparing those reared together and, thus, having similar although not identical environments to those reared apart. If those from the same environment died close together while those from different environments did not, then that would support an environmental influence. The findings suggest that longevity is largely determined by environmental factors with a minimum of 66 percent of the variance in longevity due to environmental, rather than genetic, influences (Ljungquist, Berg, Lanke, McClearn, & Pedersen, 1998). This estimate is virtually the same as that provided earlier and taken from the studies of ancestors. It is clear that environmental factors strongly influence longevity. We examine the influence of a few of the more well-known environmental factors: diet, exercise, supplements, tobacco, alcohol, and stress.

Diet

The relationship between diet and longevity has been examined in animals more than in humans. Animal studies usually compare animals who have experienced restricted diets to those who have had no restrictions while human studies usually correlate longevity with **body mass index (BMI)**. BMI is used rather than weight because it takes height and weight into account. For a description of how to calculate your own body mass index, see Box 4-1.

The research on health and longevity of animals raised under different types of diet restrictions has produced positive results for over 70 years. The restriction that results in the greatest gains in life expectancy has been calorie restriction. In these studies rats were randomly assigned to groups that were allowed to eat as much as they want or to groups that were given 25 to 60 percent fewer calories than they had eaten previously (each rat's diet is reduced according to how much that individual rat ate before). The underfed group was not malnourished; they received all the vitamins and minerals necessary for rat health. The underfed groups lived longer and calorie restriction begun in rat adulthood has nearly as great an effect as calorie restriction begun early in life. A wide range of ordinary age changes were slowed and age-related diseases were often postponed or slowed down (Masoro, 1984). The underfed rats also outperformed the well-fed rats on measures of learning and coordination (Ingram, Weindruch, Spangler, Freeman, & Walford, 1987). Some work suggests that the benefits of diet restriction were only found for rats that were not well-exercised but that exercise increases average length of life for all rats (Holloszy, 1998). The longer life benefits of restricted diet also have been found for spiders, water fleas, guppies, and protozoa (Weindruch, 1996).

BOX **4-1**

Determining Your Body Mass Index

Body mass index (BMI) is found by dividing your weight in kilograms by your height in meters squared. A relatively quick and easy way to compute BMI without converting to metric measures is to take your weight in pounds and divide by your height in inches squared. Multiply that answer by 703 and you have your BMI.

$$BMI = \frac{\text{Weight in pounds}}{(\text{Height in inches})^2} \times 703$$

For example, if you are 5 feet 3 inches then your height in inches would be 63 (i.e., 5 feet × 12 inches per foot = 60 + 3 inches = 63). Your height squared would be 63 × 63 = 3969. If you weighed 120 pounds, then your BMI would be 120/3969 × 703 or 21.25.

Recommended BMI for health and longevity is usually between 20 and 30.

If this math is intimidating, go to the website of the National Heart, Lung, and Blood Institute and your BMI will be calculated for you: *http://www.nhlbisupport.com/bmi/bmicalc.htm.*

More recent work has examined calorie restriction in a species much closer to humans than rats, monkeys. A 30 percent calorie reduction in two species of monkeys resulted in longer life expectancy. The underfed monkeys had lower metabolic rates (Sell, Lane, Johnson, Masoro, Mock, Reiser, Fogarty, Cutler, Ingram, Roth, & Monnier, 1996).

It is not possible to conduct such controlled studies with humans. Can you imagine signing up to participate in a study in which your current diet was restricted by 30 percent for the rest of your life? Probably not. Biochemist Ray Wolford and his wife and daughter have been doing exactly that. They began restricting their diets in 1987 but the results are not in yet. Of course, even if they live longer than average that will not be strong evidence in favor of calorie restriction. The Wolfords also exercise and perhaps have long-lived ancestors. Also, recent research suggests that the benefit of caloric restriction may be only in old-age. Severe dietary restriction may protect older people from the effects of degenerative disease but may increase the risk of mortality in young age by making young people more vulnerable to infectious disease (Pletcher, Khazael, & Curtsinger, 2000).

It is estimated that close to 25 percent of men and 40 percent of women are trying to lose weight for two main reasons: appearance and health. (Serdula, Williamson, Anda, Levy, Heaton, & Byers, 1994). Recommended BMI for health and longevity is between 20 and 30. Obesity is related to heart disease, adult onset diabetes, and a number of circulatory and kidney problems and is believed to shorten life. Both men and women with high BMI die sooner (Lee, Manson, Hennekens, & Paffenbarger, 1993; Manson, Willett, Stampfer, Colditz, Hunter, Hankinson, Hennekens, & Speizer, 1995). A BMI over 35 is considered dangerous. Other work has found higher death rates for those with very low BMI (less than 20) (Rissanen, Knekt, Heliovaara, Aromaa, Reunanen, & Maatela, 1991). What is your BMI?

Why do both very high or very low BMI shorten life? There seem to be other environmental factors involved (Gaesser, 1999). For example, a very high BMI may be one part of a person's overall life style. Such a person may never exercise and physical activity of any type might be limited. Perhaps lack of exercise rather than or in addition to obesity causes health problems and shorter life. Some work suggests that men and women with a BMI higher than 27 are less physically active than persons with a lower BMI (Simoes, Byers, Coates, Serdula, Mokdad, & Heath, 1995). In an examination of Harvard alumni, researchers found that men with high BMI, who were also physically active, outlived men with lower BMI who were not active (Paffenbarger, Hyde, Wing, Hsieh, 1986).

A very high BMI also could be a result of a diet high in fats and low in nutrients and/or fruits and vegetables. A low BMI also might indicate a diet without the proper nutrients. Perhaps it is eating the wrong foods rather than eating too much or too little that is responsible for the shorter lives of such people. The U.S. Department of Health and Human Services recommends a diet rich in grains and sparse in fats, oils, and sweets. The well-known food pyramid (Figure 4-1) summarizes the recommendations. Generally,

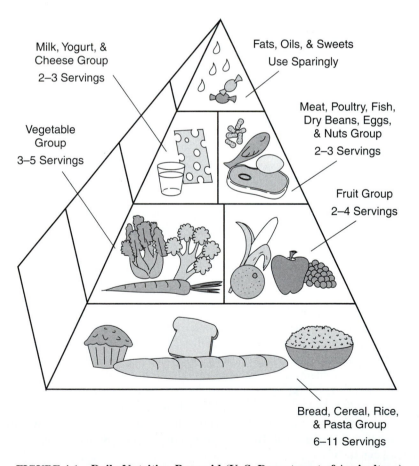

FIGURE 4-1   Daily Nutrition Pyramid (U. S. Department of Agriculture).

people should eat a lot of grains, fruits, and vegetables; some meat and dairy products, and avoid fats and sweets. Some research, however, suggests that certain sweets may not be so harmful as long as you don't overdo it. (See Box 4-2.)

Nutritional recommendations for older adults are essentially the same as for younger adults, in part, because the nutrient needs of older adults have not been well investigated. Some differences do, however, exist. For example, older adults often are advised to increase their intake of calcium (see Chapter 2). Fiber and protein recommendations for older adults are also somewhat higher while Vitamin A is somewhat lower (DiGiovanna, 1994). Studies have found that diets rich in fruits and vegetables, which have high levels of antioxidants result in lower risk of cancer, cardiovascular disease, and age-related degenerative diseases. A recent study also found that Vitamin E, eaten in foods such as spinach or taken as a supplement, results in a significant reduction in the neurological decline associated with aging (Martin, Prior, Shukitt-Hale, Cao, & Joseph, 2000).

Exercise

Exercise is important for promoting and maintaining muscle strength, strong bones, flexible joints, and a healthy heart. Exercise is believed to reduce hypertension and the risks of adult onset diabetes, heart disease, cancer, and osteoporosis. Exercise may reduce

BOX 4-2

Sweets for the Sweet

Most dieticians and nutritionists recommend avoiding too much sugar. A common assumption is that chocolates, candy, and other sweets are never good, always harmful, and should be avoided. Dentists say candy causes tooth decay, and they are undoubtedly right that candy does contribute to the growth of cavity-producing bacteria. Many people believe that sugar makes kids hyperactive, but they are wrong. Research evidence indicates no relationship between hyperactivity and sugar consumption. Perhaps these findings mean that candy in some instances may not be a bad thing. But is it ever a good thing?

One study suggests that might be true. Candy consumption was examined in 7841 men who had no heart disease or cancer when the study was initiated. Participants were between the ages of 60 and 72 and were asked about their consumption of candy, cigarettes, red meat, alcohol, vegetables, and vitamins over a year's time. Death rates were followed from 1988 to 1993 and 7.5 percent of those who did not consume candy died while only 5.9 percent of candy consumers died. Candy consumers were less likely to smoke, drank less alcohol, ate more red meat and vegetables, and were less likely to take vitamins. Both groups had the same levels of physical activity. On average, candy consumers lived almost a year longer than those who did not consume candy (Lee & Paffenbarger, 1998).

Other, more humorous work, suggests that chocolate, in particular, along with lobster and champagne, may be beneficial for those who wish to live long (Kirschbaum, 1998). Another study of chocolate suggests that dark chocolate contains flavanoids that stimulate antioxidant and blood clot-inhibiting effects in the blood (Rein, Paglieroni, Pearson, Wun, Schmitz, Gosselin, & Keen, 2000). The possible benefits of candy are not easy for many professionals to accept but we suspect the majority of folks would welcome this news.

anxiety and depression and increase cognitive abilities by increasing blood flow to the brain. Exercise is a major factor in increasing longevity (Cress, Buchner, Questad, Esselman, deLateur, & Schwartz, 1999; Lee & Paffenbarger, 1992; Vena, Graham, Zielezny, Swanson, Barnes, & Nolan, 1985).

Research suggests that the more exercise one gets, the greater the benefits. One study followed 10,224 men and 3120 women in Dallas, Texas, for eight years. All participants were healthy when the study began. Physical fitness was measured by performance on a treadmill. Based on age, gender, and treadmill performance participants were assigned to one of five fitness groups. Deaths from all causes over the course of the study were highest for the least fit group (93 deaths) and fewest for the most fit group (39 deaths). These differences in number of deaths were primarily due to lowered levels of cancer and heart disease in the more physically fit individuals (Blair, Kohl, Paffenbarger, Clark, Cooper, & Gibbons, 1989).

Adults who exercise increase their physical fitness in a number of ways and show improvement even when starting later in life. In Chapter 2 we discussed the importance of resistance training for strengthening bones, and preventing bone loss, and osteoporosis. Aerobic exercises such as biking, brisk walks, dancing, jogging, uphill hiking, cross-country skiing, and swimming, as well as aerobic machine exercisers such as cyclers, steppers, and treadmills, improve respiration and cardiovascular health (American Heart Association, 1993). A recent study randomly assigned adults 70 years of age and older to an exercise group or a nonexercise control group. The exercise group met three times a week for six months. Exercises consisted of stair-stepping, weight lifting, rowing, and other machine exercises. The exercise group showed an 11 percent increase in oxygen consumption; a 33 percent increase in muscle strength; and increases in flexibility, endurance, and coordination. The control group showed no change at all (Cress, Buchner, Questad, Esselman, deLateur, & Schwartz, 1999). Similar benefits were seen in a group of nursing home residents, including physically frail and cognitively impaired persons, who participated in a four-month comprehensive exercise program (Lazowski, Eccleston, Myers, Paterson, Tudor-Locke, Fitzgerald, Jones, Shima, & Cunningham, 1999).

People who exercise are also better able to control their weight and, perhaps, it is the lower weight that contributes more to longevity than the exercise itself. Several studies have used good research control to investigate these contributions separately and have found benefits of both, independent of one another.

Supplements

People who want to live longer lives have often sought quick and easy remedies for aging. Claims for lotions, pills, herbs, beverages, and other products that will reverse aging and prolong life will exist as long as people are willing to buy them. Manufacturers are not hesitant about offering new products containing the latest herbal remedy for some aspect of aging (Feig, 1998). Figure 4-2 on page 86, provides a fictional example of these types of products.

In Chapter 2 we looked at the claims often made for the hormones DHEA, melatonin, and human growth hormone and saw that none of these supplements reversed aging or lengthened life. (See Project 4 on page 87.) In fact, their use can be quite dangerous. The same is true for the following supplements (Schulz & Salthouse, 1999).

*Older adults participating in
the Senior Games.*

- **Pantothenic acid** is the active ingredient in royal jelly. Royal jelly is the substance fed to newborn bees to help their growth and fed continually to the Queen bee. Queen bees can live for years while other bees live for a few months at most. Since royal jelly extends the life of queen bees one might hope that it would extend the life of humans too. This substance is, however, already present in a number of whole grains and legumes and no evidence for any anti-aging or life-extending effects in humans has been found.
- **Gerovital** has been advertised as an anti-aging and rejuvenation supplement for decades but has no effect on aging. It may make you feel better because the main ingredient, procaine hydrochloride (Novocain) is a mild antidepressant.
- **Ginseng** comes from a small plant and is thought by some to be an aphrodisiac and a rejuvenator. There is no evidence to support either of these claims and large amounts of ginseng can produce anxiety, insomnia, gastrointestinal disorders, and elevated blood pressure.
- **Selenium** is found in several foods, especially nuts, and is an essential nutrient. No evidence for any effects on aging has been found but some recent work suggests that selenium may retard cancer growth in mice. Large doses can be toxic. Tests on cancer growth in humans have not been completed.

Reduces wrinkles, brow lines, sagging skin, crows feet

Grows new hair & Colors gray hair

Halts hearing loss

Improves memory & eyesight

Builds strong bones & muscles

Kindles your sexual fire

Contains Vitamins E & C, Ginseng, Melatonin, Ginger, Garlic, Zinc, Selenium, DHEA, Chromium, Calcium, Gingko, Iron, & Crocodile Tears

FIGURE 4-2   Fountain of Youth Supplements.

Other supplements may, however, have some benefits. Applications of **Retin A**, over a period of several months, reduced lipofuscins (dark spots; see Chapter 2) and some wrinkling of the skin in close to 75 percent of test participants. However, almost as many adults experienced reddening, swelling, and irritation of the skin. Most often these unwanted side effects disappear after several months of use. **Alphahydroxy acids (AHAs),** which often include citric acid, may decrease the thinning and wrinkling of the skin that occurs with aging. AHA treatments do not appear to produce the skin irritations that frequently accompany the use of Retin A, but also do not reduce lipofuscins on the skin (Rowe & Kahn, 1998). Little is known about the long-term effects of using these products. However, to keep wrinkles and/or lipofuscins at bay, one must continue using the supplement.

Aspirin is an effective agent for reducing the risk of stroke, myocardial infarction, and in some cases heart attack. One dose of 325-mg aspirin daily can reduce the risk of heart attack by 50 percent in men with high levels of C-reactive protein. C-reactive protein is an indicator of inflammation and accumulation of blockage of blood vessels in the heart and brain (Mahoney & Restak, 1998). Aspirin can, however, also increase the risk of brain

PROJECT **4**

Searching for the Fountain of Youth

Take a trip to a local health store or try a large pharmacy or department store instead. Go to the sections that have dietary supplements and cosmetics and look for **anti-aging products**. You may be surprised at how many you find. Americans spend millions of dollars every year trying to reverse, or stop, aging. Many vitamins, herbs, minerals, ointments, and other more mysterious substances are advertised for their anti-aging properties. For each product you find:

- Record the name, the company that makes it, and the specific claim(s) made.
- Which ingredient is the one that is supposed to produce the anti-aging effect?
- If the active ingredient is one of the ones discussed in this chapter (e.g., ginseng, pantothenic acid, selenium, Retin A) or in Chapter 3 (melatonin, SOD, DHEA, growth hormone, beta-carotene), then you know how valid the claims made for anti-aging benefits are; were any of the claims based on current evidence?
- If the active ingredient is not one we have discussed (e.g., lamb fetus, crocodile tears), how valid do you think the claims are? Why?

It is sad that so many people search for youth while it slips through their fingers. All of us grow older and each day should be appreciated rather than spent yearning for days already past. Old age is a time to be welcomed and celebrated. The real fountain of youth is in your mind. You are only as old as you think you are or as the great Satchel Paige asked, "How old would you be if you didn't know how old you was?"

---

hemorrhage. Aspirin also is very damaging to the lining of the digestive system and should be taken in a buffered or coated form. **Folic acid** is associated with reduced risk of heart disease and cancer in the colon and rectum. Researchers are still examining these two supplements and also have begun to look at the use of finasteride to prevent prostate cancer and tamoxifen to prevent breast cancer (Lanier, McGinnis, Sox, & Weingarten, 1999).

Tobacco

Tobacco, in the form of cigarettes, is responsible for over 3 million deaths each year, worldwide (American Cancer Society, 1994). Cigars, pipes, chewing tobacco, and snuff account for additional cancers and deaths, as does secondhand smoke. Smoking is strongly associated with cancer of the lungs, esophagus, bladder, mouth, larynx, kidneys, pancreas, and cervix. Smoking is strongly associated with heart disease, emphysema, and bronchitis (Katchadourian, 1987; Menotti, Giampaoli, & Seccareccia, 1998; U.S. Department of Health & Human Services, 1987). Tobacco smoke contains a number of harmful substances that contribute to these disorders. Nicotine is an addictive alkaloid (like caffeine, morphine, and strychnine) that causes small blood vessels to constrict while increasing heart rate. One result is an increase in blood pressure. Smoke particles and tar produce respiratory problems. Tar is carcinogenic. Toxins such as carbon monoxide and cyanide combine with red blood cells and block the transportation of oxygen to body tissues and the brain. Smokers get a constriction of small blood vessels, a racing heart, a jump in blood pressure, a block-age of oxygen, and the ingestion of cancer-causing substances with every smoke inhalation.

For men, the effects of smoking may be quite important long before the end of life. The incidence of erectile dysfuncion is far higher in smokers than in nonsmokers (Sofikitis, Miyagawa, Dimitriadis, Zavos, Sikka, & Hellstrom, 1995). For couples hoping to conceive, researchers also have found that the sperm of smokers shows lower quality than the sperm of nonsmokers (Zavos, Correa, Antypas, Zarmakoupis-Zavos, & Zarmakoupis, 1998).

Clearly smoking is very harmful. Nevertheless, it is estimated that more than one-third of men and almost one-third of women in the United States smoke on a regular basis (Zavos, 1989). These estimates mark a decline in smoking over the last two decades as society has become less tolerant of smoking. Most individuals who smoke begin in adolescence or young adulthood and between one-third to one-half of those who try cigarettes become regular users (Giovino, Henningfield, Tomar, Escobedo, & Slade, 1995). Non-smokers who live with smokers are estimated to inhale about 5 percent of the amount of smoke produced by the smoker (Matsukura, Taminato, Kitano, Seino, Hamada, Uchihashi, Nakajima, & Hirata, 1984). Research is underway to investigate the health effects of secondhand smoke.

When one quits smoking the improvements in blood circulation begin immediately. Within the first year, the risks of heart attack and stroke decline dramatically. For example, the risk of heart attack for nonsmoking women and for women who quit smoking three years ago are the same (Rosenberg, Palmer, & Shapiro, 1990). Even the likelihood of cancer returns to normal levels after ten or more years following quitting (National Institute on Aging, 1993). If you are currently a smoker, the greatest influence you can have on your own longevity and on those who breathe your smoke is to quit. If you are not a smoker, the greatest influence you can have on your own longevity is to never begin and avoid exposure to the smoke of others.

Alcohol

The relationship between alcohol consumption and longevity is U-shaped. Those who don't drink at all and those who consume excessive amounts of alcohol are at the highest risk for a number of disorders and early death while those who drink moderately are generally healthier and live longer (Williams, 1988). Red wine has been found to be associated with reduced levels of heart disease (Leger, Cochrane, & Moore, 1979). Alcohol from sources other than red wine is also associated with lower levels of heart attacks and increases in good cholesterol (high density lipoproteins), which help protect against heart disease (Johansson & Medhus, 1974; Klatsky, Friedman, & Sieglaub, 1974). The benefits of moderate consumption are reduced risk of heart disease.

Excessive use of alcohol shortens life. Alcoholism is strongly associated with liver damage and disease (cirrhosis), depression, and suicide. Some researchers believe that the relationship between alcohol use and longevity is due to factors other than alcohol. It is generally accepted that excessive drinkers endanger their health. Nondrinkers, however, may die sooner for other reasons. Both heavy drinkers and nondrinkers have a lower average socioeconomic status (SES) than moderate drinkers and, thus, might have less access to health services and lower levels of nutrition. These factors might account for their poorer health and shorter lives. Nondrinkers may have more rigid personalities than moderate drinkers and be more affected by stressful situations. Even moderate drinkers with a fair amount of stress have a drink to relax. These differences, if they exist, might also contribute to poorer health and shorter life (Ferrini & Ferrini, 1993). These are important questions for researchers to answer before the beneficial effects of alcohol are fully understood.

Stress

Stress refers to life events that produce mental and/or emotional disruption. Life is full of such events and the amount of disruption produced depends on the amount of change that accompanies the event and the individual's own coping skills. Positive events such as moving to a new home, getting a better paying job, getting married, or having a baby produce considerable amounts of disruption just as negative events do such as the death of a parent, a divorce, being fired at work, or developing a serious illness. Ratings of the stressfulness of different events place death of a spouse and divorce very high while having a baby or moving to a new home are much lower. The relationships among level of stress, coping skills, health, and mortality have been investigated, and the general finding is that people under a lot of stress, particularly those with poor coping skills, experience a decrease in health and a shorter life (Holmes & Rahe, 1976; Ruberman, Weinblatt, Goldberg, & Chaudhary, 1984; Yong-Xing, Zan-Sun, Yue, Shu-Ying, Zheng-Yan, Long, Jian-Ying, Shu-Qi, Jian-Gang, & Lin, 1998).

How do stressors produce such effects? Stress increases blood pressure and continued stress and high blood pressure increase the risk of a heart attack and ulcers (Sapolsky, 1992). Stress increases the secretion of the hormones adrenalin and noradrenaline and prolonged stress results in higher cortisol levels. Cortisol suppresses the functioning of the immune system. Persons under stress show decreased immune function (Endresen, Relling, Tonder, Myking, Walther, & Ursin, 1991–1992). Long periods of stress may produce long periods of suppressed immune system functioning. The ability to cope with stress is often decreased in older adults who may secrete higher levels of hormones and for longer periods of time after a stressful event (Lakatta, 1990). At the same time, many older adults, after a lifetime of experience with stress, have developed effective coping strategies. An interesting study comparing centenarians and young people in Italy found that genetic markers of longevity affect stress adaptation. The same genes that may be related to higher mortality in young- and middle-age may push individuals who survive those periods to a higher level of stress adaptation capacity in old-age (Yashin, DeBenedictis, Vaupel, Tan, Andrew, Iachine, Bonafe, Valensin, DeLuca, Carotenuto, & Franceschi, 2000). The old adage, that which does not kill you, makes you stronger, may be right.

Since the effects of stress can be ameliorated with good coping skills, it may be important to develop such skills before facing more stress. One of the hypothesized reasons for the long life of Hawaiians is that they have learned to relax when minor frustrations occur. One indicator of this relaxed attitude is the absence of horn blowing on the streets and expressways of Hawaii (Glatzer, 1999). Relaxing by using biofeedback, meditation, or a specific relaxation technique can be quite effective for handling stress; Box 4-3, on pages 90–92, describes some of these techniques.

BOX **4-3**

Learning to Relax

It is important for health and longevity to relax and not bottle up stress. A certain amount of stress occurs for everyone but the following techniques might help you gain some control over your response to stress.

Biofeedback

Biofeedback refers to a training technique in which people are taught to control bodily functions not normally controlled voluntarily in order to improve health and performance. Biofeedback devices provide information about heart rate, brain waves, blood pressure, and for purposes of relaxation, hand temperature. Learning to warm your hands involves redirecting blood flow from the head to the hands and can be very relaxing. One method uses a liquid crystal, or a biodot placed on the hand (Figure 4-3). The color of the dot indicates the temperature of the skin on the hand. If you can find mental strategies that increase blood flow to the hand to make it warm, the dot will turn blue. You will feel relaxed. Once you have found a mental strategy that works, the dot is no longer needed; you now know how to relax.

Biodots to help you learn to warm your hands and relax, are available from Biodot International Inc. at 1-800-272-2340. Professionals use other biofeedback techniques, as well. For people with tension and migraine headaches, biofeedback has been shown to be a very effective treatment (Schwartz & Schwartz, 1993).

Meditation

Meditation involves gaining control over attention so that a heightened state of relaxation can be achieved. The goal is to eliminate sources of distraction. It is, of course, relatively easy to find a quiet and private place to meditate and, thus, eliminate all external distractions. It is much harder to control attention and quiet continual internal noise. We tend to be always thinking about something. To eliminate this internal chatter, meditation techniques focus attention on a picture, which

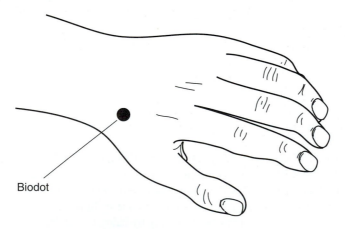

Biodot

FIGURE 4-3   Biodot on Hand.

is called a mandala (Figure 4-4), or a sound called a mantra, or some physiological function such as breathing.

　　Successful meditation focuses the individual on the present moment without evaluating or analyzing that moment. Meditation results in lowered blood pressure, a decrease in heart rate, and is more effective than just closing your eyes and relaxing (Holmes, 1987). On the other hand, meditation is not easy to learn and it requires a fair amount of practice to achieve the meditative

(continued)

FIGURE 4-4   Mandala.

BOX **4-3**   **Continued**

state. If you are interested in learning to meditate, you might consult the report provided by Michael West (1987).

Relaxation Techniques
There are a number of relatively simple relaxation techniques. These techniques are designed to relax the skeletal muscles and calm the heart and autonomic nervous system (e.g., digestion, hormone output). One of these techniques, referred to as autogenic, involves finding a comfortable place to sit, closing your eyes, and then relaxing, muscle by muscle, from your toes; up your legs, backside, back, stomach, chest, shoulders, and down your arms to your finger tips. When those muscles are relaxed, you return to your shoulders; and relax your neck, chin, cheeks, eyes, and forehead. Many find it helpful to visualize a blue light progressing up the body with each new relaxed muscle and/or to visualize all tension being pushed out the tips of your fingers and the top of your head. Some areas of the body will take longer to relax then others and this varies from individual to individual. Relaxation is an effective technique for lowering blood pressure and the levels of stress-related hormones (Taylor, 1995).

So learn to relax. We strongly encourage you to try biofeedback, meditation, or a relaxation technique if you do not already have some technique that works for you. Don't forget that exercise has been shown to dramatically reduce stress! Relax, it will help you live longer and healthier.

Other Factors

One cannot change one's gender or race/ethnic group although one could appear to make such changes. These factors influence longevity but seem to do so through social variables.

Gender

Females live longer than males and this difference in longevity is referred to as the **gender gap**. From conception onward males have higher death rates than females (Smith, 1993). This difference in favor of females occurs in species other than humans and, in humans, it occurs worldwide. The only exceptions have been several countries where female infanticide and high rates of maternal mortality have existed (Zopf, 1992). Over the last 100 years, the size of the gender gap has fluctuated and grown. Figure 4-5 shows female and male life expectancies in the United States over the last 100 years.

The gender differences in death rates are particularly high for certain forms of death. It is estimated that about 40 percent of the gender gap is due to gender differences in heart disease and stroke due to atherosclerosis. Another 33 percent of the gender gap is thought to be due to social and behavioral differences. Men have much higher rates of suicide, cirrhosis of the liver, lung cancer, and emphysema. Men tend to smoke, drink, and use guns more than women do (National Institutes of Health, 1988). It is expected that the gender gap, which was bigger in 1970 than it had ever been (when female life expectancy was 7.6

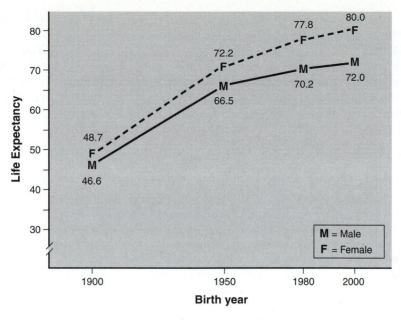

FIGURE 4-5   Gender Gap in Longevity from 1900 to 2000.

years longer than male life expectancy), will decrease, somewhat, as individuals begin eating better, exercising more, and paying more attention to their health; the gap might never, however, disappear (Kranczer, 1999). Others argue that the gap will narrow but not as a result of men becoming more health conscious. Instead, the gap may narrow as women become heavier smokers, drinkers, and risk-takers than they are at present.

Genetic/Biological Explanations.   There are several different genetic and biological explanations for the gender gap. One hypothesis is that the differences in longevity between females and males are due in part to inherited sex chromosomes. Females receive an XX sex chromosome while males receive an XY sex chromosome. This difference is known to play a role in disorders such as color blindness and hemophilia. When a gene is carried on the X chromosome, females receive two while males receive one. If the gene is recessive and codes for a negative trait (N), then females who receive that gene on one X chromosome still have a chance to inherit the healthy (H) dominant gene on the other X chromosome. Males do not since they receive only the one gene on their one X chromosome. Perhaps some negative factor(s) associated with longevity are carried on the X chromosome. While this hypothesis is interesting, no one has found any genes that code for shorter life let alone ones that are carried on the sex chromosomes. Interestingly, in birds the female receives two different sex chromosomes (ZW) while the male receives two of the same kind (ZZ). If the sex chromosome hypothesis was correct, one would expect male birds to live longer but, in fact, female birds live longer (Ricklefs, 1973).

A second genetic/biological hypothesis is that the gender gap is due to hormonal differences. Men and women have many of the same hormones but the relative amounts differ. Men have more testosterone while women have more estrogen (DiGiovanna, 1994). Testosterone is known to increase blood clotting while estrogen reduces clotting. If testosterone increases clotting, then that may account for some of the higher levels of atherosclerosis in males. Females might have some protection against atherosclerosis because of the positive effects of estrogen (U.S. Department of Health & Human Services, 1992). One way to investigate the effects of these hormones is to eliminate them. While estrogen is eliminated in women after menopause and the rate of heart attacks does increase, there are other factors involved. The women are older. Other work has eliminated testosterone in male rats by castrating them when they are young. Generally these rats live longer than usual but often not as long as well-exercised intact rats. In humans, castration was not an uncommon treatment for some forms of psychosis, certain cancers, and mental impairment during the last decades of the nineteenth century and the early decades of the twentieth century. Many years ago, researchers interested in the relationship between testosterone and longevity examined several hundred institutionalized persons with mental impairment. Some of them had been castrated. On average, the females outlived the males by just over six years while the castrated males outlived those females by about the same amount. The younger the men were when they were castrated, the longer they lived (Hamilton, 1948). Of course, there are some problems with such comparisons. Perhaps, the castrated males were treated better than other persons in the institutions because their lack of testosterone made them more docile than the other males and females. People who work in institutions often favor docile residents. Perhaps they were castrated in the first place because of some personality or health difference that was not present in the other males or females. Although we cannot be sure what factors resulted in the obtained differences in length of life, the results are very interesting and do correspond with the results from many animal studies.

Environmental Explanations. One environmental difference that may contribute to the gender gap is the difference in proportions of female and male tobacco users. Of course, the gender difference in smoking has been narrowing as the recent drop in smoking has been greater for males than for females (Centers for Disease Control, 1989; 1991a). Twelve percent of men and women under the age of 18 smoke (Centers for Disease Control, 1991b). Since tobacco use is a major factor in the production of cancer and heart disease, the gender differences in smoking must be responsible for some of the gender difference in longevity.

A second environmental explanation is that men are more likely to engage in risky behaviors, beyond smoking, than are women. More men than women drink alcohol excessively and die from cirrhosis of the liver. Men are more likely to isolate themselves socially while women are more likely to use social supports to assist them in times of trouble (see Chapter 9). Social supports are known to help buffer individuals against certain diseases and to assist individuals in getting well (Eckert & Rubinstein, 1999). Men are more likely to commit suicide than are women. Men are more likely to drive fast, jump from airplanes, wrestle alligators, and shoot guns than are women. These differences are largely cultural and some expect that the gender gap may narrow as women begin doing the same sorts of things in greater numbers than they have in the past.

An older person sky diving.

Race/Culture

There are large life expectancy differences between different racial and ethnic groups (see Chapter 1). White Americans live longer than African, Hispanic, and Native Americans but not as long as Asian Americans (Smith, 1993). Over the last decade, however, African Americans have been making greater advances in life expectancy than other groups. The average gain for White American men and women from 1990 to 2000 is about one and a quarter years while the average gain for African American men and women is more than 4 years. These recent gains also have been greater for men than for women (Kranczer, 1999). These changes suggest an improving health environment for African Americans although more needs to be done.

The major causes of death and incidence of serious diseases among various ethnic groups are not the same. Adult **African Americans** have higher rates of heart disease, cancer, stroke, diabetes, cirrhosis of the liver, pneumonia, and influenza than White Americans. The rate of infant mortality is also higher. The rate of homicide among African Americans is almost six times higher than among White Americans. White Americans, however, have higher rates of chronic obstructive pulmonary disease and suicide (Smith, 1993). Many of these differences can be attributed to poorer nutrition and less access to health care for individuals at lower SES levels and a greater proportion of African than White Americans are at those lower levels. A greater proportion of African American men smoke than White American men but a lower proportion of African American women smoke than White American women (Smith, 1993). African Americans have higher rates of hypertension, high BMI, high cholesterol, and alcohol abuse (Otten, Teutsch, Williamson, & Marks, 1990).

African Americans are far more likely to die during young and middle adulthood than are White, Hispanic, Asian, or Native Americans (U.S. Department of Health and Human Services, 1992). Older African Americans, however, have longer life expectancies (LEASA) than others. Life expectancies at 85 for White American men and women are 90.1 and 91.3 years, respectively. Life expectancies for 85-year-old African American men and women are 90.7 and 92.0, respectively (Smith, 1993).

Most of the data on **Hispanic Americans** has come from studies of Mexican Americans and, thus, might not be accurate for all other Hispanic American groups (Yee & Weaver, 1994). Heart disease, cancer, diabetes, and stroke are the most frequent causes of death and rates of hypertension are also high for Mexican Americans. The incidence of AIDS is also fairly high. The homicide rate among Hispanic Americans is more than nine times higher than among White Americans. As with African Americans, however, older Hispanic Americans have lower death rates than White Americans (Zopf, 1992).

Asian Americans have the longest life expectancies. Although Asian Americans have higher rates of tuberculosis, anemia, and hepatitis than other groups, they have lower rates of heart disease and stroke (Yee & Weaver, 1994). Fewer Asian Americans smoke and/or abuse alcohol than members of other ethnic groups and infant mortality rates are also lower. Cancer rates among Asian Americans are lower except for stomach cancer, which occurs at a much higher rate (Weisburger, 1991). As with Hispanic Americans, it is difficult to generalize the findings from one group, such as Japanese Americans, to all other Asian American groups.

Native Americans have high death rates from many of the same causes as White Americans: heart disease, cancer, stroke, pneumonia, and influenza. For Native Americans, diabetes is also a major cause of death. The incidence of diabetes in Native Americans is ten times the rate in White Americans (American Association of Retired Persons, 1993). Alcohol abuse is more frequent among Native Americans than among other ethnic groups (Yee & Weaver, 1994). On the other hand, the rate of infant mortality among Native Americans is lower than among African Americans even though their SES levels also are lower (Zopf, 1992). As with African and Hispanic Americans, older Native Americans have longer life expectancies than older White Americans. Again, one must be cautious in generalizing since there are many different Native American groups. For example, the incidence of lung cancer among Native Americans in the Southwest is very low as not many use tobacco while those in the Northwest have much higher rates (American Cancer Society, 1991).

Handedness

There are large age differences in handedness with many more younger left-handed people than older left-handed people (Coren, 1994). About 15 percent of younger adults are left-handed while only 1 percent of older adults are left-handed (Porac & Coren, 1981). The percentage of right-handers is always higher and seems to increase the older we get (Coren & Halpern, 1991). Why do you think this difference occurs? Do right-handers tend to live longer than left-handers? Some suggest that the difference is a cohort rather than an age difference. When today's older adults were young, many teachers and parents discouraged and sometimes even punished use of the left hand. The low incidence of left-handedness among these, now older individuals may, thus, be due to these early experiences. A second hypothesis suggests that the difference is due to greater risk of accidents for left-handers living in our right-handed cultures. Left-handed people simply die, on average, sooner than right-handed people because of these risks. A third hypothesis suggests that the two hemispheres of the brain develop at different rates. The slower left hemisphere, which controls the right hand, produces more frequent use of that hand as it matures. Some people who were initially left-handed would become right-handed as their left hemisphere matured (Geschwind & Galaburda, 1987). Of course, all three hypotheses could account for a portion of the obtained differences.

One recent examination of differences in handedness between old and young tested rhesus macaques. Handedness was assessed by observing which hand was used for retrieving food that was tossed into the animal home environments. Among 34 young primates, only 1 was right-handed, 21 were left-handed, and 12 showed no preference. Among 30 older primates, 16 were right-handed, 4 were left-handed, and 10 showed no preference. As with humans, left-handedness was far more prevalent among the younger macaques. Since the primate environment does not favor right- or left-handedness by discouraging, punishing, or increasing the risk for one or the other types of handedness, the findings are most consistent with the third hypothesis of different maturation rates for the two hemispheres of the brain (Westergaard & Lussier, 1999). Young left-handed macaques may become right-handed as their brain matures. More work is needed to determine whether or not young left-handers really do tend to become right-handers as they grow older. Research on brain use offers supporting evidence from another direction. Older adults tend to activate both frontal lobes when completing spatial and verbal performance tasks. This is in contrast to younger task performers who tend to use only one side of the brain (Reuter-Lorenz, 2001). The relationship between handedness and longevity is an interesting mystery.

Social Factors

A number of social factors influence longevity and, as suggested in our discussion of gender and racial/ethnic group differences, may underlie the apparent influence of these other factors. The major social factors are SES and social support. The role of religion in aging is being examined from a scientific perspective (see Chapter 9) and interesting relationships between religion and mortality have emerged.

Socioeconomic Status

The relationship between SES and longevity seems obvious. People who make less money, have low-paying and/or hazardous jobs, or, at the extreme are unemployed and generally less healthy. Such individuals often have poorer nutrition and less access to doctors, hospitals, and technology. For many, a lack of insurance is the major reason for the inaccessibility of medical care. People with lower SES may not be able to afford nutritional foods and many work long hours that prevent exercise. Exercise clubs also cost money, which may not be available. These individuals are usually less educated and may not know how to care for themselves or their families. Also, individuals at lower SES levels are more likely to use tobacco and to drink excessively. On average, they have poorer health than individuals at higher levels of SES. They do not, therefore, live as long (Atchley, 2000; Escobedo & Peddicord, 1996).

Attempts to address and correct differences in SES have a long history in many countries and cultures. No solution has yet been found. Although social security, Medicare, and Medicaid programs in the United States have helped some individuals, research suggests that the SES differences among older Americans are still greater than for any other age group (Crystal & Shea, 1990). Those most likely to be at a lower SES are African, Hispanic, and Native Americans.

Social Support

One of the most well-known longitudinal investigations of longevity began in 1965 near San Francisco. Participants were followed for 17 years. As you might expect, results showed strong influences for many of the factors already discussed. For example, smoking, not exercising, having a high BMI, and abusing alcohol were strongly associated with shorter life expectancy. Results also showed a large difference in life expectancy between those who were socially active and had a lot of social support from family and friends and those who were socially isolated. Those with social support had less than half the mortality rate of those who were socially isolated (Berkman & Breslow, 1983). Other studies using cross-sectional comparisons of individuals with and without social support have obtained the same result (House, Landis, & Umberson, 1988). People with strong social support groups live longer.

Social support can come from a number of sources. In a successful marriage husband and wife can rely on each other in times of stress or ill health and support each other in healthy habits and outlook. Married people live longer than divorced, widowed, or single people of the same age (Eriksson, Hessler, Sundh, & Steen, 1999; Pfeiffer, 1970). An unsuccessful marriage, however, offers no social support and may even worsen conditions. Maintaining close ties and interactions with family and friends and/or being socially active in religious or cultural groups or other social organizations also offer social support (Berkman, 1986; Cohen, Teresi, & Holmes, 1985). Another form of social support can come from serving as a volunteer. Volunteers typically meet new people and develop new social relationships and research suggests that a moderate amount of volunteering is associated with longer life (Musick, Herzog, & House, 1999). Interesting gender and age differences contribute to the social support and longevity relationship. Men under the age of

70 who remarry show a greater risk of mortality than do women in this same category. For women, longevity benefits occur for those with strong organizational ties and more living children, but only for women age 70 and over (Tucker, Schwartz, Clark, & Friedman, 1999). It is important to emphasize that it is the quality of the social relationships rather than the number of relationships that is most important.

How does social support contribute to longevity? A favorite hypothesis is that support serves as a buffer against stress and encourages healthy habits. As we saw earlier, high levels of stress, particularly for individuals with poor coping skills, are strongly associated with poor health and shorter life. Family, close friends, and other social groups can offer help in times of stress and so relieve some of the negative effects of stress. As a result, they contribute to health and longevity (Cobb, 1976; Hanson, Isacsson, Janzan, & Lindell, 1989). People who are alone without a network of family and friends to lend a hand in troubled times are less likely to eat well and care for themselves. Isolated individuals are more likely to turn to suicide when experiencing major depression.

Another hypothesis is that some characteristics of sociable people contribute to their high levels of social support and their longer lives. For example, people with higher levels of sociability, optimism, and religiosity are generally healthier (Antonucci, Fuhrer, & Dartigues, 1997; Oxman, Freeman, & Manheimer, 1995; Scheier, Matthews, Owens, Magovern, Lefebvre, Abbott, & Carver, 1989). In one recent study, researchers compared individuals high in trust with those low in trust over an eight-year period and found that people with high levels of trust lived longer (Barefoot, Maynard, Beckham, Brummett, Hooker, & Siegler, 1998). It is not clear, however, whether higher levels of trust, optimism, religiosity, and sociability result in more social support or if they derive from higher levels of social support.

Clearly there are no simple formulas for living longer. The variables related to longevity are numerous and influence each other as well as health and long life (Box 4-4, pp. 100–102). The quality of life for older adults is an important part of the quest for longevity.

Quality of Life

Good health is an important aspect of quality of life. Healthier people are also happier, more socially active, and more satisfied with life (Cockerham, Sharp, & Wilcox, 1983). Satisfaction with life is strongly associated with longevity (Palmore, 1985). When older adults are asked about their health, many more White Americans (70%) than African Americans (52%) or Hispanic Americans (50%) rate their health as good or excellent. Older adults with annual incomes of less than $10,000 rarely rate their health as good or excellent (10% do) (American Association of Retired Persons, 1991). It is also the case that people who perceive their health to be good live longer than those who perceive their health to be poor (Kaplan, Barell, & Lusky, 1988). Interestingly, older people who rate their life expectancy as being high live longer than those who do not expect to live as long (van Doorn & Kasl, 1998). One might expect people who live long to be relatively healthy and happy.

One recent study compared the quality of life for 38 centenarians, 38 adults age 75 to 85, and 38 adults age 86 to 99. In each of these groups, 32 participants were

B O X   **4-4**

Estimating Your Own Life Expectancy

This test is designed to estimate life expectancy for individuals with different genetic endowments and different life experiences. The number(s) that result are only estimates. Answer each question honestly.

To begin, you will need to determine your life expectancy at birth. Take, from the following, the age that is closest to your present age and use that as your starting point.

	Male		Female	
Age	*White*	*Black*	*White*	*Black*
20	73.0	67.5	79.7	75.3
25	73.5	68.1	79.9	75.6
30	73.9	68.7	80.1	75.9
35	74.2	69.4	80.2	76.2
40	74.6	70.2	80.4	76.7
45	75.0	71.2	80.7	77.2
50	75.7	72.5	81.2	78.1

Use that beginning life expectancy to add or subtract from as you answer the following questions:

1. If you are now over age 50, **add 10**.

   If you are over 60 and still active, **add 2** more.

2. If your mother lived beyond 80, **add 4**.

   If your father lived beyond 80, **add 2**.

3. If any grandparent lived to 80, **add 1** for each grandparent.

   Add .5 for each that lived beyond 70 (don't add twice for the same person).

4. If any close relative (defined as parent, grandparent, sister, or brother) died of a heart attack, stroke, or arteriosclerosis before the age of 50, **subtract 4** for each death.

   Subtract 2 for each such death before age 60.

5. If any close relative died of diabetes or peptic ulcer before age 60, **subtract 3** for each death.

   If any close relative died of stomach cancer before age 60, **subtract 2** for each death.

   If any close relative died before 60 of any cause except accident or homicide, **subtract 1** for each death.

   Women only—if any close female relative died of breast cancer before age 60, **subtract 2** for each death.

6. Women only—if you cannot or do not plan to have children or if you are over 40 and have not yet had children, **subtract .5**.

   Women only—if you have had more than 7 children or plan to, **subtract 1**.

7. If your mother was over 35 or under 18 when you were born, **subtract 1**.

8. If you are the first born in your family, **add 1**.

9. How intelligent are you? If you believe that your intelligence is superior, that you are smarter than almost everyone you know, **add 2**.

10. Are you overweight? Pick the age that is closest to your present age and **subtract the appropriate number of years**.

How Overweight?

	>30%		10–30%	
Age	Men	Women	Men	Women
20	15.8	7.2	13.8	4.8
25	10.6	6.1	9.6	4.9
30	7.9	5.5	5.5	3.6
35	6.1	4.9	4.2	4.0
40	5.1	4.6	3.3	3.5
45	4.3	5.1	2.4	3.8
50	4.6	4.1	2.4	2.8

If you have been at least 10 percent overweight at any point in your life or if your weight has fluctuated by more than 10 pounds since high school, **subtract 2**.

11. Do you prefer to eat vegetables, fruits, and simple foods to foods high in fat and sugar? If yes, **add 1**.

12. How much do you smoke? If more than a pack a day **subtract 15**; if about a pack a day, **subtract 8**; if less than a pack a day **subtract 3**.

13. How much do you drink? If you do not drink at all, then add or subtract nothing. If you are a light drinker (never drink to intoxication, have an occasional drink but almost everyday) **add 1.5**. If you are a moderate drinker (rarely drink to intoxication, have one to two drinks of whiskey or half a liter of wine or up to four glasses of beer a day) **add 3**. If you drink more than a moderate amount or are an alcoholic, **subtract 8**.

14. If you exercise at least 3 times a week at jogging, bike riding, swimming, long brisk walks, dancing, or skating, **add 3** (only exercising on weekends does not count).

15. If you sleep excessively (ten or more hours a night) or very little (five or less hours), **subtract 2**.

16. If you enjoy regular sexual activity, having intimate relations once or twice a week, **add 2**.

17. If you have regular physical examinations (including breast exam and pap smear for woman and proctoscopic exam for men) every other year, **add 2**.

18. If you have a chronic health condition such as heart disease, high blood pressure, cancer, diabetes, or ulcer, or if you are frequently ill, **subtract 5**.

19. If you have completed at least two years of college, **add 3**. If you are in your first two years of college, **add 1.5**.

20. If you are a professional, **add 1.5**. If you are a technical, administrative, or agricultural worker, **add 1**. If you are a semiskilled laborer, **subtract .5**. If you are a laborer, **subtract 4**.

21. If you are over 60 and still on the job, **add 2**; if you are over 65 and still on the job, **add 3**.

22. If you live in an urban area and have lived in or near the city for most of your life, **subtract 1**. If you have spent most of your life in a rural area, **add 1**.

(continued)

BOX **4-4** **Continued**

23. If you are married and living with your spouse, **add 1**.

    Men only—if you are separated or divorced and living by yourself, **subtract 9**; if living with others **subtract only 4.5**. If you are widowed and living by yourself, **subtract 7**, if living with others, **subtract 3.5**. If you have never been married and are past the age of 25 and living by yourself, **subtract 2** for each decade past 25. If you have never been married and are past the age of 25 but are living with family or friends, **subtract 1** for each decade past 25.

    Women only—if you are separated or divorced, **subtract 4**. If you are widowed, **subtract 3.5**. If you are separated, divorced, or widowed and also the head of a household, then **subtract only 2**. If you have never been married and are past the age of 25, **subtract 1** for each decade past 25.

24. If you are always changing things in your life (jobs, where you live, friends, spouses, your appearance), **subtract 2**.

25. If you generally like people and have at least 2 good friends in whom you can confide almost all the details of your life, **add 1**.

26. If you feel that you are under time pressure, are aggressive and sometimes hostile; if you pay little attention to the feelings of others, **subtract 2, 3, 4, or 5** depending on how much this pattern describes you.

27. If you are a calm, reasonable, relaxed person who is easy going and adaptable and you take life pretty much as it comes, **add 1, 2, or 3** depending on how much this pattern describes you.

    If you are rigid, dogmatic, and set in your ways, **subtract 2**.

28. If you take risks (drive without your seatbelt, exceed speed limits, take dares) or live in a high crime neighborhood, **subtract 2**.

    If you use seatbelts regularly, drive infrequently, and avoid dangerous parts of town, **add 1**.

29. If you have been depressed, tense, worried, or guilty for more than a period of a year or two, **subtract 1, 2, or 3** depending on how much this describes you.

30. If you are basically happy and content and have had a lot of fun in your life, **add 2**.

Source: Adapted from Perls, T., Silver, M. H., & Lauerman, J. F. (1999). *Living to 100: Lessons in Living to Your Maximum Potential at Any Age.* New York: Basic; and Woodruff-Pak, D. S. (1988). *Aging.* Pacific Grove, CA: Brooks-Cole.

women and 6 were men. Two standard questionnaires and interviews were used to assess quality of life. Centenarians reported more lost functions, such as ability to shop, maintain their finances, and use the telephone, than the individuals in the two younger groups. Seven of the centenarians were completely dependent on others for medicine, washing, dressing, and transportation. The youngest age group, however, complained of the most discomfort and the greatest number of painful symptoms. The centenarians reported the highest levels of satisfaction with their social life. Centenarians showed good mental functioning and social support. They were more satisfied with their lives than the younger participants. Researchers suggest that people who live to be very old are also likely to be people who adapt well to change, are generally optimistic, and maintain good social relationships. They remain intellectually active and work on tasks requiring use of their creativity (Buono, Urciuoli, & de Leo, 1998). A positive outlook and intellectual and social involvement are very important aspects of quality and length of life.

One good example of a person with these characteristics is Jeanne Calment (see Chapter 1). She exercised on her bicycle until she was 100 years old. Until she was 110, she lived independently and maintained her own home. She ate chocolate, drank red wine, and didn't quit smoking until she was 117. She is said to have had an excellent sense of humor and an extremely positive outlook on life. Bernadine Healy (1997) relates the story of a visitor leaving Jeanne Calment's presence and saying on the way out, "until next year, perhaps." Jeanne Calment answered, "I don't see why not! You don't look so bad to me."

Making Choices

This chapter is filled with choices that you can make to live a long and healthy life. Kaplan (2000) suggests that primary prevention programs, such as stop-smoking programs that require behavioral changes, have a much better track record of enhancing both life expectancy and quality of life than do secondary prevention programs such as medical screening for specific disease. Currently, our healthcare policy emphasizes secondary over primary prevention.

You can choose to eat a balanced diet, avoid fatty foods, and eat the appropriate number of calories for your age and height. You could also exercise regularly. The American Heart Association recommends at least 30 minutes of vigorous exercise three to four days a week, ideally every day. The 30 minutes can be accumulated over the day and can involve everyday activities such as walking to the car, climbing steps, and other routine activities. To get the most cardiovascular benefit, vigorous exercise should be done at 50 to 75 percent of your maximum heart rate. Strength-training is important too and should be done two to three times a week for as long as it takes to work your entire body. Remember that the goal of resistance or strength training is to build strong muscles, not big muscles. Use a comfortable weight to give you a good workout and increase repetitions to gain strength; increasing weight builds muscle. Additional guidelines for exercise of all types can be found on any number of websites including the American Heart Association: *http://www.americanheart.org*.

If you currently smoke, stop. Here is a sobering statistic: The Centers for Disease Control and Prevention estimates that one of every two lifelong smokers will eventually die of smoking.

Go easy on the alcohol. Learn to relax in the face of stress. Consider meditation or take a yoga or tai chi class. Men may help themselves by avoiding risky or psuedo-macho behaviors.

Choose to be socially involved with family and friends. Look at your social life now. Are you close to members of your family? Do you have close friends in whom you can confide? Do you belong to any groups, clubs, or organizations that provide you with social support? If you answer no to all of these questions, then we urge you to get involved. If you are too shy or are afraid of people, your campus counseling center can offer training and help. We are social animals and need contact with others to survive.

Two factors that we didn't discuss are wearing seat belts and having regular checkups. Seat belts save lives even though we can all imagine instances where a seat belt could interfere with escape from a damaged vehicle (as in *Final Destination*). The odds, however, are in favor of the seat belt wearer in the vast majority of cases.

CHAPTER HIGHLIGHTS

- A number of factors are thought to influence the probability of living a long and healthy life.
- People have searched for long life for ages and even today a large number of people hope for a way to reverse aging and remain healthy well into old age. In ancient Greece people believed in a place in the world, where people, favored by the gods, lived long healthy lives. Others believed in a magic potion that would reverse aging. Although there is no such place or magic potion, many continue to search and there are places on earth where people live much longer and healthier lives than they do in other places and there are foods that contribute to a longer, healthier life.
- Differences in longevity are found worldwide; people in Japan live longer than people elsewhere do and, within the United States, residents of Hawaii live the longest.
- Geographical and cultural differences in longevity suggest a role for environmental as well as genetic factors.
- Genetic influences are estimated to account for 25 to 35 percent of the variability in human longevity.
- Genes from both parents influence longevity by producing life-threatening disorders (e.g., through the apolipoproteins (APOE) producing genes), influencing body chemistry (e.g., through free radical production and mitochondria damage), and generating the stability of telomere sequences or the entire genetic code.
- Genetic influences are not yet clearly understood and may be considered to be out of our control, at least for now.
- Environmental influences on longevity are within our control.
- Healthy, low-fat diets are related to longevity; a high or low BMI is associated with a higher risk of death, perhaps, because of other factors such as lack of exercise or eating the wrong foods.
- Exercise is another important factor and seems to produce benefits relative to the amount of exercise; cancer and heart disease may be especially reduced by regular vigorous exercise.
- A number of supplements claim to have aging-reversal effects but, in fact, do not.
- Tobacco use shortens life and is dangerous for those around the smoke of others.
- Alcohol is thought to be beneficial in moderate amounts because it may reduce the risk of heart disease; the general finding of a benefit of moderate consumption over no consumption at all is, however, still questioned.
- Reactions to stress can be very unhealthy and can increase blood pressure and release immune suppressing hormones; we recommend that you learn to relax by practicing biofeedback, meditation, or some relaxation technique.
- Gender, race/ethnic group, and handedness are beyond our control but may exert their influence on longevity through social factors.
- Females live longer than males and this difference could be due to the relative differences in amount of testosterone and estrogen for men and women or sex chromosomes.
- The finding that men smoke more than women and are more likely to engage in risk-taking behaviors is thought to contribute to the gender difference in longevity.

- There are a number of differences in most frequent causes of death and life expectancy among African, Asian, Hispanic, Native, and White Americans. These differences seem to be due to social factors.
- Social factors also influence longevity; people at lower levels of SES generally are less healthy and die sooner.
- People with good social support live longer; social support may buffer individuals against stress and it may be that certain characteristics (e.g. optimism) and behaviors (e.g., volunteering) of sociable individuals are what influence length of life.
- Very-old adults who retain their health live longer and seem to be satisfied with life; they report having good quality of life.

STUDY QUESTIONS

1. What is a major theme about living a long and healthy life and why is it still fairly prevalent today? Why?

2. Describe how researchers attempt to determine whether longevity is due to genetic or environmental factors. What have researchers concluded?

3. Why does a very low or very high BMI seem to shorten life? What factors are involved?

4. Describe four types of exercise that are aerobic and beneficial. How does exercise help lengthen life?

5. Name and describe five supplements intended to reverse aging. Is there any evidence to support the claims?

6. Why is tobacco harmful; what ingredients produce the harm?

7. Why might nondrinkers die sooner than people who drink a moderate amount of alcohol?

8. Why does stress often produce poorer health and shorten life? How can one learn to handle stress (describe specific techniques)?

9. Describe four factors that might account for the gender gap in longevity.

10. Describe some of the race/ethnic group differences in longevity and possible reasons for these differences.

11. Explain how SES affects longevity.

12. Explain how social support affects longevity.

13. How high is the quality of life for people who live long lives? What factors make a difference and why?

RECOMMENDED READINGS

Allard, M., Lebre, V., & Robine, J. M. (1994). *Jeanne Calment: From Van Gogh's Time to Ours*. New York: W.H. Freeman. This is a delightful little book written by Jeanne Calment's physician and two gerontologists. We get a look into the life of the world's oldest person. Filled with Calment's humorous quips and sayings, this book makes living to 122 a wonder and a joy.

Mahoney, D. & Restak, R. (1998). *The Longevity Strategy: How to Live to 100 Using the Brain-body Connection*. New York: Wiley & Sons.

Perls, T., Silver, M. H., & Lauerman, J. F. (1999). *Living to 100: Lessons in Living to Your Maximum Potential at Any Age*. New York: Basic Books. Want to live to be 100? What are the odds and what can you do to improve your chances? These books present optimistic and easy to read reviews of relevant research and suggest specific strategies that could improve your chances for a long and healthy life.

INTERNET RESOURCES

http://www.attitudefactor.com   Offers useful information about aging but may be overly optimistic about some of the factors that influence longevity:

http://www.northwesternmutual.com/games/longevity   Givers life expectancy estimates.

http://www.deathclock.com   See how life is slipping away.

PART II   Aging and Our Minds

CHAPTER

5   Sensation, Perception, and Slowing with Age

The same space of time seems shorter as we grow older.

—*William James*

William James and others claim that our perception of time seems to change as we age. When we are very young, a year seems to take forever but as we grow older, the years seem to fly by. We will examine changes in our sensations and perceptions as we age. Perhaps the perception that time moves faster is related to our own slowing down, or because we value time more because each passing year means one less in the future.

Sensation and Perception

Many of our bodily organs and tissues change with age and senescence. Sense organs, such as the eye and ear, are likely to change and show senescence although we must emphasize that not all changes occur in all people and not all changes occur at the same time. **Sensation** refers to the stimulation of sensory cells in the body's sense organs. That stimulation is then passed on to centers in the brain. **Perception** refers to the interpretation of sensory stimulation and takes place in the brain. Perception gives meaning to sensory stimulation and may signal the organism as to which stimulation should receive the greatest amount of attention. Changes in sense organs frequently influence perception. A change in one's ability to sense the presence of a sweet taste in food is likely to influence that person's perception of sweetness in food. If you cannot taste the sugar in coffee, you may add more sugar until you are finally able to detect the sweetness. At the same time, sensory changes can take place over relatively long periods of time and, thus, enable individuals to compensate. Such compensation can result in little, or no, significant change in perception. Some changes in senses may influence perception while others may not. Some changes may be compensated for while others may not.

Senior View

Mabel Carson Davis, born in 1912, worked as a registered nurse until she retired in 1982 at age 70. Mabel lost her husband several years ago and lives alone. She says her health is good, she is strong and independent, and able to care for herself. She agreed to talk with us about changes that she has experienced in perception and slowing down.

When asked if she currently perceives things the same way she did when she was younger, Mabel said no. She said perceiving colors had been especially difficult until she had her cataracts removed. "Before that, I was arguing with everyone in the country about what color I was seeing," she said. The operation was "like a yellow sheet was

removed." In this chapter we address that yellow sheet and how it can affect perception of color.

With respect to hearing, Mabel told us that three years ago, when she was 83, she had a bad cold and sore throat with drainage. As she was blowing her nose, she went deaf in both ears. The doctors could not figure out what had happened and for about six weeks she could not hear anything. It finally got better but, after a year, she needed a hearing aid. She says it is an advantage because "when people see it, they speak more directly to me."

Mabel says that she has not noticed any change in her sense of smell or taste and that she has a very high threshold for pain. She said her breakfast that morning did not taste good so she was sure she could taste quite well. Taste and smell are important senses for a healthy diet.

As for slowing down, Mabel says she is not sure whether she has slowed down. She often cannot do as much yard work as she would like to do but says it may be because she gets tired sooner. She still drives but not as fast as she used to drive. Why? "Because I have an old car; I don't go 85 anymore," she said. When asked if her thinking had slowed down, Mabel told us that she often reread things.

Does time move faster? Mabel said, at times. "When I was young I used to think Christmas and my birthday (Dec. 27) would never get here and now on Monday it's Friday before I know it," she said. She says she would like to say "stop" to the world. As we were leaving, Mabel told us that each part of life is interesting and can be exciting if you look for the excitement. She said, "Youth is wonderful but old age is not bad at all."

Vision

A diagram of the human eye can be seen in Figure 5-1. The outer membrane covering the eye is called the **cornea**. Light rays enter the eye through the **iris** which expands or contracts depending on the level of illumination. When the light is dim, the iris opens wide to let in more light and when the light is bright the iris closes to reduce the amount entering

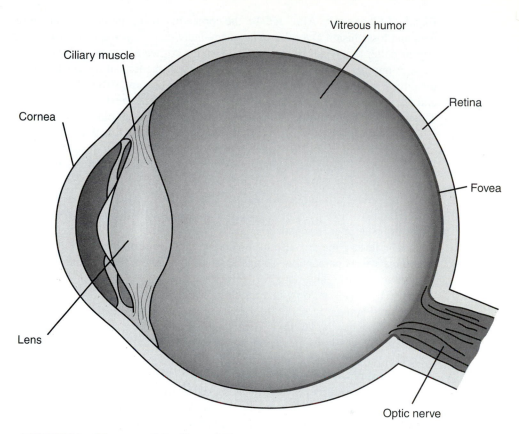

FIGURE 5-1   Diagram of the Normal Eye.

the eye. Light is focused by the **lens** onto the **retina**. The **ciliary muscles** function to change the shape of the lens to focus the image, which might be near or far from the viewer. The inside of the eye is filled with a fluid called the **vitreous humor**. The retina converts the light rays into electric impulses for the nerve cells and those impulses are carried to the visual cortex at the back of the head. The retina has a **blind spot** where the optic nerve exits the eye on its way to the brain. You may be able to see this blind spot by closing one eye and moving a picture toward and away from the eye. At some point a small portion of the picture should vanish as it focuses on the blind spot. Cells in the retina are called cones and rods. **Cones** number close to six million and respond to color and high levels of illumination; they are for daytime/light vision. **Rods** are cells distributed throughout the retina but concentrated in the periphery. They respond to low levels of illumination and number close to 120 million; they are for night/dark vision. You may have noticed that you can see better in the dark if you look out of the corner of your eye. When you look out of the corner of your eye, you are focusing the image to be seen on your rods, and rods see well in the dark.

Physical Changes.   After age 40, the cornea begins to increase in curvature and thickness and loses luster. Over the years, many individual's eyes appear to stick out more and appear duller as a result of these changes in the cornea and surrounding skin and bone.

A number of changes occur in the lens. First, the lens of the eye becomes flatter and the ciliary muscles, like other muscles in the body, become stiffer. Between the ages of 40 and 50, the result of these changes moves the point of clearest vision farther from the eye. This is called **presbyopia**. The term comes from *presby* for old or older and *opia* for eye. Older individuals often hold a book or newspaper at arm's length to read it and many purchase magnifying glasses for reading or change their glasses to bifocals. Another result of these lens and ciliary muscle changes is a decreased ability to shift back and forth between near- and farvision. This ability to shift back and forth is called **distance accommodation** and is important in many tasks, particularly driving. Some middle-age and older drivers have difficulty shifting focus from the roadway to the dashboard and back as a result of declines in distance accommodation.

The lens of the eye also turns more yellow as insoluble proteins accumulate in the lens. This affects perception. Things appear more yellow. The change to yellow, however, is so gradual that it does not affect perception in all cases. Your lenses are already turning yellow even if you are only in your early 20s but you probably won't notice this gradual change until you are in your 90s. For older adults with yellow lenses, everything does not appear yellow but the ability to distinguish certain colors, particularly in the green-blue-violet end of the spectrum, can be greatly reduced (Whitbourne, 1996). Please don't reset the color on your grandparent's television unless they ask you to. It may look "off" to you but look just fine through yellow lenses.

The lens of the eye also grows thicker as we age. This thickening, along with yellowing, allows less light to reach the retina. As a result, older adults are less able to perceive clearly when the lights are low and generally need higher levels of illumination for good visual perception. It is very important that there be adequate lighting, particularly in unfamiliar environments and on stairways, to prevent falling accidents.

As we grow older, particles of insoluble protein, called "floaters," accumulate in the vitreous humor. The longer you live, the more floaters accumulate. They appear to be harmless and do not ordinarily affect perception. They are quite normal.

Changes in Visual Perception.   The **adaptation from light to dark** is slower and less efficient for older eyes. Shifting from cones to rods takes longer because there are fewer cells. Driving at night, particularly when one must drive in and out of lighted areas, can be dangerous for older drivers. Walking into a darkened theater should be done much more slowly when one is older. Even in the daytime, driving in and out of a tunnel can be more difficult for older drivers. Having a picture taken with a bright flash has a more pronounced effect on older adults; it takes longer to recover normal vision.

With aging, **peripheral vision** also declines. Peripheral vision is measured by testing vision for objects seen at the sides while looking straight ahead. For young adults, the typical peripheral vision range is about 170 degrees. By age 50 peripheral vision range is only 140 degrees and continues to decrease as one ages (Kline & Schieber, 1985). The replacement of muscle fiber with stiffer tissue in the ciliary muscles contributes to this decline. To see things in the periphery, we must turn our heads more as we grow older.

Visual acuity refers to the ability to identify objects in space and is the ability to resolve images and then to identify them. This is what most people think of when they think of vision. Our ability to detect where one object ends and another begins underlies our ability to perceive those objects. There are two forms of acuity. **Static acuity** is the identification of stationary objects and is measured using an eye chart. This form of visual acuity and the eye charts used to measure it were first created by a Dutch physician named Hermann Snellen (Sekuller & Blake, 1994). **Dynamic acuity** is the identification of objects when they are moving or you are moving or both.

Both types of acuity decline with age especially under low light levels but the decline in dynamic acuity is greater. The decline in dynamic acuity is partly dependent on the speed of moving objects with older adults, particularly women, having more difficulty at higher speeds (Atchley & Andersen, 1998). Some research, however, suggests that older adults show virtually no deficit in static acuity, compared to younger adults, when levels of illumination are sufficiently high (Long & Crambert, 1990). Higher levels of illumination help contrast or detection of the edges of objects. Researchers have compared the static acuity of younger and older adults with 20/20 vision under conditions of high-contrast and low-contrast. In the high-contrast condition, letters were printed in black ink on a white board while in the low-contrast condition letters were printed in gray ink. The acuity of the young and old were the same in the high-contrast condition but in the low-contrast condition older adults performed much worse (Adams, Wang, Wong, & Gould, 1988). When you renew your driver's license, static acuity is tested by having you identify letters or road signs in a viewer under high-contrast conditions. While driving you are more likely to need dynamic acuity; signs must be identified while you are moving. Furthermore, contrast is frequently not very high. Since many of the changes that can affect vision are important for driving, Box 5-1 applies these changes to driving.

B O X **5-1**
Older Drivers and License Tests

Several normal changes that occur in the eyes of older adults and in their vision have implications for safe driving. Older adults are also likely to respond slower. Such changes in older adults have led to recent proposals for changes in driver's license renewal tests that are given in a number of states. We do not believe that older adults should be prohibited from driving. Anyone who can drive safely and responsibly should be permitted to drive. At the same time, changes in vision that frequently accompany aging can make driving more difficult. As a result, license renewals should be more frequent and involve more than the simple vision test given at present. Consider the following situations:

1. You are driving down the highway and looking for an exit with a gas station. This requires monitoring of signs. Monitoring is more difficult with the decline in **dynamic visual acuity** common in older adults. If it is nighttime then a decline in **contrast sensitivity** will make it more difficult.
2. You see a highway patrol officer ahead on the side of the road. Traffic is heavy. You look at the speedometer to check your speed. Shifting of vision from the road to the relatively close

(continued)

BOX **5-1**   **Continued**

dashboard and back to the road is more difficult with the decline in **distance accommodation** common in older adults.

3. You exit the highway and come to stop sign where you must look left and right before you make a left turn toward the gas station. Such monitoring is more difficult with the decline in **peripheral vision** common in older adults. Declines in dynamic acuity and contrast sensitivity may also make it more difficult to see other vehicles coming from the left and right.

4. For older adults it is more difficult to drive in and out of lighted areas at night. Everything becomes harder to see as a result of slower, less efficient **dark adaptation** common in older adults.

Older adults who experience these changes are not necessarily poorer drivers. Most are very experienced drivers and that experience offsets some of these changes. For example, as a result of extensive experience there may be less need to consult the dashboard for information. One may be able to tell how fast one is going simply by looking at the road. Older adults may also compensate for visual declines by slowing down and looking more than once. Some work indicates that older adults avoid driving after dark and/or in unfamiliar areas (Mancil & Owsley, 1988; Morgan, 1988). The statistics on average number of accidents per licensed driver show that drivers 65 and older have the lowest average number of accidents. (Barnhill, 1998). At the same time, however, older drivers have the highest accident rate per miles driven (Hooyman & Kiyak, 1996). These statistics result from the increased difficulties many older drivers have and the great reduction in miles driven by older drivers.

Future driving tests for new licenses and renewals for all adults of all ages are likely to contain some, or all, of the following (Barnhill, 1998):

1. The **Useful Field of Vision** (UFOV) **Test** requires individuals to rapidly identify car-shaped forms on a large screen. The test measures attention span. Research suggests that the UFOV is reduced in about 20 percent of drivers over age 50 and that reductions increase the risk of a crash at an intersection.

2. The **Waypoint Test** shows many letters and numbers on a blank background and requires the test taker to connect appropriate letters and numbers by drawing lines from one to the other. For example, one would connect *1* to *A, 2* to *B,* and so on. Another form has letters (or numbers) and one must draw a line from the first letter to the second, second to third, and so on (*A* to *B* to *C* to *D* to *E* and so on) as rapidly as possible. Research shows that this test successfully predicts later involvement in an accident in 80 percent of the cases.

3. **Driving Simulators** involve sitting in a mock car with steering wheel, gas pedal, brakes, and so on while navigating a street scene. Scores are based on how quickly and correctly one responds to different emergency situations. These tests are quite expensive.

Older adults are more likely than younger adults to experience serious eye problems just as older adults are more likely to experience other disorders, such as arthritis and cancer. Table 5-1 presents some serious and not normal visual problems. You might recall from Chapter 2 that 16 percent of older adults experience cataracts and another 8 percent experience one or more of the other visual disorders shown in the table. Regular eye examinations increase in importance as we age.

TABLE 5-1   Disorders of Vision and Hearing That Increase with Age

Disorder	Description	Treatment
	Vision	
Cataracts	Cloudy, opaque areas on lens, blurred vision common	Can be surgically removed
Glaucoma	Excessive fluid pressure in eye, can cause retinal damage, not noticeable by individual	Can be medicated with drops and/or marijuana if detected early
Macular degeneration	Central part of retina does not function effectively, blurred vision when reading, dark spots, distortions when viewing vertical lines	Amenable to laser treatments in some cases
Retinal detachment	Inner and outer layers of retina separate	Can be surgically reattached
Retinopathy	Small blood vessels that nourish retina do not function properly as a result of diabetes	Amenable to laser treatments
	Hearing	
Central auditory impairment	Difficulty in understanding language but external sounds are heard; nerve centers in brain are damaged.	None at present but advances in technology look promising
Conductive loss	Sound does not travel through outer or middle ear due to blockage from wax, fluid, or abnormal bone growth; sounds seem muffled while one's own voice may sound louder.	Treated by flushing ear, medication, or surgery
Presbycusis	Progressive loss of hearing for high-frequency tones due to deterioration in inner ear.	Hearing aid

Hearing

Physical Changes.   Figure 5-2, on page 114, shows a diagram of the ear. Changes in the muscles and bones, and the degeneration of sensory cells in the base of the cochlea are physical changes that contribute to hearing loss in older adults (Schneider, 1997; Whitbourne, 1996). The most typical loss is a deficit in hearing for high-pitched tones. This deficit is called **presbycusis**. Hearing impairments are one of the most frequent chronic

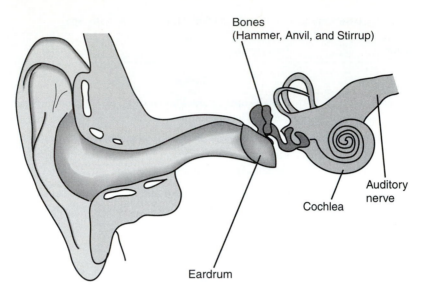

Bones
(Hammer, Anvil, and Stirrup)

Auditory
nerve

Cochlea

Eardrum

FIGURE 5-2   Diagram of the Normal Ear.

conditions of older adults and are reported in 28.6 percent of individuals aged 65 and older. Hearing loss is more frequent for men than women (Fozard, 1990). One might expect that such hearing loss would result in greater difficulty in speech perception for older adults.

There is some debate as to whether presbycusis is due to changes that occur with age or whether, it is due to a lifetime of exposure to sounds. One cross-cultural study examined hearing loss in African tribal people who were 70 years of age and older and found no decline in hearing (Bergman, 1966). Since these people lived all their lives where there is very little noise pollution the findings support the idea that hearing loss may be due to exposure to noise pollution.

Changes in Auditory Perception.   The aspect of auditory perception that has received the most attention from researchers is the perception of spoken language. Research has examined age differences in **speech perception** under a variety of conditions and found age differences under noisy conditions (Fozard, 1990). These studies used a cross-sectional approach and compared adults of different ages on their ability to perceive speech when presented by itself, or in the presence of other competing voices in the background, or in the presence of other noises such as electronic static. Results show little decline in speech perception from age 20 to 89 when speech is presented by itself but show progressively more decline in the presence of other voices and especially static noise (Bergman, Blumenfeld, Cascardo, Dash, Levitt, & Margulios, 1976; Heller & Wilber, 1990). Studies like this are often criticized for failing to consider the possibility that any obtained differences could be cohort differences.

Longitudinal studies allow one to examine this question by following the same group or groups of adults over longer periods of time and measuring the same individuals at several points. In one such study, adults ranging in age from their 20s to their 80s were tested two to six times with an average interval of three years between tests. Results showed a steady rate of hearing loss for high frequencies even in the young and an increased loss for older adults in the perception of sound frequencies at the level of speech (Brant & Fozard, 1990). Note that such longitudinal work may tell us that changes in hearing occur with age and are not simply cohort differences but do not tell us whether those changes are due to exposure to noise over one's life.

Speech for older adults is most difficult to perceive when it is interrupted, noisy, or speeded. Difficulty with speeded speech indicates general slowing as well as sensory changes as underlying causes of age differences in speech perception.

There are a number of important points to consider when talking to an older person with a hearing impairment (Cheesman, 1997). As with vision impairments, hearing impairments are more likely in older adults (see Table 5-1). Raymond Hull (1980) tells us that when conversing with a person with a hearing impairment, one should talk a little louder (do not shout) than one ordinarily would and should not speak too rapidly.

Hearing is important in social interactions.

Face the person when speaking to them so that they can see your lips move. Do not try to make the person hear you when there is a lot of other noise around. If the individual does not understand you, do not repeat what you have said. Try saying it a different way. Do not shout into a person's ear; that is insulting and takes away any use of visual cues that might help the person understand what is being said. Treat older adults who have a hearing impairment with respect; treat them as you would wish to be treated.

Smell, Taste, Touch, and Balance

The olfactory bulb in the brain is the center for **smell** and shows cell loss with advanced age. Tests of 1955 people ranging in age from 5 to 99 were conducted to see if simulated aromas such as cinnamon, cherry, pizza, mint, and lemon could be detected and named (Doty, Shaman Appelbaum, Bigerson, Sikorski, & Rosenberg, 1984). Best performance was by people between the ages of 20 and 40. After age 50 decrements appeared and after age 70 there was rapid decline. One-half of the adults over the age of 80 seemed to have lost all ability to detect aromas. As with vision and hearing, some researchers believe that this loss of smell is not the result of aging. Instead, loss of smell may be the result of a lifetime of exposure to airborne toxic substances such as car exhaust fumes, pesticides, factory waste, cigarette smoke, and other pollutants. People living in a pollution-free environment may show little or no decline with age while those living in a very polluted environment may show great loss at a relatively young age. Clearly, the total loss of sense of smell influences perception. As you might imagine, this could be a very dangerous loss in situations where one might be unable to detect a gas leak or the smell of spoiled food. One's enjoyment of foods may also decline due to a loss of sense of smell.

Humans have four types of **taste** buds on the tongue resulting in four basic taste sensations: bitter, sour, salty, and sweet. Taste buds are short-lived but are continually replaced. The total number of taste buds declines with age starting at about age 40 because the rate of replacement declines. Some individuals show a loss of nearly two-thirds of total taste buds by age 70 and the buds most frequently lost are those for sweet sensation (Aiken, 1995). Many older adults compensate for this loss by adding extra sweetener to coffee, desserts, lemonade, and other items. Have you ever had a grandparent offer you a glass of lemonade that was too sweet for your taste? It may not have tasted that sweet at all to the person who made it. At high concentrations, older adults are as able as younger adults to differentiate all tastes (Bartoshuk, Rifkin, Marks, & Bars, 1986). You might notice that older adults often put more salt, pepper, or other condiments on their food. They need what appears to be an excess amount so that they can taste it. The amount of salivation also decreases with age and saliva may become thicker. As a result, older adults often drink more fluids with a meal than younger adults do and are often less tolerant of dry foods such as potato or corn chips (Cunningham & Brookbank, 1988).

Sensitivity to **touch** also declines with age. As discussed in Chapter 2, fewer nerve cells are present to detect contact on the skin as one grows older and the skin itself has changed. Older adults may not be as sensitive to changes in temperature as a result of this loss or may not easily detect a light pressure stimulus such as a mosquito on the skin. In very cold climates, the danger of frostbite can be much greater for older adults because their skin is less sensitive to temperature. Burns are also more frequent for older adults since they may not feel the heat of a stove, match, or fire and may not pull away until the skin is burnt.

Sensory cells in the vestibular system located in the ears also decline with advanced age and can produce more difficulty in maintaining **balance**. Older adults with such decline are more likely to experience vertigo or dizziness, although dizzy experiences also may be linked to changes in vision, muscles, and the skeletal system (Whitbourne, 1996). Research has shown that reductions in lower body strength, poor vision, and cigarette smoking all contribute to loss of balance and that women over 85 have the most difficulties (Satariano, DeLorenze, Reed, & Schneider, 1996). Some work suggests that the loss of sensory cells in the vestibular system can be compensated for by relying more on other sensory information to help maintain balance. Adults in their 80s have been trained to improve their balance and strength by performing leaning exercises on balance boards and lifting sandbags with their legs. Following training, gains have been maintained by teaching adults to practice low intensity tai chi (Wolfson, Whipple, Derby, Judge, King, Amerman, Schmidt, & Smyers, 1996). **Tai chi** is a Chinese system of physical exercises that involve slow, rhythmic

Tai chi may help one's balance.

movements. Six months after learning tai chi, adults showed higher levels of balance and strength than untrained control participants (Wolf, Barnhart, Kutner, McNeely, Coogler, Xu, & the Atlanta FICSIT Group, 1996).

Stimulus Fusion

A perceptual change that seems to be related to slowing, as well as actual changes in sense organs, is the change in **critical flicker fusion** which occurs in older adults. Critical flicker fusion refers to the point at which successively presented stimuli are perceived as being a single stimulus. When we view a film, we rely on flicker fusion to make the action seem real. What is really presented to us is a series of still pictures at a rate fast enough to merge into one, to fuse. The presentation rate at which the separate images fuse is an individual's critical flicker fusion and it varies for adults of different ages. You can get a feel for this critical rate by visiting the Cognitive Development web site listed in Internet Resources at the end of this chapter. A series of still pictures that fuse into movement is presented there and you can vary the rate of presentation. The rate at which these stimuli must be presented before they fuse into a single moving image (flicker fusion) is slower for older adults. For them, fusion occurs earlier and more easily; it occurs at a slower presentation rate (Curran, Hindmarch, Wattis, & Shillingford, 1990; Weale, 1965).

Researchers have found this age difference in fusion with several different types of stimuli and for a number of different senses. An example of visual fusion occurs if one presents alternating red and green lights at an increasingly faster rate. Individuals will eventually report seeing the color yellow. Older adults report seeing yellow sooner and at a slower rate than is needed for young adults to fuse the two separate colors, red and green, into one color, yellow (Kline & Orme-Rogers, 1978; Kline & Schieber, 1985).

Age differences in fusion also have been found for sounds (Weiss, 1963). Some research found age differences in fusion for shocks presented to the skin of older and younger person's fingers. Older adults fused the two shocks into one at a rate of presentation slower than the critical fusion rate for younger adults (Axelrod, Thompson, & Cohen, 1968).

One way to explain these various findings is to assume that stimuli persist for a longer period of time (Botwinick, 1984; Coyne, Eiler, Vanderplas, & Botwinick, 1979). If an old stimulus is not replaced by a new incoming stimulus as rapidly as it used to be, then new and old stimuli are more likely to fuse. Stimulus persistence is, thus, a result of slowing. Such slowing could affect the perception of one fused stimulus from several separate stimuli. Perceptions can, thus, be influenced by a slowing in the speed with which we process stimuli as well as changes in senses.

Slowing

Measurements of response time have been made since psychologists began systematic investigations of human behavior. In 1884 at the International Health Exhibition held in London, England, Sir Francis Galton measured the response times of 9337 men and women ranging in age from 5 to 80, who paid three pence each for this privilege. Individuals responded as quickly as they could when a tone was sounded and when a light was flashed.

People responded quicker to the tone than the light and the fastest people responding were between the ages of 18 and 20. Older adults were consistently slower (Boring, 1950). This finding has been replicated many times over the last century and is one of the most certain findings in gerontology. We know, as a certainty, that people slow down as they age.

Reaction time measures are usually divided into three different types. The kind of response or reaction time measured by Galton is referred to as **simple reaction time**. One stimulus is presented and when it occurs, the person makes one response. For example, a clock might start when a light comes on and, when the light is seen, a person presses a button as quickly as they can; the button stops the clock and, over a series of trials, average simple reaction time is recorded. **Choice reaction time** refers to the situation in which two different stimuli are presented and a different response for each one is required. One might have to press the button on the right when the red light comes on and the button on the left when the green light comes on. When there are more than two stimuli and two responses, the situation is referred to as **complex reaction time**.

Think for a moment about what sorts of internal processing must go on for a person to react in one of these situations. Table 5-2 illustrates the steps involved. Sensing is the first step. *First*, you must sense the stimulus when it is presented; failure to sense that the light has come on would result in no response at all. Once the sense has registered, it must be correctly perceived as being the relevant stimulus. Then, you must decide to respond, and you must initiate the response. These components of perception, decision, and initiation are central and take place in the brain. They make up the *second* step. Third, nerve signals must be sent to the correct muscles and those muscles must move and press the button. Motor action is the *third* step.

TABLE 5-2   Three Components of Response Time: Sensory, Central Processing, and Muscle

Step 1 (Sensory)	Step 2 (Central processing in the brain)	Step 3 (Muscle response)
The stimulus must be sensed by the appropriate sense organ.	Stimulus must be perceived as the one requiring a response.	When nerve impulse reaches muscle the response occurs.
	One must decide whether to respond.	
	One must initiate the response.	
	One must determine which of two (choice) or several (complex) stimuli was sensed.	
	One must determine the correct response for the stimulus that was perceived.	

In simple, choice, and complex reaction time situations, all three steps must occur but in choice and complex situations, the second step requires more processing. In Table 5-2, the steps shown above the line always occur whether the situation is simple, choice, or complex. In choice and complex situations, however, the additional central processing shown below the line also takes place. More central processing is needed in choice and complex situations than in simple situations. In choice and complex situations, you must perceive which of the relevant stimuli has occurred and which response is appropriate for that stimulus. For example, you must decide whether the red or the green light has come on and to press the button on the right if the red light came on or the button on the left if the green light came on. Choice and complex situations involve more central processing at the level of the brain but the work of the sense organs and muscles, steps one and three, are largely the same in simple, choice, and complex situations.

If older adults respond slowly because of slowing at some central location in the brain, then we would expect them to be much slower than young adults in choice and complex situations since more central processing is required. Complex situations require more brain activity than simple situations and some work suggests that about 80 percent of total response time is central processing time (Botwinick & Thompson, 1966).

The results support the hypothesis that slowing with age is a slowing of central processing in the brain. Researchers who have compared younger and older adult response times in simple, choice, and complex situations found that older adults respond more slowly as the situation becomes more complex. Age differences in simple reaction time are much smaller than age differences in choice and complex situations (Birren, Woods, & Williams, 1980; Panek, Barrett, Sterns, & Alexander, 1978; Salthouse, 1985). The decrease in response speed, between age 20 and 60, is about 20 percent for simple situations and about 50 percent for complex situations (Welford, 1984). Related work shows very small age differences in the registration of sensory input and motor output (Botwinick, 1978; Salthouse, 1985). The major slowing is in central processing in the brain.

Recently, researchers have attempted to determine which mental processes are primarily responsible for the observed age differences in response time. The range in response times in these tasks is much wider for older rather than for younger participants suggesting that some particular aspects of central processing for older participants underlie their slower response times (Ratcliff, Spieler, & McKoon, 2000). Two recent studies had younger and older adults respond to asterisks or dots presented on a screen. Participants judged as quickly as possible whether there was a high or low number of asterisks (Experiment 1) or whether the distance between two dots was large or small (Experiment 2). Results showed that much of the slowing in these tasks for older participants was due to their setting of more conservative response criteria. That is, they tended to delay response until they were certain that they were correct. More conservative response criteria may be one aspect of central processing that contributes to age differences in response times (Ratcliff, Thapar, & McKoon, 2001).

Why does the brain respond more slowly as we age? Several possibilities have been suggested and the slowing could be due to loss of and/or damage to nerve cells and/or a decrease in blood flow to the brain (Schaie & Willis, 1991). These hypotheses have received limited support. You already know from Chapter 2 that some areas of the brain lose neurons while others seem to show little or no loss and that older neurons have fewer connective spikes, called dendrites. Perhaps the slow down in an older brain occurs as longer routes must be taken by nerve impulses when dendrites and cells are lost. Although no direct evidence supports this hypothesis, such a differential loss of neurons in different areas of the brain fits well with the finding that slowing may be present with advanced age for some aspects of certain tasks but not for other aspects of the same tasks (Sliwinski, 1997).

In terms of blood flow, we know that many older adults experience some blocking of arteries (see Chapter 2) and that even in healthy adults some decrease in blood flow is evident (Duara, London, & Rapoport, 1985; Hagstadius & Risberg, 1989). Related work shows that older adults' response times can be significantly improved by exercise and we know that exercise increases blood flow and the amount of oxygen in the blood (Spriduso & McRae, 1990). Older adults who are athletic have faster responses than young adults who are not (Spirduso & Clifford, 1978). Exercise may help offset declines in blood flow to the brain and increased blood flow may result in faster response times.

In most of the laboratory work on response time and aging, the differences found between older and younger responders are less than a second (Salthouse, 1985). Such response differences are barely visible to the casual observer and require careful measurement to be noticed. One might think, therefore, that these small slowdowns are relatively meaningless, and in many situations they are. If one seals envelopes or squeezes toothpaste a little slower it is unlikely to make much of a difference. Think for a moment, however, of all the central processing that goes on in a situation such as driving down an unfamiliar street when suddenly something appears ahead in the road. Your visual sense detects the object and now you must try to perceive what it might be. Is it a child in the road? A dog? A newspaper? A shadow? If it is a dog, is it standing still or moving? Is it in your way? Will its movement put it in your way when you arrive at that location? What, if any, response should you make? Should you blow your horn? Should you swerve to avoid a collision? Should you apply the brakes? A little bit of slowing may not be a problem but the cumulative effect of a little bit of slowing in each of these steps could make the difference between a close call and a disaster. Slowing with advanced age can, in all too many situations, make a major difference in the outcome.

Slower response rate, combined with changes in muscles and bones described in Chapter 2 and the changes in vision and balance described earlier, may make older adults far more likely to experience certain kinds of accidents, particularly falls, than younger adults. Box 5-2, pages 122–123, presents information about accident rates among different aged adults.

The slowing that accompanies old age varies from individual to individual. Just as not all older adults experience baldness, presbycusis, or osteoporosis, not all older adults show the same amount of slowing. The slowing we observe seems to be due to genetics and early environment, to exercise and experience, and much is yet unexplained (Simonen, Videman, Battie, & Gibbons, 1998). There are large and significant individual differences. Even when there is slowing, it may be in a particular type of mental processing and the amount is affected by several factors such as exercise, amount of practice, and type of response. Individuals who engage in aerobic exercise regularly tend to respond quicker than individuals who do not exercise, regardless of age (Dustman, Ruhling, Russell, Shearer, Bonekat, Shigeoka, Wood, & Bradford, 1984; Spirduso & MacRae, 1990). Individuals of all ages respond faster as they gain more practice responding (Murrell, 1970). Adults who have worked in

BOX 5-2

Aging and Accidents

Traffic accidents are a major cause of death for adults of all ages. However, older drivers taking certain medications, with reduced vision, or feeling depressed are more likely to be involved in a crash (Sims, McGwin, Allman, Ball, & Owsley, 2000). For older adults, the most typical traffic accident is being hit by a moving vehicle (Aiken, 1995). With changes in peripheral vision, hearing, and a general slowing of brain processes, older adults often step into the way of oncoming traffic, exit their own car without looking, or enter a busy intersection without seeing the traffic light, "don't walk" sign, or oncoming vehicles. When driving in any area where there are likely to be older pedestrians, drivers of all ages need to be alert.

The most frequent accident for older adults is a fall. **Falls** are the leading cause of accidental death in adults 65 and older (Morse, Prowse, & Morrow, 1985). Each year, it is estimated that close to 30 percent of older adults experience at least one fall. Nursing home residents fall at a higher rate. Falls are more likely for women, who experience close to 80 percent of these falls, and far more likely in Whites who experience close to 90 percent of falls (Peterson & Rosenblatt, 1986). Every year 200,000+ Americans fracture a hip in a fall. As many as 20 percent of older women who fall never recover and die of pneumonia within 6 months (Tinetti, 1989). It is estimated that 50 percent die this way within the first year (Peterson & Rosenblatt, 1986).

Why do falls occur? Weakening of muscles and bones and the high rate of osteoporosis among older, White women are assumed to account for much of the data. Many individuals with osteoporosis do not fall and break a bone, they fall because the bone broke. When bones are extremely fragile they may break under ordinary strain and when a fracture occurs, the person falls. Declines in vision also seem to produce falls. When moving from a room with a light-colored flooring to one with a dark-colored flooring, a visually impaired person may see the change in coloring as a change in elevation. They may raise their foot expecting to step up and lose their balance when no such elevation occurs. If one also responds slower, then that sudden loss of balance may not be corrected before one falls. Older adults are often frailer than younger adults and a fall that might not injure a younger person is often quite serious for an older person.

Preventing falls is a major concern. Some older adults fear falls so much that they walk cautiously. Such changes in gait are usually uncalled for and can increase, rather than decrease, the risk of falling (Campbell, Reinken, Allan, & Martinez, 1981). A study conducted in Australia followed 418 older adults for one year. Several measures, including a measure of fear of falling, were administered. Several analyses were restricted to persons who had not fallen in the year prior to the study or during the year of the study. Results showed that those with the highest fears of falling, were the most likely to fall in the future, declined the most in ability to perform activities of daily living, and, were more likely to be institutionalized (Cumming, Salkeld, Thomas, & Szonvi, 2000). In Chapter 12 we discuss healthy environments for older adults: so here, we mention only a couple of the major factors that can help prevent falls. It is important that stairs in particular, be well-lit and light switches located at the top and bottom of the stairwell. It may be useful to paint stairs different colors so that they are distinct. Nothing should be placed on stairs or floors that might accidentally be stepped on. Throw rugs that may slide or be tripped over should be removed. One should not walk on stairs or waxed floors wearing socks or smooth-soled shoes. Wear supportive shoes with rubber soles and low heels. Do not get up too fast or you may feel dizzy. When you feel dizzy or weak, use a cane to help maintain your balance. Many falls can be prevented.

Fires and burns are also frequent among older adults (Aiken, 1995). Fires may go out of control because older adults may not smell the fire burning in the kitchen or detect the smoke until they see it. At that point, it may be too late to gain control. Declines in sensitivity to touch may result in burns on the skin; one might not feel the hot utensil or frying pan until a burn has occurred. Stoves left on can be a hazard so setting a timer as a reminder, and/or making the "on" indicator light very noticeable are good ideas for those with some visual loss. Abandoned cigarettes may ignite chairs, beds, curtains, or rugs (Sterns, Barrett, & Alexander, 1985). Smoke alarms are important and are usually mandated by law. Check the batteries in smoke alarms for your grandparents.

Finally, **poisoning** and **drowning** also occur frequently for older adults. It is believed that food poisoning is often the result of a loss of the sense of smell. Sometimes you can tell that food has gone bad by looking at it but other times it might look fine but smell rotten. An older adult with a decreased sense of smell is likely to think spoiled food is fine until the poisoning has taken place. Drowning appears to often result from swimming out too far or not getting out of the pool before exhaustion sets in. It is important to know your own limits and to respect them (Sterns et al., 1985).

jobs demanding mental processing as opposed to physical labor tend to respond faster (Simonen et al., 1998). The age difference in response time is also smaller when a verbal rather than motor response is measured (Kaufman, 1968).

In spite of these individual differences and the qualifying factors just mentioned, it is generally the case that older adults respond slower than younger adults and that the slowing is primarily in the brain and some mental processes. When mental processes slow down they may not function as efficiently. Older persons may not be able to take in as much information in a short period of time as they did in the past. They may, however, be able to take in the same information if given sufficient time. They may have more difficulty remembering information previously presented because the search of memory operates much slower than previously. At the same time, they may be able to remember just as well if given sufficient time to remember. Slowing has implications for the ways in which we evaluate the memory, cognition, and intelligence of older adults both in the laboratory and in everyday settings. We will see in the next two chapters that one must be careful about drawing conclusions regarding changes in mental processes above and beyond the slowing that occurs in those processes.

Time

At the beginning of this chapter we quoted the famous psychologist William James who expressed the belief that time is perceived as passing more rapidly when we grow old. Mabel Davis, in this chapter's Senior View, says that time passes far too quickly for her ("on Monday, it's Friday before I know it"). It is, in fact, a common belief that time passes more rapidly as we age (Fraisse, 1984; Lemlich, 1975; Ross, 1991). Research shows that students perceive time as having passed slower when they were younger (8-to 10-years-old) and fully expect it to pass more rapidly as they grow older (Joubert, 1990). Although most of the research on time perception involves estimates of very short intervals of time during which some task was performed (Allan, 1979; Brown, 1985), there are some studies that have examined age differences in the perception of longer periods of time.

In some of these studies, individuals estimate how long a given period of time lasted in the past compared to how long the same period of time lasts now. When older adults are instructed to treat the present year as a 10 and to estimate, using the same scale, how long a year lasted at the half way point of their life (age 40 if they are now 80), they tend to give that earlier year a value of 14. It seems to have lasted longer. A year at the quarter point of their life (age 20 if they are now 80) received a value of 16. Time is perceived as having moved more slowly in the past compared to how rapidly it moves now (Walker, 1977).

It has been suggested that this difference in perception is a result of memory and novel activity (Flaherty & Meer, 1994; Pedri & Hesketh, 1993). If we do not remember much happening over the last few years, then that time may seem short compared to time in the distant past when many new things were happening. If you do the same thing over and over, year after year, time, in retrospect, seems to have passed quickly. If you move slowly and take a long time to finish a task, then later it will seem as if time flew by since you accomplished so little. Older adults may have fewer new experiences and this lack of novelty may make time seem to move faster for them (Fraisse, 1984).

In support of these ideas, work has shown that when middle-age and older adults living in a nursing home are asked to estimate the passage of time, time is generally underestimated by the oldest adults who have been in the home for the longest period of time; for them, time has flown by. Adults who are relatively new to that environment experience time as moving slower (Licht, Morganti, Nehrke, & Heiman, 1985). Other work has compared young, middle-age, and recently retired older adults who were enrolled in a campus Elderhostel program. Elderhostel participants took short, noncredit courses on campus. Results showed that the middle-age adults who were involved in the most routine and repetitive activities reported the fastest passage of time (Flaherty & Meer, 1994).

Other research has found that time perception is influenced by memory for past events and that ratings of how quickly time went by are faster for events of one year ago than of one month ago, and of one month ago then of yesterday for adults of all ages. When events are well-remembered, time seems slower than when events are not so well-

PROJECT 5

This project is based on work conducted by Michael Flaherty and Michelle Meer (1994). You will need a group of volunteers to participate. Each person is asked to estimate the passage of time using the following scale:

    1 = Very slowly
    2 = Slowly
    3 = Normally
    4 = Quickly
    5 = Very quickly

Select a few different time periods for them to estimate. For example, Flaherty and Meer used yesterday, last month, and last year. You might try the same time periods, or others.

Flaherty and Meer also used young (mean age of 19.8), middle-age (mean age of 38.4), and older (mean age of 71.2) adults. You might use the same age groups or different groups. Children, for example, might provide different estimates than adults.

Each person is told to think about the things they did and experienced during a time period, such as last month, and to estimate how they remember time as passing using the scale, ranging from very slowly (1) to very quickly (5). They are then asked to think about another time period and estimate time for that period. You should be careful to present the time periods that you are using in different orders for different people.

When you finish, calculate scale means for each time period for each group. Flaherty and Meer found means of 3.79, 4.03, and 3.80 for young, middle-age, and older adults, respectively. Time was reported as fastest for the middle-age participants. They also found means of 3.46, 3.95, and 4.22 for estimates of time passing yesterday, last month, and last year, respectively. More recent time seemed slower than more distant time. How do your means compare?

The researchers found that all three age groups rated time as passing more quickly last year than last month and more quickly last month than yesterday. They assume that this difference is largely due to memory. People remember a lot that happened yesterday but not as much for last month and even less for last year. The less that is remembered, the quicker time is perceived as having gone by. What do you think of this explanation? Can you think of any other possible reasons for the obtained difference?

They also found that time moved quicker for their middle-age group than for younger and older adults. The middle-age group was involved in the most routine of activities while the younger and older adults were experiencing new things. Did you also find age differences? If so, do they seem to be due to the routine of life?

---

remembered (Flaherty & Meer, 1994). Try a version of this study by completing Project 5.

Finally, some have found that time perception is influenced by the speed with which tasks are performed. When young adults are asked to estimate the amount of time spent on a prior task, they tend to underestimate tasks performed slowly and overestimate tasks performed quickly (Pedri & Hesketh, 1993). In retrospect, time seems to have gone by rapidly when one performed slowly.

Making Choices

There is little that individuals can do to stop the loss of sensory cells in the eyes, ears, nose, tongue, and skin if they are a result of changes that occur with aging. If, on the other hand, some of these changes are due to environmental factors, then you may be able to slow the change or make such loss less devastating. Simply choosing to stay away from very loud noise (or music) does lessen the probability of overall hearing loss. Be careful with headphones. When you use headphones all the sound is directed into your ears and can be damaging even at low levels. Protecting your eyes from intense light might lessen visual loss. Do you wear sunglasses when you go out in the bright light?

Balance can be maintained even when sensory cells are lost by practicing balance exercises. The low-intensity movements found in tai chi are beneficial for such maintenance. You might choose to learn tai chi or practice some yoga to help strengthen your movements and help your balance.

Slowing may be inevitable but the degree of slowing can be reduced by a regular program of aerobic exercise. Exercise increases blood flow to the brain and results in faster mental, as well as physical, response.

Finally, be aware of sensory loss in others and respond appropriately. Talk a little louder and a little slower to older people and try not to hold conversations with them in noisy places.

CHAPTER HIGHLIGHTS

- Some changes in senses affect perception while others do not.
- Physical changes in the eye include an increase in curvature/thickness of the cornea, and the lens become flatter, yellow, and thicker. These changes result in presbyopia (when point of clearest vision moves farther from the eye), altered perception of some colors, less light entering the eye, and reduced distance accomodation. Floaters also increase, some rod and cone cells are lost, and ciliary muscle fibers are lost.
- Adaptation from light to dark is slower and less efficient for older eyes.
- Periperal vision declines with age.
- Visual acuity declines (especially dyamic acuity). These declines make reading more difficult and driving less safe.
- Physical changes in the inner ear and/or exposure to noisy environments may produce hearing loss. The most common loss in older adults, especially men, is presbycusis (a deficit in hearing for high-pitched sounds).
- Older adults have no difficulty perceiving speech unless other talking or noise occurs at the same time.
- Loss of cells in the olfactory bulb often results in loss of smell for older adults. Such loss can be dangerous.
- The rate at which taste buds are replaced slows as one grows older and many older adults need higher concentrations of a flavor to perceive the taste.
- Sensitivity to touch declines as nerve cells under the skin are lost.
- Loss of cells in the vestibular system often occurs in older adults and can result in loss of balance. Tai chi is effective in helping adults improve and maintain balance.
- The rate at which successively presented stimuli fuse is slower for older adults and seems to be due to slowing in the rate at which stimuli are processed.
- The finding that older adults respond more slowly is one of the most certain findings in gerontology.
- Age differences in response time increase as situations change from simple to complex. These results support the hypothesis that the slowing that occurs with advanced age is in the central processing that takes place in the brain.
- The slowing of central processing in the brain may be due to the loss of nerve cell connections or decreased blood flow.
- Small amounts of slowing in a number of central processes can result in serious problems in some complex real-life situations.
- Time perception seems to change with age. Older adults frequently perceive time as passing quickly. This perception could be due to memory for events, absence of novel activities, and/or the speed with which tasks are performed.
- Sensory changes, perceptual changes, and the slowing of central processing influence many types of cognition.

STUDY QUESTIONS

1. Which of the changes in the eye, that are typical of advanced age, begin when we are very young and which do not begin until we are older?

2. Explain why perception is not always affected by changes in sense organs.

3. Name some ways in which the risk of falls can be prevented. Why do older adults fall so often?

4. Why do you think your grandmother puts so much sugar in her tea? Is it because she likes sweet tea or because of changes in her sense of taste? Explain.

5. Could changes in senses be due to exposure to our environment? What things in the environment could produce sensory decline? Can anything be done to lessen the effects of these environmental factors?

6. Older adults respond slower than younger adults but only by a fraction of a second. Explain how such a small difference could make a big difference in some real-life settings.

7. Why do we conclude that most of the slowing with advanced age is in the brain rather than in the sense organs or muscles? Explain the steps involved in responding and the research findings.

8. What factors influence our perception of time?

RECOMMENDED READINGS

Sekuller, R. & Blake, R. (1987, December) Sensory underload. *Psychology Today, 21*, 48–51. Describes ways that older adults compensate for sensory losses.

Wolf, S. L., Barnhart, H. X., Kutner, N. G., McNeely. E., Coogler, C., Xu, T., & the Atlanta FICSIT Group. (1996). Reducing frailty and falls in older persons: An investigation of tai chi and computerized balance training. *Journal of the American Geriatrics Society, 44*, 489. This article provides information on the use of tai chi as a method for helping older persons (younger too) improve and maintain their balance.

INTERNET RESOURCES

http://www.eurekalert.org/releases/better-smeller.html   For information on loss of smell due to breathing in pollutants.

http://nidcd.nih.gov/   National Institute on Deafness and other communication disorders website supporting human communication research.

http://hubel.sfasu.edu/courseinfo/agingRefs.html   A bibliography of much of the recent work in aging and perception.

http://www.152.15.20.100/cogsci   Go to the Cognitive Development module and look in the section on aging and sensation and perception for a nice cartoon for examining critical flicker fusion that allows you to alter the rate at which the individual pictures are presented.

http://macnet007.psy.uva.nl/ResEdu/PN/res/PSYCHOFYS/Locusofslowing.kok   Recent, ongoing work that is examining the source of the mental slowing that seems to occur with advanced age.

CHAPTER

6 Memory and Cognition

The true way to render age vigorous is to prolong the youth of the mind.
—*Mortimer Collins*

It is commonly believed that memory declines as we age. Older adults are said to forget things, even things that just happened. They are said to remember the "good old days" but fail to remember appointments, names of people they just met, items they were supposed to pick up at the store, and so on. Such beliefs are as common among older adults as among younger adults (Hertzog, Dixon, & Hultsch, 1990).

This chapter examines the changes that seem to occur with advanced age. Also, we try to dispel some of the false beliefs, and suggest ways to improve memory. First, we take a brief look at how memory is thought to operate.

An Overview of Memory Processing

While different views of the details of memory and processing exist, most have a common configuration. It is this common configuration, or skeleton of memory, that we use for our discussion.

This common view suggests that there are three basic components of memory processing (Figure 6-1, p. 131) and that incoming information must be processed in order to be remembered. Memory does not operate like a video camera or a tape recorder; it does not simply record events. The information that gets put into memory is information that we have thought about, reacted to, or mentally processed in some way. Memories are a result of processes that we apply to information. For example, we select items to remember or ignore, we abstract information, we condense or expand it, we associate it with other things we know, we concentrate or hardly pay attention, and the final product is as much a result of our processing (probably more) as of any actual experience. We know that three people witnessing the same event may remember it in three different ways. Each person's memory of the same event is a result of each person's processing of that event.

Senior View

We spoke with Edward and Isabelle Peltz about changes in their memories as they have grown older. Ed was 72 and Isabelle was 69 when we spoke with them. Before his retirement, Ed was a teacher, then a principal, and finally the superintendent of schools. Isabelle worked as a medical assistant and certified nurse until their children were born.

We asked Ed and Isabelle if they thought that their memories had changed as they have aged. Isabelle said that she has difficulty recalling names but, aside from that, her memory is still good. Ed, on the other hand, told us that his memory is not as good as it used to be. You will see in this chapter that the usual state of affairs for changes in memory with advanced age is somewhere between the positive view of Isabelle and the less-positive view of Ed.

Isabelle added that she had no trouble recalling events, whether they were recent or occurred in the past, except when she is under stress. Research has shown that most people, young and old, have more difficulty remembering when they are under stress. "My husband claims that I don't remember certain things; (but) that is under dispute at all times," she said. Ed chuckled and said, "What is the question again?"

We asked both to tell us what sorts of things they do to improve memories. Both told us that crossword puzzles helped keep the mind sharp. Both said that they also read a lot. Ed told us that he and Isabelle belonged to a number of organizations and that these opportunities to meet and interact with a variety of people helped them stay mentally active. Ed uses tricks to remember names by associating the new name with some familiar object. Isabelle writes down names and other things. The act of writing and looking at what has been written helps her remember. Ed told us that following a set routine is helpful in remembering to do certain things. Doing them becomes automatic.

Finally, we asked how much information was stored in their memories and whether quantity had any influence on how easy it might be to remember something or have room for new information. Isabelle thought the amount of information influenced memory for the better. When you have more information your organization may improve, she noted. Ed told us that everything you experience goes into memory and stays there but that you do not run out of room.

Both agreed that memories are not always accurate. Different people may remember the same thing in very different ways. Isabelle summed up a lot of memory research very succinctly by stating that "the way you perceive it at the time is the way it is stored in the memory, not necessarily the actual facts." It would be hard to find a cognitive psychologist who did not agree with her.

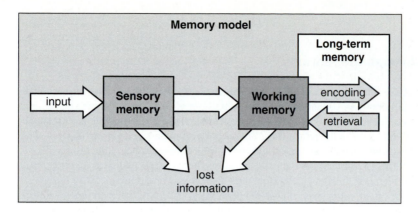

FIGURE 6-1   Illustration of the Memory System.

It is also the case that processing depends on many factors, each of which influences our memory for an event. For example, the amount of time available to process information will influence how well it is processed. Our familiarity with the information, the complexity of the situation, our physical and mental health, our knowledge of processing techniques/tricks, and so on, influence our memory for information by influencing the processing of that information. In short, memories depend on processing and processing depends upon a number of other factors. Finally, these factors may influence different aged adults in the same or in different ways.

Sensory Memory

The first part of memory is called **sensory memory** and consists of a different brief memory for each sense. For example, a visual memory (sometimes called iconic memory), is thought to store information received by the eyes; an auditory memory (sometimes called echoic memory) is thought to store information received by the ears. The amount of information coming into the sensory memories is enormous. Most of it is discarded immediately; it does not receive any conscious processing. Box 6-1 gives an example of the information that bombards our sensory memories.

Information enters and is held in sensory memory for a brief period of time. Researchers have been very successful at demonstrating the memory qualities of the eye and ear and showing this brief storage of information (Neisser, 1967). Information in sensory memory(ies) has not received any extensive processing yet, and will not unless it is attended to by working memory, the second component.

Working Memory

Working memory is assumed to be centrally located in the brain. As the name implies, this part of memory does the real work of encoding, processing, abstracting, selecting, retrieving, and so on. Working memory has been referred to by many different labels

B O X **6-1**

A Walk through the Library

To get a feel for the three components of memory imagine you are entering the library to check out a certain book. As you enter, your senses are bombarded. The walls may be covered with shelves that are filled with books of different sizes and colors. There may be paintings on the walls and tables and chairs in the room. There are people everywhere and all are different. They are wearing a wide-variety of clothing of assorted colors. The lights may be bright, dim, white, or yellow. Even though this is a library there are sounds everywhere: people whispering, copy machines running, people walking, and doors, elevators, and heaters/air conditioners quietly humming. You can feel the floor under your shoes and the temperature of the room. You can feel your backpack on your back and pen in your hand. You might detect the cologne of other students or the musty scent of books. All of this information impinges on your sensory memories but almost all of it is immediately discarded. Most information gets no further than sensory memory.

Working memory has allocated resources to finding a particular item. As you examine a row of books looking for that item you come upon a book laying on the floor. You bend to pick it up and see that it is *The Life and Times of S. V. Shereshevskii*. This information has made it past your sensory memory and into your working memory; you have noticed it but since it means nothing you discard the information from working memory and place the book on a shelf. You do not process it further. Most information is lost at the sensory memory level and some which makes it past that level to working memory is also lost.

Suppose, however, that you know that Shereshevskii is the famous memory magician described by Luria (1968). You might then open the book and examine it; you might consider borrowing it and reading about this famous mnemonist. You are processing information about the book and encoding that information into permanent episodic memory. Even if you discard the book, you are more likely to remember having seen it if you ever see it again or the next time someone talks about memory.

Try to examine all the information that is discarded at the level of working memory and the even greater amount lost at the sensory memory level the next time you enter the library or grocery store, or the next time you go to a concert, dinner, or movie. It is a good thing about memory that most information is discarded. We could stand there forever, in a daze, if everything were processed for storage in permanent memory.

(e.g., short-term store and primary memory) but for our purposes they all will refer to the same memory component. One simple way to think about working memory is to equate it with consciousness. If you are consciously aware of something then that something must be in working memory. It is best thought of as a pool or pools of processing resources that can be allocated to different tasks by a central executive (e.g, Baddeley, 1981).

Working memory is limited in the amount of processing that can be done at one time. Researchers say that the pool or pools of available processing resources are quite small. The central executive cannot allocate to all tasks demanding processing when the demands of such tasks exceed the available resources. In such cases, choices must be made. We are aware of the difficulties encountered when we are asked to do too many things at the same time. We cannot do them all at once. Some things will be lost but those that are processed in working memory are stored in long-term memory, the last component.

Long-Term Memory

The third component is **long-term memory** and is assumed to reside in the cerebral cortex as a vast interconnected network of stored memories. As working memory, long-term memory has several other names (e.g., long-term store, secondary memory, permanent memory). In fact, it is often assumed that two or three different networks of long-term memories exist and are interconnected. For our purposes we will assume that there are three major parts of long-term memory: procedural, episodic, and semantic memories (Tulving, 1985), although there are other ways to categorize these different aspects of permanent memory (Schacter, 1992).

Procedural memory refers to memory of how to do something. Permanent memories of how to tie your shoes, wash your hands, make a bed, and open a door are examples of procedural memories.

Episodic memory refers to memory for the episodes/events of your life. Permanent memories of where you grew up, your first date, where you parked your car, and what you did last night would be episodic memories.

Semantic memory refers to memory for knowledge and meaning. Permanent memories of the meanings of words, the location of Mexico, the difference between a liquid and solid, and which way is up would be semantic memories.

Most of the research conducted on memory has measured episodic memory rather than procedural or semantic memory. Research participants typically are presented with some items (e.g., a list of words, a story, face–name pairs) and then, after some period of time, tested for the items presented. They might be asked to recall or recognize the presented items. Since the presentation of the items was an event in their life, it is memory for that event that is being tested.

Long-term memory is assumed to have no upper limit to its storage capacity. Think of it as a structure being built with Legos. The bigger the structure gets, the more places there are to add on more pieces.

Memory System

It is important to think of the various components of memory as working together but the heart of the system is working memory. Working memory can be viewed as a pool of processing resources. It is a very limited pool. We can only carry on so many processing tasks at the same time. For example, you cannot sing the National Anthem while reading a book and jumping rope. You do not have enough processing resources to do all these things at the same time although you undoubtedly have sufficient resources to do any one of them, or a combination if you are resourceful.

These resources can be allocated to paying attention to new information. That is, working memory may select some of the information impinging on sensory memory and pay attention to it. It is, thus, being processed in working memory.

While in working memory the information can be encoded (e.g., rehearsed or pictured) in an attempt to lay down a permanent representation. You might try associating it with other information that you already know. In this case, you are clearly using some resources to retrieve information from permanent memory to relate to the new information. In this case you can allocate some resources to retain the new information while you allocate others to retrieving information from permanent memory.

We know that new tasks take a lot of processing resources while tasks that are very well-practiced take less. Think of the first few times that you drove a car. It took your full attention. Many new drivers have difficulty finding the wiper or light switch unless stopped at a traffic light. With more experience, however, one can flip all the switches and change channels on the radio while carrying on a conversation and still driving safely. With a lot of experience, you may find that you have driven to a familiar location with no memory at all of actually driving; it was done automatically (Hasher & Zacks, 1979).

The interactions between working memory and permanent memory can be thought of as going in two different directions. When resources are being used to place information into long-term storage they are referred to as **encoding** processes. Thus, rehearsing information or trying to form a mental image or associating information with prior information are considered forms of encoding processes. The more distinctive these encoding operations are, the better the *copy* in permanent memory. The better the copy, the easier it will be to find at another time. When resources are devoted to finding something in long-term memory and bringing it to conscious attention in working memory they are referred to as **retrieval** processes. Thus, trying to recall the name of someone you met or recognizing the correct item on a multiple-choice test are considered forms of retrieval.

Memory and Aging

Although many adults believe that memory declines with advanced age, the evidence is not convincing. Clearly, some parts of memory change while others seem to stay the same or even improve (Cerella, Rybash, Hoyer, & Commons, 1993).

Sensory Memory and Aging

While vision and hearing often decline with advanced age (see Chapter 5), evidence suggests that visual and auditory sensory memories do not decline or do so only minimally (Poon, 1985). Of course, minimal declines in sensory memory could underlie some difficulties in other components of memory (Craik & Jennings, 1992) if important information does not reach working memory and is not processed. Nevertheless, aging does not seem to result in any great decline in sensory memory.

Working Memory and Aging

Working memory does seem to change with advanced age. Research suggests that typical changes in working memory for older adults are due to a decline in available resources and a slowing in the rate at which information is processed. Thus, older adults may have more difficulty paying attention to more than one thing at a time and, typically, have to devote more effort to learning something new (Fogler & Stern, 1994).

Foos (1989a) examined working memory in young, middle-age, and older adults using a number of different tasks. For example, in one study individuals had to solve three mental addition problems, one at a time. Participants were given a problem to solve (e.g., add 46 and 28) and when they solved it, they were given another to solve (e.g., now add 14 and 37). When the second problem was solved, they were given a third (e.g., now add 84 and 91) and were only allowed to tell their three answers (e.g., 74, 51, and 175) after solving the last problem. Figure 6-2 shows the results. Young and middle-age adults performed identically and quite well. Older adults performed as well as young and middle-age adults on first and third addition problems (the difference in the graph for first and third addition problems is not significant) but poorer on the second addition problem. This suggests that older adults can process information quite well since they performed as well as other adults on the addition problems presented first and third. It is not the mental operations involved in mental addition that have declined. However, older adults seemed to have insufficient resources to hold solutions to the first two problems when the third one was presented. They tended to lose the solution to the second problem while solving the third and recalled only the first and third solutions when asked for their answers. Available resources for processing and storing information seem to decline with age. Older adults can do the work just not as much of it at the same time. Their performance on a single task is quite good. Other work (Corgiat, Templer, & Newell, 1989; Fastenau, Denburg, & Abeles, 1996) suggests

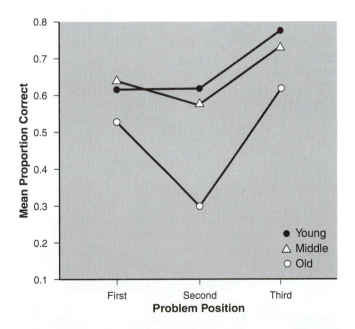

FIGURE 6-2   **Adult Age Differences on Addition Problems Presented First, Second, and Third. Figure reproduced from Foos (1989a).**

that available processing resources seem to be fewer for many older adults. They appear to have fewer resources available in working memory and, thus, process less information at any one time.

Processing speed is also an essential element in the observed decline in working memory (Salthouse, 1990; Salthouse & Babcock, 1991). For example, Fisk and Warr (1996) tested older and younger adults on several measures of working memory and perceptual speed. Perceptual speed refers to how quickly an individual can make a decision about presented materials. For example, participants were shown two strings of letters on a computer screen and had to answer as quickly as possible whether they were the same or different. They also had to answer questions about sentences that they had just read and later recall the last words of several sentences. These and other tasks showed that differences in perceptual speed accounted for many of the obtained age differences in working memory. Older adults may not only process less but they process less at a slower rate. It seems likely, as suggested by Babcock and Salthouse (1990), that resource space and speed each contribute, perhaps equally, to the deficits in working memory that are observed in older adults.

Long-Term Memory and Aging

Some work suggests that older adults have difficulty encoding information for later retrieval from permanent memory (Salthouse, 1991). Part of this difficulty is assumed to be due to the lower level of resources and slower processing speed. These changes would make distinctive encoding more difficult for older adults, especially when information is presented at a fairly rapid rate. Less distinctive encoding results in lower recall performance and more difficulty in recognizing the correct item when it is placed among related distractors (Hess, 1984; Rabinowitz, Craik, & Ackerman, 1982; Rankin & Kausler, 1979). For example, even without distinctive encoding, it might be easy to pick out a word you saw before (e.g., palm) when it is among a set of unrelated distractors (e.g., house, car, palm, baby). Perhaps all you encoded was the fact that the word was the name of a type of tree. That is not very distinctive encoding but would still be sufficient to enable you to choose the correct items from the set of unrelated distractors. Such shallow encoding would not serve you well, however, when the correct item is among a set of related distractors (e.g., maple, palm, elm, oak). In studies like these that attempt to examine the distinctiveness of encoding, researchers measure hits (i.e., picking the correct item) and false alarms (i.e., picking the incorrect item). One might expect many more false alarms in the case of related distractors especially when the encoding has been less distinct.

Isingrini, Fontaine, Taconnat, and Duportal (1995) examined recognition of highly related word pairs in young, young-old ($M = 68.25$), and old-old ($M = 83.75$) adults. An example of a highly related pair, would be "picture-movie." They found lower hit rates and higher false alarm rates for the oldest adults and concluded that encoding deteriorates with advanced age. The oldest adults had the greatest difficulty because they did not encode the original information distinctively. Other work also has found less efficient encoding for older adults. For example, Zacks, Hasher, Doren, Hamm, and Attig (1987) found no age differences in the recall of explicitly stated paragraph information but big differences when implications made from paragraph information were tested. It, thus, appears that older adults were as able as younger adults to retrieve information that required less encoding effort (i.e., explicitly stated information) but performed worse when encoding demands were greater (i.e., implicit information that required the making of connections and inferences).

In addition to less distinctive encoding, several lines of research also have found difficulties with retrieval for older adults. Older adults often have more difficulty coming up with the right word or name and seem to take longer to retrieve items even when their retrieval is successful (Fogler & Stern, 1994; Lovelace, 1990). A classic demonstration of the permanence of memory and the increased difficulties with retrieval is one conducted by Smith (1935, 1951, 1963). At age 10, Smith memorized the 107 questions and answers of the Westminister Catechism. When she was 43-, 63-, and 73-years-old, she tested her memory for those items, with the help of a friend. At each test she remembered every item, but as she grew older, she needed more prompting to aid information retrieval. For instance, at the first test, 9 items required more extensive prompting (i.e., when she was 43), 15 at the second test (when she was 63), and 34 at the third test (when she was 73). Clearly all the information was still there in long-term memory but it was more difficult to retrieve without help as she aged. Several traditional laboratory studies also show greater retrieval difficulties for older adults (e.g., Burke & Light, 1981; Schonfield & Robertson, 1966).

There are declines in both encoding and retrieval operations with advanced age. Much of the decline in encoding may be attributable to the decline in working memory resources and slower processing speed while much of the decline in retrieval may be due to those changes plus the increase in the amount of stored information that has accumulated over a long life. In some ways the decline in retrieval may be viewed as a positive change since it seems, in part, due to the wealth of knowledge stored over a long, rich life. It may be easy for a 6-year-old to recall a name since she may have stored only a few dozen names. It may be difficult for a 70-year-old to recall the same name since she may have stored more than a million names in her lifetime. Her difficulty in retrieval may be a sign of her rich store of information.

Procedural Memories.   Procedural memories appear to remain relatively intact for healthy older adults. One does not forget how to drive a car, boil an egg, swim, or brush one's teeth as one ages unless something is seriously wrong. Even tasks that are not performed on a regular schedule seem to remain strong in procedural memory.

Episodic Memories.   Episodic memories, on the other hand, are difficult to retrieve as we get older. Of course, the longer one lives, the more episodes there are to search through. It would be quite a surprise if retrieval from episodic memory did not become more difficult. Some aspects of specific episodes also are more likely to be forgotten. Spencer and Raz (1995) examined the results of 46 research studies using meta-analysis. This analysis showed greater age deficits in memory for the context of a message than for the content, although content differences also were obtained. Older individuals were better able to recall what was presented to them than to recall who presented it or where the presentation occurred. Contexts that were most relevant for message content were the ones most likely to be remembered. If you read in the paper that a good friend was wanted by the FBI you would probably remember the content but may not remember whether you read it in the paper, saw it on TV, or heard about it on the radio. If, however, the FBI came to see you and asked where your friend is, you are more likely to remember the context in which you learned that your friend was wanted. Erngrund, Mäntylä, and Nilsson (1996) also found that older adults showed lower performance than younger adults on item and source recall but that the deficits were greater on source recall. Older adults were more likely to forget where the information came from. Perhaps our limited resources, as we age, are allocated to the content of a message rather than the source because the content is usually of more importance?

A classic study of memory for real-life events was conducted by Bahrick, Bahrick, and Wittlinger (1975). They examined memory for names and faces of high school classmates by testing people ranging in age from 17 to 74. Recall of names was far more difficult than recognition. Far more retrieval effort is involved in recall (recall the name of the person quoted at the beginning of this chapter) than in recognition (was the name of the person quoted Smedlap or Collins?). Face recognition remained high, over 90 percent, until 15 years after graduation. Even the oldest group tested recognized over 70 percent of the faces. Older adults remember real-life events very well, although whether they remember older memories better than more recent ones is very doubtful. Box 6-2 may surprise you. The

BOX **6-2**

Remembering Old Memories Better Than New Memories

A common myth about older adults' memories is that older adults remember things that happened a long time ago but not things that happened recently. My grandfather remembered a lot of stories about the Great Depression but could not always remember what happened a few days, hours, or minutes ago. There are, of course, enormous difficulties with these comparisons. We know that everyone remembers more meaningful material better than less meaningful material, and the Great Depression was clearly more meaningful than yesterday's lunch. We know that everyone remembers well-rehearsed stories better than stories that have never been told. Finally, we do not have a way to estimate the total amount of stored information from which these items are being retrieved. If grandfather remembers one of the four items we had for lunch, then he is remembering 25 percent. If he remembers one of ten Great Depression stories, then he is only remembering 10 percent. We do not know how many total stories there are and so we cannot estimate the amount remembered. In spite of such difficulties, two lines of research offer some evidence on remembering old memories.

Hulicka (1982) interviewed several older adults in a congregate living facility who told her that they frequently spoke about old memories around young listeners in an attempt to increase the listener's interest. Memories of a 70-year-old might be quite unique for a 20-year-old whereas memories of recent events would be of less interest to the young listener. Hulicka recorded the conversations of one 93-year-old man to learn what memories were discussed in conversations among older adults. The tapes showed that recent (last 20 years), old (those of 60+ years ago), and in-between memories were equally likely to be brought up in conversations. Perhaps older adults discuss old memories with young listeners but discuss any memory (new or old) with their peers.

Other work has shown that when adults are asked to recall events in their lives they tend to recall recent events and then fewer older memories except for an unusually high recall of adolescent memories. This is referred to as the reminiscence bump (Fitzgerald & Lawrence, 1984; Robinson, 1976). To examine this phenomenon, Jansari and Parkin (1996) had adults in their late 30s, 40s, and 50s recall under instructions to avoid recent memories. This instruction resulted in a reminiscence bump, not just for the oldest participants, but for the younger ones as well. They then had other participants recall and rate the memories on several dimensions (e.g, vividness, pleasantness, importance, etc). Although these dimensions did not differentiate new from old memories, old memories were more often first-time or unique experiences. The authors state that "firsts are more abundant in early-life and are also easy to retrieve" (p. 89). It may not be that older adults remember old memories better; it may be that everyone remembers their first-time better (better than their eighth time or forty-second time, and so on).

Test yourself and see if you can remember your:

- first car
- first date (how about your eighth date?)
- the house you grew up in
- first job

---

myth of older adults remembering older events better than recent events does not appear to be true.

Some research has attempted to examine the rate at which episodic memory is searched by different age groups. Generally, older adults search at a slower rate than younger and middle-age adults, and even middle-age adults seem to search at a slower rate than younger adults (Anders, Fozard, & Lillyquist, 1972; Strayer, Wickens, & Braune, 1987). This slow down in the rate at which memory is searched may also be partly responsible for the observed retrieval difficulties of older adults. Older adults may end the search before the answer is found or be unable to find the answer fast enough to respond in a time-limited test situation.

Semantic Memories.   Semantic memories, like other types of long-term memory, also accumulate with age. We have much greater knowledge of more things the older we become. Think about how much more you know now than you did when you were only ten. Think about how much more your grandparents know than you do. Older adults generally perform very well on tests of world history (Perlmutter, Metzger, Miller, & Nezworski, 1980) and some kinds of common knowledge (see Box 6-3, p. 140). On the other hand, they do not perform well on tests of everyday knowledge such as memory for songs (Bartlett & Snelus, 1980), odors (Stevens, Cain, & Demarque, 1990), grocery items (McCarthy, Ferris, Clark, & Crook, 1981), proverbs (Wood & Pratt, 1987), telephones, and the U.S. penny (Foos, 1989b).

Why do older adults have difficulties in some situations but not in others? One possible reason is because researchers selected the materials and perhaps researchers do not know what older adults know. To test this possibility, Foos and Dickerson (1996) asked older and younger adults to rate how easy it would be for members of their own and the

BOX   6-3

Equal but Different (or Equal and Not)

Many items are remembered well by adults of different ages. In some of these instances, the amount of information may be the same, but the actual items remembered may be different. Foos, Clark, Booth, Myers, and Schmitz (1996) examined the recall of brand names by 65 young ($M = 21.74$), 71 middle-age ($M = 44.92$), and 64 old ($M = 67.67$) adults. They found no age or gender differences in quantity recalled. All groups remembered about the same number of brand names (the overall mean number recalled was 39.35). There were, however, many interesting group differences in which specific brands were most frequently recalled (defined as recalled by at least 25 percent of a group). For example, all groups of women recalled Liz Claiborne among their top brands while all groups of men recalled Chevrolet, Ford, General Electric, and RCA. Middle-age and older women had many items in common with each other but not with younger women. Middle-age and younger men had many items in common but not with old men. Younger adults recalled many more brands of clothing than middle-age adults and middle-age adults recalled more clothing brands than older adults. Middle-age women recalled more food brands than any other group. Men of all ages named many more automobile brands than did women. While middle-age and older men and women named the same number of electronic brands among their top brands (i.e., 4 and 2, respectively), younger men named more such brands than any other group (i.e., 9) while younger women named none. Can you explain any of these findings? Would you have predicted them?

The five most frequently named brands across the entire sample, from first to fifth, were Coca Cola, Pepsi Cola, General Electric, Levis, and Nike.

other age group to remember a number of different items. Some of those items are shown in Table 6-1. The set of items shown in the first row (e.g., U.S. geography, world geography, radio personalities, dairy items, events/people 1970–1990) are items that each age group rated as being better remembered by their own age group (thus, the first check means older adults rated all of these items as better remembered by older adults while the second check indicates that younger adults rated all of these items as better remembered by younger adults). The second set (U.S. presidents, etc.) are those items that older adults would remember best as rated by both older and younger raters. The third set of items shown (cartoon characters and planets) are those that were rated as being better remembered by younger adults by both older and younger raters and the fourth set of items (Olympic gold medal winners, etc.) are those that both older and younger raters thought would be better remembered by the other age group. No one believes that they themselves remember these latter items as well as someone in the other age group! Do you agree with these ratings?

Foos and Sarno (1998) selected 13 items from those that had been identified as remembered best by older (e.g., the first set of items in Table 6-1) or older and younger adults (e.g., the second set shown in the table) and tested them on a group of older and a group of younger adults. In all 13 cases, older adults remembered these items better. They were very good at retrieving information from their semantic memories. Other work also indicates that retrieval from semantic memory is not a problem for older adults (Mayr & Kliegl, 2000).

TABLE 6-1   Ratings of the Memorability of Different Items of Common Knowledge by Older and Younger Adults

Rated as Better Remembered by These Adults	Rated by		Sample Items
	Old	Young	
Old	✓		U.S. geography
			World geography
Young		✓	Radio personalities
			Items in a dairy case
			Events/people of the period 1970–1990
Old	✓	✓	U.S. presidents
			Broadway shows
			Instruments in an orchestra
			Events/people of the period 1910–1970
Young	✓	✓	Cartoon characters
			Planets
Old		✓	Olympic gold medal winners
			World Series winners
Young	✓		Tools in a hardware store
			Best-selling books

Older adults also were correct in their ratings; items that they said would be better remembered by older adults were better remembered by other older adults. Thus, one possible reason for lower performance on many of the materials tested in research studies (e.g., U.S. penny) is simply that older adults do not remember them as well and know that they do not. This does not mean that semantic memory has declined since other items, especially those named by older adults, are remembered very well. Older adults are better judges of what information they have available in their semantic memories than are memory researchers. They also seem to be better judges of their own memories than younger adults. It is not clear whether younger adults make bad judgments about their own memories or whether they just make bad judgments about how their memories relate to the memories of an older person. Project 6 (p. 142) gives you a chance to answer part of this question.

In those cases where older adults have performed poorly on tests of semantic memory, it is possible that some variable other than age was the important factor. It seems reasonable to hypothesize that level of education might be strongly associated with level of world and common knowledge. Since most younger adults tested are college students, they may have a higher, on average, level of education than the older adult group being compared to them. Recent work has examined the role of education and several other factors on age differences in semantic and episodic memory.

Nyberg, Bäckman, Erngrund, Olofsson, and Nilsson (1996) examined 1000 adults in ten different age groups (i.e., 100 people aged 35, 40, 45 . . . 75, and 80) to see if age, or other measured variables, predicts age differences in episodic and semantic memory. The

P R O J E C T 6

The text discusses a study (Foos & Dickerson, 1996) in which older and younger adults were asked to rate a number of items for memorability by their own age group compared to the other age group. These categories of items are listed in Table 6-1. For example, both older and younger adults claimed that their age group would be able to remember U.S. and world geography, radio personalities, items in a dairy case, and events/people of the period 1970–1990 better than adults in the other age group. When many of these items were tested, it was found that older adults performed better. This may mean that older adults know what they know and how it compares to the knowledge of younger adults. But what do younger adults know?

It may be that younger adults also know what they know but do not have a clear idea of how their knowledge relates to that of an older person. They may underestimate that knowledge. Thus, they may be correct in believing that younger adults remember things like geography (from the first set in Table 6-1) and planets (from the third set in Table 6-1) much better than presidents (from the second set in Table 6-1) and World Series winners (from the fourth set in Table 6-1). For convenience, call the former items *top* items and the latter *bottom* items.

If this is true, then younger adults should remember the items they said they would remember (i.e., *top* items) better than the items they said would be better remembered by older adults (i.e., *bottom* items). **This project involves checking this prediction to see if younger adults know what they know**. Select some *top* and *bottom* item(s) from these sets that can be easily scored as proportions correct (i.e., sets that have a limited and identifiable number of items such as U.S. states and presidents, planets, World Series winners, etc.). Proportions will allow you to make comparisons across the different item types. Ask a group of younger adults (10–20 people) to participate and give them each a pen and paper (one for each set of items being tested). Ask them to recall as many of each item set, one set at a time, as they can and then compare the recall of *top* to *bottom* items.

Did younger adults remember a greater proportion of *top* than *bottom* items? If so, that seems to confirm the hypothesis that younger adults do know what they know. If not, why not?

Do your results say anything about younger adults' knowledge of older adults' memories? What would you tell younger adults about older adults' knowledge?

---

other variables measured included gender, education, blood pressure, and level of Vitamin B_{12}. Several different measures of episodic and semantic memory were taken (e.g., free recall of sentences, name recognition, word fluency, general knowledge retrieval). The authors found that the most important variable accounting for semantic memory differences was education. Controlling for differences in the other variables did not, however, eliminate age differences in episodic memory. The authors suggest that age differences in episodic memory are due to neuronal changes that accompany advanced age. Other work also has found that the age differences in episodic memory may depend, to a large extent, on mental activity of an individual. In a six-year longitudinal study, researchers found very little decline in performance for participants who were regularly engaged in intellectually challenging activities such as learning a new language or playing bridge (Hultsch, Hertzog, Small, & Dixon, 1999). Do you remember what challenging mental activities Ed and Isabelle Peltz engage in to preserve their memories?

Metamemory

Metamemory refers to knowledge about one's own memory. Thus, metamemory is really cognition rather than memory per se. If you know how well your memory works, if you know what strategies are likely to be effective in different situations, if you can successfully predict your own performance, if you know how much you know, you probably have a very good metamemory. For example, as a student, you may know how well you perform on essay versus multiple-choice tests or in English versus math. Such knowledge, if accurate, will allow you to allocate your study time efficiently and to select more effective test-taking strategies. If your metamemory is not very good, then you may end up prioritizing tasks inefficiently and using your time and strategies ineffectively. Researchers typically measure metamemory by using a questionnaire such as the Metamemory in Adulthood (MIA) (Dixon & Hultsch, 1983), Memory Self-Efficacy (Berry, West, & Dennehey, 1989), or Memory Functioning (Gilewski, Zelinski, & Schaie, 1990). Table 6-2 provides examples of the types of questions asked on these questionnaires.

TABLE 6-2   Sample Metamemory Questionnaire Items

For each of the items listed below (1) rate how often remembering that item presents a problem for you (i.e., always, sometimes, never), and (2) for each problem item rate how serious you consider the problem to be (i.e., very serious, somewhat serious, not serious):

Names	Faces	Appointments
Where you put things	Phone numbers	Directions
Your shoe size	Words	Things people tell you
Day of the week	Date	Taking a test

Is your memory the same, worse, or better than it was . . .

One year ago?
Five years ago?
Ten years ago?

How often (always, sometimes, never) do you use the following techniques to help you remember things?

Appointment book	Reminder notes
Mental repetition	Making a list

How would you rate your memory in terms of the kinds of problems you have?

Major problems			Some minor problems			No problems
1	2	3	4	5	6	7

Source: Adapted from Gilewski, Zelinski, and Schaie (1990).

Older adults generally believe that their memories have declined (Cavanaugh & Green, 1990; Dixon, Hultsch, & Hertzog, 1988; Hertzog, Dixon, & Hultsch, 1990) even though such beliefs are not always correlated with real declines. Measures of memory performance in older adults generally show that those who complain the most, often show very little decline in actual performance while those who have the greatest declines in performance, often overestimate their own memories (Kaszniak, 1990; Smith, Petersen, Ivnik, Malec, & Tangalos, 1996). In terms of overall beliefs about their memories, older adults do not appear to be very accurate but there may be several reasons for this apparent inaccuracy.

McDonald-Miszczak, Hertzog, and Hultsch (1995) tested two large samples of older adults over two- and six-year periods, respectively. The MIA questionnaire assessed metamemory. Individuals also were asked about memory change and were given several tests of memory (e.g., recall of words, text, and general knowledge). Results showed longitudinal change in both metamemory and memory performance but the two did not coincide. Individuals who believed that their memories had worsened frequently showed no change while others who believed that no change had occurred exhibited a decline in performance. McDonald-Miszczak et al. concluded that metamemory in older adults may be based on actual performance but, to a much larger extent, on their own self-efficacy and their implicit theory about how memory changes with age. Such implicit theories seem to be negative as older and younger adults believe that memory declines with age (Kite & Johnson, 1988).

One hypothesis that has received attention recently contends that since the beliefs about memory and age vary from culture to culture perhaps the memory performance of older adults also varies. Some cultures, particularly Asian and African, have greater respect for older adults. While older adults in American culture are believed to have declined quite a bit, older adults in some of these other cultures are believed to remain quite capable and wise. An initial test of this hypothesis provided promising results (Levy & Langer, 1994) but more recent work found no differences. A comparison of younger and older Anglophone Canadians to younger and older Chinese Canadians found older adults of both cultural groups performing poorer than younger adults on a number of memory tests (Yoon, Hasher, Feinberg, Rahhal, & Winocur, 2000).

Another longitudinal study (Johansson, Allen-Burge, & Zarit, 1997) conducted on very-old adults (mean age at first testing was 86.85) found a modest relationship between metamemory assessments of memory and actual performance. More interestingly, the researchers found that low self-evaluations of memory at the first testing were predictive of decline and, in some instances, diagnosis of dementia, two to four years later. It may be that older adults can detect changes in their memories that are not easily detected by traditional tests of memory until they become more severe. Such low self-evaluations may be useful for identifying individuals at risk for further decline or possible dementia. When older adults complain about memory problems they should be taken seriously. Such complaints could be due to a general belief that older adults lose their memories. Memory problems also could be due to changes that are not easily detected by others initially but may become evident at a later date. In either case some reassurance and monitoring may be prudent.

Other work shows that older adults' evaluations of their own memories are dependent, to some extent, on how the questions about memory are asked (e.g., Cavanaugh, 1986–1987). Older and younger adults rate their memories for specific items and events

"I don't remember."

very nearly the same but when asked more general questions about their memories, older adults are less positive about their abilities. Again a general belief in memory decline with age does not seem to correlate with beliefs about specific items or with actual performance.

Although older adults tend to believe that their overall memory declines with age, but that they will do well on a number of specific tasks, the real state of affairs may be the reverse. Overall memory has not declined much with age but on a number of specific tasks, older adults do not often perform as well as younger adults. Some researchers believe that older adults need to be educated about memory in order to improve their memory self-efficacy (Cavanaugh, 1996; Welch & West, 1995). If older adults understood the changes that occur in memory with advanced age, confidence in their own memory ability might increase. As a result, memory performance might improve. These ideas await further testing but it is never too early to reassure and educate an older loved one about their memories.

Memory Improvement

Everyone can improve memory. You may be familiar with techniques for remembering items for tests or names of people you have met. Most of us are familiar with little tricks like acronyms for remembering the colors of the spectrum (i.e., ROY G. BIV) or the names of the Great Lakes (i.e., HOMES). There are many techniques (e.g., imagery, peg-words, loci) and books describing those techniques (Brown, 1989; Gose & Levi, 1988; Lapp, 1992), in addition to research that demonstrates the advantage of using them (Bellezza, 1982; Glass & Holyoak, 1986; Loftus, 1980). Some techniques and tricks of memory are shown in Table 6-3.

Camp, Foss, Stevens, Reichard, McKitrick, & O'Hanlon (1993) provide a model for categorizing the different types of techniques and memories involved in improvement. Their model is called the *E-I-E-I-O* model. The first *E* and *I* stand for the type of memory involved, explicit or implicit. Explicit memories are those that require some effortful retrieval such as remembering the name of the third president (i.e., Thomas Jefferson). Implicit memories do not require such effort (e.g., remembering your own name). The second *E* and *I* stand for the type of memory technique used, external or internal. Making a list of items to remember is an external technique but using a rhyme to remember them (e.g., "Columbus sailed the ocean blue, in 1400 and 92") is an internal technique. Those techniques mentioned previously (acronyms) are explicit, internal aids. The *O* (*oh*) stands for the realization that the information has been successfully stored and can be easily retrieved.

TABLE 6-3   Some Memory Improvement Tricks

Problem	Technique
Forget to do something when I get home.	Call home and leave yourself a message on your answering machine.
I leave the car lights on after driving in the rain.	Keep a clip in your car and attach it to the keys when you turn on the lights. You will feel that reminder when you turn the engine off.
Forget to get something when I'm out.	Create an acronym. To remember to get *m*ilk, *a*spirin, *g*reen pepper, *i*ce cream, and *c*andy at the store, remember the word *magic*.
I forget where I parked my car.	When you exit the parked car pay careful attention to where it is. Look back at the car before entering the building.
I can't remember numbers.	Convert the numbers to words by replacing each digit with a word that has that many letters. The number *549* could be remembered as *learn* (5) *this* (4) *technique* (9).
I forget new names right away.	When you learn a new name, say it out loud ("I'm pleased to meet you _____). Practice retrieving it using the implicit, internal technique described in the text.

Source: Techniques and examples taken from Foos (1997).

Older and younger adults use a number of explicit, external aids to memory such as telephone logs, appointment calendars, birthday calendars, Palm Pilots, and lists. Such aids are the most frequently reported techniques for memory improvement by adults of all ages (Foos, 1997; Park, Smith, & Cavanaugh, 1990). With the decline in working memory resources that seems to occur with advanced age, such external stores of information can be particularly helpful, especially if many things must be dealt with in a short amount of time.

Implicit, internal aids are repeated retrieval attempts with feedback. That is, one learns something and then tries to remember it (retrieve it from long-term memory); a friend or a written answer provides feedback as to the success of each retrieval. This technique has had some success in helping individuals remember to perform future tasks as well (Camp & Stevens, 1990; McKitrick, Camp, & Black, 1992). A recommended implicit, internal technique for remembering the names of people is to say their name out loud when you first meet them, and continue saying it to yourself a few minutes later, several minutes later, and even an hour or so later when you are driving home. This continued practice at retrieval over longer intervals is likely to produce the *O* experience of having learned that person's name.

Many older adults worry about their memories and complain about memory loss. However, the changes that take place in memory with advanced age are not as bad as people assume. Furthermore, the concerns that older adults have about their memories do not seem to be based on actual loss. Efforts to increase confidence and self-efficacy have

Good memory is important, if you want to win the game.

been successful but do not improve performance (Dittman-Kohli, Lachman, Kliegl, & Baltes, 1991). The reverse is also true. Memory improvement training, especially with explicit, internal aids (e.g., acronyms), has been successful but does not reduce anxiety or complaints (Scogin, Storandt, & Lott, 1985). Best, Hamlett, and Davis (1992) recommend providing older adults with memory improvement training *and* anxiety reduction. Work shows that neither alone is sufficient to improve memory and reduce complaints (Floyd & Scogin, 1997).

Studies also have shown that older adults can learn and use explicit, internal techniques to improve memory but often the techniques are not used following the training and/or have limited use beyond the specific training materials (Greenberg & Powers, 1987; Neely & Bäckman, 1995). Some other work (Foos, 1997) showed that offering older adults a variety of techniques to choose from and providing information about normal changes in memory to reduce anxiety, increased performance on novel tasks and also reduced anxiety and complaints. Four weeks after the original training, older adults still performed well on a novel task. Additionally, all reported reduced anxiety about memory changes. People seem more likely to continue using a technique and to apply it to new situations when the technique is one that they have selected.

Aside from techniques that can be categorized using the *E-I-E-I-O* model are pharmacological aids. "Memory improvers," which come in capsules or pills, are advertised in magazines, newspapers, and are even available in health food stores. Although most of these products have no proven effect on memory, one promising herbal remedy is ginkgo biloba. Ginkgo is an extract from the fan-shaped leaves of the ginkgo tree (also known as the maidenhair tree), which was once a sacred plant in China and Japan. Manufacturers of ginkgo-based products say it has been "proven to increase alertness and short-term memory." Although research has not been conducted to test these claims, initial results seem promising (Deberdt, 1994; Israel, Dell'Accio, Martin, & Hugonot, 1987). For example, Hofferberth (1994) found significant improvement in baseline performance for dementia patients receiving a special extract of ginkgo biloba compared to control groups receiving a placebo. The improvement appeared after one month of treatment (see also Chapter 11). Other work has found virtually no benefit from a number of different nutrients and drugs designed to act on certain neurotransmitters, such as acetylcholine (Lombardi & Weingartner, 1995). Whether ginkgo or some chemical will be found to improve memory reliably is still an open question.

We encourage interested readers to examine the work of Stine-Morrow and Soederberg Miller (1999). Cognition does change as one grows older but the changes are not all declines and the declines are not as severe as many believe them to be.

Making Choices

Several lines of research suggest that we can preserve our mental functioning, our memory and cognition, well into old-age if we make certain choices. In this chapter, you learned about the importance of processing and the changes that can take place with advanced age. Those changes can be offset to some extent by using memory improvement techniques to assist in the encoding of information. You can learn these techniques. There are a number of good books which describe memory improvement techniques. Researchers have examined some other choices as well.

For example, Albert, Jones, Savage, Berkman, Seeman, Blazer, and Rowe (1995) followed 1115 adults to assess what measures and choices made in life would predict changes in memory and cognitive functioning over a 2½-year period. Four important variables emerged as the main predictors. First, education was the best predictor. Higher levels of education were strongly associated with higher performance levels in old-age (see also Carmelli, Swan, & Cardon, 1995). Second, strenuous activity was associated with higher levels of cognitive functioning, and physical activity is important for mental health (see Chapter 4). Third, pulmonary peak expiratory flow-rate predicted better performance. Low flow-rate is associated with smoking and high LDL cholesterol levels. Fourth, self-efficacy also predicted better performance. People who believed in themselves scored higher.

Are you smoking and eating fatty, high cholesterol foods? DON'T. It is not just the youth of your body that you threaten by smoking and eating fatty foods, you also risk the youth of your mind and your longevity.

Do you believe in your own ability? A study by Seeman, McAvay, Merrill, Albert, and Rodin (1996) suggests that such self-efficacy beliefs, although important for everyone, may be more important for the performance of older males than females. Learn to believe in yourself.

CHAPTER HIGHLIGHTS

- All memories are the result of processing that takes place using resources held in working memory. Memory is assumed to have three major components: sensory memory, working memory, and long-term memory. Permanent memory is also divided into three components: procedural, episodic, and semantic.
- Older adults show no decline in sensory memory.
- Older adults show declines in working memory that appears to be due to a loss of resources and a slowing in processing.
- Older adults show no decline in procedural memory but very little research has been done.
- Older adults show a decline in encoding and retrieval from episodic memory. These declines seem to be due to the changes that have taken place in working memory and to the accumulation of information in permanent memory coupled with a slowing of retrieval processes.
- Older adults sometime show a deficit in semantic memory but the deficit seems to be due to the specific items tested and/or the level of participants' education. Older adults typically do very well in tests of general knowledge.
- Tests of metamemory in older adults show mixed results and the answers one gets often depend on how the questions are asked. Older adults believe their memories have declined but such beliefs do not generally correspond to beliefs about specific items or actual performance. This may be due to the common belief that memory declines with age or to the inability of our current tests to detect changes that can be detected much earlier by the individual experiencing them.
- Memory improvement techniques can be categorized with the *E-I-E-I-O* model. Both younger and older adults report frequent use of explicit, external aids such as lists. With explicit, internal aids, older adults are capable of improving their memories but are more likely to do so when they can select the improvement technique(s). Little research has been conducted on implicit, external aids but with implicit, internal aids, such as continued retrieval with feedback, older adults have performed very well.
- While most of the pharmacological agents tested have not been shown to improve memory, recent work on ginkgo biloba seems promising.

STUDY QUESTIONS

1. Describe the three components of memory and explain how they work together.

2. Describe aspects of memory that increase, and decrease, with advanced age, and also those that do not change.

3. Give an example of a procedural memory that you have. How will this memory be affected by your aging?

4. What reasons are given for the findings that older adults perform very well on some tests of semantic memory and very poorly on others?

5. Why does grandpa remember stories about the Great Depression and his adolescence when he cannot remember what he had for lunch an hour ago?

6. Explain how the decline in encoding with advanced age might be due, in part, to changes in working memory resources and speed. Could these changes in working memory also be responsible for the decline in retrieval? Why? Are there other factors that influence the decline in retrieval?

7. Older adults frequently have difficulty in coming up with the right word or name. What positive thing might you tell an older adult with this difficulty?

8. When older adults complain about their memories it could be due to two factors. What are those factors?

9. Describe memory improvement techniques using the E-I-E-I-O model.

10. What choices can you make to prolong the youth of your mind? What is the likelihood of your making such choices? Is such prolonging even possible?

RECOMMENDED READINGS

Bäckman, L., Small, B. J., & Wahlin, A. (2001). Aging and memory: Cognitive and biological perspectives. In J. E. Birren & K. W. Schaie (Eds.), *Handbook of the Psychology of Aging* (5th ed., pp. 349–377). San Diego, CA: Academic Press. This chapter reviews the latest research on memory and aging.

Cerella, J., Rybash, J., Hoyer, W., & Commons, M.L. (Eds.). (1993). *Adult information processing: limits on loss.* San Diego, CA: Academic Press. This book contains chapters by a number of experts on several aspects of memory and aging.

Kausler, D.H. (1994). *Learning and memory in normal aging.* San Diego, CA: Academic Press. This is a good overview of all aspects of memory and aging.

Lapp, D.C. (1992). *Maximizing your memory power.* New York: Barron's Educational Series. This book on memory improvement gives a number of techniques to use.

INTERNET RESOURCES

http://www.secretsofaging.com/mind/fluid.html   A website that will offer you information about changes in working memory with age and a chance to try your skill at a couple of memory games.

http://www.psywww.com/mtsite/memory.html   For information on memory techniques and mnemonics

http://www.merkle.com/humanMemory.html   Short article about the possible size of long-term memory.

7 Intelligence, Wisdom, and Creativity

Life could be compared to an embroidery of which we see the right side during the first half of life, but the back half in the latter. This back side is less scintillating but more instructive; it reveals the interpatterning of the threads.

—Schopenhauer, 1844

Schopenhauer believed that the second half of life changed our perspective. Older adults could see the interpatterning of the threads and perhaps that is what is meant by wisdom. Of course, to be wise, we assume that one must have a certain amount of intelligence. In **Senior View**, May Taylor tells us that she has slowed down and has difficulty paying attention to more than one thing at a time but that her intelligence and wisdom have increased and that she is more creative now than in the past. Jack Palis, on the other hand, says that he is much wiser than he used to be but that his intelligence and creativity are not called into play as much anymore because he no longer has to confront problems. These different perceptions of what has happened to intelligence, wisdom, and creativity are much like the research. In some cases there appear to be increases in all three while in other cases the opposite seems true. The answers to if and how intelligence, wisdom, and creativity change with age may be less clear than in any other area.

Intelligence, wisdom, and creativity are related. They all rely on similar mental processes, such as attention, encoding, and retrieval. Intelligence might be thought of as the ability to remember information and to use it effectively when necessary. One might become very intelligent in some specific area with continued experience and practice; we would say that such a person has developed expertise in that area. Wisdom might be thought of as an overall perspective on knowledge and the ability to use it in practical situations; wisdom can be viewed as expertise for matters of real life. Creativity might be thought of as going beyond what is known in an attempt to create something new. Robert Sternberg says,

"If we view existing knowledge as setting constraints much like a prison, we might view the wise person as seeking to understand this prison and just what its boundaries are, the

Senior View

May Taylor was 85 when we spoke with her in 1998. A widow living with her dog, she told us that she was in very good health when we asked her about intelligence, wisdom, and creativity.

May said that she is as smart as she ever was but that she has slowed down. It takes her a little longer and she is not as sharp after four hours of bridge as she used to be. At the same time, May said that she has grown more intelligent. She has had to learn how to handle financial matters after her husband passed away. Intelligence is "the ability to handle any crisis or anything that comes up, well," she told us. One good measure of intelligence, according to May, is the way people drive. She has seen some really stupid driving.

Regarding wisdom, May told us that she believes that she is wiser because of the experiences she has had over a long life. As we will see later in this chapter, many theorists would agree with her about the importance of the right kind of experiences.

When asked about creativity, May told us that she was still creative but in different ways than when she was younger. She has found new interests and took painting classes and now loves to paint.

Jack Palis was 82 when we talked with him. Jack is still married and he and his wife have an apartment in the city. Like May, Jack said that intelligence is "the ability, when confronted with a situation, to be able to cope with it." He says he's much wiser today than when he was young but was better at coping with situations when he was young.

Like May, Jack says his wisdom has increased because of the experiences he has had over a long life. Jack thinks that people may become more experienced with age but not necessarily become wise. He told us that "some people will never learn and they act on impulse all their lives." As we will see, this too fits well with what some theorists say about wisdom. Experiences benefit some people in terms of wisdom but do not benefit everyone.

Jack says he no longer has many opportunities to be creative and that he is less creative now then when he was young and constantly had problems to solve. Jack believes that one needs problems to solve if one is to be creative. He wanted to tell young people that "before you act on impulse, think of the possible outcomes; if the possible outcomes outweigh the gratification you may get now, then do not act on that impulse."

intelligent person as seeking to make the best of life in prison, and the creative person as seeking to escape from the prison" (1990, p. 153).

Intelligence

Age differences in intelligence and the relationship between age and intelligence have received more research attention than almost any topic in gerontology. Among lay people, there is a general belief that "you can't teach an old dog new tricks," but most researchers know better. Older animals, including humans, may seem to lose some ability to learn and remember; they may seem to lose intelligence but some aspects of memory and cognition change with age while others do not. Those that change can increase as well as decrease in efficiency. There are gains and losses at all stages of development and this is certainly the case when intelligence is measured.

What Is Intelligence?

Although there are many ways to measure intelligence and probably many different kinds of intelligence, most researchers would agree on the major aspects and might, thus, define intelligence as some overall ability. **Intelligence** is a general proficiency at cognitive tasks (Glaser, 1986). An intelligent person can be expected to perform well on most, but not all, types of tasks that demand some form of thinking and remembering. Most people are better at some tasks than others. Most people are intelligent in some ways but not all ways. This is one of the problems in defining and measuring intelligence; it seems to be more than one thing.

Intelligence was first measured by Alfred Binet who created an IQ (intelligence quotient) test to assess the learning ability of French school children. The test measured how well a child of a given age performed compared to the average child of that and other ages. It should be clear that one could not expect to calculate IQ unless one knew what the average person of a certain age knows. The IQ score is meant to give an indication of how close a person, whether a child or an adult, is to average intelligence. The problems of knowing what the average intelligence of a population is and of finding a way to measure it are described in Box 7-1 on page 154.

Louis Terman at Stanford University imported the test to this country and created the Stanford-Binet test of intelligence. Later, other tests were created including the Army Alpha (for literate recruits) and Beta (for illiterate recruits) tests during World War I and the Wechsler and Thurstone scales. These latter two tests assume that intelligence is composed of several different abilities and that each of those abilities can and should be measured by a separate subtest. The Wechsler test has 11 subtests while the Thurstone test has 5 subtests. These tests and subtests are described briefly in Table 7-1 on page 155. Attempts to assess changes in intelligence with age have generally used the Alpha, Wechsler, and Thurstone Primary Mental Abilities tests.

Age Differences in Intelligence

Evidence for Declining Intelligence.   When the U.S. Army recruited soldiers to fight in World War I, those recruits took the Army Alpha (or Beta) intelligence test. Test scores

BOX 7-1

Three Important Features of Testing

There are three important features of testing that must be met whether one is using a test to measure intelligence, personality, pathology, the effectiveness of treatment, or aptitude for college or graduate school.

The first is that we must know what the average or normal person scores on the test. If we want to use the test to help determine whether a person is average, above, or below the average, we must know what is average. Test makers determine the average by administering the test to a sample group meant to represent the larger population who will later take the test. This sample is called a **standardization sample**. When you take an IQ test, your score is compared to the standardization sample. If you scored the same as the sample average, then your IQ is 100. It is assumed that test scores are normally distributed so if you score above or below, your IQ is determined by how many standard deviations above or below the sample average you scored. It is very important that the sample used to standardize an IQ test be representative of the population of people who will be taking the test. This is often a sensitive area in the use of IQ tests. If the standardization sample did not contain approximately the same proportion of older adults as the population being tested, then that sample may not be a fair sample to use in assigning IQ scores to older adults. The same can be said by replacing the adjective "older" in the prior sentence with African American, Hispanic American, poor, disabled, or any other minority group. When an IQ score labels a person as above, below, or average, it means above, below, or average for that population but only if the standardization sample is a good representation of that population.

Tests also must be consistent in measuring what they claim to measure. Consistency of measurement is referred to as **reliability**, If you took an IQ test and received a score of 142 and then took the same test a month later and scored 78, we would assume that your intelligence did not change by that much in that short a period of time. (Of course, there are some circumstances that could result in such a radical and unfortunate change in actual intelligence.) We would be far more likely to say that the test is not very reliable. Reliability is measured using a statistical test called correlation which produces results ranging from 0.0 to 1.0. The higher the number, the higher the correlation. Tests that are consistent are reliable and give the same, or close to the same, result each time that they are applied. The reliability of IQ tests measured in this way is quite good and is usually around 0.80.

Tests must also have **validity**. That is, they must measure what they claim to measure. For example, answer these two questions:

What is your favorite color? _____
What is your favorite holiday? _____

If you were asked those same two questions a month from now, do you think your answers would change? Probably not. This two-question test is usually very reliable. It consistently gives the same values each time it is applied to the same person. If, however, we told you that this two-question test measured your intelligence, you would probably realize that it has no validity. Tests can be very reliable and still have no validity. Tests cannot, however, have validity unless they are reliable. Validity is also measured by using correlation. If IQ tests really measure intelligence, then they ought to correlate well with other measures of intelligence, and they do. The validity of IQ tests is pretty good and is usually around 0.60.

IQ tests do fairly well in meeting the three requirements of tests but they are not perfect.

TABLE 7-1   **Adult Intelligence Tests and Subtests**

The **Wechsler Adult Intelligence Scale** has 11 subtests briefly described below. The first six subtests are not timed while the last five are timed.

Subtest	Sample Item/Description
General information	How many wings does a bird have? *or* Who wrote Macbeth?
General comprehension	Why does the state require people to get a marriage license? *or* What is the meaning of "two swallows do not a summer make"?
Arithmetic	How many apples can you buy for 81¢ if each apple costs 9¢? *or* Sam had 3 pieces of candy and Joe gave him 4 more; how many did Sam have altogether?
Similarities	In what ways are a circle and triangle alike? *or* In what ways are a peach and an apple alike?
Vocabulary	What does the word fossil mean? *or* What is a silo?
Memory span for digits	Repeat digits read aloud, *9-6-5-7-3-1-0* in forward and in reverse order.
Digit-symbol	Learn a series of equivalencies, 1 = ★, 2 = ○, 3 = □, 4 = ●, and so on, and then use it to provide the correct digits for a string of symbols.
Picture arrangement	Three pictures must be put in some logical story order that can then be explained.
Picture completion	Find the missing part of a picture, such as a cup without a handle or a clock without an hour hand.
Object assembly	Complete a series of jigsaw puzzles.
Block design	Use multicolored blocks to duplicate designs from a test book. Designs become more complex as one goes through the book.

Thurstone's **Primary Mental Abilities Test of Adult Intelligence** has several subtests. The five most frequently used in investigations of age differences are briefly described here.

Subtest	Sample Item/Description
Verbal meaning	Same as vocabulary test of WAIS.
Numerical ability	Same as the arithmetic test of WAIS.
Word fluency	Name as many words as you can that contain a given letter, such as *G*, in a two-minute period (also used to measure divergent thinking; see Table 7-3).
Inductive reasoning	Figure out a rule and use it. For example, what would be the next letter in the following series: *A, E, F, H, I, K, L, M?*
Spatial orientation	Match the figure with one that is the same but rotated. For example, match this figure Δ to one of the following: ◆, ■, ∇, or ◇.

were obtained for tens of thousands of men ranging in age from 18 to 60 and the scores for officers were examined, after the war, by Yerkes (1921). Yerkes found that past the age of 25, intelligence, as measured by the Alpha test, declined. The older the recruit, the worse he did on the test. These data were recalculated years later and the original result was confirmed (Jones, 1959). These average scores for different age groups are shown in Figure 7-1. The belief that intelligence declined with age was so strong that older test takers had a constant added to their score to make up for their "constant decline."

Not every researcher, however, obtained evidence for this decline. Tests conducted on gifted adults in 1939 and again on the same adults 12 years later in 1951 showed that they improved their scores (Bayley & Oden, 1955). Many researchers assumed that the findings were a peculiarity of the gifted individuals who were tested and that they would undoubtedly decline at a slightly older age than normal persons (Jones, 1959). If you think about the work conducted on this sample of gifted adults and the type of research design conducted with the army recruits, you might notice that the type of persons tested, average versus gifted, is not the only difference between these studies. Think critically for a moment and apply what you know about the differences between cross-sectional and longitudinal research.

Evidence for Cohort and Other Effects.   K. W. Schaie and his associates understood that the decline in intelligence found with the army recruits, and in other cross-sectional comparisons, could be due to cohort rather than age differences. Individuals who en-

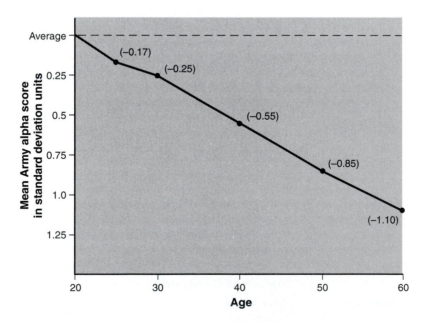

FIGURE 7-1   Graph of Age Differences in Intelligence Based on Army Alpha Data. From Yerkes (1921).

tered the army in 1917 at the age of 50 had been born in 1867, right after the Civil War, and belonged to a much older cohort than the 20-year-olds who also joined the army in 1917. Perhaps the differences that were found on the tests were due to differences in the experiences and environments of these different cohorts.

Schaie and his associates have been conducting the Seattle Longitudinal Study of Adult Intelligence for several decades now (Schaie, 1979, 1983, 1990, 1994). The study began in 1957 with a sample of 500 people selected from the roster of a prepaid medical plan. Fifty people, 25 males and 25 females, at each five-year age group from 20 to 65 participated. There were 50 people who were 20 years old, 50 who were 25, 50 who were 30, and so on up to and including 50 people who were 65 years old. Every few years those who are willing are tested again and, thus, provide longitudinal information on any intellectual changes. At each test, new samples are added providing data for cross-sectional comparisons.

Using Thurstone's Primary Mental Abilities Test of intelligence, Schaie tested these hundreds of individuals looking for differences that could be attributed to age, or cohort. Schaie's data showed that most of the obtained results on intellectual decline can be attributed to cohort, rather than age, differences. Older cohorts scored lower especially on tests of verbal meaning, inductive reasoning, and spatial orientation. Older and more recent cohorts scored about the same on tests of number and word fluency while middle cohorts, born in the 1920s and 1930s, scored higher on number but lower on word fluency. These cohort differences accounted for most of the previously assumed decline with age.

Cohort effects could be due to a number of environmental differences between generations. Younger cohorts may have more years of schooling; more exposure to information from television, movies, and the Internet; more work experience requiring thought rather than physical labor; and, probably, have taken tests recently. Undoubtedly all of these, and many other differences, play some role in the obtained cohort differences in intelligence. With no control over the environmental circumstances in which different cohorts developed, it is impossible to know for certain which factors are most important in producing the obtained cohort effects. It is, however, certain that effects due to cohort, rather than age, underlie most of the obtained differences in overall intelligence.

One factor that has received a fair amount of attention is the phenomenon known as **terminal drop**. Terminal drop refers to a relatively sudden decline in cognitive abilities shortly before death. Although terminal drop might occur in any individual close to death regardless of their age, it is assumed that many more older adults are close to death than younger adults and that terminal drop would, therefore, exert a bigger influence on the performance of older adults. Work examining terminal drop is described in Box 7-2.

Schaie (1989) found that changes due to age were minimal until the individuals tested reached their 60s. By age 80, most older adults showed some significant decline but on only one or two of the five tested abilities. Less that 10 percent showed decline on four or five of the tested abilities (Schaie, 1989). Some types of intelligence are more likely than others to change with age just as some are more likely than others to show cohort effects. Look at the tests in Table 7-1 and try to determine which types of tests you think are more likely to show age differences knowing what you do about sensation, perception, slowing, and memory in old age.

B O X   **7-2**

Terminal Drop

Terminal drop refers to a relatively sudden decline in cognitive abilities shortly before death. If terminal drop really occurs in a high proportion of individuals near death, then it may be that obtained deficits in memory, cognition, and intelligence may reflect terminal drop and not be genuine aging differences. In other words, these deficits are only an artifact of the methods we use (Jarvik & Cohen, 1973). Imagine that we conduct a longitudinal study and follow a group of 100 adults from age 20 and we measure their abilities every ten years. Imagine that we also could measure how many people at each testing were experiencing terminal drop. These imaginary figures are shown below (Baltes & Labouvie, 1973):

Age	Average IQ	Number with Terminal Drop
20	115	0
30	114	1
40	113	2
50	113	2
60	105	10
70	95	20
80	85	30

Each person with terminal drop declines enough in measured intellect to reduce the group average by 1 point. Since the person with terminal drop dies before the next test is given, the average is assumed to be at the highest level, 115, before the effects of terminal drop are subtracted. Terminal drop could, thus, produce large differences in IQ measured in the same individuals over a long period of time. If we looked at only the healthy 80-year-olds (those without terminal drop), their average IQ could be the same 115 of the 20-year-olds.

How would near death produce such changes in cognition? It may be that, with so many deaths from heart disease and other cardiovascular problems, the brain receives less oxygen as the disease worsens. Without adequate oxygen, the brain functions less efficiently.

Is there evidence for terminal drop? The first study was conducted almost 40 years ago and examined older men four times over a 12-year period. The results showed a more rapid decline for those who died compared to those who lived (Kleemeier, 1962). More recent work conducted in Sweden tested men and women aged 80 and older. Participants were tested three times over a 6-year period and much lower scores were found for those who died before the last test (Johannson & Zarit, 1997; Johansson, Zarit, & Berg, 1992). A study conducted on 1000 older adults living in Florida found a decline but only on vocabulary skills and only in adults who were younger than 70 (White & Cunningham, 1988). Other work has also shown declines on usually stable verbal skills shortly before death (Small & Bäckman, 1997). Since fluid abilities may decline with age, perhaps terminal drop is only evident, or most evident, on tests of crystallized intelligence. Another study found declines, shortly before death, on verbal meaning, word fluency, number, and spatial orientation subtests but not on inductive reasoning (Cooney, Schaie, & Willis, 1988). Finally, one study followed 2000 older adults who had been assessed for mental competence. After four years, 85 percent of those who showed no cognitive impairment were still alive while only 51 percent of those with severe impairment were still living (Kelman, Thomas, Kennedy, & Cheng, 1994). Even though a greater proportion of cognitively impaired adults died, many impaired adults were still living at the end of the four years. Furthermore, not all older adults tested who later died showed terminal drop; many died who showed no cognitive impairment. In some cases, the proportion showing a sudden decline is less than 20 percent (Siegler, 1983).

Is terminal drop responsible for the obtained age differences in IQ? At this point in time the answer seems to be no. Not all adults show terminal drop and when it does appear, it is not always on the same measures. Terminal drop may, however, account for some proportion of the obtained differences. There are still too many unanswered questions regarding terminal drop to allow us to reach any firm conclusions (Small & Bäckman, 1999). Remember our earlier example was just that, an example. Nevertheless, terminal drop clearly does occur in some people. An older adult who exhibits a relatively sudden and major loss of cognitive abilities is an older adult who needs to be examined.

Different Kinds of Intelligence.   One way of categorizing types of intelligence that has been fairly influential in gerontology, has been the division into **crystallized** and **fluid intelligence** (Horn, 1982). Crystallized intelligence refers to accumulated knowledge gathered over a lifetime of experiences. Intelligent people will have gathered and remembered more information than less intelligent people. Fluid intelligence refers to the ability to deal quickly and efficiently with new situations and unfamiliar circumstances. This is similar to the definitions given by May Taylor and Jack Palis in this chapter's Senior View. Intelligent people are able to learn new things quickly.

If we look at some of the different subtests (see Table 7-1) used to measure intelligence we see how some seem to be measuring crystallized intelligence while others measure fluid intelligence. Speeded tests, such as the digit-symbol, block design, or picture completion tests of the WAIS, probably tap into an individual's ability to deal quickly with unfamiliar items. They seem to measure fluid intelligence. Tests for vocabulary and general information, on the other hand, seem to measure some of the accumulated crystals of knowledge. Still other tests, for similarities for example, might tap into both types of intelligence. As a general rule, older adults seem to perform poorly on tests of fluid intelligence but better or no different than younger adults on tests of crystallized intelligence. Averaged across all these different subtests, we may find very little overall difference, as shown in the idealized Figure 7-2 (p. 160).

If older adults do well on some tests and not on others, maybe they have a different approach to solving problems or to achieving "proficiency at cognitive tasks." If so, then using tests designed to measure what is learned in school would not tap into this different approach. These ideas led to a whole new way of thinking about adult intelligence.

Redefining Adult Intelligence

Recently, it has been argued that the tests used to measure intelligence, most often the WAIS and Thurstone, are designed to measure those aspects of intelligence that are important for performance in school. They measure how quickly one can learn something new,

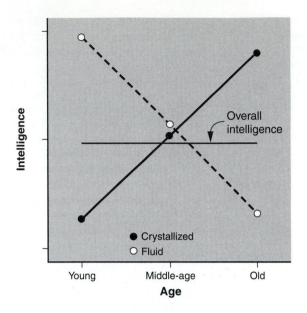

FIGURE 7-2   **Graph of Age Differences in Fluid, Crystallized, and Overall Intelligence.**

the ability to respond quickly to different kinds of puzzles, and other such tasks. They are good measures for those who are still in school, but may have little to say about adult intelligence, which is assumed to be quite different (Cornelius, 1990; Dixon & Baltes, 1988).

Adult intelligence, according to this point of view, is different because adults deal with real-world situations, get along well with diverse groups of people, are able to avoid conflict, are able to plan ahead, and are able to see things from broader perspectives. These are the things that adults, or at least intelligent adults, are good at. If this type of adult intelligence could be measured, we might expect to find older and middle-age adults scoring higher than younger adults and adolescents. Although no one has created a standardized test of these adult intelligence tasks, several investigations have been conducted on what might be considered different aspects or components of real-world adult intelligence while other work has examined qualitative changes in adult intelligence.

Aspects of Adult Intelligence.   In one study of adult intelligence, an examination of 200 bank managers, ranging in age from 24 to 58, found that older managers scored lower on standard tests of intelligence but that the best older managers scored very high on a measure of tacit knowledge. Tacit knowledge refers to knowledge gained implicitly by working on a task and may be one aspect of adult intelligence. This kind of intelligence was very high among these older adults (Colonia-Willner, 1998). One study tested 135 adults between the ages of 30 and 59. Participants took subtests of standard IQ tests and 20 knowledge tests including: American government, art, astronomy, biology, music, law, psychology, technology, tools, and world literature. Older adults performed lower than younger adults on many of the standard IQ tests but higher on all but one (chemistry) of the knowledge tests (Ackerman & Rolfhus, 1999). Age differences in intelligence depend on what aspects of intelligence are measured.

Another real-world situation in which adult intelligence might be displayed is at the race track. Researchers went to an east coast race track and solicited volunteers for a study (Ceci & Liker, 1986). Volunteers picked the top three horses (win, place, and show) for ten races. Following the races, the volunteers were divided into two groups on the basis of their performance. Those who did as well as or better than the track handicappers were the "experts" and those who did not do well were the "nonexperts." Both experts and non-experts had been coming to the track for many years. All volunteers were given the Wechsler test of intelligence (WAIS) (described in Table 7-1). No relationship between IQ score obtained on the test and ability to pick winning horses was found. The experts ranged in IQ from 81 to 128; the nonexperts ranged from 83 to 130. One of the experts picked the winning horse in all ten races and the top three horses in five of those races; his tested IQ was 85. Volunteers also were asked to think out loud while handicapping 50 other pairs of horses. Researchers found that both experts and nonexperts considered most of the same factors such as past performance by jockey and horse, conditions and nature of the track, and weather. Nonexperts considered these factors independently while experts considered interactions among these factors and combined them in complex ways to arrive at the odds of winning. This is clearly an aspect of adult intelligence that involves complex cognitive operations acquired in a certain context. Such intelligence is not tested using a standard intelligence test (Ceci & Liker, 1986).

Researchers also have measured aspects of adult intelligence by having people classify and/or finish stories. Individuals might be given several stories to read and then asked to classify them into different groups. The goal would be to look for similarities among the stories that could be used to group them into the same category. Participants could create as many, or as few, categories as they could find. It is assumed that the greater the number of stories per category, the higher the intelligence. A highly intelligent person is assumed to see relationships among stories that a less intelligent person might miss. Studies have shown that more educated and older individuals score higher on this and similar measures of adult intelligence than do less educated and younger individuals (Kramer & Woodruff, 1986). In measures of finishing stories, individuals are read the first part of a situation and then asked what would happen following some event. For example, a woman has threatened to leave her husband if he comes home drunk one more time; what might she do if he came home drunk again? It is assumed that higher intelligence will result in more complex answers to the question. The individual with higher intelligence will take into account other factors, contexts, and situations and see other possibilities besides the obvious one. Researchers have found that with this kind of test, older adults score higher than younger adults and younger adults score higher than children (Labouvie-Vief, 1985).

In these kinds of tests, the intelligence displayed by older adults seems unrelated to the intelligence measured by standard IQ tests and involves the consideration of many more factors drawn from real-life rather than from the presented materials. Going beyond the presented material is counted as intelligent behavior and results in a higher score.

Qualitative Changes in Adult Intelligence.   Another way to think about adult intelligence is to think of intelligence in terms of the stages of cognitive development described by Jean Piaget (Piaget, 1963, 1970, 1972; Flavell, 1985). Piaget's theory claims that intelligence is not simply the accumulation of more knowledge but instead is a reorganization of greater knowledge to produce a different way of thinking, a qualitative change. At certain points in life and experience, one gains a different perspective and thinks differently and more intelligently. Adults in Piaget's last stage (formal operations) are qualitatively different, in terms of intelligence, from younger individuals. Some adults may, in fact, go beyond the stage of formal operations to other qualitatively different forms of intelligence. Several researchers have attempted to examine adult intelligence in terms of Piaget's stages and the tasks intended to measure such levels of intelligence and to identify an additional stage (or stages) of intellectual development.

This work has been difficult to interpret. When older adults are given conservation tasks they often perform like very young children. For example, given two green rectangles each with a house and two red barns, individuals are asked whether the same amount of time would be spent mowing the grass. After answering yes, the buildings in one of the rectangles are moved and the question is asked again. Although the amount of green not covered by a building is still the same older adults generally answered yes, it will now take longer to mow (Hornblum & Overton, 1976). Since the total amount of grass was not affected by the arrangement of the these buildings, researchers asked them to explain their answer. Older adults pointed out that mowing would be far more difficult and time consuming when the arrangement of obstacles resulted in many small spaces, fewer long straight paths, and many corners to turn even though the total amount of grass area was the same. One would have far more weed-wacking to do in tight areas (Newman-Hornblum, Attig, & Kramer, 1980). An example of this task is shown in Figure 7-3. As above, when finishing stories, older adults are more likely to bring in real-life experiences and other factors that were not intended to be a part of the testing situation. Older adults may score low on such tests because they do not restrict their answers to the specifics of the testing situation. In these sorts of tests, going beyond the presented material is counted as an error and results in a lower score.

Moving beyond present test material seems to be a first component of adult intelligence that is not tapped by standard IQ tests. A second component that frequently

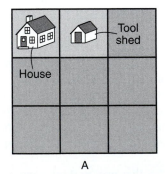
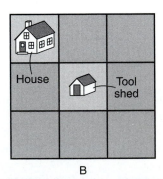

A   B

FIGURE 7-3   Conservation Task Used to Measure Adult Intelligence with House and Shed Arranged Two Different Ways in the Yard.

occurs is that adults consider their own feelings and the feelings of others when thinking about problems. They rely more on intuition. A response that may seem less intelligent on the surface might be regarded as more intelligent if it protects the feelings of other people. A third component is a greater willingness to accept ambiguity. Adolescents and younger adults may seek a right or single correct answer for a problem while older adults may believe that there is no single correct answer for real problems. All is relative; there are no absolutes. The fourth component is a tendency to seek new problems and new perspectives as opposed to attempting to solve all problems. Older adults may have a stronger tendency to seek new ways of looking at the world and their own place in it. Questions may be as important as answers. These four components may mark a qualitative, rather than quantitative, change in intelligence that occurs during adulthood and that goes beyond Piaget's final stage of formal operations (Belsky, 1999; Labouvie-Vief, 1992; Sinnott, 1984, 1991; Stevens-Long, 1990).

If it is reasonable to think that intelligence during adulthood is qualitatively different than during childhood and adolescence, and that it consists of many components that are different from younger intelligence, then it also may be reasonable to think that intelligence may be different at different stages of adulthood. The intelligence of younger, middle-age, and older adults may be as different from one another as they are from the intelligence of adolescents. One attempt to describe differences in adult intelligence comes from Schaie (1977/1978). According to this theory, it is during childhood and adolescence, that the individual is mastering the best ways of acquiring knowledge; this is the **acquisitive stage** of intelligence. In young adulthood, people turn to the application of the acquired knowledge as they begin a career and/or a family. This is the **achieving stage** of intelligence. Adults in this stage must deal with real-life situations and make important decisions. The consequences of those decisions need to be carefully monitored. Adults who achieve will become fairly independent and, during middle-age, enter the **responsible stage** of intelligence. This occurs as the individual establishes a family and has a spouse and children for whom they are responsible. Sometimes the responsibility goes well beyond the family as one must monitor an organization and might reach an **executive stage** of intelligence. These individuals have responsibility for many others. As one reaches old age, one has less need to acquire new information or to make and monitor decisions about future events; one may retire. At this point, the individual may enter the **reintegrative stage** of intelligence. Intellect is now, more than ever, a function of an individual's interests, values, and attitudes. Such adults may be unwilling to spend time on tasks that seem to them to be unimportant or uninteresting.

In sum, it seems clear that as with all aspects of development, intelligence changes with age. Some types of intelligence, such as crystallized intelligence, seem to improve while others, such as fluid intelligence, seem to decline. In addition, other aspects of intelligence may be peculiar to the adult experience and not tested in standard ways. These aspects may be part of a series of stages beyond formal operations and may even involve types of intelligence beyond our current understanding (beyond our current intelligence).

Selective Optimization and Compensation

Aspects of intelligence and all other mental and physical operations are subject to change with advanced age and that change can be positive or negative. To deal with change, successful adults may adopt a strategy referred to as **selective optimization and compensation** (Baltes, 1993; Baltes & Baltes, 1990; Mariske, Lang, Baltes, & Baltes, 1995). This three-part strategy is meant to assist adults of all ages in learning to deal with change but is usually described for older adults since they are likely to show some decline with change. Selection refers to choosing activities, mental or physical, to continue with while discarding others. Optimization refers to maintaining mental or physical capability and increasing knowledge and performance in some specific area or areas. Compensation refers to adapting to change by finding new ways or techniques to maintain a high level of performance.

One can find examples of selective optimization and compensation in all areas of human endeavor. Think of an older librarian who used to work at the circulation desk, reshelve books, and give guided tours. Now because of physical changes occuring with advanced age, the librarian has difficulty getting around as quickly and easily. This person might *select* to work exclusively at the circulation desk and give up those other duties. To *optimize* that selection, they might work hard to master all aspects of the computer system available at the desk and learn as much as possible to be able to provide useful information to patrons of the library. To *compensate*, they might need to get magnifying glasses to focus clearly on the small monitor at the desk or extra lighting to be able to see clearly. Other examples of selective optimization and compensation are given in Box 7-3.

BOX **7-3**

Examples of Selective Optimization and Compensation

Tom and Sarah have always loved camping and hiking in the woods. In their younger days they would often spend several weeks camping and hiking miles of trails in the mountains. They would set up camp by a lake or stream and do a little fishing too. Now they find hiking in the mountains to be difficult even though they both walk regularly. Steep rocky paths make it difficult for Tom to maintain his balance and he is afraid of falling and fracturing a hip. As a result, they have now **selected** fishing as their primary activity during a camping trip. To **optimize** this activity, they have been reading about different types of mountain trout and the best ways to catch them. They have talked with experienced people who fish about the best locations and the best way to cook trout. To **compensate**, they invested in new fishing gear, wading boots, and are thinking about purchasing a small boat.

Jean has been on the police force for 40 years and spent most of those years as a plain-clothes detective investigating violent crimes. She has always been in charge at the crime scene making sure that everything was dusted for prints, photos were taken, all evidence was bagged, and witnesses were interviewed and had their names and addresses taken. Now, at 60, she finds it more difficult and less rewarding to be in charge and to organize all this activity. She has **selected** witness interviewing as her primary task and has given up the rest. To **optimize** her interviewing skills she has read several reports and attended a training session where she got to meet Dr. Ronald Fisher, one of the creators of the Cognitive Interview Technique for interviewing eyewitnesses. She uses her knowledge to help guide her questioning of witnesses. To **compensate** Jean takes her time and tape records witness interviews.

Selective optimization and compensation seems like a wise strategy to use especially when one is confronted with some deficit that was not previously present. Some recent research has found evidence for the use of selective optimization and compensation in work and social settings by younger and older adults (Abraham & Hansson, 1995; Baltes & Graf, 1996).

Expertise

People may select their best intellectual areas, optimize performance in those areas, and use compensation when necessary to achieve or maintain a high level of performance. *When one develops a high level of intelligence in some area we say that that person has developed expertise.* In Chapter 6, we talked about using processing resources for different tasks and how some tasks become so well-practiced that they require very few of the available resources. Such tasks are said to become automatic. Tasks in which one has developed expertise tend to become automatic. People with expertise are faster, more efficient, and

Expertise comes with practice.

more accurate than nonexperts in their field (Hoyer, 1987; Solso, 1998). Generally, middle-age and older adults have higher levels of expertise than do younger adults because of the amount of time and experience that it takes to develop it. Expertise is dependent on extensive practice. Older adults have had more practice (Ericsson & Charness, 1994; Ericsson, Krampe, & Tesch-Romer, 1993).

A number of studies have compared the performance of experts and nonexperts in a number of different fields. Some of the earliest work was done with chess masters versus novice players (Chase & Simon, 1973). This and other work shows that experts are better able to look ahead than novices are, and they are more able to evaluate the consequences of different courses of action. That is, their knowledge about their area of expertise is better organized and cross-referenced than is the knowledge of a relative beginner (Anderson, 1993; Gober & Simon, 1996). At the same time, experts in one particular area are no better or worse than nonexperts when they perform in areas other than their own, and the skills and mental operations involved in expert performance seem to be no better than average when examined in isolation or outside of the area of expertise (Charness, 1985; Salthouse, 1984).

Older adults have more difficulty encoding new information and retrieving old information than do younger adults. One might, thus, expect that older adult experts would lose some of their expertise and advantage over nonexperts. Nothing, however, could be further from the truth. Researchers have compared younger and older experts and nonexperts in a number of different areas. Older typists who are experts are as quick and error-free as younger experts. Experts, young or old, are quicker and more accurate than nonexperts (Salthouse, 1984). Older expert pilots perform at higher levels than younger pilots or nonexperts (Morrow, Leirer, Altieri, & Fitzsimmons, 1994). Older expert baseball players maintain high levels of performance for longer periods of time and decline more slowly in baseball skills than less expert younger or older players (Schulz, Musa, Staszewski, & Siegler, 1994). Older and younger medical laboratory experts are equally proficient at identifying clinically significant information presented on a previously seen slide even while performing another task at the same time. Experts were much better than nonexpert, younger and older lab technicians (Clancy & Hoyer, 1988). Older chess experts have been found to perform as well as younger chess experts at selecting the best move from among presented alternatives (Charness, 1981). Age does not seem to diminish expertise even though some of the mental operations involved in such expert performance may have declined.

Why do many aspects of mental processing, memory, and intelligence seem to slow down and decline with age while those aspects in which we are experts do not? Three possible reasons have been suggested. First, since expertise involves a fair amount of automatic processing, perhaps automatic processes do not decline with age or decline to a much smaller extent than effortful processes (Hasher & Zacks, 1979; 1988). Second, perhaps older experts do decline in the same way as nonexperts but, because of their expertise, find ways to compensate for that decline. Older typists, for example, have been shown to compensate for slower response time by looking further ahead on the material to be typed (Salthouse, 1984). Third, experts may have developed special ways of processing the information. One recent study of expert and nonexpert *GO* game players found that experts had developed expertise at the deductive reasoning and working memory involved in playing *GO*. Researchers suggest that these expertise abilities are forms of adult intelligence not measured by standard IQ tests (Masunaga & Horn, 2001). It is clear that age does not ordinarily diminish expertise.

Wisdom

Wisdom is often regarded as the highest level of cognitive development that a person can attain and can be viewed as expertise but in matters of real-life rather than in some specific task (Dittman-Kohl & Baltes, 1990). Wise people are experts at life and wisdom is viewed as "expert-level knowledge in the fundamental pragmatics of life" (Baltes & Smith, 1990, p. 95). To be an expert in real-life, one must have lived a long time; expertise, after all, takes practice. It is, thus, quite common to believe that wisdom is a special characteristic of older adults, or at least of some older adults (Clayton & Birren, 1980). When individuals have been asked to define wisdom or to describe a wise person, they generally name such characteristics as extensive experience, being able to control emotions, considering all points of view, concentration, and going beyond the limitations of persons or situations; when asked to name wise individuals, generally older adults are named (Birren, 1985; Simonton, 1990). Besides age, two other factors also are thought to be important for the development of wisdom (Baltes & Staudinger, 1993).

Personality traits are thought to be important for the development of wisdom. Some personality types are more likely to learn from extensive experience and be more open to the relativism and uncertainties of life. A person who is very rigid or set in their ways is unlikely to learn much from experience; a person who shuns new experiences is not likely to develop wisdom.

A third factor important for the development of wisdom has to do with having the right kinds of life experiences. Someone who has had experience with personal, ethical problems and planning under difficult, complex situations is more likely to develop wisdom than someone without such life experiences. Thus, being older, having the right personality characteristics, and having experiences dealing with life should contribute to the development of expertise in life or wisdom (Baltes & Staudinger, 1993; Smith & Baltes, 1990).

Paul Baltes and his colleagues have spent the last decade attempting to find ways to measure wisdom and test hypotheses about its development (Baltes & Staudinger, 1993; 2000). According to their view, wisdom consists of five characteristics shown in Figure 7-4 (p. 168). First, wisdom depends upon **factual knowledge** about life. Second, **knowledge about strategies and procedures** is necessary for wisdom. Without factual knowledge or knowledge of strategies and procedures one cannot be wise.

A third characteristic is referred to as **life-span contextualism,** which means that someone with wisdom considers multiple contexts for problems and dilemmas. Different cultures may do things differently. The wise person is aware of differences due to context. The fourth characteristic is **relativism**, or the realization that life's goals and values are relative. What is important for one person may be less important for another. The last characteristic is **uncertainty**. The wise person has the ability to recognize and manage life's uncertainties.

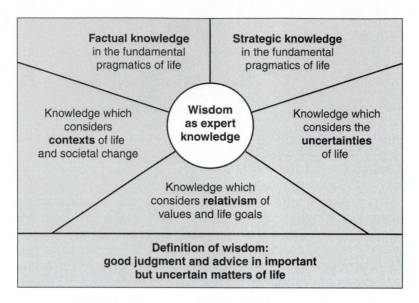

FIGURE 7-4   Five Components of Wisdom.

Source: From Baltes, P. B., & Staudinger, U. M. (1993). The search for a psychology of wisdom. *Current Directions in Psychological Science 2*, 75–80. Copyright © 1993 Blackwell Publishing. Reprinted with permission.

To test this model of wisdom, researchers have asked individuals to respond to imaginary life situations. Their responses are recorded and then observed by raters who attempt to determine how an individual rates on factual knowledge, procedural knowledge, contextualism, relativism, and uncertainty. For example, individuals might be asked to respond to the following situation: A 15-year-old girl wants to get married right away. What should she do and consider (Baltes & Staudinger, 1993, p. 77)? Think for a moment about how you might respond to this situation. Another situation that has been used includes a good friend who calls to tell you that she cannot go on and has decided to commit suicide. Participants are asked to describe what they would consider, what they would do, and/or what advice they might give in these sorts of situations (Baltes, Staudinger, Maercker, & Smith, 1995).

Generally, researchers have found no overall age differences when the responses of younger and older adults are compared. Age, by itself, does not generate wisdom. Using adults with different life experiences does, however, result in differences. Comparisons between clinical psychologists, who are assumed to have had extensive experience with life's problems, and accountants, who have had extensive experience with business problems, show that clinical psychologists score higher on the five characteristics of wisdom. Persons nominated as wise by others also score as high as clinical psychologists and nominated individuals were all older adults. The highest score on the characteristics of wisdom ratings are obtained by older persons who have been nominated as wise and older clinical psychologists (Baltes, Staudinger, Maercker, & Smith,

1995; Smith, Staudinger, & Baltes, 1994; Staudinger, Smith, & Baltes, 1992). It appears that older people and/or people with the right kinds of experiences generally score well on this test of wisdom.

Think about your response to the situation of the 15-year-old girl who wants to get married right away. A response that would score fairly low on the five characteristics of wisdom might say that she should not get married; that it is unacceptable to get married so young. A response that would score fairly high might say that special circumstances might be involved; perhaps the girl has a terminal illness; perhaps she is from another culture or historical period; more information is needed before any decision can be made. The wise response takes into account culture (which is part of lifespan contextualism), sees that the situation is relative to different times and religions, and knows that there is no single correct response. There is uncertainty.

Other researchers have attempted to look at specific and different aspects of wisdom rather than the five characteristics described by Baltes and colleagues. Baltes and Staudinger (2000) have examined ability to solve everyday problems, such as how to get a landlord to make expensive repairs or how to get friends to visit more often. Older adults performed better than younger adults on these kinds of problems (Cornelius & Caspi, 1987). These problems are assumed to tap expertise at life. Other researchers have examined what is referred to as theory of mind. Theory of mind is when an individual attributes some mental state to another person (Leslie, 1987). Having a theory of mind is considered one aspect of wisdom; a wise person takes into account what others may be thinking. In these studies, individuals are given stories and then asked to answer a question about the story. For some stories, a correct answer involves attributing some thoughts to a character in the story. Consider the following story:

> A burglar who has just robbed a shop is making his getaway. As he is running home, a policeman on his beat sees him drop his glove. He doesn't know the man is a burglar, he just wants to tell him he dropped his glove. But when the policeman shouts out to the burglar, "Hey you! Stop!", the burglar turns around, sees the policeman and gives himself up. He puts his hands up and admits that he did the break-in at the local shop. Why did the burglar do that? (Happé, Winner, & Brownell, 1998, p. 362)

Answers to the question are used to determine whether the individual is using a theory of mind. If a person says that the burglar surrendered because he thought the policeman knew that he was the robber, then that would score high on theory of mind. The response takes into account what the burglar may have been thinking. If a person says that the burglar surrendered because the policeman caught him, then that would score low. Although little research has been done to compare older and younger adults on this type of task (there is research examining children), the findings, so far, indicate that older adults score higher than younger adults (Happé, Winner, & Brownell, 1998).

Does one become wise as one grows older? The answer is that it depends. It is clear that older adults do not score lower than younger adults on most tests of wisdom and that usually they score as high or higher. Older and younger adults who have had life experiences dealing with life's problems score higher than adults with fewer such experiences. Some work even suggests that older people with such experiences or wisdom are more satisfied with their lives (Ardelt, 1997). The probability of wisdom seems to increase with advanced age but advanced age does not by itself guarantee wisdom.

Creativity

Another aspect of cognition is creativity. Creativity is different from general intelligence and wisdom and seems to be a distinct cognitive ability (Guilford, 1956, 1967; McCrae, Arenberg, & Costa, 1987). **Creativity** is defined by its newness and difference from the ordinary. Creative responses are unusual, original, and unique. They may be relevant to some problem but are out of the ordinary (Botwinick, 1984). Creativity has been one of the most difficult concepts to define clearly and is often thought to be of two different types. **Exceptional creativity** refers to the creativity of well-known persons who may be artists, authors, scientists, or other professionals and whose work is recognized as creative by experts in and out of that particular discipline. **Ordinary creativity** refers to the creativity of persons whose work is not recognized by experts although often recognized by others. Finding a new way to keep the squirrels off the bird feeder or changing the old recipe for meat loaf, if done successfully, would be examples of ordinary creativity (Weisberg, 1986). Researchers interested in the relationship between aging and creativity have used three general approaches.

One way to examine creativity, particularly ordinary creativity, has been to administer a standardized test. Just as there are standardized tests of intelligence, there are also standardized tests to measure aspects of creativity. These tests are referred to as tests of **divergent thinking** (Guilford, 1967). Divergent thinking involves coming up with multiple solutions to a problem. Problems such as what would happen if people no longer needed air to breathe, how can garden pests be eliminated, or how many uses can you think of for a hammer, have many possible answers and the number and uniqueness of such answers is regarded as one aspect of creativity. In fact, some have argued that divergent thinking is a necessary condition for creativity. If one cannot think divergently, then one cannot think creatively although the ability to think divergently may not, by itself, be enough to produce creativity (Rebok, 1987). The creative individual not only may need to come up with a wealth of divergent ideas but also be able to separate good ideas from bad ideas (Csikszentmihalyi, 1996). Table 7-2 gives examples of tests of divergent thinking.

Cross-sectional comparisons of older and younger adults on tests of divergent thinking have generally resulted in lower scores for older adults (Alpaugh & Birren, 1977; Ruth & Birren, 1985). In one study older adults performed as well as younger adults on all measures except word fluency which was a timed test (Schaie & Herzog, 1983). In a comprehensive study, with cross-sectional and longitudinal comparisons of 825 adult males ranging in age from 17 to 101, age, rather than cohort, differences were found on the five measures of divergent thinking shown in Table 7-2. Older adults performed worse than younger adults (McCrae, Arenberg, & Costa, 1987). All five tests were timed. In short, measures of divergent thinking, which are typically timed tests, show lower scores for older adults that are not due to cohort. Does this mean older adults are less creative than younger adults or only slower to make a creative response?

TABLE 7-2   Tests of Divergent Thinking

The following tests are from a set of tests used to measure different aspects of divergent thinking (Christensen & Guilford, 1957a, 1957b, 1958a, 1958b; Christensen, Merrifield, & Guilford, 1958).

Test	Example
Associational fluency	This test has two parts. Each part contains two words and you try to write as many other words that have similar meaning in the two minutes allowed. Try it. In two minutes (time yourself) write as many words as you can that are similar in meaning to the word LARGE and to the word DRY.
Consequences	This test has five parts. In each part you try to write as many consequences as you can for a new and unusual situation. You are allowed two minutes for each part. Try it. In two minutes (time yourself) write as many consequences as you can for the situation that EVERYONE ON THE PLANET IS NOW BLIND.
Expressional fluency	This test has four parts. In each part you try to write sentences made up of four words with each word beginning with the letter given. You are allowed two minutes for each part. Try it. In two minutes (time yourself) write as many sentences as you can in which the four words begin with the following letters in the following order R__A__T__B__.
Ideational fluency	This test has four parts. In each part you try to name as many things as you can that belong to a certain category. You are allowed three minutes for each part. Try it. In three minutes (time yourself) write down as many things as you can that are TREES THAT GROW FRUIT.
Word fluency	This test has two parts. In each part you try to name as many words as you can that contain a certain letter. You are allowed two minutes for each part. Try it. In two minutes (time yourself) write down as many words as you can that contain the letter *D*.

For associational fluency, a score of 7–10 is about average. For consequences, a score of 4–7 is about average. For expressional fluency, a score of 6–8 is about average. For ideational fluency, a score of 12–14 is about average. For word fluency, a score of about 23–25 is about average.

   If you scored about, or higher or lower, than average, please remember that you were not taking the tests under normal, standard testing conditions and took only one part of each test. Your scores are fun scores rather than reliable, valid measures of your divergent thinking.

   A second approach to measuring changes in creativity with age looked at the accomplishments of professionals in different disciplines. Some of these accomplishments might be regarded as truly exceptional while others might be more ordinary examples of creativity. The classic example of this approach is the work conducted over 40 years ago by Lehman (1953). Lehman examined citations of authors in key textbooks for a number of different disciplines and charted the contributions by the age at which they were made. For example, he might count how many times S. Freud was cited in a psychology textbook.

He would then compare the year of the cited reference and the age of Freud at the time of that contribution. He found that productivity rose quickly to a peak and then gradually declined as the individual grew older. For most disciplines the peak occurred in the late 30s or early 40s. An example of this general finding is shown in Figure 7-5. For heads of religious orders, the peak was in the 60s. For poets, the peak was earlier, occurring in the 20s while for authors of best-sellers, the peak was later, occurring in the late 40s. Musicians showed two peaks, one in the late 30s and a second in the early 70s. This work was taken as support for the general hypothesis that creative productivity declined with age. Creative people seemed to peak around 40 years of age and then decline, although they did not become totally nonproductive. More recent research provides less clear results.

Using Lehman's type of measurement, other researchers have found some qualifications for the claim that creativity peaks during the late 30s or early 40s. If one ignores the first two decades of life (childhood and adolescence) and expects about equal productivity for each remaining decade (20s through 70s), then about 16.7 percent of a person's total productivity should occur during those years. In the disciplines of philosophy, history, and literature, scholars produced 21 percent in their 60s and 20 percent in their 70s. In these cases more is produced in the later years than would be expected. Well-known inventors produced 53 percent of their work in these last two decades. That is far more than expected. On the other hand, artists produced only 14 percent in their 60s and 6 percent in their 70s while architects produced less than 15 percent in these last two decades (Dennis, 1966, 1968). The years of peak productivity may be close to age 40 for a large number of disciplines but there is considerable variation among disciplines. Work with professional athletes, as you might guess, has found peak performance to be in the 20s. Some of this work is described in Box 7-4 (p. 173).

The second qualification is that in all disciplines examined, more productive people are more productive at all ages and creative productivity does not decline to a level lower

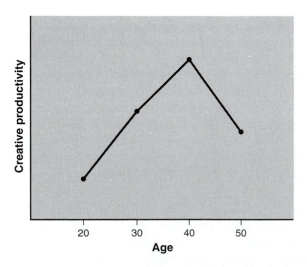

FIGURE 7-5   Example of Peak Creative Productivity Based on Data from Lehman (1953).

BOX **7-4**

Take Me out to the Ballgame

Richard Schulz, Donald Musa, James Staszewski, and Robert Siegler (1994) examined age and major league baseball performance. Data were gathered on 388 major league players who had played in the major leagues for at least ten years. A primary interest was whether an age of peak performance could be found. Results showed a rapid rise in performance for hitters/fielders between the ages of 19 and 27 followed by a decline. For pitchers, the peak was a little later, occurring around 29. A number of age peaks for different baseball statistics are shown below:

Hitting and Fielding		**Pitching**	
Baseball Statistic	**Peak Age**	**Baseball Statistic**	**Peak Age**
Batting average	27.69	ERA	29.11
Home runs	27.39	Strikeouts	27.33
At bats	27.21	Walks	30.45
Base on balls	28.10	Hits allowed	29.48
Strikeouts	29.91		
Stolen bases	27.19		
Fielding average	30.52		

These data suggest that fielding peaks later than hitting. It is also interesting that stolen bases peak around the same time as the other characteristics of good hitters. Stealing base depends on getting on base in the first place but also on careful attention to the infield and catcher as well as the pitcher. It is not simply a matter of speed. Younger players may be faster than older players but stealing base successfully depends on several factors. Pitchers peak earlier on strikeouts and later on walks than on other tasks.

Is it all over for a ball player after age 27 or 29? Of course not. The decline is gradual and there is a lot of variability with some players peaking much earlier than the average and others much later. How old were Mark McGwire and Sammy Sosa when they hit all those home runs? Mark was 34 when he hit 70 home runs during the 1998 season and Sammy was 29 when he hit 66. Barry Bonds was 36 when he sent 73 baseballs flying in 2001. Can we expect even more in the years ahead?

than about half of what it was at its peak. The lowest level of productivity is almost always in the first decade of a career when an individual is still in their 20s. The best predictor of someone's creative productivity is that person's past creative productivity rather than their age (Horner, Rushton, & Vernon, 1986). A third qualification is that it may be the number of years in a given career rather than the age of the individual that is most important. Perhaps individuals have only a finite number of ideas or contributions to make for a given field and, after peaking, they only decline unless they switch careers (Simonton, 1991). These possibilities have not been easy to test since not many people have switched careers at midlife or started their first careers very late and then had their productivity monitored.

One frequently cited example is Grandma Moses who did not begin painting until she was in her 70s and continued painting past the age of 100.

The third general approach to examining creativity and aging has involved looking at particular individuals or groups of individuals and following their work over a long period of time. This work has shown that the types of creative contribution made by an individual often changes as that individual ages (Sasser-Coen, 1993). In a study of 172 composers of classical music, research has shown that the last compositions were different from the prior compositions in several important ways. Latter compositions were shorter, often simpler, and more restrained and gained recognition among performers (Simonton, 1989). This finding has appeared in studies of authors and religious leaders (Hall, 1922) and is referred to as the "swan song" phenomenon. Legend has it that the swan sings but once in its life and that is just before its death. This line of research also has found that many exceptional contributions have been made by older individuals. Table 7-3 lists some of these prominent older contributors. Project 7, on page 176, gives you a chance to find some of your own.

What Can We Conclude?

Do intelligence, wisdom, and creativity change with age? Intelligence changes with cohort and, in some ways, with age. Attempts to measure adult intelligence as something different from the operations tested on standardized tests has generally found older adults scoring higher. Perhaps there are qualitative changes in adult intelligence. Intelligence does change with age but the changes are far from simple.

Wisdom may change with age but it seems to be one's experiences and personality type that make a difference. People with many life experiences are more likely to show aspects of wisdom than are people with few such experiences.

Creativity changes with age but not in a consistent manner. The change can be a decline in productivity but that decline is different for people in different careers. Creativity may increase with age for certain individuals who find new areas of interest. For intelligence, wisdom, and creativity there seems to be far more variation within any one age group than there is between different age groups.

Making Choices

What can a person do to maintain or increase intelligence, wisdom, and creativity while growing older? As you learned, there is a lot of variability in what happens to all three mental gifts as one ages. Some aspects of intelligence, measured by standardized tests, seem to decrease and it is unlikely that you can do a lot about that. Fluid intelligence depends heavily on speed and most older adults slow down. Crystallized intelligence, however, depends on accumulated knowledge and you can choose to continue accumulating knowledge.

Broaden your knowledge. Read, discuss matters with others, even take an occasional night class. Knowledge accumulation is a major part of intelligence. Some work suggests

TABLE 7-3   Examples of Older Creative Individuals

Person	Creative Accomplishment and Age
Maya Angelou	Continues as a best-selling novelist and poet in her 70s.
Helen Hooven Santmyer	Wrote the 1985 bestseller *And the Ladies of the Club* longhand on paper while she was a resident of a nursing home in Ohio at age 86.
Sophocles	Greek poet wrote *Oedipus Rex* when he was 75 and *Oedipus Coloneus* when he was 89.
Mae West	At age 76, published her autobiography, *Goodness Had Nothing to Do with It*.
Claude Monet	Impressionist/artist began his water lily series at age 73.
Eudora Welty	Wrote numerous novels and short stories and won a Pullitzer Prize when she was 65.
Helen Keller	Published her book, *Teacher*, the story of Anne Sullivan, at age 75.
Frank Lloyd Wright	Architect who completed the Guggenheim Museum at age 91.
Salvadore Dali	Created a new school of hyperstereoscopic painting at age 72 and continued to paint until age 79.
George Abbot	Directed a broadway musical at age 100.
Mary Baker Eddy	Founded the *Christian Science Monitor* at age 87.
Mahatma Gandhi	Began the Indian Independence Movement at age 72 and completed negotiations for India's independence at age 77.
Benjamin Franklin	Invented the bifocal lens at age 78.
Bill Cosby	Continues to entertain, acting and producing in his 60s.
Dr. Seuss (Theodore Geisel)	Published his adult bestseller *You're Only Old Once* at age 82.
Susumu Mikami	Started his own business producing artificial caviar that he created from seaweed, squid ink, and seafood; he was 66.
Jessica Tandy	Won an Oscar for her performance in *Driving Miss Daisy* at age 80.
Marian Anderson	Opera star who began a two-year world tour at age 61 and continued to teach opera until 91.
Antonio Stradivari	Created two famous violins, the *Muntz* and the *Habeneck* in his early 90s.
I. M. Pei	Designed the Rock and Roll Hall of Fame in Cleveland at age 78.

PROJECT 7

In this chapter you have learned that many older people are very creative although general trends suggest a decline in creative productivity with aging. Research also shows that the peak age of creative productivity is very different for different disciplines. For this project find someone in your major who was creative after age 65. If you have not declared a major, then choose an area in which you might be interested.

Please note that we are not looking for someone who was very creative when they were younger and who has now passed the age of 65. Find someone who did something creative *after* 65. Try to answer the following questions:

Who is this creative person? How old are they now? How old were they when they made this creative contribution? Are they still making creative contributions?

Was this person always creative or did their creativity begin late in life? If this person is someone who has always been creative, have their creative "products" changed?

Why do you consider their contribution to be creative?

Do you think that there are a lot of people in the area you have chosen who have made creative contributions during old age? Why or why not?

Most students find this project to be relatively easy to complete. Maybe that means that there are a lot of older creative persons in a number of different disciplines.

---

that word games like crossword puzzles, scrabble, and even watching Jeopardy, can improve vocabulary.

Wisdom will develop if you have the right kind of experiences and are the kind of person who is willing to accept and learn from those experiences. You can choose to have certain experiences and a good way to gain life experience is to serve as a volunteer for a local organization. Be a volunteer Big Brother/Sister, volunteer at a home for older adults, volunteer at a number of different places (not all at the same time) and you will gain valuable life experiences that will facilitate the development of wisdom. You will become an expert on life.

As for creativity, you know how creative you are. If you are fairly creative, don't ever stop. Creativity may decline as one uses up their best ideas in same area. We suggest switching areas and trying something new. If you think that you are not very creative, you are probably wrong. You just need to experiment a little; try different areas such as painting, writing, building, drawing, designing; take an elective in a subject that might be fun. Creativity needs nurturing.

CHAPTER HIGHLIGHTS

- Intelligence, defined as performance on IQ tests or subtests, was initially thought to decline with age but longitudinal and sequential design research shows that age changes are relatively modest compared to large cohort differences. When age deficits are obtained, they are typically on measures of fluid intelligence, the ability to respond quickly to a novel situation. Older adults frequently perform quite well on measures of crystallized intelligence, the accumulated knowledge of a lifetime of experience, and vocabulary increases are seen well into old age.

■ It has been hypothesized that terminal drop, the significant decline in cognition thought to occur shortly before death, may contribute to obtained age differences since more older adults are closer to death than younger adults.

■ Some researchers have argued that IQ tests do not really measure adult intelligence although they may be quite good at measuring the kinds of intelligence used in schools. Attempts to measure aspects of adult intelligence have generally found older adults doing well on tasks not correlated with standard IQ performance.

■ Expertise depends on extensive practice at some task and does not seem to decline with age.

■ Wisdom may be thought of as expertise in matters of life and, thus, develops as one gains life experiences which is more likely as one grows older. To develop wisdom one must not only have experiences, they must be of the right kind and one must have a personality to learn from such experiences.

■ Baltes and his associates define wisdom as being composed of factual knowledge, strategic knowledge, contextualism, relativism, and uncertainty. Research has found higher levels of these components in older individuals nominated by others as being wise and in persons with appropriate life experiences.

■ Other measures of wisdom, such as an ability to solve everyday problems or theory of mind, have shown better performance by older, than younger, adults. Old age does not guarantee wisdom but it may make it more probable.

■ Creativity involves unusual, original solutions to problems and has been measured in three ways.

■ Measures of divergent thinking, an important aspect of creativity, have generally found lower scores for older adults. Such tests are, however, given with limited time to respond which may unfairly bias results against older adults.

■ Measures of lifespan productivity have generally found peak performance at some age followed by a gradual decline. The peak age is quite different for different disciplines and, in some cases, the peak is during advanced age.

■ Measures of individual creative people suggest that the nature of creativity may change as one grows older and that a great many older adults have made major creative contributions.

STUDY QUESTIONS

1. Why did early researchers believe that intelligence declined with age? What research changed their minds and why?

2. Explain how terminal drop could be responsible for obtained age differences in intelligence in both cross-sectional and longitudinal designs.

3. Compare and contrast fluid and crystallized intelligence. Give an example of a WAIS subtest that measures each and a subtest that has both fluid and crystallized components.

4. If we devise special measures of adult intelligence, couldn't we also devise special measures of adolescent intelligence? If so, what sorts of things should we measure for adolescents that are not measured on standard IQ tests?

5. Describe the proposed stages of adult intelligence.

6. Why does expertise remain stable while the mental operations involved in expert performance decline?

7. Why might one older adult exhibit a high level of wisdom while another might not?

8. Describe the five characteristics of wisdom. Think of examples for each.

9. How might creativity depend on divergent thinking skills?

10. Why might poets peak early, psychologists around 40, and inventors quite late in terms of creative productivity?

RECOMMENDED READINGS

Csikszentmihalyi, M. (1996). *Creativity: Flow and the psychology of discovery and invention*. New York: HarperCollins. This book examines the creativity of 90 older adults.

Schaie, K. W. (1990). Intellectual development in adulthood. In J. E. Birren & K. W. Schaie (Eds.), *Handbook of psychology and aging* (3rd ed., pp. 291–309). New York: Academic Press. This is a good overview of Schaie's model of adult intellectual development presented briefly in this chapter.

Simonton, D. K. (1990). Creativity and wisdom in aging. In J. E. Birren & K. W. Schaie (Eds.), *Handbook of psychology and aging* (3rd ed., pp. 320–329). New York: Academic Press. This chapter presents an overview and summary of a lot of the earlier work on creativity, wisdom, and aging.

Sternberg, R. J., & Lubart, T. I. (2001). Wisdom and creativity. In J. E. Birren & K. W. Schaie (Eds.), *Handbook of the psychology of aging* (5th ed., pp. 500–522). San Diego, CA: Academic Press. This chapter is a good review of the latest research on wisdom, creativity, and aging.

INTERNET RESOURCES

http://www.apa.org/monitor/feb97/wisdom.html.   Wisdom and old age are summarized well in article from the APA *Monitor.*

http://www.newchurch.org/sermons/individualsermons/oldage.html.   A more personal view and an interesting sermon on old age and wisdom.

http://www.apa.org/monitor/may95/successb.html   Creativity and aging is also summarized in another article from the *Monitor.*

http://www.nig.nl/congres/3rdeuropeancongress1995/abstract/148-1301.html   A source of useful information from a series of meetings in Europe.

Part III   Aging and Our Selves

CHAPTER

8   Personality

We are the same people as we were at three, six, ten, or twenty years old. More noticeably so, perhaps, at six or seven because we were not pretending so much then.

—*Agatha Christie*

Agathie Christie says we do not change much as we grow older although we may appear different. While we pretend to be different; we are still the same person. Many theorists and researchers in the area of personality also claim that personality changes very little under ordinary life circumstances although major change may occur under extraordinary circumstances. In this chapter we examine what we mean by personality and whether change occurs as we age. Our view is that some aspects of personality do change while others remain stable.

An Overview of Personality

Personality is one of the broadest terms in psychology. In general it refers to those traits, behaviors, ways of thinking, motives, and emotions that make us who we are. These are all aspects of personality. To know someone's personality is to know them. We would know a person's traits such as how outgoing, how friendly, how aggressive, and how anxious they are. We would know how they acted in different situations and at different times. We would know how they think about things such as equal rights, world peace, or gun control. We would know their motivation for doing things they do and why they avoid doing other things. We would know their emotional reactions to various people and situations and how intense such reactions tend to be for them. To know someone's personality is to know a lot about them. Personality is so all encompassing that it can be difficult to even know ourselves let alone someone else. It is, as you might imagine, a difficult concept to fully measure.

Senior View

We spoke with Jane Hege and Tolly Kleckley about personality and whether or not it changes as one gets older. Jane was 69 and still employed as a receptionist and switchboard operator when we spoke with her. She has been happily married for 50 years and has three grown children. She believes that your "personality is one of the most important factors in your home life, your church life, and in every aspect of your life." She told us that a person should hold onto the personality they had when they were young because you can't change it very much anyway and that "a good personality and outlook will help you be healthy and overcome obstacles in life." Jane told us that personality is especially important in old age because older adults often depend on others for assistance. A person

with a poor personality, who complains all the time, never has a kind word, and is always "downing" everyone is likely to have difficulty finding help when help is needed.

Tolly was 77 when we spoke with him. He also is happily married and now is retired from the retail furniture business. He told us that your personality is how other people see you; it's the image you project and how you feel about yourself. Tolly said that his own personality "has pretty well stayed the same" and that "most people keep the same personality all their lives." This lack of change is not, however, total and Tolly told us that some aspects of personality can and do vary but not by a lot. Tolly said, "Most people don't change much; they have a way of being themselves and they are just that way whether they want to be or not." When you get older, the best personality to have, according to Tolly, is one that doesn't worry about the past but instead thinks "about what you're gonna do in the future."

We asked Jane and Tolly about midlife crises because some researchers believe that such crises are inevitable while others suggest that they are pretty infrequent. Tolly told us that he wasn't even sure what a midlife crisis was but that people

sometimes worry more than they used to or do things that they never did before. Jane told us that men were more prone to midlife crises than women (and research suggests she's right) because men are less mature. She said such crises tend to occur when "one partner is not attentive to the other, so one goes astray." She thinks that most men need a lot of attention.

Measures of Personality

Since there are so many different aspects of personality, there are a number of ways to measure the different aspects. No single measure can encompass them all and the measures of personality used most frequently fall into two large groupings called objective and projective measures.

Objective Measures of Personality.   Objective measures of personality are those that measure characteristics or aspects of personality by directly asking a person to list, sort, or rate typical features or behaviors. There are a number of objective measures of personality that are paper and pencil tests. Typically these tests ask individuals to respond, true or false (or agree/disagree), to a number of statements such as those shown in Table 8-1. Responses to these items are then compared to the responses made by a standardization sample that took the test when it was first developed. If the individual being tested responded the same as highly aggressive people in the standardization sample responded, then the individual would be assumed to be highly aggressive. Another type of objective test is the Q-sort. In this type of test, the person is given a stack of cards each with a different description of some characteristic of personality. For example, cards might say things like "I really enjoy

TABLE 8-1   Sample Items from an Objective Measure of Personality*

For each of the following statements answer True (T) or False (F):

1. I prefer to be by myself.   _____
2. I am a flexible person.   _____
3. Most people like me.   _____
4. I tend to avoid new places.   _____
5. Birds frighten me.   _____
6. I like to wear mittens.   _____
7. I like to meet new people.   _____
8. I control my own destiny.   _____
9. My life is full of adventure.   _____
10. I am often bored.   _____
11. I like to party.   _____
12. I read a lot of books.   _____
13. When I am angry, I try to deal with the situation immediately.   _____
14. My family thinks I'm crazy.   _____
15. I often feel sad.   _____

* These are exemplar items and are not taken from any standard test of personality.

the company of others" or "I feel lonely most of the time." The person sorts the cards into piles depending on how well each statement matches their personality. In all cases, the individual decides how true a statement is, how much they agree with it, or how well it describes them. Sometimes the measures are made by interviewing an individual and evaluating their answers to standard questions about different aspects of their personality.

Objective personality tests generally have a number of scales that examine different characteristics, such as outgoingness and typical ways of dealing with certain situations. These tests are frequently used to assist in the diagnosis of various psychological disorders. Objective measures of personality include the California Psychological Inventory (CPI), the Minnesota Multiphasic Personality Inventory (MMPI), the Myers-Briggs Type Indicator (MBTI), the Revised NEO Personality Inventory (NEO-PI-R or the more recent NEOFFI), and the Inventory of Psychosocial Development (IPD), as well as several others.

Projective Measures of Personality.   Some researchers and theorists believe that objective measures of personality are incomplete. While they may measure certain traits and habitual ways of behaving quite well, they may miss other and/or unconscious aspects of an individual's personality. Projective tests are designed to tap into these other aspects by presenting some ambiguous figure to the individual and allowing the person to project their personality onto that ambiguous figure. As the person does this, they may reveal aspects of their personality that would not be evident on an objective test (and, of course, aspects that are revealed on an objective test may not be evident on a projective test). Generally, the reliability and validity (see Chapter 7) of projective tests are lower than for objective tests.

The Rorschack Inkblot Test and the Thematic Apperception Test (TAT) are two examples of these projective tests. In the former, individuals are shown a series of ten inkblots, one at a time, and are asked to describe what they see in each one. The examiner may ask questions during these descriptions to gather more information. In the TAT, the individual is shown a series of black-and-white pictures of one or more people in an ambiguous situation. The person is asked to describe what the situation is, what led up to it, what the person or people are thinking or feeling, and what the end result will be. An example of a picture like those found in the TAT is shown in Figure 8-1.

If we were to use one or more objective tests, a projective test or two, an interview to measure an individual's personality, and if we also asked that person's family to rate them on a number of dimensions, we might expect to have a fairly complete picture of that person's personality. We would have information about several different aspects of their personality but to get a complete picture we would have to obtain much more information at several different levels. One way to combine all the information or aspects of personality is to think of a description of personality as operating on different levels.

Levels of Personality

Dan P. McAdams has proposed that we think about a person's personality as being composed of three levels of description (1994a, 1994b, 1994c, 1995). The three levels are assumed to be distinct and nonoverlapping. Knowing one level of an individual's personality may tell you nothing about that person's position on the other two levels. In this chapter we will use McAdams's proposal to organize the different aspects of personality and the

FIGURE 8-1   An Example of a Picture That Would be Part of a Thematic Appreciation Test (TAT).

findings with respect to stability and change in personality as one ages. Remember this organization is just one way to think about the different aspects of personality. Critically evaluate it as you read through our discussion in this chapter.

The first level is the level of traits. A **trait** is a distinguishing feature of a person's character and is assumed to remain the same over time and a variety of situations. Traits may be genetically determined. A person who is high on the trait of aggressiveness is likely to remain high on that trait throughout their life and to display aggressive behavior in a variety of situations. The same would be true for other persons and other traits such as dominance, extraversion, rigidity, and neuroticism.

The second level is the level of personal concerns. This level includes an individual's ways of coping, goals, values, defense mechanisms, motivations, and strivings. These aspects of personality may change over time or place or as a function of learning and social role. People learn new ways of coping; their values and defense mechanisms may change as a result of experience.

The third level is the level of identity. Identity can be thought of as the "inner story of the self that integrates the reconstructed past, perceived present, and anticipated future to provide a life with unity, purpose, and meaning" (McAdams, 1995, p. 365). It allows me to view myself as the same person that I was long ago even though I may have changed in many ways.

Throughout our examination of these levels of personality we will examine different theories that describe personality. We continually examine the evidence on stability and change in personality as one grows older.

Traits

Gordon Allport was among the first to describe personality in terms of traits or enduring characteristics (1937). An individual's personality could be described by specifying where they placed on a continuum ranging from an extremely low score to an extremely high score on each of these traits. The extremes of each trait are labelled with terms indicating their opposition, such as dominant/submissive. An individual would reflect behavior indicative of traits such as dominance-submission, extraversion-introversion, friendly-unfriendly, nervous-calm, and so on. Allport believed that there were close to 5000 different traits. Other researchers have identified smaller numbers of traits as representing personality, and there is overlap in the traits identified. Overlapping traits can be assigned to a single dimension. Research in gerontology focuses on whether identified traits or dimensions remain stable, or change, over the course of one's life. Some researchers have examined multiple traits and dimensions, while others have focused on a single dimension like rigidity/flexibility. Today, the major trait theory of personality that has been tested for age differences is the Big 5 theory.

Five-Factor Theory of Personality

Paul Costa and Robert McCrae (1994; McCrae & Costa, 1984; 1990) have argued that all important traits can be grouped into five dimensions of personality. Each dimension is composed of several different but related traits. The five dimensions are: neuroticism, extraversion (also spelled extroversion), openness to experience, agreeableness, and conscientiousness. Our position on these dimensions is measured by an objective test of personality and is thought to be due to both genetic and environmental factors.

Neuroticism refers to level of anxiety. Neurotic people are anxious, hostile, irritable, overly sensitive to criticism, and often sad and lonely. People low in this trait are secure and fairly relaxed even under stressful conditions.

Extraversion refers to how outgoing an individual is and is the opposite of introversion. Extraverted people are very sociable, enjoy being the center of attention, and seek excitement. Introverts are more serious and prefer to be by themselves.

Openness to experience refers to a willingness to try new ways of doing things. People high in this trait are imaginative, and always ready to go somewhere new or try something different. People low in openness are more traditional and set in their ways. They may be more rigid.

Agreeableness refers to being warm-hearted with a strong tendency to cooperate. Agreeable people are trusting, submissive, and may be easily persuaded by others. People low in agreeableness are skeptical of others, stubborn, proud, and often, very competitive.

Conscientiousness refers to a tendency to accomplish things. Conscientious people are well-organized, competent, and have a high level of self-discipline. People low in this trait tend to be easygoing, disorganized, and may even be careless or lazy.

Most people reside somewhere in the middle of these dimensions. We are generally calm but sometimes experience feelings of anger or sadness. We enjoy being with other people but enjoy our privacy as well. We try to balance old and new ways of doing things.

We are usually agreeable but can be stubborn too. We are fairly well-organized but do not work all the time.

Costa and McCrae, and others who look at personality traits, argue that your traits are biologically based, genetic in origin, and only slightly modified by your environment. To understand a biological base, think of how you feel when you are in front of a classroom making a presentation. Everyone is a little nervous at first. Some people calm down fairly quickly while others get more nervous and experience stage fright. They can hear their heart racing. That "gut feeling," whether you calm down or get more nervous, indicates your biological system's involvement in this reaction. Costa and McCrae claim that your personality is tied into your biological system. While we do not know the exact genetic origins of personality traits, many believe we inherit these traits. To examine genetic influences, researchers have compared identical twins who have the same genetic endowment with fraternal twins who do not. They found that identical twins are much closer to each other on each of the five dimensions than are fraternal twins (Plomin, DeFries, McClearn, & Rutter, 1997).

To examine the role of genetic and environmental factors, researchers have examined personality traits prevalent in different cultures. If traits depend to some extent on the cultural environment, then people in different cultures may show different traits or some traits may be more common in some cultures than in other cultures. Recently, researchers administered the NEO-PI-R to different age adults in Croatia, Germany, Italy, Korea, and Portugal and compared their findings to those obtained in the United States. In all six cultures, researchers found a decline in neuroticism, extraversion, and openness and an increase in agreeableness and conscientiousness when comparing young and middle-age adults. Since these same differences are found in several different environments they may be universal and due to genetic/biologic/maturational factors rather than environmental factors (McCrae, Costa, de Lima, Simões, Ostendorf, Angleitner, Marušić, Bratko, Caprara, Barbaranelli, Chae, & Piedmont, 1999). Another recent study compared scores on the CPI for adults living in the United States and adults living in China. Researchers found that older adults in both cultures scored lower on extraversion and flexibility but higher on measures of self-control and orientation toward accepted norms. These age differences were much larger among the Chinese younger and older participants than among the American younger and older participants. The obtained difference between people living in Chinese and U.S. cultures suggests that environmental factors also play a role in the expression of traits. The recent moves toward modernization and westernization in China seem to have influenced younger Chinese adults, who are now closer to their U.S. counterparts on many measures, than are older U.S. and Chinese adults (LaBouvie-Vief, Diehl, Tarnowski, & Shen, 2000). Such work suggests both genetic and environmental influences on traits.

Age Differences in Traits

There are two major research strategies that can be used to look for age differences. An investigator can conduct cross-sectional research and compare different adults of different ages. Any obtained differences could be due to age, cohort, or both. An investigator could, instead, conduct longitudinal research and follow the same individuals over a long period of time to see if they show any change. In this case, differences cannot be due to different cohorts since only one cohort was used. Such research, however, has its own set of problems (see Chapter 1). Both strategies have been used by personality researchers to determine whether personality changes or remains stable as one grows older.

A specific trait that has been tested is the trait of **rigidity/flexibility**. A common belief is that older adults are more rigid, more set in their ways, than are younger adults, who are believed to be flexible in their approach to problems. Rather than being a trait that remains constant throughout life, the trait of rigidity/flexibility might be thought of as one that changes with advanced age. If so, the notion that traits remain stable would be false, at least for this trait. Early research examining age differences in rigidity were usually cross-sectional and generally found more rigidity in older adults. In one study, adolescents (age 14 to 19), young/middle-age adults (age 20 to 49), and older middle-age adults (age 50 to 58) attempted to solve increasingly difficult problems. Early problems could be solved with a fairly simple technique but that technique did not work for later, more difficult problems. The two younger groups switched strategies when they learned that the simple technique would no longer work while the older group stuck to the simple technique for a much longer period of time. The older group seemed to be more rigid (Heglin, 1956). Some other work, however, tested rigidity and intelligence in 200 people ranging in age from 20 to 82. When age differences in intelligence were statistically removed, age differences in rigidity disappeared (Chown, 1961). Less intelligent people, regardless of their age, tend to be more rigid. Finally, in a longitudinal study of rigidity and age, researchers found that differences in rigidity were due to cohort rather than age. Older cohorts tended to be more rigid suggesting that this trait is influenced by environmental differences (Schaie & Labouvie-Vief, 1974).

This finding with rigidity is typcial. Generally, cross-sectional comparisons have found group differences although there are some exceptions (Stoner & Spencer, 1986). The two studies described earlier, which looked at adults living in different cultures, found group differences. The first found a decline in neuroticism, extraversion, and openness and an increase in agreeableness and conscientiousness when comparing young and middle-age adults (McCrae et al., 1999). The second found that older adults scored lower on extraversion and flexibility but higher on measures of self-control and orientation toward accepted norms (LaBouvie-Vief et al., 2000). Another study, using the MMPI, found higher levels of neuroticism and extraversion for younger adults and higher levels of agreeableness for older adults (Zonderman, Siegler, Barefoot, Williams, & Costa, 1993). Using a different personality scale, other researchers found older adults to be more cautious, more conforming to society's rules, and less energetic. These researchers did not, however, find the usual age differences in extraversion (Stoner & Panek, 1985). The general findings from a number of cross-sectional studies are that older adults are less extraverted, flexible, neurotic, and open to new experiences but more agreeable, conforming, and conscientious. These differences could be genuine age differences or they could be cohort differences. If they are genuine age differences, then we would expect to find the same results when we collect data longitudinally but, as we will soon see, that is not what happens.

These cross-sectional findings can be easily seen as cohort differences. Society was very different in the early years of the twentieth century and last decades of the nineteenth century than it was in the last decades of the twentieth century and is now. Level of education for the average American is much higher than previously. Very few people attended college before the end of World War II. There were fewer opportunities for travel or employment far from home for members of those older cohorts. Today, many students live far from where they grew up. Younger cohorts have lived most, or all, of their lives in a world filled with space shuttles, TV, VCRs, computers, and microwaves. Older cohorts had books and radios. It may be the younger cohort's experiences with a wide range of other people and places, as well as their higher education, that contribute to their greater openness and extraversion. Older cohorts were generally taught to be more reserved and less outgoing in social situations and this too may have contributed to their lower levels of extraversion. This wide range of experiences also may contribute to a heightened anxiety resulting in higher levels of neuroticism for younger cohorts. It may come as no surprise to you that older cohorts are generally less extraverted and open to new experiences than younger cohorts, or that they are generally more agreeable, conforming, and conscientious. They are quite often portrayed in these ways in print and electronic media.

Longitudinal research has found great stability with modest change in personality traits particularly among the oldest adults. A recent review of emotional characteristics found great stability across the lifespan. Emotionally related changes in personality are seen only when major interpersonal life events such as marriage or divorce occur (Magai, 2001). People who were relatively extraverted, open to new experiences, low in anxiety, conscientious, and not very agreeable when they were young tend to be about the same when they are older. In an examination of participants in the Baltimore Longitudinal Study of Aging, Costa and McCrae looked at personality measures given over a number of years to fairly well-educated, mostly white men ranging in age from 20 to 80. Traits of neuroticism, extraversion, and openness remained stable over periods of time as long as 45 years, although the cohort differences discussed earlier were evident (Costa & McCrae, 1988; Costa, McCrae, Zonderman, Barbano, Lebowitz, & Larson, 1986; McCrae & Costa, 1990). In an examination of over 3000 adults over a seven-year period, other researchers also found cohort but not age differences (Schaie & Willis, 1991). Among the oldest adults, some researchers have found small longitudinal changes. The oldest-old adults seem to be less energetic and more androgynous than younger old adults (Douglas & Arenberg, 1978). Adults over the age of 70 may become more agreeable and less extraverted (Field & Millsap, 1991). Perhaps older adults may be more agreeable as they rely more on others for help. The change in extraversion may be related to different mortality rates for extraverts and introverts. One study that found a longitudinal change in extraversion compared the eight adults who had died during the length of the study with matched persons (by age and gender) who were still living and found higher levels of extraversion among the people who died (Slater & Scarr, 1964). Perhaps extraverts die earlier than introverts and that is why rates of introversion are higher among older adults? Are personality traits somehow related to health habits; are people with certain personality traits more likely to become ill or even die than those with different traits? Box 8-1 (pp.188–189) takes a look at these questions.

People's perceptions of changes in their personality traits also have been studied. One study that examined the perception of stability or change tested 362 men and women over the age of 65 and living in Montreal. Researchers measured neuroticism, extraversion, social adjustment, well-being, activities, health, financial situation, and locus of control. A month later, they returned and administered the same measures under two different

BOX **8-1**

Personality and Health

Are people with some personalities healthier than others? Are people with certain personality traits more likely to become ill or even die than those with different traits? Several studies indicate a relationship between certain personality traits and healthy or unhealthy behaviors. Regardless of specific traits, the stability of traits is also thought to be a major contributor to our well being as we grow older (Costa, Metter, & McCrae, 1994).

People who score high on measures of neuroticism are far more likely to experience anxiety disorders or depression than people who score low on measures of that trait. Such people are prone to experience negative emotional states on a regular basis (Watson & Clark, 1984). One study examined personality traits in 57 depressed clients before and after therapy. Neuroticism scores decreased after treatment but were still higher than average scores for healthy adults (Bagby, Joffe, Parker, Kalemba, & Harkness, 1995). Other work strongly suggests that it is the high levels of neuroticsm in such individuals that lead to their depression rather than depression producing high levels of neuroticism (Costa, Yang, & McCrae, 1998; Shea, Leon, Mueller, Solomon, Warshaw, & Keller, 1996). Finally, some work has shown that middle-age adults who are low on neuroticism and high on extraversion and conscientiousness are more satisfied with their lives and themselves (Siegler & Brummett, 2000).

Studies conducted with personnel in the U.S. Navy and Marine Corps. found a greater tendency toward risk-taking with alcohol among individuals high in extraversion and openness to experience while individuals high in agreeableness and conscientiousness reported a greater number of wellness or self-care behaviors. Those high in neuroticism reported fewer wellness or self-care behaviors (Booth-Kewley & Vickers, 1994). Clearly these personality traits are related to health and satisfaction with life.

The traits of neuroticism and extraversion even seem to be related to oral self-care. In a longitudinal study of several hundred dental patients, researchers found that high levels of extraversion were strongly associated with flossing, use of gum stimulators, and using mouthwash. Extraverted persons seem to be concerned about the appearance of their teeth and the freshness of their breath. Individuals high in neuroticism tended to brush their teeth less often than others. It is thought that very neurotic individuals are too anxious about other things and may tend to ignore their dental health (Kressin, Spiro III, Bossé, & Garcia, 1999).

Women high in conscientiousness and extraversion are more likely to adhere to a regimen of regular breast cancer screening while women with higher levels of neuroticism (particularly depression) and introversion are less likely (Siegler & Costa, 1994).

Some work with another trait not mentioned in the text has shown a relationship between trait stability and mortality. This trait is **field independence–dependence,** which refers to a person's tendency to rely on internal (field independent) or external (field dependent) cues when orienting themselves in space (Weiten, 2000). In this study, field independence–dependence was measured by the rod and frame test (RFT) shown in Figure 8-2. In this test, individuals turn two knobs to make the rod vertical while it is positioned in a tilted frame. Field independent individuals are able to do this quite well and tend to ignore the tilted position of the frame while field dependent individuals seem unable to ignore the frame and end up with slightly tilted (not vertical) rods.

In this longitudinal study, 113 men and 79 women living in a small town in southern Sweden took the RFT at age 67, 69, 71, and 73 and were followed until age 83. Researchers found stable RFT scores for 80 percent of those tested. Field-independent people tended to remain independent while field-dependent people tended to remain dependent. Of those who changed,

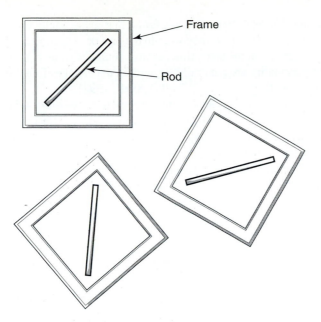

FIGURE 8-2   Rod and Frame.

more field-independent people became field-dependent on the later tests. Men and women who showed stability in their RFT scores were far more likely to survive to age 83 than those who did not. Instability was strongly associated with early death (Hagberg, Samuelsson, Lindberg, & Dehlin, 1991).

While this study suggests a relationship between mortality and stability the direction of that relationship is not clear. Perhaps people who are less stable are less healthy or perhaps people who become ill or get closer to death lose their stability on certain measures. Either way, it is clear that some personality characteristics and their stability are associated with healthy (and unhealthy) behaviors and mortality.

conditions. A control group took all the tests again while an experimental group was told to answer the questions as they would have answered them when they were 40 years of age. To help them recall where they were and what they were doing when they were 40, interviewers reviewed each person's family history and relevant objective events, such as living location, job, marital status, presence of children, and so on, that were present when the person was 40. Results indicated high levels of stability on all but a few measures for the experimental group and total stability for the control group. Many people in the experimental group perceived themselves as being a little more extraverted when they were younger (when they were 40) and as behaving in a more socially desirable way in the present. Generally they believed they were the same at age 40 as they are now (Gold,

Andres, & Schwartzman, 1987). Other work has found that many adults tend to perceive themselves as having changed from how they were in the past or expecting change to occur in their future personalities but, at the same time, always being the same person. Adult perception of changes in personality are generally larger than the changes found in longitudinal research (Fleeson & Heckhausen, 1997; Troll & Skaff, 1997).

These findings of trait stability across age are what many older adults, such as Agatha Christie, Jane Hege, and Tolly Kleckley, say about their own personality. We are the same person today as we were yesterday. Trait theorists would agree with them. It appears that personality traits do remain relatively stable across most of adulthood and, perhaps, most of our lives, although there are differences between younger and older cohorts. These age and cohort findings are illustrated in Figure 8-3.

Personal Concerns

Your biggest concerns today are probably very different from those that you had ten years ago. Your biggest concerns after you finish college and have begun a career and, perhaps, a family are likely to be different than the ones you have now. Personal concerns are likely to change although the basic traits with which you address those concerns are not. This second level of personality description, personal concerns, encompasses what individuals want and the techniques, strategies, and plans that people use to achieve those wants (McAdams, 1995). What people want can, of course, vary as a funtion of age, time of life, and social role. People with different basic traits may, of course, resort to different strategies to

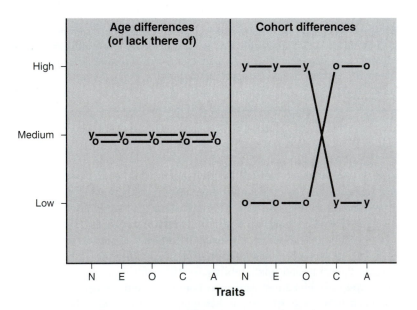

FIGURE 8-3   Age and Cohort Differences in Personality Traits.

achieve the same goal. At the level of personal concerns we expect to see some changes as people grow older. Project 8 offers the opportunity to compare the personal concerns of different aged adults and to relate those concerns to some of the theories we will discuss in this section. One way to view the level of personal concerns is to view those concerns as being a function of stage of life. At different life stages people tend to have different social roles and tend to focus on different concerns. Stage theories of personality are often good descriptions of these changing concerns.

Stage Theories of Personality

Stage theories of personality development are numerous although not all of them describe stages that occur during the adult years. For example, Freud's theory had no adult life stages

---

PROJECT **8**

Age/Cohort Differences in Personal Concerns

In this project we want you to examine the personal concerns for different age individuals. Remember, these different age individuals are members of different cohorts.

Using the rating scale shown below, rate the items on the "concerns list" for how concerned you are about them at this point in your life.

Make copies of the scale and list and ask family members and friends to rate the same items using the same rating scale. Make an effort to test people of different ages. What items do you expect them to rate almost the same as you did and what items do you expect them to rate differently? Why?

Are your expectations based on age, cohort, or specific environmental circumstances (e.g., dad's car just broke down so I know he wants a new one).

Compare the different ratings and see which items were rated differently and which were rated the same. Are the differences and similarities the ones that you might expect on the basis of things that you have learned about adult development and aging? Are the differences that Erikson might expect (in intimacy? in generativity?) or Levinson (midlife crisis?) or Guttman (mastery?) present in the ratings you obtained?

We hope you also will take the time to talk about the similarities and differences with your parents, grandparents, and/or the people that completed the ratings for you. We expect that you will learn much from your discussions with these older adults.

Use the following Rating Scale to rate how important each item on the concerns list is to you at the present time.

- Not important at all   1
- Not very important   2
- A little important   3
- Fairly important   4
- Very important   5

(continued)

P R O J E C T **8**   **Continued**

Being with my family   _____
Making money   _____
Being with my friends   _____
Travelling to new places   _____
Making new friends   _____
Nurturing my family   _____
Protecting my family   _____
Teaching younger people   _____
Maintaining my health   _____
Improving my health   _____
Changing my life   _____
Finding true love   _____
Starting a family   _____
Getting a new car   _____
Staying out of trouble   _____
Losing weight   _____
Being happy   _____
Avoiding rating scales   _____

and placed all important aspects of personality development in the first five years of life (Hockenbury & Hockenbury, 2000). Stage theories generally maintain that stages are qualitatively different and center on some major life event or crisis, are always in the same order, that the transition from stage to stage is gradual, and some say that not everyone goes through all stages. Remember our discussion in Chapter 1 on the continuity/discontinuity issue of development? Stage theories are discontinuity theories. Change is dramatic from one stage to the next. Several important stage theories have much to say about the development of personality during the adult years. We examine the theories of Erikson, Levinson, and Guttman, and then examine the evidence for age differences.

Erikson's Stages of Lifespan Development.   Erik Erikson studied with Freud but believed that personality development did not end in childhood (1963, 1968, 1982; Erikson, Erikson, & Kivnick, 1986). He proposed that adults too experience life stages that may alter aspects of their personal development. In fact, he was the first to propose a detailed lifespan theory of development in any area. His theory proposed eight stages of personality development each revolving around a psychosocial event that required some resolution. The resolution of each event resulted in a new aspect of personality. During childhood individuals were said to go through four stages and develop aspects of trust/mistrust, autonomy/doubt, initiative/guilt, and industry/inferiority. During adolescence, individuals develop self-identity or role confusion. The development of self-identity was thought to be particularly important for the first of the three adult stages. Erikson's stages are not like off/on switches. For example, an indivdual is not full of trust or mistrust or totally industrious or inferior. Most of us are somewhere between the two extremes.

The first adult stage is **intimacy versus isolation**. Erikson believed that young adults experienced social and biological pressures to merge with another human being in an intimate relationship. Such relationships typically involve courtship, marriage, and often, the beginning of a family. Of course, intimate relations may be formed with very close friends. People who do not form intimate relations with someone are expected to experience feelings of isolation. Feelings of intimacy or of isolation then become a part of that person's personality and make them different than they were before the resolution of this stage. In Erikson's view, you gain ego strength when you resolve a stage positively. This enables you to better resolve subsequent stages. Others have argued that these stages do not really change one's ego but are simply tasks that one must deal with at different points in life (Havighurst, 1972).

The second adult stage is **generativity versus stagnation**. Erikson believed that during middle-age, people became concerned about their own and future generations of people. They may strive to create something that would contribute to the welfare of humanity and that could be passed on to younger people. Generativity might be achieved by parenting strong, smart, and healthy children and/or by working hard to be a success or a role model in one's career or place of employment. It is important to point out that one cannot determine another's generativity simply by knowing the kind of work that a person does or the size of their family. It is the feeling they have about the work they do or the family they care for that determines generativity or stagnation. An artist may appear to be generative because she creates works of great beauty that attract praise from others in her own generation and that will undoubtedly be appreciated by many future generations. She may, however, feel that her work is repetitive and only done to fund her lifestyle; she may be stagnant. An auto mechanic may appear to be stagnant doing the same jobs over and over again but she may feel very generative as she works to make the repairs that keep others and their children safe on the highways and as she teaches future mechanics her trade and skills.

The last adult stage is **ego integrity versus despair**. During old age, Erikson believed that a person looks back over life and attempts to determine whether that life has been coherent, whole, and fulfilling. If so, one experiences feelings of integrity and can face decline and accept mortality without regrets. If, instead, one looks back and wishes they had made other choices in their youth and middle years, then they are likely to experience despair since it is too late to make those changes.

Levinson's Stages and Transitions of Adult Life.   Daniel Levinson interviewed a number of middle-age men and proposed a theory of adult personality development (1978). In later work, he interviewed other adult men and women and expanded on this original data base (Levinson, 1986; 1996). A version of Levinson's theory has been made popular in the "passages" books of Gail Sheehy (1974; 1996). The theory revolves around the concept of a life structure that is the relationship between one's goals and the life situations, such as job, family, and marriage, within which one lives. This life structure changes and evolves over adult life as one gains more experience and grows older. Distinct stages of adult personality development are separated by transition-to-the-next-stage periods.

During **young adulthood** one first must make the transition from adolescence to adulthood. This usually occurs when an individual moves out of the family home and establishes some distance from their parents, siblings, friends, and high school teachers. One goes to college and moves into a dorm or apartment or one gets a job and finds a place to live closer to work. Soon the individual has entered the adult world and created a tentative life structure in which their plans for career, marriage, peer relations, as well as, their values and lifestyle abide. Close to age 30, the individual again goes through a transition and examines and adjusts their tentative life structure. For some of the men interviewed by Levinson, this was a traumatic period in their lives as they attempted to make permanent the choices they had made or make permanent choices for the first time. Should I marry? Should I take a job in Miami? Should I continue to play guitar on weekends? In the late 30s individuals are assumed to have made some of these choices and to settle down and work on being successful on the path they have chosen.

In **middle adulthood,** one again makes a transition and may go through a period of examining all that has been accomplished and all that lies ahead. One may ask whether the present life structure is the correct one. People at this transition may begin to feel some physical decline and recognize their own mortality. Eventually, people make decisions and settle down after any revisions in their life structures. For the men interviewed by Levinson, many experienced significant changes in their lives during these years. Some lost a close family member, parent, or friend; others divorced; some changed occupations; others lost interest in their work or experienced a decline in the quality of their marriage. In the early 50s, another transition is thought to occur as the life structure is again examined for flaws. For others, interviewed by Levinson, this was a time of great crisis. According to this stage theory, all people are expected to experience some form of midlife crisis. In fact, individuals may experience a crisis at every transition but the one at midlife is thought to be the most serious due to the recognition of physical decline and mortality. The crisis is largely subconscious but the inner turmoil is reflected in observable behavior.

As one enters **old age,** between the ages of 60 and 65, another transition occurs. One may now view themselves as old because society views them that way. Retirement may be at hand and a transition from full-time work to full-time leisure may require alterations in one's life structure. Eventually one settles into a routine and lives life in accordance with their altered life structure. In Chapter 10 we will see that other theorists have proposed a number of different forms of transitions from work to retirement (Atchley, 2000).

Guttman's Changes in Gender Role Theory.   The third theory is one proposed by David Guttman (1975, 1977, 1987) and has posited one particular change in personal concern over the adult years. That change is in gender role and the type of mastery used by different aged men and women. A number of personality tests measure mastery in the form of the trait of masculinity/femininity. Persons high in masculinity tend to attempt to take charge, be dominant, and change the world rather than change themselves in order to meet the needs of self or others. They are said to have an **active type of mastery**. Persons high in femininity are more submissive and tend to change themselves to deal with the demands of the world and the needs of self and others. They are said to have a **passive type of mastery**.

According to Guttman, in young adulthood, men tend to be highly masculine and use tactics of active mastery while women tend to be highly feminine and use tactics of passive mastery. Guttman argues that these tendencies are due to the **parental imperative,** which calls for a division of labor and different approaches in order to successfully raise children. Young men with children have been more likely than young women to seek full employment and to make as much for their families as possible. Young women have been more likely to spend time at home and care for and nurture young children. During these years, men may hide their feminine sides while women may hide their masculine sides. When the children grow up and leave home, the need for a division of labor in the arena of child care is no longer there and both father and mother become free to express their other side. They become more androgynous. **Androgony** means being high in both masculine and feminine characteristics rather than high in one and low in the other or low on both. Some of these tendencies are changing as more women also seek active careers and, in many cases, both parents must work to adequately provide for children.

Age Differences in Personal Concerns

The above stage theories, unlike trait theories, predict that differences in personality are likely to occur as we grow older and confront new situations, meet new people, and take on new social roles. Our traits may stay the same but our personal concerns are likely to change.

Testing Erikson's Theory.   Although Erikson describes old age as the time of ego integrity or despair, not many studies have examined that last adult stage. The work that has been done suggests that, as predicted, older adults show higher levels of self-acceptance than middle-age and younger adults (Kogan, 1990). Most of the research investigating Erikson's theory has examined **generativity,** which is thought to be a major concern of middle-age adults. Most of the longitudinal research on personality and aging has

A generative act.

examined traits rather than stages and so, most of the present work is cross-sectional. Defining what is meant by generativity has not been an easy task and it is likely that there are several different types of generativity. Some researchers have suggested that obtained age differences in generativity will depend upon the type of generativity being measured. For example, the desire to be generative might be highest in young adulthood, the capacity for generativity might be highest in middle-age, and the feeling of generative accomplishment might rise throughout adulthood and be highest in old age (Stewart & Vandewater, 1998)

Researchers have attended to these different ways of measuring generativity. In a comparison of 51 young adults (ages 22 to 27), 53 middle-age adults (ages 37 to 42), and 48 older adults (ages 67 to 72), researchers used four different measures of generativity and a measure of life satisfaction and retested 70 percent of the sample six months later. The measures of generativity assessed how much each person was concerned with future generations, how committed they were to doing something to help, what actions they were taking presently that were generative (e.g., actions like donating blood or teaching somebody a new skill were classified as generative while actions such as buying a new car or going bowling were not), and how much their recall of important life events included generative themes. The results were generally supportive of Erikson's theory. On all four measures, young adults were less generative than middle-age and older adults and on measures of generative commitment and generative themes older adults also were less generative than middle-age adults. Overall, middle-age adults showed consistently high levels of generativity. Generativity was not related to an individual's marital situation or the presence of children (McAdams & de St. Aubin, 1992; McAdams, de St. Aubin, & Logan, 1993). Perhaps a reason for higher levels of generativity in middle-age compared to young age is that one becomes more generative as one spends more time in a career or in raising children. After a certain amount of experience one may be expected to share the knowledge they have gained and to teach members of the next generation. Of course, these age differences could be cohort differences. Perhaps people born between 1951 and 1956 (the people who were middle-age at the time of the study) always have been more generative.

A longitudinal comparison of three different cohorts also has examined the different stages of personality development proposed by Erikson. In this study one cohort of 99 adults was tested in 1966 when they were 20 years old, then again in 1977 and in 1988; a second group of 83 adults was tested in 1976 at age 20 and again in 1988; and a third group of 292 20-year-old adults was tested in 1988. The oldest adults at this last testing in 1988 were only 42 (they were 20 when first tested in 1966) so no older adults have been tested yet in this ongoing study. Current results support the hypothesis of consistent age, rather than cohort, differences in the resolution of some of Erikson's stages. When two different cohorts were tested at age 20 (in 1966 for one cohort and in 1977 for the other cohort) and at age 31 (in 1977 and 1988) both cohorts showed better resolution of identity and intimacy stages when they were older (Whitbourne, Zuschlag, Elliot, & Waterman, 1992). This supports Erikson's predictions. Unfortunately, some of the other findings from this study are less clear and any conclusions with regard to generativity must await future testing.

Testing Levinson's Theory.   Researchers testing Levinson's theory have often attempted to find evidence for the **midlife crisis** that is predicted. People in middle-age often make transitions in their lives, make job changes, lose a parent, move to a new location, be troubled by adolescent children, or get a divorce. Such events might occur for younger or older adults as well, but in midlife the occurrence of such events is expected to contribute to a time of serious reevaluation and major stress since it is coupled with a realization of physical decline and one's mortality. People are thought to spend time asking themselves whether they have made the right choices and are on the right track or whether some radical change in their life structure is needed. The individual might experience higher than normal levels of anxiety or depression and might behave in unusual ways as they attempt to correct mistakes or try a new path. Midlife is expected, by many people, to be a time of crisis. Researchers have developed a scale to measure midlife crisis but, when the scale has been given to middle-age adults, the scores are not high (McCrae & Costa, 1984). In fact, most research has failed to find evidence for this predicted crisis during middle age in all but a handful of adults (Chiriboga, 1989). In a study of 300 middle-age men, about 12 percent seemed to have experienced a midlife crisis while a study of 300 middle-age women showed no evidence for the expected crisis (Farrell & Rosenberg, 1981; Baruch, Barnett, & Rivers, 1983, respectively). Those who do experience a midlife crisis are often people who experience crises on a regular basis and not just during middle-age. The group that seems to have the highest probability of experiencing a midlife crisis are white, professional men (Tamir, 1989). Perhaps that is why Levinson proposed such a crisis as a part of adult development in the first place. His initial theory was built on data collected, in large part, from white, mostly professional, men.

Instead of expecting a time of crisis, some theorists argue that middle-age should be seen as a time of great relief from the strivings of young adulthood. At middle-age, men and women have raised their children, established their careers, and have money to spend on themselves (Gallagher, 1993). Middle-age could be the best time of life. Some research supports this view. In one study, a sample of women who had graduated from Smith College about 30 years ago were asked how they felt about turning 50 after the fact. Nearly half, 48 percent, had very positive feelings while only 18 percent were very negative (21 percent were neutral and 13 percent were mildly negative) (Stewart & Ostrove, 1998).

Testing Guttman's Theory.   Guttman's theory predicts that men and women will add to their style of dealing with the world as they grow older. That is, they will take on aspects of the style typical of the opposite gender. Men and women will become more **androgynous** due to a lessening of the demands of caring for their family and children. There is research to support this general prediction but other work that suggests different patterns of change.

In support of Guttman's predictions, studies of families with very young children show that the mother typically takes most of the responsibility for child care and household chores even when both partners predicted that such a division of labor would not occur (Cowan & Cowan, 1987; Rexroat & Shehan, 1987). The demands of parenthood often produce the predicted division of labor. Other work in support of the theory has found middle-age women being more assertive and masculine than young women while middle-age men are more nurturant and feminine than young men (Huyck, 1990). Keep in mind that these are cross-sectional comparisons. One cross-sectional study compared 25 women who were still active mothers with 25 women who were no longer active mothers; all women were between the ages of 43 and 51 so that parenting, rather than age, differences could be observed. An interview and several measures, including the TAT (see above), were used to assess personality differences. The women who were no longer directly involved in child care (their children no longer lived at home) showed higher levels of the masculine characteristics of assertion, aggression, and executive control (Cooper & Guttman, 1987).

These changes also have been examined longitudinally. One longitudinal study has been following women who were first tested in 1958 when they were seniors at Mills College in California. These women have been tested at ages 21, 27, 43, and 52. Several measures, including the CPI, have been used and results indicate an increase in femininity between the ages of 21 and 27 followed by a decrease. Masculinity, on the other hand, increased in these women between the ages of 27 and 52. Researchers did not, however, find any connection between this latter increase and menopause or the decrease in parenting responsibilities that accompanies children leaving home (Helson & Moane, 1987; Helson & Wink, 1992). The pattern predicted by Guttman was observed but was not related to any lessening of the parental imperative.

Other researchers have not found the pattern of change predicted by Guttman. One study followed two samples of men and women for a 10-year period and used the Bem Sex Role Inventory as the primary measure (Bem, 1974). Participants ranged in age from 13 to 81. For both samples, men increased in androgyny as they grew older while women increased in femininity (Hyde, Krajnik, & Skuldt-Niederberger, 1991). In other words, both men and women displayed more feminine characteristics as they grew older. Women did not become androgynous. In another study, mothers of the women participating in the Mills College study were given a test of their masculinity/femininity. They, unlike their daughters, did not show increased masculinity or androgyny (Helson, 1992). It appears that changes in mastery or masculinity/femininity do frequently occur during adulthood but the changes that occur are not always the same and may depend on cohort, age, and a host of other factors in addition to the demands of parenthood.

Overall, some changes in personal concerns do seem to occur as one grows older. Research supports Erikson's prediction of increased generativity during middle-age but such results depend on how generativity is measured. Levinson's prediction of a midlife crisis is generally not supported although such crises do occur and more often in some groups than in others. Guttman's prediction of a change in mastery also has received mixed support. A change frequently occurs but not always the one predicted and the parental imperative may not be the most important factor in these changes.

If a number of different changes in personal concerns occur during middle- and old-age, then it seems likely that a number of different changes in strategies for dealing with life's events and attempting to resolve personal concerns might also occur. As you recall, part of the definition of this second level of personality description includes the strategies and plans that people use to achieve the things they want (McAdams, 1995). It is, therefore, expected that those strategies and plans will often change over the course of a person's life. People with different experiences may cope differently and since experiences and personal concerns change with age, coping too should change.

Age Differences in Coping

An important part of personality is the way individual's cope with everyday situations and with high-stress situations. It may be that some of the change in masculinity and femininity are best seen as examples of a change in coping style. Of course, many other changes in coping style are also possible with advanced age. In examining these changes, there are two very different points of view as to why coping strategies change as we age: the new opportunities view and the compensating for loss view.

New Opportunities.   The new opportunities view suggests that old age is a time when individuals are released from many of the responsibilities and obligations of middle-age. It should be noted that new does not mean better or worse; it simply means opportunities that were not available previously. Older adults are usually retired and, thus, no longer have work obligations. Children are gone from the home and older adults, like most middle-age adults, are released from direct child care. They have the freedom to do things that they may have wished to do for quite some time. Rather than planning and working toward a distant future, older adults can focus on the present and devote time to becoming more socially and emotionally involved with family, friends, and community. Middle-age and older adults may change their goals and priorities as they realize that they have less remaining time (Carstensen & Freund, 1994). They may deal with problem situations differently because they value outcomes differently than they once did, or they focus more on emotional and social aspects of problems, or simply because they can.

A part of the new opportunity view has to do with experience. Older adults typically have greater experience with both everyday and high-stress situations than younger adults. They may have learned effective coping strategies not yet known to younger, less experienced, adults and be better at selecting an appropriate strategy. Their coping may vary more than that of young adults because they have a wider variety of strategies to choose from and they need not be as cautious in certain kinds of situations. For example, a 60-year-old worker may be more able and willing to confront an employer than a 40-year-old worker. A 60-year-old is a senior worker with more experience, and is closer to retirement. A 40-year-old worker may still have children living at home and may fear job loss. Older adults may have new opportunities, as a result of changes in their social roles, to use different coping strategies.

Differences in coping strategies also depend, to some extent, on the situation that the individual is confronting. Some situations can be solved more easily than others and a coping strategy that attempts to find and implement a solution may be the best strategy. The emotional content of the situation can vary from fairly low to very high and this also may affect coping strategy (Blanchard-Fields, 1986). In some cases the feelings of others may need to be considered or protected. Finally, some situations are expected and happen to most people while others are not. Unexpected situations may result in different ways of coping (Neugarten, Moore, & Lowe, 1965; Neugarten & Neugarten, 1987). It has been suggested that older adults have fewer unexpected and more expected situations than do younger adults. Situations such as the sudden loss of a job, an unexpected divorce, or a terminal illness are more unexpected for young and middle-age adults than for older adults.

For older adults loss of a job may not be so unexpected (as we will see in Chapter 10), divorce is unlikely after so many years of marriage, and cancer may be more expected. Some examples of different situations that have relatively easy or relatively difficult solutions and that vary in emotional content and expectedness are shown below:

- You are wandering down the hall in your dorm when you notice a small party going on. The people at the party invite you into their room and offer you alcohol. They are all drinking but you, and perhaps some of them are not old enough to legally consume alcohol. What should you do?
- A woman married a man who was 35 years older than she. She is now close to finishing her college degree and is eager to start her career in the town in which they currently live. He will retire from his career next year and would like to travel and move to a new location. What should they do?
- A young couple planned to marry next June so that his parents could attend. The parents live in France, can only get to a June wedding, and are very eager to attend. Her mother also wants to attend but has been diagnosed with a terminal illness that gives her only until March to live. What should the young couple do?
- When you took the midterm exam in biology, you saw two students cheating. They had their notebooks open on their laps. What should you do?

You probably found some of the situations easier to solve than others and you may have used different styles for solving different problems. Researchers have attempted to look at the coping strategies used by older and younger adults by presenting similar situations that are easy or hard to solve and have high or low emotional content.

This research has shown lower levels of performance by adolescents compared to young and middle-age adults when the emotional content is high but not when it is low (Blanchard-Fields, 1986). The wedding example has higher emotional content than the midterm in biology. For adults, researchers found no age differences when the emotional content was fairly low but when the emotional content was high, older adults tended to change strategy more often than younger adults, and to use more emotion-managing strategies (Folkman, Lazarus, Pimley, & Novacek, 1987; Blanchard-Fields & Camp, 1990). In one such study all four groups, adolescents, young adults, middle-age adults, and older adults were compared. Everyone received vignettes that were low in emotional content (e.g., a teenager's use of the family car), medium (e.g., a sibling's accusation of stealing), or high (e.g., a spouse's affair) and wrote their proposed resolutions to each vignette. Resolutions were scored by independent raters. A problem-solving style, which involves taking direct action, was used most often across all age groups. As the level of emotional content rose, however, older adults were more likely than other age groups to use an emotion-managing strategy, or one that attempts to suppress emotions and to focus attention away from the central issue. Older adults were, thus, more willing and/or better able to alter their strategy depending on the situation and, the researchers suggest, that older adults may possess a broader range of coping strategies (Blanchard-Fields, Jahnke, & Camp, 1995).

Other work also shows that problem-solving is the most frequent choice of strategy across all age groups even when the individual has a wide variety of available strategies. For example, one choice a person could make would be to avoid the situation altogether. In one study, men were asked to describe real situations that had happened in their lives and the strategy that they used to solve the problem. Older men were less likely than middle-age men to use avoidance strategies in situations that occurred in their lives when the situation involved confronting an authority or making an important decision. The research also showed that both middle-age and older men had and used a wide variety of strategies. Older men, who did not have to worry about the same repercussions in the workplace that middle-age men did, tended not to avoid confrontation as often as middle-age men (Feifel & Strack, 1989). Again, older adults, including middle-age adults, appear to have a wide variety of coping strategies and select an appropriate strategy based on a number of relevant factors.

In related work, researchers have examined the preferences for different kinds of social interactions among younger and older adults. In one study 75 young, 208 middle-age, and 97 older people between the ages of 11 and 92 participated in a phone survey. They were asked in two different situations whether they would rather be with (1) a member of their immediate family, (2) a person that they recently met and who they appeared to have much in common with, or (3) an author of a book that they had read. In one situation they chose who to be with if they had a half hour open and could spend it with the person they chose. In the second situation they chose who to be with if they were moving across country with no accompanying family or friends. In both situations older adults tended to select a member of their immediate family. Younger adults tended to select a recently met person or an author in the first situation but a member of their immediate family in the second situation. When the situation is one in which it may be a last chance to be with someone for quite some time, as in the second situation, all persons are more likely to select loved ones. Older adults may always select familiar loved ones because for them it could be the last time they see them (Fredrickson & Carstensen, 1990). In old age we may more fully realize the importance of these emotional and social ties and find new ways to use the opportunites that become available to us. Part of our coping in old age involves being close to family and friends.

Compensating for Loss.   As we become adults we gain new freedoms, abilities, and knowledge but lose some of the security and regularity of childhood. As we age we continue to gain and lose, but it is commonly thought that the losses begin to outweigh the gains. This view of coping suggests that the changes that occur in coping strategies are due to an attempt to compensate for these increasing losses.

One loss that is thought to contribute to a change in coping is a loss of independence and an increased dependency on others. One may feel a loss of control over many of the events in their own lives (Hyde, Krajnik, & Skuldt-Niederberger, 1991). Older adults who have retired have lost some of their prior prestige as a working, contributing member of society and some or most of their prior income. They may view themselves as having lost some of their power and influence and, as a result, may modify the strategies they use in interacting with the world. Older adults also may recognize the changes that have occurred in their own abilities. As you know from Chapter 2, older adults are less likely to have the strength and energy they once had. They may not see or hear as well. Older adults are likely to be a little slower (Chapter 5) and have more difficulty learning something new or retrieving information from memory (Chapter 6). These physical and mental changes may lead older adults to believe that they have less control and, as a result, they may resort to less assertive ways of handling both everyday and high-stress problem situations. Perhaps that is why some research has found increases in feminine characteristics and passive mastery for both men and women in old age (see Hyde, Krajnik, & Skuldt-Niederberger, 1991).

To examine this hypothesized change in the ways in which people cope with different situations, researchers have looked at the control perceived by older and younger adults to determine whether or not older adults really do believe that they have less control. Perceived control is typically measured as **locus of control**, which was originally thought to be a personality trait and was proposed by Rotter (1966). Locus of control refers to one's beliefs about how rewards are obtained and punishments avoided. Locus of control has two extremes, which are referred to as internal and external locus of control. A person high in internal control believes that their successes and failures depend primarily on their own actions. A person high in external control believes that such things are largely due to chance and/or the actions of others. These two forms of external control, chance and "powerful others," are usually measured separately (Levenson, 1974). Contrary to expectations, a lot of early cross-sectional research found higher levels of internal control among older adults (Staats, 1974; Strickland & Shaffer, 1971; Wolf & Kurtz, 1975) although other studies showed the opposite (Ryckman & Malikioski, 1975). Older cohorts, or older adults, believed they were more in control than did younger cohorts or, perhaps, they are just more willing to accept responsibility. The few longitudinal studies were conducted over short periods of time ranging from two to six years and have shown mixed results (Lachman, 1983; 1985; Siegler & Gatz, 1985).

In a series of three studies Margie E. Lachman (1986) tested 188 younger adults and 192 older adults on overall locus of control and on control in two specific domains, intellectual and health. Individuals rated their agreement or disagreement with a series of statements that expressed a belief in chance, powerful other, or internal locus of control. Examples of chance, powerful other, and internal statements in the intellectual domain might be "I have little control over my mental state," "I wouldn't be able to figure out the postal rates on a package without a postal worker's help," and "it's up to me to keep my mental faculties from deteriorating," respectively. Chance, powerful other, and internal statements in the health domain might be "no matter what I do, if I'm going to get sick, I will get sick," "regarding my health, I can only do what my doctor tells me to do," and "if I take care of myself, I can avoid illness," respectively. Although she found no overall difference between the two age groups, older adults were more external when it came to both the intellectual and health domains. It may be that older adults do show lower perceptions of internal control in some specific areas, but maintain high levels of internal control in other areas. It is also possible that some of these obtained differences are due to cohort rather than or in addition to age.

Control can be thought about in terms other than internal and external. Another way to think about coping and control is to think in terms of primary and secondary control (Schulz & Heckhausen, 1996). **Primary control** refers to exerting influence on the external world. If the environmental situation is not acceptable, a person using primary control changes that environment. **Secondary control** refers to change within the individual. If the environmental situation is not acceptable, a person using secondary control changes him or herself. Figure 8-4 illustrates the expected availability and use of these two types of control over the course of a person's life. During childhood, adolescence, and young adulthood, we learn both strategies but we mainly use primary control as we explore and shape our environments. All through our lives we strive for primary control. In middle adulthood we use both strategies but in different situations. In late adulthood our ability to change the environment and exert primary control declines and we rely much more heavily on secondary control strategies. At the same time, we become much more selective in our choice of goals and use primary control strategies whenever possible. In very old age, we may have to rely entirely on secondary control. Some research shows that very old adults strive to avoid problems whenever possible and to accept what they cannot change (Aldwin, Sutton, Chiara, & Spiro, 1996). Older adults often rely more heavily on religion which is seen as a form of secondary control (McFadden, 1999). In one examination of the coping strategies reportedly used by older adults, religion was named more frequently than any other strategy (Koenig, George, & Siegler, 1988).

In one test of this model of coping, younger, middle-age, and older adults answered questions about their life goals and took standardized measures of tenacity and flexibility. Researchers found that older adults were less optimistic about attaining their goals and believed that they had less control over that attainment. Older adults were more concerned with health, leisure, and community goals than were the other groups but less concerned with family, financial, and work goals. Older adults strove for primary control but were more flexible in their approach and more willing and likely to use secondary

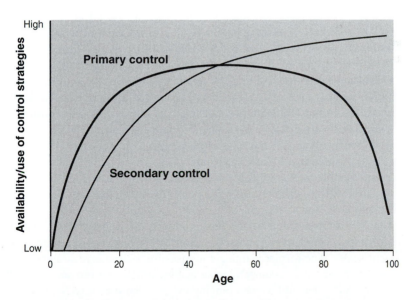

FIGURE 8-4   Primary and Secondary Control Across the Lifespan.

Source: Reprinted with permission from Schulz, R. & Heckhausen, J. (1996). A life span model of successful aging. *American Psychologist, 51,* 702–714.

control strategies (Heckhausen, 1997). Other studies also have found that older adults use secondary control in many situations and more often than younger adults (Wrosch & Heckhausen, 1999).

Recently, 1013 younger adults, 1650 middle-age adults, and 827 older adults participated in a half-hour phone survey and provided, by mail, ratings for their well-being, control strategies, and their current level of stress in health and financial matters. Control strategies were evaluated by having people rate three types of control statements on a scale ranging from "not at all" (a 1 on the scale) to "a lot" (a 4 on the scale). An example of a primary control statement is "Even when I have too much to do, I find a way to get it all done." Secondary control was measured in two forms, positive reappraisal and lowering aspirations. The former is described as seeing the good side of a bad situation. A statement characteristic of this strategy is "I find I usually learn something meaningful from a difficult situation." The latter type of secondary control refers to changing goals or giving up. A statement characteristic of this strategy is "When I can't get what I want, I assume my goals must be unrealistic." Researchers found that primary control was positively related to well-being for younger adults while the positive reappraisal form of secondary control was positively related to well-being for middle-age and older adults. Lowering aspirations was negatively related to well-being for adults of all ages. These findings were particularly strong for individuals who had relatively high levels of health or financial stress. Older adults also showed a higher level of reliance on primary control strategies than did younger adults suggesting that older adults rely more on all control strategies than do younger adults (Wrosch, Heckhausen, & Lachman, 2000).

One final way to think about the changes in coping strategies that occur in older adults is to view them as attempts to protect the older adult's self-image, which may be threatened by a loss of physical health, financial security, social support, and other losses. According to this model, three types of coping strategies are available. The first are **assimilation strategies** in which the individual modifies her/his behavior to meet certain goals. For example, you wish to live a long time so you quit smoking. The second are **accommodation strategies** in which the individual modifies the goal that is being sought or substitutes an alternative goal. For example, you can no longer be the star on the softball team so you switch and learn line dancing. The third are **immunization strategies** in which evidence of some decline in or threat to one's self image is interpreted in a more positive way or regarded as irrelevant. For example, you frequently forget appointments but you claim that you had far more important things on your mind. The use of these three strategies are thought to change as we grow older. Younger adults are thought to rely more on assimilation while older adults rely more on accommodation and immunization (Brandtstädter & Greve, 1994).

In studies designed to test the predictions of this model, individuals were asked to respond to two standard measures, the Tenacious Goal Pursuit and the Flexible Goal Adjustment scales. The former is thought to measure assimilative strategies while the latter is thought to measure accomodative strategies. Findings from several studies and responses from 3689 men and women ranging in age from the early 20s to the late 70s has shown a consistent decline in scores on the assimiliative measure and an increase on the accomodative measure as the age of respondents increased. No gender differences were found (Brandtstädter, 1992; Brandtstädter & Greve, 1994). Other cross-sectional work also

Coping strategies change with age.

has found higher, although not very high, levels of accomodation in older adults (Coleman, Ivani-Chalian, & Robinson, 1999).

It appears that personal concerns tend to change as we grow older. We tend to become more concerned with generative issues in middle-age. In old age our concerns may shift to issues of health, leisure, and community. The strategies we use to cope with various situations also seem to broaden and change and our beliefs in how much control we have and how much we are able to exert also seem to shift with advanced age for certain domains. We may become more focused on social and emotional ties and worry less about the future. At this point in our exploration of personality it appears that traits tend to remain stable and personal concerns tend to change.

Identity

The third level of personality description is one of identity. **Identity** refers to our continuing and coherent sense of self over time. Even though our concerns and strategies for coping with various situations may change, we still see ourselves as being basically the same person that we have always been. Do you think this is true? Are you the same "person" that you were ten years ago? One factor that helps us to maintain a coherent and lasting identity is the stability of the traits that we discussed earlier. This stability is thought to be a major contributor to our well being as we grow older (Costa, Metter, & McCrae, 1994). Seeing our characteristics remain the same helps contribute to a sense of continuity but a more holistic view of ourselves gives us a better sense of who we are. Examining this broader sense of self in terms of continuity and change is the focus of the third level of personality.

Identity can be revealed in a life story that allows people to view themselves as the same person, the same identity, that they were long ago even though they may have changed in some or many ways. The life story is a person's description of who they are, where they have come from, and where they are going. It is the individual's telling of the important events in their life and has a beginning and an anticipated end. This life story is thought to be revised, perhaps many times, as one grows older and confronts new problems and finds new strategies for dealing with problems (McAdams, 1995). Nevertheless, the same identity, the same person, is the "star" of the whole life story. Others have examined identity in other ways without looking at life stories.

Identity as Revealed in a Life Story

In this section we look at studies of identity that have examined the life stories told by individuals and the factors that are likely to produce revisions in those stories. It is important to keep in mind that identity itself is not the life story. The life story is a way for the individual to maintain a coherent identity and also a way for the researcher to examine that identity. Since it is expected that these life stories are revised as one's life changes, some research has focused on the factors that might produce such revisions.

Although it is possible for any major life event, such as starting a new job or confronting major loss, to produce revisions in one's life story, it is important to remember that our identity remains the same (Kaufman, 1986). Researchers have suggested that revisions are most likely to occur at three or four major points in life (Cohler, 1982). The first revision point is thought to occur between the ages of five and seven when one enters the world of school, spends much of the day outside the family home, and develops concrete operational thought as described by Piaget (Inhelder & Piaget, 1958). Some, however, question whether children as young as five to seven are able to construct a coherent life story and argue that such construction most often begins in adolescence (Habermas & Bluck, 2000). In adolescence, abstract reasoning develops and one's social and sexual world becomes more complex. One now thinks seriously about the future. The third is when individuals enter middle-age, during their 40s, and realize the limits of life and the reality of their mortality. While this may seem to imply a form of midlife crisis, remember the research we discussed earlier on the very low prevalence of such crises. A possible fourth point of revision is when one enters old age and prepares to confront death.

Whether these periods of life really are points when life stories tend to be revised is not yet known but some findings seem to suggest that some changes occur at some of these points. For example, researchers have found that people in their 40s are more preoccupied with their past than they were in their 30s (Livson & Peskin, 1980). Other studies have found major differences between memories of adolescence reported during the college years and later during middle-age, or between early life memories reported by people in their 30s and again later in their 40s (Runyan, 1980; Vaillant & McArthur, 1972). A change in a life story might change the way the past is remembered or, perhaps, a change in the way the past is remembered results in a change in the life story. Other researchers have suggested that the continuity of identity provided by a life story might undergo major change with a major life event. Continuity might not be found when an individual becomes seriously ill. In such cases, people may find it difficult to view themselves as being the same person that they were in the past when they were healthy (Warren, 1998). At present, we do not know the answers to many of these questions.

The collection of people's life stories and any subsequent analysis of collected stories are not easy tasks. People may be reluctant to tell such stories if indeed they have them, and once such stories are told, what does the researcher do with them? It has been suggested that analysis must look at themes, images, plots, scenes, characters, and other elements (special effects?) more common to students of literature or theatre than social science (McAdams, 1995). The analyses that are used for literature are not easy or familiar to researchers trained in experimental methodology and so other types of more familiar analysis have been sought. Peter G. Coleman (1999) has suggested four important characteristics for examining life stories. The first characteristic is **coherence**. Stories must have a linking thread that makes them whole, and not just a sequence of events. The second is **assimilation**. Stories must interpret the events that are presented rather than just present events (please note that this is a different form of assimilation than the assimilation strategies for coping that were discussed earlier). The third is **structure**. Stories need some beginning, middle, and anticipated end. None of us, of course, know for certain how our stories will end. The fourth is **truth**. Stories should be like histories rather than works of fiction. They should tell the truth from the viewpoint of the person constructing the story. These four characteristics are much easier to measure and are closer to the kinds of analyses social scientists are used to doing.

Using some of these characteristics, Coleman and his colleagues have begun to examine life stories. In one study, 18 men and 25 women ranging in age from 80 to 98 were interviewed about the course of their lives. Of these 43 people, 28 (65 percent) saw their life course as a story and many (27) thought it worth telling or writing about. Story coherence was most typically maintained by long-term relations with family and friends who provided the links between past and present. For others, work provided this important link. Ten of the individuals interviewed (23 percent) saw their life course as disconnected or as a series of events rather than as a story. Eight of these ten individuals without life stories were women. Three years later, 10 men and 17 women of the first sample were interviewed again. The majority of these individuals still reported life stories with family relationships as the main theme for both men and women (Coleman, Ivani-Chalian, & Robinson, 1998). In a continued investigation involving these same people, five individuals were selected for a more intensive case analysis. These individuals have maintained their life stories even in very old age and have used these stories "not only in making sense of the past but interpreting the present as well" (p. 843). The results from these case studies suggest that perceived control is an important factor in whether one constructs a life story. As you might expect from our earlier discussion of control, people who believe they have little or no control are more likely to perceive their lives as disconnected events (Coleman, Ivani-Chalian, & Robinson, 1999). Perhaps women of that older cohort (these people were born between 1895 and 1913) grew up and lived in times when women perceived little control over their lives. Would women in the present cohort be more likely to construct life stories?

In looking at life stories it may be that the very same life events would be presented very differently by different storytellers and different storytellers might include different events in their stories (McAdams, 1998). Box 8-2 presents another way to conceptualize different types of storytelling based on different personality styles.

BOX **8-2**

Personality Styles and Life Stories

These are excerpts from a life story told by an imaginary person. As you read through the personality styles described below, see if you can determine which style fits this particular client.

> All of my life has been a struggle against incompetence. When I was in elementary school I had to be in the same class with a bunch of dolts and most of the time I was treated as if I also was a dolt. My fifth grade teacher, Mrs. Markey, however, recognized my talent and gave me the chance to join the honor society. I joined and was very excited and happy for the rest of the year but the next year I figured out that most of the other kids in the society were really as selfish and stupid as all my other classmates. Over the course of twelve years of school and four of college I rarely found anyone I really respected or liked very much. I've had to do most things by myself. After college I got my first job working for Norris Inc. I worked hard and was promoted to assistant manager of technical operations by the end of the first year. Soon I learned that some of the other workers over whom I had been promoted were out to get me. I saw them plotting at breaktimes and at lunch and once after work at a bar where they often met. I followed them there one evening and saw five of them sitting together at the same table. They ignored me for a while but eventually one of the women asked me to come on over and join them. I said no, I was leaving and so I left. Two weeks later, the boss told me he had to let some people go and, sure enough, I was one of them. Later I developed my own website and, as you know, made a lot of money helping to advertise products for Larrabie and Sons and a few other big corporations. I'll be glad to retire in a few years and get away from all the dolts in my life.

Five personality styles which might be taken as five types of life stories have been described in one theory (Silver, 1992). The first type is the person with **paranoid style** who is always concerned with some external threat and may become more suspicious with advanced age. Worries about being robbed, cheated, or assaulted may lead to distrust of even close family members and friends who are then blamed for any problems that occur. As a result, family members and friends may stay away and the individual may be isolated. The life stories of these individuals are likely to be full of the deceit of others and conspiracies against themselves.

The second type is the person with **obsessive-compulsive style** who strives to maintain control over the environment and prefers to be alone rather than with others. Such individuals are thought to be quiet, socially isolated, and uninvolved emotionally while, at the same time, remaining intellectually active. Their life stories may be full of their own achievements and the frequent interference of others.

The third type is the person with **hysterical style** who may view aging as a period of growth and a time to freely express emotional needs. These individuals seek social contacts and interactions with others and are often the "life of the party." Their life stories may be filled with the many people they have known and social/cultural events in which they have participated.

The fourth type is the person with **impulsive style** who may behave recklessly, oppose authority, and confront aging directly. These individuals are likely to continue to do the same sorts of things they have always done, such as sky diving, skiing, or swimming, until they can no longer do so. At that point they may become very angry. These people are often well-liked and form friendships, with little emotional attachment, to achieve their own ends. Their life stories may be action packed and quite exciting.

The fifth type is the person with **narcissistic style** who may fear aging and spend considerable time and money trying to look young. These individuals seek attention and positive regard from others. They may strive to spend as much time as possible with children and grandchildren who will tell them how good they look. Their life stories may be filled with events from their youth.

It is thought that the hysterical and impulsive styles are those most likely to receive needed social support from family, friends, and medical personnel. Which style do you think matches our imaginary person? Paranoid or obsessive-compulsive are most people's guess. Our person presents aspects of both of these styles. It should be pointed out that most individuals are thought to be a mix of several different styles rather than being only one particular style. Do you think these mixes should be called a personality style of their own? Do you have aspects of any of these styles? Perhaps there are many other styles not described in this theory. At present, the life stories constructed by these different personality styles have not been carefully examined but are expected to be quite different.

Finally, some research has attempted to compare the stories told by people with different traits or different personal concerns. In one study, researchers examined the life stories told by highly generative and less generative adults who ranged from 25 to 72 years of age. Generativity was measured by scores on a test of generative concern, a test of daily generative acts, and the individual's professional and/or volunteer activities. Unpaid volunteers were regarded as highly generative. Interviews were conducted to gather the life stories of 40 adults who were highly generative and of 30 adults who scored low on generativity. Stories were scored by independent raters. The life stories told by highly generative adults showed a sensitivity to the feelings of others early in life, a stable morality, a tendency to obtain good outcomes even from bad situations, and the setting of future goals that were intended to benefit the greater society rather than the self (McAdams, Diamond, de St. Aubin, & Mansfield, 1997). The life stories of generative adults were quite different from the life stories told by less generative adults.

The work on life stories has just begun and many additional studies will be needed before we can be sure how often such stories are used to maintain identity and how other factors such as the components of the first two levels of personality, health, age, gender, and ethnic group relate to the types of stories created by people. Nevertheless, the intitial work suggests that many individuals maintain a coherent identity by using a life story. Some interesting relationships (e.g., with perceived control and generativity) and some new directions for personality researchers interested in human aging are emerging from this line of research.

Other Ways of Studying Identity

Examing life stories is not the only way to study identity and not the only way for individuals to maintain a coherent identity. As we saw earlier, many adults report no life story but we believe they still have an identity.

One other way of examining identity is to ask individuals to respond to specific questions about their sense of identity. In longitudinal examinations of the students who graduated from Mills College (Helson, 1993), Radcliffe (Stewart & Vandewater, 1993), Smith College, and from the University of Michigan (Tangri & Jenkins, 1993; Cole & Stewart, 1996) researchers examined responses to scales that measured identity certainty, which is the "sense of having a strong and clear identity" (p. 1189). The results showed an increasing awareness of self-identity as these individuals aged through their 40s and up to age 50 (Stewart & Ostrove, 1998). At present, few of these graduates are much older than 50 so it is not clear whether this identity certainty will continue to increase. Other work has found similar changes in sense of identity by comparing measures of identity given to men and women when they were in college and again ten years later. In this study, sense of identity was higher on the later measure (Whitbourne, & Waterman, 1979). It seems clear that one's awareness of or, perhaps, concern with self-identity changes as one grows older at least through middle-age.

Earlier we said that the events in one's life play a role in revisions made to one's life story. One's identity might, however, remain the same. Another view is that these life events play a role in the formation of and changes to one's actual identity, regardless of how that identity is measured. Susan Whitbourne's (1985; 1989; 2001) theory proposes that identity is one's sense of how their life has gone so far, how it is going now, and how it will go in the future. Our view of our past can be thought of as a life story but our view of the present and future is referred to as our **scenario**. The scenario part of our identity can change as a result of the events that occur in our life or the events that occur can be interpreted in terms of our identity and, thus, our identity is maintained.

Maintenence and changes in identity rely on two processes. When we attempt to fit life events into our preconceived view of who we are and where we are going, that process is called **identity assimilation** (yes, yet another type of assimilation). One's life story might be considered a prime example of identity assimilation as one includes events that fit well and confirm one's sense of identity and leaves out or downplays events that are not consistent with one's view of self. One example of such assimilation was found with older psychiatric patients. These individuals greatly downplayed, and in some cases even denied, that they had spent major parts of their lives in the hospital. Spending time in the hospital did not fit well with their self views (Whitbourne & Sherry, 1991). Sometimes events will happen that cannot be fit into our scenario. When we must alter our scenario because life events will not assimilate, the process is called **identity accommodation**. If I believe that I will never marry and then find myself taking those vows, some accomodation is clearly necessary. In the course of identity development and maintence, both processes play a role and healthy development occurs when a balance between the two processes is present.

Another view is that the formation of identity, which Erikson included as the stage during adolescence (self-identity versus role confusion), also takes place during adulthood. A stage of career consolidation versus self-absorption, between Erikson's stages of intimacy and of generativity, has been proposed to describe one's development of an identity with one's career (Vaillant, 1993). Identity with a career occurs when a major part of one's view of self is what one does for a living. The individual may go to work not because of the money earned but because that is who they are. In answer to the question, "who are you?" you might respond by first naming your career. I am a doctor. I am a firefighter. I am a computer programmer. I am a college student. Failure to develop a sense of identity with a career may result in overabsorption with self.

Some researchers have compared the identities held by older adults in different cultural groups to see if cultural environment leads to different ideas about who we are. One such study examined identity in Spanish and Dutch adults over the age of 60. Identity was measured by having individuals complete sentence stems with truthful statements about themselves. Sentence stems included: "I am best at _____;" "Others think I am _____;" "My life's goal _____;" and so on. Although the two groups responded similarly to many of these stems, an important difference was found in the number of responses that related to family and to personal activities. Spanish older adults responded more frequently with reference to members of their families when completing sentences while Dutch older adults responded more frequently with reference to their own free-time activities. Researchers suggest that this difference is a result of the more collectivist Spanish culture in contrast to the more individualistic Dutch culture (Katzko, Steverink, Dittmann-Kohli, & Herrera, 1998). The culture in which we live seems to influence the identity we form for ourselves.

Another cross-cultural study looked at attitudes toward older adults and views of one's self-identity in China, Japan, and the United States. Older adults are not viewed very positively in any of these cultures although they are treated more favorably and with greater respect in China and Japan. Japanese culture maintains a strong distinction between the outer and inner self that the other two cultures do not. The outer self in Japan is the identity that interacts with the world while the inner self is free from influences of the material and social world. Other studies have shown that success or failure in social situations seems not to affect the self-esteem of the Japanese because the inner self is not affected by such external events (Kitayama, Markus, Matsumoto, & Norasakkunkit, 1997). In this study of attitudes, older adults in these three cultures were asked what the first five words or phrases were that came to mind when they thought about themselves and when they thought about an older person. The results showed that in China and the United States, views of self and of an older person were mostly the same and fairly negative. The negative stereotypes of older people in these cultures is related to the negative views that older adults have of themselves. In Japan, however, older adults also viewed an older person negatively but viewed themselves very positively. The cultural emphasis on an inner and an outer self seems to protect the identity of older adults in Japan from any damaging influences of attitudes toward older persons (Levy, 1999).

As with the work with life stories, other research on identity also suggests that life events are very important and that culture plays a role in identity. Our conceptions of past events and our plans for the future depend on our total situation and what we make of it.

Stability, Change, and Satisfaction with Life

Does personality change as we grow older or does it remain the same? The answer seems to be that it does both if you think of personality as being made up of different levels. If by personality you mean traits, then personality shows great stability, although some changes may occur under some circumstances. If by personality you mean personal concerns and coping strategies, then personality tends to change, but some stability also may be found. If by personality you mean identity maintained by life stories, then some changes in life stories are expected but identity is thought to remain stable.

With stability in traits that may or may not be favorable to well-being; with changes in personal concerns and coping strategies that may or may not be effective; with declines in physical abilities, health, and cognition; and with retirement and loss of status and income, one might expect to find many older adults having problems in old age. Of course, some adults do have problems and difficulty adjusting to old age (see the description of the narcissistic personality style in Box 8-2). Most research, however, shows that older adults are generally as satisfied or even more satisfied with their lives than are younger and middle-age adults (Diener & Suh, 1998; Lawton, Kleban, Rajagopal, & Dean, 1992).

Perhaps older adults are simply reluctant to express dissatisfaction. Members of that older cohort may have learned to grin and bear it. Perhaps people in these older cohorts need to be asked several times or in different ways before being willing to talk about their troubles. In an attempt to determine whether this is the case, one group of researchers pushed (coaxed?) adults to respond about their troubles and problems. In this study 1052

I'm quite happy with my life, thank you for asking.

men first received a standard stress and coping interview and many denied having any problems. Interviewers then asked them to "identify the most serious problem or concern they had had in the past week and to describe it briefly" (p. P181). If an individual still did not respond with a problem, the interviewer told them that the problem did not have to be major but could be anything that bothered them during the past week. For those who still did not report a problem, the interviewer then asked about any problems at work or home, with their family, health, or even their automobile. This intensive interviewing and repeated asking about problems resulted in a higher level of reported problems for every group. In other work, 70 to 80 percent of adults usually report some problem(s) (Aldwin & Revenson, 1987), but in this study 90 percent reported a problem. It was still the case, however, that the oldest adults (those over 75) reported the fewest problems. Only 3 percent of the middle-age men reported no problems while 17 percent of the oldest men reported no problems. For those who did report a problem, the most frequent category of problems reported by middle-age men were problems at work while the most frequent category of problems reported by the few older men who reported a problem, were problems with health (Aldwin, Sutton, Chiara, & Spiro III, 1996).

What have we learned about adult personality? Some aspects are likely to change (Level 2) while other aspects are likely to remain the same (Levels 1 and 3). As we grow older and gain more experience we appear to acquire and use a greater variety of coping strategies. We are better equipped to handle many stressful situations. We either have fewer problems or we see situations that might once have been viewed as problems as being no problem at all. Old age, for those who reach it, is far more likely to be a time of peace and satisfaction rather than a time of stress and worry.

Making Choices

One choice that you should consider is not to jump to conclusions in judging another person's personality. There are so many aspects of personality that even trained professionals cannot easily know them all for any one individual. If you judge someone on the basis of a few aspects, you may miss the chance to know somebody who might have been well-worth knowing or end up knowing someone you wish you did not.

Another choice you can make is to be open to new possibilities during your college years and the early years of your career (if not your entire life). Levinson has recommended that people take care not to shut too many doors during the early years of their adult lives and we tend to agree with him. The things you learn may serve you well in the future.

Finally, you might choose to record the life stories of your older relatives or to begin documenting your own life story by keeping a journal. It is a bit of extra work now but imagine how interesting it will be to read when you are out of college, middle-aged, or old.

CHAPTER HIGHLIGHTS

■ We examined personality, one of the broadest terms in all of psychology. Because of this breadth, it is difficult to measure and researchers have had to use techniques that measure only some aspects of personality. These measures are typically divided into objective and projective assessments.

■ To examine personality we, like McAdams (1995), divided the aspects into three levels. The first

- level, traits, are characteristics assumed to have a genetic component, although environmental factors also play a role.
- Traits include rigidity/flexibility and the five factors described by Costa and McCrae (1994). These five are neuroticism, extraversion, openness, agreeableness, and conscientiousness. These traits tend to remain relatively stable across the adult years although a number of cohort differences have been found.
- The second level, personal concerns, is assumed to show change as we grow older or our circumstances change.
- We examined the stage theories of Erikson, Levinson, and Guttman and the research that has been conducted to test these theories. Several lines of evidence support Erikson's generativity stage in middle-age. Middle-age adults do seem to be more generative than younger adults and, depending on how generativity is measured, than older adults too. Levinson's notion of a midlife crisis is not well supported although such a crisis does seem to occur in some cases, particularly for white professional men. Guttman's hypothesis of increases in masculinity and femininity in younger adults followed by increased androgyny in middle-age and older adults due to the parental imperative is not well supported. Such changes do frequently occur, but so do other changes, and the parental imperative may be only one of several underlying factors.
- Age differences in coping could be due to new opportunities or to compensations for loss.
- With respect to new opportunities, it appears that middle-age and older adults have and use a wider range of coping strategies that do younger adults. Older adults also seem to have greater concern for and desire to be with close family members under a variety of circumstances while younger adults preferences depend upon the circumstances.
- With respect to compensations for loss, evidence suggests that older adults are more likely to use secondary control and accommodation strategies than are young adults. Older adults also seem to vary in their locus of control depending upon the specific domain being asked about.
- Research on the third level of personality description, the level of identity revealed in life stories, shows that revisions to these stories can occur at several different points in life and as a result of several changes in one's situation. Stories seem to depend on a sense of control and are different for generative and nongenerative people. Identity as a scenario or future view can be assimilated or accomodated depending on one's situation and the culture in which one lives influences one's views of self.
- Some aspects of personality, such as traits and identity, remain stable while other aspects, like personal concerns, change. Regardless of stability or change, older adults seem as or more satisfied with life than younger and middle-age adults and report fewer problems.

STUDY QUESTIONS

1. Name some characteristics of a person that do not fit under the broad heading of personality.

2. Compare and contrast objective and projective measures of personality.

3. Define each of the following traits: neuroticism, extraversion, openness, agreeableness, conscientiousness, and rigidity. Which of these is not one of the five factors?

4. Do traits change with age? With cohort? What factors account for these differences?

5. Describe Erikson's three stages of adult development. Are these stages supported by research?

6. What is meant by a midlife crisis? How often does this occur?

7. Describe Guttman's theory.

8. Why might both men and women become more feminine as they get older? How do such changes relate to changes in coping styles?

9. How does the emotional level of a situation change the coping strategies used? Who are influenced most by emotional levels when selecting a coping strategy? Why?

10. Describe age differences in locus of control overall, and for specific domains. Why do such differences occur?

11. Explain the differences in primary and secondary control. Which is used most often? Under what circumstances might the other strategy be used?

12. Explain what is meant by the three kinds of assimilation described in this chapter.

13. What is a scenario and how is it affected by changes in one's life situation? Give examples.

14. Do older adults present more problems when they are asked several times in several different ways? Do they present more problems than other age adults?

15. Describe some of the cultural differences that have been found with respect to adult identity.

RECOMMENDED READINGS

McCrae, R. R., & Costa, P. T. (1990). *Personality in adulthood*. New York: Guilford Press. This book is a very readable description of the five-factor model and argues that personality is stable across adulthood.

Ryff, C. D., Kwan, C. M. L., & Singer, B. H. (2001). Personality and aging: Flourishing agendas and future challenges. In J. E. Birren & K. W. Schaie (Eds.), *Handbook of the psychology of aging* (5th edition, pp. 477–499). San Diego, CA: Academic Press. This chapter is the latest review of theory and research in the personality of aging.

INTERNET RESOURCES

http://users.rcn.com/zang.interport/personality.html   Personality test that is fun but of questionable reliability.

http://www.grc.nia.gov/branches/lpc/pscs.htm   For views of personality, stress, and coping in older adults.

http://www.issid.org/issid.files/research.html   For links to personality research.

9

Relationships

Though you are in your shining days,
Voices among the crowd
And new friends busy with your praise,
Be not unkind or proud,
But think about old friends the most;
Time's bitter flood will rise,
Your beauty perish and be lost
For all eyes but these eyes.

—W. B. Yeats

Grow old along with me
The best is yet to be

—Robert Browning

Yeats and Browning both express something important about lasting relationships. Yeats tells us that as we change with age, perhaps growing less beautiful in the eyes of many, our beauty is always visible to the eyes of those closest to us. Browning asks us to stay close with those we love and promises that the future will be even better than the present.

Social Relations across the Lifespan

Think about the relationships you have had with people in your life. What are the common factors across those relationships? What things are different? How are the relationships you have today like or unlike the ones you had ten or fifteen years ago? What do you think your relationships will be in like ten, twenty, fifty, or eighty years from now? These are the kinds of questions that researchers in the field of social development have not addressed well. Considerable time and effort has been spent on identifying what different kinds of relationships look like or what they do for an individual, but broader theoretical questions are still unanswered (Antonucci, 2001; Levitt, 2000). Recall our discussion of theories and issues that guide development in Chapter 1. The developmental perspective embodied in

Senior View

There are many different kinds of relationships that we enter into over the course of our lives. In this Senior View we tried to talk with older adults about all the main relationships discussed in this chapter. We asked one couple and one married man to talk about marriage with us. Both the couple, Pauline and Lester Hopkins, and the married man Tom Mc-Nair, were married for 46 years when we spoke with them. We spoke with Eleanor McNair about sibling relationships. We spoke with Reverend Edwin Schmidt about his relationships with his children and grandchildren. Finally we spoke with Carol Milheim about friends.

Marriage

Pauline Hopkins was 70 and Lester was 74 when we interviewed them. Pauline told us that "Bat" (Lester's nickname) came over to her parent's farm to help in the wheat field when they were both young, met her, and "didn't leave me alone until he got me." He served in the army and when he returned he told her "we'll get married if you want to," and they did. They eloped and when they returned from their wedding, each went to their respective homes and lived with their parents for the next five months. During that time Lester made a downpayment on a house and furnished it before they told their parents they were married. "He put the ring on my finger and looked at momma and said "she's mine now," Pauline said. They have lived happily together in that same house since. They told us that their marriage has been very stable with few ups and downs.

When the Hopkins were asked what the best years of their marriage were, they both agreed that it was when they were raising their two children. As you will learn in this chapter, that is quite different from the usual pattern of marital satisfaction. When asked about their worst time, both agreed that they had none. We reminded them of the time they were apart after eloping and Pauline said, "That was just like nothing had happened; we were just surrounded with our families." When asked if anything about their relationship has

changed over the 46 years they told us that they know each other so well that they talk less.

Tom McNair was 81 and Eleanor was 70 when we interviewed them. We spoke with Tom about marriage and with Eleanor about her siblings. Tom and Eleanor met when both were teachers in Iran; they knew each other for close to two years before getting married. Tom remembers getting caught one night by the police in Iran, who pulled a gun on him, while he was sneaking out of the compound to be with Eleanor. They were married in Tehran and drove to a number of Iranian cities during their honeymoon. While they were gone, Iranian friends slept on the floor in their place "guarding their presents." Tom told us that their marriage has been very stable and that they have had some very good times. They have three children and seven grandchildren and some of the best times are when the whole family visits at

Christmas. Their worst time was when Eleanor was working in Phoenix on an election, had to count votes all night, and did not get back until noon the next day. This was the only real anxiety Tom has felt during their long relationship. The McNairs are very close.

We asked Tom about the longevity of their marriage and the high rate of divorce. He told us that marriage is a lifelong commitment. This is one reason for longevity given by many couples who have been married for a long period of time. On the night before he and Eleanor were married, he told her, "it's done now" and they have been together ever since. Tom said that today, "There are a number of people who enter into marriage and, for some reason or other, don't fully accept the spouse for who he or she is; they have an ideal in mind and they want to change the other person to meet their ideal rather than changing themselves and accepting the individual for who they are." Tom told us that when you marry you must accept your spouse as they are and not hope to change them at some later time.

Siblings

We spoke with Eleanor about her relationship with her siblings. She is the oldest child and has two

younger brothers and one sister. She told us that her youngest brother is a lot like her. They "are both proactive and want to get things done." He is a salesperson, is very outgoing, talks loud, and has a very loving heart. She said that her other brother "is slower than molasses in January." She described her sister as a worrier. Do these very different people get along with one another? She told us that there was never any real sibling rivalry. The worst time was when she and her sister had to share a bed when they were very young. "Now that we're all grown up, we're friends," she said. Eleanor also told us that they all became even closer when their father died a year ago. The comfort and support she received from her siblings and that she gave to them helped all to cope with this loss. Times of loss often serve to bring siblings closer together.

Children and Grandchildren

We spoke with Edwin R. Schmidt about children and grandchildren; Reverend Schmidt was 69 when we interviewed him. Edwin has two daughters, two sons, and six grandchildren. His four children live all over the country with one each in Illinois, Minnesota, North Carolina, and Oregon. He told us that he found it challenging to raise four children and that "you can't treat them like possessions." He said, "The hardest part was knowing when to discipline, and come down hard, not abusively but hard, and knowing when to let them loose and let them make their own mistakes; we always told them we loved them." We asked Edwin about the "empty nest" which is thought by some to be a difficult time for parents. He told us that he missed his children when they left but that "he only owed his children two things, roots and wings." That is, they need a solid base and the ability to find their own way. Today he sees most of his children only once a year but those visits are filled with much happiness.

Edwin told us that he sees most of his grandchildren once a year but for about ten days. He said, "With grandchildren you don't feel quite as responsible; you can spoil them and not feel bad; you try and teach some values but you don't impose; what you do teaches them more than what you say." Many other grandparents would

(continued)

Senior View   Continued

agree with these comments. The worst thing about having grandchildren he told us, was that they are not always there. He also told us that he expects that his grandchildren will not be as close to him when they are adolescents but that they will be close again once they become young adults. He said, "When they get older, they realize how much you knew."

Friends

Carol Milheim was 68 when we interviewed her. She told us that she has several friends but two very close friends who she can trust with anything. These individuals have been friends for a long time and over the last 20 years have shared the caring for a sick parent, bereavement, and divorce. "One friend is like a sister that I never had; I have no siblings and neither does she; this has

been an important part of our relationship," she said. Carol told us that she has moved many times in her life and has had to leave friends behind and find new ones. She said that making new friends is often difficult but that she has been successful at finding friends who have different religions, belong to different ethnic groups, and have different backgrounds. Diversity, she told us, is rewarding and educational.

When we asked how important it is to have a close friend, Carol told us that "it fills a tremendous need to have a close personal friend." Friends, she said, shop together, eat together, discuss grandchildren, generally socialize, and most important, confide in each other. "Friends, are people I would trust with anything I said to them," she said. She told us that her friendships were balanced with each person giving and receiving support when needed. About her closest friend, she said, "If I needed her tomorrow she would be here without question and vice versa." The last thing we asked Carol was whether family or friends were most important. She said, "I value and need them both."

As you read about relationships with family and friends you will discover that the research strongly supports the views of these seniors.

these theories is missing in social relation research. Mary Levitt (2000) has proposed one concept from social relation research that might provide a unifying framework for the disparate research in this area. That concept is social support.

Social Support

Social support refers to assistance received from other persons who are close to us, it is assistance received from or given to those in our social network. Our **social network** is that group of friends and family who are close to us. Social support and social networks are, thus, fundamentally connected. Human beings are social creatures and it appears that an important part of being social is the support we give and receive from others.

Support is typically divided into two general types: instrumental and emotional. **Instrumental support** is usually help with specific tasks, such as shopping, transportation, repairs, or housework. **Emotional support** is help that is intended to lift our spirits, relieve our sadness, or comfort us in time of need. Some researchers also discuss informational support, which is knowledge provided to us by people in our network. When support is needed, friends are more likely to give emotional forms of assistance while family members are more likely to give instrumental forms of assistance (Antonnucci, 1990). Spouses tend to provide both types of assistance.

Social support is typically measured using a standardized test such as the Interpersonal Support Evaluation List (Cohen, Mermelstein, Kamarck, & Hoberman, 1985). Networks also are measured using standardized tests such as the Lubben Social Network Scale (Lubben, 1988) or the hierarchical mapping technique using the concentric circles diagram shown in Figure 9-1 (p. 222). This latter measure has been used frequently in research investigating the convoy model of social support (Antonucci, 1986; Kahn & Antonucci, 1980). The convoy model is based on the proposal that people are involved in a dynamic network of close relationships with a small group of family and friends and that those relationships, the members of that network, travel with the individual throughout their life. Just as a group of trucks in a convoy travel together down the interstate watching out for one another, the convoy or network also travels together through life, giving and receiving assistance and social support. Figure 9-1 shows the concentric circles used for the convoy model. The center circle in the diagram is labeled *you* and the individual then reveals their support network by placing others in the surrounding concentric circles. Thus, in the very closest circle, are the very closest person or people; those who you could not live without and in whom you can confide virtually everything. In the next outer circle are those people who also are very close but not quite as close as those in the inner circle. In the last circle are people who you like and are friendly with but not people who are as close as those are in the two inner circles. Circles can be full or empty or anywhere in between. Researchers using this technique compare the responses made by men and women or adults of different ages or compare the responses made by the same people when they were young to their responses when they are old. Try using the convoy model of measuring social networks in Project 9 (p. 222).

Using these measures, researchers have found that people place close to twenty people in their convoy with five to ten people in the inner circles. The number of close members remains relatively stable when examined longitudinally although older adults do lose

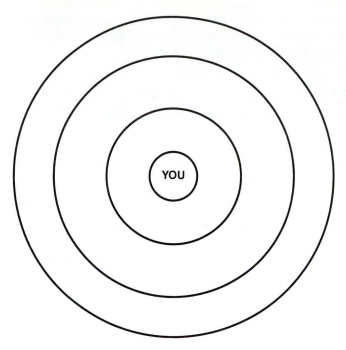

FIGURE 9-1   Diagram of social networks as concentric circles.

members in their outer circles, (Antonucci, 2001). Consistent with the notion of a convoy, people who are included in an individual's network at one point in time tend to be included at later points as well, especially those who are closest (Kahn & Antonucci, 1980). It is the support from these close relationships that is most linked to our well-being.

    Although there are relatively few age changes in social support networks, a number of other factors such as gender, sexual orientation, race, and culture contribute to differences in social support.

PROJECT 9

Social Networks

This project will allow you to get an idea about your own social support system using a modified version of the scale developed by Kahn and Antonucci (1980). Keep in mind the characteristics of social support and what friends versus family do for one another when you consider your own convoy of social support. One other thing that you might find interesting is to identify the different types of support provided by various network members. Kahn and Antonucci's convoy model suggests that social support has three different components: aid, affect, and affirmation. Aid is the physical help given and received, affect is the emotional support shared, and affirmation are the things people do to make you feel good about yourself, make you feel worthwhile. Start thinking about the folks in your life and see how they all fall into place in the convoy model.

Look at the concentric circle diagram in Figure 9-1 and recreate it on a piece of paper. Put yourself in the very center. Now beginning with the first circle out from you (considered your inner circle), write the names of all of those people in your life who you feel so close to that you cannot imagine life without them. People who you do not feel quite *that* close to but who are still very close go in the second circle. People to whom you feel less close, but are still important to you go in the third circle. Circles can be full, empty, or anywhere in between.

Now answer the following questions about the people in your network. Write the names of the people who fit the description in each question.

Are there people who reassure you when you are feeling uncertain about something?
Are there people who make you feel respected?
Are there people who would make sure that you were cared for if you were ill?
Are there people you talk to when you are upset, nervous, or depressed?
Are there people who you talk to about your health?
Are there people who you talk to about your family?
Are there people you confide in about things that are important to you?

Now compare your answers above to your answers on the next set of questions:

Are there people who you reassure when they are feeling uncertain about something?
Are there people who you make feel respected?
Are there people who you would make sure were cared for if they were ill?
Are there people who talk to you when they are upset, nervous, or depressed?
Are there people who talk to you about their health?
Are there people who talk to you about their family?
Are there people who confide in you about things that are important to them?

One last set of questions to consider.

Would you want to have more people, fewer people, or do you think you have the right number of people in your network?

Would you want to have more people in your network that you could depend on?

Now you have a clearer understanding of how the concentric circle diagram is used in measuring social networks and social support. What did you learn about your own network and support that you did not realize before doing this project?

One important difference seen in social support networks is between men and women. Women tend to report larger networks and to place more family members in their convoy than men do (Antonucci & Akiyama, 1991). Women also place more people in their inner circle than men do although the number of people in the outer circle is about equal. Those placed in the inner circle by women but not by men are often sisters; men tend to place siblings of either gender in the second circle (Antonucci & Akiyama, 1997). As we note several times throughout this chapter, women tend to maintain close confiding relationships with people other than their spouses while men are more likely to confide only in their spouses. One interesting recent finding is that gender differences disappear after the age of 70.

The support networks of gay and lesbian couples tend to be about the same as the convoys of heterosexual couples with the exception that their convoys contain more gay or lesbian people or people with an awareness of the individual's orientation. Awareness of the individual's gay or lesbian orientation is regarded as the single most important factor in the individual's overall satisfaction with the support received (Grossman, D'Augelli, & Hershberger, 2000).

Race and ethnicity have been examined in relation to social support revealing considerable commonality across groups. Differences stem more from customs that affect relationships than from group membership, per se. Those holding to traditional customs tend to have similar social support networks that differ slightly from others. The role of family, friends, and church as support providers is very important in the African American elderly community. More relatives are in African American networks than networks of Whites, but being married predicts this more than race. Race emerges as a difference because fewer African Americans elders are married. Hispanic American elders tend to have a lot of people in their networks including nuclear and extended family members. Older Chinese Americans rely primarily on their children for support, especially their daughters (Antonucci, 2001).

Researchers have attempted to determine whether the social networks and support found in the United States are similar to those found in other cultures. One recent study compared social support in Liverpool (United Kingdom) with that found in Beijing (China). Researchers interviewed 495 British and 165 Chinese adults age 60 and over about their living arrangements, health, marital status, number of children, and sources of instrumental and emotional support. One major difference bewteen the two cultures is that three generations and other relatives are more likely to live in the same household in China than in the United Kingdom. Like residents of the United States, older residents of Liverpool tended to live alone or with a spouse. The primary similarity in social support between Beijing and Liverpool was in the people named as sources of instrumental and emotional support. In both, very different cultures, the most frequently named source of these types of support was the spouse, followed by the daughter (or daughter-in-law), followed by a friend (Wenger & Jingming, 2000). The two cultures have social support patterns very much like those found in the United States.

The social support that one has is strongly related to one's physical and mental health. You might recall some of the research we discussed in Chapter 4, which found that adults with strong ties to family and friends lived longer than those who were socially isolated. Social support appears to have a significant protective effect. Over 80 studies have examined the relationship between social support and health and have found a strong positive relationship. Those with more support have healthier cardiovascular, endocrine, and immune systems. Strong social support seems to slow some aspects of the biological aging that accompanies old age (Uchino, Cacioppo, & Kiecolt-Glaser, 1996). Related work shows that people who express high levels of satisfaction with the individuals they have placed in their inner circle tend to have high levels of psychological well-being (Antonucci, Fuhrer, & Dartigues, 1997). In a study of 271 women between the ages of 65 and 93, researchers found that low levels of well-being were strongly associated with low levels of contact with family members or friends. Well-being did not differ depending on whether the social contact was with family members or friends; both types of relationships were beneficial (Thompson & Heller, 1990).

Physical impairments, life satisfaction, and depression also are related to social support. Measures of these factors and several others were taken from 4734 adults who were 65 and older. Physical impairments were measured in several ways such as the ability to prepare food, walk, lift, climb steps, or shop. Social support measures looked at both family and friend networks and at how much instrumental and other (e.g., emotional, informational) support the individual perceived themselves as giving and receiving. Results indicated that physical impairments were associated with lower levels of contact with family and friends, and that people with impairments perceived themselves as receiving and giving less instrumental assistance. Lower social support seemed to be responsible for lower levels of life satisfaction. Symptoms of depression resulted from lower levels of instrumental support. This latter finding may be related to age changes in primary and secondary control (see Chapter 8). Older adults with impairments must rely on instrumental support from others in order to maintain some level of primary control over their environments and when that support is lacking they may exhibit signs of depression, as well as lower life satisfaction (Newsom & Schulz, 1996).

Social support is, thus, very positive and lack of such support can result in lower levels of physical and mental health. It is important, however, to point out that social support from family and friends can, in some instances, create, rather than relieve, negative

Support from others is invaluable during times of stress.

feelings and depression. This can result from continual arguments, or emotionally negative interactions, or if a person believes that some other person is taking away their independence. Imagine how you might feel if some other person entered your life and made all decisions about what you could do, where you could go, what you would wear, who you would socialize with, and so on. It would be like being a child again. You would probably be quite unhappy with this situation and seek to change it. When this happens to an older adult, particularly one with some disability, changing the situation can be very difficult and depression can result. Older adults must decide what support they need and who should provide it if they are to fully benefit from such support. (Krause, 1995b).

The relationships between the different measures of physical and psychological health and life satisfaction on the one hand, and social support on the other, are quite strong and several possible reasons have been suggested for these associations. Some believe that the important factors fall into three categories: social, psychological, and behavioral (Cohen, 1988). Social factors include the buffering of stress provided by family and friends. Stress is easier to handle if there is an ally close by to hold your hand. Stress shared with others may mean less stress for us. As we saw earlier (Chapter 4) stress reduction is very important for healthy functioning. Psychological factors refer to the positive emotions that family and friends engender. Contact with those in our social network is most often in the context of good times as family members visit on holidays or friends accompany us to concerts. They make us feel good. Social support seems to encourage positive feelings and discourage negative emotions (Cohen & Herbert, 1996).

The role of control fits in with psychological factors. Recent research has emphasized the role of control in social support (Antonnucci, 2001; Krause, 2001). Having a sense of control in your life is important and social support stimulates feelings of control and self-efficacy. When people support you, you get the message that you are a worthwhile and competent person, which helps you face the challenges of life. It may be a sense of control, received through social support, that produces better health and well-being and lower mortality. Behavioral factors refer to healthy and unhealthy behaviors that are thought to be influenced by those in our social networks. Our friends and family may nag us to quit smoking, drive slower, exercise more, eat healthier, and so on. They watch out for us. In a major review of articles that examined physical health and social support, researchers found that social support may produce many of its positive effects by reducing an individual's blood pressure, lessening reactivity to stress, decreasing body chemicals that influence heart rate and hormone levels, and improving functioning in humoral and cellular immune systems. Family and emotional support seem particularly important for these effects while changes in healthy (and unhealthy) behaviors did not seem to play a major role (Uchino, Cacioppo, & Kiecolt-Glaser, 1996).

One last thought about social support. We identified the different types of support provided by our network members. The person receiving the support also has different types of reception. We receive the actual help, or hug, or words of encouragement from our network. But we also receive what is called perceived support. This is how we view the help that others provide. If we think help is genuinely and lovingly given, we tend to think of the giver as a major support provider. On the other hand, if we think someone is helping us out of obligation or is coerced in some way, we do not feel like we have been helped. This perceived or subjective support can differ dramatically from the actual objective support provided. Moreover, it is the perceived support that is more highly related to health and well-being than objective support. This is important to remember when helping those we love. If we are helping because we "have" to help, we may not be really helping at all.

In sum, humans need strong social relations with others. Social relations provide social support and are related strongly to physical and psychological health and longevity. Our spouses, children, parents, grandparents, siblings, and friends are our most valuable asset. Think about how each of these types of people has provided you or your loved ones with social support across the lifespan.

Family Relationships

Family relationships have received more attention from researchers than any other type of relationship. This makes sense since most of the relationship types that we experience in our lives are those with various family members and such relationships are usually quite long-lasting. We have a set of caregivers, most typically one or two parents; we may have one or more siblings; we have extended families in our grandparents, aunts, uncles, cousins, and in-laws; we usually marry and have one or more children; and, most of us eventually become grandparents. In this section we examine the major types of family relationships including marriage, divorce, sexual relations, elder abuse, siblings, and grandparenting.

Marriage, Gay/Lesbian Unions, Divorce, and Remarriage

Marriage.   **Marriage** is the legal union of a man and woman as husband and wife. Of all relationships, marriage has been studied the most. There is some controversy about broadening the definition of marriage to include unions between same-sex couples. Most people get married at least once. In fact, about 95 percent of U.S. residents have been married at least once.

While many marriages last, almost 50 percent end in divorce. Divorce is the legal dissolution of a marriage. The divorce rate was at its highest in 1980 but has gone down since then. In 1980, close to 60 percent of marriages ended in divorce while in present times about 45 percent are expected to end in divorce (Whitbourne, 2001). If you add all the different lengths of marriages, counting some that last for 50 or more years while others last for less than 50 days, the average length of a marriage in the United States is only about 9.2 years (U.S. Bureau of the Census, 1997). Usually, divorce happens within the first three years of the marriage; men are usually in their early 30s and women in their late 20s at the time of this first divorce (Clarke, 1995).

These statistics have prompted researchers to investigate the factors that are responsible for long-lasting marriages and those responsible for divorce. Why do some marriages last while others do not? One factor is marital satisfaction. Marital satisfaction is usually measured by asking individuals to rate their overall satisfaction with a number of different aspects of their marriage. Figure 9-2 (p. 228) illustrates what has become known as the curvilinear pattern of marital satisfaction for couples who have remained married. The early years of the marriage, during young adulthood, are generally quite high in mar-

FIGURE 9-2   Curvilinear pattern of marital satisfaction over the course of a long-term marriage.

ital satisfaction—this seems reasonable. If satisfaction were not high the marriage might never have taken place or could end in divorce soon after the marriage. Marital satisfaction then declines with the birth of the first child. This also seems reasonable. That very high level of satisfaction during those early years could only change in one direction and typically declines as the couple settles into a routine and begins to raise a family. Middle-age couples, particularly those with children, often face increased financial obligations and less interaction with each other. Following the departure of the last child from home, marital satisfaction usually rises again. Financial obligations decline and interactions between husband and wife increase. This frequent pattern has been found in a large number of studies. The next most frequent pattern is one of relatively high marital satisfaction at all ages, with no decline in middle age (Anderson, Russell, & Schumm, 1983; Atchley, 2000; Weishaus & Field, 1988; White, Booth, & Edwards, 1986). In a survey of over 3000 married adults over the age of 50, 85 percent reported being satisfied and happy with their marriage (Brecher, 1984).

Another way to examine the factors that underlie long-lasting marriages is to compare couples who have been married for different numbers of years. The differences between middle-age and older married couples and between satisfied and dissatisfied married couples have been examined by Carstensen and her colleagues. One major study observed 35 satisfied middle-age couples, 47 dissatisfied middle-age couples, 43 older satisfied couples, and 31 older dissatisfied couples. The middle-age couples had been married for at least 15 years and had an average length of marriage of 44 years. Older couples had been married for at least 35 years and had an average length of marriage of 63 years. A video recording was made of each couple while they discussed three topics: the events of the day, an agreed-upon pleasant topic, and a problem that caused continued disagreement over the years of their marriage. Couples also were asked about specific problem areas such as money, children, communication, recreation, sex, and in-laws. Independent raters coded each videotape. Three major comparisons were made.

In comparing satisfied and dissatisfied couples, researchers found that satisfied couples had higher levels of physical and psychological health than did dissatisfied couples. As you might expect, satisfied couples were happier during their discussions and showed more affection while dissatisfied couples displayed more anger, sadness, and belligerence. In a comparison of husbands and wives, researchers found that wives in dissatisfied marriages reported higher levels of physical, psychological, and functional health problems than did their husbands. The researchers believe that marital dissatisfaction leads to lower levels of health rather than poor health causing dissatisfaction.

In comparing middle-age and older couples, researchers found that older couples had lower levels of disagreement and higher levels of affection than middle-age couples even when discussing problem areas. For older couples, children and grandchildren were

Still together after all these years.

a major source of pleasure while for many middle-age couples children were a problem area. Older couples seemed to approach their problems with more humor and affection for one another and negative emotions were rare (Carstensen, Gottman, & Levenson, 1995; Levenson, Carstensen, & Gottman, 1993). Although these comparisons were all cross-sectional, they suggest that older couples may have learned more effective ways of coping with life's problems, as we discussed in Chapter 8. We must, however, be cautious. These results do not tell us whether couples who have been married for a long time learn to use more affection and humor in dealing with problems or whether couples who were that way in the first place tend to stay married for longer periods of time.

Another approach taken by researchers has been to ask couples who have been married for a long time to explain why their marriage has lasted. Researchers Jeannette and Robert Lauer have taken this direct approach a couple of times. In one study they interviewed 351 couples who had been married for at least 15 years and found that husbands and wives agree on the top seven reasons for their long lasting relationship. The number one reason given was that "my spouse is my best friend." Other reasons included "I like my spouse as a person," "marriage is sacred," "we agree on aims and goals," "my spouse has grown more interesting," and "I want the relationship to succeed." Fewer than 10 percent mentioned sex as a major reason. In a second study, 100 older married couples who had been married for at least 45 years were interviewed to see if they would give the same reasons as middle-age couples. Once again, husbands and wives agreed on the major reasons for their long-term relationship and the reasons given were essentially the same as the ones given earlier by middle-age couples, with the addition of humor as an important part of a long-term marriage. Couples said they laughed together everyday, kissed each other daily, and confided in one another (Lauer & Lauer, 1985; Lauer, Lauer, & Kerr, 1990). It is important to note that as more longitudinal research is conducted with long-term relationships, many factors are emerging that are varied and unique to many couples (Bachand & Caron, 2001). It is clear that most husbands and wives are major sources of social support for one another.

As happily married as these couples may be, many must have had some times when satisfaction was lower. Remember that the most frequently found pattern is the one shown in Figure 9-2. Some research suggests that our memories of prior marital experiences might predict our future marital happiness and be influenced by our present level of satisfaction. Older adults may tend to alter their memory in favor of the choices they made (Grote & Freize, 1998; Mather & Johnson, 2000). If we are happy now, we may remember being happy in the past or that we are even happier now than we were previously. In one longitudinal study, a series of interviews conducted with older married couples, ages 75 to 95, found that few reported any dissatisfaction with their marriage and that those who had reported serious problems 40 years earlier tended not to remember those problems (Erikson, Erikson, & Kivnick, 1986).

In a more recent longitudinal study, 98 wives who were still married were interviewed and completed questionnaires in 1970, 1980, and 1990. At each point they were asked questions about their spouse's sensitivity, how much he confided in them, and how much they confided in him. At the last two interviews, they also were asked to remember how sensitive and confiding their spouse had been ten years earlier. Results showed that these wives tended to remember the past as worse than they had originally rated it. Their husbands were remembered as being less sensitive and confiding ten years ago than at present. They saw their marriage as being at the same high level of satisfaction or even better than it was in the past although though their ratings ten years ago were often higher than their present ratings (Karney & Coombs, 2000). People view their past through the eyes of the present. If things are fine now then they must have been fine then, although not quite as fine as now.

There are, of course, couples who have stayed together for most of their lives in less than satisfactory relationships. Many cases of spousal abuse continue into old age. Box 9-1 presents some of the research that has examined the abuse of older spouses and other older adults.

BOX **9-1**

Elder Abuse

The abuse of older adults, and of many other groups, occurs too often and has only begun to receive serious attention from researchers over the last 12 to 15 years. These researchers have described four different types of elder abuse. **Physical abuse** involves actual hitting, pushing, grabbing, assault with some weapon (such as a gun or knife), or other physical activities that cause pain. **Psychological abuse** is typically verbal insults or threats that often result in humiliation or fear in the older adult. **Financial abuse** involves withholding money or stealing money from an older person. **Neglect** means depriving the older person of some needed assistance, such as transportation, medicine, or nutrition. Elder abuse is believed to occur in 4 to 10 percent of adults aged 65 and older (Wolf, 1998).

The first large study of elder abuse was conducted in the late 1980s and used a random sample of 2020 older adults living in the Boston area. Interviews were conducted and researchers found that 2 percent reported physical abuse, 1.1 percent psychological abuse, and 0.4 percent neglect. Financial abuse was not examined. Most frequently the abuser was the individual's spouse and older men were abused as frequently as older women (Pillemer & Finkelhor, 1988). A similar study conducted in Canada found an overall abuse rate of 4 percent and the highest category was financial abuse at 2.5 percent (Podnieks, 1992). It is thought that many instances of elder abuse, particularly when the abuser is a spouse, go unreported.

A study of 5168 couples who were 19 years of age or older examined variables associated with abuse. Respondents were divided into young and old (over 60 years of age) groups. Elder abuse was far more likely in situations where the husband had a lower level of education (wife's education did not seem to play a role), when family income was low, when depression was present, and when abuse had occurred earlier in the relationship (Harris, 1996).

Other researchers have looked at adult responses to different scenarios to determine when abuse is or is not perceived to be present. One such study presented six different scenarios to 105 college students and asked them to rate whether abuse was present in the scenario, whether the caregiver or the older adult was the abuser, and how justifiable the abuse was. Scenarios included a situation where a daughter throws a frying pan at her mother, where a daughter threatens to poison her mother's food, where a daughter withholds money belonging to her mother, and where a daughter refuses to take her mother to a doctor's appointment. Students also answered questions

(continued)

BOX **9-1**   **Continued**

about their relationships with their grandparents. Results showed that students found caregiver abuse to be more justifiable when the older adult was portrayed as being agitated or senile but less so when the older adult was helpless. Students who reported closer contact and more involvement with their grandparents over the course of their lives found more instances of unjustifiable abuse on the part of the portrayed caregivers in the scenarios than did students who were not as close to their grandparents (Mills, Vermette, & Malley-Morrison, 1998). Is abuse okay if the older person is being annoying? Is it okay to slap older adults, children, and even babies if they cry too much? How close are you to your grandparents?

Other work has examined cross-cultural differences in the perception of elder abuse and the prevalence of such abuse. In one study older African, Korean, and White American women aged 60 to 75 were interviewed and asked to respond to 13 scenarios created by the researchers (six of these same scenarios were used in the study above). For each scenario, women were asked if there was any abuse, to rate its severity, and to tell whether they would call for help if they witnessed such a situation. Although no differences were obtained between African and White American women's responses, Korean American women were less likely to perceive a situation as abusive and less likely to call for help. Korean American women told the interviewer that they would not want to bring shame to the family or to create conflict (Moon & Williams, 1993).

A study of elder abuse in Japan analyzed 235 cases of reported abuse and found neglect to be the most frequent type of abuse occurring in more than half the cases. The most frequent abuser was the daughter-in-law. In many Japanese families the son and his family live with his parents, the son is not expected to help with any household work, other sons and daughters also are not expected to participate, and the burden of caring for his aging parents falls fully on the daughter-in-law(s) (Soeda & Araki, 1999). This situation is quite different from the one found in U.S. culture where the spouse is the most frequent abuser.

What can be done to decrease elder abuse? Part of the answer is assumed to be education. The more people who know about elder abuse, the more likely it is to be detected, reported, and stopped. Forty-two states now have laws that require healthcare workers to report suspected instances of elder abuse (Lachs & Pillemer, 1995). Several large cities also have special programs that are funded by grants and/or local human services agencies to deal with cases of elder abuse (Wolf & Pillemer, 1994). Unfortunately, it is probably the case that elder abuse goes undetected, unreported, or reported but ignored in too many cases. We hope you will be watchful and willing to report any instances of elder or other abuse to the appropriate authorities.

Gay and Lesbian Unions.   Although marriage between gay and lesbian partners is not often legally sanctioned, there are many long-term relationships of homosexual couples (Peplau, 1991). However, research has failed to include this population in studies of older marriage or long-term relationships. It may not, however, be the fault of researchers. Older gay and lesbian couples may have been difficult to find. It is important to remember that today's cohorts of gay and lesbian older adults grew up in a time of strong hostility against homosexuals. They were forced to hide their sexual orientation and their relationships. Most gay couples kept their relationships secret to avoid discrimination from employers, family, friends, and society. Not all gay and lesbian older couples have remained in hiding. But those who have been open about their relationships have had to develop coping strategies to deal with discrimination. In a study of how older homosexual couples have adapted to societal expectations, researchers found that the experience of "coming out" strengthened the resources for meeting late-life challenges (Quam & Whitford, 1992).

Not having legal status has presented gay older couples with many obstacles. Adoption of children by unmarried couples was not allowed so many long-term gay couples are childless, unless one partner brought children from a previous marriage. Typically this was frowned upon. Healthcare systems still routinely discriminate against gay couples. When one partner is hospitalized, the other partner is often denied access to areas restricted to "next of kin." Without a power of attorney, hospital personnel do not recognize the authority of gay partners to make healthcare decisions. Finally, even with a will, many older gay survivors find that family members successfully contest their right to inheritance.

Although no study yet has examined relationship satisfaction longitudinally in gay and lesbian couples, some insights are provided by a few studies of gay and lesbian relationships. Raymond Berger interviewed 92 male gay couples ages 24 to 70 years to determine how their relationships began and how they were maintained. Similar to the findings for heterosexual couples, communication was an important factor in staying together. Major conflicts focused on finances and relations with family members (1990). Other work suggests that long-term companion relationships of gay men and lesbians are most successful when the couple has created a supportive network of friends and family (Kimmel, 1992). A review of the literature on family lives of lesbians and gay men concluded that the picture of lesbian and gay relationships emerging from the research is one of positive adjustment, even in the face of stressful conditions (Patterson, 2000).

We need more research to examine long-term gay and lesbian relationships. Stoller and Gibson (2000) caution about generalizing findings from heterosexual couples to all couples. We do not yet have a true and complete picture of how all older families meet the challenges of aging. Those gay and lesbian elders in long-term relationships may be the hardy.

Divorce.   The probability of divorce is higher for people who marry at a younger age, people who live together before marrying, and people who had parents who divorced (Bumpass, Martin, & Sweet, 1991; Axinn & Thornton, 1992). Many are surprised that couples who lived together before marrying have a higher divorce rate but the finding seems to be reliable. African American women are most likely to divorce (Clarke, 1995). One factor that plays a role in this latter finding is the probability of remarriage. All of these general findings do not, however, tell us what goes wrong or goes wrong more often in these particular marriages. To examine the underlying factors, researchers have had to use similar approaches to those used in studying long-lasting marriages.

One way to investigate the factors underlying divorce is to ask divorcees why they divorced. Using this strategy, one study surveyed 275 men and 336 women who had divorced. The average age of respondents was 33.6, the average length of marriage before the divorce was 11.5 years, and all divorcees had minor children. The three most frequently named problems were the same for men and women: communication, basic unhappiness, and incompatibility. Men named their own abuse of alcohol and the women's liberation movement more often than women named these causes, while women named emotional abuse, husband's infidelity, and physical abuse more often than men. Children were rarely mentioned as a problem (Cleek & Pearson, 1985). Other research also has found infidelity to be a frequent cause of divorce occurring in as many as one-third of examined cases (South & Lloyd, 1995). One problem with this type of research is that individuals may remember things differently once they have decided to divorce or actually experienced a divorce. Perhaps some of the factors named are those that were revealed during the divorce proceedings but that did not actually cause the proceedings. To solve this problem, researchers examined the problems reported before a divorce is considered.

One study examined the marital problems reported by over 2000 married people and then followed those individuals for 12 years. After the 12 years, those reported problems were examined as causes for divorce in those couples who had divorced or permanently separated. In reporting problems, wives reported more total problems than husbands did and named themselves as often as they named their husbands as the source of the problem. Husbands, however, tended to name themselves as the source of the problem more often than they named their wives. The problems that were the strongest predictors of a future divorce were jealousy, infidelity, foolish spending, irritating habits, and the use of drugs or alcohol (Amato & Rogers, 1997). A shorter longitudinal study also examined problems among 47 married couples and observed their interactions. Three years later several of these couples had divorced and an analysis was done to see which factors measured at the beginning of the study were most predictive of these divorces. Researchers found that when husbands had low levels of affection for their wives, when both husband and wife expressed negative feelings and disappointment in the marriage, and when both acted as individuals rather than as a couple, divorce was predicted correctly in all seven couples who divorced. These factors, however, also predicted divorce in three of the 40 couples who remained married (Buehlman, Gottman, & Katz, 1992).

The consequences of divorce can be quite severe for some people. Women are more likely to suffer economic hardship following a divorce than are men. Some of this difference is due to the fact that many divorced men avoid paying alimony and/or child support. It is typical for a man's standard of living to increase after a divorce while a woman's is most likely to decrease. Men are more likely to lose custody of their children than are women. In 72 percent of divorce cases where children are involved, the woman is granted custody while only 9 percent of such cases result in the man receiving custody. Divorced individuals show higher rates of emotional and physical disturbances than single, married, or remarried persons. They are more likely to die from cancer, heart disease, cirrhosis of the liver, or in an accident (Clarke, 1995; Heatherington, 1979; Heatherington, Stanley-Hagan, & Anderson, 1989; Wallerstein & Kelly, 1976).

These findings suggest that, as with long-lasting marriages, there are a number of factors that play an important role in divorce. Infidelity and the inability or unwillingness to communicate with one another seem to be the most significant factors.

Remarriage.   "Well I'm glad that's over. Whew, what a relief to be away from that *%$#*#. I'll never make that mistake again. The next time I marry I'm going to make sure that they're the right choice." Many people who divorce, remarry with exactly this belief. "I'll do it right the next time." The probability of a divorce is, however, actually higher for a remarriage than for a first marriage (Martin & Bumpass, 1989). Furthermore, second marriages, on average, last about one year less than first marriages and third marriages are shorter, on average, than second marriages (Clarke, 1995). Instead of getting better, do things get worse with each subsequent marriage? People who have been divorced may find it easier to choose divorce when marital satisfaction declines and may even turn to divorce for fewer reasons than they did the first (or second) time. Things may not really be worse in a second, or subsequent marriage, but remarried people may be less willing to take as many bumps as they did the first time.

Many more men than women remarry and many more younger divorcees than older divorcees remarry (U.S. Bureau of the Census, 1997). One reason for the high rate of divorce among African American women, that we mentioned earlier, is that their exhusbands are far more likely to remarry than they are. On average, a remarriage follows a divorce by about three years (Furstenberg, 1982; Glick & Ling-Lin, 1986). In a longitudinal study of 2180 Canadians ages 67 to 102, gender differences emerged in the effect of marital status on life satisfaction. Men losing a spouse had a much larger drop in life satisfaction than did women and the same amount of increase in life satisfaction when they gained a spouse. Women showed a decrease in life satisfaction if they remained unmarried or married, they became less satisfied with their lives over time. Men showed no change over time in stable marital conditions (Chipperfield & Havens, 2001). Think back to our discussion of social support to explain these results.

Alfred Tennyson said it is "better to have loved and lost, than never to have loved at all." People who have divorced may have experienced love once while those who have never married may never have experienced love at all. Do you think Tennyson was right? Research suggests that he may have been wrong. In a survey of 3390 adults age 55 and older, researchers examined relationships such as marriage, divorce, remarriage, widowhood, and being single and the overall loneliness of the people in these various relationships. Several interesting results were obtained. People with an intimate partner, whether in marriage or cohabitation, were less lonely than all other groups. People in their first marriage were less lonely than those who were remarried. This difference in loneliness may be a contributing factor to the higher divorce rate for remarried couples. More loneliness was found for men without a partner than for women without a partner but no differences were found for women and men with partners. Both men and women benefit from a loving relationship but without such a relationship, men are lonelier than women. Finally, with respect to Tennyson, those who never had a partner were less lonely than those who once had a partner but no longer did (Peters & Liefbroer, 1997). Having loved and lost resulted in more loneliness. Keep in mind, however, that those with a partner had the very lowest levels of loneliness. It is better to love. It is losing that is not good.

Sexual Relations

Sexual relations are not mentioned frequently as a factor in long-lasting marriages or as a problem that led to divorce. Nevertheless, sex is an important part of life for most younger people but not for very many older people. Did you believe that last statement? Although it is a common belief that once you are old you are no longer sexually active, it just is not true. Do you think of your parents or grandparents (or great-grandparents) as being sexually active? Most likely they are.

Sexual Activity.   Sexual activities are almost always examined by use of a survey and typically quite a large number of people respond. It is not easy, however, for researchers to decide what to ask. Does one ask about sexual activity without specifying which activities count? Is masturbation an activity to be included or are we only interested in intercourse? What about oral sex? Is frequency enough information or should we also ask about the quality of the experience? Various surveys have answered these questions differently and this may contribute to some differences in obtained results. It is also the case that in a survey we must always rely on what people tell us although there is always the chance that some proportion of respondents are less than truthful about their sexual relations and activities. Data on sexual activities obtained via surveys are nearly always cross-sectional making it difficult to determine whether obtained differences are due to age, cohort, or both.

In surveys comparing the reported frequency of sexual activities among younger, middle-age, and older adults, the general and typical finding is that of less activity the older the respondents are (Pfeiffer, Verwoerdt, & Davis, 1972). For example, in one such survey, younger adults (18 to 39 years of age) reported having intercourse 78 times a year, middle-age (40 to 49 years) 67 times a year, older middle-age (50 to 59 years) 46 times, and young-old (60 to 69 years) 23 times (Seidman & Rieder, 1994). While the frequency of activity decreases, research shows that satisfaction with that activity does not. In a study

Your kiss is still so sweet.

of 800 adults between the ages of 60 and 91, 36 percent said that their sexual activities were better now than when they were younger (Starr & Weiner, 1981).

One survey of 807 adults over the age of 60 asked about sexual activity, education, health, self-esteem, religion, marital satisfaction, and shared activities. Sexual activity was measured by asking "about how often did you and your husband/wife have sex during the past month?" Results showed that the frequency of sexual activity was lower for the oldest adults with 65 percent of those age 60 to 65 reporting at least one instance of sex with a spouse (or significant other) during the past month, 55 percent of those 66 to 70, 45 percent of those 71 to 75, and 24 percent of those 76 and older. For those who did report sexual activity, 72 percent reported having had sex between one and four times during the past month while 7 percent reported having had sex ten or more times. No differences were found between men and women or African and White Americans in terms of sexual frequency. In another survey of 800 older adults age 60 to 91, close to 80 percent reported that they were sexually active and most had intercourse at least once a week (Ade-Ridder, 1990; Starr & Weiner, 1981). Health and self-esteem are related to frequency. Those with better health and healthy spouses and those with higher levels of self-esteem have more frequent sexual relations (Marsiglio & Donnelly, 1991).

In a more recent survey, people were asked about sexual activity and satisfaction. Satisfaction was measured on a 5-point scale. Results showed that those with better mental health reported higher levels of satisfaction than those with lower levels of mental health even when the level of sexual activity was the same. Married women were far more likely to have sexual activity than unmarried women while marital status made little difference for men. Two-thirds of those who reported sexual activity said that they were satisfied or very satisfied with such activities (Matthias, Lubben, Atchison, & Schweitzer, 1997).

Research on sexuality in older gay or lesbian individuals has not been very extensive. Those studies that have been done have obtained similar results to those found with heterosexuals. Older homosexuals tend to report that they are still active although often to a lesser degree than when they were younger, still find sexual relations satisfying, and, in many cases, regard sex as less important than it was previously, although still important. Older lesbians seem to be more likely than older gay men to discontinue sex altogether just as older heterosexual women are less likely than men to engage in sexual activities. Older gay men tend to prefer partners who are about the same age as they are but are less likely than heterosexual partners to have sexual relations with only one other person (Adelman, 1990; Berger, 1982; Christenson & Johnson, 1973; Pope, 1997; Pope & Schulz, 1990; Van-de-Ven, Rodden, Crawford, & Kippax, 1997).

The last survey that we will discuss was given to very old adults. Respondents were 100 men and 102 women ranging in age from 80 to 102. This survey asked 117 questions about health, marital status, and sexuality. Sex questions used a 7-point rating scale and asked about sexual interest, daydreaming about sex, intimacy with a partner, past and present importance and frequency of sex, touching/caressing without intercourse, intercourse, and masturbation. Results showed that although these older adults rated sex as having been more important in their past lives than in the present, two-thirds of the men and 38 percent of the women still regarded sex as important. At the time of the survey, only 14 percent of the women and 29 percent of the men were still married. Nevertheless, 25 percent of the women and 53 percent of the men reported having a regular sex partner. Activities with this partner included intercourse for 62 percent of the men and 30 percent of the women and touching/caressing without intercourse for 83 percent of the men and 64 percent of the women. Finally, 29 percent of the men and 50 percent of the women did not answer the questions regarding masturbation. Of those who did, 72 percent of the men and 40 percent of the women reported occasional masturbation. One important finding related to the decreases in frequency that are usually found with advanced age is that no significant decreases in frequency past the age of 80 were found in this survey (Bretschneider & McCoy, 1988).

In summarizing these results, it seems clear that interest in sexual relations, sexual activity in different forms, and certainly sexual satisfaction continue into very old age for both hetero- and homosexual men and women. At the same time, it appears that interest in and amount of activity decrease for many as they enter older age around the age of 60. That decrease may not, however, continue but may instead level off around age 80. Sexual interest, activity, and satisfaction are generally higher for those who are healthy, married, confident, educated, and well-tuned into their social networks. Remember the benefits of social support and you may see a link with these factors.

Explanations for Changes in Sexuality. The most frequently found change in sexual activity for older adults is a decrease in frequency although that decrease may level off past the age of 80. Although we feel obligated to express some caution since these data were obtained in cross-sectional comparisons, it is also true that these data were collected at several points in time and, as a result, a number of different cohorts have been compared. This suggests an age, rather than cohort, difference. The most frequent explanations for this decrease are changes that occur in hormones, physiology, health, availability of a partner, and social acceptability.

As you learned in Chapter 2, men and women experience changes in the relative quantities of male and female sex hormones as they grow older. For women these changes are more abrupt as they go through menopause while for men the changes are more gradual. Menopause does seem to exert some influence over the sexual activities of women. One study found that close to 30 percent of women reported a decline in sex drive associated with menopause (Sheehy, 1992). Rather than being a direct cause for this decline in interest in sex, it is thought that menopause is an indirect cause. Many women report that menopause means that you are now an old woman and old women are not expected to have sexual desires (Wilk & Kirk, 1995). For men, the decline in hormones does not seem to play a major role in decreased sexual activity (Segraves & Segraves, 1995).

Some changes in physiology with advanced age do seem to be involved in the obtained decreases in sexual activity. For men, reduction in nerve cells in the peripheral nervous system that frequently occur in older adults (see Chapter 2) seem to contribute to difficulties in obtaining and maintaining an erection. Some work has reported more frequent problems with obtaining and longer time to obtain an erection for older than for younger men (Mulligan & Katz, 1989). The older penis is not as sensitive (Berger, Rothman, & Rigaud, 1994). Reduced blood flow to the penis is another major factor in reduced sexual activity for men, reductions in blood flow are frequently the result of smoking (Rieske & Holstege, 1996). Constriction of smaller blood vessels are a result of the intake

of nicotine (see Chapter 4). For women, the thinning of the vaginal wall that frequently occurs with advanced age after menopause and a reduction in lubrication often leads to pain
during intercourse and, thus, lower levels of such activity. One study found this problem
in 12 percent of women 60 years of age and older (Masters & Johnson, 1981).

Health factors seem to exert considerable influence on the sexual activities of older
adults but the influence may be indirect. In one study, 1290 men between the ages of 40
and 70 provided information about their health and their sexual activities. Diabetes, heart
disease, and hypertension were associated with the difficulties that several older men had
in obtaining an erection. The medications used to treat these disorders rather than or in
addition to the disorder itself may, however, have been responsible for these difficulties
(Goldstein & Hatzichristou, 1994). Psychiatric medications also have been implicated as
a contributor to sexual dysfunction in both men and women, and women with multiple
sclerosis seem to have difficulty in achieving orgasm (Segraves & Segraves, 1995).

For women, but not men, the decreased availability of a partner in older age is
another factor in decreased sexual activity. Women tend to marry older men, live longer,
become widowed, and outnumber older men, their most likely partners, by more than two
to one. Even when male partners are present, they may be unable to perform for reasons
such as those given above (Roughan, Kaiser, & Morley, 1993).

The social acceptability of sexual activities in older adults is still another factor that
seems to influence the prevalence of such behaviors. Most people do not realize that older
adults are still sexually active. In fact, a number of people think that the idea of older adults
having sex is repulsive. Still others regard the idea of older adults having sex as a joke. A
large proportion of jokes about aging are jokes about the loss of ability to perform sexually (Palmore, 1971). Sexual activity or even affection between older persons is frequently
seen as being only "cute" or even "dirty." Even college students often hold such views and
are surprised to learn that most older adults are still sexually active. In one survey, one-
quarter of students believed their parents never had sex anymore and one-half believed that
their parents had sex very infrequently (Pocs, Godrow, Tolone, & Walsh, 1977).

These false beliefs about and negative attitudes toward sex and old age are thought
to influence a number of older adults and lead them to give up sex prematurely (Hooyman
& Kiyak, 1996; Teitelman, 1990). If sex was mostly kept behind closed doors in your cohort; if you see that sex among older adults is regarded as comical, rare, and socially unacceptable; or if you believe that sex is dangerous to your health or simply not possible
after menopause and other physical changes, then you might tend to quit engaging in such
activities. Giving up sexual activity is especially prevalent among residents of nursing
homes where staff may have very narrow views about sexual activities among older residents and may actively inhibit any sexuality on the part of residents (Glass, Mustian, &
Carter, 1986). Some researchers have compared the responses of staff and older residents
of long-term care facilities to questions about their knowledge of and attitudes toward sexuality among older adults. When asked how important sexuality was, 75 percent of the
staff but only 50 percent of older residents responded that it was very important. On other
questions, more older adults than staff agreed that sex improved quality of life, that relationships among residents should be encouraged, and that sexuality promotes well-being.
When asked whether members of the staff should help get erotic videos or magazines
for residents, 43 percent of the residents but only 10 percent of the staff said yes (Walker,

Osgood, Richardson, & Ephross, 1998). Sex may not be regarded as very important compared to the other things that residents of such facilities must deal with but it is viewed as a significant contributor to well-being and quality of life and, clearly, is desired by a number of residents.

Siblings

Siblings are usually the longest social relationship that individuals have. Your older siblings have known you since you were born and your younger siblings have known you since their own birth (or shortly thereafter). Siblings, like parents, are not a social relationship that we choose. Having siblings is beyond our control. Like them or not, they are still our siblings.

Most people have at least one sibling and close to 80 percent of older adults have at least one living brother or sister. When asked how close they felt to the sibling(s) that they see most often, most older adults report being close or very close while a small minority, only 5 percent, report not being close at all (Atchley, 2000; Bedford, 1996). Close relationships can be of several different kinds and researchers have attempted to characterize these different kinds of close and not-so-close sibling relationships.

Deborah T. Gold and her colleagues (1989, 1990; Gold, Woodbury & George, 1990) have provided the most commonly used typology of sibling relationships. These types were arrived at by interviewing 30 men and 30 women who were 65 years of age or older and who had at least one living sibling. Transcripts of the interviews were rated for evidence of feelings such as closeness, envy, resentment, emotional support, approval, amount of contact, and other factors. Five types of sibling relationships were revealed and are summarized in Table 9-1. Intimate siblings are very close and are friends that one can confide in at any time. Congenial siblings are also close and friendly but not as close as spouse or adult child. Loyal siblings are close because they belong to the same family; they may or may not like one another. Apathetic siblings do not like or dislike one another; they are indifferent. Hostile siblings avoid one another and are resentful and/or angry with each other. In a later analysis of these relationship types, four rather than the original five, types of relationships were identified. Later analysis showed that the apathetic and hostile relationship types were very much the same on several measures, such as amount of contact between siblings.

Research on the proportion of older sibling relationships that fall into each of these types for African and White American older adults shows significant group differences. For White Americans congenial (30 percent) and loyal (34 percent) relationships are most common. Intimate relationships occur infrequently (14 percent) but apathetic (11 percent) and hostile (11 percent) relationships occur too often. Nearly one-quarter of White American sibling relationships were classified as negative. For African Americans loyal relationships (55 percent) are the most common, followed by congenial (20 percent) and intimate (20 percent) relationships. Apathetic (2 percent) and hostile (3 percent) relationships are very uncommon. Negative relationships were found in only 5 percent of African American siblings. The most positive emotional relationships for both groups tended to be sister to sister (Gold, 1990).

Your relationship with your sibling(s) and how often you contact one another are undoubtedly influenced by a number of factors, and this is true for all adults. Research has

TABLE 9-1   Type of Sibling Relationships Identified by Gold (1989)

Type	Characteristics
Intimate	Strong feelings of love and trust; may regard each other as best friends; have frequent contact (through visits, letters, e-mail, phone); provide support and whenever it is needed without being asked.
Congenial	Feelings of love and trust; may regard each other as good friends; contact is less frequent; feel closer to their spouse or children; provide support if asked; get along well with one another.
Loyal	Relationship is based on beliefs about family ties and responsibilities that siblings have to be a good brother or sister; may not have much contact except at traditional family gatherings.
Apathetic	Rarely contact or even think about each other; no strong positive or negative emotions about each other; it is as if they have no sibling(s).
Hostile	Feelings of resentment, anger, and occasionally envy toward each other; no intentional contact and effort to avoid each other; usually a result of some specific event (battle over an inheritance, feeling less loved by a parent, and so on).

revealed several life events and situations that generally improve but can worsen these relationships under some circumstances. In one study extensive interviews were conducted with 120 adults ages 20 to over 80 who had at least one living sibling. Results showed that marriage and having children usually had little effect on the sibling relationship while divorce, widowhood, illness, or death of a close family member usually strengthened the relationship (Connidis, 1992). Other work suggests that these same events can, in some circumstances, result in renewed antagonism between siblings. The death of a parent may eliminate any perceived obligation to remain quiet about perceived injustice and siblings may confront or avoid one another following the funeral. Generally, however, sibling relationships grow stronger as siblings grow older and in cases where there were earlier disagreements and negative feelings, they tend to lessen (Schulman, 1999).

Frequency of contact also is influenced by several factors. Siblings are more likely to remain in contact with one another when they are emotionally close to one another, feel responsibilities to the family, and live in close proximity. Women, particulary sister-sister pairs, are more likely than men to maintain contact and people without children tend to feel more obliged to maintain contact than those with children. People with children feel more obligation toward their children than toward their siblings (Lee, Mancini, & Maxwell, 1990).

When help is needed, those without a spouse or children are more likely to turn to a sibling for help than are those with a spouse or children (Connides, 1994). Most older adults are confident that they could call on a sibling for help if needed but that spouse and children, if present, would be called on first (Cicirelli, 1985). Siblings may be the next line of support following an individuals own nuclear family but fewer than 5 percent of older adults are cared for by siblings (Coward, Horne, & Dwyer, 1992). We saw earlier that social support is important at all ages. Given the length of the sibling relationship, you might think that these individuals would provide an important lifespan source of social support. In fact, many people report just that. But siblings may be more likely to play a role in lifelong psychological support, which is not often reported in the research. More research on the role of siblings and lifelong social support is needed.

Intergenerational Relationships

Intergenerational relationships are relationships between parents and adult children, grandparents and grandchildren and, of course, children, parents, and grandparents. Other relationships exist. Most people have some aunts, uncles, and cousins, but these other relationships have received little attention from gerontology researchers.

Parents and Children.   Relationships between parents and young children or adolescents are a topic for courses in child or adolescent development or lifespan development. Our discussion will, thus, be limited to parents and their adult children. Recall our earlier discussion of how marital satisfaction increases when young adult children leave home. This is in contrast to the belief that women, particularly, and parents in general, have a great deal of trouble when their nest is empty. **Empty nest** refers to the transitional state of parenting when the last child leaves the home. In fact, only a few parents have difficulty when children leave. Women who have invested the majority of their time in parenting, to the exclusion of other activities, do have some trouble adjusting when the last child is gone. Some fathers regret that they did not spend more time with their children. But the vast majority of parents see the empty nest as a relief from the constant pressure and work of childraising, and a normal transition in the life of parenthood (Rubin, 1979).

Over the last 20 years, more adult children have continued to live with their parents or returned to their parents' home after residing elsewhere for some brief period of time. For example, an adult might return to a parents' home following a divorce. One national survey found that 30 percent of parents had an adult child between the ages of 22 and 24 living with them, 19 percent had a child between the ages of 25 and 29, and 10 percent had a child 30 years of age or older (Hamner & Turner, 1996). Two-parent homes are more likely to have an adult child living with them than are homes with only one parent or homes in which a remarriage has taken place. The adult child who is most likely to live with parents is one attending a school that is within commuting distance from the parents' home. These situations require careful consideration of parent-child division of labor, differences in lifestyle, economic issues, and setting of rules. Who does the laundry, cooking, and cleaning? Does the child pay rent? Can friends be invited over anytime or only at certain times? Is staying out all night acceptable? Most families deal successfully with these issues. The opposite situation, a parent moving in with an adult child, usually occurs because of a crisis involving a parent's health and the need for care. These relationships are typically handled quite well but do sometimes deteriorate because the child did not fully understand the demands of caregiving, conflicts between caregiving and employment, or a need for professional caregiving that arises as the health of the parent grows worse (Brackbill & Kitch, 1991). You will learn more about these situations in Chapter 12. In most situations parents and adult children do not live together.

The amount of contact between parents and adult children who do not live together varies as a function of number of adult children, proximity, and affection. Parents with only one adult child do not have contact as frequently as parents with more than one adult child but still 75 percent have contact at least once a week with their one child (Uhlenberg & Cooney, 1990). Parents and children who feel strong affection for each other maintain contact even at great distance and most parents and children report strong positive feelings. Parents remain concerned about their child's welfare regardless of that child's age. Having a child with serious problems is a major cause of parent depression (Pillemer & Suitor, 1991).

The quality of the parent-adult child relationship is influenced by a number of events. An examination of some of these events was conducted by surveying several thousand adult children in 1988 and again in 1994. These surveys were part of the National Survey of Families and Households (NSFH). Close to 60 percent of the relationships did not change over that time period while 20 percent improved and another 20 percent got worse. Relationships tended to improve when a parent's health improved, when the child got married, when a son's work hours increased, or when a son (but not a daughter) had an additional (not a first) child. Relationships tended to worsen when parents divorced, when a daughter got divorced (but not when a son did), or when a daughter's work hours increased. Having a first child or remaining single had no consistent effect on the quality of the relationship. Women who remained single were among those reporting either improved or worsened relationships with their mothers (Kaufman & Uhlenberg, 1998). One can imagine both of these cases as some parents support their single child while others show great impatience. While there are many reasons for remaining single, one may be competence in managing a romantic relationship. Some recent work suggests that the success of romantic relationships for adult children is strongly influenced by the nurturance they received from their parents when they were much younger. Those who had very nurturant parents were seen to be supportive and warm toward romantic partners and to show far less hostility than those from less nurturant parents (Conger, Cui, Bryant, & Elder, Jr., 2000).

Grandparents and Grandchildren.   Unlike becoming a parent, becoming a grandparent is not something that an individual can choose to do. Your children decide for you and, usually, they decide to have children. Using data from 10,008 people interviewed in the NSFH, researchers estimate that about 67 percent of adults with children of childbearing age are grandparents and that 95 percent of those with children age 40 and older are grandparents. The older your children are, the more likely you will have grandchildren. Most individuals become grandparents before reaching age 50 and, with the increasing numbers of older adults and longer life expectancy, it is estimated that 50 percent are great-grandparents. On average, African Americans become grandparents at a younger age than White Americans because they tend to marry earlier and bear children at a younger age. Most grandparents in the survey had more than one grandchild and the average number of grandchildren was between five and six (Kivnick & Sinclair, 1996; Szinovacz, 1998).

Grandparents play a number of different roles in the family depending on the family itself and particular situations that arise. Grandparents may serve as historians telling grandchildren stories of the family's history and keeping track of extended family members, as mediators when conflicts arise between parents and children or siblings, as sources of values and role models for younger members of the extended family, and even as surrogate parents for grandchildren when parents are unable to fill that role themselves (Atchley, 2000). Table 9-2 gives examples of some of the more common roles played by different grandparents. You may be able to characterize your own grandparents as filling one, or more, of these roles. The number of grandparents raising grandchildren has increased over the last decades of the twentieth century and is now just over 5 percent of all families (*Population Today*, 1999). That is close to 4 million children and adolescents being raised by their grandparents. Box 9-2 describes some of the issues and problems involved in these grandparent as parent situations.

As with parents and adult children, research on grandparents and grandchildren has focused on many of the same issues. Of great interest has been contact between grandparents and grandchildren and the quality of the relationship. Contact between grandparents and young grandchildren is controlled by parents and is influenced by such factors as number of grandchildren and proximity. The portrayal of grandparents in young children's literature has shown that they are generally shown in stereotypic ways: being gray, balding, and wrinkled; wearing out-of-style clothing; and needing help from others, rather than as independent, up-to-date older persons (McElhoe, 1999). When young children, ages 3 to 11, have been asked to categorize older adults, they tend to say that older adults are ugly, sick, and tired all the time (Taylor, 1980). Some of these perceptions, undoubtedly, come from the literature that young children read and have read to them. However, when children have been asked about their own grandparents they tend to view them positively, particularly when contact is frequent. They are not seen in the same way as ordinary older adults or as the grandparents portrayed in childrens' stories (Creasey & Kaliher, 1994). A description of grandparents written by a 9-year-old girl exemplifies some of the positive views of grandparents:

> A grandmother is a lady who has no children of her own, so she likes other people's little ones. A grandfather is a man grandmother . . . they drive us to the market where the pretend

TABLE 9-2   Examples of Roles Filled by Grandparents

Companion or fun-seeker	See grandchildren at least 4 to 5 times a year; very affectionate and playful; enjoys activities with grandchildren
Remote or formal	See grandchildren infrequently, interactions are reserved and formal; limited assistance provided to parents
Involved or surrogate	See grandchildren at least 4 to 5 times a year; frequent exchange of services and may watch grandchildren regularly or even assume parenting responsibilities
Reservoir of family wisdom	Authoritarian; dispenses advice, information, and resources to grandchildren

Source: Based on the work of Cherlin & Furstenberg, 1985 and Neugarten & Weinstein, 1964.

BOX **9-2**

Grandparents as Parents Again

A great many grandparents find themselves in the role of parent again as they open their home and arms to their grandchildren. In 1970, 3.2 percent of children under the age of 18 lived with their grandparents but in 1999, that figure had grown to 5.4 percent (*Population Today*, 1999). More than 10 percent of grandparents have raised one or more grandchildren for at least six months and most of these have been parents again for more than three years. About 12 percent of African American grandparents have had this experience and about 4 percent of White American grandparents (Thomas, Sperry, & Yarbrough, 2000). Grandmothers who are younger and who never completed high school are the most frequent grandparents to find themselves raising their grandchildren (Minkler & Fuller-Thomson, 2000). The family situations most likely to need grandparents to raise grandchildren are when there is some form of substance abuse on the part of the grandchildren's parents, when the parents are unable to care for the child, when there has been child neglect, and when the parent has psychological (e.g., clinical depression) or financial problems (Sands & Goldberg-Glen, 2000). A number of recent studies have looked at the effects this situation has on the well-being of grandchildren and grandparents.

In an examination of 3111 participants in the National Survey of Families and Households who were grandparents, it was found that 158 were the primary caregivers for their grandchildren at the time of data collection. These caregivers were twice as likely as other grandparents to exhibit symptoms of depression. Grandmothers showed higher levels of depression than grandfathers and those who recently became parents for their grandchildren showed higher levels of depression than those who had been fullfilling that role for a longer period of time. Grandparent caregivers who were older and in good health had lower levels of depression but these levels were still higher than grandparents who were not caring for their grandchildren (Minkler, Fuller-Thomson, Miller, & Driver, 1997). Grandparents with chronic arthritis perceive themselves as having great difficulty serving as primary caregivers and, as a result, tend to feel angry, frustrated, guilty, and depressed (Barlow, Cullen, Foster, Harrison, & Wade, 1999). One interesting study found different effects for grandmothers and grandfathers while raising grandchildren. Grandmothers showed more depression when grandchildren first moved into their home but grandfathers showed more depression when grandchildren moved out. It is thought that grandfathers may be less involved in actual custodial care but benefit from the companionship and being viewed as a wise elder when the grandchildren are in their home. When they leave, grandfathers lose these benefits (Szinovacz, DeViney, & Atkinson, 1999).

Grandchildren living with their grandparents are more likely to have some behavioral, emotional, school-related, or neurological problems than those living with their parents. The presence of such problems create more difficulties for the grandparents and result in poorer grandparent-grandchild relationships (Hayslip, Shore, Henderson, & Lambert, 1998). At the same time, grandchildren raised by grandparents are at about the same levels of overall health and performance in school as those raised by their own parents (Solomon & Marx, 1995).

Clearly, these family situations are ones that result from some crisis in the nuclear family. Grandparents acting as parents to their grandchildren may find themselves in that role for relatively short or relatively long periods of time. Negative effects of this situation, when found, are far greater for grandparents than for grandchildren and for grandmothers than for grandfathers. Much of the research on grandparents as parents again is quite recent and a number of questions are as yet unanswered.

horse is and have lots of dimes ready. Or, if they take us for walks, they should slow down past things like pretty leaves and caterpillars. When they read to us, they don't skip or mind if it's the same story again. Everybody should try to have one, especially if you don't have a television, because grandmas are the only grown-ups who have got time. (McElreath, 1996)

With adult grandchildren, contact is in the hands of the grandparents and grandchildren. Most of the research investigating this contact has surveyed younger adults, usually college students, and found that, on average, contact occurs once a month or less. This is not surprising since college students usually live away from home. Younger adults report more shared activities with grandmothers than with grandfathers and report that their relationships with their grandmothers are stronger than with their grandfathers. Grandmothers are usually reported to have had more influence on the grandchild's development (Roberto & Stroes, 1992). Adults generally report that contact with their closest grandparent(s), whether a grandmother or a grandfather, is very important and that contact with this grandparent has had great influence on their lives (Boon & Brussoni, 1996). A majority of college students say that contact with a grandparent positively influenced their own values, goals, and the choices they made in their lives (Franks, Hughes, Phelps, & Williams, 1993). Contact with grandparents, although not very frequent, is usually more frequent than contact with great-grandparents who also are likely to live farther away (Roberto & Skoglund, 1996). When asked about the activities that they shared with their grandparents during a visit, adult grandchildren most frequently named being together at family events or just messing around, eating out or just eating and spending the night at a grandparent's house, watching TV together, discussing recent events in each other's lives, playing games, and going shopping (Kennedy, 1992).

Other researchers have examined contact with adult grandchildren from the point of view of the grandparents. The AARP conducted a national survey of 823 grandparents age 50 and over (1999). In this survey, 82 percent of the grandparents reported that they had seen a grandchild in the past month, 85 percent had talked to a grandchild on the phone in the past month, and 53 percent had sent a card to a grandchild. Of those with contact, most reported sharing a meal with their grandchildren and one half said their grandchildren spent the night and that they enjoyed watching TV together. Clearly, grandparents report having substantial contact with their grandchildren. Grandparents report strong affiliation with their grandchildren in college and great pride in the achievements of these grandchildren. Grandparents feel especially loved when a grandchild visits or calls unexpectedly. These same grandparents reported enjoying being asked for and then providing advice, especially when they believe that the grandchild took their advice seriously (Harwood & Lin, 2000).

Do grandparents find grandparenting enjoyable? The AARP study (1999) and others suggest that for many the answer is *absolutely*. AARP asked grandparents to rate their relationship with any one of their grandchildren on a scale of 1 to 10, with 10 reflecting a strong and very enjoyable relationship. The average rating for this survey sample was 8.7. When asked what they wanted to pass on to their grandchildren, they listed, in this order, morals or integrity, success or ambition, and religion.

One classic study investigated whether grandparents found their role rewarding and, if so, what factors contributed to those feelings. A sample of 286 grandparents completed a lengthy survey and their answers were analyzed to determine how many felt good about

Grandparents may experience a form of immortality when they are close to their grandchildren.

grandparenting and what factors were most responsible for those good feelings. Generally, grandparents under the age of 50 or older than 80 found the role less rewarding than those between the ages of 50 and 80. Those under the age of 50 were frequently still very involved in careers and work and had little time for grandparenting. Those over 80 were often less healthy than younger grandparents and were, therefore, less able to be actively involved in grandparenting. For those who found grandparenting to be the most rewarding, four important factors were identified. First was the opportunity to spoil and indulge grandchildren without any burden of parental responsibility. Second, grandparents experienced a sense of immortality by seeing their children, then grandchildren, and, in some cases, great-grandchildren carrying on their lineage. Third, being regarded as a valued elder and a wise older person by the grandchildren was a very important contributor to a rewarding grandparenthood. Being asked for advice was very rewarding. Finally, the experience of being reinvolved in one's own past also was important. Being with grandchildren tended to bring back happy memories of being with one's own grandparents. Most grandparents surveyed reported that their activities with their grandchildren were of central importance to them (Kivnick, 1982).

African American grandparents are more likely than White grandparents to be involved with their grandchildren (Strom, Strom, Collinsworth, Strom, & Griswold, 1996). The authors conducted a study comparing 204 African American and 204 White grandparents regarding their views of grandparenting. African Americans rated their performance as grandparents significantly higher than did White respondents. This may be an effect of time spent since African American grandparents reported spending more time with their grand-children. Grandparents of either race who spent more time with their grandchildren perceived themselves as being better at the job. In Kivett's study comparing African American and White American grandparents (1991), African Americans saw their role as more meaningful and important than did Whites, this was especially the case for grandfathers. African American grandparents had higher expectations for their grandchildren, gave them more assistance, and reported more interpersonal closeness than their White counterparts. In a study of the very old (over age 85) Barer (2001) found that most African American grand-, great-, and great-great-grandparents continued to spend a significant amount of time when possible with grandchildren and reported significant emotional benefits and a great deal of pride from their role. An interesting finding from this study was that for some interviewees, they could report only the number of grand-, great-, and great-great-grandchildren, not their names, Nevertheless, they were quite proud of their role and their descendants.

Isolation and Loneliness

Isolation and loneliness are regarded by some as major problems for many older adults. As we grow older we are more likely to lose friends and close members of our families and/or to become ill or disabled and have difficulty maintaining contacts with others. As a result, our chances of isolation and loneliness increase. Isolation and loneliness are not, of course, the same thing. Isolation refers to lack of contact with other people and is often described as being of two different types, social and emotional. **Social isolation** is defined as the state of having minimal or no contact with other people. **Emotional isolation** is defined as minimal or no contact with a loved one. **Loneliness** refers to a negative emotional state of dejection or even depression that can occur when one feels alone or isolated (Dugan & Kivett, 1994; Wenger, Davies, Shahtahmasebi, & Scott, 1996). Being isolated does not always result in loneliness and one can be lonely without being isolated. You have undoubtedly heard that one can be lonely in a crowd of others or you might know people who treasure their time alone without feeling lonely at all. The relationship between the types of isolation, feelings of loneliness, and other factors is complex.

Social isolation is related to health. People in poor health have less contact with other people. Whether that loss of contact is a result of their poor health or whether their health declined as a result of loss of contact is not clear (Wenger et al., 1996). Probably both occur. It is easy to imagine friends and family being reluctant to spend time with an older person who is very ill or terminal. They may feel depressed or think that care in such a case is better provided by professionals. All but close family may avoid an unhealthy person. In this case, illness increases isolation. On the other hand, an unhealthy individual may not want contact with others or want others to see them in such a state. An unhealthy person may be unable to get around on their own and so all contact must rely on others. Furthermore, one also can imagine the case where an individual with little social contact becomes lonely and depressed. We are, afterall, social beings and need contact with others. Depression itself is an illness known to result in reduced functioning of the immune system, often resulting in more illness. A person's isolation can result in poor health.

Social isolation is related to education and income. In one study of 640 people age 55 and over, researchers found that those with lower education were more likely to have lower income and to live in run-down, dilapidated urban neighborhoods. Run-down neighborhoods are ones with buildings in poor physical condition, high levels of noise pollution, low air quality, and lower levels of safety due to higher levels of crime. People living in these neighborhoods showed higher levels of distrust for others. They tended to think that others would take advantage of them and that they had to be very careful in dealing with others. These distrustful individuals also reported the lowest levels of contact not only with neighbors, but with family and friends. They were socially isolated (Krause, 1993). These factors associated with social isolation are not ones easily controlled by individuals.

Emotional isolation is more common for older women than for older men, simply because older women are more likely to become widowed (Carey, 1977). At the same time, emotional isolation may last longer for men who lose a wife than for women who lose a husband because women tend to have closer social support from their children and siblings than men. Widowed men may take longer to find a new emotional attachment (see Chapter 13). The social networks of men are smaller and contain fewer close members than those of women. Older adults who have never married or who are divorced or separated also tend to have higher levels of emotional isolation (Wenger et al., 1996). These individuals, who have no spouse, are less likely than married persons to have a close, emotional attachment to someone they can confide in and count on for social support.

Another possible reason for higher levels of emotional isolation among those who never married is that such persons are less likely to have children. Children may provide emotional attachments for older parents that are unavailable to those who never fostered any children. Even for those who do have children, contact between parents and children is, to some extent, a function of the number of children. Parents with only one adult child do not have contact as frequently as parents with more than one adult child. Since birth rates have dropped following the birth of the baby boom generation (1946–1965), some gerontologists have predicted that there will be more social/emotional isolation for future generations of older adults because these generations have fewer children. One study that examined this prediction looked at living arrangements and social contact for 1400 Canadians ages 65 and older. Of prime interest were those who had lost or never had a spouse and the amount of isolation these individuals experience as a result of having none, one or two, or three or more children. The percentage of those living alone in these three-child conditions were 64 percent, 71 percent, and 62 percent, respectively. They did not differ. When asked about daily contact with other people, 34 percent of those without children had no daily contact while 29 percent of those with children had no daily contact. They did not differ. It appears that children are a good source of social and emotional support for parents but people without or with few children find others, usually friends, to provide that same support (Marcil-Gratton & Légaré, 1992). There may not be more social/emotional isolation for future generations afterall.

Emotional and social isolation are related to one another. A person who is socially isolated also is isolated emotionally. If there is no contact with other people than there certainly is no emotional contact with other people. One who is emotionally isolated may or may not be socially isolated. A widowed person still may have a great many social contacts but be emotionally isolated following the death of a spouse. A person who avoids emotional attachments to other people also may have less social contact with others. Recent work has examined this possibility.

Emotional attachments to other people can be of several different types and are frequently measured by standardized tests such as the Relationship Scales Questionnaire (RSQ) (Bartholomew & Horowitz, 1991). This scale can be used to classify individuals as having a secure, a dismissive, or an ambivalent attachment style. A secure style is characterized by warm, close ties to other people while a dismissive style is characterized by self-reliance and a tendency to avoid warm, close ties. Several studies suggest that older cohorts have far greater proportions of people with dismissive styles than do younger cohorts (Diehl, Elnick, Bourbeasu, & Labouvie-Vief, 1998). One recent study examined social isolation, income, perceived discrimination, immigration, and attachment style using the RSQ, and several other factors in 573 African American and 228 White American urban adults over the age of 65. Results showed a dismissive attachment style in 83 percent of the African Americans and in 65 percent of the White Americans compared to rates of less than 20 percent in prior studies of younger adults. People with a history of lower income, recent immigration, and/or perceived discrimination showed the highest rates of dismissive style. While a secure style was positively associated with strong ties to family and friends, a dismissive style was related negatively to such ties. Their dismissive style is probably responsible for the higher levels of social isolation among these older individuals. Although attachment styles can change with age, these differences between younger and older adults are more likely to be cohort differences. Older cohorts were taught to be more self-reliant and undoubtedly experienced more overt discrimination than more recent cohorts. It is feared that as members of these older cohorts who have dismissive attachment styles become less able to care for themselves, they will avoid seeking the help they need and that those who do obtain such help will be a great burden on those who care for them (Magai, Cohen, Milburn, Thorpe, McPherson, & Peralta, 2001). Remember, however, that isolation may or may not lead to feelings of loneliness.

Most older adults do not report experiencing loneliness. In an examination of 15 different studies of adults over the age of 65, about 10 percent of the participants in these studies reported being very or often lonely, 20 percent lonely sometimes, and 70 percent never or rarely lonely. Perhaps the relatively large proportion of older adults in older cohorts with a dismissive attachment style tend not to feel lonely. Other research has examined the amount of time spent alone and how that time might relate to loneliness. For each hour spent alone, older adults reported lower levels of loneliness than younger adults (Malatesta & Kalnok, 1984). Even though social isolation does not necessarily result in loneliness, socially isolated people are more likely to be lonely than are those with good social contacts. Emotional isolation is even more strongly related to loneliness than is social isolation. People who desire emotional attachments that they are unable to obtain report high levels of loneliness. Loss of a spouse is, as you might expect, strongly related to loneliness and visits from friends and neighbors seem to have little effect on these lonely feelings (Dugan & Kivett, 1994; Wenger et al., 1996).

In sum, social and emotional isolation does occur for older adults under some circumstances and those circumstances are largely beyond our control. Even when such conditions do occur, however, loneliness is relatively infrequent. This may in part be a cohort effect and younger cohorts may report more loneliness when they grow old.

Social and emotional support not available from spouse and/or children is frequently available from friends.

Friends

How many friends do you have? In answering this question you probably responded as most people do and counted individuals who are and are not all that close to you. If asked how many good friends you have, you would undoubtedly give a smaller number. For researchers interested in friendships it is good friends that are of most interest and very little research has examined differences between different types of friends, good friends, best friends, or close friends, even though such types are common categories used in everyday speech (Atchley, 2000).

Friends, of all types, are important in a number of ways. Long-term close friends tend to be placed in the inner circle of older people's social support network. They are a major source of social support as are family members. Older adults in need are sometimes more willing to ask a friend for support than a child because the help of a child may produce a loss of independence or, at least, the perception of such loss (Lee, 1985). Friends are less likely to take away your feelings of independence. People with friends, regardless of their age, have more social support and, as a result, seem to enjoy better health and lower mortality rates (Berkman, 1995; Penninx, van Tillburg, Kriegsman, Deeg, Boeke, &

My friends know who I am.

van Eijk, 1997). Friends help each other cope with stress (Cavanaugh, 1998). Friends play a more important role in older adult's well-being and life satisfaction than income and marital status (Siebert, Mutran, & Reitzes, 1999). And, older friends serve as important caretakers of our memories. They share with us a large part of our lifetime and bring back happy memories, cushion sad memories, and reminisce as no others are able. (Stowe, Rosenblatt, & Foster, 1997).

By now you have witnessed the shattering of so many common myths about older adults that it will not surprise you to learn that older adults do not have fewer friends than other aged adults. The number of close friends that most people have remains relatively stable over the course of their adult years (Antonucci, 1990; Babchuck, 1978–1979). People who have a large number of close friends when they are young tend to have a large number of close friends when they are old, while those with fewer close friends when young tend also to have fewer close friends when old. Of course, the chances of losing a friend are higher for older adults than for younger adults, but older adults are usually quite successful at forming new friendships when older ones are lost (Johnson & Troll, 1994). Older adults most often lose close friends as a result of relocation, retirement, or death. On average, adults of all ages have five to six persons that they name as close friends (Stowe, Rosenblatt, & Foster, 1997).

There are, however, age differences in the number of acquaintances and casual friends; older adults have fewer of these types of friends (Antonucci, 2001; Carstenson & Charles, 1998). Remember our earlier discussion of the reduction, with age, in the number of persons in the outer circle of the social support convoy. You also probably recall our discussion of the research by Carstensen and her colleagues in the section on marriage. The results of those studies and other extensive investigations into friendship led Carstensen to develop a theory of why older people have fewer casual or nonclose members in their social support network. The socioemotional selectivity theory holds that older people develop an increased attention to emotional factors in relationships due to the awareness that time may be limited. They explain the results on decreased negative emotions and increased positive emotions in marital discussions and a general increase in complexity of emotional experiences as indication of this increased focus on emotions in older age. Regarding the social support network, Carstensen suggests that older people reduce the number of people in their lives who do not provide emotional closeness and focus more on those who do. She and her colleagues have collected some impressive supporting data (Carstensen, 1992, 1995; Carstensen & Charles, 1998).

While there are no age differences in average number of close friends, there are certainly large individual differences. Some people are more outgoing or extroverted than others, and this personality trait remains relatively stable over the adult years (see Chapter 8). Extroverted people are more likely than introverted people to report a large number of friends although the number of close friends may be about the same.

There also are gender differences in friendships. Men tend to be friends with other men while women tend to be friends with other women. As we saw with the social support network placement, women tend to have more close friends in whom they confide than men. Men are more likely to confide only in their closest friend, their spouse (Shumaker & Hill, 1991). Men exert less effort to maintain friendships than women. Women have more emotional ties with their friends and share their feelings and concerns while the friendships of men more often are built around activities that they share with one another. Men who are friends tend to do things together (Cavanaugh, 1998; Wright, 1989). These gender differences in friendships disappear in adults 85 and older, particularly when one member of a pair of friends is disabled (Johnson & Troll, 1994).

A number of factors are regarded as important aspects of friendship. Friendships are voluntary. Unlike family relationships into which you are born or adopted, friends are selected. You can be friends with members of your family but the friendship part of that relationship is selected. Friendships are reciprocal. Each member gives as well as receives. When a friend needs help, a friend is ready to help. Friends self-disclose to one another. They share secrets that they would not share with other people, they know each other's likes and dislikes, they confide in one another. It is the mutual nature of this self-disclosure that is most important. Women are more likely than men to have more than one friend in whom they confide. Friends are equals in the relationship. One is not always the leader while the other is always the follower. They may alternate these roles or never engage in them at all. Friends have an emotional attachment to one another; they care about each other. Friends have overlapping interests. They enjoy many of the same things and like to do things together (Atchley, 2000; Matthews, 1986; Schulz & Salthouse, 1999). Close friendships have all or most of these characteristics. Thinking about some of the people you regard as friends, you might try the friendship scale in Table 9-3 and see if researchers also would regard them as your friends. Do they meet most (or all) of the criteria we have just presented? The scale also includes a few other common characteristics, such as physical appearance and intelligence. Friends tend to be close to each other in terms of these latter two characteristics.

Some of these aspects of friendship are the same in the friendships of younger and older adults while other aspects differ. Both younger and older friends maintain a strong emotional attachment. Younger and older friends trust and understand one another. These aspects of friendship always seem to be present and are found in cross-sectional and longitudinal comparisons. Reciprocity and equality may, on the other hand, be different for older than for younger friendships. One study that interviewed older adults about their friendships found that satisfaction with friends was not related to reciprocity or equity in the relationship (Jones & Vaughn, 1990). Unfortunately no direct comparisons to younger adult friendships was made. To examine changes in friendships with aging it is necessary to collect longitudinal data and several studies have done that. In one of these studies, 90 adults, age 85 and over, were interviewed three times over a 31-month period. Between the first and second interviews, 59 percent of the men and 42 percent of the women lost a friend. By the time of the third interview, 53 percent still had at least one close friend and 78 percent reported weekly contact with a friend. New friends had been found by 45 percent of these older adults. Older adults lose friends but often replace them with new friends. Most of the people interviewed who had close friends often did not confide in those close friends. Many expressed an unwillingness to bother others with their troubles since others, who also were old, tended to have troubles of their own. Common gender differences found in young friendships were not found in this study of very old adults (Johnson & Troll, 1994). The friendships of men and women were essentially the same.

A second longitudinal study interviewed 74 women who were in their early 60s in 1978 and again when they were in their mid 70s in 1992. At both times, the women

TABLE 9-3   Are Your Friends Really Friends?

Think about and answer the following questions about your relationship with a person who you regard as being a close friend. Add up your score and see if your friendship also would be regarded as a friendship by those who conduct research on friendships.

1. If you truly regard this person as a close friend, **start off with a score of 1**; afterall, you're probably right.
2. Do you and this person get together even when you don't have to? If you only see this person in class or in church or at gatherings held by family or some social organization, that does not count. If you can answer "yes" to this questions **add 2**.
3. When is the last time you did something to help this person? How important was the thing you did? If you did something to help within the last six months and the thing you did was important, **add 1**.
4. When is the last time this person did something to help you? How important was the thing he or she did? If this person helped you within the last six months and the help was important, **add 1**.
5. Think of your three biggest secrets. How many of these have you told this person? **Add 1 for each secret you revealed**. If you have not yet revealed any of these secrets to this other person but you plan to tell sometime soon, **add 1**. If you think that you will never reveal any of these secrets to this other person, **subtract 2**.
6. Has this other person told you any of their secrets? If "yes" **add 1**; if "no" **subtract 1**.
7. Are you or the other person the boss in your relationship? If either of you is the boss, **subtract 3**.
8. How strong are your feelings for this other person? If you rate them as very strong and positive, **add 2**.
9. How strong are this other person's feelings for you? If you rate them as very strong and positive, **add 2**.
10. Think of your five most favorite things to do. How many of these are favorites for this other person? **Add 1 for each thing that is a favorite for both of you**. If none of the five things you thought of are favorites for this other person, **subtract 3**.
11. Do you and this other person like the same music? The same movies? The same books? The same sports? If you answered "yes" to at least two of these categories, **add 1**. If you did not answer "yes" to any of the categories, **subtract 1**.
12. Is this other person as physically attractive as you are or are they better or worse? If you think that they are about the same as you, **add 1**.
13. Is this other person as smart as you are or are they smarter or not as smart? If you think this other person is as smart as you or smarter than you, **add 1**.
14. Do you have other close friends in addition to this person? If "yes" **add 1**; if "no" **subtract 1**.

If your total score is 12 or higher, most researchers would agree with you that the person you thought of is a close friend. Try the scale again thinking of a different person.

were asked whether they agreed or disagreed with 11 statements about different aspects of their friendships. At both times, women agreed that confiding in one another, expressing intense feelings, and having similar attitudes/values were important aspects of their friendships. On the other hand, women tended to agree less that they shared mutual interests (Roberto, 1997).

Dorothy Field compared friendship patterns for young-old and old-old individuals enrolled in the classic Berkeley Older Generation Study, a longitudinal study of development begun in 1928 with young adults. She found that there was more continuity than change in the amount of contact that older people had with their friends. She found a distinct difference in the type of contact at all ages that older adults had with both close and casual friends. Interactions with casual friends tended to be in the context of group activities while close friendship interactions involved confidence exchange, sharing experiences and thoughts, and helping. With regard to gender differences with age, Field found similar results as others have found. Men decreased in number of new friends and in desire for close friendship while women changed little with age. Changes were most pronounced for casual friends with little change in close friendships. An important point that Field makes is in how we define and how we measure friendship. She emphasizes the need for better measures and more longitudinal studies of friendship before drawing firm conclusions (1999).

One final longitudinal study interviewed 71 older adults in 1979 and then again in 1995 when the youngest person was 81. Many had lost friends over this time period and many made new friends. In 1995, 70 percent still had good friends and were satisfied with their friendships while 10 percent had good friends and wished for even more. Another 15 percent had no good friends and did not wish for friends; they were largely self-reliant and did not report being lonely. The remaining 5 percent had no good friends but wished they did. They often had feelings of loneliness. This finding is a slightly lower incidence of loneliness than that we reported earlier (10 percent average over 15 different studies). A striking difference between the friendships reported by these older adults, compared to other studies of younger adults, was that more older friendships were between men and women. Younger adult friendships are far more likely to be between men or between women. The researchers suggest that this finding may indicate a more pragmatic approach to friendships among older adults. To make new friends when you are older, you must be less picky and take who is available (Jerrome & Wenger, 1999). Older adults who have lost friends, feel lonely, and who wish for new friends may benefit from programs that emphasize pragmatic factors, teach specific skills, and allow participants to practice those skills in role-playing sessions. One recent study found that such a program greatly reduced the loneliness and increased the friendships of a number of older women (Stevens & van Tilburg, 2000).

Religion

If you are or have ever been a member of a religious group, you know that the religious beliefs held and the rituals practiced by members of that group can serve as social connections even when members may know very little else about one another. They share their religion. **Religion** is a community of individuals who share common beliefs and participate in common activities or rituals. Thus, Buddhists, Catholics, Hindus, Jews, Muslims, Protestants, and other religions provide links among their members that would not otherwise be available. These links are another form of social relationship. Religion is the public and social side of theological belief systems and is different from spirituality. **Spirituality** is the private emotional and/or intellectual connection that one makes to an accepted higher being. People who are members of a religion may or may not be spiritual and people with spirituality may or may not be members of some religion. Research on religion typically has measured attendance at services and participation in organized rituals while research on spirituality more often has measured belief. Most of this research has involved cross-sectional comparisons and has been done recently. In the past, religion was not frequently regarded as a topic for scientific investigation.

It is estimated that about 50 percent of the adult population regularly attend the services held by an organized religion. A higher proportion of women than men attend and those with higher income, education, and who have lived in the same place for a longer period of time are more likely to attend (Cutler & Hendricks, 1990). Religion seems to play a more central and important part in the cultures of many African and Mexican Americans than for White Americans (Levin, Chatters, & Taylor, 1995; Levin, Markides, & Ray, 1996). Hispanic Americans are more likely to turn to their own family or church for support before seeking any public assistance.

Age differences in religion and spirituality are less clear. Some cross-sectional studies have found age differences in attendance with higher rates for older adults. Data obtained from a number of Gallup polls, conducted over a number of years, consistently have found higher rates for older adults (Krause, 1997). This suggests that obtained differences may truly be age rather than cohort differences since the same finding has been obtained from a number of different older and younger cohorts. When people are asked whether they believe in God, about two-thirds of those between the ages of 15 and 34 answered yes while 87 percent of those 55 and older answered yes (Jacobs & Worcester, 1990). These differences could still be cohort differences. Older cohorts grew up in times when religion was a more central part of life and this is true for many older cohorts. The differences could be cohort differences involving many cohorts. Some assert that although participation in religion is less evident in younger cohorts/younger adults, spirituality still remains high (Davie & Vincent, 1998). One longitudinal study followed a large group of adults for 20 years and found that attendance at services was the highest during early old age, between 60 and 75. Past the age of 75 attendance was lower. While some of the lower attendance was due to increased illness and disability in some older adults, others who became ill or disabled actually increased their attendance. Many who had no apparent disability attended less often than they had previously (Atchley, 1999). It is clear that participation in religion is different for older adults and/or older cohorts. Differences in spirituality are less clear.

Religion and spirituality have been associated with a number of benefits for adults of all ages. In a review of over 200 prior studies and three national surveys, Jeffrey Levin found that religion was strongly and positively related to health and that a large number of health problems were less frequent among adults who reported more religious involvement (1994; 1998). Psychological well-being and life satisfaction also have been associated with religion (Johnson, 1995). In this case, however, the association is *U* shaped. Those with higher involvement in religion and those with no involvement in religion tend to have higher levels of psychological well-being than those with moderate levels (Krause, 1995a). Finally, religion also is related to mortality. In one recent study, 2023 California residents, ages 55 and older, were asked about their attendance at religious services. As in other studies, attendance was higher for women than men and lowest for the youngest (middle-age) and oldest (old-old) adults in the sample. Over the next five years, mortality data were collected by continual reading of obituary notices in newspapers and attempts to contact participants for later interviews. The death rates were highest for those who had earlier reported no attendance at religious services and lowest for those who had reported weekly attendance (Oman & Reed, 1998).

These relationships between religion and health, well-being, and mortality are thought to be due to a number of factors. One factor is the set of rules or demands made by some organized religions. In some cases, religions prohibit members from drinking alcohol, using drugs, smoking, or other behaviors that can be dangerous to one's health. The demands of Buddhist, Hindu, Muslim, Mormon, Seventh Day Adventist, and several other religions are such that many unhealthy behaviors are not acceptable. A second factor may be relaxation as a manager of stress. People high in spirituality, whether members of an organized religion or not, may spend considerable time in a form of meditation. People may read the Bible, spend time praying, or listen to religious or spiritual programs. In one study of 1300 adults 60 and older, more than half reported reading the Bible and one-third listened to or watched religious programs many times each week; 60 percent reported praying everyday (Koenig, 1995; Koenig, George, Blazer, & Pritchett, 1993). Such activities are similar to more traditional types of meditation and relaxation through meditation can be a powerful technique for reducing stress. Remember from Chapter 8 that religion has been named more frequently than any other strategy for coping with stress (Koenig, George, & Siegler, 1988). Part of the beneficial effect of religion also may be due to its role as a source of continuity in one's identity. Some researchers have found that religion, work, and family serve as major themes in the life stories of older adults and that religion plays a particularly prominent role in the life stories of older African American adults (Nye, 1992–1993).

Finally, religions offer a social support network beyond that offered by family and friends alone. In one survey of older African Americans, researchers found that 60 percent reported receiving support from members of their religion, 50 percent from family members, and 80 percent from a good friend (Taylor & Chatters, 1986). Krause (2001) suggests that support in religious settings looks very similar to support in other settings but perceived support, as we discussed earlier, may be different. The support from others in religious settings may be perceived as more genuine and honestly offered since most religions advocate care and concern for others.

Religions also provide opportunities to form new friendships through sponsored activities. Box 9-3 (p. 258) describes Shepherd's Centers, which provide activities for older adults at a number of religious organizations across the country. In a series of cross-sectional and longitudinal comparisons, researchers have found that involvement in religious activities is highly associated with a number of healthy behaviors, such as regular exercise, lower levels of smoking, less alcohol consumption, lower BMI, and more social involvements with family and friends. When a group of over 900 adults were followed for 12 years, researchers found that those with strong family relationships, healthy behaviors, and attendance at religious services during the early years of the study showed far fewer and less serious disabilities during the later years of the study. Furthermore, the influence of religion went beyond the factors of healthy behaviors and close family relationships suggesting that there are other influences at work (Idler & Kasl, 1997a; 1997b).

A group of researchers in North Carolina attempted to control for several of the factors that might underlie the findings regarding religion and lowered mortality. They followed a group of 3968 people age 64 to 101 for six years. They controlled for size of

BOX **9-3**

Shepherd's Centers

Religious groups in your community may sponsor a number of activities managed by **Shepherd's Center**. Shepherd's Center was founded in 1972 by Dr. Elbert Cole as a way for older adults to provide services for other older adults. The national headquarters in Kansas City offers assistance to those interested in beginning a local center. There are now over a 100 local centers in more than half the states and over 100,000 members (Atchley, 2000). Space for activities is usually provided by a religious group that has ample space available and funding is donated by a number of local religious groups and participants. Shepherd's Center activities are open to older adults regardless of religion. Centers provide classes on a number of different topics, companion aide service, transportation for grocery shopping or doctor's appointments, handyperson services, hot meal deliveries, and other activities.

Available activities at our local Sheperd's Center include information on income tax assistance and travel; transportation and aides; and classes on bridge instruction and play, creative writing, current events, line dancing, memory improvment, music appreciation, origami, portrait drawing, romantic poetry, water exercise, and wood carving. Classes are usually taught by older adults or by volunteers from the community who have some expertise in the topic. A different variety of classes is offered each fall and spring and usually meet once a week for 6 to 7 weeks. Participants pay $15 to participate in one morning and one afternoon class.

---

social support networks, health and health care behaviors, depression, smoking, and drinking. Even with all of these factors controlled, lower mortality rates still were found for those who attended religious services at least once a week. The effect was stronger for women than men (Koenig, Hays, Larson, George, Cohen, McCullough, Meador, & Blazer, 1999). In a related study, researchers conducted a 28-year follow up of 5286 persons, ages 21 to 65, also controlling for many potentially confounding factors. With this control, the mortality decrease due to weekly attendance (the same result found several times now) only remained for women in their sample (Strawbridge, Cohen, Shema, & Kaplan, 1997). Can you think of why women might benefit from religious participation more than men? Do you think all confounding factors have been controlled? At present, it is not clear which factors are most responsible for the strong relationship between good health and religion but it is clear that people with religion tend to be healthier and live longer than those without religion.

Making Choices

One choice that you can make as a result of information learned in this chapter is to maintain close ties with family members and/or friends. A strong social network can provide strong social support, which is associated with good health and well-being. Of course, you also learned that there are individual differences in our ability and, perhaps, willingness to build and maintain close ties with others. Most people desire and form these close ties but

Three generations of social support.

some people are very self-reliant and tend to avoid such close ties while other people desire close ties but have difficulty forming and/or maintaining them. If you are of the latter type, seek assistance in learning how to build close ties and to form good friendships with others.

People with higher levels of education and, thus, higher income are better equipped to avoid social isolation. Isolated people are more likely to become lonely.

We hope you will choose to contact your grandparents as soon as possible. A card, call, or, best of all, a visit to say hello can make a big difference for them and, as you will discover, for you too. If you have a problem of some sort ask them for advice. In fact, while you are at it, contact Mom and Dad too. Tell them you love them. You and they will feel better.

CHAPTER HIGHLIGHTS

- Social support from family and friends seems to remain stable across the adult years and to be a major factor in physical health, psychological well-being, and longevity.
- Family relationships begin at birth for most people and relationships with parents and siblings are typically the longest relationships in an individual's life.
- Most people marry at least once in their lives and close to half of these marriages end in divorce.
- Generally, marital satisfaction is relatively high in the early years of a marriage, declines somewhat during the years in which children are present, and rises again following the departure of the last child from home.

- Long-lasting marriages tend to be those in which the couple agrees on many important topics, where marriage is regarded as a major commitment, where humor and affection reside, and where spouses are regarded as best friends.
- Divorce tends to occur when there is lack of or minimal communication between partners and/or infidelity.
- Many more men than women remarry and such second, third (and so on) marriages are less likely to succeed than first marriages.
- Sexual relations continue into very old age but at a reduced rate. A number of reasons are thought to underlie this lower activity level.
- Most parents become grandparents before reaching age 50.
- Grandparents generally enjoy being grandparents for a number of reasons including the chance to spoil the grandchildren.
- Between 10 and 20 percent of older adults experience loneliness sometimes. The probabilty of loneliness is related to a number of factors, including type of isolation.
- Friendships are characterized as being voluntary relationships in which each person gives and receives. Friends typically confide in one another and are equals in the relationship. Friends have close emotional attachments and share common interests.
- The number of friends does not seem to change with age. For older adults friendships are more often cross-gender, less confiding, and less reciprocal.
- Religion plays an important role in social relationships and is related to health, well-being, and mortality. Several factors are known to underlie this relationship while others are, as yet, unclear.

STUDY QUESTIONS

1. Describe the convoy model of social networks and social support. Are there age and gender differences in social networks and support?

2. How does social support exert an influence on physical health, psychological well-being, and mortality?

3. What are the similarities and differences between social relationships with family and with friends?

4. What factors play a role in long-lasting marriages? In divorce?

5. People view their past through the eyes of the present. What does this mean and what evidence supports such a view?

6. What are the types of elder abuse? How frequent is such abuse?

7. Is it better to have loved and lost than to have never loved at all? Explain the reasons for your answer.

8. Describe/discuss changes in sexual activity with age and the reasons for these changes. Are the reasons the same for men and women?

9. Describe the different types of sibling relationships. Do sibling relationships change with age? With the loss of parents? With changes in health?

10. What factors influence the relationships between parents and adult children?

11. What are the similarities and differences in the relationships between grandparents and young versus adult grandchildren? What factors play a role?

12. Do grandparents enjoy being grandparents? What factors play a role? Do grandparents enjoy acting as parents again? What factors play a role? Do grandchildren benefit or suffer when they are parented by their grandparents instead of their real parents? Do grandparents benefit or suffer?

13. How likely is it that older adults will experience periods of extended loneliness? Social isolation? Emotional isolation? How do these different states relate to one another? What factors produce these states?

14. What criteria do researchers use when defining a friendship? In your opinion, which of these criteria are most/least important?

15. Are the friendships of older adults different than those of younger adults? Of men than those of women?

16. What is the difference between religion and spirituality?

17. What accounts for the relationship found between religion/spirituality and health/mortality?

18. How do you think that social support might bring all of the aspects of social relations together in a comprehensive view of lifespan social development?

RECOMMENDED READINGS

Hanson, W. (1999). *Older love*. Minneapolis, MN: Waldman House Press. This very short book or very long poem (36 pages) is a description of the love that resides in a long-lasting marriage.

Krause, N. (1999). *The Healing power of faith: Science explores medicine's last great frontier*. New York: Simon & Schuster.

Lee, J. A. (Ed.). (1991). *Gay midlife and maturity*. Binghamton, NY: Harrington Park Press. If you are interested in learning more about older gay persons and their adjustment to aging this older book is a good place to start.

Werking, K. (1997). *We're just good friends: Woman and Men in Nonromantic Relationships*. New York: Guilford. This book examines cross-gender friendships and their survival in our culture.

INTERNET RESOURCES

http://www.census.gov   Find some of the latest statistics on marriage, divorce, and other relationships.

http://www.shepherdcenters.org   Learn more about Shepherd's Centers of America and the activities offered, how to start a local center, and other information.

CHAPTER

10

Work and Retirement

Talking about retirement: You'll wonder how you ever had time to work.
—Grace Holden

As our friend Grace Holden suggests, retirement can be very busy. That same sentiment is expressed by many others such as Peter Strasser (1997) who said, "I have often wondered how I had time to go to work." Many retired individuals report the same feeling of a life full of rewarding activities. A few, however, have quite a different experience and may even return to work. Others experience a lot of activity, followed by a letdown, and finally a regular routine. We examine these patterns of retirement in this chapter after we examine work. As you will learn, work is a very important component of our lives that influences and is influenced by many other components.

In Senior View, Pat Shelley tells us how she chose her work as an elementary school teacher and why she retired. Like Grace Holden, Pat Shelley has kept very busy in retirement by volunteering, working in her yard, and visiting with family and friends. Keeping busy is a very important part of a successful retirement.

Work

If you want to get ahead in this world, you need to have a certain amount of money. Friends and family, taking care of your health, finding intellectual stimulation, and feeling safe and appreciated are very important. Money, however, buys food, shelter, clothing, medicine, and can contribute substantially to overall well-being. For most people, money comes from work and the majority of us will work most of our lives. Even people who inherit great wealth and have no real need to work often do so anyway. Work is a part of human existence and the work ethic is a strong part of our American culture. Our focus here is on how work is related to adult development and aging. The work we do influences many aspects of our lives including our eventual retirement. The work we do influences our physical and mental health, our intellectual attainment, and the relationships we form with other people.

Senior View

It was not easy to schedule an interview appointment with Pat Shelley, an 83-year-old former schoolteacher. She stays busy with her hobby of taking care of old folks during the week. Pat Shelley has a set routine of visiting shut-ins in the community and driving folks to the store and doctor's appointments. We also had to schedule meetings around the baseball games, as she is a stalwart fan of the Atlanta Braves. We caught up with her after a game one afternoon to ask her some questions about her views on work and retirement. Pat said she has been very happily retired for about 12 years after an enjoyable 39 years of teaching third and fourth grade children. She said one of the best parts about her former teaching career is that she still gets notes, letters, and messages from her former pupils. She loves to hear from them and especially loves it when they come to visit, even those who remind her, sometimes in public, about having spanked them so many years ago!

When we asked her why she chose teaching as her career, she said simply, "I always knew I wanted to be a teacher." She added that career decisions were very easy for women in the early decades of the twentieth century. If she wanted to

be a professional, she had a choice of being either a teacher or a nurse. She said her parents encouraged her to teach and she had older sisters who also went into teaching.

When asked if she had any advice for young people on choosing a career, she said, "You have to go with your personality." We asked her to explain this and she said that she has always been a very happy, energetic person, and loved children. These are perfect traits for working with children. She also advised, "If you aren't happy in a job, you should leave." She feels that a good job must reward you for what you have done and one that does not, is not one to keep you happy.

We asked Pat Shelley a few questions about retirement. With regard to planning, she said that she and her husband, a barber, always saved for the future, including for their retirement. She said they made it a priority and learned to do without things occasionally so they would have what they needed later. Those later things included college money for their children, money to help her husband through an illness that eventually took his life, and money for retirement. By the time Pat retired at age 71, a few years after her husband had retired, their house and car were paid for so she and her husband had money to cover their bills and a little extra for traveling to visit their children and grandchildren. Social Security and her small teaching pension have provided her with enough to live comfortably. Pat told us that she is lucky to live in a small town where expenses are low. In addition to her passion for baseball and college basketball, she loves to garden. She has a beautiful yard that she says takes more sweat equity than monetary capital to maintain.

We asked her how she made the decision to retire. "I knew it was time to retire. It was time to let younger teachers take over," she said. When asked if she had any advice about retirement, she said, "If you can't do it right, don't do it." Then she added with a grin, "You want to be sure to leave enough time to do some other fun things." Pat seems to fill her days with fun things and is thoroughly enjoying her retirement.

Jobs

Most people begin working during the summer while still in high school. Such jobs might be formal with regular hours at a place of business or informal baby-sitting, yard mainte- nance, and so on. Part-time work during school is also common for many college students and many work full time out of necessity. More frequently people with careers and full- time work return to school to advance in their current career or to change careers. When one finally leaves school, whether high school, college, or graduate/professional school, a career path begins. Generally, higher status and higher paying jobs are more readily avail- able to persons with more years of education.

Not everyone sticks with their first career. They may become dissatisfied, ill or disabled, attracted to other opportunities, bored, or downsized. Students are encouraged to take advantage of campus placement offices and/or career center. Since your development will not end when you complete college, you might expect that what is a suitable career and job for you will change as you change. Midlife career change may be a purposeful choice for many, however good data to verify this trend are not currently available. We do know that millions of people in midlife were let go or offered incentives to retire early as corporations resorted to downsizing to cut costs starting in the last decade of the twentieth century (Atchley, 2000). We do not know how many of these individuals might have re- tired to seek alternative employment anyway. The individuals most frequently downsized were the older workers since they were typically paid the highest salaries. As we will see, many employers have treated older workers as a separate class that can no longer keep up and should retire as soon as possible.

Older Workers

The average age of the American worker has increased over the last several years and is expected to continue to increase for several more years. In 1996, the average worker was 38 years old and by 2006 the average worker will be 41 years old. Younger workers tend to have a great variety of jobs as they develop their careers while the jobs that are held by older workers are, to a great extent, the same as those held by middle-age workers. The jobs held by men and women of any age tend to be quite different. Table 10-1 (p. 266) lists the most frequent jobs for middle-age and older men and women in the United States. For women in both age groups, clerical and service jobs are the most frequent types of jobs held. For men, management and professional/technical jobs are frequent for both age groups. You also might notice that men have a greater variety of job types than women. The vast majority (80 percent) of middle-age women have clerical, service, or profes- sional/technical jobs. The top three jobs for middle-age men are held by only 57 percent of those men. For older men three job types are most frequent while for older women only two job types occupy the same proportion of people (Czaja, 2001). These results should not surprise you as the job opportunities for older cohorts of women were far more limited than those for older cohorts of men.

Many changes occur in our bodies and minds as we age. Older adults typically lose some physical strength and stamina (see Chapter 2), are more likely to have chronic ill- nesses such as arthritis (also Chapter 2), may show sensory declines, especially in seeing and hearing (see Chapter 5), almost always respond slower (also Chapter 5), and have

TABLE 10-1 Percentage of Middle-Age and Older Men and Women in Different Job Types

Men Age 45–64		Women Age 45–64	
Crafts	21%	Clerical	40%
Management	19%	Service	21%
Professional/Technical	17%	Professional/Technical	19%
Total	57%	Total	80%
Men Age 65+		**Women Age 65+**	
Management	18%	Clerical	25%
Professional/Technical	15%	Service	21%
Service	13%		
Total	46%	Total	46%

Source: Adapted from Czaja, 2001.

more difficulty with some cognitive tasks, especially those which demand responding quickly to a host of new stimuli (see Chapters 6 and 7). Because of these changes, several beliefs are common among employers, fellow workers, and even some older workers themselves. It is thought by many that older workers have more injuries, are more frequently absent from work, are less productive, cannot learn new skills, and cost more than they are worth to the employer (Wegman, 1999). None of these beliefs are supported by data and many are refuted. An examination of the health and ability of older adults to work has shown that older workers are healthier than ever before. For example, there was a higher percentage of able workers at age 67 in 1994 (80.9 percent) than there was at the younger age of 65 in 1982 (76.4 percent) (Crimmins, Reynolds, & Saito, 1999).

In terms of injuries and absences from work, older adults have fewer of each but their injuries, when they do occur, are thought to be more severe and, as a result, may require longer absence from work (Doering, Rhodes, & Schuster, 1983; Giniger, Dispenzieri, & Eisenberg, 1983; Laflamme & Menckel, 1995; Mitchell, 1988). Unhealthy workers of all ages are more likely to be absent from work. As for accidents, the highest rate is for workers under age 24; workers from age 25 to retirement have about the same low rate (Cleveland & Shore, 1996). Severity of injury often is measured by time absent and time absent is usually determined by management and the attending physician as well as the injured worker (Wegman, 1999). Beliefs about older adults may influence recommended time away from the job; for the same injury, older workers may be told to take more time than younger workers. If a manager believes that it will take an older worker longer to heal then the older worker may be given more time off. Was the injury severe? The older worker took more time off so it must have been. Older workers have had more experience than younger workers and accidents are less likely for an experienced worker. Finally, older adults who are injured at work are more likely to ignore minor accidents.

Some injuries that occur in older workers are attributed to the amount of time on a particular job rather than to the age of the worker. Older workers have been on the job for a longer time than younger workers and are, thus, more likely to experience these types of injuries. Cumulative trauma disorders and repetitive strain injuries result from performing a job while standing in an awkward posture, repeating the same motions, and/or having to exert excessive force. The longer you do this sort of work, the more likely you are to suffer, and some of these strains, such as carpal tunnel syndrome, can be quite severe. Generally, the incidence of such disorders are about the same for younger and older workers but the prevalence rates are higher for older workers. For example, problems of pain in the lower back are as likely to first occur (incidence) among younger workers as among older workers, but more older workers have such pain (prevalence) because they have had it for a long time (de Zwart, Broersen, Frings-Dressen, & van Dijk, 1997). The effects of continual standing at work and repetitive motions decrease work ability especially for older workers who are more likely to have decreased muscle strength and who have been at the job for a longer period of time (Tuomi, Ilmarinen, Seitsamo, Huuhtanen, Martikainen, Nygård, & Klockars, 1997).

The beliefs that older workers have more injuries and are more frequently absent from work are false but when older workers are absent, they may be absent for a longer period of time than younger workers. Of course, this longer absence may often be due to the recommendations made by management rather than severity of the injury. For most

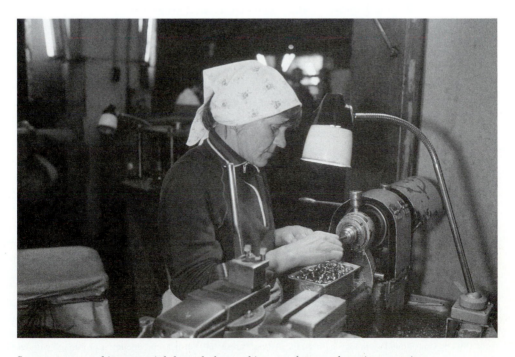

Seamstresses pushing material through the machine can damage the wrists over time.

companies, injuries and absences are important to the extent that they affect productivity and cost. Age differences in injuries and absences do not, however, seem to contribute to any deficits in productivity or cost.

Job Performance.   Research has examined the relationship between worker age and performance on the job. The general finding is that there is no relationship between worker age and job performance although some individual studies have found positive (older workers perform better) or negative (older workers perform worse) relationships on specific jobs (Sterns, Sterns, & Hollis, 1996; Waldman & Avolio, 1986). To examine the overall relationship, a meta-analysis was conducted on the results from 96 different studies with 38,983 workers. Workers ranged in age from 17 to over 60 and were employed in a variety of professional (e.g., engineer, scientist, manager, nurse) and non-professional (e.g., clerical, sales, bank teller, blue-collar) jobs. The results showed no overall relationship between worker age and job performance except for very young workers. Workers age 17 to 22 showed a small positive relationship between age and performance; 22-year-olds performed better than 17-year-olds. Older workers, on average, perform their jobs as well as workers of any other age (McEvoy & Cascio, 1989).

When one looks at specific jobs and age, relationships are sometimes evident. As you can see in Table 10-2, the expected relationship depends on whether the job requires skills that are likely to decline with advanced age and whether performance on

TABLE 10-2   Effects of Experience and Age on Expected Productivity

Basic job skills decline with age?	Performance improves with experience?	Example of job skills or activities	Expected relation between age and productivity
Yes	Yes	Skilled manual work such as carpentry.	None; age decline is offset by experience.
Yes	No	Rapid processing of new, often unexpected information such as an air traffic controller.	Negative; older workers are less productive.
No	Yes	Making decisions based on knowledge such as a judge.	Positive; older workers are more productive.
No	No	Activities that depend on personality or social skills such as a host.	None; age and experience are not very important.

Source: Modified and reproduced by special permission of the Publisher, Consulting Psychologists Press, Inc., Palo Alto, CA, from *Handbook of industrial and organizational psychology* by H. C. Triandis, M. D. Dunnette, and L. M. Hough, Eds. Copyright 1994 by Consulting Psychologists Press, Inc. All rights reserved. Further reproduction is prohibited without the Publisher's written consent.

the job is improved by experience (Warr, 1994). In most cases we expect no relationship between age and job performance. However, in cases where the typical changes
that occur with age do not influence job performance but experience does, we expect a
positive relationship; older workers are more experienced and should perform better. In
cases where the typical changes that occur with age do influence job performance and
where experience provides little or no benefit, we expect a negative relationship; older
workers should perform worse. It is important to keep in mind that the physical or mental changes that can occur with age might only influence work performance when the
specific job depends upon those particular physical and mental abilities (Westerholm &
Kilbom, 1997). Even in cases such as these, older workers are likely to have found ways
to compensate and maintain performance. As you have learned, people can develop expertise at a task from extensive practice and that such expertise offsets any deficits in
performance with advanced age (see Chapter 7).

One can think of a number of jobs that could be more difficult for older workers because of the typical physical and mental changes that were described in Chapters 2, 5, 6,
and 7. It is unusual to see a professional baseball player, basketball player, figure skater,
football player, or gymnast who is over 40. Airline pilots, firefighters, police officers, bus
drivers, and those serving in the foreign service are still required to retire at age 60 (Hoyer,
Rybash, & Roodin, 1999), although some researchers question the legitimacy of such requirements (Landy, 1994; Stuck, Van Gorp, Josephson, & Morgenstern, 1992). Close to 7
percent of older workers are required to retire because of their age (Binstock & George,
1996). The job of an air traffic controller is another job thought by some to be more difficult for older workers unless sufficient technical support is available (Becker & Milke,
1998). All of these jobs are ones where the benefits of experience are not thought to offset
the changes that can occur with aging.

Other jobs could be easier for older workers because of their greater experience and
accumulated knowledge. Most judges, managers, and politicians are older. A greater percentage of older workers are self-employed (about 25 percent) compared to younger workers (about 8 percent) (AARP, 1991). Artists and musicians often do their most creative work
when they are older (see Chapter 7). Older workers are actively recruited by companies for
some positions. For example, making reservations at national reservation centers for guests
at Days Inn and Ramada Inn, serving customers for Travelers Insurance Corporation, working for the hardware store B & Q in Great Britain, and working for large discount stores
such as Home Depot or Wal-Mart because, in part, of their greater experience.

Even jobs that seem to rely heavily on good sensory abilities, muscle strength,
and stamina might be influenced less by age and more by other factors. One study examined the performance of fishers in Okinawa and Japan and hunters in Papua, New
Guinea. On average, younger fishers tended to make more money from their catch than
older fishers but the most productive fisher was one of the oldest at age 52. For hunters,
those who were younger and unmarried were the least successful even though they spent
the most time at it. The most successful hunters were older and married and also spent
less time at it (Ohtsuka, 1997).

Older workers perform as well as younger workers in part because of their greater experience on the job but what if the job itself changes? As the use of technology increases
and jobs are automated, as computers become more sophisticated and widespread, training

may be more necessary and more frequent. If a job requires use of a computer then the person in that job may need to be retrained on new software every few years. Are older workers as willing to undergo training and as able to benefit from training as younger workers? Older workers seem far more willing to undergo training when they have experienced training previously and the new job continues to be interesting for them (Yeatts, Folts, & Knapp, 2000). From the information presented in Chapters 5 and 6 you might expect older workers to learn well but to take longer than younger workers. Some work shows exactly that. Older workers are as able to learn new skills as younger workers but it often takes older workers more time (Siemen, 1976). Compared to younger workers, older adults are frequently slower, need more assistance, and make more mistakes when learning computer skills (Charness & Bosman, 1992), although some studies have found no differences between older and younger trainees (Garfein, Schaie, & Willis, 1988). Older workers are sometimes reluctant to participate in training for fear that they will not perform as well as younger trainees. Some desire age-separated training groups while others prefer not to be treated as special. Older workers are likely to have many of the same false beliefs that others have and so expect to have difficulty with training (Plett, 1990). In short, older workers may need to be encouraged to participate in training and may need more time to learn than younger workers. However, once trained, older workers perform as well as younger workers when they return to their jobs. Employers are, however, less likely to recommend or provide training for older workers. Training opportunities for workers age 55 and older occur at a rate about one-third that for workers age 35 to 44 (Erber & Danker, 1995; Simon, 1996).

Older workers may learn faster when certain training methods are used. The discovery method involves presenting tasks to learn and problems to solve in a continuous series of steps; this method may be particularly effective for older workers (Belbin, 1970). In teaching computer skills such as word processing or spreadsheets, the most effective techniques for older and younger learners are those that reduce the demands on working memory by modeling procedures or providing menus (Gist, Rosen, & Schwoerer, 1988; Kelly, Charness, Mottram, & Bosman, 1994). Older workers also learn to perform computer tasks quicker and perform better when specific goals are set during training. Goal setting benefits a wide range of individuals with different intelligence levels and personality types (Hollis-Sawyer & Sterns, 1999). In general, older workers learn new computer skills quicker when the demands on memory are reduced, specific examples and tasks are modeled, and specific goals are set (Czaja, 2001).

Job Satisfaction.   Workers who are satisfied with their jobs are likely to perform better and older workers generally have higher job satisfaction, more employer loyalty, and report being more involved with their jobs than do younger workers (Doering, Rhodes, & Schuster, 1983; Rhodes, 1983).

A number of hypotheses have been suggested as explanations for this relationship between age of worker and job satisfaction. One, the **grinding down hypothesis,** suggests that after decades in the workplace, the expectations of older workers have been lowered (ground down) and so they are satisfied with less, than new, younger, more idealistic workers. Older workers have a more realistic view of life and so have learned to be satisfied with less. A second hypothesis, the **Lordstown hypothesis,** suggests that the differences in job satisfaction are cohort rather than age differences. Younger cohorts grew up with television, battery-powered toys, handheld calculators, much more than older cohorts and, therefore, expect more. The hypothesis is named for Lordstown, Ohio, where General Motors opened a plant staffed entirely by younger workers. During its first ten years, the plant was the source of more worker unrest than all other General Motors plants combined. The third hypothesis, the **job change hypothesis,** suggests that older workers have better, more fullfilling jobs than younger workers. Older workers have had more time to examine the different jobs available to them and to find one that is most congruent with their own abilities and desires. Younger workers have not yet found that position and, so, are less satisfied. To test these hypotheses, 496 city and county managers in Florida, ranging in age from 23 to 73, were surveyed. The results strongly supported the job change hypothesis. The effects of age on job satisfaction were due to older workers having jobs congruent with their needs, higher salaries, and more perceived control. They had found the jobs they wanted while younger workers were still searching (White & Spector, 1987).

Age Discrimination.   Why would any place of employment turn away workers who have fewer injuries on the job, are less likely to be absent from work, perform as well as any other age group, and are more satisfied with their positions even if they may take a little longer to train? The answer would seem to be because they are old. Older workers are still believed by many to be less capable than younger workers. You can test the influence of such beliefs by doing Project 10 (p. 272). The Age Discrimination in Employment Act (ADEA) was designed to protect workers age 40 and older from this sort of discrimination. People are protected from being fired, forced to retire (this amendment was added in 1986), discriminated against in hiring decisions, or being paid lower wages because of their age. This law applies to any place of employment with 20 or more employees. In spite of this law, age discrimination still exists and may even be increasing (Ilmarinen, 1997; Schatz, 1997).

With respect to being fired and rehired, older workers are at a disadvantage. When companies close, merge with other companies, reorganize, or attempt to cut costs, workers are fired; this is sometimes referred to as downsizing. Close to 25 percent of those let go are age 55 and older (Markey & Parks, 1989). The unemployment rate is higher for those between the ages of 55 and 64 than for those ages 25 to 54 (Hayslip & Panek, 1993). After being released by a place of employment, older workers take longer to find another job and take a bigger cut in salary than younger workers who have been downsized (Quinn & Burkhauser, 1990). Some research has found that older workers are particularly disadvantaged when younger workers are available for the same job (Lee & Clemons, 1985). Other work has examined the onset of and increases in alcohol consumption following loss of a job for an older worker. This research found no increase in alcohol consumption for those who drank alcohol before losing their jobs but 12 percent of nondrinkers began consuming alcohol after losing their jobs. The individuals who began drinking did not, however, drink heavily after their job loss and averaged less than one drink per day (Gallo, Bradley, Siegel, & Kasl, 2001). Perhaps older workers have other more effective coping strategies to deal with involuntary job loss (see Chapter 8 for a discussion of coping strategies).

When manufacturing jobs declined in the 1970s and 1980s, many older and younger workers were forced to search for new jobs. For those 55 and older, less than half (about 40 percent) were successful while for those in their 20s, 70 percent found new jobs

PROJECT **10**

Discrimination against Older Workers

A major study that looked at discrimination against older workers recruited 142 younger business students (Rosen & Jerdee, 1976b). Students were asked to make decisions about workers in six different situations and in each of the six cases, some were led to believe that the worker was young while others were led to believe that the worker was old. Prior work showed that managers and students held the same typical stereotypes about older workers (see text for some of these stereotypes) in situations like those used in the study (Rosen & Jerdee, 1976a). The following are three of those situations:

- A shipping room employee who was hired only three months ago appears to be unresponsive to customer calls for service according to the foreman. How much difficulty is expected in getting the employee to improve and be more responsive?
- A candidate is up for possible promotion to a marketing job that requires "fresh solutions to challenging problems" and "a high degree of creative and innovative behavior." Should the candidate be promoted?
- A position is open that requires a person "who not only knows the field of finance but who is capable of making quick judgments under high risk." Should the applicant be hired?

In addition to receiving one of the three situations described above, participants also were told that the employee, candidate, or applicant was an older or a younger person and in some conditions a picture of an older or younger person accompanied the description.

For the first situation, 65 percent of the students recommended talking to a younger employee but 55 percent recommended replacing an older employee. For the second situation, 54 percent recommended promoting a younger candidate while only 24 percent recommended promoting an older candidate. For the third situation, 25 percent recommended hiring the younger applicant while only 13 percent recommeded hiring the older applicant. As discussed in the text, people tend to have negative views about the abilities of older workers.

For this project use some of the situations described above (or look at the other three from Rosen & Jerdee, 1976b) or write some of your own. In some cases describe the individual in question as being younger and in other cases as being older. Ask people from different majors or careers and of different ages to make a decision and to explain the basis for their decision.

Did you find age discrimination? If so, were the reasons given for not helping, promoting, or hiring the older person the ones that you expected?

If you did not find age discrimination could it have to do with the sample you used? Did you use business majors, psychology majors, sociology majors, or a mix of many different majors? Do you expect students in different majors, who have certainly taken many different courses, to have different views about the qualifications and abilities of older workers? What about those in different careers? What about people in different age groups? Why or why not?

(Atchley, 2000; Barlett & Steele, 1992). In one study, workers were followed after a plant closing. Those 55 and older took, on average, 27 weeks to find another job while those under age 45 took only 13 weeks. When older and younger workers seeking a new job were matched on education level, marital status, job tenure, and willingness to relocate, older workers still took four more weeks than younger workers to find a job.

When jobs were found, older workers earned, on average, 16.5 percent less than younger workers (Love & Torrence, 1989). Older workers who are rehired are paid less.

Employers argue that these differences are not due to worker age (Johnson & Johnson, 1982). Older workers are more likely than younger workers to have been on a particular job and/or working for a specific company for an extended period of time. Such people may be unaware of new techniques and new opportunities and this unawareness may make it harder for them to find a new job. The job that an older worker performed for a plant that closed may no longer be available anywhere. That job may be done by robots, managed by computers, or just not necessary and, perhaps, that is one reason why the older worker was let go in the first place. Such older workers may need to be retrained, and retraining of older workers takes longer and may, thus, cost more. Workers who have not looked for a job for 20 to 30 years may not have good resumé preparation skills, job search skills, and interview skills. Older workers looking for a new job may be far less willing to relocate than younger workers. Employers argue that older workers take longer to find a job and when hired often are paid less because their work skills are outdated and they do not search efficiently or interview successfully.

With conflict between the evidence that shows no decline in the performance of older workers on one side and the beliefs that older workers have outdated job and job search skills and are costly to the company on the other side, you might expect that lawsuits based on the ADEA are quite frequent. In the early 1980s, there was a threefold increase in the number of cases and more than 5000 older workers were awarded close to $25 million (Atchley, 1996). In the early 1990s the number of cases continued to increase to over 15,000 but the number of actual prosecutions declined (Atchley, 2000). In the mid-1990s, more than 20,000 cases were filed annually (Hannson, DeKoekkoek, Neece, & Patterson, 1997). Most recently, however, the number of cases has declined to 14,000 in 1999 and a little over 16,000 in 2000 (Ormsbee, 2001). Recent court decisions have made it more difficult to prove age discrimination and employers are more careful, subtle, or, perhaps, ruthless about their dismissal of older workers. Older workers are less willing to file a case when the odds of winning seem so low (Nicholson, 2000). Many prosecutors seem to believe that age discrimination is not caused by a dislike of older people or an intention to discriminate but, instead, by a lack of knowledge about the relationship between age and job performance (Eglit, 1989). Companies are not thought to be biased against older workers but simply uninformed. The company did not have bad intentions but may have made an honest mistake. When cases do go to court, companies win almost two-thirds of the time (Snyder & Barrett, 1988). It is hard to prove age discrimination and so litigation may be seen as not worth the effort by some older workers. Many other older workers are not even aware of the protection that is meant for them. It is probably the case that far more age discrimination takes place in hiring and firing decisions than is currently documented.

Since mandatory retirement is no longer permitted for most workers (see exceptions above), companies have had to find other ways to encourage older workers to leave. Many employers believe that they can cut costs more by getting rid of ten older workers than by getting rid of ten younger workers simply because older workers are, on average, paid more than younger workers. They are paid more because they have more seniority and, if you also believe that they are not as productive, then getting them to retire seems like a good economic decision. Sometimes such encouragement to retire is done in a negative manner and involves transfer to a less attractive, lower status job or providing less consideration of requests made by older workers (e.g., for vacation time). In one such case, older workers were far more likely to retire early after being assigned to work the night shift (Harma, Hakola, & Laitinen, 1992). Older adults have more difficulty in shifting their circadian rhythms and tend to perform better in the morning than at night. At night, they are more likely to experience reduced alertness that can affect their performance and safety and they take longer to adjust (Reilly, Waterhouse, & Atkinson, 1997).

In other cases, the encouragement to retire early is done more positively by providing incentives. Incentives are usually in the form of changes in the pension plan offered by the company. For retiring early, an older worker might be given extra years credit. For example, if 30 years with the company are needed for full pension benefits and the worker only has 25, the five additional years might be purchased if the individual agrees to retire now. Administrators seem to expect, in spite of data to the contrary, that replacing older workers with younger workers will increase productivity. Employers may in some cases save money.

An examination of such expectations and actual results was conducted in the late 1980s on a retirement incentive program for university faculty in Ohio. A questionnaire was used to obtain data from 240 department heads, deans, and provosts. Administrators expected that the university system would save money by getting rid of overpaid full professors and would increase productivity by bringing in younger, vital faculty. Retirement incentives were three to five years credit purchased toward full benefits and many faculty took advantage of this offer and retired early. Administrators were very positive about the program and over 80 percent claimed that it was good for faculty morale and higher education in Ohio. At the same time expected salary savings did not occur because new faculty were paid at nearly the same rate as retiring older faculty and they cost money to recruit. Faculty who retired were just as likely to have been highly productive and be some of the most valuable members of their departments as to have been nonproductive. Results showed that most of the expected benefits of early retirement for the universities simply did not occur. At the same time, administrators still believed incentives for early retirement were a good thing and 89 percent said that they would recommend use of such a program again (Seltzer & Karnes, 1988). It is very hard to overcome entrenched beliefs even when such beliefs are not supported by the data.

Transitions to Retirement.   Two common transitions to retirement from working full time are bridge (to retirement) jobs and retirement planning. Planning may be quite informal or may be through participation in some formal program.

A common belief is that most adults work at a job until age 65 and then retire. In fact, most workers do not fit this pattern. Quite a large number, anywhere between 42 and 78 percent, work at a different job or the same type of job for a different employer before retirement and after leaving their longest held job. These other jobs, **bridge jobs**, serve as a transition to full retirement. They are particularly sought by farm and nonfarm laborers who may need to find a less physically demanding job with the declines in muscle strength and sense organs that can occur in old age. These transition jobs are also sought by those who have been fired but who have not yet given up the search for a new job. The most likely workers to continue in a career job until retirement are professionals, although 29 percent of them also find other employment before retiring (Hayward, Friedman, & Chen,

1998; Ruhm, 1990). Professionals who do not seek a different job, such as doctors and lawyers, often make their career job into a bridge by reducing the number of hours that they work so that their longest held job becomes a part-time job. Close to 60 percent of self-employed professionals take this transition to full retirement (Quinn, 1981).

Bridge jobs are frequently lower pay and lower status jobs than the individual's longest held job. On average, individuals work at a bridge job for about five years before retiring. In many cases bridge jobs are part-time jobs. Part-time work before retirement is often desired by older workers but can be hard to find. In one survey, 21 percent of older men and 54 percent of older women, still in a full-time job, expressed a strong desire to work part time if such work were available. These workers often expect to stop working before they wish to simply because part-time bridge jobs are fairly hard to find; so many people want them and so few companies offer them. Over 50 percent of workers who have left their longest held job are employed part time; this trend is especially true for older women workers (American Association of Retired Person, 1991; Quinn & Burkhauser, 1993).

It is easy to imagine why a part time bridge job would be desirable before giving up work entirely. It is difficult to quit work, cold turkey, and plunge into retirement without some transition and a part-time bridge job fills that role nicely for a very large number of older adults. It is unfortunate that more companies do not offer such a transition to their older full-time employees instead of attempting to get rid of them altogether through early retirement incentives. Of course, from the company's point of view, it is expensive to allow older full-time workers to become part-time workers and still continue with full benefits.

Older worker.

Retirement planning, both formal and informal, is another type of transition to full retirement. It appears that most older workers do some informal planning as they get closer to retirement. One recent survey of 2500 working men and 2300 working women between the ages of 51 and 61 found that 74 percent had a particular retirement date (age or year) in mind, 13 percent believed that they would never retire, and only 12 percent had not thought about it. Of those who said they would never retire, 29 percent said they would not work full time after age 65; they will be looking for some of those hard to find part-time jobs. Of those who thought about retirement, over 60 percent said they thought about it some or a lot and had discussed it with their spouse. As you might expect, the closer to retirement, the more they thought about it and planned for it (Ekerdt, Kosloski, & DeViney, 2000). People who do less planning for retirement tend to be those who have very positive social relations at work and place high value on their work. One recent survey found that people who responded very positively to items such as "the people I work with are helpful and friendly" and "even if I didn't need the money, I would probably keep on working," were the least likely to be planning for retirement (Kosloski, Ekerdt, DeViney, 2001).

Informal retirement planning can, of course, take many different forms and can range from an individual doing some thinking about income after retirement to full family planning of finances, recreation, travel, and where to live after retirement. To assess informal planning among older workers living in a rural community, researchers surveyed 66 adults between the ages of 45 and 64. Participants were asked, among other things, to list retirement issues that were important to them and to list any actions they had taken regarding these important issues. More than half of those responding said that the most important issues were being able to share their experiences with others after they retired, knowing more about Social Security and financial benefits, learning how to adjust to the physical changes that would probably accompany old age, and finding ways to spend time with their children after retirement. In terms of actions taken, more than half had started saving money, determined beneficiaries for insurance, and selected an executor for their estate. Their informal planning had made them aware of the issues that were most important to them but they seemed to take action only on financial matters. Researchers found no gender, age, race, health, or education differences in this pattern of results. One reason for the lack of action on many important issues other than financial matters may be the paucity of information about these issues (Glass & Flynn, 2000). Participants believe these other issues are very important but do not know how to deal with them or where to find assistance.

While informal planning occurs frequently, only about 5 to 10 percent of older workers participate in formal retirement planning programs. These participants generally have higher income and more educated older male workers who have already done a fair amount of informal planning (American Association of Retired Persons, 1986; Atchley, 2000). Formal programs are far more likely to be offered by larger places of employment and very unlikely in small places or self-employment settings. Even when such programs are offered, however, only about 10 percent of those invited to participate actually do participate (Campione, 1988). It also seems to be the case that the people who most need formal preparation are the least likely to get it. For example, lower income workers are likely to have lower income after retirement and might benefit from some form of financial planning well before retirement. Single people will receive less income from Social Security than married people after retirement. Women may receive less income and/or lose a husband after retirement (see Chapter 13). All of these groups are less likely to have access to formal retirement planning programs (Dennis, 1989; Perkins, 1992). Adults who have a mental impairment or learning disorder often view their work as the major focus of their lives and find it particularly difficult to retire and stop going to work. Training programs have been shown to be especially useful for such individuals who can learn to replace work with recreational activities and to view retirement as a reward rather than punishment (Heller, Factor, Sterns, & Sutton, 1996). Unfortunately, such programs are rare for impaired older adults. Although the number of older workers who have such programs available to them and use these formal programs is small, those who do participate do seem to benefit and make the transition from work to retirement more easily (Glamser, 1980; Kamouri & Cavanaugh, 1986).

Formal retirement planning programs always address financial matters such as pension plans but only rarely cover some of the other topics that we have seen are important to older workers. To assess the value of formal programs and the importance of various topics that could be covered, 478 adults ranging in age from 50 to 84 and who had already retired were surveyed. The vast majority, 77 percent, thought such programs would be useful while only 5 percent thought they would not be useful (15 percent were not sure and 3 percent did not respond). Retired adults thought that financial information was very important but that information about leisure activities, traveling, creative endeavors, social participation, self-care, and psychological and physical well-being were also very important (Marcellini, Sensoli, Barbini, & Fioravanti, 1997). The transition to retirement would be easier if more information about these other topics were provided although the information that is provided is helpful. Figure 10-1 (p. 278) illustrates some of the issues that older workers and retirees would like to see included in preretirement planning programs.

People who participate in formal planning programs have done a fair amount of informal planning too. However, the reverse is not true since formal planning programs frequently are not available and when they are available frequently are not used. It could be that the obtained benefits of formal programs are, in fact, due to the informal planning that individuals do on their own. To assess the benefits of formal and informal planning, researchers examined 34 university faculty and staff before and after a formal retirement planning seminar. Results showed that both formal and informal planning were beneficial but in different ways. Both had benefits for participants' expectations about retirement. Informal planning, however, also increased self-efficacy. Self-efficacy, in this case, referred to the individual's confidence in successfully making the transition to retirement. The difference in benefits between the two types of planning is attributed to the belief that it takes longer to change self-efficacy and that informal planning usually goes on for an extended period of time (Taylor-Carter, Cook, & Weinberg, 1997). Both formal and informal planning, particularly when important issues beyond the financial ones are a part of the planning, are beneficial in helping the transition to retirement.

Retirement

Retirement refers to a self-determined or voluntary withdrawal from work. Being fired or downsized is not retirement because it is not voluntary. If one is unable to find a new job after being downsized, becomes discouraged, and quits searching, that counts as retirement

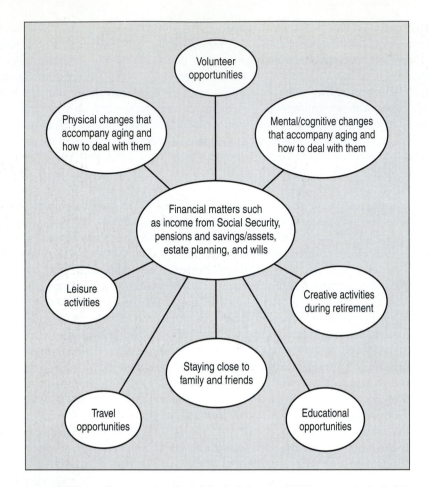

FIGURE 10-1   Some topics that older adults would like to see included in preretirement programs. The inner circle shows programs offered at present while the outer circles indicate kinds of topics that many older adults would like to have included.

because quitting is self-determined. Such a retirement would, of course, be an unhappy one while most retirements are more pleasant.

Demographics of Retirement

Chancellor Otto von Bismarck of Germany first established 65 as the retirement age late in the nineteenth century by supplying a pension for people over that age. Of course, not many adults lived to be age 65 in the late nineteenth century so the cost of providing pensions was fairly low. Before the twentieth century in the United States, retirement was rare and short because there were no government financial supports for retired people and people did not live as long. In 1900, the average number of years spent in retirement was 1.2

and retired people were typically supported by their families. People usually retired because they could no longer work. When the U.S. Social Security Act was passed in 1935 it designated 65 as the age of retirement. A prime impetus for Social Security and retirement was to lower the number of people actively looking for a job during the years around the Great Depression in the 1930s (Atchley, 2000). Social Security created jobs for younger workers by vacating positions previously held by older workers. Since then, unemployment has become less of a problem and retirement has come to be an expected event in the lives of most workers and, generally, people look forward to it. Retirement is viewed as the reward one receives for a lifetime of work (Ash, 1966). It is a chance to share in the nation's wealth that you helped to create.

Who Retires?   Who retires? The answer is most people retire. It is a easier to answer questions about who does not retire. Professionals are more likely to remain at work for longer periods of their lives than are nonprofessionals. People who like their work and are dedicated to their careers are more likely to remain at work for longer periods of their lives than those who do not like and are not dedicated to their work. People who fear, do not like, or find the idea of retirement repugnant are more likely to remain at work for longer periods of their lives than those who look forward to retirement (Adams, 1999; Mutran, Reitzes, & Fernandez, 1997). One longitudinal study followed 5000 working men, age 45 to 59, for 25 years. When they were between the ages of 69 and 74, 20 percent were still working and past the age of 75, 12 percent were still working. The vast majority had retired. In each age group, about two-thirds of those who were still working had part-time jobs and one third had full-time jobs. Those who were working past the typical age of retirement had good health, negative attitudes about retirement, higher education, and surprisingly low incomes. Many of those still working may need to continue to work for monetary reasons (Parnes & Sommers, 1994).

People who are no longer in good health, have been injured at work, or acquire some disability are likely to retire. In many instances withdrawing from work because of a disability is not counted as retirement since the withdrawal was not self-determined. About 25 percent of the population between the ages of 55 and 64 may be considered too disabled to hold a job and the majority of these individuals are women (Greenblum & Bye, 1987). The most common disabilities among these older workers are circulatory disorders, bone diseases (such as osteoporosis), and mental dysfunctions (McCoy & Weems, 1989).

Laborers all over the world have higher rates of disability than other types of workers (Iams, 1986). A study of 350 French coal miners found that those who worked longer, used more physical effort, carried heavier loads, used vibrating equipment, and worked in wet conditions (among other examples of occupational strain) suffered more impairment in use of their arms and shoulders, greater lower back pain, and had more difficulty getting around even after retiring (Calmels, Ecochard, Blanchon, Charbonnier, Cassou, & Gonthier, 1998). Construction workers, plumbers, and printers commonly come into contact with chemicals thought to be harmful. A study of 8000 German construction workers between the ages of 25 and 64 found that high levels of aspartate transaminase (AST) doubled the probability of early retirement and tripled the death rate compared to those rates for men with low levels of AST (Arndt, Brenner, Rothenbacher, Zschenderlein, Fraisse, & Fliedner, 1998). The same types of effects occur in United States. Although most people retire because it is viewed as a reward for a lifetime of work, too many retire because they have become disabled in their lifetime of work.

When Do Most People Retire?   Although 65 was the established retirement age, people today retire much earlier. This trend toward earlier retirement has been happening since 1970 in Germany, Japan, and Sweden, as well as the United States (Gendell, 1998). In the United States, the median age for retirement is 60.6 years (Hooyman & Kiyak, 1996). That means half of the people who retire do so before reaching 60.6 years of age. Only 24 percent of women and 44 percent of men still work full time after age 62, which is the lowest age at which one can receive Social Security benefits (Woodbury, 1999). After age 65, these percentages drop to 9 percent of women and 16 percent of men (Parnes & Sommers, 1994). The majority of people over age 62 get Social Security benefits and 75 percent of new recipients every year are retiring before age 65 (U.S. Bureau of the Census, 1992; U.S. Senate Special Committee on Aging, 1992). Since average life expectancy is now over 75, people who retire around age 60 can expect to spend about 15 years in retirement, or 20 percent of their life. A person who lives to be 100 may spend 40 years in retirement, or 40 percent of their life. Most people will probably *only* spend between 20 and 30 percent of their lives in retirement if the tendency to retire early and live long continues (Monk, 1994).

Although several factors play a role in the decision of when to retire, health and finances are the two reported most frequently (Fronstin, 1999). If an older worker is not healthy or has become disabled, retirement may be the only choice. Even without a specific disability or chronic disorder, people in poor health generally retire a couple of years earlier than those in good health. Some work suggests that health is a more influential factor in retirement decisions than are finances (Dwyer & Mitchell, 1999; Siddiqui, 1997). For men, cancer, diabetes, and heart attacks are the most frequent and serious health problems leading to early retirement while for women, hypertension is the leading health-related cause for early retirement (Colsher, Dorfman & Wallace, 1988). Health problems account for 60 percent of retirements that occur before the individual is truly ready to retire (Ozawa & Law, 1992).

If an older worker has sufficient funds built up in equity and/or savings and has a good pension as well as Social Security, retirement may be quite appealing. If sufficient funds are not available, retirement may be avoided. About 80 percent of older workers are well aware that their income will be significantly less after they retire but expect no major financial difficulties (Atchley, 2000).

People who are satisfied with their job and dedicated to their careers retire later than those who are not. Satisfaction and dedication are composed of a number of factors, all of which can influence the retirement decision. If the individual's immediate supervisor is fair and reasonable, perhaps even likeable, job satisfaction will be higher. If the commute to work is not too long and arduous, satisfaction will be higher. If the job itself is interesting and occasionally challenging, satisfaction will be higher. If one's fellow employees are friendly and helpful, job satisfaction will be higher. If the rate of pay is good with raises every year, job satisfaction will be higher. In most jobs, you will find some of these factors but not others. It is a lucky worker who finds all of these positive aspects in a job. Such a worker is likely to retire later than the worker who has few or none of these aspects.

Married couples report that their spouses are major influences on the decision of when to retire. Men say their wives influenced their retirement mainly by discussing it with them while women say their husbands influenced their retirement by also retiring. Recently, however, many more women are naming financial planning as a major reason for their retirement and are less likely to retire simply because their husband retired. Close to half of 228 couples (43 percent when the man retired and 45 percent when the woman retired) agreed that the retired person's spouse had equal or more influence on the decision (Smith & Moen, 1998). This makes sense since the retirement of one person is certain to influence the life of their marriage partner. Couples almost always discuss retirement as it gets closer.

Researchers have attempted to assess the importance of age for retirement. In one study, 319 adults ranging in age from 18 to over 65 were asked a number of questions about the age at which working men and women should retire. Close to half of the respondents argued that age is not a relevant factor for retirement. Those who thought that age was important were more often nonprofessionals, without college degrees, members of a minority group, and younger (or members of a more recent cohort). The average age they gave for when men should retire was 61.3 and for women 59.3 (the average of these two is 60.3, which is almost the same as the median age of retirement of 60.6). When respondents were asked whether there were any important consequences of working beyond or well beyond the expected age of retirement, most said there were none (Setterstein, 1998). In another study, 60 students between the ages of 20 and 25, 60 workers between the ages of 40 and 45, and 60 retired people between the ages of 60 and 65 were asked what the minimum (and maximum) ages for retirement would be for workers in 30 different occupations. They also were asked about important factors influencing performance in each of those occupations. Table 10-3 (p. 282) presents some of these data. Generally, retired people gave older minimum retirement ages than middle-age workers, and middle-age workers gave older retirement ages than younger students. Occupations that were perceived to require more physical capabilities were given younger retirement ages (Joulain, Mullet, LeComte, & Prévost, 2000).

Where Do People Go When They Retire?   Do people who retire move to Arizona or Florida? A survey of adults age 55 and older found that 84 percent do not want to move (American Association of Retired Persons, 1992). Sometimes, however, people must consider the option of moving. Relocating to a new home, a retirement community, or some form of care facility is likely to be considered at two points, and retirement is the first. When a person retires, they no longer need to live close to work and may consider moving to a location that offers opportunities and housing that is unavailable in their present location. Most, however, do not move when they retire and continue to live in single-family homes in mixed age neighborhoods (Gibler, Lumpkin, & Moschis, 1997). Those who do move (about 5 percent) often move into a smaller home. About half of these moves are in the same county while one quarter are to a different state (U.S. Bureau of the Census, 1994). An examination of 1990 Census Bureau data compared the moves of veterans and nonveterans over age 60, since veterans are believed to be more likely to migrate than nonveterans. When you divide the older population into veterans and nonveterans, you find, of course, that veterans are far more likely to be male (about 95 percent of the sample of veterans),

TABLE 10-3   Average Minimum Age for Retirement from Different Occupations Given by Young, Middle-Age, and Older Adults

	Age Group of Respondents		
Occupation	*Young*	*Middle-Age*	*Old*
Firefighter	49.6	54.2	55.2
Nurse	52.9	55.8	57.4
Sales representative	55.3	57.8	59.0
Social worker	54.5	57.4	58.4
Bus driver	53.8	56.0	55.9
Dentist	57.1	58.2	58.9
Judge	59.3	58.9	62.2
High school teacher	55.5	57.6	57.0
Politician	58.7	60.9	61.9
Clergy	63.3	60.9	64.6

Source: Data sampled from Joulain, M., Mullet, E., LeComte, C., & Prévost, R. (2000). Perception of appropriate age for retirement among young adults, middle-age adults, and elderly people. *International Journal of Aging & Human Development, 50,* 73–84.

married, and have higher income than nonveterans who are frequently widows. Veterans also have had more experiences away from home than nonveterans and, thus, might be more eager to relocate after retiring. Survey results confirmed this expectation. Six percent of veterans but only five percent of nonveterans had moved within the last five years. Even among veterans, the vast majority do not move after retirement. The most frequent destinations for those who moved out of their home state were Florida, Arizona, Texas, and North Carolina (Cowper, Longino, Kubal, Manheim, Dienstfrey, & Palmer, 2000).

As people retire at an earlier age and families live at greater distances from one another than they once did, many believe that postretirement moves will increase. Retired people may move closer to family who were not nearby during their working years. If neither work nor family hold a retired couple to a specific location then they may look for places that offer skiing, bike trails, or other outdoor activities. They may look for the lower living costs of a small town that is not too far from the part-time employment opportunities and culture of a big city (Howells, 1998). Box 10-1 (p. 284) provides some examples of popular places.

The second point at which movement may be considered is when one loses a spouse or because of serious illness (such as Alzheimer's disease) or disability (such as blindness) that requires family or professional assistance or institutionalization (Bogorad, 1987; Litwak & Longino, 1987). Moving to a retirement community is a likely option for people who experience a decrease in their ability to care for themselves and who live alone with no children living near by (Silverstein & Zablotsky, 1996). There are many retirement communities and care facilities available for people who find themselves in such circumstances and we examine them in Chapter 12.

Older retirees.

Why Do People Retire?   Why would anyone retire when they could continue going to work five days a week? As we have already discussed, workers may retire because of injury or poor health, a dislike of work or working conditions, or an inability to find another job after being dismissed. Workers may retire because they believe they have earned it and look forward to it. Family and friends also influence the decision to retire. If your spouse is eager for you to retire then you also may be eager to retire. On the other hand, if your spouse does not want you around then you may avoid retirement. If friends and neighbors frown on retirement and view retired people as over the hill, then an individual might be discouraged from retiring. On the other hand, if many friends are retired already or retiring soon and if retirement is viewed as the reward earned for a lifetime of work, then an individual might be encouraged to retire. If one believes that life would be empty without work or that it would be impossible to make ends meet on retirement income alone, then one is unlikely to retire. On the other hand, if Social Security, pension, and savings seem to be adequate, then one is likely to retire. If one has plans to remain busy in retirement, then retirement may be more attractive than if one has no such plans. Up to 40 percent of older workers hope to obtain another job after retirement and to continue contributing to their community (Lewis, 1999). Clearly many factors are involved and these factors interact as they influence the decision to retire.

Some of the interactions among factors that influence the decision to retire are illustrated in a recent longitudinal study of 897 older workers and retirees. One finding was that individuals who had financial responsibility for children were far less likely to retire.

BOX **10-1**

The Top Retirement Locations in the United States

There are many places to retire to in the United States but some locations are excellent for those who (1) are not tied down by work, family, or other connections to their present location, (2) want a new and different place that offers recreational activities and cultural opportunities, and (3) do not want to spend their entire savings and income on housing. John Howells (1998) of *Consumers Digest* rates the following as among the very best.

Ashland, OR. Ashland is a small college town with relatively mild winters (only eight inches of snow on average). Southern Oregon State College is well-known for its theater and specialization in the works of Shakespeare.

Bloomington, IN. This is a small friendly community with Indiana University offering music and theatre almost every night of the week. The town is surrounded by gentle hills and many homes sell for less than $80,000.

Columbia, MO. There are four universities located in Columbia with many musical, theatrical, or sporting events taking place. The city is big enough to offer many of the opportunities of larger cities but with a lower crime rate.

Green Valley, AZ. More than half of the people who live in this small town are retired. The desert and mountains are beautiful for exploration and the elevation makes the weather a little cooler. Green Valley is only 25 miles from Tuscon.

Hot Springs, AK. This small town is in the foothills of the Ozark mountains. Most recreational activities take place in the mountain forests or nearby lakes and rivers, including actual hot springs.

Kerryville, TX. Almost a third of the residents of this small community are adults age 65 and older. The town is in hill country and not too far from Austin and San Antonio. Kerryville attempts to assist older adults seeking employment with an annual Senior Job Opportunity Fair.

Oxford, MI. Oxford is a small university town with a university culture. An old southern town square provides shopping, quality restaurants, inexpensive entertainment, and a bookstore. Retirees from all over the country can be found here.

Palm Coast, FL. This small town is on the Atlantic midway between Daytona and St. Augustine. Golf, tennis, water skiing, and boating opportunities are everywhere and a number of neighborhoods have canals and marinas.

Paradise, CA. Paradise is located in the woods of the Sierra Nevada mountains. Opportunities for hiking, camping, fishing, and hunting are ample and most homes sit on large lots surrounded by trees.

Ruidoso, NM. This town is located in a canyon filled with pine, oak, and aspen trees and a crystal clear river. Horse racing is available in the summer and skiing in the winter.

Savannah, GA. Old southern culture is abundant and downtown and river walk are filled with restaurant and shopping opportunities. Most retirees live away from the central city and close to beautiful woods, rivers, or beaches.

University Triangle, NC. The University of North Carolina at Chapel Hill, North Carolina State University in Raleigh, and Duke University in Durham comprise this triangle with an abundance of cultural and intellectual events and part-time job opportunities.

Howell also praises Aiken, SC, Boise, ID, Durango, CO, Gainesville, FL, Georgetown TX, Hendersonville/Brevard, NC, Las Vegas, NV, Mena, AK, Ozark/Enterprise, AL, Rio Rancho, NM, San Luis Obispo, CA, Sedona, AZ, and Vancouver, WA. He strongly recommends that planning begins long before actual retirement.

Researchers point out that this may mean that such people continue working to support their children or, in other cases, workers who are not even considering retirement might choose to continue supporting their children because they are still working. Unmarried men with no children and women with children who saw them infrequently were unlikely to retire. At the same time, men with children who saw them infrequently often tended to retire so that they might have more time to spend with their children. Results showed that caring for a sick spouse or a disabled family member was not related to retirement decisions even though other research has found that men are more inclined to retire when they are taking care of a sick wife (Szinovacz & De Viney, 2000). In this study, caregiving sometimes led to a decision to retire while in other cases the individual continued to work in order to pay for caregiving (e.g., medical supplies, equipment, professional help). African American women who had one child living at home were likely to retire while White American women and African American men in the same situation were less likely to retire. Researchers suggest that this complex interaction may have to do with caregiving and/or a working child's support of a parent. The factors involved in the decision to retire can exert different influences on different people and different people have different attitudes toward retirement (Szinovacz, De Viney, & Davey, 2001).

Attitudes toward Retirement.   Most older workers have positive attitudes toward retirement and look forward to it (Atchley, 1999; Cockerham, 1991). Retired persons are no longer viewed as being unable to care for themselves, incompetent, too old to work, or close to death. Retirement is a reward. However, the American work ethic places high value on being a productive worker. Theorists suggest that people have resolved this apparent discrepancy between the work ethic and retirement by adopting a *busy ethic*. Retired people who stay busy are regarded as valuable members of society even though they are no longer productive workers (Ekerdt, 1986). They are busy with nonwork activities including recreation, leisure, hobbies, and serving as volunteers.

Some psychologists believe that retirement is a new life challenge for older individuals and that is why many retire. For younger adults, major challenges include finding the right career, job, and mate. For middle-age adults, major challenges include providing for your family by succeeding in work and making a mark. As children leave home and find their own careers, jobs, and mates, older adults no longer need to achieve recognition in the workplace. Their attention may now shift to those closest to them, their family. The challenge then becomes one of personally caring for family members. A high salary is less important after the children are on their own and/or have completed college. Continued work takes time away from family while retirement offers the opportunity to increase the time spent with family (Belsky, 1999; Carstensen, 1995). Perhaps this change in perspective offers a new challenge and is another reason why many people retire.

The view that retirement brings new opportunities or challenges and is a reward to be treasured is not a view shared by all individuals or all groups. Although women and minorities frequently have this view, others do not.

Gender and Ethnic Group Differences.   A major factor influencing the decision to retire is whether it is financially feasible. If sufficient funds are not available from Social Security, pensions, and savings, then a person may avoid retirement. We learned that formal planning for retirement is more available for those with white-collar jobs working for larger companies. Women and members of minority groups are less likely to have sufficient funds to support retirement and less access to formal planning than do white-collar White American men. There are health differences among different ethnic groups. Members of minority groups are more likely to work in more hazardous, as well as lower paying jobs and, thus, be more likely to suffer injury, disability, or ill health from such work. The major gender group differences with respect to retirement are financial while the major ethnic group differences are both in the areas of finance and health.

Gender and ethnic group financial differences at retirement stem from gender and ethnic group differences at work. Although women have made great advances in the workplace and more women work now than they did 25 years ago, the gender difference still exists. At every age, a greater proportion of men than women are employed (U.S. Bureau of the Census, 1997). Women who are working make less, on average, than working men and tend to be in lower level jobs. Look at the most frequent jobs for men and women shown in Table 10-1. Over 90 percent of the top management positions are held by White men (Rieske & Holstege, 1996). Women are more likely than men to retire involuntarily or to discontinue work at one or more times during their careers as they give birth (perhaps more than once) or leave to care for an aging parent. Workers caring for an older parent are more likely to have difficulties sleeping, frequent headaches, increased anxiety, and be absent from work (Lee, 1997). Both time away from work and changing jobs reduce the opportunity to invest funds in retirement pension plans. Income from pensions following retirement is the largest single gender difference. The pensions of retired women are, on average, only about 60 percent as large as the pensions of retired men and many more men receive pensions than do women (Belgrave, 1988; O'Grady-LeShane, 1996). Furthermore, only about 25 percent of women over the age of 65 receive a pension from a former employer and the median income from a pension is less than $5000 compared to a median of nearly $8000 for men (Richardson, 1999).

It is expected that these gender differences will diminish but not disappear as today's working women reach retirement age. Many more women are employed now than in the past and close to one-third are covered by plans that allow them to designate how their pension funds are invested (compared to about 40 percent of working men) (Sundén & Surette, 1998). Surveys of working women indicate that they are less likely than older cohorts to rely exclusively on their husband's retirement benefits and more likely to evaluate their own earned benefits (Honig, 1998). At the same time, men are more likely than women to plan for retirement in terms of finances and lifestyle factors. It is estimated that over 70 percent of working women have not planned for retirement (Meinecke & Parker, 1997). Fewer women than men, regardless of hours at work, receive retirement information (Onyx, 1998). In terms of allocating pension funds to high-risk (and potentially high-benefit) stocks versus low-risk (and lower benefit) bonds, marital status as well as gender plays a role. Single men are the most likely to choose investments in stocks. Single women and married men are the least likely to choose high-risk investments. A middle-risk investment could be to invest some assets in stocks and some in bonds. This strategy is more likely to be chosen by men than women, especially married women (Sundén & Surette, 1998). Single working women may be risking a high retirement pension by investing too little and too conservatively.

Older African and Hispanic American workers of either gender are more likely to be forced into involuntary retirement than are older White American workers. They are more likely to lose their job as they age and to have greater difficulty in finding a new job. Part of this is due to the physical demands of the jobs held by minority workers compared to the less physically demanding jobs held by most White Americans. Many unemployed minority workers, thus, retire because they have no other choice (Flippen & Tienda, 2000). Members of minority groups are more likely to have lower paying jobs and have a number of different jobs during their work lives. For African American men, the rate of employment has been lower than the rate for White American men since the 1940s, but the relative wages of African American men have been increasing (Welch, 1990). Those who work earn more than previous generations of African American men, but on average African and Hispanic American men earn only about 60 percent as much as White American men (Hogan, Kim, & Perucci, 1997). African and Hispanic American workers are more likely to be disabled, and unable to continue work and to be less healthy. They also have more difficulty finding a new job once they are ready to begin work again than are White American workers (Choi, 1997). Members of minority groups are less likely to stay in one job for most of their work lives and workers with discontinous work experiences are less likely to think of themselves as retired, more likely to be disabled, and less likely to have a pension (Gibson, 1991). Over the course of their lives, African Americans typically spend more time working and more time disabled than White Americans while White Americans spend more time retired (Hayward, Friedman, & Chen, 2000).

Those least likely to be well prepared for retirement are women and members of a minority group. These groups are said to experience *double jeopardy*. Women and members of minorities have less opportunity to begin or to build up an adequate pension for retirement. This is due to discontinous work, lower pay, and lower status jobs. Older African American women are more likely than any other group to work in cleaning or cooking jobs in private households. Such jobs rarely pay much or offer opportunities to invest a portion of earnings in retirement plans and rarely offer benefits such as health insurance (Rieske & Holstege, 1996). For such disadvantaged workers, retirement may hold no benefits. Such individuals may be forced to work until they can work no longer.

In countries less technologically advanced than the United States, Japan, or those in Europe, the pattern of retirement can be quite different than the pattern we have been examining. Box 10-2 (p. 288) describes some aspects of retirement in several of these places.

Phases of Retirement

There is a strong tendency for social science researchers to look for patterns of and regularities in human behavior when major life events occur. The most well-known description of phases of retirement is provided by Robert Atchley (2000), who is quick to point out that not all retired people go through these phases. Phases of retirement are only meant "to organize ideas about the issues people face in taking up, playing, and relinquishing the retirement role." (p. 253) Brief case studies of retired people in these phases are presented in Box 10-3 (p. 289).

The first phase is known as the **honeymoon**. Immediately following retirement many retirees experience an elevated mood. All of the things that had to wait for retirement

BOX **10-2**

Cultural Differences in Retirement

Retirement in fully developed countries such as the United States is the type with which most of us are familiar. In less developed countries, retirement frequently does not exist as an official time of life and, when it does exist is very different.

One examination of cultural differences involved older adults in Botswana, Ireland, and Hong Kong and compared retirement in these places to that in the United States (Keith, Fry, Glascock, Ikels, Dickerson-Putnam, Harpending, & Draper, 1994). Retirement was viewed and experienced differently in the four countries. In Botswana, the typical features of aging seem to occur earlier and are more obvious. Most work is hard labor which takes a toll on workers sooner than the less demanding jobs frequently found in other parts of the world. Furthermore, there are fewer opportunities to obtain hearing aids, false teeth, and other assistive devices to maintain functioning or the appearance of youth. Adults retire when they can no longer work but generally remain active in their families. In Zimbabwe, many older adults are very poor and must live in special housing provided by church groups. This housing can be very restrictive or function more like a co-op. Co-op arrangements are generally preferred (Holmes & Holmes, 1995). In Clifden, Ireland, adults are generally self-employed or work at farming or fishing. Here people never really retire; they simply work less as they grow older and begin to receive a pension to assist them in meeting their needs. In Hong Kong a retired person is an older person who is unable to find or continue steady work and many older adults are unable to find any work at all. Pensions are small and most older retired adults must rely on their children for housing and support. Community homes for older adults in Hong Kong often are crowded and older residents sometimes cease writing to relatives believing it would be better to be thought of as dead than as a resident of one of these old age homes (Holmes & Holmes, 1995). Retirement has more negative connotations in these other cultures. Patterns of retirement in the United States, as you know, are similar to these places in some ways but different in many others.

Another study examined retirement in Chile, the Dominican Republic, Sri Lanka, and Thailand (Kaiser, 1993). Older adults in all of these countries were still actively involved in domestic activities. The most frequently named domestic activity in Chile and Sri Lanka was household cleaning while in the Dominican Republic it was food preparation and in Thailand it was childcare. The most frequently reported source of retirement income was a pension in Chile; retired adults in the other three countries named their children as their primary source of income. In all four countries, retired adults listed finances as their major problem and health was a close second. Their concerns are similar to retired adults in the United States.

to occur can now be done. One no longer has to go to work and may feel truly free for the first time in a long time. Many retirees travel during this early phase. This is a time of much activity and great joy. The length of the honeymoon phase is usually not long and depends to some extent upon the individual's preparation for retirement and having sufficient funds.

Instead of an active, joyous honeymoon phase, some people begin retirement with a joyful phase of **rest and relaxation**. After working all their lives, some want nothing more than to take it easy. In this phase, overall activity level declines. This period of relaxation

BOX **10-3**

People in Different Phases of Retirement

Pat is a 64-year-old retired dentist who seems to be in the **honeymoon phase**. He and Jeanne, his retired spouse, have enrolled in a literature class at the university. Class begins when they return from a three-week tour of Europe. Pat and Jeanne take tennis lessons at a local health club. Pat says, "Now I can do all those things that I've waited for years, no decades, to do; we've never felt so alive and haven't been this happy since our first honeymoon, forty-two years ago."

Miranda is a 66-year-old retired manager who currently is in the **rest and relaxation phase**. She worked over 40 hours a week in a high-stress position and is simply tired. After Miranda retired she terminated her membership in a health club and spends most of her time at home. Fellow workers bought her a new bicycle as a retirement gift six months ago but she has not used it.

Janine is a 59-year-old retired nurse who never made any retirement plans. She left work after becoming dissatisfied with her chances for promotion and the relatively low salary increases she was receiving year after year. Now she cannot find anything to do that she enjoys and all of her friends are still employed. She wishes she had stuck it out, at least for a few more years. Retirement is the biggest mistake she ever made. She is in the **disenchantment phase**.

George and Peggy are both 72 and have been retired for several years. They are in the **retirement routine phase**. Every morning they get up at 8:00, have a relaxed breakfast, and then go for a walk around the nearby park. When they return George reads the morning paper while Peggy wraps herself in a novel. Lunch is at noon and then they each work on chores for a few hours. Every Monday afternoon they go out to a movie, Tuesdays are for their favorite TV shows, Wednesday is the day for bridge with friends, Thursdays are when each plays poker with their own friends, Fridays are for resting at home, Saturdays are for bingo at the church, and Sundays are for church and a variety of activities.

Allen is a 61-year-old retired man who is in the **termination phase**. He is looking for a new job because he needs to make more money before he can retire in the way he hoped he would be able to once he turned 60. He searches the want ads in the local paper daily, has applied to about a dozen jobs, and has had two interviews but no offers.

can last for a couple of years before some restlessness sets in and the person resumes activity (Atchley, 1982).

After a honeymoon or a rest and relaxation period, many retirees settle into an **initial routine** and organize all the activities that they planned to do while they were still working. The high activity level of the retiree who was in a honeymoon phase now slows down while the low activity of the retiree who was in a rest and relaxation phase increases. This initial routine usually undergoes several modifications but generally evolves into a regular, permanent **retirement routine**. The retired couple may get up at the same time every morning; have regular daytime activities such as exercise and chores, or activities every few days or a couple of times a week such as shopping, or once a month activities such as an outing or tour. They may do certain chores like cleaning, laundry, or gardening at a regular time on certain days; get together with family or friends on a regular schedule; attend religious services at the same time every week; watch the same TV shows and go to bed after the evening news. Such a routine can be very comfortable and typically changes little unless or until some other major life change, such as loss of a spouse or serious illness, occurs.

Some retirees are thought to go through a phase of **disenchantment** before achieving a retirement routine. Their hopes and plans for retirement may have been unrealistic and the reality of their situation and the inability to do all the things they had hoped to do may lead to mild or even major depression. One's plans may be dashed if one becomes disabled or loses a spouse or if available funds are insufficient to finance all the activities dreamed of in the years preceding retirement. A retired person may find that they have nothing to do and that life has become uninteresting without work. However, it is thought that very few retirees actually experience disenchantment. In one longitudinal study, over 300 people were followed from 1975 to 1995 and not one experienced a disenchantment phase following retirement (Atchley, 1999).

With or without disenchantment, some retirees enter a **termination** phase and return to work, become disabled, or become full-time caregivers for an ailing spouse. Of course, returning to work can be difficult since many employers favor younger workers. In many cases, retirement is not completely terminated but only dimished by the need to perform other required activities. All of these phases relate to how well one is adjusting to retirement.

Adjustment to Retirement

Adjustment to retirement is generally very positive for the majority of older adults (Rosenkoetter & Garris, 1998). People tend to look forward to retirement even though they anticipate less income; most people are prepared and have gone through informal, if not formal, planning; and, disenchantment is rare. Worries about retirement and even about broader issues, such as the destruction of the environment, the numbers of homeless people, and the corruption in government, are generally lower for retired people than for those still working and higher for women than men (Skarborn & Nicki, 2000). Many retirees seem to be happy. At the same time, you might expect those who are forced into retirement to be less positive in their adjustment to retirement.

Financial Adjustment.   Those who have good income after retirement have better financial adjustment to retirement than those with poor income. Income during retirement is traditionally described as a *three-legged stool*. One leg stands for income from Social Security, one for retirement pensions, and one for personal savings and assets (Gale, 1997).

Economists and financial planners say that an individual's preretirement standard of living can be maintained after retirement as long as the three-legged stool replaces at least 60 percent of preretirement income (Atchley, 1997). After retirement, less income is needed to maintain the same standard that the person had while working. With more leisure time, the retiree can perform tasks that others may have been paid to do in the past; there are fewer people living at home and needing support; expenses are lower (there is no longer a need to maintain a wardrobe for work); often the mortgage is paid off; there are no payroll taxes; and income tax is lower (Gale, 1997). In cases where medical expenses, housing, or transportation costs may be higher than normal, one may need 70 to 80 percent (or more) of preretirement income to maintain the same standard of living.

The first leg of the three-legged stool, **Social Security**, makes up 40 percent of all income for older adults and is received by 95 percent of older, retired people (American Association of Retired Persons, 1994). Social Security replaces about 44 percent of preretirement income (National Academy on Aging, 1994). Social Security benefits include cost-of-living adjustments. At present, one must be at least 62 years old and have been continuously employed and contributing to Social Security for at least 8 years to be eligible for Social Security benefits. To receive full benefits, one must be at least 65 years old when retiring. One who retires and receives benefits before the age of 65 never receives full benefits. Social Security benefits are based on average earnings during an individual's working years and are higher for lower income workers. While this may seem unfair at first, it makes sense if you think about it. People with higher incomes are able to put more of their income into savings and are more likely to have jobs providing pensions while those with lower incomes have little or no money left for savings. Those with low incomes need more money from Social Security after retirement just to meet the basic costs of living. It also is important to know that Social Security money comes from current working adults and not from funds contributed by retired adults. There is a cap on the amount of income taken for Social Security. Although you pay more into Social Security as you earn more (because it is taken as a percentage of wages), you pay no additional Social Security once your income reaches a certain level. Some argue that removal of this cap would help make Social Security available for future retirees since those who make large amounts of money would then contribute more to Social Security.

As the number of retired adults increases with the baby boom generation, the number of working adults that support retired adults will decrease and some fear that Social Security taxes will have to greatly increase or the system will go bankrupt. In 1970 there were 410 working adults contributing to Social Security for every 100 retired adults. That number dropped to 320 workers for every 100 retirees in 1980 and is expected to be about 200 workers for every 100 retirees in 2025. To help offset this trend, the age of eligibility will increase over the next several years until 2027 when one will have to be at least 72 to receive Social Security benefits (Hooyman & Kiyak, 1996). It is expected that the increase in minimum age to receive benefits will result in an increase in the average age of retirement and so lessen some of the cost of Social Security. It will be important to watch these changes over the next decade. The National Committee to Preserve Social Security and Medicare keeps a close eye on issues important for health and retirement and issues a monthly report as do several other organizations. Others believe that Social Security will have no problems meeting the needs of future retirees (Rosenblatt, 1999).

The second leg, **pensions**, make up 18 percent of all income for older adults and are received by 66 percent of older, retired people (Quinn & Smeeding, 1994). Pensions are income paid to the retired person through their place of employment. Pensions replace about 25 to 30 percent of preretirement income (Gale, 1997). About 90 percent of federal, state, or local government workers and 50 percent of private company workers have pension plans available to them. To be eligible for benefits, however, one must work for a required number of years and/or reach a certain age before retiring. Most pension plans do not include any cost-of-living increases after retirement and so the income received remains the same regardless of inflation.

The third leg, **savings and assets**, makes up 23 percent of all income for older adults and also are held by 66 percent of older, retired people. However, income from assets is less than $500 a year for one-quarter of these people and is over $5000 for only a third (Radner, 1991). The proportion of preretirement income replaced by savings and assets is highly variable. The biggest asset for most retired people is their home which may comprise almost half of their net worth (National Academy on Aging, 1994). About 76 percent of older, retired people own their home or are close to paying off their mortgage. Of course, home repairs, utilities, and property taxes are continual expenses for home owners and must be paid from Social Security and pensions. Home equity counts as a major portion of the assets of older adults but is not income that can be used to pay expenses.

Social Security, pensions, savings and assets make up 81 percent (40 + 18 + 23) of all income for older adults. Another 17 percent comes from earnings usually from those difficult-to-find, part-time jobs (American Association of Retired Persons, 1994). These averages hide the racial, ethnic, and gender group differences that lead to higher rates of poverty among African and Hispanic American older adults than among White American older adults and among females than among males (Choi, 1997). For many retired adults, Social Security is the primary or only support received during retirement. For those over 85, 85 percent receive half (or more) of their income from Social Security; for those over 65, 62 percent are in this situation (Aleska, 1994). Those who receive a smaller percentage of their total income from Social Security are those who obviously receive more income from pensions, savings, and assets. These wealthier persons tend to be White American men.

The income gap between African and Hispanic Americans on the one hand and White Americans on the other is larger in retirement than in the working years. Table 10-4 shows average annual income for retired minority and White Americans from Social Security, pensions, and assets. These data were gathered by Richard Hogan, Meesook Kim, and Carolyn C. Perrucci from 3422 married men and show that White Americans earn more in every category but that the biggest gap is in earnings from assets. Social Security earnings by minorities are 72 percent of White American earnings; minority earnings from

TABLE 10-4   Average Income for Retired Men from Social Security, Pensions, and Assets

Racial group	Average income from		
	Social Security	*Pensions*	*Assets*
White Americans	$8767	$3984	$5596
African and Hispanic Americans	$6300	$2491	$ 825

Source: Data from Hogan, R., Kim, M., & Perrucci, C. C. (1997). Racial inequality in men's employment and retirement earnings. *Sociological Quarterly, 38*, 431–438.

pensions are 62 percent of White Americans; but minority earnings from assets are only 15 percent of White Americans. Other work shows that for White Americans, 19 percent of total retirement income comes from assets while for African and Hispanic Americans the percentage from assets is only four and seven percent, respectively (Choi, 1997). Although all Americans showed increased income over the last 30 years, the increases were greater for White Americans. Minority Americans have had difficulty acquiring assets to boost their retirement income and to pass on to their children and grandchildren (Hogan, Kim, & Perrucci, 1997).

Married retired couples have higher income than single retired adults. Women are more likely to be single in old age than are men since women live longer than men. About 15 percent of older women but only eight percent of older men are below the poverty level (American Association of Retired Persons, 1994). Women who are also African or Hispanic Americans are doubly disadvantaged. Only four percent of White older couples are below the poverty line while 18 percent of African and 22 percent of Hispanic American couples are below that line. For singles, especially women, the rates are much higher. The poverty rates for single White, African, and Hispanic retired men are 14, 48, and 44 percent, respectively. Those rates for single White, African, and Hispanic American women are 26, 61, and 59 percent, respectively (Choi, 1997).

Will the retirement picture get better for minorities and women who work through the twenty-first century and as baby boomers begin to retire ten to twenty years from now? We expect that the current differences in retirement finances will diminish as differences in the workplace have diminished and availability of pensions has increased but we expect that it will take time before equality is the norm. For a look at how well baby boomers are preparing for retirement and how well they are likely to do when they reach retirement, see Box 10-4 (p. 294).

Health and Life Satisfaction.   Researchers examining health among older adults have generally found lower stress levels among the retired than among those still working (Midanik, Sokhikian, Ransom, & Tekawa, 1995). In one longitudinal study of satisfaction with retirement, 117 men were followed from preretirement to seven years after retirement. Researchers measured amount of distress that people felt, energy level, financial and interpersonal satisfaction, feelings of being in control, and overall satisfaction with life. All measures showed an increase after retirement and peaked at about one year. After seven years of retirement, most measures decreased but not as low as they were at preretirement. With retirement, people experienced a gain in perceived control over the events in their lives (Gall, Evans, & Howard, 1997). Other work has found the same general pattern after retirement although some cross-sectional comparisons have found lower perceived control (Ross & Drentea, 1998).

Of course, the adjustment to retirement is more difficult for those who are forced to retire or who do so for reasons of health or disability (Lehr, Jüchtern, Schmitt, Sperling, Fischer, Grünendahl, & Minnemann, 1998). Comparisons of measures of distress between those who retire voluntarily and those who retire for health reasons or because they were let go show show higher levels of distress, anxiety, and depression among the latter (Sharpley & Layton, 1998; Gallo, Bradley, Siegel, & Kasl, 2000). Those who retire involuntarily show lower levels of life satisfaction (Schultz, Morton, & Weckerle, 1998).

B O X **10-4**

Will the Boomers be Ready for Retirement?

Baby boomers are people born between 1946 and 1965. They should begin to retire in large numbers between the years 2010 and 2020. Members of the baby boom generation have higher annual incomes than prior generations and are, thus, expected to have higher average incomes after retirement than today's retired adults (Manchester, 1997). They should benefit from Social Security just as today's retirees do.

Currently, about 57 percent of boomers own their own home. This number is expected to increase as younger boomers (those born between 1960 and 1965) begin to buy homes. About 50 percent of this generation is currently enrolled in a pension plan for retirement and this number is expected to increase over the next several years. Inflation, however, could easily erode large portions of income from pensions since pensions do not usually include any adjustments for cost of living. It is expected that baby boomers will have more expenses than today's retired adults because they tend to have higher standards of living. Boomers also are expected to have more expenses associated with caring for older parents than today's retirees do since their parents are expected to live longer than their grandparents and great grandparents (Dennis & Migliaccio, 1997). These expectations mean that savings and assets will be absolutely critical if members of the baby boom generation are to maintain their current standard of living after retirement.

Are boomers saving enough? It is estimated that baby boomers are saving only about one-third of what they will need (Dennis & Migliaccio, 1997; Gale, 1997; Glass & Kilpatrick, 1998). Currently, married couples are saving more than singles and men are saving more than women but most are not saving enough (Glass & Kilpatrick, 1998). Those who are worst off, in terms of investing in assets and saving for their future retirement, are those who have lower levels of education, are single, and who have not been able to buy a house (Manchester, 1997).

Of course the future could hold low levels of inflation, which would mean that income from pensions would not suffer so much. More boomers could marry and/or buy houses within the next few years and increase their savings and assets. The best estimate seems to be that, as things are now, about one-third of boomers are doing fine in preparing for retirement, about one-third are in terrible shape, and about one-third could go either way depending on a number of economic factors, such as inflation and future health costs (Gale, 1997).

An old myth that is incorrect is that retirement increases stress and leads to poor health. Retirees were once thought to deteriorate rapidly. Findings like those described above show that there is less stress following retirement. Retirement does not lead to poor health but poor health often leads to retirement. Retired people generally do not report a decline in their health but often report increased concern about maintaining the good health that they have (Mein, Higgs, Ferrie, & Stansfield, 1998). Good psychological resources before retirement, such as high self-efficacy and good social support, facilitate a successful adjustment to retirement. Improvements in healthy behaviors, such as eating better and exercising more, result from such resources and increase following retirement (Midanik, Sokhikian, Ransom, & Tekawa, 1995; Wells & Kendig, 1999).

Social Support.   It is likely that when you stop going to work everyday, your contacts with friends from work will diminish. One might expect to find a lower level of social support for retired people than for people still on the job. Generally, contacts with friends from work do seem to decline with retirement but the quality of friendships and contact with close friends does not (Bossé, Aldwin, Levenson, Spiro, & Mroczek, 1993). Retirement may affect some members of the individual's social network but family and close friends are unaffected. The support of close family members and the worldview of family members are important factors in adjustment to retirement. Families with a strong, positive outlook are better able to deal with potential problems and the social support they provide enables the retiree to succeed in overcoming unforseen difficulties (Smith, 1997). Some retired people move to retirement communities and lose contact with friends outside of that community. Research shows that those who move to these communities, but maintain close contact with friends outside the retirement community, maintain better mental health and show less depression (Potts, 1997). Losing contact by moving to a retirement community can decrease social support from persons in the inner circles (family members and close friends) and result in more difficulties. Thus, positive social support, which comes mainly from the closest members of a social support network, is not influenced by retirement but may be influenced by a move away from home following retirement. Perhaps that is one reason why so few people move after retiring.

For a married adult, a prime source of social support is the spouse and this is especially true for men (see Chapter 9). Before retirement couples frequently worry about the effects that retirement will have on the quality of their marriage and are often more concerned about those effects than about income and health (Hilbourne, 1999). Research, however, indicates that the quality of married life and overall marital satisfaction does not decline when individuals retire and may, in some instances, improve (Atchley & Miller, 1983; Vinick & Ekerdt, 1989). Retired couples have fewer complaints than preretirement couples (Kulik, 2001). After retirement, married couples have more time to spend together. Married retirees tend to spend more time doing the household tasks that they did before retirement and to help their partner more with her or his tasks (Kulik, 2001; Szinovacz, 2000). A closeness that may have diminished in the childrearing years may be renewed. Next to the early years of a marriage, the retirement years are frequently reported to be the happiest of all (Rieske & Holstege, 1996).

Activity.   To feel good about themselves and to adjust well to retirement, it may be important for Americans to stay busy. Staying busy does not necessarily mean physical activity. After retirement, one might stay busy with a wide variety of activities.

In a telephone survey of 2592 people, retirees and workers were asked about their typical activities. When retirees were asked what activities they participate in during the day, about 50 percent reported engaging in household chores and family care tasks such as cooking, cleaning, and laundry. Also mentioned was serving as a sitter for grandchildren or as a caregiver for an older relative or spouse. Leisure activities were named by 21 percent and included watching TV, playing golf, walking, playing cards, and visiting friends. These activities are probably closer to what you might expect to find retired people doing. Close to 12 percent reported activities that maintained the house and/or yard, eight percent did unpaid work for a family business, four and one half percent did school work, and four percent reported working as a volunteer. The activities of retirees involved far less problem solving than the activities of those still working and retirees did not have higher levels of stress (Ross & Drentea, 1998). Other studies have found that the most common activities for retirees are reading, watching TV, walking, playing games, arts and crafts, visiting, gardening, traveling, touring, and participating in club events (Harris, 1976; McAvoy, 1979; Nystrom, 1974; Roadberg, 1981).

Some retirees wish they had spent more time in school or completed higher levels of **education**. It is estimated that close to 35 percent of older adults are functionally illiterate. The Adult Education Act was passed to help older adults develop reading skills, complete high school, and improve their education, but less than five percent of those who participate in programs supported by this act are over 60 years of age (U.S. Senate Special Committee on Aging, 1991).

Retired adults who want to further their education often attend classes at nearby community colleges, four-year colleges, and universities. Many of these places offer older adults the opportunity to audit classes. Classes that attract the greatest numbers of retired adults are in arts and crafts, literacy training, computers, humanities and social sciences, performing arts, career counseling, and exercise (Atchley, 2000).

There are also educational opportunities outside of the traditional school settings. Shepherd's Centers across the country offer numerous adult education classes on a wide variety of topics. Elder Hostel offers many classes in a variety of settings in the United States and abroad. In the United States and Canada there are now over 200 separate institutes that cater to retirees and specialize in peer-led learning where students are actively involved in group learning activities (Linnehan & Naturale, 1998).

Serving as a **volunteer** is regarded as one of the more rewarding activities for retirees. It is estimated that close to 40 percent of retired adults are actively involved in volunteer work (Chambre, 1993). These volunteers play an important part in the lives of children, adolescents, and adults of all ages. Surveys of isolated older adults have shown that they benefit greatly from visits and support from retired volunteers (Cheung & Ngan, 2000). An excellent description of volunteer opportunities is provided by Robert Riekse and Henry Holstege (1996) and a sampling of volunteer opportunities are shown in Table 10-5.

TABLE 10-5   A Selection of National Volunteer Organizations for Retired Adults

Program	Description
Foster grandparent program	Low-income older adults receive wages for providing support for children who have disabilities.
Retired senior volunteer program	Volunteers over 60 years of age serve as tutors, counselors, and caregivers for children, adolescents, and all age adults.
Senior companion program	Low-income older adults receive wages for helping other older adults who are vulnerable and frail.
Service Corps of Retired Executives (SCORE)	Retired business people offer help to community organizations and small businesses with management problems.
Volunteers in Service to America (VISTA) and Americorp	Volunteers of any adult age commit at least one year to aid the handicapped, homeless, jobless, hungry, and illiterate.

Making Choices

People are generally more productive and satisfied with their jobs when they are doing work that they enjoy. If you are unsure about what work would be most enjoyable for you, visit your Career Center, read about job opportunities for people with your major, or speak with people who have the kind of job that you think you might like. Sometimes students discover that a particular job is really quite different from what they expected.

Register for an internship or practicum experience for a semester in order to sample a work environment. Such an experience allows you to network with important people in that profession. Internships are an important step to getting a job after graduation.

It is never too early to start planning for retirement. Begin to invest in a good pension program and assets. Many planners recommend that individuals diversify their investments. Talk to retired friends or relatives and gather information on what they have found to be positive and negative about retirement.

CHAPTER HIGHLIGHTS

- We examined work and retirement. Most people begin work when they are fairly young with weekend and/or summer jobs in high school and college. Most individuals hold several different jobs before finding their longest held career job.
- Older workers are often viewed negatively by employers but research shows that such views are mistaken.
- Older workers have fewer injuries and accidents than do younger workers. Time away from work following an accident is often longer for older workers but a large part of this is management's expectation that older adults need longer to heal.
- Older adults in most jobs perform as well as younger adults. Job performance does not always depend on the physical abilities that may decline with age and, in many cases, job experience offsets any declines.
- Older workers are generally more satisfied with their jobs than are younger workers, perhaps because they have found the job that is best suited for their abilities and interests.
- In spite of all of these data on older workers, age discrimination in the workplace occurs frequently. The ADEA bars such discrimination and several formal complaints and prosecutions have taken place. Companies, however, win about two-thirds of all cases and many prosecutors and judges seem to believe that even when discrimination occurs, it is unintentional. Companies are misinformed about the usefulness and value of older workers. Formal complaints declined in 1999 and companies have become more subtle in the procedures used for removing older workers. Both positive (lowering age required to receive full pension) and negative (transfer to the night shift) techniques are used to encourage early retirement for older employees.
- Workers preparing to retire frequently seek a bridge job after leaving their longest place of employment. Part-time bridge jobs are attractive but difficult to find.
- Most people do informal planning before retiring but few people do formal planning, which is less available to women and members of minority groups. Many of the topics that people would like to learn about in formal planning sessions are not included although financial matters are always included.
- Most people choose to retire. For others, retirement is a result of poor health or disability. Those who delay retirement are more likely to be professionals or people who expect less retirement income.
- The median age of retirement is 60.6 years.

- The decision on when to retire is influenced by finances, health, job satisfaction, spouse, and friends. The factors that influence the decision to retire interact with one another differently for different groups.
- Most people do not move after retirement. Movement is more likely after the loss of a spouse or the onset of serious illness.
- Most people look forward to retirement and welcome it as a reward for a life time of work. Some researchers believe that retirement is the means of meeting the life challenges of old age.
- There are huge gender, social, and ethnic group differences in retirement. Members of minority groups are more likely to become disabled and forced to leave work. Members of minority groups have less retirement income from Social Security and pensions than do White Americans but the biggest gap is in savings and assets. Women have significantly lower retirement income than men and single people have significantly lower retirement income than married couples. Single women who are members of minority groups have the highest poverty rates in old age.
- It is thought that retired individuals go through various phases of retirement. Initially, some experience a honeymoon phase in which their activity levels increase as they try to do all the things that they planned to do. Others may go through a rest and relaxation phase in which their activity levels decline as they take it easy. Eventually retirees may reach a phase of routine in which most activities are carried out at specific times on specific days. Such routines are thought to be quite comfortable and unlikely to change much until some major event (e.g., loss of a spouse) occurs. Some retirees are thought to go through a phase of disenchantment regretting their retirement but this phase is rare. Some go through a termination phase and end their retirement for a period of time as they return to work or become a full-time caregiver for an ailing spouse.
- Although most retirees expect their income to decline after retirement, most are not bothered by this eventuality and adjust to the finances of retirement with little difficulty.
- The three-legged stool, income from Social Security, pensions, and savings and assets, is sufficient for most married White Americans but less likely to be sufficient for all other groups.
- Health is not affected by retirement nor is quality of social support; most marriages show no change in satisfaction after retirement although some show improvement.
- Retired adults report being involved in a number of different activities including working around the house and yard, visiting friends and relatives, engaging in various leisure pursuits, furthering their education, and participating in volunteer work. Retirement is a busy time for many retired adults.

STUDY QUESTIONS

1. What accounts for the finding of fewer injuries for older workers than for younger workers? What might account for the finding of more time off when an older worker is injured?

2. Older adults often show deficits in physical abilities, sensory abilities, and cognitive abilities, yet, they perform well on the job. Why?

3. Why are younger workers often less satisfied with their jobs than older workers?

4. Describe some of the evidence that suggests that employers discriminate against older adults. What claims do companies make in defense of their actions? Would you recommend that an older worker file suit under the ADEA? Under what conditions? Why or why not?

5. Do you think a presentation of the information in this chapter regarding older workers would be an effective way to reduce age discrimination in business? Why or why not? What other information would you add to employer training?

6. Describe gender and ethnic group differences in formal retirement planning, disability rates, and income after retirement.

7. Describe an older worker who is likely to retire and one who is unlikely to retire. What factors influence the differences between these workers. Describe an interaction of two or more factors.

8. Describe the phases of retirement.

9. How much preretirement income must be earned after retirement to support an individual's standard of living? Why is less income needed? How is this income received (describe the three-legged stool)?

10. How is social support from friends, family, and spouse affected by retirement? How is retirement affected by social support?

11. Retired people often claim to be very busy. What is it that they do?

RECOMMENDED READINGS

The following two short essays will give you a glimpse of life as a servant in a private household.
Brooks, G. (2000). At the Burns-Coopers. In E. P. Stoller & R. C. Gibson (Eds.), *Worlds of difference: Inequality in the aging experience* (pp. 187–188), Thousand Oaks, CA: Pine Forge Press.
Childress, A. (2000). Like one of the family. In E. P. Stoller & R. C. Gibson (Eds.), *Worlds of difference: Inequality in the aging experience* (pp. 189–190), Thousand Oaks, CA: Pine Forge Press.

If you are interested in learning more about the finances involved in supporting retirement and the difficulties people frequently encounter you might try the following book.
Schulz, J. H. (1995). *The economics of aging* (6th ed.). Westport, CT: Auburn House.

An interesting view of adaptation to old age and to retirement is given in the following book by Robert Atchley.
Atchley, R. C. (1999). *Continuity and adaptation in aging: Creating positive experiences*. Baltimore, MD: Johns Hopkins University Press.

INTERNET RESOURCES

http://www.eeoc.gov   For information about the ADEA and equal employment opportunities and information concerning Social Security, Medicare, healthcare issues, and age discrimination in employment.
http://www.ssa.gov, http://www.pbgc.gov, and *http://www.dol.gov/dol/pwba*   For information on Social Security, pensions, or welfare benefits for older adults. The National Committee to Preserve Social Security and Medicare also has a website with the latest information on congressional plans to alter these programs and tips on how to talk with your representatives.
http://www.retirement-living.com   For information about finances, housing options, entertainment, and health care for retired adults living in the mid-Atlantic region.
http://www.retirementnet.com   For information on different types of retirement communities ranging from those for very active retired adults to those providing care.
http://www.energizeinc.com   Information about opportunities for volunteers.

Part IV Aging and Our Survival

11 Psychopathology

While the sick man has life there is hope.

—Cicero

Cicero had a higher level of optimism than many physicians, researchers, and caregivers do when the sick person is an older person. While it may be true that the older you are, the closer to death you are, that is still no reason to assume that sick older people should be left to die. Older adults with a serious medical condition frequently seem beyond help and, indeed, many of the disorders that we examine in this chapter are irreversible. There is no cure. Nevertheless, we hope that at the end of this chapter you will be optimistic that in the near future many of these disorders will be treated successfully and that even when a cure is not available, caring always is.

In Senior View, Edna Carpenter and Wanda Washburn told us about several of the disorders that we examine in this chapter including depression, Parkinson's disease, and Alzheimer's disease. They and everyone we interviewed knew someone who had Alzheimer's disease; a large part of our discussion will be centered on this disorder about which Wanda said "a fate worse than death, to me, is Alzheimer's."

Overview

The disorders we look at in this chapter are listed in the 1994 edition of the *Diagnostic and Statistical Manual of Mental Disorders* (DSM-IV) published by the American Psychiatric Association. This latest edition, the DSM-IV, places disorders in several different categories such as psychotic disorders, anxiety disorders, mood disorders, substance-abuse disorders, and cognitive disorders. Many disorders are more frequent in young adulthood while others are more frequent in old age; we concentrate on the latter.

The study of the distributions of various illnesses in different times, places, and populations and of the factors that influence these distributions is **epidemiology**. Distributions are typically determined by examining two important statistics, **incidence** and **prevalence**.

Senior View

Edna Carpenter, 71, is a widow who agreed to talk with us about psychopathology. She worked as a full-time executive secretary until three years ago. She now works only two days a week. She says her own health is about average because she has emphysema. She says it probably resulted from 40 years of smoking.

Wanda Washburn, age 73, was widowed 17-years ago when she was working as a real estate broker. She now works part-time at Hertz and says she will keep on working "as long as I can make it up the office steps." Wanda says she is in fairly decent health but has osteoarthritis that is frequently painful.

When asked about depression and old age, neither women believed that older adults were any more depressed than younger adults unless there was something seriously wrong with them. Edna said that, "people are more depressed if they let themselves" be. Wanda knew a man who had been depressed and commited suicide because he had many things wrong with him and couldn't take the pain. The experiences of both of these women seem to be validated by the data. Depression may not be more frequent among older adults but the highest suicide rate is for older white men.

Both women knew of others who had Parkinson's disease and of several with Alzheimer's disease. Wanda said her daughter-in-law's mother has Parkinson's and has been able to eliminate some of the tremors with medication but still has great difficulty swallowing. Edna told us about a friend who has Alzheimer's disease and now "doesn't know she is in this world; she is not aware of anything." This friend knew she had Alzheimer's disease when the doctor diagnosed it and she and her husband made plans to care for her until she had to be institutionalized about two years ago. Edna said, "Of course now . . . I don't think anything makes any difference to her."

When asked what advice they would offer to younger people, Edna immediately said, "Please don't smoke." Both women agreed that it is important to eat right and get enough exercise. Wanda was particularly optimistic about the future. "The way they're replacing joints and hearts, they'll have everything taken care of" by the time you reach old age, she said.

Incidence refers to the number of new cases of some disorder divided by the population at risk. Incidence rates are for some period of time. For example an annual incidence rate of two percent means that every year two percent of the population being considered is diagnosed with this particular disorder. If we found different incidence rates for different age groups then that would tell us that some age groups are more prone to develop that disorder and that finding might offer clues as to the causes of the disorder. Prevalence refers to the total number of cases with a certain disorder divided by the population at risk. As we will see later, incidence and prevalence rates for certain disorders can be very different for men and women, old and young, and different cultural groups.

How does one determine whether an individual has a psychopathology? The best procedure involves the administration of several different kinds of tests or measures. A medical doctor may examine blood work to look for nutrient deficiencies or a brain scan to look for evidence of a stroke; a mental health professional may administer a personality inventory and interview the individual, family, and friends; and the individual's behavior might be observed in certain situations. Ordinarily, several measures are made in an attempt to determine whether there is a problem and, what that problem might be. This is an especially important consideration when older persons are undergoing testing because of the existence of multiple medical conditions that can cloud diagnosis. For example, an older adult who goes to the doctor complaining of memory problems actually may be experiencing a result of drug interactions resulting from treatments for high blood pressure, arthritis, and/or some other condition(s). This is why multiple assessment is so important. Several measures can more effectively identify multiple symptoms and multiple conditions.

Schizophrenia

Schizophrenia is characterized by a total, or near total, break with reality and affects between one and two percent of the total population. Schizophrenics seem to live in their own private world but not necessarily 24 hours a day. Many can function fairly well for varying periods of time. Common symptoms include auditory hallucinations, delusions, autism, and an inability to sustain a train of thought or carry on normal speech. That is, the schizophrenic may hear voices that are not there, believe that others are out to get them, be preoccupied with an inner fantasy, and totally ignore the concerns, questions, or behavior or others in the same environment. Schizophrenia is largely a disorder of adolescence and young adulthood (Gleitman, Fridlund, & Reisberg, 1999). Both incidence and prevalence rates are the highest for these age groups with men more likely to show the disorder in their early 20s and women in their late 20s (Black & Andreasen, 1994). Rates are also different for different cultural groups with African Americans showing higher prevalence rates than Asian, Hispanic, or White Americans (Lefton, 1997; Snowden & Cheung, 1990). Few individuals develop schizophrenia past the age of 45 and development in old age is so rare that it is sometimes referred to separately as **paraphrenia**. Schizophrenia is not a disorder of old age although schizophrenics certainly often do live to become older adults.

Anxiety Disorders

Anxiety is a feeling of apprehension, nervousness, worry, and fear. The anxious individual may have difficulty sleeping, eating, and concentrating and may even experience panic attacks. In a panic attack, the person may have difficulty breathing, have heart palpitations, hot or cold flashes, or feel dizzy or faint. Anxiety disorders can be general where the feelings just described come and go almost unpredictably. In other cases, the anxiety is associated with a particular object or situation and is called a **phobia**. For example, fear of high places is called acrophobia, and fear of enclosed places is called claustrophobia. Another type of anxiety takes the form of recurring thoughts that cannot be stopped or repetitive actions; this is called obsessive-compulsive disorder (OCD). Prevalence and incidence rates for most anxiety disorders are lower for older adults than for younger adults (Flint, 1994). Older and younger adults have about the same rates for OCD (Sheikh, 1996).

Mood Disorders

As the name implies, mood disorders are present when one's mood or emotional state is out of proportion to one's circumstances. It is normal to be excited when something exciting is going on and normal to be depressed when something sad happens. These states of excitement and depression are disorders when there are no appropriate circumstances or the mood persists well beyond a normal period of time.

Depression

Major depression is characterized by continual sadness, lack of energy, difficulty sleeping, weight gain or loss, aches and pains that will not go away, feelings of helplessness and hopelessness, and, in many cases, thoughts of death or suicide (Lefton, 1997). These symptoms must last at least two weeks to be considered clinical depression. Depression is one of the more common disorders among adults of all ages. A milder form of depression characterized by low self-esteem, difficulties concentrating and making decisions, low energy, sleep difficulties, and feelings of hopelessness is referred to as **dysthymic disorder**.

A common belief among many younger people is that depression increases with old age because older adults have more things to be depressed about. For example, older adults are more likely to become seriously ill with life-threatening diseases such as cancer and cardiovascular disease; to lose major portions of their income with retirement from an active role in the work place; to lose status as a respected member of the working community; to lose friends and relatives to disease and death; to lose their ability to see well, hear well, and move well; and so on.

In spite of this belief, the general finding has been a lower, rather than higher, rate of major depression among older adults (Blazer, Hughes, & George, 1987; Gatz & Hurwitz, 1990; Hendrie, Callahan, Levitt, Hui, Musick, Austrom, Nurnberger, & Tierney, 1995; Lyness, Cox, Curry, Conwell, King, & Caine, 1995). The prevalence of major depression among adults 65 and older is about one percent which is the same as or even lower than the prevalence among younger and middle-age adults (Mirowsky & Ross, 1992; Regier, Boyd, Burke, Rae, Myers, Kramer, Robins, George, Karno, & Locke, 1988).

There are some age differences, however, in causes of depression for different age groups. Many older adults, for example, show increased levels of depression after they stop driving (Fonda, Wallace, & Herzog, 2001). Some other work has found that an impairment in activities of daily living, something that also rarely happens to younger adults, can lead to depression in older adults but that those who believe that they have adequate social support from family and friends show far less depression (Oxman & Hull, 2001). Older and younger adults seem to experience depression as a result of the same kinds of life events and older adults most at risk are those who have accumulated both stressful events and daily hassles (Kraaij, Arensman, & Spinhoven, 2002; Nolen-Hoeksema & Ahrens, 2002).

Depression can occur at any age.

The prevalence of milder depression or dysthymic disorder may be higher in older adults. Table 11-1 shows a depression scale used to assist diagnosis of depression. Using data gathered from scales like this, researchers have found relatively high rates of mild depression among adults 65 and older (Beekman, Deeg, van Tilburg, & Smit, 1995). In one such study, 27 percent of the participating older adults were found to be mildly depressed

TABLE 11-1   Sample Depression Scale

Answer *yes* or *no* to each of the following questions:

1. Much of the time, do you feel:
   Sad?
   Lethargic?
   Pessimistic?
   Hopeless?
   Worthless?
   Helpless?
2. Much of the time, do you:
   Have difficulty making decisions?
   Have trouble concentrating?
   Have memory problems?
3. Lately, have you:
   Lost interest in things that used to give you pleasure?
   Had problems at work or in school?
   Had problems with your family or friends?
   Isolated yourself from others, or wanted to?
4. Lately, have you:
   Felt low energy?
   Felt restless and irritable?
   Had trouble falling asleep, staying asleep, or getting up in the morning?
   Lost your appetite, or gained weight?
   Been bothered by persistent headaches, stomachaches, backaches, or muscle/joint pains?
5. Lately, have you:
   Been drinking more alcohol than you used to?
   Been taking more mood-altering drugs than you used to?
   Engaged in risky behavior such as not wearing a seat belt or crossing streets without looking?
6. Lately, have you been thinking about:
   Death?
   Hurting yourself?
   Your funeral?
   Killing yourself?

If you answered *yes* to three or more of these questions, you may be depressed.
You should consult your physician or a mental health professional.

Source: From *http://www.depression.com/health_library/quiz/index/htm* and adapted from materials created by the National Institute of Mental Health's Depression Awareness, Recognition, and Treatment Program, Rockville, MD.

(Koenig & Blazer, 1992). This is as high as younger adults and together these two groups show much higher rates than adults in their middle years. Across all of these age groups, more women than men are diagnosed with depression. This gender difference, however, seems to vanish after age 80 as the number of depressed men increases from age 60 to 80 until the proportion of depressed men and women is about the same (Barefoot, Mortensen, Helms, Avlund, & Schroll, 2001). Older adults may, thus, show mild depression frequently but rarely show major depression and gender differences in the rate of depression, major and minor, may vanish by age 80.

Several reasons have been offered for the differences in the prevalence of major and minor depression among older and younger adults. One possibility is that older adults, as members of an older cohort, grew up in times when mental illnesses, such as depression, were a stigma; people tended to keep mental problems to themselves. Thus, members of these older cohorts may be less willing to ask for help when they need it or answer items on a depression scale honestly. If this were, however, the major reason for obtained differences, then it is not at all clear why dysthymic disorder would be high among older adults. A second possibility is that older adults have learned how to deal with depressing events and do not experience depression as deeply. Their high rates of dysthymic disorder may be due to those depressing events and situations that can accompany old age and their better coping strategies learned from experience. They may get depressed as often as young adults but not as deeply. A third possibility is that major depression is under- or misdiagnosed in older adults because it consists of a different set of symptoms missed by standard diagnostic procedures. Perhaps there are many older adults suffering with major depression that are simply missed when data are collected using standard methods (Baldwin, 1994). One study found that about half of a group of older adults who showed signs of depression on a standard measure (similar to the one in Table 11-1) were not detected as being depressed by their physicians (Garrard, Rolnick, Nitz, Luepke, Jackson, Fischer, Leibson, Bland, Heinrich, & Waller, 1998). At present it is not clear which, if any, of these three hypotheses might play a role in the obtained age differences on measures of depression.

The relationship between health and depression is fairly strong. Depressed individuals tend to die earlier and, frequently, from heart disease (Schulz, Martire, Beach, & Scheier, 2000). The relationship between health and depression seems to operate in both directions. Individuals who experience a physical illness or impairment often become depressed. Individuals who have depressed personality characteristics tend to become physically ill or impaired (Meeks, Murrell, & Mehl, 2000).

Regardless of age or cause of depression, it is treatable. Depressed older adults, like younger adults, often receive prescribed antidepressant medication. While the rate of use for such medication is reasonably high for institutionalized older adults (36 percent), it is very low (4.2 percent) for depressed older adults living in the community (Newman & Hassan, 1999). Different modes of therapy are, of course, more or less successful with different groups of people (Aponte, Rivers, & Wohl, 1995). For example, some recent work suggests that self-reinforcement, which is the ability to control pleasant events, is an effective treatment component for White and Asian American older adults who are depressed. On the other hand perceived control, which is a perception of one's own ability to reduce aversive and increase positive events, is effective for White but not for Asian

Americans (Wong, Heiby, Kameoka, & Dubanoski, 1999). Other work suggests that older African Americans are less likely to report mild depression than are White Americans but far more likely to report thinking about death (Gallo, Cooper-Patrick, & Lesikar, 1998). Unfortunately, many adults, young and old, do not seek treatment and attempt suicide.

Suicide

Major depression is strongly related to suicide; about 15 percent of those who have experienced major depression or bipolar disorder (see below) end their own lives. This is 15 times higher than the suicide rate in the overall population. More than half of those who commit suicide are depressed when the suicide is committed (Andreasen & Black, 1994). This is especially true of older adults. People who commit suicide under the age of 40 are more often schizophrenic. Between the ages of 40 and 60, alcoholism is the most frequent diagnosis; for those over 60, depression is the most frequent diagnosis (Conwell, 1995). About 30,000 Americans commit suicide every year.

Suicide rates are quite different for men and women and for adults of different ages. Many more women attempt suicide than men; about 75 percent of suicide attempts are by women. Many more men succeed at suicide than women; about 67 percent of completed suicides are by men (Mynatt & Doherty, 1999). Part of the reason for this difference is the method used. Women tend to use sleeping pills or other drugs and often are found while still alive. Men tend to use more instantly lethal means such as guns or hanging and are usually found after they are dead. Suicide rates for women tend to remain fairly stable and fairly low from young to old adulthood with a slight rise between the ages of 40 and 60. White females have slightly higher suicide rates than African American females. For men, suicide rates vary as a function of both race and age. Such gender and ethnic group differences in suicide are important but it is the relationship between suicide and age that is most striking.

Overall, older adults are more successful at suicide than are younger adults. It has been estimated that about five percent of suicide attempts among younger adults are successful while about 25 percent of attempts among older adults are successful (Kastenbaum, 1995). For African American men, the highest suicide rates are at age 20 and at age 80 but are never as high as for White men of any adult age. For White men, the suicide rate starts high in young adulthood and increases dramatically with age. The highest rate of suicide is for older, White men. As you can see from Figure 11-1 (p. 309), no other group comes even close to this high rate which continues to increase until the mid 80s.

Since some suicides are not detected, the rates are probably higher for all of these groups. An older (or younger) adult who simply stops taking important medication may die and be pronounced dead from the disease. A person may do just the opposite and take too much medication and end their life. Then they may be thought of as forgetful rather than suicidal. An older (or younger) adult may intentionally take part in some hazardous activity and be pronounced dead from accidental causes. Regardless of these factors, it is clear that older, White men commit suicide far more often than others.

This finding is not a cohort effect. Older White men have had the highest suicide rate since the turn of the century and, thus, many cohorts have shown this effect (Posner, 1996). One hypothesis frequently mentioned has to do with loss of power and prestige. White

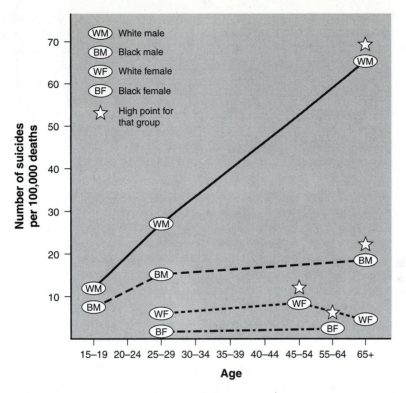

FIGURE 11-1 **Graph comparing suicide rates for old and young, male and female, and White and African Americans.**

Source: Adapted from U.S. Census data, 1991, 1995.

males who are still working have more power and prestige than Black males and White or Black females. With retirement, one may lose that workplace power and prestige and, thus, White males have more to lose than do the other gender and racial groups (McCall, 1991). This loss may result in feelings of worthlessness, depression, and lead to suicide.

Individuals who contemplate and attempt suicide often give warning signs to family, friends, and professionals such as their family doctors. Warning signs include talking about death, giving away valuable possessions, avoiding activities that one ordinarily enjoyed, neglecting personal appearance, and apparent changes in personality or habits. One might, for example, become much more anxious or begin drinking heavily. Such warning signs should be taken seriously.

Other Mood Disorders

There are two other mood disorders, mania and bipolar disorder. **Mania** is characterized by exaggerated elation often mixed with intense irritability (Lefton, 1997). Mania is not more frequent among older adults, and may be less frequent (Butler, Lewis, & Sunderland, 1998).

Bipolar disorder is characterized by severe swings in mood from deep depression to exaggerated elation. Bipolar disorder most often occurs before age 30 and occurs equally often for men and women. People with this disorder may live to be old but the disorder itself is not a disorder of old age (Butler, Lewis, & Sunderland, 1998).

Substance-Use Disorders

A **substance-use disorder** occurs when an individual uses some substance that causes harm that they are aware of and/or uses the substance in high-risk situations such as driving and continues to use the substance for over a month (American Psychiatric Association, 1994). For older adults the most frequent substance-use disorder is **alcoholism**. Alcohol abuse can lead to more severe **alcohol dependence**, also called alcoholism. Dependent individuals show at least three of the following symptoms: tolerance or a need to increase the amount of alcohol to achieve the same effect previously achieved by less alcohol; withdrawal symptoms (such as delirium tremors, hallucinations) when alcohol is discontinued for a period of time; using more alcohol or using it longer than originally intended; not being able to control the use of alcohol; avoiding important work-related, family, or social activities because of alcohol use; and using alcohol even when such use worsens physical or psychological difficulties already present (American Psychiatric Association, 1994). It is estimated that about seven percent of the U. S. population abuses alcohol or is alcohol dependent (Grant, Harford, Dawson, Chou, Dufour, & Pickering, 1994). Alcoholism is far more prevalent among men than women. Close to 20 percent of men will develop alcohol abuse or dependence at some point in their lives; the estimate for women is less than 10 percent (Kessler, McGonagle, Zhao, Nelson, Hughes, Eshleman, Wittchen, & Kendler, 1994). Different cultural/ethnic groups also show different levels of alcohol abuse and dependence. Box 11-1 describes some of the differences in more detail.

The rate of alcoholism among older adults is less than that among younger adults. About three percent of adults over 65 abuse alcohol or are dependent. Over all ages of adults, however, the highest rate is for widowers who are 75 and older (Glass, Prigerson, Kasl, & Mendes de Leon, 1995; Gurland, 1996). It is also the case that older residents of nursing homes are more likely to be alcoholics than older adults living in the community (Horton & Fogelman, 1991). Older alcoholics fall into two general categories. Many are people who began drinking when they were much younger and have continued drinking in their later years. Others are people who began abusing alcohol when they reached old age. These late-onset alcoholics are more often women and are estimated to comprise about one-third of older alcoholics (Dupree & Schonfeld, 1996; Lichtenberg, 1994).

The relatively low rate of alcohol abuse that has been found for older adults is thought to have three important qualifications. The first is an assumed underreporting of alcoholism in older adults. Some older adults are fairly isolated from others who may not detect their alcoholism. Families may often hide or ignore a grandparent's excessive drinking believing that it is no one else's business, that the older adult needs alcohol to get by, or that the cost of treatment in terms of money and time would not be worth the effort for someone who may not live much longer anyway. It is thought that doctors often may ignore signs of alcoholism in older patients that they would otherwise attempt to treat in

BOX **11-1**

Alcoholism and Ethnicity

Different ethnic groups in this country show different patterns of alcohol abuse and dependency. The highest rate of alchoholism occurs in the majority, White American group but a close second goes to African Americans who have higher rates than Hispanic and Asian Americans (Aponte, Rivers, & Wohl, 1995; Atkinson, Ganzini, & Bernstein, 1992). Most researchers suggest that patterns of alcoholism are closely tied to patterns of underemployment, unemployment, poverty, substandard housing, and discrimination. How do you think this relationship works for minorities? What about White Americans who have the highest rate of alcoholism?

The general pattern of lower levels of alcoholism for older adults than for younger adults is found for White Americans but not for African or Hispanic Americans. African and Hispanic Americans show about the same rate of alcholism throughout the adult years (Bucholz, 1992). African Americans, perhaps as a result of this continued rate of alchoholism throughout adulthood, show higher rates of death from liver disease than do White Americans. Among different Hispanic American groups, different rates of alcoholism also are found. Cuban Americans show a relatively low rate throughout middle- and old age while Mexican American and Puerto Ricans living in the United States show consistently higher rates (Black & Markides, 1994).

Prohibition may have had a major influence on the consumption of alcohol of older White Americans and may, in part, be responsible for their lower rates of alcoholism at present. Perhaps Prohibition did not exert this strong influence on African Americans who in those days were often excluded from significant participation in American society or Hispanic Americans who are, in large number, more recent immigrants. If this is the case, then we might expect newer cohorts of White Americans to begin to show the more continued high rate of alcoholism even into old age.

---

younger patients. They may assume that alcoholism is the least of their patient's worries and can be safely ignored in the face of cancer, stroke, or Alzheimer's disease (Adams & Waskel, 1993; Ankrom, Thompson, Finucane, & Fingerhood, 1997; Atkinson, Ganzini, & Bernstein, 1992).

A second qualification for the low rate of alcoholism found among older adults is that many alcoholics die before reaching old age. Some may perish in auto accidents while others may die of cirrhosis of the liver or Korsakoff's syndrome. Cirrhosis is a degeneration of the liver that most often results from alcohol abuse or dependency (Gallant, 1987). Korsakoff's is a dementia in which the person suffers disorientation, confusion, and irreversible loss of memory. The brain deteriorates and the individual eventually dies. Alcoholics are an unhealthy group of people who typically die earlier than nonalcoholics (Eberling & Jagust, 1995).

The third qualification is that the current low rate of alcoholism among older adults may be a cohort effect. Many of the older adults who are in the low rate of alcoholism group lived through Prohibition (1920–1933). During those years alcohol use was considered a social stigma; it was illegal. Women were especially tainted if they drank. Since most alcoholics begin drinking when they are young (67 percent of older alcoholics began when they were young), the cohorts who were young during Prohibition may have had unusually low rates of alcoholism. Over the next 20 years the lower rate of alcoholism for older adults may increase to the level found for younger and middle-age adults (Ganzini & Atkinson, 1996). Some evidence for this prediction comes from longitudinal studies of alcoholism which have found no change in alcohol use for any age adults (Dufour, Colliver, Stinson, & Grigson, 1988; Glynn, Bouchard, LoCastro, & Laird, 1985). As today's younger and middle-age adults reach old age, they are likely to bring their current higher rate of alcoholism with them unless deaths from alcohol-related diseases and accidents offset this expected cohort effect.

Cognitive Disorders

Cognitive disorders are ones in which the individual displays one or more of five major disruptions of cognition (American Psychiatric Association, 1994). Most cases of cognitive disorders are organic brain syndromes in which there is real damage to the brain. The five major disruptions are:

■ *Impaired memory:* Deficits in working memory, such as being unable to remember what just occurred, are usually first followed by deficits in the ability to retrieve information from permanent memory. Usually episodic permanent memory, rather than semantic or procedural, is affected.

■ *Impaired intellect:* Person has difficulty in understanding or comprehending presented information and/or in learning new behaviors. The person may seem to have lost some of their intelligence.

■ *Impaired judgment:* Person cannot make plans or decisions and/or understand the plans and decisions made by others. The individual cannot differentiate between a good and a bad plan or decision.

■ *Impaired orientation:* Person is confused about where they are, what time/date it is, and the identities of others even those who are familiar to them.

■ *Impaired emotionality:* Person displays excessive or very shallow emotions out of proportion to circumstances.

When an older adult shows one or more of these symptoms, one must be careful not to assume that it is an irreversible organic brain syndrome (OBS) or dementia, such as Alzheimer's disease. Although the term **dementia** frequently is used in conversation to refer to many types of cognitive declines it actually refers to irreversible cognitive declines that result from some organic brain disorder. Too many families, professionals, and older adults are too quick to assume the worst. An older adult who begins to have difficulty keeping track of appointments or forgets things may begin to suspect Alzheimer's disease. Alzheimer's disease is feared among older adults and an individual may begin worrying about having it. Worrying disrupts memory and it may lead to more forgetting and more worrying and so on until the person is convinced that they have Alzheimer's disease. We must try to avoid this downward spiral by first examining other possible causes of changes in cognition before we arrive at a diagnosis of Alzheimer's disease or any other dementia

(Centofanti, 1998). The first step is to determine whether the cognitive changes are a part of normal aging or whether they are one or more of the five symptoms of a cognitive disorder.

There are a number of tests that are used by clinicians to determine whether there is a cognitive disorder and what the source of the disorder might be. To measure cognitive impairments, one of the most widely used tests is the Mini-Mental Status Examination (MMSE; Folstein, Folstein, & McHugh, 1975). This test asks questions about orientation (what is the date, day, month?), registration (name three objects), calculation (count by seven's), recall (recall the three objects previously named), and language (follow a command such as, "close the book, put it on the floor, and stand up"). This test has, however, been criticized for falsely diagnosing individuals with low education or short attention span as having a cognitive disorder and for missing mild cases of genuine cognitive disorders (Kukull, Larson, Teri, Bowen, McCormick, & Pfanschmidt, 1994). If education level is not considered, the test may falsely diagnose members of some minority groups as having a cognitive disorder (Murden, McRae, Kaner, & Bucknam, 1991). Once a cognitive disorder is detected, however, scores on the MMSE seem equally useful for measuring the degree of impairment for African American and White patients (Ford, Haley, Thrower, West, & Harrell, 1996).

The Mattis Dementia Rating Scale (Coblenz, Mattis, Zingesser, Kasoff, Wisniewski, & Katzman, 1973), CAMCOG (Huppert, Brayne, Gill, Paykel, & Beardsall, 1995) which is a part of the Cambridge Examination for Mental Disorders of the Elderly (Roth, Huppert, Tym, & Mountjoy, 1988), and the Short Test for Mental Status (Fleming, Adams, & Petersen, 1995) are also used frequently and are similar to the MMSE in format. These latter tests may be somewhat better at detecting milder cases of cognitive disorder. Recently, diagnosticians have tried to create even shorter, quicker tests. The Time and Change Test takes only a couple of minutes to administer but has reliability. In this test, individuals look at a clock and tell what time it is and then attempt to make a dollar in change from a number of coins (quarters, dimes, and nickels) placed on a table (Inouye, Robison, Froehlich, & Richardson, 1998). Other tests are designed to screen only for fairly specific cognitive difficulties. For example, to assess visuospatial and construction deficits that frequently are associated with various cognitive disorders, individuals may be asked to draw a clock. People who are able to draw a "normal" clock rarely show other cognitive impairments (Siu, 1991). Difficulties in drawing a clock correlate well with severity of cognitive disorder but do not distinguish among the various types of disorders (Hill, Bäckman, Wahlin, & Winblad, 1995). Some examples of clocks drawn by a normal person and persons with some cognitive disorder are shown in Figure 11-2 (p. 314).

If the behaviors displayed by the individual are among the symptoms of a cognitive disorder, then one can attempt to determine which of several possibilities are responsible. These include disorders such as depression pseudo dementia, focal brain damage, and types of acute OBS. Only after all of these have been ruled out should one turn to the chronic organic brain disorders, the irreversible dementias.

Pseudo Dementia

Depression can produce many of the cognitive symptoms typical of a cognitive disorder. When an apparent OBS is in fact depression, the disorder is often referred to as **depression pseudo dementia (DPD)** although some researchers balk at the use of the term

FIGURE 11-2   **Sample clocks as drawn by a normal person and victims of cognitive disorders.**

pseudo (Nussbaum, 1994). An older adult who is depressed may have difficulty concentrating, be uninterested in making plans or learning new behaviors, and show great sadness seemingly disproportionate to observed circumstances. It has been estimated that close to 30 percent of older adults diagnosed with OBS are, in fact, depressed with no brain damage at all (La Rue, Dessonville, & Jarvik, 1985). Table 11-2 presents some of the differences between depression and a cognitive disorder (Safford, 1992). Physicians and clinicians are advised to test for depression in older adults before advancing to tests for types of organic brain syndrome.

Focal Brain Damage

A second possible cause for symptoms of a cognitive disorder is **focal brain damage**. **Focal brain damage** refers to damage that occurs in one specific segment of the brain often

**TABLE 11-2   Cognitive Disorder or Depression: Some Guidelines for
Distinguishing the Two**

Cognitive Disorder	Depression
Slow onset	Rapid onset
Fluctuating mood	Continual mood
Person conceals problem(s)	Person highlights problem(s)
Stable cognitive loss	Fluctuating cognitive loss
Near-miss answers	No answers
Memory loss occurs first	Depressed mood occurs first
May be irreversible	Can be successfully treated

Source: Adapted from Safford (1992).

due to a head injury, a stroke, or a brain tumor. These problems are often amenable to treatment with medication and/or surgery. Excellent and amazing examples of focal brain damage can be found in the books of neurologist Oliver Sacks (1985; 1996). Focal brain damage typically can be treated and does not usually spread to other areas in the brain.

Acute Organic Brain Syndrome

If DPD and focal brain damage have been ruled out, then the cognitive disorder is likely to be a form of OBS. There are two broad categories of OBS, acute and chronic. As the name implies, acute OBS shows relatively rapid onset and is reversible. It is not dementia; it is a form of delirium. **Delirium** is a temporary state of mental confusion. It is estimated that about 15 percent of OBS cases are acute. Persons with an acute OBS get better and frequently show full recovery. An **acute OBS** is typically the result of a disturbance in the metabolism of the brain which results in various cognitive impairments. Brain metabolism can be disturbed in several different ways.

Medications taken in the wrong quantity or interacting with other medications can result in an acute OBS. These interactions can result from **polypharmacy** which is the condition of taking many medications simultaneously. Some medications produce very different effects when they are taken at the same time as other drugs. Medications include over-the-counter drugs such as aspirin and laxatives in addition to prescriptions. About one-half of all prescription medications are for older adults and more than one-third of older adults take three or more prescription drugs (Park, Morrell, Frieske, & Kincaid, 1992). Drug dosage must be carefully monitored for older adults because their liver and kidneys may not function as well, especially under stress, as they did when they were younger. Medications can be present in the body for longer periods of time and, thus, increase the chances of a drug interaction. Even over-the-counter medications can produce symptoms of a cognitive disorder. For example, some types of laxatives disrupt cognition and memory. This type of OBS is easily remedied when it is detected. Medications or dosages can be changed resulting in a return to that person's normal level of cognitive behavior.

Nutritional deficiencies also can produce an acute OBS. Of particular concern are the B vitamins; B_6 deficiency can cause depression, anxiety, delusions, hallucinations, and even death. Good dietary sources of Vitamin B_6 are chicken, fish, pork, eggs, rice, soybeans, peanuts, and whole wheat products. A B_{12} deficiency can cause insomnia, irritability, extreme lassitude, and disturbed memory and concentration. Good dietary sources of Vitamin B_{12} are red meats. Both vitamins are available in capsule form and as part of numerous multiple vitamins. Some older adults who take vitamins may, however, still not get enough of these particular vitamins because of changes in the stomach lining. These changes can result in lower levels of stomach acid and, as a result, decreased absorption of B vitamins (Rowe & Kahn, 1998). Some older adults find it necessary to have injections of B vitamins to relieve the symptoms of this acute OBS.

A third cause of acute OBS is an electrolyte imbalance in the body sometimes produced by malnutrition or toxic levels of various drugs. This form of delirium is frequently seen soon after major surgery and can be effectively treated by restoring the electrolyte balance.

Acute OBS can be remedied if it is detected and treated at an early stage. Unfortunately, often it is not and close to 40 percent of acute OBS cases are thought to end in death from exhaustion, pneumonia, or the underlying cause.

Chronic Organic Brain Syndromes

Chronic OBS is usually slow onset and results in permanent damage to the brain; it is not reversible. Another name for chronic OBS is **dementia**. Since chronic OBS produce damage in the brain, it is important to know some of the areas of the brain (Figure 11-3) and where damage occurs. Different areas of the brain use different chemical neurotransmitters. Acetylcholine areas are located in the cerebral cortex and the hippocampus (as well as other brain areas). The cortex is assumed to house the higher mental functions of thinking and memory while the hippocampus is known to be crucial for the formation of new memories. An important dopamine area is in the substantia nigra which is a crucial brain area for movement (Kossyln & Koenig, 1995).

The incidence and prevalence rates for chronic OBS are much higher in older adults and increase the older one gets. The prevalence of mild dementia may be as high as 12 percent in adults age 65 and older and the prevalence of moderate to severe cases may be as high as six percent (Schulz & O'Brien, 1994). In early old age, prevalence rates are much higher for males but past the age of 75, the rates are higher for females (Kay & Bergmann, 1982). Table 11-3 shows these prevalence rates. A recent study conducted in Denmark examined the rate of different forms of dementia in 276 adults who were 100 years of age and older. Results showed that 37 percent of these very old adults showed no signs of any cognitive disorder while 51 percent did. Some of those showing signs of dementia actually had an acute organic brain disorder (a deficiency of B vitamins) that could be treated. Most of those showing signs of dementia were, however, chronic (Andersen-Ranberg, Vasegaard, & Jeune, 2001).

There are a number of different kinds of dementia besides Alzheimer's disease. In fact, a number of animals besides humans show dementia and different forms of OBS. A

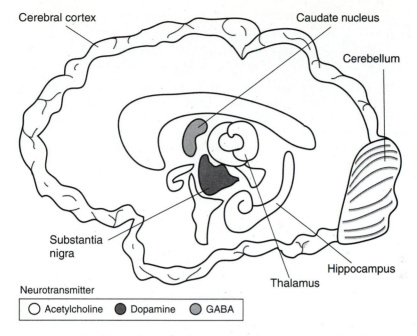

FIGURE 11-3   Areas of the brain and neurotransmitters involved in chronic OBS.

sampling of some of these animal dementias is given in Box 11-2 (p. 318). Three of the less frequent human dementias are briefly described in Box 11-3 (p. 319).

AIDS Dementia.   AIDS dementia is a result of HIV infection in the brain (Price, 1998). The infection is responsible for the death of nerve cells in several areas of the brain. The person may show cognitive symptoms and have difficulty concentrating, show memory

TABLE 11-3   Male and Female Dementia Prevalence Rates with Advanced Age

Proportion of Chronic Organic Brain Syndrome Cases as a Function of Gender and Age

Age	Male	Female
65	0.039	0.005
70	0.041	0.027
75	0.080	0.079
80	0.132	0.209

BOX **11-2**

Animal Dementias

Dementia is not a disease of humans alone; probably all animals with brains can experience some form of dementia. Dog dementia or canine cognitive dysfunction syndrome (CDS) frequently occurs in older dogs. Some estimate the prevalence to be as high as 62 percent of older dogs. Such dogs may act confused, not always recognize their owners, bark at night for no reason, turn away when petted, mess in the house, and not wag their tails very frequently. While the exact cause of CDS is not clear, there are treatments available. The drug Anipryl is often prescribed by veterinarians for CDS. Cinder, shown here, suffered from canine CDS.

Another recent concern, particularly of hunters and those who eat venison, is mad deer disease or chronic wasting disease (CWD). Like mad cow disease, CWD seems to be caused by a virus which eats away at the brain and results in a form of Creutzfeldt-Jakob disease (see Box 11-3). Some work suggests that a prion, rather than a virus, is responsible for this disease. A prion is a twisted piece of microscopic protein that is thought to invade nerve cells and convert ordinary proteins into more invading prions. Thus far, CWD has only been found in elk and deer in Wyoming and Colorado but is expected to spread to the nearby states to which deer migrate. Although no human cases have been confirmed, there is suspicion that two recent human deaths may have been due to consumption of CWD-infected venison (Miniter, 1999).

---

loss, and struggle with complex sequential mental tasks. An example of a complex sequential mental task would be to: (1) start with the number 4, (2) subtract 3, (3) add 12, (4) subtract 3, (5) give the answer. The answer, 10, is not often given by individuals with AIDS dementia (or Alzheimer's disease either; see below). Other symptoms include clumsiness, weakening in the limbs, apathy, and social withdrawal. Eventually the person

B O X **11-3**

Three Less Frequent Chronic OBS

Although all chronic OBS occur too often, the following three conditions are less frequent than those presented in the text.

Creutzfeldt-Jakob disease is a rare disorder that has a rapid rate of decline, unlike other chronic OBS. Death typically occurs within two years after diagnosis and about 250 to 300 Americans die every year from this disease. Creutzfeldt-Jakob is thought to be caused by a prion which is a small, infectious protein. The prion is contracted years or even decades before any symptoms appear. Such a prion is known to result in the disease *Scrapie* in sheep. In some countries, sheep parts (e.g., brains) are mixed with grain and fed to cattle. You may have heard of Mad Cow disease which is thought to result when cows eat infected sheep (DeArmond, 1998). The disease eats away at the cow's brain making it look like a sponge and the cow dies. Humans who eat meat from such cows may be at risk for this form of Creutzfeldt-Jakob, the brain destroying disease. At this writing, there have been about 80 cases in England of this form of Creutzfeldt-Jakob, one case in France, and, so far, none in the United States. The American Red Cross has urged the government to ban blood donations from any person who has lived for more than six months in Europe. Blood from such persons could carry the deadly virus which would then be passed to individuals receiving transfusions.

Pick's disease is also rare and seems to be determined by a single dominant gene. The disease damages nerve cells particularly in the frontal and temporal lobes of the brain. In the early stages, symptoms include social inappropriateness, loss of modesty, and uninhibited sexual behavior. An example of inappropriate behavior occurred when Dr. Allan Zarkin carved his initials into the abdomen of a mother after successfully delivering her baby by Cesarean section. The mother, Liana Gedz, sued the doctor and the case was settled for $1.7 million. Dr. Zarkin's lawyer says he suffers from Pick's disease. The doctor's right to practice was suspended following the incident (Dobnik, 2000; Singleton, 2000). Only later do the cognitive, symptoms of memory and intellectual impairment appear and death is inevitable (Haward, 1977).

Huntington's disease also is caused by a single dominant gene. Symptoms usually appear during middle adulthood, 35 to 50 years of age. The disease produces a shortage of the neurotransmitter GABA in the caudate nucleus of the brain's basal ganglia. This brain area is shown in Figure 11-3. Symptoms include involuntary flicking movements of the arms and legs, an inability to sustain a motor act such as sticking out one's tongue, mood swings similar to bipolar disorder, hallucinations, paranoia, and depression. The cognitive impairments do not usually appear until late in the disease and eventually the individual dies.

cannot walk without assistance and loses bowel and bladder control. Finally the individual is confined to bed and eventually dies. In the early 1990s, it was estimated that about 10,000 Americans over age 60 had AIDS dementia.

Parkinson's Disease. **Parkinson's disease** (or Parkinsonism) was named for James Parkinson who first described the symptoms in 1817. This OBS develops slowly with a slowing down of movement. Eventually the person develops a stooped posture with the head forward and elbows flexed. People with Parkinson's disease walk with a shuffling gait and show tremors in their fingers, forearms, eyelids, and tongue. Their face may lack emotional expression, speech is often slurred, and the voice becomes a monotone. The probability of cognitive symptoms increases as the age at which motor symptoms first appear increases. The probability of cognitive symptoms for a Parkinson's disease patient is still, however, only 65 percent by age 85 (Chun, Schofield, Stern, Tatemichi, & Mayeux, 1998).

Although Parkinson's disease usually appears in people over 60, it can appear as early as 30. Actor Michael J. Fox, developed Parkinson's before his 30th birthday. Close to 400,000 Americans have Parkinson's disease and the disorder occurs with equal frequency among men and women and people of different races (DiGiovanna, 1994). Without treatment, Parkinson's disease can cause severe disability within five years of onset. Increased levels of depression and/or anxiety often accompany Parkinson's (Brod, Mendelsohn, & Roberts, 1998).

In Parkinson's disease, cells in the substantia nigra area of the basal ganglia near the center of the brain (see Figure 11-3), begin to die. These cells produce and use a neurotransmitter called **dopamine**. As cells die, the quantity of dopamine diminishes and the remaining cells work harder to produce more. This increased production leads to the buildup of toxic substances resulting in the death of more cells and a continual decline. The cause of Parkinson's disease is this downward spiral produced by some initial death of cells in the substantia nigra. The causes of that initial death are assumed to be multiple and environmental rather than genetic. Studies of families and identical twins seem to rule out a genetic cause (Marsden, 1987).

One probable environmental cause of Parkinson's disease is encephalitis. Encephalitis is an inflammation of the brain caused by a virus. An excellent description of Parkinson's disease resulting from encephalitis can be found in Oliver Sack's book (1999), and movie of the same name, *Awakenings*. A second probable cause comes from some synthetic drugs, such as synthetic heroin, which may contain a contaminant (MPTP) that produces Parkinson's disease (Schneider, Pope, Simpson, Taggart, Smith, & DiStefano, 1992). A third probable cause is pesticides. In Quebec, researchers compared areas subjected to heavy pesticide spraying with areas that were pesticide-free. Residents of the sprayed areas had a seven times higher incidence of Parkinson's disease (Barbeau, Roy, Cloutier, Plasse, & Paris, 1986). A fourth probable cause are the seeds of certain plants found in Guam. Eating these seeds seem to result in Parkinson's disease (Hirano, Kurland, Krooth, & Lassell, 1961; Spencer, Nunn, Hugon, Ludolph, Ross, Roy, & Robertson, 1987). A fifth probable cause is severe injury to the brain. Champion Muhammed Ali appears to have acquired Parkinson's disease from repeated injuries. It appears that a number of environmental events can produce the beginnings of the downward spiral in dopamine production which is Parkinson's disease.

If the symptoms of Parkinson's disease result from the ever decreasing availability of dopamine in the brain, then the clearest treatment is to find ways to increase dopamine levels. Dopamine itself cannot be given because it will not cross into the brain from the bloodstream but a precursor of dopamine, L-dopa (also called Levodopa), will and, thus, is one treatment. Unfortunately, maintaining the correct dosage of L-dopa is very difficult since the downward spiral in the brain continues even with such treatment. Too much L-dopa (and dopamine in the brain) produces psychotic, schizophrenic-like symptoms. Because of these difficulties, L-dopa is often a last resort treatment. The mild, antidepressant drug deprenyl inhibits a brain enzyme that breaks down dopamine. Inhibiting this enzyme results in an increase in available dopamine and can slow the progress of Parkinson's disease by as much as 83 percent per year (Pearce, 1992). Some individuals with Parkinson's disease have an electronic device implanted under the skin with a wire attached to the crucial area in the brain. When tremors or rigidity begin, the individual turns on the device by passing a magnet over it. Signals are sent to the brain to stop the tremors and rigidity (Neergaard, 1997). Finally, implants of dopamine-producing tissue from the individual's own adrenal glands or from the brains of human fetuses also have been attempted. This approach has not produced satisfactory results yet. Implanted fetal tissue takes some time to develop and noticeable changes may take several years. Implants seem to be moderately effective for relatively younger patients but may not benefit adults older than 59. In older patients, the implants frequently produce negative side effects such as uncontolled movement (Freed, Greene, Breeze, Tsai, DuMouchel, Kao, Dillon, Winfield, Culver, Trojanowski, Eidelberg, & Fahn, 2001). While often successful, such treatments are also controversial (DiGiovanna, 1994).

Vascular Dementia.   **Vascular dementia** is also known as multi-infarct dementia. An infarct is an area of dying or dead brain cells. These cells die from numerous small strokes in which small blood clots cut off the blood supply to the dying area. Over time, more small strokes produce more dead areas in the brain. Vascular dementia is more common in men than in women and usually results in death from a major stroke, heart disease, or pneumonia. About 20 percent of deaths from chronic OBS are from vascular dementia.

The early symptoms of vascular dementia include dizziness, headaches, and even passing out. Sometimes the individual will suffer a sudden attack of confusion or even hallucinations. Because of the presence of hallucinations and delusions, older schizophrenics are sometimes misdiagnosed with vascular dementia. Weakness and fatigue are common but cognitive impairments usually do not occur until late in the disorder. Some individuals experience difficulty in swallowing, episodes of laughing or crying, and show kidney failure and/or scarring of the retina. After each occurrence of symptoms, rapid and steady improvement usually takes place, but with each succeeding stroke, recovery becomes more difficult and is never quite complete. The typical pattern for a person with vascular dementia is interspersed good and bad days with the good days becoming less frequent and less good as the disease progresses (Desmond & Tatemichi, 1998).

Vascular dementia results from clogging of and clotting in the blood vessels. Almost all cases come from hypertension and atherosclerosis (see Chapter 2) and, thus, the most successful treatments involve medications and procedures designed to reduce blood pressure and restore blood flow. Such treatments can slow the progress of the dementia but cannot reverse it.

Alzheimer's Disease.   **Alzheimer's disease**, also known as senile dementia of the Alzheimer's type (SDAT), was first described by Alois Alzheimer in 1906–1907 in a woman patient named Auguste D. who was in her fifties. This does not mean that this dementia did not exist before 1900 but rather that it had not been identified in the medical literature before this time. There are indications that some form of Alzheimer's disease occurred in the earliest records of human existence. It was generally believed that those cognitive symptoms were simply a result of getting old. Old people were expected to lose their memories and intellects. Now we know that such severe loss is an illness and not the normal expected state of affairs. Today Alzheimer's disease is the most frequent chronic OBS accounting for close to 60 percent of those cognitive disorders. An estimated four and one-half million Americans have Alzheimer's disease. Prevalence and incidence rates increase with old age and slightly more females than males are affected. About one percent of the population under age 65 have Alzheimer's while seven percent of those over 65 show this disorder. After age 80, the rate increases to over twenty percent (DiGiovanna, 1994; Sayetta, 1986; Schulz & Salthouse, 1999). Alzheimer's disease is clearly a disorder of old age.

The chances of getting Alzheimer's disease are greater for individuals with low education, low occupational attainment, or both. It may be that Alzheimer's disease is more difficult to detect in individuals with higher education and/or occupational levels or that these individuals have greater reserve mental power that delays the onset of some symptoms (Gurland, Wilder, Cross, Phil, Lantigua, Teresi, Barrett, Stern, & Mayeux, 1995; Stern, Gurland, Tatemichi, Tang, Wilder, & Mayeux, 1994). There also are large differences in incidence and prevalence rates for different races even when the influence of age, education, and gender variables are removed. African Americans have nearly four times the rate of White Americans and Hispanic Americans have two times the rate of White Americans up to age 90 (Gurland, Wilder, Lantigua, Mayeux, Stern, Chen, Cross, & Killeffer, 1997; Tang, Stern, Marder, Bell, Gurland, Lantigua, Andrews, Feng, Tycko, & Mayeux, 1998).

Alzheimer's disease affects major areas of the brain resulting in all five cognitive impairments and eventual loss of procedural and semantic, as well as episodic, memory. Some of the most frequent symptoms for individuals with Alzheimer's disease, in addition to the cognitive impairments, are apathy (72%), agitation (60%), anxiety (48%), irritability (42%), dysphoria (38%), delusions (22%), and hallucinations (10%) (Mega, Cummings, Fiorello, & Gornbein, 1996). The decline seems much like infant and child development only in reverse order and is referred to as **retrogenesis**. Children learn to smile before they learn to walk, walk before they talk, talk before they can toilet themselves, and so on. Alzheimer's victims lose their ability to toilet themselves before they lose talking, talking before they lose walking, walking before they lose smiling, and so on. The first areas of the brain that are developed seem to be the last to be lost while those developed somewhat later seem to be the first to be lost (Reisberg, 1999). There is no recovery from Alzheimer's disease; things only get worse until the person dies. Alzheimer's disease is a leading cause of death among older adults and kills about 100,000 people every year.

Diagnosis.   One attempts to rule out all other possibilities, such as depression, focal brain damage, an acute OBS, and other chronic OBS disorders, before a diagnosis of Alzheimer's disease is made. This is done because there is currently no accepted test for Alzheimer's while the individual is still living. The only way to be absolutely certain that the disorder is Alzheimer's disease is to perform an autopsy. At autopsy, Alzheimer's disease is indicated by three primary findings (Ball & Murdoch, 1997). First, there is major loss of nerve cells that produce and use the neurotransmitter, **acetylcholine**. These areas are marked in Figure 11-3 and up to 90 percent of these cells can be gone in some areas of the brain. As the disorder progresses, other neurotransmitter areas, such as dopamine areas, also are lost (Chan-Palay & Asan, 1989; Zubenko, Moossy, Martinez, Rao, Classen, Rosen, & Kopp, 1991). Second, many of the remaining cells contain paired and twisted filaments of proteins called neurofibrillary **tangles** which are thought to disrupt the functioning of the cell. Tangles seem to result from the actions of an aberrant form of a brain protein called *tau*. Third, the brain contains a number of **amyloid plaques** surrounded by masses of degenerating nerve tissue. These plaques are composed of one type of amyloid (β-amyloid) which is a protein byproduct of metabolism that does not ordinarily accumulate at such high levels. Research has shown no age differences in the presence of an important precursor of this form of amyloid suggesting that it is not age by itself that leads to increases in this form of amyloid (Niederwolfsgruber, Schmitt, Blasko, Trieb, Steger, Maczek, Hager, Bobak, Steiner, & Grubeck-Loebenstein, 1998). Sometimes tangles and plaques, and certainly cell loss, are found in normal brains at autopsy and occasionally the level of tangles and plaques is quite high even in persons who showed no signs of a cognitive disorder (Skoog, Blennow, & Marcusson, 1996).

Even though the only sure way to diagnose Alzheimer's disease is after the person has died, Alzheimer's disease is diagnosed often and with 80 to 90 percent accuracy later confirmed by autopsy (Victoroff, Mack, Lyness, & Chui, 1995). The diagnosis is typically made after ruling out other possibilities and measuring the cognitive impairments involved. Unfortunately, many primary care physicians engaged in general practice, family practice, and internal medicine are not well trained to diagnose any of the cognitive disorders. A survey returned by 403 practicing physicians found that their average score on a test of knowledge about Alzheimer's disease was a relatively low 75 percent and that many did not follow published guidelines in making the diagnosis. Some individuals with reversible and acute OBS or other types of chronic OBS would be misdiagnosed as having Alzheimer's disease by a number of these practicing physicians. Patients with disorders that could be treated properly will, if misdiagnosed, never receive treatment and be more likely to perish (Brown, Mutran, Sloane, & Long, 1998). Families of older adults diagnosed with Alzheimer's disease are advised to seek a second opinion.

Several new diagnostic tests are under investigation and it may not be long before a reliable indicator of Alzheimer's disease, that can be used while the person is still living,

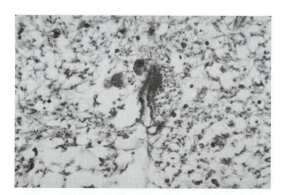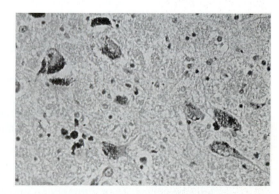

Alzheimer's disease (on the left) is diagnosed by high levels of tangles and amyloid plaque.

is found. One possibility involved examining pupil dilation. Later research, found that the pupil dilation may occur in healthy individuals with a certain form of protein (Verghese, 1999; Scinto, Rentz, Potter, & Daffner, 1999). A blood test for a specific precursor of the amyloid that accumulates in the brain of Alzheimer's patients is also under investigation and seems promising (Luca, Pastorino, Bianchetti, Perez, Vignolo, Lenzi, Trabucchi, Cattabeni, & Padovani, 1998). A third possible test involves having individuals identify common road signs including stop, merging traffic, no U turn, pedestrian crossing, and cattle crossing. An initial study found that persons with no signs of dementia scored significantly higher on this test than did those with mild to moderate levels of dementia (Carr, LaBarge, Dunnigan, & Storandt, 1998). Finally, one recent case study found severely impaired, classic eyeblink conditioning in an individual six years before other standard tests revealed any signs of Alzheimer's disease. Perhaps eyeblink conditioning can serve as an early detection device for impending dementia (Woodruff-Pak, 2001). All of these potential diagnostic tools, and several others, are still being tested to assess their reliability and accuracy. A good test can not miss too many patients who do have Alzheimer's disease and must certainly not misdiagnose Alzheimer's in persons who do not have the disorder.

Progression.   Alzheimer's disease is believed to be present in the brain long before any noticeable symptoms appear. The brain is quite efficient at recovering from minor injury and is fairly redundant in neural pathways for different mental tasks. Since no symptoms are present, it is difficult to determine how long this initial period might be; it may be years or even decades. Once symptoms appear, they are very difficult to distinguish from normal memory changes with advanced age. The individual may begin having difficulties in recalling words, well-known names, and the locations of familiar things. These difficulties are indistinguishable from the retrieval difficulties of many healthy older adults (see Chapter 6). As the disorder progresses, persons may have greater retrieval difficulties and a number of working memory problems. The person may forget what was just read and be unable to remember new names. Objects of value may be lost or misplaced. It is still unlikely that anyone besides the individual or very close family members would even notice these changes. As time goes on, the individual loses track of recent events, has difficulty remembering parts of their own personal history, and may find it very difficult to handle finances, travel plans, and even daily meals. Sequential mental tasks, such as the ones described in our discussion of AIDS dementia, are now very difficult for the individual. Sometimes a phenomenon known as sundown syndrome appears at this level. **Sundown syndrome** refers to an increase in agitation and confusion after dark and is only found in some individuals. After dark, the afflicted adult may wander and be unable to sleep. The noncognitive symptoms mentioned earlier also may begin to be noticeable at this point in the disorder and most families report knowing for certain that something is wrong. Once treatment is sought and if a diagnosis of Alzheimer's disease is made, the life expectancy is still 8 to 18 years (Barclay, Zemcov, Blass, & Sansone, 1985). Families may face a long time of caring. Some examples of treatments used by these families for adults with Alzheimer's disease are described in Box 11-4 (p. 325).

   With further deterioration of the brain, the individual loses memory for major aspects of their lives. Their address and phone number of many years, the names of close family members such as grandchildren, and the name of the high school and/or college that they at-

BOX **11-4**

Dementia Treatments Used by Families

Families who care for a relative or spouse with Alzheimer's disease or some other form of OBS often devise effective treatments to deal with potential problem behaviors and to calm the confused and/or agitated individual. Here are some examples of a few of those treatments described by the caring family members:

- At night, mother gets out of bed and wanders. We fear that she may go to the kitchen and turn on the stove or that she may go outside, wander off and be unable to find her way home. Every evening, after she goes to bed, we place a basket of clean laundry beside a chair in the hall near her bedroom. She cannot get to the kitchen or an outside door without going past the laundry and, as a result, she never does. She comes out of her bedroom, sees the laundry, and sits down and folds it all. Once that task is complete, she goes back to bed secure in the feeling that she has accomplished what she set out to do.

- Several times a week grandpa decides it is time that he went home; he has been visiting long enough and has things to do. He is, of course, already at home but no amount of arguing will convince him of that. We deal with this by saying goodbye to him and thanking him for coming over to visit. One of us then offers to walk home with him. We walk down the street a short way then turn around and head back. When we get back, grandpa feels comfortable at home. Sometimes he will thank us for coming over to visit him.

- Nearly every evening my wife and I watch the eleven o'clock news before going to bed. During the news she will turn to me and say, "You'd better go now; Larry will be home soon and I don't think it's a good idea for you to be here so late." I am Larry but she doesn't recognize me. I learned quickly not to argue with her and play along. I will say that Larry knows I am here and he said it was fine. I will be a perfect gentleman and offer to sleep on the couch because I have no where else to go. Larry should be home any minute and I will clear it with him when he returns. She says, okay and heads off to bed. After a short time, I can go to bed without disturbing her.

- We have placed a recorder near the TV and it clicks on and delivers messages to Mom at various times throughout the day. At 11:45 AM it comes on and Dad's voice says, "It's just about lunch time honey; I'm feeling hungry, how about you?" Mom will answer and go to the kitchen and fix lunch. It's always the same lunch but it's pretty tasty. Dad always comes home for lunch so when he arrives at noon, lunch is ready and waiting.

- Here in the nursing home we have a number of Alzheimer's patients who can become quite agitated. We try to avoid drugs and restraints whenever possible and have found that a recorded message from a close family member can usually calm most individuals. When Leo gets agitated we hand him the phone and tell him it's for him. The recorded message from his brother Tommy always calms him and he'll listen and talk as if he really were on the phone. The same recording can be used again. This is a nice friendly deception that works very well in most cases and is referred to as simulated presence therapy (see text).

tended may be lost. The individual may not be able to determine where they are in terms of city or country or what day, date, or year it is. Performance on the MMSE and other tests designed to detect cognitive impairment is usually quite poor at this level. Many have difficulty counting backward by more than one (count backward from 40 by 4's or from 20 by 2's). Difficulties getting dressed are quite common. Some families use techniques like the pictures shown in Figure 11-4 (p. 327) to assist the person in dressing themselves.

As the end nears, afflicted individuals forget even the names of their spouse and children. Past experiences are only partly remembered and the person may be totally unaware of time and place. Counting backward by ones is now very difficult and some experience delusions and hallucinations. Individuals at this stage cannot take care of themselves as they cannot prepare meals, bathe themselves, or even toilet themselves without assistance. Finally, all verbal abilities are lost and the individual loses the ability to walk or even sit up. The brain seems no longer able to tell the body what to do and death is inevitable.

Our description of this decline may suggest that it is quite regular but it is not. There are great individual differences in the progression through the disease and differences in the rate at which different mental abilities decline (McCarty, Roth, Goode, Owen, Harrell, Donovan, & Haley, 2000). Quite often Alzheimer's disease is classified as early-onset or presenile (senile means old) dementia for those who are diagnosed before age 65 or late-onset or senile dementia for those diagnosed at age 65 or older. Those who are diagnosed younger than age 65 progress through the decline at a faster rate than those who are older when first diagnosed (Wilson, Gilley, Bennett, Beckett, & Evans, 2000).

While the above progression is typical there are some notable exceptions and some interesting data on the possible length of the disorder. Some victims of Alzheimer's disease retain certain abilities and cognitions long beyond the point at which everything else has been lost. A musician may, for example, still be able to play quite well but only when the musical instrument is placed in their hands (Beatty, Brumback, & Vonsattel, 1997). Not everything is lost. One of the most interesting cases is that of Sister Mary. Sister Mary was a nun in the Catholic order, Sisters of Notre Dame, and one of many nuns who are participating in a major longitudinal study of Alzheimer's disease. That study suggests that Alzheimer's disease may be present in the brain for a long period of time before any symptoms are ever noticed. Sister Mary was one of several nuns who did not show any symptoms of Alzheimer's disease and continued to have high scores on measures of cognition until she died at age 101. At autopsy Sister Mary showed all the signs of Alzheimer's. She had cell loss, tangles, and plaques. It is believed that she may have retained her memory because of the location of the disease in her brain but it is not clear at present (Snowdon, 1997). Perhaps many more people have Alzheimer's disease than those who actually show the cognitive impairments. Some other interesting results of these studies of nuns are presented in Box 11-5 (p. 328).

Possible causes.   What causes Alzheimer's disease? The answer is we do not know but there are a number of hypotheses under investigation and, undoubtedly, a number of factors involved. Diseases such as Alzheimer's and Parkinson's may have multiple causes. One strong hypothesis is that Alzheimer's disease is genetic. The genetic components that seem to be involved are not, however, simple or obvious. Five different chromosomes are implicated because genes on all of these are associated with increased susceptibility (Butler,

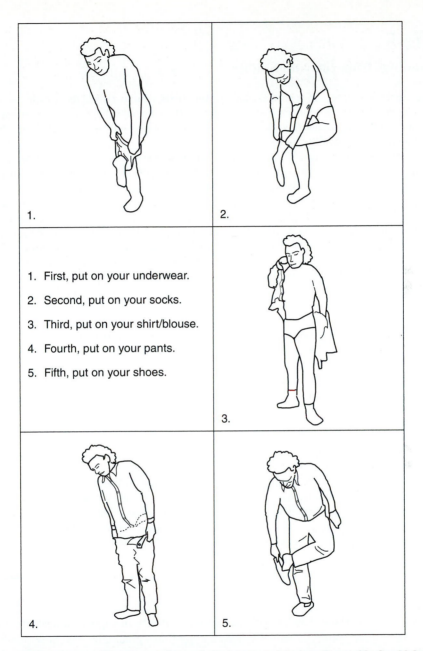

1. First, put on your underwear.

2. Second, put on your socks.

3. Third, put on your shirt/blouse.

4. Fourth, put on your pants.

5. Fifth, put on your shoes.

FIGURE 11-4 How to get dressed; A picture and instruction guide for Alzheimer's victims and family caregivers.

BOX **11-5**

Some Findings from the Nun Studies

A group of researchers have been examining over 1000 Catholic nuns of the teaching order, Sisters of Notre Dame. These volunteers take various tests (like the MMSE), have regular physical examinations, and submit to autopsy after death. It is hoped that they will reveal much about Alzheimer's disease and other cognitive and physical disorders.

One study examined 93 nuns to look at differences in the incidence of Alzheimer's between women who were very active mentally, they worked as teachers, and women who were less active mentally, they worked as domestics. No differences were found between these two groups in terms of the incidence of Alzheimer's disease which was close to one-third of the sample. The study did, however, find frightening evidence concerning the possible length of the disorder. All of the women wrote autobiographies when they were in their 20s and first joined the order. Those autobiographies predicted later Alzheimer's disease, 40 to 60 years later, with close to 90 percent accuracy. The crucial measure was the density of ideas expressed in average sentences. Sentences that contain many ideas are high density while those with few ideas are low density. Low density predicted later Alzheimer's disease. The researchers found no changes in the density of writing for the nuns over the course of their lives (Snowdon, Greiner, Kemper, Nanyakkara, & Mortimer, 1999). Can it be that Alzheimer's disease was already in their brains while they were in their 20s? Do students who write low density essays and papers have higher risk of Alzheimer's disease? Do they already have Alzheimer's disease? These questions are not yet resolved.

Another study examined self-rated function and self-rated health and how these self ratings might relate to the actual health of the brain after death. Self-rated function measures ask the individual to say how able they are to take care of themselves while self-rated health asks the individual how healthy they are compared to others their age. Researchers found that low levels of self-rated function were associated with high levels of brain infarcts. Brain infarcts seem to be experienced as a loss of ability to function rather than as a sign of illness. Both self-rated function and perceived low health were associated with all causes of mortality (Greiner, Snowdon, & Greiner, 1996; Greiner, Snowdon, & Greiner, 1999).

Another interesting finding showed that the decline in function with advanced age was steeper in nuns without a bachelor's degree up to age 95. After age 95, the two groups were similar. It has been hypothesized that less educated individuals may show earlier decline or that the less educated who actually survive to very old age are quite hardy compared to those who do not survive (Butler, Ashford, & Snowdon, 1996). Although the probability of decline may be the same, less educated individuals seem to experience it earlier.

Lewis, & Sunderland, 1998; Schulz & Salthouse, 1999). In support of a genetic influence, the risk of developing Alzheimer's disease is six times greater among close relatives of an individual with the disorder than among the general population and this is particularly true of early-onset Alzheimer's disease (Clark & Goate, 1993; Gatz, Pedersen, Berg, Johansson, Mortimer, Posner, Viitane, Winblad, & Anlbom, 1997).

A gene on another chromosome codes for a protein, Apolipoprotein E, which functions to transport cholesterol in the body. One form of this gene is inherited from each parent. There are three different forms: ApoE-2, ApoE-3, and ApoE-4. White persons who inherit two ApoE-4 genes, one from each parent, are almost eight times more likely to develop early-onset Alzheimer's disease than those who inherit two ApoE-2 genes (Roses & Pericak-Vance, 1995). Those with only one ApoE-4 gene are no different than those with no ApoE-4 genes (Blacker, Haines, Rodes, Terwedow, Harrell, Perry, Bassett, Chase, Meyers, Albert, & Tanzi, 1997). Since the presence of ApoE-4 only has a major influence on the development of Alzheimer's disease before age 65 to 70 only about 10 percent of the cases are involved. Because of this, screening for ApoE genes may have limited value (*Aging Research & Training News*, 1997). African and Hispanic Americans have a high risk of Alzheimer's regardless of the ApoE forms that they have inherited (Tang et al., 1998). Some recent work has compared African-Americans to residents of Yoruba (in Africa) and found much lower rates for Yoruba residents who also have much lower levels of cholesterol. Since ApoE functions to transport cholesterol there may be a genetic/environmental interaction underlying some forms of Alzheimer's disease (Hendrie, 2001). It is hypothesized that environmental conditions may, in some cases, outweigh the effects of ApoE inheritance.

Some researchers believe that a genetic predisposition may be inherited but that Alzheimer's disease needs an environmental trigger of some sort to initiate the dementia. Aluminum has been a much discussed possible trigger. Early research showed that injecting aluminum into the brains of cats produced tangles like those found in Alzheimer's victims (Wisniewski & Klatzo, 1965). A study of 6600 miners in Canada found that those who were exposed to aluminum were twice as likely to experience cognitive impairment as those without exposure and that the degree of impairment was correlated with the length of exposure. At the same time, no differences in reported diagnoses of cognitive disorders for the two groups were found (Rifat, Eastwood, McLachlan, & Corey, 1990). More work is needed to determine whether aluminum plays a role in the onset of Alzheimer's disease (Rifat, 1994). Perhaps one effect of Alzheimer's disease is to allow aluminum to enter the brain and produce tangles. Another possibility is that Alzheimer's disease interferes with the elimination of aluminum in the body. It does not appear that aluminum by itself causes the disease.

Possible prevention. Some ongoing research suggests that soon we may find a technique to immunize persons against Alzheimer's disease. Preliminary work with mice shows that the accumulation of amyloid plaques might be prevented by getting the mouse immune system to regard amyloid as an invader that should be attacked by injecting amyloid combined with chemicals to excite the immune system. Mice that received such injections showed very little amyloid accumulation compared to mice not receiving the injection. Researchers have begun efforts to test this technique with humans (Schenk, Barbour, Dunn et al., 1999).

An enzyme, referred to as β-secretase, believed to be responsible for the production of amyloid plaque in the brain was recently identified. Researchers have spent considerables time searching for this enzyme and its identification is considered a major discovery. The enzyme is believed to clip the ends off certain protein molecules resulting in the release of toxic substances which then accumulate as a form of amyloid plaque (Vassar, Bennett, Babu-Khan, et al., 1999). If chemical inhibitors of this enzyme can be found, then a method for reducing the accumulation of amyloid in the brain may be close at hand.

Other work has examined the use of a nonsteroidal anti-inflammatory drug, ibuprofen, on the risk of getting Alzheimer's disease in humans. In a major study of 2300 persons over a 20 year span, those who used ibuprofen for long periods of time reduced their risk of Alzheimer's disease by 60 percent. Even shorter use reduced the risk by up to 35 percent (Stewart, Kawas, Corrada, & Metter, 1997). Recent research with mice strongly suggests that drugs such as ibuprofen are effective agents for blocking the accumulation of those toxic precursors of amyloid plaque which are produced by the actions of β-secretase (De Strooper & König, 2001; Weggen, Eriksen, Das, Sagi et al., 2001). We may be close to finding ways to prevent or at least slow down the progression of Alzheimer's disease.

Current treatments.   Like all other chronic OBS, there is currently no cure for Alzheimer's disease. Treatments have, however, been found that are far more effective than those used in the past. For example, in 1927 Julius Wagner von Jauregg was awarded a Nobel prize in medicine for treating dementia by giving patients malaria to induce a fever (*Time*, 2000). This is no longer considered an effective or ethical way to treat Alzheimer's disease, or any other disorder. Today, three drugs are typically prescribed for patients with Alzheimer's disease. All are designed to increase the relative amount of acetylcholine in the brain by inhibiting the enzyme that normally diminishes excess acetylcholine. **Cognex** (or tacrine) has been used for quite a while and was the first drug approved for use by the FDA. Unfortunately, Cognex often results in damage to the liver. A second drug, **Aricept** (or donepezil), has come into widespread use because it does not have the liver-damaging side effects of Cognex. Clinical studies of Aricept have found it to be an effective treatment in improving functioning and cognitive performance in all but severe cases (Rogers, Farlow, Doody, Mohs, & Friedhoff, 1998). The third drug, **Exelon** (or rivastigmine), also is not toxic to the liver and is fairly effective in mild and moderate cases of Alzheimer's disease (Khalsa, 1998). None of these drugs can cure Alzheimer's disease but they can be effective in slowing down the progression of the disease.

The hormone **estrogen** has received a fair amount of recent attention as a possible treatment (Giacoboni, 1998). Estrogen injections in rats have resulted in increased neural connections in areas of the brain associated with learning and memory; the action of estrogen in producing these increased connections is linked to apo-E proteins in the brain (Henderson, Williams, & Einstein, 1996; Stone, Rozovsky, Morgan, Anderson, & Finch, 1998). Some work suggests that women with family histories of Alzheimer's disease and who are receiving hormone replacement therapy after menopause are less likely to get the disease than untreated siblings (Paganini-Hill & Henderson, 1996). Estrogen patches also have been used and have been found to increase the cognitive performance of women in the early/mild stage of the disease (Asthana, Craft, Baker, Raskind, Birnbaum, Lofgreen, Veith, & Plymate, 1999; Henderson, Watt, & Buckwalter, 1996). In one study, six of twelve women diagnosed with mild to moderate levels of Alzheimer's disease wore estrogen replacement patches while the other six women wore placebo patches. Within the first week, women receiving estrogen performed better on tests of attention and verbal memory and continued to perform better for the eight weeks of the treatment. When treatment was discontinued, their scores declined. Other work has not, however, found such benefits when following persons for longer periods of time. In one such study, 97 women with mild to moderate Alzheimer's disease were randomly assigned to receive low or high doses of estrogen or a placebo. Researchers monitored their progress at two, six, twelve, and fifteen months and found that 80 percent of those taking estrogen got worse while only 74 percent of those taking the placebo worsened (Mulnard, Cotman, Kawas, van Dyck, Sano, Doody, Koss, Pfeiffer, Jin, Gamst, Grundman, Thomas, & Thal, 2000). Perhaps estrogen produces some short-term benefits that vanish after a more extended observation period.

Vitamin E is also under investigation and in the laboratory has been shown to modulate the toxic effects of amyloid plaque because of its action as a strong antioxidant (see Chapter 4) (Butterfield, Koppal, Subramaniam, & Yatin, 1999; Yatin, Yatin, Aulick, Ain, & Butterfield, 1999). Some work has found that vitamin E seems to slow down the progression of the disease (Sano, Ernesto, Thomas, Klauber, Schafer, Grundman, Woodbury, Growdon, Cotman, Pfeiffer, Schneider, & Thal, 1997).

Gingko biloba, which we briefly mentioned in Chapter 6, results in some improvement on cognitive measures for individuals in the early levels of Alzheimer's disease. In a review of the effects of gingko on cognitive performance due to various forms of dementia, gingko was found to be effective in 39 of 40 trials (Kleijnen & Knipschild, 1992). Gingko is frequently recommended although one must be cautious as bleeding under the skin or in the eye has been observed; usage must be monitored (Wincor, 1999).

While vitamin E and gingko seem promising, skepticism remains high for the benefits of any hormone, nutrient, or vitamin supplement especially when the disease process has advanced to later stages (Lombardi & Weingartner, 1995).

Alzheimer's disease often is referred to as the cruelest disease because it kills the victim twice and devastates family and friends with long periods of agony. The person is thought to die when they lose their mental ability. They die again when the brain can no longer run the body's life support system. With Alzheimer's, as with all diseases, the effects on family and friends are very serious.

Caregiving

Most Alzheimer's victims, and the victims of other functional and organic disorders, are cared for by their family rather than in an institution at least in the early and mild stages (Cantor, 1983; Haley, Brown & Levine, 1987; Zarit & Zarit, 1983). This places tremendous pressure and strain on the family members who must devote a major part of their lives to caring for an individual who, in many cases, has no hope for recovery. Caregivers for Alzheimer's sufferers know that, as time goes by, they will not even be recognized by the person for whom they care. Between 46 and 83 percent of such caregivers experience major episodes of depression (Alspaugh, Zarit, & Greene, 1999; Gallagher, Rose, Rivera, Lovett, & Thompson, 1989). These caregivers are often the forgotten people, not even recognized by the people they care for when those people are in the last levels of Alzheimer's disease and not supported or recognized by the community in which they live.

Caregivers, especially spouses, have begun to receive more attention from researchers with the increased attention focused on Alzheimer's disease. Some work shows that the style of coping (see Chapter 8) that caregivers adopt when caring for a relative with Alzheimer's disease is a function of the level of stress that they are experiencing. Caregivers with high levels of stress tend to adopt more emotion-managing strategies while those with

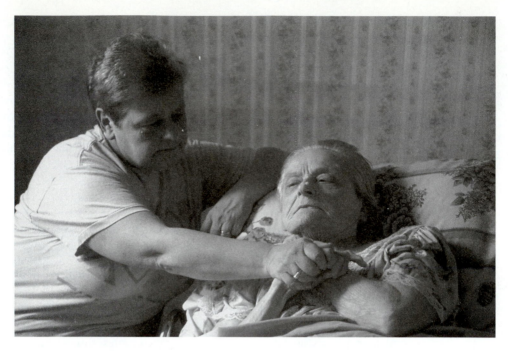

Caregiving can be a very stressful job.

lower levels of stress tend to adopt more problem-solving strategies (Ross, Strauss, Neun-dorfer, Smyth, & Stuckey, 1997). Other work has shown that spouse caregivers are very good at rating changes in increased neuroticism and lower extraversion, openness, and con-scientiousness in the Alzheimer's person that has been under their care. Agreeableness tends to remain stable even for people with Alzheimer's disease (Siegler, Dawson, & Welsh, 1994). Finally, some recent work shows that caregivers are very accurate when estimating the cognitive abilities of those who have little or no impairment but tend to over-estimate the abilities of impaired individuals (Loewenstein, Argüelles, Bravo, Freeman, Argüelles, Acevedo, & Eisdorfer, 2001). Perhaps this latter finding contains a bit of wishful thinking on the part of those caregivers.

Grandchildren are especially vulnerable when a grandparent is diagnosed with a severe dementia such as Alzheimer's disease. Even young grandchildren seem able to un-derstand and deal with the decline of a grandparent produced by heart disease, cancer, or se-vere arthritis. With Alzheimer's disease, however, the grandparent may appear to be quite healthy but in interactions may be unable to remember the grandchild's name, may lose their temper very easily, may act strange, confused, agitated, and forgetful. This is difficult for young grandchildren who may believe that they are doing something to cause the grand-parent to act in this way. Adolescent grandchildren are likely to feel anger, shame, or guilt when around a grandparent with Alzheimer's disease. They may feel very embarrassed by the behavior of a once respected and loved grandparent. Grandchildren need to be told about the disorder, that the grandparent is not intentionally behaving badly, and that the disease is not contagious. The Alzheimer's Association has a number of brochures and suggestions that can be helpful for children and adolescents and younger grandchildren. Providing children and grandchildren with tips on how to talk to and deal with the behavior of relatives with dementia can be very beneficial and produce more positive interactions.

One important support for family caregivers is respite care. **Respite care** occurs when the family caregiver(s) is(are) freed from the burden of caring while the older adult in need of care is placed in a care center or a hired home-worker comes to the home to provide the necessary care. Typically this respite lasts for two or more weeks. The caregiver receives a well-earned vacation and this time off is very effective in relieving some of the stress of caring for another and seems also to improve the functioning of the dependent older adult (Knight, 1993).

In many cases, the individual with dementia is finally institutionalized. A number of different therapeutic approaches are used in these institutions and also in homes. **Validation therapy** focuses on talk about past experiences and the communication of feelings by the patient. The practitioner may rephrase what the individual has just said and repeat it back, reminisce about past events, maintain good eye contact, use a clear and loving tone of voice, gently touch the person, and even use music as a form of communication (Fell, 1993; Toseland, Diehl, Freeman, Manzanares, Naleppa, & McCallion, 1997). **Music therapy,** in which older, familiar songs are played, is sometimes used to relieve agitation and to help bring back pleasant memories for patients with dementia. Sometimes music will evoke humming, laughing, and even singing of familiar songs (Brotons, Koger, & Pickett-Cooper, 1997; Whitcomb, 1992). **Simulated presence therapy** is the use of a personalized audiotape of a family member's side of a phone conversation with soundless spaces for the patient's side of the conversation. An example of this therapy can be found in Box 11-4 (p. 325). Videotapes of family members also can be used. These techniques improve problem behaviors such as agitation or confusion over 90 percent of the time (Woods & Ashley,

PROJECT 11

Be a Volunteer

Most of the disorders presented in this chapter will not be witnessed by most of our readers. We expect, however, that you have had some personal experience with at least one of the disorders. Perhaps you know of an older friend, relative, or neighbor who has abused alcohol. You may have or have had a grandparent with some form of dementia. You may have witnessed depression in a parent or grandparent who has lost a close family member or spouse.

If you have not had any of these experiences, then we recommend that you volunteer in a senior center, for the Alzheimer's Association, or for an adult daycare center to gain some firsthand knowledge of some of these disorders.

Another way to help out is by participating in or helping to organize the raising of funds to support research on these conditions or care for those afflicted. For example, many local Alzheimer's Associations hold an annual Memory Walk to raise funds and would be glad to have your help.

1995). **White noise audiotapes**, usually with the sounds of the ocean or gentle mountain streams, have been used to quiet agitated residents of nursing facilities (Burgio, Scilley, Hardin, Hsu, & Yancey, 1996). An increasingly popular approach in some institutions is **person-centered care**. This approach grew out of the work of psychologist Tom Kitwood (1990; 1993; Kitwood & Bredin, 1992) and involves focusing on the behavior and expressed emotions of the patient and treating the dementia sufferer as a person as in validation therapy. The caregiver attempts to accept all actions as meaningful and to cooperate fully in facilitating communication. These are by no means the only treatments that are attempted and, as you might guess, different approaches work well for different people.

Making Choices

In this chapter we learned that too many clinical practitioners diagnose Alzheimer's disease and other chronic OBS without carefully examining other possibilities. If you or your loved ones are ever confronted with a diagnosis as serious as Alzheimer's disease, get a second opinion. Thorough testing is important and many lives can be saved with a correct diagnosis.

We also talked briefly about the possibility of aluminum acting as a possible environmental side effect of Alzheimer's disease that may cause some of the damage in the brain. Although this is still an open question, you might choose to be safe rather than sorry and avoid aluminum. Every morning many Americans wake up, take a quick shower, and then rub aluminum on their bodies. Aluminum is found in antiperspirants. Many deodorants do not contain aluminum. You might choose to read those ingredient labels and avoid products containing aluminum. Keep an eye on the ongoing research, particularly if you have a family member who has experienced some psychopathology. New treatments emerge continually.

CHAPTER HIGHLIGHTS

- In this chapter we examined several types of psychopathology and the incidence and prevalence of these disorders for different aged persons, males and females, and different ethnic groups.
- Schizophrenia, a disorder characterized by a break with reality, is far more frequent among younger adults than older adults.
- Anxiety disorders, characterized by high levels of nervousness, are higher for younger adults in the cases of generalized anxiety and phobias but about the same for younger and older adults in the case of obsessive-compulsive disorder.
- Mood disorders are characterized by moods out of proportion to the existing circumstances and take three forms. Mania, or exaggerated elation, has about the same prevalence among younger and older adults. Major depression which is less prevalent among older adults while milder depression or dysthymic disorder, is as frequent among older as younger adults. Bipolar disorder is less prevalent among older adults.
- Several hypotheses that attempt to explain these differences in rates of depression include social stigma, better coping strategies, and different symptoms for older adults. All of these mood disorders are treatable.

- Females make more suicide attempts but males are more successful at suicide. The highest rate of suicide is for older white men. This is clearly not a cohort effect and may be due, in part, to the loss of power/money that occurs for older white men.
- Alcoholism is currently higher among younger and middle-age adults than older adults but this difference may be due to a low level of alcoholism among members of the cohort that came of age during prohibition, the underreporting of alcoholism by family and doctors of older adults, and the unhealthy lifestyle and early death of many alcoholics.
- Cognitive disorders are characterized by symptoms of impaired memory, judgment, intelligence, orientation, and emotionality.
- Diagnosing a cognitive disorder is difficult and requires administration of several tests.
- To diagnose Alzheimer's disease with 100 percent certainty requires an autopsy. Because of this, physicians try to rule out all other possibilities before reaching a diagnosis of Alzheimer's disease. Depression and focal brain damage must first be ruled out before an organic brain syndrome can be diagnosed. Organic brain syndrome (OBS) is far more frequent among older adults than younger adults. Acute OBS is reversible and is caused by an upset in brain metabolism due to drug interactions, vitamin deficiencies, or electrolyte imbalance and must be ruled out next. Chronic OBS or dementia is not reversible. AIDS dementia, Parkinson's disease, and vascular dementia should be ruled out before diagnosing Alzheimer's disease.
- The prevalence of Alzheimer's disease is much higher in African and Hispanic Americans than in White Americans.
- The progression of Alzheimer's is unique to each individual but generally starts with unnoticeable small cognitive decline and ends with severe cognitive impairment. Alzheimer's disease may be present for a long time before any symptoms appear.
- Many possible causes of Alzheimer's disease have been proposed. Genetic causes have strong support and current research has implicated five different chromosomes and the genes that code for apo-E proteins in cases of early-onset Alzheimer's. Environmental triggers for genetic predispositions also have been suggested.
- Prevention efforts have focused on reducing amyloid plaque. These efforts include injecting chemically treated amyloid to boost the immune system and taking certain nonsteroidal anti-inflammatory drugs that may block the accumulation of proteins that result from the actions of the enzyme β-secretase.
- Treatments for Alzheimer's disease include medications designed to increase the amount of acetylcholine. These work well for mild and moderate levels of the disease. Estrogen is being examined and the results are mixed suggesting that estrogen may be effective for a short period of time but not, perhaps, in the long run. Vitamin E and gingko biloba are promising treatments in mild cases.
- Caregivers of Alzheimer's patients experience a great deal of stress. Respite care has been shown to be one effective way of temporarily relieving the burden of these caregivers.
- A number of therapies have been used with Alzheimer's patients in institutions and in homes. The most popular of these therapies are validation therapy, music therapy, simulated presence therapy, and person-centered care.

STUDY QUESTIONS

1. Which disorders discussed in this chapter are most likely to have a genetic cause and which are most likely to have an environmental cause? Is it ever the case that the cause is entirely genetic or entirely environmental?

2. Why do many people believe that older adults are more likely to be depressed than younger adults? What does the evidence on prevalence rates show?

3. What are some of the signs of a possible suicide attempt?

4. If older adults have lower rates of alcoholism in part because of prohibition, then what would you expect to happen to other types of drug abuse if drugs were no longer illegal? If it turned out that prohibition had no effect on alcoholism rates (that is, they don't change as other cohorts enter old age), does that suggest any effect of illegality on rates of use? What do you expect the data to show when it becomes available?

5. If an older relative shows a sudden loss of memory and fears Alzheimer's disease, is there anything that you now know that might help to reassure this person?

6. What is the controversy surrounding the use of fetal brain tissue to treat Parkinson's disease? What do you think should be done? Is this type of treatment effective?

7. Describe the steps recommended to reach a diagnosis of Alzheimer's disease. Why are these steps necessary?

8. Describe the three physical changes evident at autopsy in the brain of a person with Alzheimer's disease.

9. What is the cause of Alzheimer's disease? Genetics? ApoE? Aluminum? Other? Does it depend on whether the disease is early or late onset?

10. Describe some of the treatments used for Alzheimer's disease including family treatments, drugs and talk therapies.

RECOMMENDED READINGS

Mace, N. L. & Rabins, P. V. (1999). *The 36-hour day* (3rd ed.). Baltimore, MD: Johns Hopkins University Press. This book is a standard for caregivers and provide very valuable information and tips for successful caregiving.

McGowin, D. F. (1993). *Living in the labyrinth: A personal journey through the maze of alzheimer's.* New York: Delta (Dell Publishing). This is a book written by a woman in the earlier stages of Alzheimer's disease. This is an excellent description of some of the cognitive difficulties encountered and the emotional impact of this dreaded disease on the person who has it.

Shenk, D. (2001). *The forgetting alzheimer's: portrait of an epidemic.* New York: Doubleday. This book is a very readable and interesting description of Alzheimer's disease from its first description, through past lives, and into the most current research.

INTERNET RESOURCES

http://www.nami.org   The National Alliance for the Mentally Ill.
http://www.nimh.nih.gov   National Institute of Mental Health.
http://www.aagpgpa.org   The American Association for Geriatric Psychiatry.
http://www.alz.org   The Alzheimer's Association provides the latest information on Alzheimer's disease, research, and education.
http://www.alzheimers.org   Alzheimer's Disease Education & Referral Center.

12 Healthy/Helpful Environments: Places and People

Home is where the heart is.

—Pliny the Elder

There's no place like home.

—Dorothy in The Wizard of Oz

Oh, we have a home—we just need a house to put it in.

—10-year-old homeless girl

Close your eyes and think about home. What comes to mind? Do you picture one place, or several places? What makes up that place? Do you see people as well as buildings, yards, sidewalks, furniture, knick-knacks on shelves? What about the feelings that you have? Is home where your heart is? Is there no place like home? Many of us have warm and fuzzy feelings about places we call home. Others may have negative feelings about some of the places where they have lived. By the time we reach old age, we have lived in many places and probably have a very complex view of what "home" means.

In this chapter we explore where older people live, what their options are when they need more help, and who the caregivers are for our frail elders.

How Spaces Become Places or How We Fit in

The right environment is the one in which we feel comfortable. But what exactly does that mean? We are comfortable when we fit with our surroundings. Powell Lawton and his colleagues at the Philadelphia Geriatric Center have proposed an explanation of this fit. (Lawton, 1977, 1980; Lawton & Nahemow, 1973; Nahemow, 1997). Their theory of **person–environment congruence**, called the ecological theory of aging, explains fit in

Senior View

We spoke to two different women about their deliberations about moving. Both Lydia Lagomasino and May Lee Wong lived alone and considered moving in with their adult daughters, who very much wanted them to move in with them. As you will see, these women made different decisions, each one the right one for them.

We asked Lydia to tell us about where she has lived in her life and her ideas about what makes a home. Lydia, who wouldn't tell us her age ("I learned that a woman never tells her age, weight, or salary, so I never have!") but says she is over 65 and thus qualifies as a senior citizen, was born in a small town not far from Havana, Cuba. In 1960, she and her husband did not want to raise their children in a communist country so they decided to emigrate to the United States. Because of restrictions, her husband came first and she and her children followed months later. Her husband found a job and family to stay with when he arrived in Miami, making the move easier for Lydia and the children. When we asked how long it took for Miami to feel like home, Lydia answered, "It never did. I only had one friend, distant family, and we only stayed there for five months." The family moved to Raleigh, North Carolina, where they lived for 36 years. She said Raleigh did feel like home to her.

We asked her to tell us about how Raleigh became a home for her. She said that at first she was very homesick as she only spoke Spanish and knew no one in this new city. She had to rely on her husband to translate everything. But she was determined to make a home for herself and her family so she learned English, was trained as a pharmacist, and began working in a small drug store. Another thing that helped her feel more comfortable in Raleigh was meeting other Cuban couples. "I really learned to love Raleigh through my work and friendships. We had frequent parties, dancing until 3 A.M. to old Latin music. It was a great time," she said.

Lydia no longer lives in Raleigh. She now lives in a duplex house in Charlotte, beside her daughter, also named Lydia. We asked her how and why she moved. She said that once she retired and her husband died and her friends were dying, she started feeling quite lonely. She made some new good friends through her church and probably would have stayed in Raleigh because she owned and loved her house. But ten years ago she was mugged in a grocery store parking lot and thrown to the ground resulting in a fractured hip. She has had difficulty moving around ever since. Then she had to have a heart valve replacement, which further affected her mobility. Her children convinced her that she should no longer live by herself.

We asked her if she had ever considered an independent or assisted living facility and she said, "Absolutely not! In Cuba, we do not put our loved ones away. My unmarried sister lived with us until she died and my sister in Cuba took in an older neighbor who needed help. That is what you do. After spending five weeks in a rehabilitation center after my hip surgery, I knew I would never live in one of those depressing places. I told my children, you can't put me in one of those places because I am not going to go!"

We asked her how she made the decision to live with her daughter. She said her son wanted her

to buy a condo near his home, a small town outside of Raleigh and her daughter wanted her to move in and rent the other side of her home in Charlotte. Lydia said it was a hard decision but she felt that her son was so busy he might not be able to help her in an emergency. She felt that her daughter would be able to help her more. She agreed with our suggestion that society expects daughters to help more than sons and that maybe that was why she too chose her daughter. We asked her if she felt that her children had an obligation to take care of her. She said that she did not feel that children *have* to take care of parents in old age nor is caring a payback situation for taking care of them when they were young. She said that in her culture it is an honor to care for older relatives and that children take on caregiving because they are good children, not out of obligation.

We asked Lydia of all of the places she has lived, which one most felt like home. We thought for sure she would say Raleigh but we were surprised by her answer. She quickly replied, "My heart is in Cuba. There I was young and alive. I flirted with the boys, fell in love and married, and gave birth to my wonderful children. It was an incredibly beautiful place. Havana is where my heart is." You too might see this joy in the photo Lydia allowed us to print here, at her heart and home in Havana.

May Lee agreed to be interviewed only because her daughter is a colleague and she will do anything to help her daughter and her work. She wasn't sure that she could tell us anything that we would find interesting or helpful but as we expected, we had a delightful and informative visit.

May Lee was born in Savannah, Georgia, and is an 80-year-old second-generation Chinese American. She has lived in many different places in her life, for a short while in Brooklyn, New York, as a child, and in several homes in Savannah. She grew up in a large family and continued that tradition by having six daughters. We asked May Lee where she liked living most and she said Savannah, primarily because it is familiar, comfortable, and feels most like *home.*

May Lee quit school and started working in her mother's grocery store at age 16. We asked her why she quit school and she said that her family couldn't afford for her to go anymore. This was a typical solution for many of her friends so she was not upset. She married at age 21 and helped her husband in his laundry. We asked her if there was a time when she didn't work and she said no that they needed the money so she bought and operated a small grocery store. When we asked about how she handled working and raising a family she laughed and said that her daughters raised themselves. After her husband died, she eventually sold the store to the housing project of which it was a part. She no longer felt safe there due to the rising crime.

We asked May Lee to tell us a little bit about what she was thinking in terms of her future home. She currently lives alone in a house that she owns and proudly says, "is completely paid for." She doesn't drive and must rely on family to help her get to church, doctors, and the grocery store. We asked her if she missed not being able to drive. She said that she never learned to drive but the only time she ever felt like she needed to was when the children were young. She often takes the bus and really enjoys the area where she lives.

A little more than two years ago, May Lee had an operation to repair a ruptured aneurysm.

(continued)

Senior View   Continued

After that operation, she had a stroke. She still has a little difficulty moving which prompted her daughters to encourage her to move in with one of them. Her daughter Jo Ann (our colleague) very much wanted her mother to live with her. When we asked May Lee if this was a good idea she said that she was considering it since Jo Ann was alone and she felt sorry for her. We had to chuckle since that was exactly how Jo Ann described her mother!

We asked May Lee to talk a little about her perspective on how elders are cared for in the Chinese culture. She said that Asians treat their elders with a great deal of respect. The oldest son usually takes his mother to live with his family when she gets old. She thinks that there is much more respect for elder family members in Asian families. She said that if she could give one message to young people it would be, "respect your elders, after all they did raise you!"

We ended our interview by following up on the feeling we had that May Lee was not convinced that moving in with her daughter was a good idea. We asked her if and when she was ready to move and she said, "I think I would miss my grandchildren in Savannah too much if I moved, and I have a very nice house all paid for." We asked one last question, "Do you think you have a good life?" To this May Lee laughed and said, "yes, all I do is eat and sleep and the girls come and take me places. I don't worry about old age, I can't think as fast or remember as well but if I can't remember something, I don't worry about it." The last we checked with JoAnn, her mother was still living alone in Savannah, enjoying her life, and not worrying about anything.

terms of a how a person operates in any given environment. The theory holds that the ability to complete a task is a result of the congruence between what the environment demands of us (which they call environmental press or demand) and the capabilities of the person attempting the task (which they call competence or person capability). For example, if you have to sit in a hard metal chair for a three-hour lecture thus requiring you to sit in a certain posture and pay attention, and your back, legs, and brain allow you to do that then you fit this environment, or have person–environment congruence. Lawton and his colleagues base their theory on an existing concept in psychology called adaptation level theory, which states that individuals are continually adapting to external stimuli. For example, you ignore the buzzing of the lights or the air conditioner or the music from your neighbor's stereo while you read this chapter. But if the noise were turned up, you would have difficulty concentrating. On the other hand, if the stimuli were reduced by turning off the lights, air-conditioning or heat, and music, you would not be able to read. The point is that people adapt to most environments which are at a middle-level of stimulation. However, environments that have high press or demand or that have very intense or very low levels of stimulation are impossible for most people to function well in or complete routine tasks.

But the environment is only one part of the equation. On the personal side, each individual brings a certain level of competence or ability to any given task. To go back to our reading example, if you are very tired when you start to read, chances are you will need a lot more stimulation (more light or a cooler room or moving around more often) to complete reading the chapter. If you have vision problems, you may need more light or larger print to be able to see the text. Your abilities predict not just how well you adapt to the environment but how long it takes you to do so and complete your task. So taken together, successful task completion is an interaction between what the environment demands or presses on you and what capabilities or competence you bring to the task. Most people have a fairly broad range of capabilities and thus adapt to a wide range of environmental stimulation. Older persons with reduced abilities or disabilities take longer and adapt best to lower levels of environmental demand. Figure 12-1 illustrates the notion of the range of adaptation or person–environment congruence as it applies to everyone.

As you can see in this graph, there are areas that represent a mismatch between competence and press and areas of comfort and challenge. Lawton and colleagues suggest that we like both comfortable and challenging environments. In fact, after working in a challenging environment, it becomes comfortable and we often seek new challenges to stimulate us. We are unhappy in environments that have too little or too much stimulation. While frail elders tolerate less environmental demand before reaching stress levels, we must be careful not to reduce their demands too low. Living in a nursing home for someone with mild arthritis and good capabilities would probably not be stimulating enough.

Powell Lawton's work has served as the basis for extending the idea of congruence beyond the physical space. It also has spurred much work in the design and modification

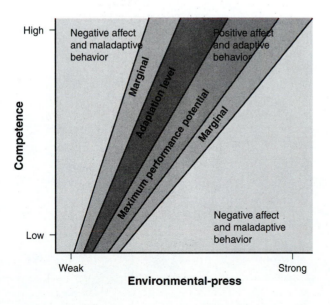

FIGURE 12-1   The Competence-Press Model of Person-Environment Congruence.

Source: Lawton & Nahemow, 1973.

of environments to reduce demand, to improve person capabilities, and to replace tasks for older persons in order to improve person-environment congruence.

Types of Person–Environment Congruence

We operate in environments on a number of levels, so we can fit or not fit on as many levels. (Weisman, Chaudhury, & Moore, 1997; Rubenstein & Parmelee, 1992). These include fitting in with other people (**social congruence**), being able to move around or work in a given space (**physical congruence**) and feelings about a place and your identity in that space (**psychological congruence**). We go through life choosing environments that fit us on all these levels or change environments to adapt to our competencies. As you read the next section, think about how well your competencies or capabilities helped or hindered you to fit into the various environments in which you have lived.

Social Congruence.   Social relationships and the importance of social support were discussed in Chapter 9. Social congruence refers to many of the issues discussed there. We are comfortable in environments that allow us the right level of access to people with whom we share good interactions. Many people in old age choose their living arrangements based on where their friends or family are and how easily they will be able to facilitate their social interactions. Some people fit in many social environments, they like all kinds of people. Those who are more social and outgoing might be considered higher in

Entertaining friends at home is fun at any age.

social competence and have a wider range of environmental adaptation. Others who prefer to be alone, who don't make friends easily, are shy, or have hearing or other disabilities may have more trouble adapting to new social environments.

Psychological Congruence. Researchers have examined the many ways in which we turn spaces that we occupy into places to which we are attached. Think about the places in your life that hold special meaning for you. Some may be specific buildings, such as the house in which you grew up or your high school. Others may be geographic locations or terrain such as the beach, the mountains, or the vacant lot where you played ball with your friends. When a space that we have lived in becomes a place, part of our identity is defined there. Events occurred there that help define who you are now (Rubenstein & Parmelee, 1992). You have memories of places that make up your personal history and for many of us; the objects in these places have further given us a sense of well-being. Think about your stuffed animal or trophy on a shelf or other reminders of important events in your life. Those items make up your attachment to a place. As we age, our attachment to old places remains with us as we add the new spaces we occupy. Attachment to place may be more important in old age than any other time in our life. Attachment to place serves to keep the past alive or provide a sense of continuity. It also strengthens the sense of self and maintains self-image. Finally it represents independence and continued competence (Weiss & Bass, 2002).

Physical Congruence. The most research and writing on person–environment congruence is in the area of the physical, or what is often called the built, environment. The example we discussed earlier, the contribution of light available and your vision ability, which predicts completion of your reading task, illustrates physical congruence. Work in aging, and specifically in human factors and aging has focused on the declining physical strength and stamina in advanced age and how that results in a mismatch with an environment made for younger, stronger people. It is important to know that the physical environment can play a very important role in well-being and remaining independent in old age. If you have difficulty getting around, due to arthritis in your knees and hips, everyday tasks are affected. Cooking, cleaning, and shopping can be difficult since they require a good deal of standing and walking. Furthermore, you may have difficulty getting out and interacting with friends and family, which can isolate you and significantly affect your well-being. Depression may result and further jeopardize your ability to remain in your own home. The physical environment impacts us in significant ways. Fitting into an environment that matches our capabilities and allows us to complete our everyday tasks is important at every age.

Where We Live in Old Age

When we discuss where older people live, most demographic profiles and research programs distinguish between those who live independently in the community (noninstitutionalized) and those who live in nursing homes (institutionalized). Table 12-1 (pp. 344–345) presents a detailed breakdown of the types of places where older people live. Ac-

TABLE 12-1 Housing Options for Older Persons

Independent Living Options
- 77 percent of older adults living in the community live in single-family detached homes
- 8 percent live in mobile homes
- 5 percent live in semi-detached homes
- 9 percent live in multi-unit buildings such as apartment buildings.

Independent or Semi-Independent Housing Options
- *Senior apartments*
  Senior retirement communities or senior apartments are specially designed to accommodate the needs of older residents who prefer to live independently. Rents vary considerably and services can include meals in a central cafeteria, easy access to public transportation, and housekeeping services, all for an extra cost. If income and assets are minimal, a person may qualify for government-subsidized housing or services. There are three major types of federally funded housing.

- Public and assisted housing is operated under programs run by the U.S. Department of Housing and Urban Development (HUD) or the Rural Housing Service. They usually require that a low-income family pay no more than 30 percent of their income on rent.

- Section 8 vouchers are given to low-income families to cover the difference in rent above 30 percent of the family's income.

- Section 202 provides housing to low-income seniors and usually includes other support services like meals and transportation.
  Federally-funded housing is scarce and there are often long waiting lists to gain admittance to a program. Seniors must compete with all low-income individuals and families and preferences based on need (for example, families with children being displaced from their homes are given preference). This can further extend the waiting period. Seniors who are interested are well advised to contact local housing offices early to place their names on the waiting list.

- *Homesharing*
  Two or more people choose to share a living environment. Generally, each person has a private bedroom and shares other living spaces and household chores. Many faith-based groups are helping elders with homeshare arrangements.

- *Accessory apartments*
  A separate apartment is constructed within a home for an elderly resident. Often children or other family members will turn their basement or garage into an apartment for an elder relative. Costs for constructing such apartments can range from quite high to minimal depending on the size and placement of the apartment.

- *Elderly cottage housing opportunities (ECHO)*
  These are small portable homes or cottages that can be located in the back or side yard of a single family home. A number of companies and contractors now offer a variety of portable units that cost upward from $25,000.

- *Continuing care retirement communities (CCRC)*
  In recent years, CCRCs or retirement communities, have emerged as a popular option for older persons looking for a range of housing options and services in one place. This option is different from many others because it offers a long-term contract and provides a wide array of housing, services, and health care all in one location. A typical CCRC includes independent housing in detached homes or apartments, assisted-living units, specialized dementia units, and a skilled nursing home unit. An individual can move in at any level and move to another if needed. Most CCRCs offer impressive entertainment and recre-

TABLE 12-1   Continued

ational programs for residents and access to community activities. Unfortunately, there is usually a large entrance fee (ranging from $20,000 to $400,000) and monthly charges (ranging from $200 to $2500) making CCRCs out of the financial range of individuals with low or moderate incomes and assets. Contracts vary considerably from one CCRC to the next.

Dependent or Supportive Options

■ *Assisted living facilities*
More than 28,000 assisted living residences in the United States house more than one million people. Assisted living facilities provide a range of services for those who need help with daily tasks including three meals a day, housekeeping, transportation, laundry, help with dressing and grooming, and some assistance with medications. Services are delivered based on need; a resident can get just what is needed or wanted and not be overwhelmed with care. On the other hand, for those who need a great deal of care, these facilities are not appropriate. Assisted living facilities are also referred to as personal care homes, residential care, or domiciliary care. These residences may be part of a nursing home, a CCRC, retirement community or some other arrangements or may stand alone. Prices range considerably based on location, services and other factors. When not part of a larger CCRC or community, there is typically no entrance fee for assisted living residences and the average monthly cost in 1998 was $1807.

■ *Board and care homes*
These homes are typically smaller than assisted living facilities. A room, meals, and help with daily activities are usually provided. These homes can be licensed or unlicensed and are only occasionally monitored by state health and human service departments. Costs range from $300 to 3000 a month and federal subsidies are available to help pay for low-income elders. These homes are often not monitored by state or local government agencies. Many social and faith-based organizations run board and care homes. They are good options for many people.

■ *Foster care*
Foster families volunteer to take an older person into their homes in this option. The foster family provides whatever services are contracted and the older person often receives additional emotional support and companionship as well as housing. Costs range from $500 to 3000 per month. Federal subsidies are available.

Complete or Extended Care Options

■ *Nursing home facilities*
Nursing homes provide medical care, personal services, and meals. Many nursing homes now have special self-contained units for residents with dementia. These units typically have a higher staff-to-resident ratio and provide specialized care for those with dementia. Nursing homes are licensed facilities and can be run as for-profit or not-for-profit facilities. A trend in the nursing home industry is away from independently owned facilities to corporate owned and managed nursing homes. Most nursing homes today are owned and operated by one of just a few large companies. Nursing home care can be very expensive and is considered a last resort by many elders. Costs range considerably for nursing home care and currently average about $56,000 a year. You can read a more detailed description of who pays for nursing homes and other long-term care health needs in Box 12-1. As you see in this discussion, Medicare provides only short-term coverage, typically as part of a rehabilitation program and must follow a hospitalization. Medicaid offers coverage for low-income residents and those with few assets. The financial picture for many older persons needing extensive care is not positive. Planning for long-term care needs is an important step all adults can take.

Source: Adapted from AARP (2000b) and the American Association of Homes and Services for the Aging (2001).

cording to the 2000 U.S. census, of the almost 35 million people age 65 and over, approximately 33.5 million (95.7 percent) live in the community and 1.5 million (about 4.3 percent) live in nursing homes (AOA, 2001). You may already be asking yourself, where do people who live in assisted living or retirement communities fit in? It is an interesting question with a vague answer. In most surveys, nursing home residents include just that, people living in skilled nursing facilities. All other specialized senior housing is usually grouped into the community dwelling category. However, as you will see, some housing residences for older persons include a skilled nursing home within a continuum of services. It is unclear whether people in these nursing homes are included only in one category, and which one, or are sometimes doubly counted. Furthermore, people living in assisted living seem to be counted in the noninstitutionalized category, but that is not the case in every study or report. Because of this confusion, the numbers of residents in various housing options is just an estimate. What is important is what these numbers tell us about the general picture of where older persons choose to live in old age.

As you can see in Table 12-1 most older people living in the community live in single family homes. Frail elderly most often are cared for in their own homes or move in with a relative or friend. But many choose, or have chosen for them, nursing homes as an institutional option. While nursing homes provide extensive care for those in need, they are expensive and may not be the best option for care from a financial perspective. Box 12-1 discusses several aspects of the problem of financing long-term healthcare.

Older people can choose from a variety of housing options, although as is the case at any age, finances most often limit these options.

B O X **12-1**

Financing Long-Term Health Care

Barb and Tom Nellis, who worked hard all of their lives, made modest incomes. After buying their home, raising and putting their children through college, and helping their young adult children, they found themselves in their early 70s with small pensions and little in savings. They did not mind because their joy was their family. They lived simply enough that their retirement savings and Barb's income from cleaning a few houses a week paid for all they needed and gave them a bit of extra spending money for an occasional drive to the mountains or the beach. They assumed that they would be fine in old age. But, when Tom developed heart problems and required surgery, they had difficulty paying their part of the medical bills. Tom's health worsened requiring more trips to the doctor, more surgery, more medication, more nursing services, in short, a lot more money. When Tom passed away after a massive stroke and six months in a nursing home, Barb found herself with no savings and many bills to pay from a now smaller amount of Social Security and pension income. Barb is worried that the only way she can pay Tom's medical bills is to sell her house and move in with her daughter or to an apartment. Long-term healthcare costs devastated Barb's security in old age.

This is, unfortunately, an all too common story. Financing long-term healthcare has become a big concern in our country. Many older people are worried about what might happen if they become debilitated and need extensive care. Many younger and middle-age adults are beginning to consider, not just the needs of their parents in old age, but what types of plans they might make to ensure that their own old age is secure. The concerns focus on how to pay for extensive health-care needs, called long-term care, which might arise. These include hospital, doctor, and medication bills as well as the need for rehabilitation, home healthcare, assisted living, and nursing home services. No one wants or expects to get this sick and as we have seen in this chapter and in Chapter 4, there are many things we can do to stay healthy in old age. The reality, however, is that there are a number of people with chronic and debilitating conditions in old age. Using census data on functional disability and institutionalization rates, the U.S. Department of Health and Human Services estimates that as many as 40 percent of persons over the age of 65 will need long-term care at some point in their lives (Congressional Budget Office, 1999). How do people pay for their long-term care? There are several mechanisms for paying for long-term healthcare, briefly summarized below.

Private Insurance
Most of you are familiar with this mechanism for paying for healthcare. It is the most common way that Americans under the age of 65 pay for their healthcare needs. Comprehensive private insurance is usually tied to employment so, after you retire, this source of healthcare payment often disappears. You can pay for health insurance on your own but it is very expensive. Moreover, standard healthcare insurance does not pay for nursing home care and many other long-term care needs. In the last several years, specialized long-term care health insurance policies (LTCI) have been developed to cover expenses not covered by Medicare. A few policies are offered through the federal government and Medicare; these are called Medigap policies and are designed to fill the gaps in Medicare coverage. The cost of LTCI policies range widely, depending on the age of the insured and the benefits chosen. For example, a fairly comprehensive policy purchased at age 55 may cost $1000 per year, but if purchased at age 75 could cost up to $6000 a year. The younger you are when you purchase LTCI, the less expensive it is. Many older people do not plan ahead and end up having to balance the possible costs of care versus the costs of long-term care insurance, with no good solutions. Deductibles and co-payments can make private insurance even more costly. Despite the cost, more people are covered by LTCI policies, up from 1.7 million in 1992 to 4.1 million in 1998 (HCFA, 2001).

Medicare
Medicare is a federal health insurance program for people age 65 and over and some younger adults with certain disabilities. Medicare provides near-universal coverage for older Americans. There are two parts to Medicare, A and B. Part A is called Hospital Insurance and covers in-patient hospital care, 100 days of skilled nursing home care or rehabilitation following hospitalization, skilled nursing care provided in the home and prescribed by a physician, and fairly comprehensive hospice care for terminally ill persons (six months or less to live as diagnosed by a physician). Part B, Supplemental Medical Insurance, covers doctor visits paying 80 percent of physician and outpatient service after an annual $100 deductible. Medicare recipients also must pay a monthly premium, which is applied to Part B services. You may notice that prescription costs, dental costs, hearing aids and eyeglasses, assistive technologies described in the text, and most long-term care in nursing facilities or at home are not covered. These other costs can be extensive. In 1994, older persons on the average spent $2519 on healthcare costs not covered by Medicare or other insurance. This does not include nursing home costs of which Medicare covers only 9 percent of the total costs (HCFA, 2001). Unfortunately, many people do not realize that Medicare does not cover long-term nursing home stays. A telephone survey of 1800 persons over the age of 45 revealed that 58 percent thought that Medicare covered all

(continued)

BOX **12-1**   Continued

nursing home stays; and, 25 percent planned to rely on Medicare to pay for any nursing home need that might arise (AARP, 2001b).

Medicare is considered an earned benefit and separate trust funds are used to finance both parts. Part A trust fund is financed through current employee and employer contributions (HI on your payroll check is your contribution to the Part A trust fund). Part B is financed by the insurance premiums paid by Medicare recipients (25%) and from general federal revenues (75%). You have to enroll in Medicare once you reach 65 and your premium is then automatically deducted from your Social Security check. If you do not yet receive Social Security, you must pay the premium to Medicare.

Medicaid

Medicaid is a state and federal cooperative insurance program for people of all ages who are poor. Medicaid is considered a means tested program, referring to the fact that you must meet the requirement of having little or no money (means) in order to receive Medicaid services. The requirement is a fairly complex formula based on size of family, income, assets, and living expenses. Eligibility requirements are set by each state with some overall guidelines established by federal law. Federal law also sets broad limits on type and costs of services but leaves the specifics and management to each individual state. As long as the state complies with the federal regulations, the federal government must match whatever money the state spends on healthcare services for its citizens. Medicaid eligibility, services, and costs vary greatly from state to state. Those states with higher proportions of poor and older residents spend more of their state budgets on Medicaid health costs. Medicaid pays approximately 52 percent of nursing home costs nationally. Why does it pay so much? The average daily cost of nursing home care is about $153 (with a range of about $90 to $350 a day); very few people can afford to pay for nursing home care on their own, even with substantial savings (AARP, 2001b). Older people often end up spending all of their savings and assets, either before or after they enter a nursing home, and then become eligible for Medicaid. We should note here that eldercare lawyers and financial planners now specialize in helping older people shelter their assets in order to become eligible for Medicaid but yet still be able to pass those assets on to their children. Needless to say this practice has sparked a lot of controversy. Regardless, most people do not have sufficient private funds for extensive nursing home stays and thus must rely on Medicaid funds. This reliance has put a strain on state budgets as the older population has grown.

Out of-Pocket-Expenses

Earlier we discussed the high cost of healthcare for older adults and they must assume much of the cost. Without a good long-term care policy, healthcare costs for frail elderly can be a substantial burden. You may recall our discussion from Chapter 10 about sources of income in old age and see that many people do not have enough money to cover costs if their health is poor. Prescription drug coverage, not covered by Medicare, is a substantial cost for elders. Many older people report not filling essential prescriptions or cutting their dosages because of finances. Those people with higher incomes obviously fare better than those with low incomes. Also not covered is nonskilled care for frail elderly. Unfortunately, this too can create a financial and psychological burden on older persons and their families. Assisted living is not covered by any except some LTCI plans at this point. Neither is companion care, homemaker services, or daycare programs for frail elders. If your mom is still fairly independent but needs some help cooking or remembering to take her medication, or needs someone to sit with her for a few hours a day, you must pay for this care out of pocket, or do without. Clearly, we have a great number of elderly going without that needed care.

On the bright side, a number of organizations are working to bring these issues to the forefront of state and federal lawmakers. At this writing, the president and his staff are discussing prescription care coverage options for older Americans. The federal government is considering a major overhaul of Medicare and states are studying ways to improve Medicaid coverage for their elder citizens. Managed care has impacted federal programs in the same way as it has impacted all of the healthcare world, some say for better, some say for worse. You may be wise to do two things. Consider purchasing LTCI while you are young. The policies are inexpensive. Take an active interest in the federal and state discussions of long-term care coverage. Write to your representatives and tell them how you feel. Decisions made now can significantly impact your healthcare options in the future. For more information about Medicare and Medicaid, visit their respective pages on the Health Care Financing Administration website: http://www.hcfa.gov.

Living Arrangements

Another way to look at what older people call home is to look at whom they live with. Remember our discussion of social congruence earlier and our discussion of social support in Chapter 9. An important aspect of being comfortable involves the people around us. Data from the Census Bureau (1998) indicate that the majority (67 percent) of older noninstitutionalized persons live in a family setting. About 80 percent of older men and 58 percent of older women live with their families. This includes individuals living with a spouse (73 percent of older men and 41 percent of older women) and those living with children, siblings, or other relatives (7 percent of older men and 17 percent of older women). About 31 percent, or 9.9 million, older persons in the community live alone. The gender differences are greatest for those living alone, representing 41 percent of older women and 17 percent of older men. Can you explain this difference based on what you now know about longevity and widowhood in old age? The Census Bureau reported that about one-half of the women over 65 years of age in the United States in 1997 were widows and about seven in ten of these women live alone (U.S. Census Bureau, 2001). Box 12-2 (pp. 350–351) takes a crosscultural glimpse at living arrangements. You can see the similarities and differences in where elders across the world live.

Homeownership.   Another way to look at where older people live is to examine who owns their home and who rents. This is important when you talk about renovations, modifications, or are considering a move. As anyone who has ever lived in a dorm or rented an apartment knows, it is difficult to make even minor changes in a home owned by someone else. On the other hand, anyone who owns a home knows that all maintenance and repairs fall on the owner. Furthermore, when you move out of an apartment or dorm, you have no more money, and usually, less than you did when you moved in. If you own your home, you can build up equity; the money that you paid into your home over the years can provide you with capital to move or to make major modifications. These are important issues to consider as you plan for old age, as we will see later.

BOX **12-2**

Cultural Perspectives on Housing for Older Adults

Elderly residents in the United States have a number of housing alternatives and a number of formal care options that they utilize. This is not the case for all elderly citizens, worldwide. The tradition in most societies has been for elderly family members to reside with their children. In fact, lifelong coresidence of extended families has been the norm in most cultures up until the mid-twentieth century. With modernization and industrialization, this pattern is changing. Over the past 50 or so years, most industrialized countries have seen a downward trend in the number of older parents and adult children living together (Aykan & Wolf, 2000). As a result, countries in Europe, Australia, the Mideast, and urban areas in Asia and the Far East have seen a decrease in coresidence and an increase in the number of older adults living alone or with a spouse (Brink, 1998). For example, in Israel in 1985, 27 percent of individuals over 65 lived with children or other family members. However, in 1991 only 2 percent lived with family members (Katan & Werczberger, 1998). Similar changes have been seen in other countries with a concomitant increase in the need for formal care. For example, Japan, with the fastest growing older population in the world, has set housing for the elderly and increasing formal social services as government priorities (Kose, 1998).

Just because families are living separately, this does not mean that families are abandoning their elderly. As we saw in the text regarding families in the United States, adult children all over the world are still very much in contact with their parents and other older relatives and involved with their care. Treas and Chen (2000) observed urban Chinese families and found that very close ties were maintained with parents living separately. They found lots of economic, social, and emotional interdependence. This is a pattern that repeats itself in many countries.

There are a number of countries in which coresidence or extended family living is still the norm. This is most frequently seen in less modernized or developing countries, such as those in South and Central America, Africa, and in many rural areas of Europe and Asia (Brink, 1998). A combination of traditional cultural family values and economic necessity seem to drive the continuation of this time-old practice. In Korea, 82 percent of older adults live with their adult children, citing the responsibility of younger members to take care of elders as the reason why (Kim, 1998). In India, the extended family is the predominant housing arrangement for elders. Indian sons consider it a duty to take care of their parents and an extreme embarrassment to allow their parents to be sent to nursing homes (Ara, 1998). Aykan and Wolf (2000) suggest that in Turkey, economic well-being is the primary driving force allowing elders to live separately from their adult children.

Keith, Fry, Glascock, Ikels, Dickerson-Putnam, Harpending, & Draper (1994) conducted a large-scale study of aging in a number of different countries. Some of their most interesting observations were of the !Kung (also called the Bushmen) and Herero peoples of Botswana. In both tribes, elders live either with families or in huts a few feet away from their children. Because of this close proximity, they consider that no elder lives alone. In fact, it is not at all uncommon for elders to share their beds with young children on a regular basis, regardless of where they live. Family members provide the most care for elders in these tribes. The Herero have a very practical tradition in which children from other families are fostered to elders to help provide care. These children and their families consider it a privilege to serve a revered elder. The elders in these situations often include these fostered children in their numbering of extended family members.

Finally, we would like to add a note from a group of indigenous women in rural Guatemala. The group *Hearts of Women* is made up of Kakchiqel women whose families were decimated and the survivors displaced by civil war. They have joined together for economic and social support in their recovery efforts. In a discussion of cultural differences in the role of mothers at a recent mother's day celebration, they asked about the practices of family living arrangements in the United States (Personal communication, 2001). On hearing that few extended families live together, they were shocked. They said that they could not imagine living more than two or three houses away from their children, siblings, and parents. Moreover, they felt that their job as mothers extended to their grandchildren and that it would be repaid in their old age when they could be assured of care. It gave everyone at the table something to consider.

In 1997, there were 20.9 million households headed by older persons (AOA, 2001). Of these, 79 percent were owners and 21 percent were renters. It is interesting to note that for these individuals, the median income of homeowners was $20,280 while the median income of renters was $10,867. Another interesting fact is that about 50 percent of homes owned by older persons in 1997 were built before 1960 and 6 percent of these homes had significant physical problems. Older homes continue to have repair and maintenance needs compared to younger homes. On a positive note, about 77 percent of older homeowners in 1997 owned their homes free and clear.

Choosing Where to Live.   We have seen the housing choices available to older persons and where people are living now. But are they living where they want to live? Do the places older people choose to live, fit them?

We learned that most older people live in single-family homes and that these are long-term residences for most of them. In many surveys, older respondents report the desire to remain in their homes as long as they possibly can, preferably until death. In Chapter 10 we saw that only 5 percent of people choose to move from their homes after retirement. This has been referred to as **aging in place** and reflects attachment to a place and the comfort or fit they have in these homes. Fogel (1992) pointed out that many elderly stay in their homes despite deteriorating neighborhoods, economic hardships, and health-related declines. He suggested that the elderly remain in their homes because of the benefits associated with staying at home, particularly psychological benefits. They like their independence, privacy and the control they have over the physical environment. Home is familiar, the place where friends are entertained; it is a part of a neighborhood social network. Home is where important family events have taken place. Home is an expression of who you are. Finally, Fogel suggests that many people find meaning or purpose through home maintenance. These all encourage strong emotional attachments, which encourage homeowners to stay.

Does this mean that individuals who move are less attached to their homes? Kahana and Kahana (1996) have been investigating relocation in healthy older persons to determine their reasons for moving. They suggest that for some older people, moving is an adventure which enhances their feelings of personal control and life-satisfaction in late life. For these individuals, the stimulation of new environments is more attractive than the security of a familiar place. Furthermore, for many, the objects in their homes, not the home itself, are the focus of attachment. They can remain attached to their "home" through favorite objects that can be moved and help make a new space feel like an old home (Koenig & Cunningham, 2001).

For many frail and sick elderly, the ability to remain functional in their home is often compromised and they decide to live with family or in an institution (Worobey & Angel, 1990). Functional ability, or how well a person can manage daily tasks, appears to be the primary factor leading to an individual's decision to move from home to more supportive care. While we emphasized in Chapter 1 that we are living longer and healthier than ever before, there are still a substantial number of elders who experience difficulty.

According to the Department of Health and Human Services (AOA, 2001), more than half of the older population (52.5 percent) reported having at least one disability in 1997. **Activities of daily living (ADLs)** are very basic physical tasks or motions that we do in the course of everyday life, such as bathing, eating, getting around, getting in and out of chairs or bed, and toileting. **Instrumental activities of daily living (IADLs)** are more complex everyday tasks that require a combination of physical and mental ability. IADLs include tasks such as preparing meals, shopping, cleaning, managing medications, arranging transportation, and using the telephone. Over 4.4 million people (14 percent) had difficulty carrying out ADLs and 6.5 million (21 percent) had problems with IADLs. For the old-old, those numbers dramatically increase with the percentage of those age 80 and over with ADL and IADL problems doubling those of the 65 and over population in total. IADLs tend to be affected first and can be hampered by minor disabilities. For example, if you sprain your ankle, you may have difficulty shopping and cleaning the house. On the other hand, if it is a mild sprain, you may just rearrange your life to complete necessary tasks when you are able. It is usually when daily tasks are interrupted, especially ADLs, that we turn for help.

In an AARP housing survey (2000a), many respondents expressed concern about their ability to stay in their homes due to problems they were experiencing. Eight percent of the survey participants reported that they had difficulty getting around their home with 63 percent of those saying this is a frequent problem. The most common physical functional problem reported was climbing stairs (35 percent). Even so, 82 percent preferred to stay in their homes even if they needed help in caring for themselves (AARP, 2000a). It is not, however, simply physical impairment that determines the need for more support. Stuck and colleagues (Stuck, Walthert, Nikolaus, Bula, Hohmann, & Beck, 1999) found that a number of factors can predict functional decline and the need for help. These include cognitive factors, depression, low social contact, low levels of physical activity, number of chronic conditions, low and high BMI, mobility problems, and vision impairment.

Gender and race play a role in decisions to move or remain at home. Older women are more likely than men and African Americans are more likely than Whites to remain at home alone (Rubenstein, Kilbride, & Nagy, 1992). Hispanic elderly are much more likely to live with family members than to live alone or be institutionalized. Furthermore, older minority and older single-person households (primarily single women) are more likely than other older households to involve substandard housing and require excessive housing costs. For those with functional difficulties the burden of home maintenance and repair is even higher because they cannot do many repairs themselves.

Quality of Life in Institutional Environments

People who enter an assisted living facility or a nursing home are there because they need help with daily tasks. This in itself is difficult for many people to accept. Older adults in residential settings may feel a strong loss of autonomy, choice, and decision making (Kane, 1991). Kane and Caplan (1990) found that the areas of choice most desired by assisted living residents were choice of roommate, food, visiting rights, and phone privileges. Autonomy in these areas was associated with well-being and better health. In several studies, quality of life also has been shown to be better when residents have good relationships with other residents and staff, participation in social activity, and ability to physically operate in the environment (Mitchell & Kemp, 2000, Ball et al., 2000). Kane and Wilson (1993) conducted a study of residents of assisted living and concluded that despite the higher level of impairment in this group, good adaptation could occur when there was a good fit between the physical and social needs of residents and the resources of the facility. In other words, person–environment congruence predicted well-being.

The goal then is for all facilities to recognize the need to take into consideration the abilities, needs and desires of residents in their design and provision of services. Resident rights committees are now ubiquitous in assisted living facilities and in many nursing homes resulting in more satisfied and happier residents.

Due to changes in longevity of the very old population coupled with the impact of managed care on the healthcare system, nursing home residents are older, sicker, and more frail than they have ever been. By definition, a frail elder is one who is experiencing a great deal of limitations due to chronic illness and disability. Studies of quality of life in frail populations have focused on nursing home residents despite the fact that most frail elders are still cared for in their own or their relatives' homes. This is no doubt due to the easy access to institutionalized persons for research studies. Examining quality of life in the community is more difficult. Much of the literature has focused on the negative effects of institutionalization, including increased dependence, isolation, learned helplessness, and not being allowed to make decisions (Cohn & Sugar, 1991).

A closer look at these negative effects reveals that they are reinforced by the environment. Baltes and Wahl (1992) examined dependency behaviors in frail elderly in institutions and living in the community. Dependency behaviors are ones that encourage other people to do things for you like asking for help or giving up trying to do a task. The authors found that in both settings dependent behaviors were immediately reinforced. Little reinforcement existed for independent behaviors. They also found that staff and family members expected frail elders to be incompetent. Nursing staff and family caregivers felt that they were doing the right thing by providing as much care as they could. The frail elders in this study saw themselves as incompetent and reinforcement from caregivers further encouraged low competence. The cycle is hard to break but changing how staff and

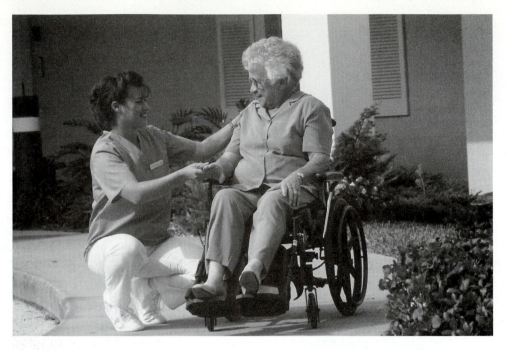

Providing the right amount of assistance is key to well-being in nursing home residents.

family view frail elders is important. Also, it is critical to set up the environment with supports so frail elders can do more things on their own or with minimal help.

Improving the psychological environment is one important way of enhancing competence and independence. Numerous studies have shown that competence and well-being increase by expanding the amount of control institutional residents have in their lives. Giving more control may seem the obvious answer, but it is difficult to run an efficient institution caring for many people and, at the same time, give individuals control over their routines. However, several studies in the 1970s (Langer & Rodin, 1976; Schulz, 1976) showed that having even a little control such as caring for a pet or plant, or determining when visitors would arrive, greatly enhanced well-being in institutionalized frail elders. More recently, Harvey and Lawler (2001) demonstrated that when residents and staff work to maintain respect for one another, including improving communication between staff and residents, enhancing the rights of individuals to determine as much of their care as possible, and encouraging control over daily life, nursing home residents have greater feelings of autonomy, lower depression rates, and greater well-being. While many perceive that nursing homes can be depressing places, and there are some very bad nursing home facilities, they also can be positive places that can be made to feel like home. Little things, such as the terminology used to refer to institutionalized persons, for example, residents not patients, can produce a more positive attitude and make life a little better for those in need of care and support.

Caring for Frail Elders at Home: Who Are the Caregivers?

Who are the people providing care for our elders? Most often it is family. But there is a network of people who support or sometimes replace families. Care can be categorized as formal or informal. **Formal care** is that provided by professional people and/or organizations. These include some of the housing options discussed earlier in Table 12-1 and services offered to individuals in their homes by federal, state, or community government programs, and nonprofit organizations. These services are usually provided on a contract basis and are usually paid for by the client. Some organizations provide significant subsidies to underwrite the costs and a few programs are covered by Medicare, Medicaid, or private insurance reimbursement (see Box 12-1, pp. 346–349). A description of the typical community service programs available for older persons in need can be found in Box 12-3.

BOX 12-3

Services for Elders at Home

There are a number of programs and services available for elders who need help with daily activities. A wide range of public and private organizations provides these services. The more common programs include:

General Care

Information and referral (I&R)—These are locally operated, often by the local Area Agency on Aging, and provide a central location to obtain information about aging services and programs available in the community. This is almost always a free service.

Companionship services—These can include friendly visitors in the home or over the phone or any combination. Typically these services run about $5 to 15 per hour but may be offered on a sliding scale basis or free through faith-based and volunteer organizations.

Help around the house—This is typically a chore service but may include help with ADLs and IADLS. These services run from $8 to 18 per hour depending on the help needed and the level of skill of the provider. Home care aides charge more than unskilled care providers.

Home modification—This is a range of services aimed at making modifications in the home to improve accessibility for those in need. Services can range from simple tasks like rearranging furniture to enhance mobility to installing ramps and grab bars to major structural changes. Prices range considerably based on the skill of the providers and the degree of modification desired.

Transportation—Special transportation for those with mobility difficulty is usually provided by local public transportation systems or through volunteer organizations.

(continued)

B O X **12-3**   **Continued**

Transportation is often free or low-cost but can be very costly depending on the provider and distance traveled.

Nutrition programs—These include a range of services from meals provided in a group setting to meals delivered in the home. Nutrition programs are run by a number of government social service organizations as well as faith-based, volunteer, and private business. Costs range from zero to quite high depending on who is providing the service and qualifications of the person in need.

Geriatric case management—This is a relatively new service in which a geriatric specialist, usually a social worker, provides assessment and ongoing management of the care for an older person in need. Assessment costs range from $200 to 300 and on-going case management ranges from $60 to 150 per hour depending on the degree of help needed. These are usually paid by the individual and can be provided through social service, health care or community organizations, or by individuals in private practice.

Healthcare Programs

In-home health aides—These are minimally trained but licensed individuals who provide personal and low-level healthcare tasks such as giving medications. Costs run approximately $10 to 30 per hour and may be covered by Medicare, Medicaid and private insurance. There are typically long waiting lists for in-home aides.

Hospice care—This is a comprehensive program for individuals who have a physician's diagnosis of a terminal illness with six months or less to live. The program is designed to provide comprehensive support to individuals to allow them to live out their remaining days in their home. Insurance programs cover hospice care. Read more about hospice care in Chapter 13.

In-home nurses and therapists—These are licensed professionals who deliver specialized care in your home or in an outpatient clinical setting including skilled healthcare, occupational therapy, physical therapy, mental health therapy, and so on. Prices range from $85 to 150 per hour with insurance covering some of these costs, sometimes.

Adult daycare—These programs typically fall into two categories, adult day social care and adult day healthcare with the latter including more extensive services. Both are half-or whole-day programs that include supervision, recreation, meals, and some healthcare and counseling for individuals in a group setting. The typical cost is $150 per day with higher costs for programs with more services. For example, adult daycare for dementia patients can run as much as $200 per day.

Respite programs—These are specialized services for individuals with dementia. Services are designed to give caregivers a break from the daily burden of caring for someone with intense needs. Respite can be provided in the home, in a day program, or in a residential facility for a longer period.

Source: AARP (1995–2001). Caring for Parents at Home Family Caregivers Alliance, 1996 Fact Sheet on Community Care Options.

Informal care includes the help a person receives from family, friends, neighbors, and religious or other organization members. This is the most frequent type of help older people receive. Results from a national survey of caregivers (The National Alliance for Caregiving & The AARP, 1997) estimated that over 22 million family caregivers, or a little over 23 percent of all households provided assistance to noninstitutionalized older people. The percentage of caregiving households is higher for Asian (31.7 percent) and Black (29.4 percent) families than for Hispanic (26.8 percent) or White (24 percent) families. Figure 12-2 presents the ethnic and race breakdown of caregiving for a sample of **sandwich generation** adults, adults between the ages of 45 and 55, simultaneously caring for aging parents and children (AARP, 2001a).

Of the 22 million caregivers, 73 percent are women, most often adult daughters (29 percent) followed by wives (23 percent) and then by other female relatives, for example granddaughters, sisters, or nieces (20 percent). Research has continued to show that when available, spouses are most likely to be the caregivers and when they are not available, adult daughters pick up the care. Sons typically assume caregiving tasks only when there

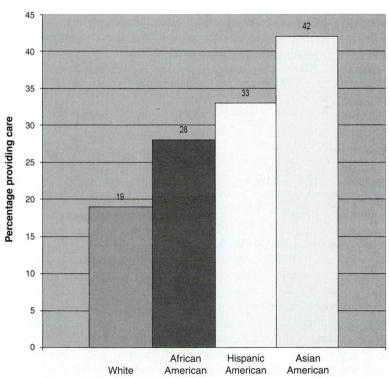

Ethnic differences in adult children caring for parent

FIGURE 12-2   **Ethnic differences in caregiving by Sandwich Generations Adults.**

is no available female sibling. Of those sons who provide caregiving, 88 percent are only children, have only male siblings, or are the only one available geographically. In addition, sons are more likely to rely on their own spouse to help provide care. In her seminal work on caregiving, Brody (1990) found that women were much more likely than men to be doing care work as they age and also were more likely to experience the strain of caregiving. Interestingly, Asian caregivers are more evenly split between men and women, 52 percent and 48 percent, respectively, than any other race; 77 percent of Black, 74 percent of Whites, and 67 percent of Hispanics caregivers are women.

Women and men are more likely to perform different types of caregiving tasks. Dwyer and Coward (1991) controlled a number of potentially confounding variables and found that daughters were a little more than three times more likely than sons to provide ADL assistance and 2.5 times more likely to provide IADL assistance. Harevan (2001) found that men tend to perform managerial and maintenance tasks and provide financial support while women are more likely to do hands-on caregiving tasks. Finally, in the AARP sandwich generation survey (2001a), results confirmed earlier findings but with a twist. Sons and daughters both estimated that they provided about the same amount of help. But when asked what type of help they provided, women reported helping with activities that consume greater amounts of time and energy, like dressing, bathing, eating, toileting, and other time-consuming tasks.

Effects of Caregiving on the Caregivers

Most research on caregiving has focused on the effects on caregivers of providing care for older persons with extensive impairments. Caregiving in these situations is very time consuming and emotionally difficult. In her review of the caregiving research, Rachel Pruchno (2000) points out that a consistent finding in the literature is that caregiving demands are stressful, disruptive, and put caregivers at risk for serious mental health consequences. Elevated rates of depression, including high rates of clinical depression are a common characteristic of caregivers. We saw in Chapter 9 that Asian American daughters-in-law in particular reported great strain in their lives from caregiving tasks. Women appear to be more negatively affected by caregiving duties than men. Furthermore, spouses seem to be more affected than are adult children.

What is it about caregiving that makes it so stressful? Several researchers have investigated the role of specific stressors in predicting poor physical and mental health of a caregiver. One longitudinal study was conducted with caregivers of individuals with advanced dementia. Objective or primary stressors were separated from subjective or appraisal stressors (see Chapter 8 for a more detailed discussion of stress and coping). Objective or primary stressors are things such as the degree of impairment of the care recipient, the number of difficult behaviors exhibited, and the amount of help received. Subjective or appraisal stressors are the degree of strain or burden experienced. They found that both objective and subjective stressors predicted risk for depression in caregivers. Specifically, when care recipients had more behavior problems and caregivers felt overloaded and caught in their caregiving role, they experienced more depression. Furthermore, caregivers who felt more trapped or captured in their role were more likely than those caregivers who did not feel trapped to experience depression over the entire year of the study (Alspaugh, Stephens, Townsend, Zarit, & Greene, 1999).

Several other recent studies found similar results (e.g., Beach, Schulz, Yee, and Jackson, 2000; D'Rourke & Tuokko, 2000). The notion of role overload is probably most felt by those experiencing multiple roles. For example, the daughter caring for a frail mother who also works full time, is married, and is raising children obviously has a lot on her plate. Very little research has examined caregiving in the context of multiple roles while this is a frequent situation. The need for more research here is obvious (Pearlin, Pioli, & McLaughlin, 2001).

Caregiving does not automatically result in negative outcomes for the caregiver. In fact, some people derive a lot of satisfaction from helping (Walker, Aycock, Bowman, & Li, 1996). Powell Lawton and his colleagues (Lawton, Moss, Kleban, Glicksman, & Rovine, 1991) proposed a model to explain contradictory findings among the many studies in which negative effects are not universally seen in caregivers. They suggest that for many, being able to help a spouse or parent can counterbalance the difficulty of watching that person decline. For these people, the more they help, the greater the burden they feel but the greater satisfaction they derive.

Interventions for Caregivers.   Several studies have examined the effects of different interventions on reducing rates of depression in caregivers who experience this problem. Programs that include teaching of coping strategies have reported lower levels of depression in participants (Gallagher-Thompson, Arean, Rivera, & Thompson, 2001). Interestingly, social support has not consistently been shown to mediate stress (Pruchno, 2000). As we saw in Chapter 9, it seems that the perception of support is more important than the actual amount of help provided by others. The use of adult daycare and respite services would seem to help alleviate burden. In fact, studies have shown that while these programs do not reduce the amount of time caregivers have to spend in caregiving tasks, nor the feelings of captivity, they do reduce the feelings of stress. The only thing that reduces the amount of care and the feelings of being imprisoned by the caregiving role is institutionalization of the care receiver. (Zarit, Zarit, & Rosenberg-Thompson, 1990). However, Mittleman and colleagues have shown that institutionalization does not reduce depression in caregivers (Mittleman, Ferris, Shulman, Steinberg, Ambinder, Mackell, & Cohen, 1995). When a loved one is in need of a lot of care, it is sad no matter whom does the caregiving. For many, it is depressing and disheartening to realize that they cannot provide all the care and support needed.

Helpful or Enabling Environments

Think back to our discussion of person–environment congruence and you can see that so far we have been discussing the consequence of what happens when older people and their environments do not fit. When we can no longer function well in an environment, we need more support. Traditionally this has meant that we enlist the help of others. We either use our family and friends or pay someone else to help us in our homes or we move to more supportive environments. This type of assistance is most often geared toward replacing task performance rather than providing a person in need with help to complete the task himself or herself. For most older people, a better approach would be to help them perform their tasks so that they can maintain control over their lives and remain independent. Mismatches in physical congruence are the most frequent reason that older people seek more support. There are alternatives to moving.

Human Factors Approach

How can we set up our homes so that we can function better in our old age? The **human factors approach** is uniquely suited to address questions such as these. Human factors engineering is an interdisciplinary field that examines task performance from the perspective of human–environment interaction. The goal is to identify problem areas in tasks as humans perform them and suggest interventions to maximize task performance. Since it is usually easier to change the design of an environment or machine rather than to change the characteristics of a person, most human factors research and applications emphasize the design of products and environments to fit the capabilities of people; this is called **ergonomic design**.

Until the 1980s, human factors research focused almost exclusively on the military or civilian work environment. While a few researchers examined task performance by older workers, no one considered that task performance by older persons in the home was a ripe area for human factors intervention. Martin Faletti was a pioneer in this area. He looked at the work world of most older adults (i.e., the home environment) and proposed using human factors research to identify areas of intervention to bring the home environment more in line with the capabilities of older adults. He and his colleagues (Faletti, 1984; Faletti & Clark, 1984; Czaja, Weber, Nair & Clark, 1993) conducted an extensive study of the performance of IADLs by older persons in order to identify the movements necessary to complete a given task (task demands of the home and grocery stores), the capabilities older persons have relevant to their tasks, and areas of possible intervention to improve the everyday task performance of older adults. An example from this research is the finding that 60 percent of IADLs performed by older persons involves lift/lower and push/pull movements while standing (Czaja et al., 1993). Barr (1994) points out that with these data, specific interventions could be identified to focus on a combination of strength training to improve person capabilities and redesign of the kitchen environment to reduce the stamina demands.

Home Modification

Most homes have been built using data collected in the military from younger, taller, stronger persons with excellent vision, hearing and other senses. For example, think about the kitchen cabinets in your home. The top shelf is usually fairly high. This presents no problem for a person who is six feet tall. But most older persons (particularly the oldest cohorts) are significantly shorter than that. You may remember from our discussion of functional height changes in Chapter 2 that for the elderly usable or reachable space is greatly reduced. Another example is the thermostat control for heating and cooling the house. It is often located high on the wall and has a small display. There are numerous examples of aspects of home design that do not take into consideration the changing capabilities associated with normal aging, and which further compromise frail elderly. See Project 12 on p. 364 for more information.

There are a number of modifications that have been well-researched that can make a home more livable for those with reduced capabilities. Table 12-2 (p. 362) presents an example of a few typical problem areas and changes that can be made to improve design.

Home modification includes structural as well as add-on changes. Examples of structural improvements might include widening doorways to accommodate a wheelchair, lowering shelves to improve access, or replacing hard to turn knob handles with lever handles, as you can see in the photos here. Add-on features can range from low-tech assistive devices like grab-bars or reacher sticks (see photo on p. 363) to high-tech use of computers to more easily operate lights, appliances, or any electrical system (Grayson, 1997). Modifications to enhance cognitive performance can be enormously helpful. Medication reminders, alarm systems for appliance controls, devices to monitor and prevent wandering into unsafe areas are some examples. Examine your own home or your parents' or grandparents' homes with an eye toward enabling design by trying out the project for this chapter.

An important thing to remember is that the design change itself can add demands that are beyond the physical or psychological capabilities of users. For example, a computer-operated thermostat control might be too difficult for someone with cognitive problems. Although older people embrace the use of technology, it can take them longer to learn complex systems (Czaja, 2001) and they are unlikely to consider a change that does not appear useful. Gadgets may be part of baby boomers' lives and will be taken into old age with them but the older generation now is more hesitant to adopt new products (Clark & Gaide, 1986). A relatively new field is providing some guidelines here. **Gerontechnology** (Fozard, Rietsema, Buoma, & Grafsmans, 2000) is a blend of gerontology and technology with the goal to use technology to prevent, delay, or compensate for declines and to support or enhance opportunities for communication, leisure, learning service, and artistic expression. Gerontechnology promises to bring some interesting changes for future aging.

Many people consider building new homes for retirement or old age. Architects are becoming much more aware of the needs and desires of older homebuilders and are often willing to generate clever designs that incorporate supportive features. A change in the building and product design fields is for universal design of new homes and products. Universal design represents a shift in thinking from adding accessibility features onto standard designs to infusing accessibility into the design of spaces and products so that all people can use the same products and building elements (Connell & Sanford, 2000).

The Eden Alternative (Thomas, 1994) is an interesting new environmental design proposed for nursing home environments. The Eden Alternative is a plan to create a functional and caring nursing home environment by focusing on people living with pets, plants, and younger people. Nursing homes who wish to *Edenize* agree to change their environments so that pets and plants coexist with people and children visit regularly. A recent evaluation of Edenized homes (Drew & Brooke, 1999) found a number of positive benefits. Residents are more interactive, take less medication for depression, experience fewer bed sores, and fall less frequently. Staff turnover and absenteeism in these facilities were also greatly reduced. Although the research on the beneficial effects of pets on health and

TABLE 12-2   Examples of Home Modifications

This table illustrates just a few common problems and modification solutions to enhance performance.

Difficulty	Current Design	Better Design	Assistive Device
Problems turning door, stove or cabinet handles (due to arthritis, stroke, general frailty)	Knob handles on doors, stoves, cabinets, etc.	Replace with lever handles	Knob turners
Difficulty seeing controls (due to low vision, cataracts, glaucoma, macular degeneration, etc.)	Controls with small displays (e.g., thermostats—also often mounted high on a wall, telephone dial pads, stove controls)	Replace controls, telephones with models that have larger display faces; mount controls lower on the wall; add additional lighting near controls.	Snap-on large control adapters or magnifiers
Trouble getting in and out of the bathtub (due to arthritis, fatigue, other mobility related problems)	Standard high wall bathtub/shower combinations	Replace standard configuration with a shower separate from the bathtub or a shower only.	Bath rails and grab bars installed securely and at appropriate locations and heights
Difficulty reaching (due to shorter stature with age, arthritis or bursitis in shoulders or arms)	Cabinets with top shelves that are quite high	Install movable cabinets	Reacher sticks—be sure to rearrange items on shelves so that lightweight objects (cereal boxes) are on top shelves
Inability to maneuver stairs with a walker or wheelchair	Stairs in entryways and top floor changes; raised thresholds in entryways; deep pile carpeting, scatter rugs	Live in one story homes; install ramp entryways; remove thresholds from entryways; replace carpeting with smooth surface flooring; remove scatter rugs.	Electric chairlifts in stairways; large-wheel walkers or wheelchairs that maneuver easily on uneven surfaces; environmental control units (ECUs) for remote access of all electric devices.
Problems using objects that require a tight grip or precision grip (due to arthritis or hand tremors)	Small-handled utensils, writing instruments, toothbrushes, keys, etc.	Use large grip designs that replace a small tight grip with a larger more comfortable hand grip	Build up handles on objects using rubber tubing, tape, or purchased handle enlargers.

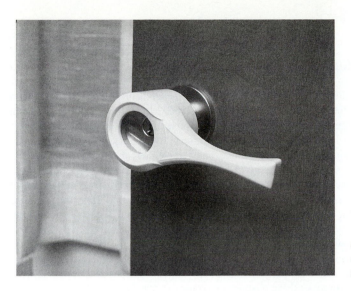

Lever handles are much easier to operate than traditional door knobs.

well-being for the general population is inconclusive, some evidence does point to positive health benefits for institutionalized persons or those experiencing a major stress in their life, such as bereavement (Tucker, Friedman, Tsai, & Martin, 1995).

An exciting area of research in design is that of environments to enhance function in persons with Alzheimer's disease and other dementias. A number of studies have

A grab bar can provide security in dangerous places.

PROJECT **12**

Check Out Your Home

Perhaps your home fits you well, perhaps not. Consider your parents' and grandparents' homes. What aspects of these homes may be poorly designed? In addition to function declining as a result of poor design, accidents also increase. You can improve function and reduce accidents for the elders in your life with simple home alterations. You can start this process by using a simple home checklist. There are several available, and a good, easy-to-use checklist can be found on the AARP website at *www.aarp.org/universalhome/checklist.html*.

Use the checklist to go through the homes of your elder relatives and identify areas for improvement. You can then sit down with your relative and discuss areas that are problematic and generate ideas for modification. The AARP has a number of suggestions for modification as do several other websites and resources listed at the end of this chapter. Do not be shy about generating your own ideas for improvements. Necessity is the mother of invention and many well-respected home modification ideas have come from older folks and their younger family members making changes to enhance daily living. Once you have generated your to-do list for improvements, you can help make these changes or arrange for professionals (e.g., home repair persons, contractors, engineers, etc.) to make some of the changes. Now you can feel assured that you have made an important difference in the safety and well-being of your loved ones.

---

shown that the environment can play a major role in preventing further problems, and increasing overall function and feelings of independence and well-being in persons with Alzheimer's disease living at home or in institutions (e.g., Lawton, 2001; Charness & Holley, 2001). For example, improving the general ambience, decreasing noise, and increasing lighting in dining areas has been shown to improve the nutritional intake of Alzheimer's patients (McDaniel, Hunt, Hackes, & Pope, 2001). Incorporating design features to allow for safe wandering, enhanced sensory experiences, and decreased confusion have led to some very innovative facilities (Charness & Holley, 2001) and designs for home environments (Silverstein & Hyde, 1997). An example of a clever intervention in a dementia unit in a nursing home is described in Box 12-4 (p. 365).

In order to remain in their homes, older people with lower function do what they can do to modify their home or behavior. Most people change their behavior or the way they do tasks before making major changes in the environment (Wylde, 1998), although many make small affordable changes such as using higher wattage light bulbs or installing night lights (AARP, 2000a). Lawton (1982) observed that very frail elders at home make a kind of center of operations, such as an easy chair in front of a TV and surround it with everything that they need, minimizing the need for excessive mobility.

There is a need to encourage service providers and payers (primarily private insurance and Medicare) to incorporate structural modifications, assistive technology, and other environmental interventions to standard care. Currently, there is little to no reimbursement or financial support for environmental changes to accommodate normal changes with age. Programs that include environmental and home management adaptations are more cost-effective over the long run than nursing home care (Heumann, 2001).

BOX **12-4**

When Is a Door Not a Door?

As part of her master's degree in gerontology at the University of North Carolina at Charlotte, Cynthia Kincaid conducted a study on behavioral management using an environmental intervention with nursing home residents with dementia. She first observed residents in the special care unit for dementia at Courtland Terrace Nursing Home in Gastonia, North Carolina. Residents with dementia exhibit a number of problem behaviors that can make caring for them frustrating and difficult. Ms. Kincaid focused on door testing, or the repeated attempt to open and exit a door.

Door testing can be a problem when residents become anxious, agitated, and even aggressive when the door cannot be opened or worse when they escape through the door to a dangerous location such as outside or a housekeeping or medicine room. She observed residents at the nursing home and recorded a number of door testing and agitation behaviors. She then designed a very clever intervention. She disguised the exit door. She enlisted the help of art students at the local Gaston Community College who painted an underwater fish scene on the wall, covering the problem door (see below for the before and after photos of the nursing home wall).

In her comparison of premural and postmural behaviors, she observed a significant drop in door testing behaviors after the mural was painted. Additionally, she observed a decrease in agitation and aggressive door testing. Another interesting finding was that premural, one resident repeatedly enlisted the help of other residents resulting in a team effort to open the door. After the mural was painted, she continued to enlist others to walk with her to the door, but the other residents ignored the now disguised door. It seems clear that using the environment to disguise dangerous or unsafe areas can be an effective and inexpensive intervention with persons with dementia.

A door in a nursing home before it was disguised with a painting, and the same nursing home door disguised by an underwater scene.

When we start to see aging as a normal part of life rather than a disease or infirmity to be cured or treated, we can begin to treat ourselves in old age with the same respect we do at other stages of our lives.

Making Choices

We become attached to the places where we live. You can become aware of this attachment and how it affects your decisions about where to live. When you are considering a move for a new job, be sure to look at social, psychological, and physical congruence in your potential new home, neighborhood, and community. If you choose wisely, you can be more assured of positive attachment and good experiences. You can also help your parents and grandparents consider all of these issues in their decisions about future moves.

Knowing about the options for care can serve you well in helping elder relatives make decisions about care services. Too many people are unaware of the options and the differences among options. And far too many people are not aware of the benefits and range of home modifications and technology solutions available to improve function in old age, or at any age. In addition, as new services and programs are added in your community, you can comment to your local and regional policy makers from an enlightened position about the needs, desires, and gaps in services for elders.

An important choice you can make now is to talk to your parents about their desires for housing and care in their old age. A recent AARP survey found that most adult children see the need to talk to parents about these issues but fail to do so. They just do not know where to start and do not want to make their parents feel disabled or in need of help. If you start talking now about these issues, it will be much easier and long-term plans can be made and even enjoyed by all.

CHAPTER HIGHLIGHTS

- How we fit in our environments is called person-environment congruence.
- There are three types of congruence, social, psychological, and physical.
- We become attached to places and in old age this leads to a tendency to want to age in place or remain in the home as long as possible.
- Older people live independently in single homes, apartments, mobile homes.
- Elders in need live in a variety of settings including with their children or other relatives, in places like board and care homes, assisted living facilities, continuing care retirement communities (CCRCs), in foster care, and in nursing homes.
- The environment can affect quality of life of frail elders, particularly if it restricts autonomy or encourages dependency, a fact common in institutional settings.
- Frail elders living at home receive care from formal (professional) and informal (family and friends) sources.
- Wives and daughters provide more caregiving than men but all caregivers experience great strain in the process. Many caregivers, though, get great satisfaction from caregiving.
- Interesting ethnic, race, and cultural differences exist in caregiving.
- Helpful or enabling environments are those designed to augment the capabilities of persons and enhance task performance.

- Human factors look at task performance and generate products and environments that fit human capabilities; for elders, capabilities regarding ADL and IADL tasks are considered.
- Home modification to enhance task performance for elders includes changing architectural features or structural features as well as adding on assistive technology that can range from low-tech gadgets to robotics and sophisticated electronics.
- Gerontechnology is new field that blends principles of gerontology and technology to generate ergonomic designs for homes and products for older adults.
- The Eden Alternative is a rapidly spreading philosophy of care in which nursing homes are designed to facilitate people living with plants, animals and having frequent visits from children.
- A holistic approach to achieving person–environment congruence in old age incorporates human services, ergonomic design of products and environments, and public policy and funding solutions.

STUDY QUESTIONS

1. What is person–environment congruence? What are the three different types? Identify the capabilities and demands you are currently bringing to your task of reading and studying. What kind of fit do you have with your environment?

2. What is the difference between younger and older persons in terms of person–environment congruence?

3. What do we mean when we say we have an attachment to place? Give an example of your own attachments to place.

4. Identify the various housing options available to older persons.

5. Where and with whom do most older persons live?

6. Describe the difference between continuing care retirement communities, assisted-living facilities and nursing homes.

7. What are the advantages and disadvantages of homeownership for older adults?

8. What is meant by the term *aging in place*?

9. Describe the findings regarding the effect of environment on quality of life of frail elders.

10. Who is most likely to care for older persons in need?

11. Describe the difference between formal and informal caregiving. Give some examples of each.

12. Describe the positive and negative effects of caregiving on the caregivers.

13. Identify ethnic, race, and cultural differences in caregiving.

14. What is a helpful or enabling environment?

15. What is the human factors approach and how has it been applied for older adults?

16. What is ergonomic design? Give a few examples.

17. Define ADL and IADL tasks.

18. Provide some examples of problems older people may experience with daily tasks and some environmental solutions for these problems.

19. What is gerontechnology?

20. What do you do when you *Edenize* a nursing home?

RECOMMENDED READINGS

AARP. (1992). *The Doable renewable home: making your home fit your needs*. Washington, DC: Author. This is an excellent step-by-step guide for making ergonomic changes in the home.

Carter, R. (1994). *Helping yourself help others: A book for caregivers*. New York: Times Books. A beautifully written and very helpful guide for those caring for loved ones.

Mace, N., & Rabbins, P. (1991). *The 36-hour day*. Baltimore, MD: Johns Hopkins University Press. A classic book on the demands of caregiving; includes a wealth of practical advice.

Pynoos, J., & Cohen, E. (1997). *Home safety guide for older people: Check it out/fix it up*. Washington, DC: Serif Press, Inc. An excellent checklist and guide for improving the safety in your home.

INTERNET RESOURCES

http://www.aarp.org   The AARP website has information on caregiving and housing, including descriptions and guides for choosing assisted living, CCRC, and nursing home facilities. Also, it has links to all their studies.

http://www.caregiver.org   The Family Caregiver Alliance.

http://www.carepathways.com   CarePathways provides information on caregiving and facilities.

http://www.caregiving.com   For information on helping caregivers.

http://www.carescout.com   Provides information, ratings, research, and data on eldercare living situations.

http://www.nfcacares.org   The National Caregivers Association.

http://www.1sn.com/homehealthcare/   For information on medical supplies.

http://www.directdme.com/pposcripts/dme_home.asp   Web-retailer for home healthcare supplies.

http://www.exnet.iastate.edu/Pages/housing   Information about assistive devices and ordering a gadget kit.

http://www.aoa.org   Good information about national policy on housing, caregiving and anything dealing with aging can be found at the Administration on Aging website.

13 Death and Bereavement

The art of living consists of dying young—but as late as possible!

—Anonymous

Death is a part of all life. It is something we face when those close to us die and, certainly, when we ourselves die. Death is never pleasant to talk about and is avoided as a topic of conversation. Even chapters on death in books like this one are often felt to be depressing and perhaps not even necessary. We try to make our presentation of death and bereavement less depressing than most; we believe it is a necessary part of life and a major part of adult life and aging. Understanding death and facing it may be the best way to prepare for future experiences with death.

In Senior View, Tat Kleckley talks about the loss of her parents when she was very young and the loss of other close relatives now that she is older. She says it is very important to have people to talk with after the death of someone close—we will see that the research strongly supports her views. The support of others is crucial at such times.

Death

The study of death, dying, and grief is referred to as **thanatology**. Research in thanatology greatly increased in the early 1970s following the publication of Elizabeth Kübler-Ross' book, *On Death and Dying* (1969). Most of this work has involved cross-sectional comparisons; there are not many longitudinal studies. Widows have been extensively studied while some other populations, such as survivors of major catastrophes or individuals with disabilities, have not (Rando, 1992). The oldest-old, our fastest growing population, those over 85, also have received little research attention as of yet. They are more likely to suffer the loss of a child than any other group since their children also are old and they are likely to have their own set of difficulties since many of the oldest-old are more frail than their younger relatives (Stroebe, Hansson, & Stroebe, 1993). Thanatology is an important field of investigation with many research questions still calling for investigation.

Senior View

Tat Kleckley was 69 years old when we talked to her about death and bereavement. She lives with her husband and reports that they are both healthy. When she has thought about her own life and death, she says she'd like to go on living as long as she is able to take care of herself and is "mentally able to think through things." When she gets to be a vegetable, she does not want to live anymore.

Tat told us that she would prefer to die at home unless it were more comfortable for her family and friends for her to be in a hospital. She has already made the arrangements to be cremated when she dies.

When she was only 3½ years old, both her mother and father died. Her father's brother and his wife took her and her older sister to live with them and raised them as their own children. She also lost some aunts who were very close and her mother-in-law. She says these losses are never easy and time, more than anything else, took care of the grief. It took her a year to get over the "deep part of grieving because during that first year you think at this time last year we were doing something together." After that first year, you have memories of at least one event, a Christmas or a 4th of July, that you spent without the deceased. It's a little easier but "you still grieve within; you still remember the people and you miss them."

When asked what she would recommend to people who are grieving, Tat said that they should get out and do things. Don't stay inside by yourself. Most important of all, "Talk about it; part of the healing process is being able to talk about it; have friends who will listen."

What is death? When is a person dead? You might think that the answers to these two questions are obvious. Death is the absence of life and a person is dead when they no longer show any signs of life; they are not breathing, the heart has stopped, the brain is no longer functioning. Death is obvious in many cases but in some it is not. In the United States there are two legal–medical definitions of death. Clinical death is when a person's heart and breathing cease and there are no reflexes. In such cases, resuscitation is a possibility. Brain death is when one's brain cells die and a flat EEG (electroencephalogram) is shown for a period of time (usually 24 hours). The person may still be breathing. Over the last century these distinctions have become important.

Before the early 1900s, the most frequent deaths occured in children. Many died during childbirth and those who survived often died from measles, influenza, whooping cough, and other diseases during their early years. Few adults reached old age. Death was much quicker in those days since early detection of a heart problem, cancer, and so on was unlikely given the diagnostic tools and tests available in those years (Lynn, 1991). Treatments were unavailable or fairly ineffective. Since disorders often were not detected until the person was close to death and no effective treatments were available, death was quick. Now, however, disease can be detected much earlier and often treated. People may live with heart disease or cancer for long periods of time after initial diagnosis. A result of our advances in medicine is that we live longer and death now occurs more slowly and more frequently in older adults than in children. An older adult is more likely to experience the degeneration that accompanies many diseases and to live for a long time with declining function. In our times, the most frequent deaths occur in older adults.

Causes of Death

Medical advances have prolonged life and resulted in significant changes in the leading causes of death over the span of the twentieth century. Table 13-1 shows the top ten causes of death during 1900 and during 1995. (Death rate numbers in this table are deaths due to a certain cause per every 100,000 total deaths.)

You will see from the data that, first, it is clear that medical advances have had great success in lowering the death rate from pneumonia, influenza, tuberculosis, diarrhea, diptheria, meningitis, and nephritis. Most of these top ten causes of death in 1900 are no longer among the leading causes of death. Second, of those causes that are on both lists, the ranks and the number of deaths associated with these causes have changed. Heart disease and cancer were once ranked fourth and eighth but are now first and second. In 1900, 137 out of 100,000 died of heart disease while in 1995, 281 out of 100,000 died of heart disease. This change in rank is not just due to medical success in fighting other disorders. Together heart disease and cancer now result in 2.4 times more deaths than they did in 1900. This is largely due to the increase in longevity. Heart disease and cancer strike many more older than younger adults. Third, many new leading causes of death are found on the 1995 list including AIDS and suicide, both of which are preventable.

In addition to these historical differences in causes of death, there are gender and age differences. For men but not women, suicide and homicide are among the top ten causes of death; for women, but not men, accidents are among the top ten causes of death. The death rate from suicide in men and accidents in women are so high that suicide and accidents make it to the top ten overall. There are also a number of age differences in the adult population in leading causes of death. Table 13-2 (p. 373) shows the leading causes of death for different age groups of adults.

As you can see, HIV infection and AIDS are a major cause of death for younger and middle-age adults but not for older adults. Homicide is among the top ten for younger adults before age 45 while Alzheimer's disease and septicemia are among the top ten for those 65 and older. Accidents, heart disease, cancer, stroke, pnemonia, and influenza are among the leading causes for adults of all ages.

Some recent attention has been paid to factors that might predict mortality in older adults. You will remember our brief discussion of terminal drop in Chapter 7. Generally, poor performance on most cognitive variables and dissatisfaction with aging predict mortality (Anstey, Luszcz, Giles, & Andrews, 2001; Maier & Smith, 1999).

TABLE 13-1   Leading Causes of Death in 1900 and 1995

1900

1.	Pneumonia, influenza	202*
2.	Tuberculosis	194
3.	Diarrhea, enteritis	143
4.	Heart disease	137
5.	Stroke	107
6.	Nephritis (kidney diseases)	89
7.	Accidents	72
8.	Cancer	64
9.	Diptheria	40
10.	Meningitis	34

1995

1.	Heart disease	281*
2.	Cancer	204
3.	Stroke	60
4.	Chronic ostructive pulmonary disease	40
5.	Accidents	34**
6.	Pneumonia, influenza	32
7.	Diabetes	22
8.	HIV/AIDS	16
9.	Suicide	12
10.	Chronic liver diseases (e.g., cirrhosis)	10

* Numbers reflect deaths due to this cause per every 100,000 deaths.

** Of 34 accidents, 16 are motor vehicle.

Sources: National Center for Health Statistics (1996). *Monthly Vital Statistics Report.* Washington, DC: U.S. Department of Health and Human Services and U.S. Bureau of the Census (1979), *Statistical Abstract*, 100th edition, Washington, DC.

Advance Directives

Since today, many more people die in old age and death is frequently the end result of some chronic, degenerative disorder, dying can take some time and the decision to live or die has become quite important. If you slip into the last stage of Alzheimer's disease and are unable to communicate with others, unable to think, unable to feed or toilet yourself, unable to breathe without a respirator, would you want to continue on life support for as long as possible or would you want someone to pull the plug and let you die? The answer to this question is not as simple as it may first appear because a number of factors are involved and there are several available options.

One factor is the state of mental competence that the individual is in when the question is answered. Persons who are conscious and mentally competent may refuse

TABLE 13-2   Leading Causes of Death for Different Age Groups of Adults

Age Group			
15–24	25–44	45–64	65+
1. Accidents	HIV/AIDS	Cancer	Heart disease
2. Homicide	Accidents	Heart disease	Cancer
3. Suicide	Cancer	Accidents	Stroke
4. Cancer	Heart disease	Stroke	Chronic pulmonary diseases
5. Heart disease	Suicide	Chronic pulmonary diseases	Pneumonia and influenza
6. HIV/AIDS	Homicide	Diabetes	Diabetes
7. Congenital abnormalities	Chronic liver diseases	Chronic liver diseases	Accidents
8. Chronic pulmonary diseases	Stroke	HIV/AIDS	Alzheimer's disease
9. Pneumonia and influenza	Diabetes	Suicide	Nephritis
10. Stroke	Pneumonia and influenza	Pneumonia and influenza	Septicemia*

* Systemic disorder resulting from pathogens and/or their toxins in the blood stream.

Sources: U.S. National Center for Health Statistics (June, 1997). *Monthly Vital Statistics Report, 45*(11); and Cook, A. S., & Oltjenbruns, K. A. (1998). *Dying and grieving: Life span and family perspectives.* New York: Harcourt Brace College Publishers.

treatment if they wish. The doctor may tell you that a cancer might be removed with surgery and that without such surgery you will surely die, but the decision is yours. You can accept surgery, seek a second opinion, or refuse to undergo treatment. However, when a person is not mentally competent, as judged by a court of law or when a person is not conscious to make a decision, then those options are not available to them. Mental competence and/or consciousness may be lost in the advanced stages of dementia or when the individual is in a coma.

The state of being in a coma with severe brain damage and no detectable signs of awareness but a sleep–wake cycle and functioning of the autonomic nervous system, for at least a month is referred to as a **persistent vegatative state** or **PVS**. Such a state can result from a number of different disorders or injuries and may be only temporary although the probability of recovery is small and grows smaller the longer the state persists. People who remain in a PVS are expected to live close to seven years with care. If feeding tube and water are removed, death usually occurs within two weeks. The cost of care for someone in a PVS is very high, averaging $150,000 for the first three months and about $100,000 for every year thereafter (Multi-Society Task Force on PVS, 1994a, 1994b). Should such a person be kept alive? Should costs be a consideration in the decision? If they regain consciousness will any of their prior cognitive functioning and memories remain? Such people are kept alive as long as the costs are paid unless there is some prior or advanced directive, a written statement that specifies actions to be taken or not to be taken in the event of such circumstances. Prior directives also might be used in the case of an individual in the later stages of dementia or whenever the individual is not competent or not conscious to make a decision. These prior or advance directives have been recognized by the Supreme Court. A person can clearly specify in an advance directive that they wish to have life support systems continued or stopped (*Cruzan vs. Director,* Missouri Department of Health, 1990) and all states recognize the legality of various advance directives (High, 1993). Advance directives take several different forms.

A **living will** is a legal document that specifies the types of treatments that an individual wants and those the person does not want if that individual becomes comatose or enters a PVS and death is imminent. Living wills are not simple statements saying that no artificial life support is desired; they are frequently more complex and require the individual to make decisions about treatments wanted or not wanted in a number of different situations. Table 13-3 (p. 375) gives an example of a living will.

The **durable power of attorney** document specifies another individual as the decision maker for emergency and any other care and fiscal decisions when and if the individual is unable to make their own decisions. A document of this type applies to many more situations than the living will, which only takes effect when the person is in danger of dying. Also, with a durable power of attorney document, there is no need for specific situations to be spelled out in advance since the document, unlike the living will, is applicable to any number of situations. For example, the individual with durable power of attorney can make decisions concerning medical treatment and monetary transactions. A more restrictive type is the healthcare power of attorney which applies only to health decisions. An attorney can help craft almost any type of power of attorney that the individual desires. It is very important for the unhealthy individual to chose a person who will honor their wishes. Most often the person chosen is a close family member and the risk of conflict with other family members in the event of a life and death decision can be high. There is real concern that the person chosen may often make durable power of attorney decisions based on their own needs or be pressured by other family members to ignore the wishes of the person whom they represent (Zweibel & Cassel, 1989). It is easy to see why this is an important decision and not an easy one to make.

Two other types of advance directives are the **do not resuscitate (DNR)** and **do not hospitalize (DNH)** orders. The former specifies that no procedure should be performed to save the person's life in the event of a medical emergency: The DNR can refer only to CPR or to any extraordinary or emergency resusication procedures (such as tracheotomy and open heart massage). A DNR is never assumed but must be in writing and in the record. Hospitals will not take verbal DNR instructions. The DNH order specifies that the individual should not be taken to the hospital for treatment in the event of an emergency. The DNH does not rule out lifesaving techniques that might be used where the person resides.

The percentage of older adults with one or more forms of advanced directive is small and is estimated to be about 18 percent (High, 1993). This percentage varies for different socioeconomic status and cultural groups. The people who are most likely

TABLE 13-3   An Example of a Living Will

In this living will, each of the following decisions must be made for each medical procedure in each of four possible situations.

Decisions

I want the treatment.

I want the treatment tried but if there is no clear improvement then I want it stopped.

I do not want the treatment.

I am undecided.

Medical Procedures

Cardiopulmonary resuscitation

Mechanical/artificial respiration

Artificial nutrition and hydration

Major surgery

Minor surgery

Kidney dialysis

Blood and/or blood products

Invasive diagnostic tests

Simple diagnostic tests

Antibiotics

Pain medication

Situations

I am in a coma or persistent vegetative state with no known hope of regaining awareness or higher mental functions.

I am in a coma or persistent vegetative state with a small probability of full recovery, a slightly higher probability of permanent brain damage, and a much higher probability of dying.

I have brain damage or brain disease that cannot be reversed and I am unable to recognize people or to speak intelligibly. I also have a terminal illness that is very likely to cause my death.

I have brain damage or brain disease that cannot be reversed and I am unable to recognize people or to speak intelligibly. I do not have a terminal illness and may live in this condition for a long period of time.

Try going through each of the four situations and making one of the four decisions for each of the 11 medical procedures. You have 44 decisions to make. Do your decisions depend on the particular situation? Are your decisions different for different medical procedures? In different situations? If so, you have a clearer idea of the complexity involved in preparing a living will.

to have such directives are those who are fairly prosperous, well-educated, and not members of minority groups (Sachs, 1994). The whole idea of an advance directive is contrary to some cultures that regard any talk about death or approaching death as forbidden. Traditional Chinese culture, for example, forbids such talk (Dubler, 1994). Attempts to increase the use of advance directives have had limited success. In one study, educational intervention only increased the percentage of older adults with advance directives from 22 to 32 percent. Some of the most frequent reasons given for not having an advance directive are deference to others and the difficulties involved in executing such documents (High, 1993). The Patient Self-Determination Act requires that all healthcare institutions receiving Medicaid funds inform patients about advanced directives and the patient's rights to refuse treatments when the patient first receives care. Nevertheless, the proportion of people with such directives remains fairly small. One reason is socioeconomic status. Because of the difficulties involved in execution and the often associated legal fees, advance directives are not an option readily available to individuals of lower SES. Many of these individuals also do not have access to the better hospitals and life-sustaining technology as do individuals with higher SES. Cynics often suggest that such individuals have no need for an advanced directive since they have no access to life-sustaining technology in the first place.

Even when an advance directive has been signed, one cannot be sure that it will be followed. Sometimes the person signing the directive never discusses it with family members or doctors who may then not realize that such a directive even exists (Dresser, 1994). Sometimes the existence of an advance directive or its specifics are known by one doctor or department in a hospital but not effectively communicated to professionals in other departments who may care for the individual (Hansot, 1996). Taking time to search a patient's chart for an advance directive in a time of crisis is not generally considered high priority and in some emergencies, charts are not even available. If a patient is in imminent danger of death and transported from an accident at home to a hospital emergency room, heroic efforts to save the individual's life may be undertaken long before the patient's own doctor, lawyer, or family can intervene and make known the contents of the patient's living will, DNR, or DNH orders or the fact that another person with durable power of attorney is supposed to make all decisions in times like these. Even when such orders are known, physicians sometimes ignore them and proceed with every effort to save the individual's life in spite of the individual's wishes (SUPPORT Principal Investigators, 1995). Physicians may fear the possibility of a lawsuit brought by surviving family members or feel that is goes against the Hippocratic oath to let a patient die. Medical personnel have been trained to sustain life and it is often difficult for them to withhold available treatments (Brody, Campbell, Faber-Langendoen, & Ogle, 1997).

Perhaps most troublesome of all is that individuals with advance directives are often unsure about treatments even though they were sure when the directive was originally signed. In one study of competent individuals undergoing kidney dialysis, the majority believed that their directives could and should be ignored if the doctor decided that it would be best to do so (Sehgal, Galbraith, Chesney, Schonfeld, Charles, & Lo, 1992). If one intends to rely on the doctor to make such decisions, then there is no need for an advance directive.

Advance directives raise many questions that are not yet resolved but should directives be ignored because of these unsolved problems or should they be followed? Should advance directives be made available to all Americans? Will the use of advance directives increase as the present older cohorts are replaced by today's middle-age and younger cohorts? What do you think? Do you think your views will change as you grow older? Why?

Regardless, you are never too young to discuss your current wishes with your loved ones and also know theirs.

Euthanasia

Euthanasia, also known as mercy killing, means *good death* and takes two different forms. One form is the refusal to accept life-sustaining technology and efforts by medical personnel or the discontinuing of such technology and efforts already in place. Such refusal is embodied in many of the advance directives that we have just examined and is often referred to as passive euthanasia. Passive euthanasia refers to cases where nothing is done to prolong life. Passive euthanasia is legal and generally accepted by most, but not all, people.

Active euthanasia, on the other hand, refers to cases where specific actions are taken to end life. There are three general forms of active euthanasia.

One form of active euthanasia is when someone kills another person because they believe that other person would be better off dead. It is not the case that the suffering person has asked to die; the killer has decided for them that it would be merciful to hold the pillow over their face, administer poison, or end their life in some relatively painless way. This form of mercy killing is murder and is not legal or acceptable, although one occasionally hears of such cases.

A second form of active euthanasia is suicide. We talked briefly about suicide in Chapter 11 when we talked about depression. As you might remember, most people who commit suicide are depressed and the group with the highest suicide rate is older, White men. Although the most frequent diagnosis for older adults who commit suicide has been depression (Conwell, 1995), many also have had a life-threatening and/or terminal illness. Some of these illnesses are more likely to lead to suicide than are others. The incidence of suicide is higher for individuals with cancer, AIDS, epilepsy, and Huntington's chorea than for individuals with blindness, multiple sclerosis, and various forms of dementia (Mishara, 1999). Terminal illnesses like cancer can cause great pain and misery and many argue that suicide should be viewed as an acceptable alternative in such cases. In 1975, 41 percent of those surveyed in a Gallup poll thought that suicide was an acceptable right of individuals who were in severe pain with no chance of recovery. That percentage jumped from a minority to a majority (66 percent) by 1990 (Ames, 1991). These suicides are, however, ones in which the individual acts alone. Public opinion is not so accepting when the person committing suicide is assisted by another.

Over the last 20 years a third form of euthanasia has gained much attention and that is **physician-assisted suicide**. Physician-assisted suicide refers to cases where a doctor prescribes or administers some drug(s) or assists in some other way to end the life of a person who wishes to die. Although it remains illegal for any nonphysician to assist a person in committing suicide, physician-assisted suicide is legal under some circumstances in the Netherlands and in the state of Oregon (Cutter, 1991; Simons, 1993). In the Netherlands the conditions under which a physician can assist in an individual's suicide are when at least two physicians have reviewed the case and agree that suicide is a reasonable request given the circumstances, that the patient's circumstances are not reversible and are unbearable, that no remedy is forseeable, that the patient is mentally competent to make such a request, and that the request has been made many times over an extended length of time (Cutter, 1991). It is estimated that several hundred patients participate in physician-assisted suicide in the Netherlands every year (Simons, 1993). Those most likely to seek suicide assistance are those with high levels of pain and suffering and low quality of life (Mishara, 1999). The first such case in Oregon occured in March of 1998 when a woman in her 80s, suffering from breast cancer, took barbiturates prescribed by a physician. She died in the presence of family members and the physician who assisted her (Murphy, 1998). By October of that same year (1998), a total of eight persons and by the end of the year, 16 had used physician-prescribed medications to end their own lives (Karr, 1998). In 1999, the number increased to 27 (Sullivan, Hedberg, & Fleming, 2000). Researchers estimate that about one in six requests for physician-assisted suicide in Oregon are currently granted (Ganzini, Nelson, Schmidt, Kraemer, Delorit, & Lee, 2000). The Oregon law is being fought by several churches, disability groups (see www.Notdeadyet.org), and Right to Life groups in that state while other groups (the Compassion in Dying Federation) fight to keep the law in place. Physician-assisted suicide is the subject of intense debate, and not just in Oregon.

No one has played a more important role in bringing physician-assisted suicide to the front page than Dr. Jack Kevorkian, a 70-year-old Michigan pathologist. Dr. Kevorkian has been charged a number of times for his role in assisting persons committing suicide and had his license to practice medicine revoked in 1991. Most frequently the individuals committing suicide have used a device designed by Dr. Kevorkian that administers an anesthetic followed by a lethal dose of potassium chloride. Death is very quick. He has assisted patients with Alzheimer's disease, terminal cancer, multiple sclerosis, severe pain, and amylotrophic lateral sclerosis (ALS), also known as Lou Gehrig's disease. His last case was a man named Thomas Youk with ALS and the suicide was televised. Because Mr. Youk could no longer control his fingers to manipulate the buttons on Dr. Kevorkian's device, the doctor gave the lethal injection himself. As a result, in 1999 he was arrested, tried, and found guilty of second degree murder and sentenced to 10 to 25 years in prison plus an additional three to seven years for delivery of a controlled substance. Dr. Kevorkian could not legally handle potassium chloride without his medical license. His practice and his trial have brought out strong arguments on both sides of the physician-assisted suicide debate (Basta, 1996; Hoyer, Rybash, & Roodin, 1999; Robinson, Kennedy, & Stevenson, 2000).

Those in support of physician-assisted suicide argue that it is truly unmerciful to allow dying patients to suffer needlessly. The agony, misery, pain, and suffering could be stopped easily if physicians were permitted to assist competent persons who wanted to die by helping them commit a quick and painless suicide (Morrison & Meier, 1994). At present, even pain medications often are withheld or given in smaller doses than needed because physicians fear being accused of murder or sued for malpractice. The line between how much morphine is needed to relieve pain and how much will depress respiration to the point of death can be a very fine line and physicians usually shy away from that line. Oregon, the only state with legalized physician-assisted suicide, now leads the country in physician prescriptions of morphine (Karr, 1998). Without some relief, patients suffer needlessly and many long for death. Physician-assisted suicide, in such cases, where suffering is unbearable, there is no hope of recovery, and the individual asks for help to die,

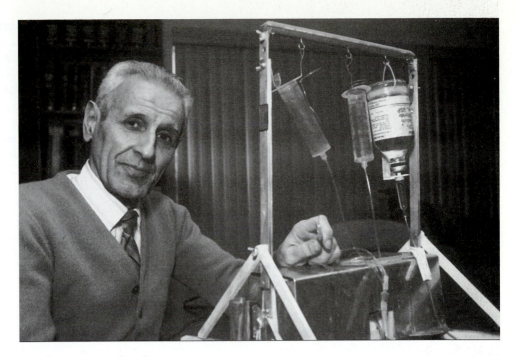

Was this man a murderer?

would be the right thing to do. In this argument, physician-assisted suicide is viewed as a way to end needless suffering.

A second argument in favor of physician-assisted suicide is that it is the right of every individual to exert as much control as they can over the time, place, and manner of their own death (Epstein, 1989). Persons who are unable because of physical inabilities (like Thomas Youk) have the right to receive assistance in their suicide just as individuals who have physical disabilities have the right to be assisted when necessary. People who suffer and wish to die but do not know anything about the quickest and least painful techniques should be permitted to receive assistance from a competent professional. The Hemlock Society USA has been a strong voice for the legalization of physician-assisted suicide for the terminally ill. They argue that those with a terminal illness are denied the right to choose a peaceful, dignified death. Doctors are outlawed from quickly and painlessly ending the suffering of these individuals even though they are allowed to permit a slow death from suffocation or starvation as a result of refusal of treatments specified in an advance directive. The Hemlock Society also has provided information about how to committ suicide (Humphrey, 1991). They argue that it is the right of any competent, suffering individual to receive assistance in ending their suffering.

Those who argue against physician-assisted suicide say that all life is sacred and that no one has the right to end their own or anyone else's life. To permit physician-assisted suicide in a few special cases is seen as a dangerous step on a slippery slope. If physician-assisted suicide is permitted then it will be difficult to control and the most likely people to suffer are those who are the most vulnerable. The old and poor who may already have limited access to the latest treatments may be the most likely to be led toward suicide by doctors who have no time for them, know they can not be cured, and know that they can legally help them die. Rather than being given a right to die, they may end up with a duty to die and to get out of the way of wealthier, healthier individuals (Brock, 1989). Legalization of physician-assisted suicide in some special cases could soon lead to physician-assisted suicide whenever suicide is desired. People who suffer from depression often choose death (see Chapter 11). Depression, however, can frequently be treated successfully. If such people are assisted in committing suicide, then they have no chance to live the remaining time of their life free from depression (Hendin, 1994). Physicians will be healers for some and executioners for others. Instead, physicians should make every effort to comfort dying patients. Even when they can not be healers, they should never be executioners (Quill, 1993).

Another argument is that physician-assisted suicide goes against the purpose of medicine and detracts attention from what is truly important. The easy way out is to help a patient end it all when we should instead focus on improving the care provided for terminally ill and suffering patients (Latimer, 1992). Research efforts should focus on providing dignity and improved relief from pain and seek remedies for the maladies that cause death and suffering. Major efforts toward better care for terminally ill patients are already taking place and will be discussed when we look at hospice.

At present, 46 states prohibit physician-assisted suicide while only one has legalized it. Public opinion, however, seems to be shifting. Gallup polls conducted between 1973 and 1996 have shown a steady increase in the percentage of people who support physician-assisted suicide when the patient is suffering a terminal illness and requests such assistance. Figure 13-1 shows this trend. A number of other surveys also have found majority support among patients and physicians as well as the public for some form of physician-assisted suicide (Blendon, Szaley, & Knox, 1994; Cohen, Fihn, Boyko, Jonsen, & Wood, 1994; Emanuel, Fairclough, Daniels, & Clarridge, 1996).

We encourage you to take a few minutes to think about these issues. They are not ones that can be settled by conducting research. What other arguments in favor of or against physician-assisted suicide do you think are important? What do you think about the arguments you have just read?

Hospice

One program advocating and providing better care for the terminally ill is hospice. **Hospice** provides palliative care for terminally ill patients and their families. This approach stems from the work of Dr. Cicely Saunders in England who served as medical director of St. Christopher's Hospice in London. The hospice philosophy is to allow the person to continue to live until they die (Saunders, 1977). Hospice makes every effort to maintain the dignity of the dying individual. In this country, the cost of hospice care is covered by Medicare and by many private insurance companies. To qualify for hospice, a person must have been diagnosed by two physicians as having no more than six months to live and be willing to give up all life-sustaining technology and heroic lifesaving efforts. A hospice team composed of a physician, a nurse, a counselor and/or social worker, and sometimes a lawyer

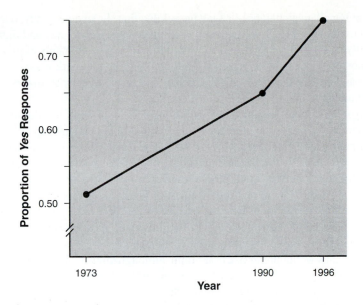

FIGURE 13.1   Proportion of people in nationwide Gallup polls who answered "yes" to the question: Should doctors be allowed by law to end a patient's life if the patient has a terminal illness and requests it?

Source: based on proportions reported in *USA Today*, April 12, 1996.

and/or volunteer worker then assume responsibility for the person's care under the direction of the physician. Most typically, one or more family members are also very involved in caring for the dying person. The family member most likely to be involved is the spouse (Bass, Garland, & Otto, 1985–1986).

Most patients enrolled in hospice programs are older adults (70+ percent) while very few (7 to 8 percent) are under age 45 (National Center for Health Statistics, 1995). Most are dying from cancer (70 to 80 percent) while the remainder typically have AIDS or heart disease (Papalia, Camp, & Feldman, 1996). A survey of 1700 hospice programs showed that few patients have some form of dementia, such as Alzheimer's disease, as their primary diagnosis (less than 1 percent) although some of those with cancer or heart disease also have a form of dementia as a secondary diagnosis (7 percent). Directors of hospice programs often believe that they do not have the necessary resources to care for late stage dementia patients and it is far more difficult for physicians to be sure that a dementia patient is within six months of dying (Hanrahan & Luchins, 1995).

Hospice is not always an easy choice to make and at present it is a choice not made by most although the numbers are growing (Levine, 1995; Sachs, 1994). The individual not only must be close to death but also must be willing to give up several rights in addition to the right to engage in life-sustaining technology and efforts. For example, the patient cannot switch doctors without permission from the team. The team makes all decisions regarding care. If an emergency occurs, the team, rather than the individual patient or family, decides whether or not to call an ambulance or seek hospitalization. In an emergency, one dials the hospice team rather than 911. Since the team is on 24-hour-call every day and family members are usually involved, dying patients may find it hard to find moments of privacy while enrolled in hospice. One may experience feelings of guilt for putting family members through tasks and ordeals that might more comfortably be handled by strangers working in a hospital or nursing home.

A dying person gains several things from hospice. Pain medication is readily given whenever the individual feels the need for it and frequently the patient is granted complete control of all pain medication. Medications that allow the person to continue functioning consciously are preferred by hospice and most patients. The hospice team attempts to lessen the isolation that dying persons sometimes experience by involving willing family members in all aspects of care. The direct involvement of family members in caring for a dying relative is thought to be important for total quality of care and family well-being after the death occurs (Andershed & Ternestedt, 1998). In this country most hospice caregiving takes place in the home and home is, for most, a preferred location. Surveys show that close to 90 percent of Americans would prefer to die at home, although almost 75 percent end up dying in a hospital or nursing home (Glasheen & Crowley, 1998). Counseling is available continually for the patient and family members while the person still lives and counseling continues for family members for at least a year after the death. Hospice helps with all postdeath activities (Cohen, 1979; Kastenbaum, 1993; McCracken & Gerdsen, 1991).

There have been attempts to compare the quality of the experiences for patients, families, and professionals involved in hospice programs with the experiences of those in more traditional settings. Caution must be exercised in drawing any firm conclusions from such comparisons since it is possible, perhaps even likely, that those participating in hospice may have been different from nonparticipants well before any participation began. They may, for example, already have been closer to dying family members or more accepting of an inevitable death. Bearing this in mind, a number of studies have found that those involved with hospice are better able to cope with death (Robbins, 1992); caregivers are able to relieve death anxiety (DePaola, Neimeyer, Lupfer, & Fiedler, 1992); patients exhibit less depression, anxiety, and hostility and say they appreciate the opportunity to talk about their own death (Lack & Buckingham, 1978); and surviving family members cope with the loss better (Seale, 1991).

The Dying Experience

One of the better known descriptions of the dying experience is the one originally provided by Elizabeth Kübler-Ross (1969, 1981). She described dying as a series of five stages that the terminally ill person experiences. Later work has shown that many terminally ill persons do not go through all of these, some do not go through any, and that, unlike stages, these temporary emotional states can occur in very different order and even occur more than once and together (Antonoff & Spilka, 1984–1985; Baugher, Burger, Smith, & Wallston, 1989–1990; Kastenbaum, 1981; Shneidman, 1992). Nevertheless, the emotional states she described are ones that do occur with some frequency in terminally ill patients and are described in Box 13-1.

BOX **13-1**

Kübler-Ross' Stages of Dying

Elizabeth Kübler-Ross (1969) wanted to interview a dying patient for a medical school seminar but found when she searched the 600 bed hospital, not one could be found. Although deaths occured everyday, hospital staff were unable to identify even one dying person. Only when she asked about specific patients would doctors admit that some were, in fact, terminally ill and dying. Based on thousands of hours spent interviewing patients facing death, she developed a stage theory of dying. As with all stage theories, Kübler-Ross believed that these stages were ordered. That is, people went through them one by one, could not skip a stage, and always completed them in the same order. The stages were thought to characterize the process of dying for all terminally ill patients but later work showed that was not the case (see text). The five stages, now more typically referred to as emotional states, are:

1. **Denial.** When one first hears that they have a terminal illness, they may experience denial. People say, "no, not me; it can't be true." The doctors must be wrong, the charts have been mixed up, the tests need to be done again, and a second opinion is sought. Denial can, of course, be more subtle. People may ignore the message they have been given and attempt to go on with their lives without showing any concern. The denial stage is usually not very long as further tests and second opinions confirm the intitial diagnosis.
2. **Anger.** Anger is often the most difficult stage for the individual's family as the person lashes out at doctors, nurses, and even family members. "Why me?" or "life is so unfair" are often heard. Anger may even be directed at an unfair God. It is hard to talk with such a very angry person.
3. **Bargaining.** In this state, the dying individual attempts to strike a bargain with God or the fates to let them live longer. If God did not respond favorably to my anger, God may be more favorable if I ask nicely. "I'll be very good and go peacefully if I'm only allowed to" finish raising my children or complete a major project. Sometimes a bargain that seems to be met leads to additional bargaining. After bargaining to live through the Christmas holiday and making it, one may now bargain to live through Easter. This stage also is thought to be relatively short.
4. **Depression.** Depression can last for quite some time and is frequently inititated by some turn for the worse. Depression is characterized by symptoms of great sadness, hopelessness, loss of appetite, loss of sleep, and thoughts of ending it all. The risk of suicide is greatest in this stage.
5. **Acceptance.** Finally, the person accepts the inevitability of their death. This is not a state where the person is eager to die but simply ready. It is a calm, even emotionless, state. The inevitability of death is obvious and, although not welcomed, accepted.

Some individuals experience positive emotions, along with the more negative emotions, when confronting death. Dying individuals and their families often find that impending death allows the display of emotions that were previously kept in check and bonds with others may be strengthened. Disagreements that may have festered for years might be resolved in the face of oncoming loss. Some develop insights about others and the world and grow stronger in the face of this hardship (Mead & Willemsen, 1995). The process of dying may be different for people of different ages if their attitudes toward dying are different.

Attitudes toward dying do seem to change with aging. Older adults are thought to be more accepting of death than younger adults (Shneidman, 1992) but not necessarily of dying (Vining, 1978). However, this is not always true. Some older adults are as unaccepting of death as are younger adults and believe that they still have a long life to live even at age 70 or 80 (Howarth, 1998). It may be that the attitudes of older adults toward death are the attitudes of their cohort and that, rather than attitude changing with age, different cohorts have different attitudes (Kastenbaum, 1999). Middle-age and older adults are more likely than younger adults to think about the process of dying rather than death itself (deVries, Bluck, & Birren, 1993; Kastenbaum, 1992). People of all ages typically express a desire to go quickly, without pain, and while asleep. This type of dying, unfortunately, is not very frequent. Attitudes toward dying may, however, influence the time of actual death.

Some work suggests that the ways in which people cope with death and dying influence how long they remain living. People who remain active socially, who are more forceful and determined to keep going, who are not depressed, and who avoid guilt and self-criticism tend to live longer (Viney & Westbrook, 1986–1987; Weisman & Worden, 1975). Other work, however, has failed to find such an effect (Schulz & Schlarb, 1987–1988).

Some research suggests that people can prolong their life beyond a certain point in time, usually an important date. A person may, for example, live long enough to celebrate one more birthday or Christmas (Phillips, 1992). An examination of deaths for Jews and non-Jews showed that deaths dipped below normal level right before Passover but rose sharply after the holiday. There were no such changes in the death rates for non-Jews (Phillips & King, 1988). A comparison of Chinese and non-Chinese showed the same pattern around the Harvest Moon Festival. Chinese deaths dropped by 35.1 percent before the holiday and then rose again, by the same amount, after the holiday; no changes were observed in death rate for non-Chinese participants (Phillips & Smith, 1990). The finding that deaths decrease before some important date but then increase right after strongly supports the notion that individuals are able to deliberately postpone their death for some period of time. How long this period of postponement might be extended is not yet known. Of course, if one can postpone one's death, one might also be able to hasten it. Some work indicates that people who believe that they are about to die do die quicker than comparable people without such a belief (Phillips, Ruth, & Wagner, 1993). How quickly death might be hastened by such beliefs is not known at present.

How might this happen? It seems likely that a fatalistic belief might lead to risk-taking behavior that would then account for the quicker death. In one study, risky behaviors, such as not following treatment programs, abusing medication, and improper eating or drinking were observed in older patients who were chronically ill and who believed that they would die soon. They died before a comparison group that did not have such beliefs and did not engage in risky behavior (Reynolds & Nelson, 1981). The effects of attitudes seem to be through overt behaviors.

Finally, the very same event might produce different effects in different groups. Men are more likely to die right before their birthday while women are more likely to die right after their birthday (Phillips, 1992). Does this mean that women regard birthdays as positive and happy occasions while men regard them as dreadful?

Eventually, of course, we all die. Dying is a part of living. In some ways, dying might be regarded as a great adventure since we cannot be certain what lies on the other side of death, if indeed anything lies there, until we ourselves go.

Bereavement

Bereavement refers to survival. The bereaved are those who have survived the death of another. Bereaved individuals are expected to go through the rites of mourning and to experience and show grief. Rites of mourning have been found by anthropologists in every culture they have examined (Leming & Dickinson, 1990).

Mourning

Mourning refers to the socially accepted ways for the bereaved to express grief and to acknowledge that a life has ended. There are enormous cultural differences in mourning and in ways of behaving following the death of another. In some cultures, the dead are immediately removed for burial and not spoken of again. In others, mourning is open and continues for an extended period of time; people may wear black or just black armbands for up to a year after the death. Some of the better known customs for religious groups in this country are briefly described below (Irish, Lundquist, & Nelsen, 1993; Sweet, 1994).

Buddhist funerals burn candles and incense near the body until the body is taken for burial. Prior to the funeral, one night of viewing for family and friends is permitted. Family members wear white while others wear black. Family but not visitors participate in the actual ceremony and may visit the body individually. At the funeral service all bow together at the end before the body is taken for burial.

Christian funerals may involve a service at the funeral home, a chapel near the funeral home, at the church, or at the cemetery and usually occur within three days of the death. Caskets are typically open and the body is available at a funeral home for viewing for a couple of days and evenings. Family members wear black and are usually very solemn. Only family and very close friends are expected to attend the burial service at the cemetery. Cremation is acceptable. Flowers and other gifts are quite appropriate.

Hindu custom is to dispose of the body before sundown on the day that death occurred. The funeral service is conducted, if possible, by the firstborn son. Family members wear white to show respect while others wear dark clothing. Flowers are appropriate and family members may individually place flowers on the deceased. All bodies are cremated. Formal grieving takes place for at least 13 days following the funeral.

In Islam, the custom is also to bury the dead as quickly as possible. Services are at the mosque, where family and visitors remove their shoes and men and women sit separately. Members of the family dress in black. The Imam reads from the Koran and chants. Following the service, people file by the body and pay their last respects before the burial. Following this, a meal is served, usually at the mosque. Flowers are considered appropriate.

In Jewish culture, the mourning rites and funeral are conducted as soon as possible after the death. Mourners wear black or a piece of black cloth or ribbon attached to their clothing. Caskets are traditionally kept closed and cremation is frowned upon although not forbidden. At the burial, each person places some dirt on the casket. A meal is held following the burial and for a week of mourning, called shiva, the family will receive visitors. Mirrors are all covered during shiva. For 30 days, a period called sheloshim, the mourning continues but is diminished. Flowers are considered inappropriate.

Some form of funeral and removal of the body as soon as possible are typical for most individuals despite differences in religious beliefs or ethnic origin. In the United States it is typical for a viewing of the body to occur; in 70 to 80 percent of funerals the body is viewed (National Funeral Directors Association, 1997; Riekse & Holstege, 1996). Funerals, body viewing, and burials are expensive. The average cost of a funeral is estimated to be over $5000 in large part due to the average cost of a casket which is $2200. Burial and a burial plot may cost an additional $2500. Tombstones can be quite costly depending on size, type of stone used, and engravings. Table 13-4 shows the range of average prices for professional services, use of facilities, caskets, outer containers, and cremation service at a typical funeral home. Outer containers are required by some cemeteries in an attempt to keep the ground from subsiding over the casket but are not required by others (Baker & Reyes, 2000).

At the time of death, the family is often far too stressed, troubled, and busy to shop around for the best prices on funeral services. It is thought that many funeral homes take advantage of this situation and charge more than they might if the funeral industry were more competitive or more closely regulated. Funeral directors may try to embarrass or shame families into spending more than they should. "I know you want the very best for your mother," is a phrase heard all too often. Many of these abuses were first brought to light, decades ago, by Jessica Mitford (1963). Funeral home directors argue that abuse does occur but very infrequently. Today Lisa Carlson and the Funeral and Memorial Societies Association work to protect consumers from such abuse (Baker, 1999). In 1994, the Federal Trade Commission adopted standards for funeral practices and ruled that bereaved family members in charge of the funeral must receive written and itemized accounts of all expenses, must not be sold unneeded products or services, and must not be billed for services never rendered (Federal Trade Commission, 1994). In a survey conducted by the American Association of Retired Persons, only 8 percent of the general public knew of these rules (Baker & Reyes, 2000). Over the last decade, four large corporations have begun purchasing individual and family owned funeral homes across the country (Mulder, 1997). At present it is not clear what effect if any this will have on funeral costs.

More families and individuals have begun making funeral arrangements ahead of time (see Project 13 on p. 388). Burial plots frequently are purchased long before death is imminent. Much or all of the expenses can be paid at these prior-to-need times (American Association of Retired Persons, 1992). Although arrangements made ahead of time avoid the rush and stress of making arrangements at the time of death, it appears that they often cost just as much. Carlson says that a common ploy is to tell survivors that the preselected casket is no longer available, then switch to a more expensive substitute (Baker, 1999, p. 18). Cremation is being used more often than in the not-so-distant past. Cremation, on average, costs about 13 percent as much as a more traditional funeral and burial. Many funeral homes will attempt to convince families who select cremation that embalming should still

TABLE 13-4   **Estimated Funeral Costs**

Professional services

Minimum (facilities and staff, coordination with cemetery, securing of documents, sheltering remains, and overhead)	$850
Additional services (direction of funeral service, attendants for visitation periods, arrangement of floral and other tributes, attendants for graveside service)	347
Embalming (required by law if body is to be viewed)	335
Other preparation of body for viewing (dressing, cosmetology, hair)	175
Use of facilities for viewing (charge per day)	196
Use of funeral coach to cemetery	111
Acknowledgement cards	33
Memorial folders (100)	53

Casket

48-ounce solid bronze	$10,778
32-ounce solid bronze	4783
48-ounce solid copper	5340
32-ounce solid copper	4160
16-gauge metal	3604
19-gauge metal	2404
Wooden	1765
20-gauge metal	890

Outer container

Copper	$9828
Concrete (with seamless liner, nameplate, and handcrafted design cover)	2875
Concrete (with seamless liner and nameplate)	1127
Wood	196

Cremation

Adult and container provided by purchaser	$1200
Disposal of cremated remains	33
Bronze urn	983
Marble urn	315
Vault for urn	315

Prices are based on averages from a number of different funeral homes in Feb., 2000. Many additional caskets, outer containers, and urns are available; those selected include the most and least expensive.

be done and a casket should be purchased for the journey to the crematory (Baker & Reyes, 2000). There is no need for embalming unless there is a viewing and purchasing a casket for a trip to the crematory is absurd. In Japan, over 90 percent of individuals choose to be cremated (Aiken, 1991). You can now purchase caskets, urns, vaults, and other items over the Internet. They are shipped immediately and you can save costs.

PROJECT **13**

Plan Your Own Funeral

For this project, we want you to think carefully and seriously about the events that might follow your own death if it were to occur soon. We know that this is not a happy thought but this project can often help people develop important insights into their own desires and preparation for what will one day happen. Try to answer each of the following questions:

- Do you have life insurance to help pay the costs?
- Who would you like us to notify first of your death? Why did you choose that person?
- Would you rather be buried or cremated or both (in some cases cremation urns are buried)? If you choose burial, do you have a particular spot or cemetery in mind? If you choose burial, do you want a tombstone? What would you like your tombstone to look like? What, besides your name and dates of birth and death, would you like to have inscribed on the stone? If you wish to be cremated but do not wish to be buried, where and how would you like your ashes to be placed? Why have you chosen as you have?
- Would you like a funeral? If not, why not? If so, who should attend? Will the funeral be in the funeral home, a church, a home, outside, or somewhere else? Will there be a religious service? Why or why not? Will there be music? What songs would you most like to have played at your funeral? Why? Will attendees be expected to do anything special (e.g., say a word or two about you; what do you think they would say)? Should people send flowers or give donations to some organization(s)? Which one(s)? Should attendees accompany you to your burial if that is what you have chosen? Why or why not? Should they bring a flower, toss some dirt into the grave, or perform some other action?
- Do you expect the answers you have given now to be different for you when you have grown old?

You should put this plan away somewhere safe and let someone close to you know where it is. This could save some anguish and concern on the part of your loved ones. They can rest assured that your needs are met and that they have done the right thing for you.

Mourning rites are the socially accepted and expected ways in which the bereaved behave. For the bereaved, those rites are only the public display of their grief and although mourning is thought to help relieve some of that grief, grief is a very powerful emotion.

Grief

Grief refers to the emotions experienced and the ways in which one copes with loss. The loss of a close loved one is considered the most stressful event that humans have to face and responses to that loss are extremely variable. Nevertheless, researchers have attempted to discern themes and patterns of grieving that might be common to most bereaved persons.

Bowlby (1980) and others (Parkes, 1972; 1998) have proposed four phases and patterns of grieving. *Numbing* is the first. Persons in this phase are unable to fully comprehend that the death has occurred. They do not believe it can be happening. The grieving person might carry on the normal daily activities of eating and sleeping but seem to do so automatically, without conscious awareness. They may appear to be like a robot. This first phase is usually short, lasting only a couple of days and rarely lasting longer than a month.

The second phase is one of *yearning and searching* for the departed loved one and usually is most intense toward the end of the first month following the death. This phase may last as long as a year or even two. Denial is common. Hallucinations may occur or the person may think the deceased is still alive somewhere and can be found if only great effort is made. The bereaved might think that they see or hear the deceased, particulary when alone at home. The desire to find and be with the lost loved one may even lead the bereaved to consider suicide as a way to be together. Any talk of suicide or of joining the deceased should be taken very seriously. Anxiety often appears in this phase as the person strives to be with the lost loved one but is frustrated repeatedly. Anxiety may grow out of the need to perform tasks that were once the domain of the departed loved one. Survivors may have difficulty in learning how to manage household finances or chores.

The third phase is one of *disorganization and despair*. The individual may lose their appetite and their ability to concentrate on any task or conversation. The loss is now accepted as being real. Depression is very common in this phase and the individual may withdraw from others and fail to take care of themselves. The survivor may become irritable. Anxiety and guilt are fairly common (Stephenson, 1985; Zisook, Schneider, & Schucter, 1990). The events that led up to the death may be continually thought about as if the person is searching for a clue as to what went wrong and why death had to occur. One may want to relive the last moments, hours, or days in order to do or say the right things. Feelings of anger at the deceased for leaving or guilt for failing to have done more to save the lost loved one frequently occur. The deceased may now be seen through rose-colored glasses as having been near perfect, a saint. As time passes the intensity of these emotions decreases with peaks occurring on important dates such as a birthday or anniversary.

Reorganization is the final phase and also can be very emotional as the bereaved individual attempts to construct a new life. Appetite is usually one of the first things to return to normal (Rosenbloom & Whittington, 1993). The bereaved may begin to care again about appearance and seek social contacts. Social activities become a major part of life again. Sometime in the second year of grieving, most individuals notice that they are finally recovering. Some survivors take on some of the mannerisms and habits of the deceased and make them a part of their new self (Stephenson, 1985). This last phase may start toward the end of the first year or as late as three to four years after the death.

Although these four phases are reasonably good descriptions of the grief experienced by many survivors, other descriptions also have been proposed. Worden (1982) has proposed four tasks involved in recovering from grief; accepting the reality of the death, feeling the pain, adjusting to the new life, and emotional reinvestment. Some may complete the tasks sooner than others but grieving is not complete until the tasks are completed. Kübler-Ross' stages of dying also have been proposed as stages of grieving (Cook & Oltjenbruns, 1998). As was pointed out previously, individuals may experience the emotional states of denial, anger, bargaining, depression, and acceptance but not as stages. It should be kept in mind that none of these models are literally true and that different people grieve in different ways. Some may experience all of the emotions and difficulties described above while others feel very different emotions and have very different difficulties. Some may seem to go back and forth between one phase and another while others show no signs of going through any of these phases (Bugen, 1979). There is no one correct and healthy way to grieve; there are many. As each person is unique, so is their way of grieving.

The emotions experienced during grief have received a fair amount of attention from researchers interested in how long such emotions last and how often they are experienced. Guilt over not having done enough to save the lost loved one, blaming oneself for not working hard enough, being guilty for not being present when needed, or failing to show enough love was once thought to be a very common emotion for the bereaved (Parkes, 1972). Research, however, indicates that guilt occurs in only about 25 percent of survivors and when experienced it is usually quite mild (Breckenridge, Gallagher, Thompson, & Peterson, 1986).

Anxiety (see Chapter 11), unlike guilt, seems to occur with some frequency among survivors although estimated frequencies seems to depend upon the measures used and type of anxiety under consideration. Phobic symptoms occur in less than 10 percent while feeling tense, nervous, and unable to get things done occur in more than 25 percent (Zisook, Schneider, & Shuchter, 1990). Anxiety measured as longing may occur in close to 75 percent (Zisook, Shuchter, & Lyons, 1987).

Depression (see Chapter 11) is very common among bereaved individuals (Breckenridge, Gallagher, Thompson, & Peterson, 1986) and actually may increase during the first year and be maintained well into the second year of grieving (Kastenbaum, 1999). Depression is most likely to begin when periods of denial end and the loss is fully recognized (Clayton, Halikes, & Maurice, 1971). Some say that the depression never really ends although it subsides enough to permit normal functioning (Lund, 1993).

There also is evidence of positive emotions and change associated with grieving. In some individuals a profound spiritual change "construing a new understanding of the meaning of human existence and revising assumptions about one's place in the universe" may take place (Balk, 1999). Confidence and even a certain amount of pride at having survived such a painful loss are often found in those who have gone through a period of grieving (Schulz, 1978). Bereavement may often be a time of growth as survivors learn to take on new challenges. Survivors may report feeling stronger, more independent, and more capable of facing new crises should they come (Calhoun & Tedeschi, 1989–1990). Those who grieve the most may, in some instances, experience the most growth in redefining their own goals and understanding their personal existence (Edmonds & Hooker, 1992).

Loss of a Spouse.   The largest group of bereaved individuals are widows. Several factors contribute to this. As you will remember from Chapter 4, women have a longer life expectancy than men and, on average, live 7 to 8 years longer. Woman also tend to marry men who are older than they are. Together these factors frequently result in situations in which a younger wife loses an older husband. The average age of widowhood for a White woman is 56, for an African American woman is 49, and for a Hispanic woman is 48. After age 65, almost half of women are widowed while only 14 percent of men are. Past age 85, 80 percent of women and 43 percent of men are widowed (U.S. Bureau of the Census, 1990). Widows also are likely to be widowed for much longer periods of time than are widowers because

Those in grief need support.

they live longer and are much less likely to remarry. Because this is such a large group of individuals, both widows and widowers have received considerable research attention.

With the loss of a spouse, particularly a spouse of a long time, many unwelcome changes occur. The survivor has lost *a*, perhaps *the*, major role in their life. They are no longer a husband or a wife. Couples who were close friends with the couple before the death may attempt to continue including the bereaved spouse in activities but the spouse may feel out of place with intact couples and may tend to stay away after the funeral. In any marriage, there are shared tasks and tasks that are primarily handled by one or the other spouse. After the loss of a marriage partner, the survivor is faced with no one to share tasks with and many tasks to take on that were the other person's domain. One may have to learn to pay the bills and organize finances, to cook, do the laundry and keep the house clean, tend to the automobile, and so on.

Widowhood changes the income for the surviving spouse. If both were working at the time of loss, up to 30 to 70 percent of total income might be lost. If only one worked and that one died, then all income might be lost. If only the survivor worked, then income can be lost paying strangers to take over the tasks that the loved one once performed. Even retirement benefits are often lost or greatly diminished when a spouse dies. Income is estimated to drop 44 percent on average following the death of a husband or wife (Healy, 1983) and, in most instances, a widow loses far more than a widower (Bound, Duncan, Laren, & Oleinick, 1991).

Sidney Zisook and his colleagues have been conducting a longitudinal investigation of grieving in 350 men and women living in San Diego who have lost a spouse. They examined anxiety, depression, changes in immune function, and increased use of medications, alcohol, and cigarettes. Anxiety is more frequent among younger than older survivors, more frequent among women than men, and more frequent when a loss of income accompanies the loss of spouse. Among widows, 85 percent lost major income following the death of a husband. Younger women who lost a spouse and, thus, a major source of income were the most likely to experience severe anxiety. Anxiety did not decline significantly during the first seven months of grief (Zisook, Mulvihill, & Shuchter, 1990; Zisook, Schneider, & Shuchter, 1990).

In terms of depression, Zisook and colleagues found 24 percent showed significant depression two months after the loss of a spouse. That incidence barely changed at seven months (23 percent) but dropped to 16 percent at 13 months. Even over two years after the death, 14 percent of bereaved widows and widowers still showed some symptoms of depression. Those most likely to experience depression were younger survivors, men and women, who had a past history of depression (Zisook & Shuchter, 1991, 1993; Zisook, Paulus, Shuchter, & Judd, 1997).

Other studies that have examined depression in bereaved men and women have obtained higher or lower estimates depending on the severity of the depression. In an examination of major clinical and minor depression (see Chapter 11) in 181 widows and widowers, major clinical depression was found in only 5 percent but minor depression was found in 66 percent up to 18 months after the loss (Faletti, Gibbs, Clark, Pruchno, & Berman, 1989). A ten year, longitudinal study of 2104 Swedish twins, ages 26 to 87, looked at depression, loneliness, and life satisfaction. Cross-sectional comparisons were made between twins where one was widowed and the other was still married, and longitudinal comparisons were made between an individual's depression, loneliness, and life satisfaction before and after the death of a spouse. Both comparisons showed increased depression and loneliness and lower life satisfaction for up to three years following the death. These effects were diminished in the oldest-old, those over age 80 (Lichtenstein, Gatz, Pedersen, Berg, & McClearn, 1996).

In other comparisons of men and women who have survived the loss of a spouse, researchers have found that both tend to show depression (Quigley & Schatz, 1999) but men seem to remain depressed for a longer period of time (Siegel & Kuykendall, 1990; Umberson, Wortman, & Kessler, 1992). Men seem to spend more time alone, and experience more boredom and less affection from others than women during the early years of bereavement but eventually those differences disappear (Nieboer, Lindenberg, & Ormel, 1998–1999). In one comparison of married men and women and bereaved men and women, all over 65, it was found that bereaved women were adjusting quite well and only a little more depressed than married women while bereaved men were far more depressed than married men because married men were the least depressed of all four groups. Married older men lose a major part of their relatively happy lives when they lose a wife (Lee, DeMaris, Bavin, & Sullivan, 2001). Most men and women do recover from depression and loneliness and recover some satisfaction with life, but it may take years.

Physical health also might decline after loss of a spouse. Bereaved individuals use more medication, call in sick more often, and have more doctor visits than comparable married persons. You already know that bereaved individuals lose their appetite and fail to eat very well for some time after the loss (Rosenbloom & Whittington, 1993). To see if widowhood or depression influenced functioning of the immune system, researchers compared 21 middle-age widows to 21 married women matched on age, length of marriage, physical and mental health, and no current or recent alcohol or drug abuse. All women were evaluated for 13 months. Impaired immune system functioning was found but only for the six widows who had major depression (Zisook, Shuchter, Irwin, Darko, Sledge, & Resovsky, 1994). Depression, resulting from widowhood, can lower the efficiency of the survivor's immune system possibly producing increased risk for serious illness. Finally, research has shown that alcohol and medication use and cigarette smoking are likely to increase for 6 to 13 months after the loss of a spouse before returning to prior levels of use (Zisook, Shuchter, & Mulvihill, 1990). Increased medication, alcohol, and cigarette use are very unhealthy. Changes in physical health are most likely to occur in middle-age bereaved adults (Wolinsky & Johnson, 1992).

Since health decreases for some period of time after the loss of a spouse, one might expect to find higher levels of **mortality** among the bereaved than among those still married and that is exactly what a number of studies have found. Bereaved individuals are more likely to die than comparable married persons of the same age. This greater liklihood of death lasts for close to 12 months and is greater for men than for women (Bowling, 1987; Rees & Lutkins, 1967; Rowland, 1977; Stroebe & Stroebe, 1993). Several explanations have been offered for this finding.

The homogamy hypothesis argues that healthy people tend to marry other healthy people while unhealthy people tend to marry other unhealthy people. When someone dies, it is more likely that they are unhealthy and their also unhealthy spouse also is more likely to die than other, still married, healthy people. It is the health of the couple that accounts for the finding. A *second* hypothesis claims that the important factor is the health of the living environment. Couples who live together in unhealthy environments are more likely to die, one soon after the other, than those who live in healthy environments. Neither of these hypotheses, however, are supported by the findings. Controlling for initial health and environmental risk does not change the findings (Schafer, Quesenberry, & Wi, 1995); bereaved individuals still have a higher death rate than comparable, still married individuals.

A *third* hypothesis claims that genetic factors are responsible. Those factors influence marriage in that people who are similar genetically tend to marry one another. Genetic factors also influence longevity. Thus, people with genetic factors influencing longevity, either for a long or short life, tend to marry one another and die close to one another. This hypothesis has been ruled out by a study of 1993 Swedish twins. Widowed and still married twins were compared to determine whether genetic factors influenced the death of bereaved individuals. They did not. Bereaved individuals showed a higher mortality rate than their still married twins for the first years after the death of a spouse. Mortality rates then returned to normal for men but for women, mortality rates actually decreased four years after the loss of a husband (Lichtenstein, Gatz, Pedersen, & Berg, 1998).

A *fourth* hypothesis addresses the gender differences in the mortality of bereaved individuals and claims that gender differences in social support are responsible for the obtained differences in increased mortality (see Chapter 9). Women are known to have more close social relationships with people other than their spouse while men rely more on their spouse for social support (Belle, 1987). This higher level of social support may help to protect women from some of the unhealthy aspects of losing their husband and, thus, contribute to better health and the difference in mortality rates (Morgan, 1984). This hypothesis also is not supported by the findings. In a comparison of 30 widows and 30 widowers with 60 married men and women of the same age, length of marriage, and SES, the expected differences in depression and loneliness (men more depressed and lonely) and social support (women more supported) were obtained. Findings showed that those with higher levels of social support, both men and women, experienced lower levels of depression and loneliness. When, however, the effects of social support were controlled for, the gender differences in depression and loneliness remained (Stroebe, Stroebe, & Abakoumkin, 1999).

What factors might then account for the higher mortality rate in survivors, especially widowers? Several have been suggested (Stroebe, 1998). As we have already noted, the bereaved eat less well and tend not to take care of themselves for a period of time. Without support from a spouse, the bereaved may neglect certain important tasks besides eating, such as taking necessary medication, keeping doctor's appointments, dressing warmly in winter, wearing a hat in the hot summer sun, and so on. It is assumed that men are more likely to neglect such tasks without a wife to remind them. Use of some medications, alcohol, and cigarettes tend to increase for a period of time after the death of a spouse. Death from accidents and cirrhosis of the liver are especially high among bereaved men (Rogers, 1995) and one can easily imagine how these might relate to increased alcohol use. Bereaved indivuals are frequently depressed and those who are severely depressed are more likely to attempt suicide. Older men have the highest suicide rate and men who have recently lost a wife are at very high risk for suicide (Li, 1995). Depression produces decreased immune system functioning. Depressed men and women may, thus, be more susceptible to bacterial, fungal, and viral infections for that period of time. Since men generally experience the depression of loss for a longer period of time than women (Siegel & Kuykendall, 1990; Umberson, Wortman, & Kessler, 1992) they are more susceptible to such risks for a longer period of time. Finally, the stress of caring for a dying person before the death actually occurs may be partly responsible for decreased health and the higher mortality rate found soon after death (Norris & Murrell, 1987).

All of these suggested factors relate to the desolation experienced by many bereaved who, for a period of time, just give up. These bereaved, especially those who do not survive, give up caring for themselves, become severely depressed, may increase their bad habits, may be careless, and are, to a great extent, lost without the departed loved one. These are, however, the extreme cases.

Most survivors regain control of their lives and many do so fairly quickly. Within two years of the death, 82 percent are getting along with considerable success (Lund, Caserta, & Dimond, 1993). In some studies, significant differences between bereaved individuals and married persons have all but disappeared within a year or two (Thompson, Gallagher-Thompson, Futterman, Gilewski, & Peterson, 1991; Stroebe & Stroebe, 1993). The coping skills of older adults have had many decades and opportunities to develop and seem to serve most older adults well in times of major stress (McCrae & Costa, 1993).

One final factor influencing recovery from grief for a lost spouse is **remarriage**. Bereaved individuals who remarry show an increase in life satisfaction and a reduction in stress levels (Burks, Lund, Gregg, & Bluhm, 1988). Men are more likely than women to remarry, in part because there are so many more older women than older men (see Chapter 4 & 9). Among bereaved individuals, widows outnumber widowers by five to one and among those over age 85, the ratio is fifteen to one (Zick & Smith, 1988). Men are thought to be more interested in remarrying than are women because men may rely more on a spouse for social support (Belle, 1987; Parkes & Weiss, 1983). Men who have lost a spouse have higher rates of physical and psychological disorders (Fitzpatrick, 1998) while those who remarry experience better health and live longer than those who do not (Helsing, Szklo, & Comstock, 1981).

Other work has found that some of the best predictors of who will remarry are different for men and women. In a longitudinal study of 249 widows and 101 widowers, researchers found that 25 months after the loss of a spouse, 61 percent of the men and 19 percent of the women were remarried or seriously involved in a new relationship likely to lead to marriage. Women who were younger than 65 were more likely to remarry than those over 65. For men, those with higher income and education were more likely to remarry (Schneider, Sledge, Shuchter, & Zisook, 1996).

Most widows and widowers recover from the devastation of loss and build new lives for themselves. Remarriage is only one way of coping. Support of family and friends is very important in helping this recovery.

Loss of a Child or Grandchild.   The loss of a child, particularly a young child, can be devastating for parents and some never recover (Rando, 1991). The loss of an adult child also is very intense (DeSpelder & Strickland, 1992) and some evidence suggests it may be more intense than the loss of a spouse (Moss & Moss, 1995). Husbands and wives may offer the necessary support for each other but many marriages simply fall apart from such loss (Brandt, 1989). The feelings of anxiety, guilt, and depression discussed earlier can be very intense. The likelihood of guilt and self-blame occurs most often when the death is accidental, and accidents are the leading cause of death in children and young adolescents (ages 1 to 14). Almost 12 percent of deaths in children and young adolecents are due to accidents and half of those involve motor vehicles (National Center for Health Statistics, 1997). In a comparison of 44 bereaved spouses, 40 adult children who lost a parent, and 36 parents who lost a child younger than 18, several measures of images/thoughts, acute separation, and grief were taken at one month, ten weeks, seven months, and thirteen months after the death. The most severe reactions were for parents who lost a child. Those who lost a spouse showed more grief than adult children who lost a parent (Middleton, Raphael, Burnett, & Martinek, 1998). A part of this difference may be due to the fact that the death of a child, especially one under 18, is usually unexpected.

Some researchers have examined the reactions of grandparents when their grandchild dies. The strongest reactions seem to be a blunting of emotion and feelings of guilt. Grandparents feel numb, confused, restless, and struggle with the belief that it was their time, not their grandchild's time, to die. Grandparents report a strong need to remain in contact with their own child, the parent of the lost grandchild (Fry, 1997). In comparisons of the reactions of parents and grandparents to the death of a child (grandchild), researchers have found depression among both but among grandparents feelings of grief for their own children were particularly strong (Ponzetti, 1992; Ponzetti & Johnson, 1991).

The most likely persons to lose a child are the oldest-old since their children also are old. In such cases, one can easily envision the heartbreak that comes when one's child, particularly in the absence of any grandchildren, dies. One may then feel truly alone with no link to the future. There may be nothing left to live for particularly if the spouse also is gone. Unfortunately, this group has not yet received much research attention.

The loss of a child is more intense in some cultures and less intense in others. In many parts of the world, the death of an older person is viewed as a greater loss. A mature person has goals that finally may be within reach and has entered into many relationships with other people. All of that will be lost with the death of a mature person (Jecker & Schneiderman, 1994; Kilner, 1990).

> In Africa, people are sadder about the death of an old man than about that of a newborn baby. The old man represented a wealth of experience that might have benefitted the tribe, whereas the newborn baby had not lived and could not even be aware of dying. In Europe, people are sad about the newborn baby because they think he might well have done wonderful things if he had lived. On the other hand, they pay little attention to the death of the old man, who had already lived his life anyway. (Werber, 1998, p. 227)

In our culture, however, the death of the young is seen as more severe and unfair than the death of an older person. The young are viewed as having great potential and being the future whereas older people already have lived a full life (Jecker & Schneiderman, 1994). They may have no more potential. Parents may see their own children as a way of attaining immortality. After the parents are gone, their children and children's children will live on. Loss of an older parent is sad but is only the loss of a part of the past (Yalom, 1989).

The loss of an older adult is an expected loss while the loss of a child, particularly a young child, is unexpected. Infant mortality is the lowest it has ever been and children who live to celebrate a first birthday are more likely to live to old age than they have ever been (U.S. Department of Health and Human Services, 1995). The death of a child, even an adult child, is out of the ordinary and not in the correct order. Those who are born earlier should be those who die earlier; it is only fair (Raphael, 1983).

Loss of a Parent.   Most people lose their parents before they themselves retire. Half have lost both parents by the time they are in their 50s and 75 percent have lost both parents before age 65 (Winsborough, Bumpass, & Aquilino, 1991). Although the loss of a parent is not usually as severe as the loss of a child or spouse, it still presents many difficulties that are unique. *First*, loss of a parent is usually the loss of the oldest relationship in an individual's life. Your parents have been a part of your life since your birth. *Second*, loss of a parent may be seen as a signal that your turn is next. Parents may represent the cohort just before yours and their loss means that death is on its way. *Third*, loss of parents means loss of a household and perhaps the very house where you grew up and were raised (Dainoff, 1989). Such losses may be felt for quite some time.

Surveys of adult children who have lost a parent show that 25 percent report continuing social and/or emotional problems one to five years after the death. Physical disorders, such as frequent fatigue, aches and pains, and illness, are common in half of the survivors (Scharlach & Fredriksen, 1993). A comparison of 68 older men with major depression to 40 older men with no history of depression found that the fathers of the depressed men had died at a much younger age than the fathers of the nondepressed men. Thus, the age of the survivor when the the parent is lost is an important factor (Furukawa, Takeuchi, Hirai, Fujihara, Kitamura, & Takahashi, 1998). Loss of a parent when the bereaved is still a child is thought to influence that person well into their own old age (Krause, 1993).

Other losses, such as loss of a sibling or close friend, have not yet received much attention from researchers. It is clear to us that the loss of such close relationships would have a lasting impact. All losses result in a period of grief for the bereaved and as we said earlier, the expression of grief is different in different cultural settings. Box 13-2 (p. 398) illustrates a few more diverse ways of expressing grief. Clearly the extent and nature of the grief depends on the bereaved person, their coping skills, and type of loss. The type of death also plays an important role.

Unexpected Death. One might think that a sudden, unexpected death would result in more severe grief reactions than a slower, expected death. In the case of an expected death, one has time to prepare for the loss and to say goodbye to the dying person. One might understand the cause of death. In the case of an unexpected death there is no time to prepare or say goodbye. The death may not make sense to the survivors (Epstein, 1993). Generally, these predictions are supported. Survivors of relatives lost to sudden death report far more anger, guilt, and physical disorders than survivors of those lost to long- or short-term (less than six months) chronic illness (Sanders, 1982–1983). In one major study, 224 survivors who had not expected a relative or close friend to die were compared to 173 who expected the death of a relative or close friend. Unexpected deaths were defined as death from murder, suicide, car accident, stroke, heart attack, drowning, fire, aneurysm, or plane crash. Expected deaths were defined as death from cancer, AIDS, diabetes, or other chronic disorders. Again, individuals in the unexpected death group had more bereavement difficulties than those in the expected death group. This was especially true for individuals who lost a person to murder, suicide, or accident. Age also played a role in the findings as more younger survivors lost a loved one unexpectedly while more older survivors had expected to lose a loved one. Age did not, however, interact with the effects of type of death. Unexpected death was more severe for both older and younger survivors (Hayslip, Ragow-O'Brien, & Guarnaccia, 1998–1999).

One aspect of unexpected death that might, in part, account for increased feelings of anger or guilt is that such deaths are often viewed as having been preventable. One might think "If only I had not let Sarah drive after knowing she had been drinking"; or "If only I had paid more attention to the signals that Jeff sent about his intended suicide"; or "If only I had warned Tameka and Simon not to take the short cut through that part of town." When bereaved individuals rate the preventability of a loss, those who rate the death as preventable show much higher levels of irritability, sleep problems, crying, missing the person, and anger and guilt (Guarnaccia, Hayslip, & Landry, 1999).

When the death is from suicide, feelings of guilt and anger and the belief that the death was preventable are typically very strong. Survivors may become obsessed with thoughts about how they could or should have prevented the tragedy. In such a situation, where help is often needed the most, help is frequently absent. The comforting support of

BOX **13-2**

Bereavement and Mourning in a Sample of Diverse Cultures

The culture in which one lives or has been raised helps define what is appropriate at the time of death and for the period of bereavement. There is tremendous variety in the rituals of mourning and the expression of grief (Rosenblatt, 1993). In the text we have briefly described some of the mourning rituals for Buddhist, Christian, Hindu, Islam, and Jewish cultures in the United States. Here are a few more:

Some cultures view death as the real beginning of one's life and a time of joy as well as sorrow. Japanese Buddhists give a new name to the deceased as a way of marking this new beginning (Morgan, 1986). In parts of Japan, many homes maintain an altar to honor and remember the lost relative. Food and candles may be placed there on a regular schedule (Mandelbaum, 1959).

In Micronesia, the Kapingamarangi begin the funeral ritual with a high-pitched wailing performed by the women. As people hear the wailing, they are drawn to the site of the ceremony. When all those who are mourning have assembled they are only then permitted to weep for the first time. Weeping must be soft and intermittent. Later at night a low chanting is performed (Lieber, 1991).

The Hmong of southern Asia sacrifice animals, including oxen, to feed the family and the departed between the time of death and burial. The night before the day of burial, a survivor will sing all night. All burials are conducted in the afternoon and for the next three days, food is taken to an agreed upon spot for the deceased spirit while it is being oriented to the afterlife. For an additional ten days, an extra place is set at the family table in case the spirit is still present and needs nourishment (Bliatout, 1993).

In India, Hindu cremations often take place on the banks of the Ganges river which is regarded as the holy river. Cloth-wrapped bodies are brought there and burned by family members. As they burn, they are slowly moved down marble or concrete slabs until the ashes can be swept into the river (Jaffrey, 1995).

In South Africa, people in the Xhosa culture believe that the deceased watch over the living. A head of household who has died is buried on his or her own land and facing the family home so that the deceased person can keep an eye on the living. The dead may protect the family or even send some misfortune if he or she becomes annoyed. The living believe that the dead are always present (Gijana, Louw, & Manganyi, 1989).

The Athabasken people in Alaska believe that the whole community must support the bereaved and to accomplish this, they hold a three-day ritual called a "potlatch." The ritual includes dancing, singing, story telling, feasting, and the giving of gifts to the bereaved family members (Simeone, 1991).

Among Native Americans, the Hopi culture views any contact with death to be tainted and dangerous for the living. One must break all ties with the deceased as soon as possible and get on with life. Grieving is strongly discouraged. The dead are to be forgotten (Mandelbaum, 1959). The Lakota, on the other hand, encourage the open and full expression of grief. Men will sing songs filled with emotion and women will loudly wail and sob (Brokenleg & Middleton, 1993).

others is often diminished when a suicide has occurred because families may restrict funeral services and withdraw from all but the very closest friends. Suicide carries a social stigma and neither survivors nor friends may want to talk about it. Friends and family members themselves may avoid contact with the immediate survivors of a suicide because such contact is unpleasant and people may not know what is appropriate to say and do. Friends may even blame the immediate family for failing to prevent the death. As a result, survivors may be abondoned (Hauser, 1987; Stillion, 1996). Survivors also may doubt their own self-worth feeling that they were not important enough for the deceased to go on living to spend more time with them. In one study, persons who lost a spouse to suicide were compared with those who lost a spouse to a more natural death and to those who were still married. While survivors of the natural death showed great grief, they also showed some recovery at 6 and 18 months. Survivors of a suicide, still showed intense grief at 12 months with no sign of any recovery until 18 months after the death. Only 2.5 years after the death, the grief reactions of those who survived a suicide were essentially the same as those who survived a natural death (Farberow, Gallagher-Thompson, Gilewski, & Thompson, 1992). Survivors of a suicide experience greater levels of depression, anger, anxiety, guilt, and the other emotions of grief for a longer period of time and with less social support. As one father said of his daughter who committed suicide: "Suicide is not a solitary act. A beloved person thinks that she is killing herself, but she also kills a part of us" (Bolton, 1986, p. 202).

One aspect of expected death that might, in part, account for lower levels of grief in some individuals and which has received a fair amount of attention is **anticipatory grief**. Anticipatory grief refers to grieving that begins while the dying person is still alive. The concept originally was proposed by Lindemann (1944). Since the grieving began early, it is assumed that much of it will be over by the time death actually occurs and those bereaved persons will have a shorter time of and perhaps less intense grieving when measured from actual time of death. Some work has found that the anticipatory grief that occurs while the loved one is still alive can be as intense as the grief that comes after the death (Wheeler, 1996). If anticipatory grief does lessen the grief occuring after the death, then that could play a major role in the finding that survivors of an expected death show less grief than survivors of an unexpected death since they will have already spent some of their grieving in anticipation of the death (Lundin, 1984).

The research findings are not, however, very supportive of this hypothesis. Some work shows that widows do benefit from the opportunity to prepare funeral arrangements and to deal with insurance and pensions with their spouses before they die but that after the death, they are as filled with grief as others without such opportunity to prepare (O'Bryant, 1990–1991). Other work has found no less grief and no better adjustment to the loss for those who experienced anticipatory grief before the death (Hill, Thompson, & Gallagher, 1988; Stephenson, 1985). It has been suggested that a reason for this may be that anticipatory grief is an entirely different kind of grieving from that which follows death and, therefore, cannot lessen the grief that follows death (Duke, 1998).

One recent study, however, suggests that in certain cases the expected death can have less of an impact when the surviving spouse has acted as a caregiver. In this study 40 bereaved individuals who had not acted as caregivers were compared to 89 who had acted as caregivers. The caregivers were placed in one of two groups depending on how much physical, mental, and emotional strain their caregiving produced in them. Results showed that caregivers who were very strained by the tasks of caregiving before their spouse died did not show as much of an increase in depression as noncaregivers or caregivers with little strain. They also did not increase health risk behaviors such as failing to take medication, not getting enough rest, or missing appointments with physicians as the other two groups did following the death. The loss of their spouse may have lessened their burden (Schulz, Beach, Lind, Martire, Zdaniuk, Hirsch, Jackson, & Burton, 2001). It may not be anticipatory grief that lessens grieving but grieving may be lessened when the physical, mental, and emotional strain that was borne before the death was very great on the caregiver. Such bereaved caregivers may know that they have done everything they could for the person and, thus, feel no guilt following the death.

Support for the Bereaved

What can be done to support the bereaved? What kinds of support are most welcome and what kinds are not? Clearly the answers to these questions depend to some extent upon the bereaved person, type of loss, and type of death. What helps one individual may not help another. It is estimated that close to 25 percent of the bereaved could, however, benefit from professional intervention. In a study of 350 newly bereaved widows and widowers, researchers found that 10 percent were experiencing the symptoms of posttraumatic stress disorder (PTSD) two months after the death and that 7 percent were still experiencing PTSD 25 months after the death. A diagnosis of PTSD is reflected in the individual spending a lot of time thinking about the loss, feeling that the lost person is with them at times, being numb, feeling lonely even when others are around, having no interest in anything, finding visits to the cemetery or looking at pictures to be too painful, having trouble falling asleep, having trouble concentrating, and feeling tense. The incidence of PTSD is highest (36 percent) in those who lose a loved one to an accident or suicide (Zisook, Chentsova-Dutton, & Shuchter, 1998).

Besides a diagnosis of PTSD, other behaviors on the part of the bereaved may predict a future need for counseling. Individuals who show the most conspicuous reactions are thought to be at very high risk for mental breakdown (Zisook & Shuchter, 1990). In addition to early and very strong emotional reactions, some individuals experience excessive confusion and lowered self-esteem. Those who avoid help and activity, who avoid keeping busy, and who show excessive crying may need counseling (Lund, Caserta, Connelly, Dimond, Johnson, & Poulton, 1985). Poor recovery has been associated with marriages in which conflict and ambivalent feelings were present before the death (Parkes & Weiss, 1983). It is important to keep in mind, however, that grief is an individual experience and that even when these behaviors are present, it may or may not signal a need for professional intervention. Most bereaved individuals do not need professional help and are able to cope quite well with their loss (O'Bryant & Hansson, 1995).

Intervention, professional or not, may, of course, take many forms including support from friends and family, to conventional therapeutic techniques, to drug therapy. Some work, however, suggests that antidepressant medications that reduce the symptoms of depression do not seem to reduce the intensity of grief (Prigerson, Frank, Kasl, & Reynolds, 1995). In addition to the more conventional techniques, some interventions are thought to be particularly useful for bereaved individuals. They are bibliotherapy, writing, self-help groups, and continued support from family and friends.

Bibliotherapy, which refers to the use of literature in therapy, has frequently been used with children and is beginning to be used with older adults (Brett, 1992; Cook & Olt-jenbruns, 1998). It is thought that reading about others who have had similar experiences may help the bereaved develop insight into their own situation and develop effective coping strategies. For family and friends, reading may help them understand and emphathize with some of the grief being experienced by the bereaved (Klingman, 1985).

For some, **writing** may serve as an effective way to cope with the grief of losing a loved one. The expression of grief by writing about it, even if only for oneself, can help the individual develop insights into their own reactions. By rereading writings done closer to the actual death and comparing them to current writings, one may see the signs of recovery.

Bibliotherapy.

Writings shared with others may help to open the lines of communication to aid the healing process (Lattanzi & Hale, 1984).

Self-help groups are typically composed of people who share some common experience, such as the loss of a spouse, and generally meet regularly to assist each other in coping with that experience (Lieberman, 1993). Many churches and communities offer such groups and the American Association of Retired Persons (AARP) has a program of peer support called the Widowed Persons Service (WPS). This program pairs widows or widowers with another person or persons of the same gender who also lost a spouse but not as recently. The person who has already survived the same loss is usually very empathetic and able to offer helpful tips on coping with the loss. This program grew out of Silverman's (1986) Widow-to-Widow program. Comparisons of survivors who participate in self-help groups with those who do not has shown that the bereaved in a self-help group seem to go through the same process of grieving but in a shorter period of time. Their return to normal functioning is quicker (Vachon, Sheldon, Lancee, Lyall, Rogers, & Freeman, 1980). Other work indicates that self-help groups are most helpful for those who have lower self-esteem, poorer mental health, and less life satisfaction. Those with higher self-esteem, better mental health, and more life satisfaction often become more depressed when in a self-help group (Caserta & Lund, 1993). Support groups on the Internet have more recently been used by many bereaved individuals. They are, of course, very convenient and one can use these chat support groups as frequently as one desires. No systematic research has yet been conducted to evaluate their effectiveness.

Finally, the continued **support of family and friends** can be most helpful for grieving survivors. Persons without such support are thought to suffer grief more intensely and for a longer period of time. In interviews conducted with 115 widows, six months after the loss of a spouse, the 20 percent who reported a need for help were those who also reported few friends and not being close with their children (Goldberg, Comstock, & Harlow, 1988). In a survey of 66 bereaved families, other family members were identified as being the most helpful during the crisis (Stinnet, Knorr, DeFrain, & Rowe, 1981). When bereaved individuals have been asked about the support of family members, the behaviors that were named as most helpful were others being available when needed; others expressing their concern by asking how the bereaved was doing, staying in touch by visiting, phoning, or writing; offering invitations to social gatherings; providing physical work, transportation, financial, or legal assistance; and giving care packages containing food and other needed items (Rigdon, Clayton, & Dimond, 1987). Unfortunately, for many of the bereaved these helping behaviors are discontinued soon after the funeral. It is important for families and friends to realize that grieving is not over so soon and social support is most helpful when it continues.

Bereavement, and grief are not often the topics of everyday conversation in spite of the widespread presence of loss. As you know, it is not just older adults who lose close loved ones. For college students, it is estimated that more than 25 percent are in the first year of grief following the loss of a family member and 30 percent following the loss of a friend, no matter when the measure is taken (Balk & Vesta, 1998). If you are among these bereaved or among friends or family of bereaved individuals we hope that the information we have provided in this chapter will be of some help to you in coping with your loss or helping others cope with theirs.

Making Choices

One choice you have is to legally declare your living will and/or durable power of attorney. If you feel strongly about the medical procedures that should or should not be used if you are no longer able to express your desires (perhaps because of a persistent vegetative state) then make those desires known. Granting decision making powers to another is a wise thing to do. Many people insist that there is plenty of time, we are still young, but none of us know how much time truly remains.

You can choose to set the arrangements for your own funeral, cremation, or burial before dying. Perhaps you already completed this chapter's project. This removes the stress of having to deal with such arrangments from your survivors and could even save some money.

CHAPTER HIGHLIGHTS

- This chapter examined death and bereavement. Today death is far more likely to occur for older adults whereas in the past children were the more likely to die. This is a result of our extended life-expectancy; the major causes of death today are different than they were 100 years ago and different for different aged adults. Younger adults are more likely to die of AIDS, older adults of Alzheimer's disease, and both young and old of heart disease and cancer.
- Advance directives, such as living wills, durable power of attorney, DNR, and DNH orders are legal in all states but are not yet used very frequently. Family members and physicians often resist such orders even when they are aware of them.
- Euthanasia takes several different forms and physician-assisted suicide is the most controversial.
- Hospice programs for the terminally ill serve family as well as patient and seem to be beneficial although the research which has been conducted has certain problems. People who choose hospice may be different in important ways (more accepting of death?) from those who they are compared with when hospice programs are evaluated.
- Positive (reuniting with love ones) and negative emotional states (anger, depression) are experienced during the dying process. Attitudes toward death and means of coping may actually influence the time of death by either delaying or hastening it. Specific behaviors on the part of the dying individual, such as failing to take medication, seem to underly this finding.
- There is much variety and many cultural differences in funeral/mourning rituals. Funeral, burial, and cremation costs are quite high. Federal law and consumer advocates urge caution when purchases are made in such a time of stress.
- The process of grieving is individual but some theorists have proposed stages. The emotions of anxiety and depression are very common and, in many cases, anger and guilt also occur. The effects on grief when the lost person is a spouse have been frequently studied. Such grief can last a very long time and be associated with decreased health and increased mortality for the surviving spouse during the first year. Several hypotheses for this finding have been offered but most were found wanting. Remarriage is one coping mechanism for the widowed. Loss of a child, loss of a grandchild, and loss of a parent are all difficult. The former, however, is often regarded as the worst loss possible in this country but not in other cultures. The influence of an unexpected death on the grief of survivors is far worse and accompanied by more anger and guilt than in cases of expected death. The perceived preventability of the death seems to be a factor in this finding but the anticipatory grief of the expected death does not. Those who have experienced much physical, mental, and emotional strain as caregivers for a now deceased spouse seem to experience less grief.
- At the end of the chapter we looked at the probability that a bereaved individual might experience PTSD and require professional intervention. Bibliotherapy, writing, and self-help groups have been

proposed as special means of dealing with grief. The continued support of family and friends is the most frequent support available for the bereaved.

STUDY QUESTIONS

1. Describe some of the differences in leading causes of death for different aged adults and the changes in leading causes over the last 100 years. What factors are responsible for the differences and changes?

2. Describe the types of advance directives and the difficulties that can occur when life and death decisions must be made.

3. Describe the arguments for and against the legalization of physician-assisted suicide. Where do you stand on this issue?

4. What is hospice? What benefits does one gain and what rights does one lose when enrolling in hospice?

5. There are risky behaviors that seem to hasten death for people who believe that death is un-avoidable and will happen soon. Describe some of those behaviors. People also seem able to postpone their death until after some major event. What behaviors might people engage in to help postpone death?

6. Describe the funeral rites practiced in seven different cultures.

7. What are the stages of grief proposed by Bowlby?

8. Describe the negative and postive emotions that are often a part of grieving.

9. What hypotheses have been proposed to account for the higher mortality rate for widowed men and women? Are any of these hypotheses supported by research findings?

10. What factors influence the likelihood of remarriage after the loss of a spouse?

11. When might the death of a mature person be considered a greater loss than the death of a child? Why is the death of a child considered the greater loss in our culture?

12. What factors make an unexpected death more difficult for survivors? What factor, expected to play a role, does not and why?

13. Discuss the likelihood of a bereaved individual requiring professional help to cope with their loss and the types of help, professional and otherwise, that might be available.

RECOMMENDED READINGS

Albom, M. (1997). *Tuesdays with Morrie: An old man, a young man, and life's greatest lesson.* New York: Doubleday. A young man meets on Tuesdays with his old college professor, Morrie, who is dying of amylotrophic lateral sclerosis (Lou Gehrig's disease). Morrie teaches many worthwhile lessons before dying.

Mannino, J. D. (1997). *Grieving days, healing days.* Boston: Allyn & Bacon. This workbook provides an abundance of exercises, activities, and insights for those who have lost or wish to help someone else who has lost a close loved one.

Phillips, K. (1996). *White rabbit*. Boston: Houghton Mifflin. An amusing last day on earth for Ruth Hubble is described.

INTERNET RESOURCES

http://www.funerals.org/famsa   Information about consumer's rights and affordable and meaningful funerals, from the Funeral and Memorial Societies Association.

http://www.aarp.org/confacts/money/funeral.html   AARP site.

http://www.ftc.gov   A brochure published by the federal government that is intended to protect consumers who are shopping for funerals. From the homepage, click on Consumer Protection, then on Seniors' Issues, and you will find the brochure under Funerals: A Consumer Guide.

http://www.nho.org/   The National Hospice Organization.

http://HemlockSociety.com or *http://NotDeadYet.com*   If you're interested in the issues surrounding euthanasia.

http://www.katsden.com/death/index.html   A number of different topics related to death and bereavement are presented at WEBster's Death, Dying, and Grief site.

http://rivendell.org   Grief Net, sponsored by Rivendell Resources is available for discussion of topics related to death and bereavement. They also provide discussion/chat groups for widowed persons, parents who have lost a child, adults and adolescents who have lost a sibling, and any individual who has lost a parent.

http://ethics.acusd.edu/euthanasia.html   The ethics of euthanasia in all forms (living will, physician-assisted suicide, and so on) is presented and discussed at this site that also provides links to many related sites.

Aging and You

14

Looking to the Future

Light tomorrow with today.

—Elizabeth Barrett Browning

As we come to the end of this text, the words of Elizabeth Barrett Browning seem clearer than ever. You now know what aging is like for most people; you know quite a lot about older people; you know how cultural, environmental, and genetic factors influence aging; and you know what choices you can make to improve your own chances of aging successfully.

In this chapter we examine the well-being of today's older adults and describe some of the variables that play an important role in their life satisfaction. Living for a long time is not the most important factor. One wants to live a quality life and be happy. Although we have examined quality of life for older adults in several other chapters, in this chapter we focus specifically on happiness. Are older adults happy? We then try to foresee how things might be when you reach old age. Of course, we do not know how old you are right now so you must give us some leeway in our projections. You know by now that we are fairly optimistic about most things having to do with human aging. We tend to see the future as being better than the present.

Age and Well-Being

After examining all the gains and losses that can occur with aging, you might wonder how well older adults cope with these changes and whether they are as satisfied with their lives as are younger adults. Do you feel satisfied with your life? Do older adults have positive emotional experiences and feel happy or do they have more negative emotional experiences and feel sad? Adults of all ages have both positive and negative emotional experiences; they feel happy sometimes and sad other times. Older adults are in many ways better equipped to cope with life's changes than are younger adults. They have had many more experiences, positive and negative, than those who are younger. In spite of such

Senior View

Since this chapter focuses on future aging we thought it might be appropriate to have you, our young readers, be the subjects of this last senior view. We would like you to sit back and relax and complete the following interview. Thank you, and please feel free to share your answers with us, we would love to hear from you!

Before you read the questions below, we would like you to think forward about 60 or 70 years into the future. Think about what life will be like, how society will look, where you will be, and finally what aging will be like for you.

Interview about Your Future

How will you look?

How healthy will you and your friends be?

What physical activities will you undertake?

What will be your overall physical condition?

What will be your best and worst aspects of memory?

Will you be wise in old age?

Who will be in your immediate and extended family? How often will you see them?

Who will you live with and where will you live?

How many friends will you have and what will you do together?

How often will you get together with friends?

What will your religious or spiritual life be like?

What roles will you hold?

When will you retire?

What will you do in retirement?

How will you get around?

What will driving be like for you and others?

What recreational activities will you enjoy, how will this change?

What will TV and movies be like?

How, when, and where will you die?

Do you think society will treat older persons differently, if so, how?

Now go ask these same questions to a few of your friends and see how answers may differ among people; you should see a big difference in your response compared to others who are not "aging smart" as you are now.

knowledge, the view that older adults are crotchety, angry, depressed, and have lower levels of overall well-being is still prevalent.

In fact, any finding of greater happiness or well-being among older adults has been regarded as surprising by some. In fact, this finding has even been referred to as the **paradox of well-being**. A paradox is a statement that seems to contain a contradiction; it runs counter to our expectations. In this case, how could well-being or happiness be so high for older adults when older adults should be experiencing events that would seem likely to lower their well-being? Older adults lose income with retirement, lose prestige and power, lose friends and family to death and disease, lose some of their own physical and mental capabilities, and grow closer to death everyday. It seems paradoxical that they should show such high levels of happiness. Happiness or well-being, is, of course, influenced by a number of factors some of which are external, such as income or education and some of which are internal, such as personality or emotional expressiveness (Lyubomirsky, 2001). Nevertheless, it seems as if internal factors should be about the same for younger and older adults while external factors may be viewed as worse for older adults. To understand this paradox, researchers have attempted to examine different aspects of well-being to see if some decline while others rise and to isolate the effects, if any, of other important factors such as personality, income, religion, marriage, and education.

Three components of well-being that have been examined are life satisfaction, pleasant emotions, and unpleasant emotions. Life satisfaction is measured by asking people how satisfied they are with their present situation, how much they desire a change, and so on. Pleasant emotions are feelings of joy, affection, commitment, and happiness among others. Unpleasant emotions are guilt, anxiety, anger, envy, and others. You may note at this point that expression of emotions is considered both a component of well-being as well as a factor affecting well-being. Factors internal to a person are often considered to play multiple roles in explaining behavior. Table 14-1 (p. 410) provides an example of how positive and negative emotions were measured in studies. In a major review of the literature and an examination of data collected in a number of different cultures, researchers looked at the relationship between a number of important factors and life satisfaction, pleasant emotions, and unpleasant emotions (Diener & Suh, 1998; Diener, Suh, Lucas, & Smith, 1999). These studies showed that one internal factor, personality, is one of the strongest correlates of well-being. Traits such as extraversion and optimism are related to the presence of pleasant emotions while neuroticism is related to unpleasant emotions. One external factor, income, is not strongly related to any of the measures of well-being within a culture. People with low incomes are nearly as happy as those with much higher incomes. People living in wealthy countries, however, are generally happier than those living in poorer countries. Religion and spirituality are positively related to overall well-being. Very religious or spiritual people are generally happier. Men are typically happier than women and show more pleasant emotions. Women report more unpleasant emotions than men. People with higher levels of education report slightly higher overall levels of well-being, which are probably due to their higher status in society. As you already know, married men and women are happier than single, divorced, separated, and widowed people. In all these studies under review, life satisfaction did not decline with age and in many studies, as reported above, was frequently found to increase. However, some studies have found well-being differences favoring younger people.

Pinquart and Sörensen (2001) conducted a meta-analysis of 300 studies examining gender differences in older and younger people on a number of variables including happiness and well-being. They found significant cohort differences in subjective well-being (their ratings of their own well-being) with older cohorts reporting lower well-being than younger cohorts. With regard to gender differences, older women had lower subjective well-being than older men, this gender difference was much less in younger persons. However, once they took into consideration marital status, health and socioeconomic status, gender differences dramatically decreased.

The studies we have discussed are, of course, cross-sectional so one must be cautious in concluding that such differences are age or cohort or both differences. Nevertheless, it is clear that for the most part, overall well-being, measured in a number of different ways, does not seem to decline with age.

TABLE 14-1   **Measuring Positive and Negative Emotions**

Use the following scale* to answer the questions below:

    1 = none of the time
    2 = a little of the time
    3 = some of the time
    4 = most of the time
    5 = all of the time

During the past 30 days, how much of the time did you feel

    a. worthless   _____
    b. that everything was an effort   _____
    c. full of life   _____
    d. joyful   _____
    e. hopeless   _____
    f. loved   _____
    g. in good spirits   _____
    h. anxious   _____
    i. commitment to another   _____
    j. guilty   _____
    k. sad   _____
    l. calm and peaceful   _____

Add up your scores for the positive emotion items (c, d, f, g, i, and l) and then for the negative emotion items (a, b, e, h, j, and k). Which score is higher, the positive or negative emotions? A higher score means more of that type of emotion over the last 30 days. Remember that this is not a valid or reliable measure but rather an example of the types of questions used to measure emotions. As with all of our examples, it is designed to give you an idea about your emotions, not a true score. Measures similar to this one are the way in which researchers often assess positive and negative emotional aspects of well-being.

* Components of this sample scale were adapted from the work of Mroczek & Kolarz, 1998.

Another major cross-sectional study focused on positive and negative emotions in a group of 2727 adults in the United States, ranging in age from 25 to 74. Researchers examined the influence of personality, marital status, education, health, and stress and obtained the same basic findings as other studies but also looked at men and women separately. Both gender and marital status were strongly related to negative emotions. Older married men showed the lowest levels of negative emotions while women and unmarried men showed very little change in their negative emotions over the range of ages examined. Both gender and personality traits were strongly related to positive emotions. Both older men and women showed higher levels of positive emotions but women, in particular, showed an increase not only in positive emotions but also in the rate of increase. People scoring high on extraversion showed higher levels of positive emotions but very little change from young to old. People scoring medium or low on extraversion, however, showed great increases in positive emotions the older they were. More introverted people tended to be more positive the older they were. These differences indicate that a number of different factors play some role in our feelings of happiness and that some of these factors operate differently for different people. Overall, however, researchers tell us "older people are happier than other adults" (Mroczek & Kolarz, 1998, p. 1346).

If this greater happiness is a cohort difference rather than an age difference it might be that today's younger cohort will not be so happy in old age. There have been few longitudinal studies that have looked at well-being but one well-known study examined close to 5000 men and women, ranging in age from 25 to 74, over a nine-year span. Positive and negative emotions and overall well-being were examined. At the time of the last measurement, a cross-sectional comparison was made with a new group of 5000 participants. These results indicated no overall age differences. The oldest adults reported the same high levels of well-being as adults of all other ages. Small cohort and gender differences were obtained. Men showed higher positive and lower negative emotions than women probably, in part, due to the effect of marriage discussed above. Older cohorts showed lower positive and lower negative emotions (Costa, McCrae, & Zonderman, 1987; Costa, Zonderman, McCrae, Cornoni-Huntley, Locke, & Barbano, 1987).

Before you read on, take a short break and try the autobiography project on p. 412. After completing the project, read the next section and see how your autobiography compares to what the literature has to say about this topic.

Is having positive emotions a good thing? You might think this is a silly question with an obvious answer; of course, everyone wants to be positive. But if you think about it, you know that this is not a universal desire. There are some people who seem quite content to be negative and who see no reason to be positive. They express few positive emotions. So we ask again, is there any benefit to being positive? The answer from a few research studies appears to be yes; people, who express more positive emotions, live longer.

You might remember in our discussion of Alzheimer's disease that we told you about the Nun study being conducted by Snowden (1997). Remember that he examined autobiographies that nuns wrote when they first joined their convents in their early 20s and 30s and then he related their writing styles to rates of Alzheimer's disease in their 80s and 90s. Along with colleagues (Danner, Snowden, & Friesen, 2001), he used those same autobiographies to look more generally at longevity patterns in late life related to emotional content in early life. They found that women whose autobiographies contained more positive emotions lived significantly longer than women who used few positive emotions in their life stories. By itself, this finding could mean that people with positive experiences while they are young live longer or that people with positive feelings about their experiences live longer. Some closely related work suggests that it is our attitude toward our experiences rather than the experiences themselves that is most important. Researchers looking at another aspect of positive emotions developed an optimism–pessimism scale to be used with the MMPI (Maruta, Colligan, Malinchoc, & Offord, 2000). In a longitudinal examination of survival rates, they found that there was a lower risk of death, over a 30-year period, for those scoring higher in optimism.

It appears that not only does it feel good to express positive emotions and be happy, but also it is good for you. Researchers suggest that being positive may affect

P R O J E C T   **14**

Autobiography Project

For this project, we want you to think about your life. Write a short sketch of your life. This account should not contain more than 200 to 300 words. Include:

- Your place of birth
- Information about your parents and grandparents
- Interesting and edifying events of your childhood
- The schools you attended
- Influences that led you to pursue a college degree
- Influences on your choice of major/career field
- Any outstanding events in your life.

Do not read any further until you write your autobiography!

Now we want you to analyze the content of your autobiography for the presence of emotions. Carefully go through your autobiography and identify each word that reflects an emotional experience. Underline or highlight these words to make the next step easier to do. Be sure to include only those words that reflect an emotion you experienced, not what elicited the emotion or what you did in response to the emotion. For example, let's say you wrote, "When I was 10-years-old, my grandmother passed away. I was so sad that I cried for several hours." The only word that you would underline or highlight here is the word *sad*.

Now classify each underlined word as having a positive, negative, or neutral connotation. For example, happiness, amusement, hope, love, and accomplishment, are all positive words. Anger, contempt, fear, sadness, and shame are examples of negative words. Surprise is an example of a neutral emotion word. If you have trouble identifying or classifying words, ask a friend to help. Now add up the number of positive words that you have written in your autobiography.

Now you can go back and read the rest of this section in your textbook.

What you have done in this project is very similar to what the nuns and the researchers did in the Nun study of positive emotions and longevity described in the text. The instructions for writing your autobiography were only slightly modified from those given to the nuns when they entered the convent in the 1930s. The scoring method that you used to classify emotion words also is very similar to that designed by Danner, Snowdon, and Friesen (2000).

Look at the number of positive emotions in your autobiography. The researchers found a linear relationship between the number of positive words in the autobiographies of nuns and longevity. In other words, the more positive words they used, the longer they lived. There was a difference of 9.4 between those using the fewest positive emotional words and those using the most. If you used few positive emotions in your autobiography, you might want to think about how you can change to be a bit more positive in your reflections and interpretation of daily life and increase your chance of living longer.

Be happy, live longer.

your physiology in ways that are beneficial over your lifespan. A recent intervention study with sedentary older adults showed that a group exercise program resulted in better health and well-being. The researchers concluded that the social environment that accompanies exercise groups is a good way to increase happiness in older adults (McAuley, Blissmer, Marquez, Jerome, Kramer, & Katula, 2001). Findings from another recent study examining the role of social support and well-being in old age (Liang, Krause, & Bennet, 2001) suggest that giving may be better than receiving; volunteering or providing support to others is an important activity resulting in well-being for the helpers. We must be careful not to provide too much assistance to older persons as this often results in lower well-being. These authors also suggest, based on their data, that simple social exchange is not nearly as important to well-being in old age as is minimizing negative interactions and reinforcing the fact that support is available when needed.

The Future

As you know from Chapters 1 and 4, life expectancy has increased dramatically over the past 100 years. Some gerontologists caution that as people live longer they may become less happy because they will have seen, heard, and done everything that there is to do. Older adults will be able to say in every situation "been there, done that." They also will be less unhappy because they will have had numerous sad experiences. They will become somewhat bland and may even hope for death when everything around them appears to be a repeat. We think this is an absurd belief. It could possibly occur if all progress ceased and one could have been everywhere and done everything. New discoveries, opportunities, and knowledge, however, become available continually. Older adults have plenty to do. In this section, we look at some opportunities and expected changes for the eventually older adults of today's younger cohorts. However, we do not know what the future holds. This section presents our best guesses—some are clearly more probable than others.

Our Future Bodies

Many researchers believe that the first person to live to be 150 years old is alive right now. Why do you think they believe this? Our discussion of increases in longevity in Chapter 4 may help you answer this question. Perhaps that first person to reach 150 is you. Jean Calment's record of 122 (see Chapter 1) will be broken a number of times over the next few decades, and before the year 2050, someone will live to be 150. Because the gender gap in longevity appears to continue to increase (see Chapter 4), this person will undoubtedly be a woman. Most expect the gender gap to continue but to diminish somewhat. To be fair, other researchers believe that we are approaching a plateau in life expectancy, which should not increase much beyond 85 years of age.

What about a possible limit in life span? There is a great controversy in the scientific literature about whether or not there is a real upper limit on how long we can live. Wilmoth (1997) critically reviewed demographic statistics and concluded that we just do not have enough data to know the answer yet and it may be some time before we will. He concludes that there is no reason to assume that there is an upper limit and that we may be better off if we plan for the possibility of more people living to very advanced ages. What do you think?

Life expectancy, or average length of life, also will be higher than it is today. This is a rather common prediction although how much longer life expectancy might be by 2050 varies. The Social Security Administration projects a life expectancy of 77.5 for men and 82.9 for women born in 2050. Other estimates run as high as 81.6 for men and 87 for women (Wilmoth, 1998).

Why will life expectancy be longer in the future? A number of factors play a role in this projection. We expect longer lives because we expect people to be in better health. We expect better health because we expect people to eat more nutritionally and to exercise on a regular basis. We expect the proportion of adults who use tobacco to continue to decline and would like to see tobacco use disappear entirely by 2050. It probably will not but a smaller proportion of people than today will participate in this very dangerous habit. We expect medical science to find more effective treatments for many of the disorders that cause so many deaths today. Heart disease, cancer, AIDS, and Alzheimer's disease may be treated successfully over the next few decades and some of those treatments may depend on advances in genetic engineering. With the rapid gains in knowledge of the human genome and cloning, we may soon be able to replace vital organs and tissues with body parts grown from our own cells. Each successful treatment will add a bit more to average life expectancy. Of course, cloning and gene manipulation or replacement are highly controversial procedures so it may be quite a while, if ever, that we see any impact of these new biotechnology revolutions on life expectancy. If you are interested in this area, we urge you to pay special attention to both the scientific and the political news to see what changes may occur in the future. We must be realistic about the possibility of the threat of new and old viruses and infections that mutate rapidly to become resistant to antibiotic treatments. If these increase (we have already seen some new strains of pneumonia, staph infection, and HIV/AIDS that show this resistance), or new medications are not developed, the effect on life expectancy could be to halt or slow the predicted increase. Again, keeping a eye on the scientific literature can make us all better health consumers at best and more knowledgeable at the least.

Another area of controversy in the literature has to do with the notion of more people living healthier into old age. **Morbidity** refers to declining health and disability. Several researchers, most particularly Fries (1980) have suggested that we can expect more people to live healthier into old age, in other words, morbidity will decline. Fries proposed the "compression of morbidity" hypothesis to predict this state in old age. He suggests that life expectancy will plateau and hold fairly steady at around 85, citing as evidence that life expectancy over the age of 85 has remained fairly constant for about six years. What this means is that rather than live many years with chronic conditions and in a morbid condition, more people will be pretty healthy until around 85 when they will decline fairly quickly until death. Morbidity would be compressed to a short period of time. Most people would like this state of affairs in old age. No one wants to live a long life if it means they would live in a disabled, unhealthy condition for those extra years. Fries cites data from recent longitudinal studies of people who exercise and have low risk behaviors to show that they postpone disability for a decade or more compared to controls (1999). Not everyone agrees with Fries, particularly those who disagree with an upper lifespan limit. If we increase the lifespan, but still decline starting after 85, perhaps we just delay morbidity rather than compress it. Fries would counter that we could extend health further than we currently do; we just have to try harder. In counter to this however, are the findings from several studies that failed to induce older institutionalized and noninstitutionalized elderly to exercise more and eat healthier (Leventhal, Rabin, Leventhal, & Burns, 2001). Do you think that older adults are just not interested or that an effective way to motivate them has not yet been found? The resolution of this controversy is important as it has great relevance for healthcare and social planning. Should we count on an increased aging population that is healthy or one in need of services? It seems to us that exercising, eating right, and engaging in low-risk behaviors can only make our lives better at all ages.

We also are optimistic about the quality of life for older adults. As more people learn about aging more positive attitudes will be engendered. We expect negative stereotypes of aging to greatly diminish although we still expect a lot of humor about aging to remain. We expect that the humor about aging will be more positive than it is today.

Exercising may extend our nation's life expectancy.

Our Future Minds

As you know from our discussion in Chapters 5, 6, and 7, a number of changes in cognition and thinking occur as we grow older. Some of these changes can be linked to the mental slowing that takes place in older brains that we discussed in Chapter 5. Some of these changes are gains, such as higher levels of knowledge and, in many cases, wisdom (Chapter 7). By 2050, we expect older adults to perform at much higher levels on most measures of cognition than older adults do today. We believe, however, that this difference will be a result of cohort rather than age. Members of younger cohorts will know much more in their older years than members of older cohorts, today's older adults, ever knew. We are in the Information Age. Television, radio, telephones, computers, and the Internet have delivered an enormous amount of knowledge that is easy to access. The technology will only improve as will our ability to sift through the *junk* and quickly concentrate on real fact. At the same time, we expect cross-sectional comparisons to continue to find age differences. When you are in the older cohort in 2050, the younger cohort of that time (those born in 2030) will probably perform better than you will on any timed test and on many measures of episodic memory. You, however, will know more and be an expert at some tasks and, perhaps, at life itself. You may be wise.

We believe that more effective measures of adult intelligence than those discussed in Chapter 7 will be created and in use by 2050. Standard IQ tests will probably still be used to measure some aspects of intelligence for young and old but measures of specific adult abilities also will be available. Those abilities include getting along well with diverse groups of people, avoiding conflict, planning real-world activities/events, being able to argue a position effectively, being persuasive, being able to take another's point of view, and having a broad perspective. We are confident that psychologists will create standardized tests to measure many of these adult abilities.

You will benefit from the results of the many studies looking at improving intelligence into old age. New games and other recreation outlets will capitalize on the desire we all have to remain mentally sharp. **Elderhostel**, a very popular program for adults over the age of 60 offers educational classes combined with social opportunities in settings around the world. This and Shepard Centers, discussed in Chapter 10, are two examples of very successful programs aimed at enhancing intellectual abilities in elders. We expect that there will be more opportunities to use our mental skills.

Our Future Selves

With advances in methodology and our understanding of the role of genetics (see Chapter 3), we expect to have a much firmer grasp on the concept of personality that we discussed in Chapter 8. Furthermore, we will be better able to identify the role of personality in everyday life and behavior. With this understanding, we can better see what is under our control and what we need to learn to live with. For example, if we find that temperament is a life-long, genetically linked propensity to behave in certain ways (what we believe to be true now but lack the genetic proof) *and* we develop definitive ways to measure it, we can make a lot of progress in adjusting to life. We can help our children from a young age to understand their propensities and to identify environments that complement these temperaments rather than work against them. Learning how to do this early in life can make doing it in adulthood and old age a habit.

We do not expect any major changes in the quality of social relationships over the next few decades. As we saw in Chapter 9, people will still be close to and value their relationships with family members as they have for all of recorded history. People will still make and value friends. We do, however, expect a greater proportion of individuals to participate in Internet communities. You may not lose touch with your college roommates or classmates as so many other cohorts have done in the past. It will be easy to keep up via email. Older and younger adults in 2050 will have friends all over the world connected by the Internet. It will become a small world (after all).

We expect that by 2050, most societies and most individuals will have far greater respect for diversity. Part of this will result from worldwide friendships via the Internet and part of it will result from efforts at integration in our own country. This is an important goal to strive for and we believe that your generations may be our best hope in achieving tolerance and peaceful co-existence.

We expect to see great changes in the work world. We saw in Chapter 10 that already the nature of work has changed and it is expected to continue to evolve. Particularly interesting to the study of aging is the move to more individuals working for themselves and out of their own homes. If this trend continues, it will be ideal for older adults as they can work part-time and still travel and enjoy different versions of retirement. We also expect to see much better personal planning for retirement as changes in government and employer provided financial support in old age evolve. Politics will play a strong role here and older voters are a strong voting block. As their numbers increase, their influence on political outcomes will probably increase. There may be some very interesting things happening in legislation benefiting elders in the next 20 to 40 years. It would be wise to pay attention and continue to vote.

Our Future Survival

We are optimistic that an effective treatment for slowing, if not halting, the progression of Alzheimer's disease will be found soon. While we discussed the results of the latest research on causes and treatments for Alzheimer's disease in Chapter 11, we need and expect to see more. The number and proportion of older adults will balloon over the next few decades.

Again, as we saw in Chapter 11, advances in the field of genetics will provide a much better picture of the origins of Alzheimer's disease and many other psychopathologies of adulthood and old age. This knowledge will help us with prevention as well as treatment programs. By the time you approach old age, you may have a good idea of your risk for these conditions and may be able to take appropriate preventative measures, such as gene therapy, behavioral programs, pharmacological treatments, or some combination of these.

While we all accept that death is inevitable, the most frequent causes of death will probably change. As we saw in Chapter 13 that we no longer die from the frequent killers of 1900s the current number one and number two causes of death, heart disease and cancer, respectively, will probably slip lower on the list. We expect this to occur as science makes great strivings towards prevention, treatment, and cure. Already, physicians view heart disease and many cancers as chronic, not terminal, and acute diseases. We can live with these conditions, not die from them. What do you think will be the biggest causes of death in 2050?

We hope to see a better understanding and treatment of death and dying. As we stated in Chapter 13, these processes are a part of life and need to be discussed openly. Euthanasia and physician-assisted suicide continue to make news as we struggle with these important ethical decisions. One important step in that direction is the growing knowledge of advanced directives or living wills. As more people understand these documents, life and death decisions can be made long before they become too difficult emotionally to make. We expect the percentage of people having advanced directives will rise from 18 percent, currently, to a majority of the population. Finally, we expect to see changes in burial customs as people consider land use issues now and in the future.

Based on the research and progress we have seen and discussed in Chapter 12, the environment that we build will undergo significant changes and become more ergonomic for us in our old age. Universal design of buildings and products will provide us with more livable environments at all ages. We suspect that technology will play an important role in our home environments over the next few decades. The **Smarthouse** is already in production. You may have seen prototypes of this house if you have ever gone to Disneyland or Disneyworld and visited their future exhibits. The Smarthouse is a joint public and private venture that has resulted in a home design that incorporates a central wiring system hooked to an electronic gateway system. All devices that are currently electronic, and many that can be converted to electronic operation, are run from the central gateway system. Terminals in every room and remote access will allow you to operate virtually everything in your home from one place. You can use your computer at work or your handheld remote device to lock a door, turn on the oven, see who is at the door and talk to them via a video cell phone, for example. Even more important for frail elderly is the ability to monitor several aspects of health using the electronic health checker. You and your doctor can be automatically alerted

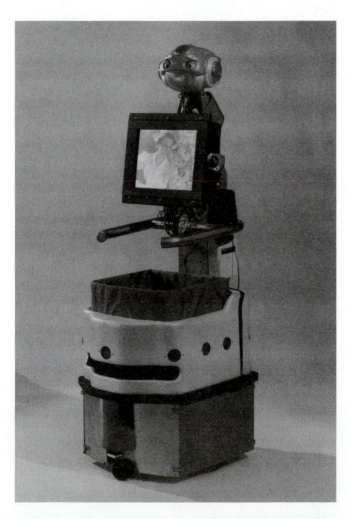

Nursebot, *Carnegie Mellon University's robot nurse.*

to any potential problems. The Smarthouse and other variations will prove that technology can improve our lives at all ages, if it is designed with everyone in mind.

In the future, housing for older adults in need of assistance will be better than it is today. Homes for older adults will be more like private homes rather than institutions. Incorporation of human and environmental supports to enhance independence will be routine. Residents will have more freedom to come and go as they please, eat when they wish, and have sexual relations in private. Technology will play an important role in facilities for frail elders, including private homes. Technology, such as Smarthouse-type monitoring, can make it possible for elders to remain in their own homes if they choose to do so. In residential facilities, technology will enhance healthcare delivery and help alleviate the anticipated shortage in nursing and care staff. For example, Carnegie Mellon University is piloting the use of a healthcare robot, the **Nursebot**, in nursing homes in the Pittsburgh area.

Making Choices

We believe that learning about aging will enhance your own aging. Table 14-2 presents a compilation of the major choices that you can make which have been discussed in this text. How many of these have you made since beginning this course in aging?

TABLE 14-2   A Compilation of Making Choices

The following are the choices that you can make to improve your life now and when you are old. We have pulled them all together here so you can look at them once again; consider keeping this list with you as you travel through your life.

Continue your education	Find a job you like
Stay informed	Invest for your future retirement
Have frequent checkups	Make a living will or durable power of attorney
Be vaccinated while young	
Watch what you eat	Think through and write out your funeral arrangements
Don't smoke	
Don't drink alcohol excessively	Get a second opinion (Alzheimer's disease)
Exercise—aerobic and resistance	Avoid aluminum
Relax	Maintain close ties with family members and friends
Believe in yourself	
Choose to experience life (volunteer)	Contact your grandparents (and parents) today
Try something new	
Don't jump to conclusions when judging others/personality	Complete a home checklist to determine person–environment fit
Begin a journal	Assess your environmental stimulation level

CHAPTER HIGHLIGHTS

- Overall feelings of happiness increase throughout life into old age when the highest levels are reported.
- The paradox of well-being is a seeming contradiction that well-being or happiness is quite high for older adults when older adults should be experiencing events that would seem likely to lower their well-being.
- Three components of well-being, life satisfaction, positive emotions, and negative emotions have been examined in their relationship to internal and external factors.
- Both internal and external factors affect well-being at all ages; internal factors related to well-being include religion/spirituality, gender, and most strongly, personality, but not age; external factors related only slightly to well-being include education and marital status but not income.
- Early results from sequential studies of age and well-being find overall similar levels of high well-being at all ages with small cohort and gender effects; younger cohorts and men showed higher levels of positive and negative emotions, however, this latter finding may be due to marital status not gender.
- Life-long happiness appears to be good for you. The Nun study found that nuns who used more positive emotions in autobiographies written in their younger years lived longer than nuns who used fewer positive emotions.
- Future predictions about aging are fun and optimistic but must be tempered with caution as no one can predict the future.
- Life expectancy will continue to increase in the future, although some researchers believe we may plateau at around an average life expectancy of 85 years of age.
- There is a great controversy about whether there is an upper limit on lifespan or how long we could possibly live; some believe it has and will continue to hold steady at 120 to 125 years of age while others predict the first person to live to 150 years of age is alive right now and that we may live even beyond that age.
- Another controversy is whether we can continue to live healthier into old age and show compression of morbidity or shorten the length of time we are unhealthy in old age; some believe we can and will live very healthy right until we die in very old age; others believe we will not and that we may just postpone morbidity into very advanced age and still live even longer.
- We expect an increase in knowledge and better understanding and use of memory processes in old age in the future.
- Better measures of adult intelligence will shed greater light on any possible age differences in the future.
- We expect to see refined definitions and better measures of personality, which will shed more light on the relationship between personality and age.
- Social relationships may strengthen as access to friends and family improves through the use of the Internet, email, videophones and other technology.
- The work world will undergo significant changes that bear close watching.
- Advances in science and healthcare research and treatment will increase our knowledge about, prevention of, and treatment of Alzheimer's disease and other pathologies and psychopathologies that are seen in late life.
- The most frequent causes of death in old age will probably change as once terminal diseases like cancer and heart disease transform into curable or chronic conditions.
- The built environment will undergo changes as designs better suited to our abilities are incorporated in homes and institutions, including the use of advanced technology.

STUDY QUESTIONS

1. Describe any age differences in happiness.

2. What is the paradox of well-being and what does research say about this contradiction?

3. What are three components of well-being and how are they typically measured?

4. Describe the relationship between well-being and internal and external factors.

5. Identify results from studies regarding age and well-being including the role of positive and negative emotions, and optimism/pessimism.

6. What are the benefits of being happy?

7. What are some predictions regarding life expectancy, life span, and health in old age in the future?

8. What are some predictions about the future regarding memory and intelligence in old age?

9. What are some predictions regarding personality, social relationships and the work world for future elderly?

10. What are some predictions regarding psychopathology, death and dying, and the built environment for future older persons?

RECOMMENDED READINGS

Rowe, J. W. & Kahn, R. L. (1998). *Successful aging*. New York: Pantheon Books. This book presents a very readable, optimistic view of how individuals can control their own health and experience successful aging. There is an emphasis on the lifestyle choices that we all can make right now. The information presented comes from a major study conducted and supported by the MacArthur Foundation.

Qualls, S. H. & Abeles, N. (2000). *Psychology and the aging revolution: How we adapt to longer life*. Washington, DC: American Psychological Association. This is an edited book with a number of different authors who write about the expanding number of years spent in retirement, changes in needs and abilities with advanced age, and the likelihood of successful aging in our changing culture.

INTERNET RESOURCES

http://psychiatry.medscape.com/Medscape/features/ResourceCenter/PNGeriatrics/public/RC-index-PNGeriatrics.html   An excellent site for some of the latest information on health and aging.
http://www.aoa.gov   For information on aging in the new century.
http://www.smart-house.com   For some of the latest in Smarthouse technology.
http://www-2.cs.cmu.edu/~nursebot   The Nursebot Project site at Carnegie Mellon University.

REFERENCES

Abraham, J. D. & Hansson, R. O. (1995). Successful aging at work: An applied study of selection, organization, optimization, and compensation through impression management. *Journals of Gerontology: Psychological Sciences, 50B*, P94–P103.

Ackerman, P. L. & Rolfhus, E. L. (1999). The locus of adult intelligence: Knowledge, abilities, and nonability traits. *Psychology & Aging, 14*, 314–330.

Adams, A. J., Wang, L. S., Wong, L. & Gould, B. (1988). Visual acuity changes with age: Some new perspectives. *American Journal of Optometry & Physiological Optics, 65*, 403–406.

Adams, G. A. (1999). Career-related variables and planned retirement age: An extension of Beehr's model. *Journal of Vocational Behavior, 55*, 221–235.

Adams, S. L. & Waskel, S. A. (1993). Late onset alcoholism: Stress or structure. *Journal of Psychology, 127*, 329–334.

Aday, R. H., Evans, E. & Sims, C. R. (1991). Youth's attitudes toward the elderly: The impact of intergenerational partners. *Journal of Applied Gerontology, 10*, 372–384.

Adelman, M. (1990). Stigma, gay lifestyles, and adjustment to aging: A study of later-life gay men and lesbians. *Journal of Homosexuality, 20*, 1–7.

Ade-Ridder, L. (1990). Sexuality and marital quality among older married couples. In T. H. Brubaker (Ed.), *Family relationships in later life* (2nd ed., pp. 48–67). Newbury Park, CA: Sage.

Administration on Aging. (2001). A profile of older Americans: 2000. Washington, DC: U.S. Department of Health and Human Services. Available from *http://www.aoa.gov/aoa/stats/Census2000/*. Accessed September 25, 2001.

Aging Research & Training News. (1997). Alzheimer's gene found to be primary factor in only 10 percent of cases. Author, *20*, 33.

Aiken, L. (1991). *Dying, death, and bereavement.* Boston: Allyn & Bacon.

Aiken, L. R. (1995). *Aging: An introduction to gerontology.* London: Sage.

Albert, M. S., Duffy, F. H., & Naeser, M. (1987). Nonlinear changes in cognition with age and their neuropsychologic correlates. *Canadian Journal of Psychology, 41*, 141–157.

Albert, M. S., Jones, K., Savage, C. R., Berkman, L., Seeman, T., Blazer, D., & Rowe, J. W. (1995). Predictors of cognitive change in older persons: MacArthur studies of successful aging. *Psychology & Aging, 10*, 578–589.

Albom, M. (1997). *Tuesdays with Morrie.* New York: Doubleday.

Aldwin, C. M. & Revenson, T. A. (1987). Does coping help? A reexamination of the relationship between coping and mental health. *Journal of Personality & Social Psychology, 53*, 337–348.

Aldwin, C. M., Sutton, K. J., Chiara, G., & Spiro, A. (1996). Age differences in stress, coping, and appraisal: Findings from the Normative Aging Study. *Journal of Gerontology: Psychological Science, 51B*, P179–P188.

Aleska, K. (1994). *Income among older Americans in 1992.* Washington, DC: AARP.

Allan, L. G. (1979). The perception of time. *Perception & Psychophysics, 26*, 340–354.

Allport, G. W. (1937). *Personality: A psychological interpretation.* New York: Holt, Rinehart, & Winston.

Alpaugh, P. & Birren, J. E. (1977). Variables affecting creative contributions across the life span. *Human Development, 20*, 240–248.

Alspaugh, M. E. L., Zarit, S. H., & Greene, R. (1999). Longitudinal patterns of risk for depression in dementia caregivers: Objective and subjective primary stress as predictors. *Psychology & Aging, 14*, 34–43.

Alspaugh, M. E., Stephens, M. A., Townsend, A. L., Zarit, S., & Greene, R. (1999). Longitudinal patterns of risk for depression in dementia caregivers: Objective and subjective primary stress as predictors. *Psychology and Aging, 14*, 34–43.

Amato, P. R. & Rogers, S. J. (1997). A longitudinal study of marital problems and subsequent divorce. *Journal of Marriage & the Family, 59*, 612–624.

American Association of Homes and Services for the Aging. (2001). Factsheets on living facilities for older persons. Available from *http://www.ahsa.org*. Accessed September 24, 2001.

American Association for Retired Persons. (1985). *The AARP grandparenting survey: The sharing and caring between mature grandparents and their grandchildren.* Washington, DC: Author.

American Association of Retired Persons. (1986). *Work and retirement: Employees over 40 and their views.* Washington, DC: Author.

American Association of Retired Persons. (1991). *A profile of older Americans 1990.* Washington, DC: Author.

American Association of Retired Persons. (AARP). (1992a). *A profile of older Americans.* Washington, DC: Author.

American Association of Retired Persons. (1992b). *The doable renewable home: Making your home fit your needs.* Washington, DC: Author.

American Association of Retired Persons. (1992c). *Understanding senior housing for the 1990s.* Washington, DC: Author.

American Association of Retired Persons. (1993). *A portrait of older minorities.* Washington, DC: Author.

American Association of Retired Persons. (1994). *A profile of older Americans.* Washington, DC: Author.

American Association of Retired Persons. (1995). *Images of aging in America*. Washington, DC: AARP.

American Association of Retired Persons. (1995–2001). Caring for parents at home. Available from *http://www.aarp.org/confacts/caregive/parentshome.ht ml*. Accessed July 21, 2001.

American Association of Retired Persons. (2000a). *Fixing to stay: A national survey on housing and home modification issues*. Washington, DC: Author.

American Association of Retired Persons. (2000b). Housing options for older people. Available from *http://www.aarp.org/confacts/housing/housingoptions.html*. Accessed September 8, 2001.

American Association of Retired Persons. (2001a). *Life in the middle: A report on multicultural boomers coping with family and aging issues*. Washington, DC: Author.

American Association of Retired Persons. (2001b). *The costs of long-term care: Public perceptions versus reality*. Washington, DC: Author.

American Cancer Society. (1991). *Cancer facts and figures for minority Americans–1991*. Atlanta, GA: Author.

American Cancer Society. (1994). *Cancer facts and figures–1994*. Atlanta, GA: Author.

American Heart Association. (1993). *Exercise and your heart: A guide to physical activity*. Dallas, TX: Author.

American Psychiatric Association. (1994). *Diagnostic and statistical manual of mental disorders* (4th ed.). Washington, DC: Author.

Ames, K. (1991, August 26). Last rights. *Newsweek*, 40–41.

Ancoli-Israel, S., Kripke, D. F., Mason, W., & Kaplan, O. J. (1985). Sleep apnea and periodic movements in an aging sample. *Journal of Gerontology, 40*, 419–425.

Ancoli-Israel, S., Kripke, D. F., Mason, W., & Messin, S. (1981). Sleep apnea and nocturnal myoclonus in a senior population. *Sleep, 4*, 349–358.

Anders, T. R., Fozard, J. L., & Lillyquist, T. D. (1972). Effects of age upon retrieval from short-term memory. *Developmental Psychology, 6*, 214–217.

Andersen-Ranberg, K., Vasegaard, L., & Jeune, B. (2001). Dementia is not inevitable: A population-based study of Danish centenarians. *Journal of Gerontology: Psychological Sciences, 56B*, P152–P159.

Andershed, B. & Ternestedt, B-M. (1998). Involvement of relatives in the care of the dying in different care cultures: Involvement in the dark or in the light. *Cancer Nursing, 21*, 106–116.

Anderson, J. R. (1993). Problem solving and learning. *American Psychologist, 48*, 35–44.

Anderson, S. A., Russell, C. S., & Schumm, W. R. (1983). Perceived marital quality and family life-cycle categories. *Journal of Marriage & the Family, 45*, 127–139.

Ankrom, M., Thompson, J., Finucane, T., & Fingerhood, M. (1997). *Gender differences in alcohol use and abuse in the homebound elderly and their caregivers*. Paper presented at the 50th annual meeting of the Gerontological Society of America.

Anstey, K. J., Luszcz, M. A., Giles, L. C., & Andrews, G. R. (2001). Demographic, health, cognitive, and sensory variables as predictors of mortality in very old adults. *Psychology & Aging, 16*, 3–11.

Antonoff, S. R. & Spilka, B. (1984–1985). Patterning of facial expressions among terminal care patients. *Omega, 15*, 101–108.

Antonucci, T. C. & Akiyama, H. (1991). Social relationships and aging well. *Generations, 15* (1), 39–44.

Antonucci, T. C. & Akiyama, H. (1997). Concerns with others at midlife: Care, comfort, or compromise? In M. E. Lachman & J. B. James (Eds.), *Multiple paths of midlife development* (pp. 147–169). Chicago: University of Chicago Press.

Antonucci, T. C. (1986). Social support networks: A hierarchical mapping technique. *Generations, 10*(4), 10–12.

Antonucci, T. C. (1990). Social supports and social relationships. In R. H. Binstock & L. K. George (Eds.), *The handbook of aging and the social sciences* (3rd ed., pp. 205–227). New York: Academic Press.

Antonucci, T. C. (2001). In J. E. Birren & K. W. Schaie (Eds.). *The handbook of the psychology of aging*. (5th ed., pp. 427–453). New York: Academic Press.

Antonucci, T. C., Fuhrer, R., & Dartigues, J. F. (1997). Social relations and depressive symptomatology in a sample of community-dwelling French older adults. *Psychology & Aging, 12*, 189–195.

Aponte, J. F., Rivers, R. Y., & Wohl, J. (1995). *Psychological interventions and cultural diversity*. Boston: Allyn & Bacon.

Ara, S. (1998). Housing facilities for the elderly in India. In S. Brink (Ed.). *Housing older people: An international perspective* (pp. 87–94). New Brunswick, NJ: Transaction Publishers.

Ardelt, M. (1997). Wisdom and life satisfaction in old age. *Journal of Gerontology: Psychological Sciences, 52B*, P15–P27.

Arndt, V., Brenner, H., Rothenbacher, D., Zschenderlein, B., Fraisse, E., & Fliedner, T. M. (1998). Elevated liver enzyme activity in construction workers: Prevalence and impact on early retirement and all-cause mortality. *International Archives of Occupational & Environmental Health, 71*, 405–412.

Ash, P. (1966). Preretirement counseling. *Gerontologist, 6*, 127–128.

Asthana, S., Craft, S., Baker, L. D., Raskind, M. A., Birnbaum, R. S., Lofgreen, C. P., Veith, R. C., & Plymate, S. R. (1999). Cognitive and neuroendocrine response to transdermal estrogen in postmenopausal women with Alzheimer's disease: Results of a placebo-controlled, double-blind, pilot study. *Psychoneuroendocrinology, 24*, 657–677.

Atchley, P. & Andersen, G. J. (1998). The effect of age, retinal eccentricity, and speed on the detection of optic flow components. *Psychology & Aging, 13*, 297–308.

Atchley, R. C. (1982). The process of retirement: Comparing women and men. In M. Szinovacz (Ed.), *Women's retirement* (pp. 153–168). Beverly Hills, CA: Sage.

Atchley, R. C. (1996). Retirement. In J. E. Birren (Ed.), *En-*

cyclopedia of gerontology, Vol. 2 (pp. 437–449). New York: Academic Press.

Atchley, R. C. (1997). Retirement income security: Past, present, and future. *Generations*, 9–12.

Atchley, R. C. (1999). *Continuity and adaptation in aging: Creating positive experiences.* Baltimore, MD: Johns Hopkins University Press.

Atchley, R. C. (2000). *Social forces and aging: An introduction to social gerontology.* Stamford, CT: Wadsworth.

Atchley, R. C. & Miller, S. J. (1983). Types of elderly couples. In T. H. Brubaker (Ed.), *Family relationships in later life* (pp. 77–90). Beverly Hills, CA: Sage.

Atkinson, R. M., Ganzini, L., & Bernstein, M. J. (1992). Alcohol and substance-use disorders in the elderly. In J. E. Birren, R. Sloane, & G. D. Cohen (Eds.), *Handbook of mental health and aging* (2nd ed., pp. 515–555). New York: Academic Press.

Axelrod, S., Thompson, L. W., & Cohen, L. D. (1968). Effects of senescence on the temporal resolution of somesthetic stimuli presented to one hand or both. *Journal of Gerontology, 23*, 191–195.

Axinn, W. G. & Thornton, A. (1992). The relationship between cohabitation and divorce: Selectivity or causal influence. *Demography, 29*, 357–374.

Aykan, H. & Wolf, D. A. (2000). Traditionality, modernity, and household composition: Parental-child coresidence in contemporary Turkey. *Research on Aging, 22*, 395–421.

Babar, S. I., Enright, P. L., Boyle, P., Foley, D., Sharp, D. S., Petrovich, H., & Quan, S. F. (2000). Sleep disturbances and their correlates in elderly Japanese American men residing in Hawaii. *Journal of Gerontology: Medical Sciences, 55A*, M406–M411.

Babchuck, N. (1978–1979). Aging and primary relations. *International Journal of Aging & Human Development, 9*, 137–151.

Babcock, R. L. & Salthouse, T. A. (1990). Effects of increased processing demands on age differences in working memory. *Psychology & Aging, 5*, 421–428.

Bachand, L. L. & Caron, S. L. (2001). Ties that bind: A qualitative study of happy long-term marriages. *Contemporary Family Therapy: An International Journal, 23*, 105–121.

Baddeley, A. D. (1981). The concept of working memory: A view of its current state and probably future development. *Cognition, 10*, 17–23.

Bader, G., Zuliani, G., Kostner, G. M., & Fellin, R. (1998). Apolipoprotein E polymorphism is not associated with longevity or disability in a sample of Italian octo- and nonagenarians. *Gerontology, 44*, 293–299.

Bagby, R. M., Joffe, R. T., Parker, J. D. A., Kalemba, V., & Harkness, K. L. (1995). Major depression and the five-factor model of personality. *Journal of Personality Disorders, 9*, 224–234.

Bahrick, H. P., Bahrick, P. P., & Wittlinger, R. P. (1975). Fifty years of memory for names and faces: A cross-sectional approach. *Journal of Experimental Psychology, 104*, 54–75.

Baker, B. (1999, November). *AARP Bulletin, 40*, 18–20.

Baker, B. & Reyes, K. (2000, March-April). R.I.P. off: Now that death has become big business, who can you trust? *Modern Maturity*. 60–67, 73.

Baldwin, R. C. (1994). Is there a distinct type of major depression in the elderly? *Journal of Psychopharmacology, 8*, 177–184.

Balin, A. K. (1982). Testing the free radical theory of aging. In Adelman & Roth (Eds.), *Testing the theories of aging.* Boca Raton, FL: CRC Press.

Balk, D. E. & Vesta, L. C. (1998). Psychological development during four years of bereavement: A longitudinal case study. *Death Studies, 22*, 23–41.

Balk, D. E. (1999). Bereavement and spiritual change. *Death Studies, 23*, 485–493.

Ball, M. J. & Murdoch, G. H. (1997). Consensus recommendations for the postmortem diagnosis of Alzheimer's disease. *Neurobiology of Aging, 18*, S1.

Ball, M. M., Whittington, F. J., Perkins, M. M., Patterson, V. L., Hollingsworth, C., King, S., & Combs, B. (2000). Quality of life in assisted living: Viewpoints of residents. *Journal of Applied Gerontology, 19*, 304–325.

Baltes, M. M., & Wahl, H. W. (1992). The dependency support script in institutions: Generalization to community settings. *Psychology & Aging, 7*, 409–418.

Baltes, P. B. (1987). Theoretical propositions of life-span developmental psychology: On the dynamics between growth and decline. *Developmental Psychology, 23*, 611–626.

Baltes, P. B. (1993). The aging mind: Potential and limits. *The Gerontologist, 33*, 580–594.

Baltes, P. B. & Baltes, M. M. (1990). Psychological perspectives on successful aging: The model of selective optimization with compensation. In P. B. Baltes & M. M. Baltes (Eds.), *Successful aging: Perspectives from the behavioral sciences.* (pp. 1–34). New York: Cambridge University Press.

Baltes, P. B. & Graf, P. (1996). Psychological aspects of aging: Facts and frontiers. In D. Magnussen (Ed.), *The life span development of individuals: Behavioral, neurobiological, and psychosocial perspectives.* (pp. 427–459). Cambridge, England: Cambridge University Press.

Baltes, P. B. & Labouvie, G. V. (1973). Adult development of intellectual performance: Description, explanation, and modification. In C. Eisdorfer & M. P. Lawton (Eds.), *The psychology of adult development and aging.* Washington, DC: American Psychological Association.

Baltes, P. B. & Smith, J. (1990). Toward a psychology of wisdom and its ontogenesis. In R. J. Sternberg (Ed.), *Wisdom: Its nature, origins, and development.* (pp. 87–120). Cambridge, England: Cambridge University Press.

Baltes, P. B. & Staudinger, U. M. (1993). The search for a psychology of wisdom. *Current Directions, 2*, 75–80.

Baltes, P. B. & Staudinger, U. M. (2000). Wisdom: A metaheuristic (pragmatic) to orchestrate mind and virtue toward excellence. *American Psychologist, 55*, 122–136.

Baltes, P. B., Staudinger, U. M., Maercker, A., & Smith, J.

(1995). People nominated as wise: A comparative study of wisdom-related knowledge. *Psychology & Aging, 10*, 155–166.

Barbeau, A., Roy, M., Cloutier, T., Plasse, L., & Paris, S. (1986). Environmental and genetic factors in the etiology of Parkinson's disease. In M. D. Yar & K. J. Bergman (Eds.), *Advances in neurology* (pp. 299–306). New York: Raven Press.

Barclay, L. L., Zemcov, A., Blass, J. P., & Sansone, J. (1985). Survival in Alzheimer's disease and vascular dementia. *Neurology, 35*, 834–840.

Barefoot, J. C., Maynard, K. E., Beckham, J. C., Brummett, B. H., Hooker, K., & Siegler, I. C. (1998). Trust, health, and longevity. *Journal of Behavioral Medicine, 21*, 517–526.

Barefoot, J. C., Mortensen, E. L., Helms, M. J., Avlund, K., & Schroll, M. (2001). A longitudinal study of gender differences in depressive symptoms from age 50 to 80. *Psychology & Aging, 16*, 342–345.

Barer, B. M. (2001). The "grands and greats" of very old black grandmothers. *Journal of Aging Studies, 15*, 1–11.

Barker, J. C. (1997). Between humans and ghosts: The decrepit elderly in a Polynesian society. In J. Sokolovsky (Ed.). *The cultural context of aging*, (pp. 295–314). New York: Bergin & Garvey Publishers.

Barlett, D. L. & Steele, J. B. (1992). *America: What went wrong?* Kansas City: Andrews & McMeel.

Bartlett, J. C. & Snelus, P. (1980). Lifespan memory for popular songs. *American Journal of Psychology, 93*, 551–560.

Barlow, J. H., Cullen, L. A., Foster, N. E., Harrison, K., & Wade, M. (1999). Does arthritis influence perceived ability to fulfill a parenting role? Perceptions of mothers, fathers, and grandparents. *Patient Education & Counseling, 37*, 141–151.

Barnhill, W. (1998). On the road: Older drivers under closer scrutiny. *AARP Bulletin, 39*, 1, 14, 18.

Barr, R. A. (1994). Human factors and aging: The operator-task dynamic. In R. P. Abeles, H. C. Gift, & M. G. Ory (Eds.). *Aging and quality of life* (pp. 202–215). New York: Springer.

Bartholomew, K. & Horowitz, L. M. (1991). Attachment styles among young adults: A test of a four-category model. *Journal of Personality & Social Psychology, 61*, 226–244.

Bartoshuk, L. M., Rifkin, B., Marks, L. E., & Bars, P. (1986). Taste and aging. *Journal of Gerontology, 41*, 51–57.

Baruch, G., Barnett, R., & Rivers, C. (1983). *Lifeprints*. New York: McGraw-Hill.

Bass, D. M., Garland, T. N., & Otto, M. E. (1985–1986). Characteristics of hospice patients and their caregivers. *Omega, 16*, 51–68.

Basta, L. L. (1996). *A graceful exit: Life and death on your own terms*. New York: Insight Books, Plenum.

Baugher, R. J., Burger, C., Smith, R., & Wallston, K. A. (1989–1990). A comparison of terminally ill persons at various time periods prior to death. *Omega, 20*, 103–115.

Bayley, N. & Oden, M. (1955). The maintenence of intellectual ability in gifted adults. *Journal of Gerontology, 10*, 91–107.

Beach, S. R., Schulz, R., Yee, J. & Jackson, S. (2000). Negative and positive health effects of caregiving for a disabled spouse: Longitudinal findings from the caregiver health effects study. *Psychology and Aging, 15*, 259–271.

Beatty, W. W., Brumback, R. A., & Vonsattel, J-P. G. (1997). Autopsy-proven Alzheimer diseases in a patient with dementia who retained music skill in life. *Archives of Neurology, 54*, 1448.

Beck, C., Heacock, P., Mercer, S., Walton, C., & Shook, J. (1991). Dressing for success: Promoting independence among cognitively impaired elderly. *Journal of Psychosocial Nursing, 29*, 30–34.

Becker, J. T. & Milke, R. M. (1998). Cognition and aging in a complex work environment: Relationships with performance among air traffic control specialists. *Aviation, Space, & Environmental Medicine, 69*, 944–951.

Bedford, V. H. (1996). Sibling relationships in middle and old age. In R. Blieszner & V. H. Bedford (Eds.), *Aging and the family: Theory and research* (pp. 201–222). Westport, CT: Praeger.

Beekman, A. T. F., Deeg, D. J. H., van Tilburg, T., & Smit, J. H. (1995). Major and minor depression in later life: A study of prevalence and risk factors. *Journal of Affective Disorders, 36*, 65–75.

Belbin, R. M. (1970). The discovery method in training older workers. In H. L. Sheppard (Ed.), *Toward an industrial gerontology*. Cambridge, MA: Schenkman.

Belgrave, L. L. (1988). The effects of race differences in work history, work attitudes, economic resources, and health in women's retirement. *Research on Aging, 10*, 383–398.

Belle, D. (1987). Gender differences in the social moderators of stress. In R. Barrett, L. Biener, & G. Baruch (Eds.), *Gender and stress*, New York: Free Press.

Bellezza, F. S. (1982). Updating memory using mnemonic devices. *Cognitive Psychology, 14*, 301–327.

Belsky, J. (1999). *The psychology of aging*. Pacific Grove, CA: Brooks/Cole.

Belsky, J. K. (1999). *The psychology of aging: Theory, research, & interventions*. Pacific Grove, CA: Brooks/Cole.

Bem, S. L. (1974). The measurement of psychological androgyny. *Journal of Consulting & Clinical Psychology, 42*, 155–162.

Bengston, V. L. & Schaie, K. W. (Eds.). (1999). *Handbook of theories of aging*. New York: Springer.

Berger, R. M. (1982). *Gay and gray: The older homosexual man*. Chicago: University of Illinois Press.

Berger, R. M. (1990). Men together: Understanding the gay couple. *Journal of Homosexuality, 19*, 31–49.

Berger, R., Rothman, I., & Rigaud, G. (1994). Nonvascular causes of impotence. In A. H. Bennett (Ed.), *Impotence: Diagnosis and management of erectile dysfunction* (pp. 106–123). Philadelphia: W. B. Saunders.

Bergman, M. (1966). Hearing in the Mabaans. *Archives of Otolaryngology, 81*, 75–79.

Bergman, M., Blumenfeld, V. G., Casardo, D., Dash, B., Levitt, H., & Margulios, M. K. (1976). Age-related decrement in hearing for speech: Sampling and longitudinal studies. *Journal of Gerontology, 31*, 533–538.

Berkman, L. (1986). Social networks, support, and health: Taking the next step forward. *American Journal of Epidemiology, 123*, 559–562.

Berkman, L. & Breslow, L. (1983). *Health and ways of living: The Alameda County study*. New York: Oxford University Press.

Berkman, L. F. (1995). The role of social relations in health promotion. *Psychosomatic Medicine, 57*, 245–254.

Berry, J. M., West, R. L., & Dennehey, D. M. (1989). Reliability and validity of the Memory Self-Efficacy Questionnaire (MSEQ). *Development Psychology, 25*, 701–713.

Best, D. L., Hamlett, K. W., & Davis, S. W. (1992). Memory complaint and memory performance in the elderly: The effects of memory skill training and expectancy change. *Applied Cognitive Psychology, 6*, 405–416.

Biesmann, H. & Mason, J. M. (1997). Telomere maintenance without telomerase. *Chromosoma, 106*, 63.

Binstock, R. H. & George, L. K. (Eds.) (1996). *Handbook of aging and the social sciences* (4th ed.) New York: Academic Press.

Birren, J. E. (1985). Age, competence, creativity, and wisdom. In R. N. Butler & H. P. Gleason (Eds.), *Productive aging: Enhancing vitality in later life.* (pp. 25–41). New York: Springer.

Birren, J. E. & Clayton, V. (1975). History of gerontology. In D. S. Woodruff & J. E. Birren (Eds.), *Aging: Scientific perspectives and social issues*. New York: Van Nostrand.

Birren, J. E., Woods, A. M., & Williams, M. V. (1980). Behavioral slowing with age: Causes, organization, and consequences. In L. W. Poon (Ed.), *Aging in the 1980s*. Washington, DC: American Psychological Association.

Bishop, J. M. & Krause, D. R. (1984). Depictions of aging and old age on Saturday morning television. *The Gerontologist, 24*, 91–94.

Bjorkstein, J. (1974). Crosslinkage and the aging process. In M. Rockstein, M. L. Sussman, & J. Chesky (Eds.), *Theoretical aspects of aging*. New York: Academic Press, 43.

Black, D. W. & Andreasen, N. C. (1994). Schizophrenia, schizophreniform disorder, and delusional paranoid disorder. In J. A. Talbot, R. E. Hales, & S. C. Yudofsky (Eds.), *American psychiatric press textbook of psychiatry* (pp. 411–463). Washington, DC: American Psychiatric Press.

Black, S. A., & Markides, K. (1994). Americans, Cuban Americans, and Mainland Puerto Ricans. *International Journal of Aging & Human Development, 39*, 97–103.

Blacker, D., Haines, J. L., Rodes, L., Terwedow, H., Harrell, L. E., Perry, R. T., Bassett, S. S., Chase, G., Meyers, D., Albert, M. S., & Tanzi, R. (1997). ApoE-4 and age of onset of Alzheimer's disease. *Neurology, 48*, 139–147.

Bladbjerg, E. M., Andersen-Ranberg, K., de Maat, M. P. M., Kristensen, S. R., Jeune, B., Gram, J., & Jespersen, J. (1999). Longevity is independent of common variations in genes associated with cardiovascular risk. *Thrombosis & Haemostasis, 82*, 1100–1105.

Blair, S. N., Kohl, H. W., III, Paffenbarger, R. S., Clark, D. G., Cooper, K. H., & Gibbons, L. W. (1989). Physical fitness and all-cause mortality: A prospective study of healthy men and women. *Journal of the American Medical Association, 262*, 2395–2401.

Blanchard-Fields, F. & Camp, C. (1990). Affect, individual differences, and real world problem solving across the adult life span. In T. Hess (Ed.), *Aging and cognition: Knowledge organization and utilization* (pp. 461–497). Amsterdam: North Holland.

Blanchard-Fields, F. (1986). Reasoning on social dilemmas varying in emotional saliency: An adult developmental perspective. *Psychology & Aging, 1*, 325–333.

Blanchard-Fields, F., Jahnke, H. C., & Camp, C. (1995). Age differences in problem-solving style: The role of emotional saliency. *Psychology & Aging, 10*, 173–180.

Blazer, D. G., Hays, J. C., & Foley, D. J. (1995). Sleep complaints in older adults: A racial comparison. *Journal of Gerontology: Medical Sciences, 50A*, M280–M284.

Blazer, D., Hughes, D. C., & George, L. K. (1987). The epidemiology of depression in an elderly community population. *Gerontologist, 27*, 281–287.

Blendon, R., Szaley, U. S., & Knox, R. A. (1994). Should physicians aid their patients in dying: The public perspective. *Journal of the American Medical Association, 267*, 2658–2662.

Bliatout, B. T. (1993). Hmong death customs: Traditional and acculturated. In D. P. Irish, K. F. Lundquist, & V. J. Nelsen (Eds.), *Ethnic variations in dying, death, and grief: Diversity in universality* (pp. 79–100). Washington, DC: Taylor & Francis.

Blick, K. A. & Howe, J. B. (1984). A comparison of the emotional content of dreams recalled by young and elderly women. *Journal of Psychology, 116*, 143–146.

Bogorad, L. (1987). Emerging trends in rental retirement housing. *Journal of Real Estate Development* (Winter), 7–17.

Bolton, I. (1986). Death of a child by suicide. In T. Rando (Ed.), *Parental loss of a child* (pp. 201–212). Champaign, IL: Research Press.

Boon, S. D. & Brussoni, M. J. (1996). Young adults' relationships with their "closest" grandparents: Examining emotional closeness. *Journal of Social Behavior & Personality, 11*, 439–458.

Booth-Kewley, S. & Vickers, R. R. (1994). Associations between major domains of personality and health behavior. *Journal of Personality, 62*, 281–298.

Boring, E. G. (1950). *A history of experimental psychology*. New York: Appleton-Century-Crofts.

Bossé, R., Aldwin, C. M., Levenson, M., Spiro, A. III, Mroczek, D. K. (1993). Changes in social support after retirement: Longitudinal findings from the normative aging study. *Journal of Gerontology: Psychological Sciences, 48*, P210–217.

Botwinick, J. & Thompson, L. W. (1966). Components of reaction time in relation to age and sex. *Journal of Genetic Psychology, 108*, 175–183.

Botwinick, J. (1978). *Aging and behavior.* New York: Springer Publishing Co.

Botwinick, J. (1984). *Aging and behavior: A comprehensive integration of research findings.* New York: Springer.

Boucher, N., Dufeu-Duchesne, T., Vicaut, E., Farge, D., Effros, R. B., & Schächter, F. (1998). CD28 expression in T cell aging and human longevity. *Experimental Gerontology, 33*, 267–282.

Bound, J., Duncan, G. J., Laren, D. S., & Oleinick, L. (1991). Poverty dynamics in widowhood. *Journal of Gerontology: Social Sciences, 58*, S115–S124.

Bowlby, J. (1980). *Attachment and loss: Loss, sadness, and depression, 3.* New York: Basic Books.

Bowling, A. (1987). Mortality after bereavement: A review of the literature on survival periods and factors affecting survival. *Social Science & Medicine, 24*, 117–124.

Brackbill, Y., & Kitch, D. (1991). Intergenerational relationships: A social exchange perspective on joint living arrangements among the elderly and their relatives. *Journal of Aging Studies, 5*, 77–97.

Brand, F. N., Kiely, D. K., Kannel, W. B., & Myers, R. H. (1992). Family patterns of coronary heart disease mortality: The Framingham longevity study. *Journal of Clinical Epidemiology, 45*, 169–174.

Brandt, B. (1989). A place for her death. *Humanistic Judaism, 17*(3), 83–85.

Brandtstädter, J. & Greve, W. (1994). The aging self: Stabilizing and protective processes. *Developmental Review, 14*, 52–80.

Brandtstädter, J. (1992). Personal control over development: Some developmental implications of self-efficacy. In R. Schwarzer (Ed.), *Self-efficacy: Thought control of action* (pp. 127–145). Washington, DC: Hemisphere.

Brant, L. J. & Fozard, J. L. (1990). Age changes in pure tone thresholds in a longitudinal study of normal aging. *Journal of the Acoustic Society of America, 88*, 813–820.

Brecher, E. M. (1984). *Love, sex, and aging.* Boston: Little, Brown.

Breckenridge, J. N., Gallagher, D., Thompson, L. W., & Peterson, J. (1986). Characteristic depressive symptoms of bereaved elders. *Journal of Gerontology, 41*, 163–168.

Bretschneider, J. G. & McCoy, N. L. (1988). Sexual interest and behavior in healthy 80- to 102-year olds. *Archives of Sexual Behavior, 17*, 109–129.

Brett, D. (1992). *More Annie stories: Therapeutic storytelling techniques.* New York: Magination Press-Brunner/Mazel.

Brink, S. (1998). *Housing older people: An international perspective.* New Brunswick, NJ: Transaction Publishers.

Brock, D. (1989). Death and dying. In R. M. Veatch (Ed.), *Medical ethics* (2nd ed., 329–356) Boston: Jones and Bartlett.

Brod, M., Mendelsohn, G. A., & Roberts, B. (1998). Patients' experiences of Parkinson's disease. *Journal of Gerontology: Psychological Sciences, 53B*, P213–P222.

Brody, E. M. (1990). *Women in the middle: Their parent-care years.* New York: Springer.

Brody, H., Campbell, M. L., Faber-Langendoen, K., & Ogle, K. (1997). Withdrawing intensive life sustaining treatment: Recommendations for compassionate clinical management. *New England Journal of Medicine, 336*, 652–657.

Brokenleg, M. & Middleton, D. (1993). Native Americans: Adapting, yet retaining. In D. P. Irish, K. F. Lundquist, & V. J. Nelsen (Eds.), *Ethnic variations in dying, death, and grief: Diversity in university* (pp. 101–113). Washington, DC: Taylor & Francis.

Brooks, G. (2000). At the Burns-Coopers. In E. P. Stoller & R. C. Gibson (Eds.), *Worlds of difference: Inequality in the aging experience* (pp. 187–188), Thousand Oaks, CA: Pine Forge Press.

Brotons, M., Koger, S., & Pickett-Cooper, P. (1997). Music and dementias: A review of literature. *Journal of Music Therapy, 34*, 204–245.

Brousset, P., Saati, T. A., Chaouche, N., Zenou, R. C., Mazerolles, C., & Delsol, G. (1997). Methods for detection of telomerase activity in tissue samples: Diagnostic and pronostic value. *Annales de Pathologie, 17*, 364.

Brown, A. S. (1989). *How to increase your memory power.* Glenview, IL: Scott Foresman.

Brown, C. J., Mutran, E. J., Sloane, P. D., & Long, K. M. (1998). Primary care physicians knowledge and behavior related to Alzheimer's disease. *Journal of Applied Gerontology, 17*, 462–479.

Brown, S. W. (1985). Time perception and attention: The effects of prospective versus retrospective paradigms and task demands on perceived duration. *Perception & Psychophysics, 38*, 115–124.

Bruce, P. R., Coyne, A. C., & Botwinick, J. (1982). Adult age differences in metamemory. *Journal of Gerontology, 37*, 354–357.

Bühler, C. (1953). The curve of life as studied in biographies. *Journal of Applied Science, 19*, 405–409.

Bühler, C. (1968). The general structure of the human life cycle. In C. Bühler & F. Massarik (Eds.), *The course of human life* (pp. 12–26). New York: Springer.

Bühler, C. (1982). Meaningfulness of the biographical approach. In L. R. Allman & D. I Jaffe (Eds.), *Readings in adult psychology: Contemporary perspectives* (pp. 30–37). New York: Harper & Row.

Bucholz, K. K. (1992). Alcohol abuse and dependence from a psychiatric epidemiologic perspective. *Alcohol Health & Research World, 16*, 197–208.

Buehlman, K. T., Gottman, J. M., & Katz, L. F. (1992). How a couple views their past predicts their future: Predicting divorce from an oral history interview. *Journal of Family Psychology, 5*, 295–318.

Bugen, L. A. (1979). *Death and dying: Theory/research/practice.* Dubuque, IA: Wm. C. Brown.

Bumpass, L. L., Martin, T. C., & Sweet, J. A. (1991). The impact of family background and early marital factors on marital disruption. *Journal of Family Issues, 12*, 22–42.

Buono, M. D., Urciuoli, O., & de Leo, D. (1998). Quality of life and longevity: A study of centenarians. *Age & Ageing, 27,* 207–216.

Burgio, L., Scilley, K., Hardin, J., Hsu, C., & Yancey, J. (1996). Environmental "white noise": An intervention for verbally agitated nursing home residents. *Journal of Gerontology: Psychological Sciences, 51B,* P364–P373.

Burke, D. M. & Light, L. L. (1981). Memory and aging: The role of retrieval processes. *Psychological Bulletin, 90,* 513–546.

Burks, V. K., Lund, D. A., Gregg, C. H., & Bluhm, H. P. (1988). Bereavement and remarriage for older adults. *Death Studies, 12,* 51–60.

Butler, R. N. (1969). Ageism: Another form of bigotry. *Gerontologist, 9,* 243–246.

Butler, R. N., Lewis, M. I., & Sunderland, T. (1998). *Aging and mental health: Positive psychosocial and biomedical approaches* (5th ed.). Boston: Allyn & Bacon.

Butler, S. M., Ashford, J. W., & Snowdon, D. A. (1996). Age, education, and changes in the Mini-Mental State Exam scores of older women: Findings from the nun study. *Journal of the American Geriatric Society, 44,* 675–681.

Butterfield, D. A., Koppal, T., Subramaniam, R., & Yatin, S. (1999). Vitamin E as an antioxidant/free radical scavenger against amyloid β-peptide-induced oxidative stress in neocortical synaptosomal membrane and hippocampal neurons in culture: Insights into Alzheimer's disease. *Reviews in the Neurosciences, 10,* 141–149.

Calhoun, L. G. & Tedeschi, R. G. (1989–1990). Positive aspects of critical life problems: Recollections of grief. *Omega, 20,* 265–272.

Calmels, P., Ecochard, R., Blanchon, M. A., Charbonnier, C., Cassou, B., & Gonthier, R. (1998). Relation between locomotion impairment, functional independence in retirement, and occupational strain resulting from work carried out during working life. Study of a sample population of 350 miners in the Loire valley in France. *Journal of Epidemiology & Community Health, 52,* 283–288.

Camp, C. J. & Stevens, A. B. (1990). Spaced-retrieval: A memory intervention for dementia of the Alzheimer's type (DAT). *Clinical Gerontologist, 10,* 58–61.

Camp, C. J. (1998). Memory interventions for normal and pathological older adults. In R. Schulz, G. Maddox, & M. P. Lawton (Eds.), *Annual Review of Gerontology & Geriatrics, 18* (pp. 155–189). New York: Springer.

Camp, C. J., Foss, J. W., Stevens, A. B., Reichard, C. C., McKitrick, L. A., & O'Hanlon, A. M. (1993). Memory training in normal and demented elderly populations: The *E-I-E-I-O* model. *Experimental Aging Research, 19,* 277–290.

Campbell, A. J., Reinken, J., Allan, B. C., & Martinez, G. S. (1981). Falls in old age: A study of frequency and related clinical factors. *Age & Ageing, 10,* 264–270.

Campione, W. A. (1988). Predicting participation in retirement preparation programs. *Journal of Gerontology: Social Sciences, 43,* S91–S95.

Cantor, M. (1983). Strain among caregivers: A study of experience in the United States. *The Gerontologist, 23,* 587–604.

Carey, R. G. (1977). The widowed: A year later. *Journal of Counseling Psychology, 24,* 125–131.

Carmelli, D., Swan, G. E., & Cardon, L. R. (1995). Genetic mediation in the relationship of education to cognitive function in older people. *Psychology & Aging, 10,* 48–53.

Carnes, B. A., Olshansky, S. J., & Grahn, D. (1996). Continuing the search for a law of mortality. *Population & Development Review, 19,* 231–264.

Carnes, B. A., Olshansky, S. J., Gavrilov, L., Gavrilova, N., & Grahn, D. (1999). Human longevity: Nature vs. nurture—fact or fiction. *Perspectives in Biology & Medicine, 42,* 422–441.

Carr, D. B., LaBarge, E., Dunnigan, K., & Storandt, M. (1998). Differentiating drivers with dementia of the Alzheimer's type from healthy older persons with a traffic sign naming test. *Journal of Gerontology: Medical Sciences, 53A,* M135–M139.

Carskadon, M. A. (1982). Sleep fragmentation, sleep loss, and sleep needs in the elderly. *Gerontologist, 22,* 187.

Carstensen, L. L. & Charles, S. T. (1998). Emotion in the second half of life. *Current Directions in Psychological Science, 7,* 144–149.

Carstensen, L. L. & Freund, A. M. (1994). The resilience of the aging self. *Developmental Review, 14,* 81–92.

Carstensen, L. L. (1992). Social and emotional patterns in adulthood: Support for socioemotional selectivity theory. *Psychology and Aging, 7,* 331–338.

Carstensen, L. L. (1995). Evidence for a lifespan theory of socioemotional selectivity. *Current Directions in Psychological Science, 4,* 151–156.

Carstensen, L. L., Gottman, J. M., & Levenson, R. W. (1995). Emotional behavior in long-term marriage. *Psychology & Aging, 10,* 140–149.

Carter, R. (1994). *Helping yourself help others: A book for caregivers.* New York: Times Books.

Caserta, M. S., & Lund, D. A. (1993). Intrapersonal resources and the effectiveness of self-help groups for bereaved older adults. *The Gerontologist, 33,* 619–629.

Cavanaugh, J. C. & Green, E. E. (1990). I believe, therefore I can: Self-efficacy beliefs in memory aging. In E. A. Lovelace (Ed.), *Aging and cognition: Mental processes, self-awareness, and interventions.* (pp. 189–230) Amsterdam: North Holland.

Cavanaugh, J. C. (1986–1987). Age differences in adults' self-reports of memory ability: It depends on how and what you ask. *International Journal of Aging & Human Development, 24,* 241–277.

Cavanaugh, J. C. (1996). Memory self-efficacy as a key to understanding memory change. In F. Blanchard-Fields & T. M. Hess (Eds.), *Perspectives on cognitive changes in adulthood and aging.* (pp. 488–507). New York: McGraw-Hill.

Cavanaugh, J. C. (1998). Friendships and social networks among older people. In I. H. Nordhus, G. R. Vanden Bos, S. Berg, & P. Fromholt (Eds.), *Clinical geropsychology* (pp. 137–140). Washington, DC: APA.

Ceci, S. J. & Liker, J. K. (1986). A day at the races: A study of IQ, expertise, and cognitive complexity. *Journal of Experimental Psychology: General, 115,* 255–266.

Centers for Disease Control. (1989). Tobacco use by adults. *Morbidity and Mortality Weekly Report, 38,* 685–687.

Centers for Disease Control. (1991a). Cigarette smoking among adults—United States 1988. *Mortality and Morbidity Weekly Report, 40,* 757–759, 765.

Centers for Disease Control. (1991b). Cigarette smoking among youth—United States 1989. *Mortality and Morbidity Weekly Report, 40,* 712–715.

Centofanti, M. (1998). Fear of Alzheimer's undermines health of elderly patients. *APA Monitor, 29,* 1 & 33.

Cerella, J., Rybash, J., Hoyer, W., & Commons, M. L. (1993). *Adult information processing: Limits on loss.* San Diego, CA: Academic Press.

Chambre, S. M. (1993). Volunteerism by elders: Past trends and future prospects. *Gerontologist, 33,* 221–227.

Chan-Palay, V. & Asan, E. (1989). Alterations in catecholamine neurons of the locus coeruleus in senile dementia of the Alzheimer's type and Parkinson's disease with and without dementia and depression. *The Journal of Comparative Neurology, 287,* 373–392.

Charlotte Observer. (January 7, 1995). 6A.

Charness, N. (1981). Search in chess: Age and skill differences. *Journal of Experimental Psychology: Human Perception & Performance, 7,* 467–476.

Charness, N. (1985). *Age and expertise: Responding to Talland's challenge.* Paper presented at the George A. Talland Memorial Conference on Aging and Memory, Cape Cod, MA.

Charness, N. & Bosman, E. A. (1992). Human factors and aging. In F. I. M. Craik & T. A. Salthouse (Eds.), *The handbook of aging & cognition* (pp. 495–551). Hillsdale, NJ: Erlbaum.

Charness, N. & Holley, P. (2001). Human factors and environmental support for Alzheimer's disease. *Aging and Mental Health, 5,* 65–3.

Chase, W. G. & Simon, H. A. (1973). The mind's eye in chess. In W. G. Chase (Ed.), *Visual information processing.* (pp. 215–281). San Diego, CA: Academic Press.

Cheesman, M. F. (1997). Speech perception by elderly listeners: Basic knowledge and implications for audiology. *Journal of Speech-Language Pathology and Audiology, 21,* 104–110.

Cherlin, A. & Furstenberg, F. (1985). Styles and strategies of grandparenting. In V. L. Bengston & J. Robertson (Eds.), *Grandparenthood.* Beverly Hills, CA: Sage.

Cheung, C. & Ngan, M. (2000). Contributions of volunteer networking to isolated seniors in Hong Kong. *Journal of Gerontological Social Work, 33,* 79–100.

Childress, A. (2000). Like one of the family. In E. P. Stoller & R. C. Gibson (Eds.), *Worlds of difference: Inequality in the aging experience* (pp. 189–190), Thousand Oaks, CA: Pine Forge Press.

Chipperfield, J. G., & Havens, B. (2001). Gender differences in the relationship between marital status transitions and life satisfaction in later life. *Journal of Gerontology: Psychological Sciences, 56B,* p176–186.

Chiriboga, D. A. (1989). Mental health at the midpoint: Crisis, challenge, or relief? In S. Hunter & M. Sundel (Eds.), *Midlife myths: Issues, findings, and practical implications* (pp. 116–144). Newbury Park, CA: Sage.

Choi, N. G. (1997). Racial differences in retirement income: The roles of public and private income sources. *Journal of Aging & Social Policy, 9,* 21–42.

Chown, S. (1961). Age and the rigidities. *Journal of Gerontology, 16,* 353–362.

Christensen, P. R. & Guilford, J. P. (1957a). *Associational fluency I, Form A.* Redwood City, CA: Mind Garden Inc.

Christensen, P. R. & Guilford, J. P. (1957b). *Ideational Fluency I, Form A.* Redwood City, CA: Mind Garden Inc.

Christensen, P. R. & Guilford, J. P. (1958a). *Expressional Fluency, Form A.* Redwood City, CA: Mind Garden Inc.

Christensen, P. R. & Guilford, J. P. (1958b). *Word Fluency, Form A.* Redwood City, CA: Mind Garden Inc.

Christensen, P. R., Merrifield, P. R., & Guilford, J. P. (1958). *Consequences.* Redwood City, CA: Mind Garden Inc.

Christenson, C. & Johnson, A. B. (1973). Sexual patterns in a group of older never-married women. *Journal of Geriatric Psychiatry, 6,* 80–98.

Chun, M. R., Schofield, P., Stern, Y., Tatemechi, T. K., & Mayeux, R. (1998). The epidemiology of dementia among the elderly: Experience in a community-based registry. In M. F. Folstein (Ed.), *Neurobiology of primary dementia* (pp. 1–26). Washington, DC: American Psychiatric Press.

Cicirelli, V. G. (1985). The role of siblings as family caregivers. In W. J. Sauer & R. T. Coward (Eds.), *Social support networks and the care of the elderly* (pp. 93–107). New York: Springer.

Clancy, S. M. & Hoyer, W. J. (1988). Effects of age and skill on domain specific search. In V. L. Pateri & G. J. Groen (Eds.), *Proceedings of the tenth conference of the Cognitive Science Society.* (pp. 398–404). Hillsdale, NJ: Erlbaum.

Clark, M. C. & Gaide, M. S. (1986). Choosing the right assistive device: A capability-demand approach. *Generations, 11,* 18–21.

Clark, M. C., Foos, P. W., & Faucher, M. H. (1995). You can touch this: Simulation exercises for aging and disability. *Educational Gerontology, 21,* 643–651.

Clark, M. C., Foos, P. W., Boone, D., Haught, C., Hicks, J., Murphey, C., & Vagnone, N. (2001, March). *Dream a little dream: Age and gender differences.* Paper presented at the annual meetings of the Southeastern Psychological Association, Atlanta, GA.

Clark, R. F. & Goate, A. M. (1993). Molecular genetics of Alzheimer's disease. *Archives of Neurology, 50,* 1164–1167.

Clarke, S. (1995). *Advance report of final divorce statistics, 1989 and 1990, 43*(9). Hyattsville, MD: National Center for Health Statistics.

Clayton, P. J., Halikes, J. A., & Maurice, W. L. (1971). The bereavement of the widowed. *Diseases of the nervous system, 32,* 597–604.

Clayton, V. P. & Birren, J. E. (1980). The development of wisdom across the lifespan: A reexamination of an ancient topic. *Life-Span Development & Behavior, 3,* 103–135.

Cleek, M. G. & Pearson, T. A. (1985). Perceived causes of divorce: An analysisn of interrelationships. *Journal of Marriage & the Family, 47,* 179–183.

Cleveland, J. N. & Shore, L. M. (1996). Work and employment. In J. E. Birren (Ed.), *Encyclopedia of Gerontology, 2,* (pp. 627–639). New York: Academic Press.

Cobb, S. (1976). Social support as a moderator of life stress. *Psychosomatic Medicine, 38,* 300–314.

Coblenz, J. M., Mattis, S., Zingesser, L. H., Kasoff, S. S., Wisniewski, H. M., & Katzman, R. (1973). Presenile dementia: Clinical aspects and evaluation of cerebrospinal fluid dynamics. *Archives of Neurology, 29,* 299–308.

Cockerham, W. C. (1991). *This aging society.* Englewood Cliffs, NJ: Prentice Hall.

Cockerham, W. C., Sharp, K., & Wilcox, J. (1983). Aging and perceived health status. *Journal of Gerontology, 38,* 349–355.

Cohen, C., Teresi, J., & Holmes, D. (1985). Social networks, stress, and physical health: A longitudinal study of an inner-city elderly population. *Journal of Gerontology, 40,* 478–486.

Cohen, J. S., Fihn, S. D., Boyko, E. J., Jonsen, A. R., & Wood, R. W. (1994). Attitudes toward assisted suicide and euthanasia among physicians in Washington state. *New England Journal of Medicine, 331,* 89–94.

Cohen, K. P. (1979). *Hospice: Prescription for terminal care.* Germantown, MD: Aspen.

Cohen, S. (1988). Psychosocial models of the role of social support in the etiology of physical disease. *Health Psychology, 7,* 269–297.

Cohen, S. & Herbert, T. B. (1996). Health psychology: Psychological factors and physical disease from the perspective of human psychoneuroimmunology. *Annual Review of Psychology, 47,* 113–142.

Cohen, S., Mermelstein, R., Kamarck, T., & Hoberman, H. M. (1985). Measuring the functional components of social support. In I. G. Sarason & B. R. Sarason (Eds.), *Social support: Theory, research, and applications* (pp. 73–94). The Hague: Martinus Nijhoff.

Cohler, B. J. (1982). Personal narrative and life course. In P. Baltes & O. G. Brim (Eds.), *Life span development and behavior* (Vol. 4, pp. 205–241). New York: Academic Press.

Cohn, J. & Sugar, J. A. (1991). Determinants of quality of life in institutions: Perceptions of frail older residents, staff, and families. In J. E. Birren & J.E Lubben (Eds). *The concept and measurement of quality of life in the frail elderly* (pp. 28–49). San Diego: Academic Press.

Cohn, L., Feller, A. G., Draper, M. W., Rudman, J. W., & Rudman, D. (1993). Carpal tunnel syndrome and gynecomastia during growth hormone treatment of elderly men with low circulating IGF-I concentrations. *Clinical Endocrinology, 39,* 417–425.

Cole, E. R. & Stewart, A. J. (1996). Meanings of political participation among Black and White women: Political identity and social responsibility. *Journal of Personality & Social Psychology, 71,* 130–140.

Coleman, P. G. (1999). Creating a life story: The task of reconciliation. *Gerontologist, 39,* 133–139.

Coleman, P. G., Ivani-Chalian, C., & Robinson, M. (1998). The story continues: Persistence of life themes in old age. *Ageing & Society, 18,* 389–419.

Coleman, P. G., Ivani-Chalian, C., & Robinson, M. (1999). Self and identity in advanced old age: Validation of theory through longitudinal case analysis. *Journal of Personality, 67,* 819–849.

Colonia-Willner, R. (1998). Practical intelligence at work: Relationship between aging and cognitive efficiency among managers in a bank environment. *Psychology & Aging, 13,* 45–57.

Colsher, P. L., Dorfman, L. T., & Wallace, R. B. (1988). Specific health conditions and work-retirement status among the elderly. *Journal of Applied Gerontology, 7,* 485–503.

Comfort, A. (1964). *Ageing: The biology of senescence.* New York: Holt, Rinehart, & Winston.

Conger, R. D., Cui, M., Bryant, C. M., & Elder, G. H., Jr. (2000). Competence in early adult romantic relationships: A developmental perspective on family influences. *Journal of Personality & Social Psychology, 79,* 224–237.

Congressional Budget Office. (1999). Projections of expenditures for long-term care services for the elderly. Available from *http://www.cbo.gov.* Accessed August 9, 2001.

Connell, B. R. & Sanford, J. A. (1999). Research implications of universal design. In E. Steinfeld & G.S. Danford (Eds.). *Enabling environments: Measuring the impact of environment on disability and rehabilitation* (pp. 35–57). New York: Plenum Press.

Connides, I. A. (1992). Life transitions and the sibling tie: A qualitative study. *Journal of Marriage & the Family, 54,* 972–982.

Connides, I. A. (1994). Sibling support in older age. *Journal of Gerontology: Social Sciences, 49,* S309–S317.

Conwell, Y. (1995). Suicide among elderly persons. *Psychiatric Services, 46,* 563–564.

Cook, A. S., & Oltjenbruns, K. A. (1998). *Dying and grieving: Life span and family perspectives.* New York: Harcourt Brace College Publishers.

Cooney, T. M., Schaie, K. W., & Willis, S. L. (1988). The relationship between prior functioning on cognitive and personality variables and subject attrition in longitudinal research. *Journal of Gerontology: Psychological Sciences, 43,* P12–P17.

Cooper, K. L. & Guttman, D. L. (1987). Gender identity and ego mastery style in middle-aged, pre- and post-empty nest women. *Gerontologist, 27,* 347–352.

Corgiat, M. D., Templer, D. I., & Newell, T. C. (1989). The effects of presentation modality, task demand, and content structure on age-related memory differences for prose. *International Journal of Aging & Human Development, 29,* 53–65.

Cornelius, S. W. (1990). Aging and everyday cognitive abilities. In T. M. Hess (Ed.), *Aging and cognition: Knowledge organization and utilization* (pp. 411–459). Amsterdam: Elsevier.

Cornelius, S. W. & Caspi, A. (1987). Everyday problem solving in adulthood and old age. *Psychology & Aging, 2,* 144–153.

Costa. P. T., Jr. & McCrae, R. R. (1988). Personality in adulthood: A six year longitudinal study of self-reports and spouse ratings on the NEO Personality Inventory. *Journal of Personality & Social Psychology, 54,* 853–863.

Costa, P. T., Jr. & McCrae, R. R. (1994). Set like plaster? Evidence for the stability of adult personality. In T. E. Heatherton & J. L. Weinberger (Eds.), *Can personality change?* (pp. 21–41). Washington, DC: American Psychological Association.

Costa, P. T., Jr., McCrae, R. R., Zonderman, A. B., Barbano, H. E., Lebowitz, B., & Larson, D. M. (1986). Cross-sectional studies of personality in a national sample: 2. Stability in neuroticism, extraversion, and openness. *Psychology & Aging, 1,* 144–149.

Costa, P. T., Jr., Metter, E. J., & McCrae, R. R. (1994). Personality stability and its contribution to successful aging. *Journal of Geriatric Psychiatry, 27,* 41–59.

Costa, P. T., Jr., Yang, J., & McCrae, R. R. (1998). Aging and personality traits: Generalizations and clinical implications. In I. H. Nordhus, G. R. VandenBos, S. Berg, & P. Fromholt (Eds.), *Clinical geropsychology* (pp. 33–48). Washington, DC: American Psychological Association.

Costa, P. T., McCrae, R. R., & Zonderman, A. B. (1987). Environmental and dispositional influences on well-being: Longitudinal follow-up of an American national sample. *British Journal of Psychology, 78,* 299–306.

Costa, P. T., Zonderman, A. B., McCrae, R. R., Cornoni-Huntley, J., Locke, B. Z., & Barbano, H. E. (1987). Longitudinal analysis of psychological well-being in a national sample: Stability of mean levels. *Journal of Gerontology, 42,* 50–55.

Cowan, C. P. & Cowan, P. A. (1987). Men's involvement in parenthood: Identifying the antecedents and understanding the barriers. In P. W. Berman & F. A. Pedersen (Eds.), *Men's transitions to parenthood: Longitudinal studies of early family experience* (pp. 79–109). Hillsdale, NJ: Erlbaum.

Coward. R. T., Horne, C., & Dwyer, J. W. (1992). Demographic perspectives on gender and family caregiving. In J. W. Dwyer & R. T. Coward (Eds.), *Gender, families, and elder care* (pp. 18–33). Newbury Park, CA: Sage.

Cowper, D. C., Longino, C. F., Jr., Kubal, J. D., Manheim, L. M., Dienstfrey, S. J., & Palmer, J. M. (2000). The retirement migration of U. S. veterans, 1960, 1970, 1980, and 1990. *Journal of Applied Gerontology, 19,* 123–137.

Coyne, A. C., Eiler, J. M., Vanderplas, J., & Botwinick, J. (1979). Stimulus persistence and age. *Experimental Aging Research, 5,* 263–270.

Craik, F. I. M. & Jennings, J. M. (1992). Human memory. In F. I. M. Craik & T. A. Salthouse (Eds.), *The handbook of aging and cognition* (pp. 51–110). Hillsdale, NJ: Erlbaum.

Craik, F. I. M. & Salthouse, T. A. (Eds.). (1992). *The handbook of aging and cognition.* Hillsdale, NJ: Erlbaum.

Creasey, G. L. & Kaliher, G. (1994). Age differences in grandchildren's perceptions of relations with grandparents. *Journal of Adolescence, 17,* 411–426.

Cress, M. E., Buchner, D. M., Questad, K. A., Esselman, P. C., deLateur, B. J., & Schwartz, R. S. (1999). Exercise: Effects on physical functional performance in independent older adults. *Journal of Gerontology: Medical Sciences, 54A,* M242–M248.

Crimmins, E. M., Reynolds, S. L., & Saito, Y. (1999). Trends in health and ability to work among the older working-age population. *Journal of Gerontology: Social Sciences, 54B,* S31–S40.

Cruzan vs. Director, Missouri Department of Health, 110S. Ct. 2841 (1990).

Crystal, S. & Shea, D. (1990). Cumulative advantage, cumulative disadvantage, and inequality among elderly people. *Gerontologist, 30,* 437–443.

Csikszentmihalyi, M. (1996). *Creativity: Flow and the psychology of discovery and invention.* New York: Harper-Collins.

Cumming, R. G., Salkeld, G., Thomas, M., & Szonyi, G. (2000). Prospective study of the impact of fear of falling on activities of daily living, SF-35 scores, and nursing home admission. *Journal of Gerontology: Medical Sciences, 55A,* M299–M305.

Cunningham, W. R. & Brookbank, J. W. (1988). *Gerontology: The Psychology, Biology, and Sociology of Aging.* New York: Harper & Row.

Curran, S., Hindmarch, I., Wattis, J. P., & Shillingford, C. (1990). Critical flicker fusion in normal elderly subjects: A cross-sectional community study. *Current Psychology: Research & Reviews, 9,* 25–34.

Cutler, S. J. & Hendricks, J. (1990). Leisure and time use across the life course. In R. H. Binstock & L. K. George (Eds.), *Handbook of aging and the social sciences* (3rd ed., pp. 169–185). New York: Academic Press.

Cutter, M. A. G. (1991). Euthanasia: Reassessing the boundaries. *Journal of National Institute of Health Research, 3,* 59–61.

Czaja, S. J. (2001). Technological change and the older worker. In J. E. Birren & K. W. Schaie (Eds.), *Handbook of the psychology of aging* (5th ed., pp. 547–568). San Diego, CA: Academic Press.

Czaja, S. J., Weber, R. A., Nair, S. N., & Clark, M. C. (1993). A human factors analysis of ADL activities: A capability-demand approach (Special Issue). *Journal of Gerontology, 47,* 44–48.

Dail, P. W. (1988). Prime-time television portrayals of older adults in the context of family life. *The Gerontologist, 28,* 700–706.

Dainoff, M. (1989). Death and other losses. *Humanistic Judaism, 17,* 63–67.

Danner, D. D., Snowdon, D. A., & Friesen, W. V. (2001). Positive emotions in early life and longevity: Findings from the Nun study. *Journal of Personality and Social Psychology, 80,* 804–813.

Davie, G. & Vincent, J. (1998). Progress report religion and old age. *Aging & Society, 18,* 101–110.

Davies, R., Lacks, P., Storandt, M., Bertelson, A. D. (1986). Countercontrol treatment of sleep-maintenance insomnia in relation to age. *Psychology & Aging, 1,* 233–238.

de Benedictis, G., Rose, G., Carrieri, G., de Luca, M., Falcone, E., Passarino, G., Bonafé, M., Monti, D., Baggio, G., Bertolini, S., Mari, D., Mattace, R., & Franceschi, C. (1999). Mitochondrial DNA inherited variants are associated with successful aging and longevity in humans. *FASEB Journal, 13*, 1532–1536.

De Strooper, B. & König, G. (2001). An inflammatory drug prospect. *Nature, 414*, 159–169.

de Zwart, B. C., Broersen, J. P., Frings-Dresen, M. H., & van Dijk, F. J. (1997). Repeated survey on changes musculoskeletal complaints relative to age and work demands. *Occupational & Environmental Medicine, 54*, 793–799.

DeArmond, S. J. (1998). Prion diseases: The spectrum of etiologic and pathogenic mechanisms. In M. F. Folstein (Ed.), *Neurobiology of primary dementia* (pp. 83–118). Washington, DC: American Psychiatric Press.

Deberdt, W. (1994). Interaction between psychological and pharmocological treatment in cognitive impairment. *Life Sciences, 55*, 2057–2066.

Dement, W., Richardson, G., Prinz, P., Carskadon, M., Kripke, D., & Czeisler, C. (1985). Changes of sleep and wakefulness with age. In C. E. Finch & E. L. Schneider (Eds.), *Handbook of the biology of aging* (2nd edition). New York: Van Nostrand Reinhold, 692–717.

Demos, V. & Jache, A. (1981, September 22). Return to sender please. *Women's Day*, 20.

Dennis, H. (1989). The current state of preretirement planning. *Generations, 13*, 38–41.

Dennis, H. & Migliaccio, J. (1997, Summer). Redefining retirement: The baby boomer challenge. *Generations*, 45–50.

Dennis, W. (1966). Creative productivity between the ages of twenty and eighty years. *Journal of Gerontology, 21*, 1–18.

Dennis, W. (1968). Creative productivity between the ages of twenty and eighty years. In B. L. Neugarten (Ed.), *Middle age and aging*. Chicago: University of Chicago Press.

DePaolo, S. J., Neimeyer, R. A., Lupfer, M. B., & Fiedler, J. (1992). Death concerns and attitudes toward the elderly in nursing home personnel. Special issue: Death attitudes. *Death Studies, 16*, 537–555.

Desmond, D. W. & Tatemichi, T. K. (1998). Vascular dementia. In M. F. Folstein (Ed.), *Neurobiology of primary dementia* (pp. 167–190). Washington, DC: American Psychiatric Press.

DeSpelder, L. A., & Strickland, A. L. (1992). *The last dance: Encountering death and dying*. Mountain View, CA: Mayfield Press.

deVries, B., Bluck, S., & Birren, J. E. (1993). The understanding of death and dying in a lifespan perspective. *The Gerontologist, 33*, 366–372.

Dickey, M. (1996). Melatonin: Does it work? *The Washingtonian, 31*, 33.

Diehl, M., Elnick, A. B., Bourbeasu, L. S., & Labouvie-Vief, G. (1998). Adult attachment styles: Their relations to family context and personality. *Jour-nal of Personality & Social Psychology, 74*, 1656–1669.

Diener, E. & Suh, M. E. (1988). Subjective well-being and age: An international analysis. In K. W. Schaie & M. P.

Lawton (Eds.), *Annual review of gerontology & geriatrics, 17* (pp. 304–324). New York: Springer.

Diener, E. & Suh, M. E. (1998). Subjective well-being and age: An international analysis. In K. W. Schaie & M. P. Lawton (Eds.), *Annual review of gerontolgy and geriatrics: Vol. 17. Focus on emotion and adult development* (pp. 304–324). New York: Springer.

Diener, E., Suh, E. M., Lucas, R. E., & Smith, H. L. (1999). Subjective well-being: Three decades of progress. *Psychological Bulletin, 125*, 276–302.

DiGiovanna, A. G. (1994). *Human aging: Biological perspectives*. New York: McGraw-Hill.

Dinsmoor, R. (1996). Elixers of youth: Which work, which don't, which might? *Diabetes Self-Management, 13*, 51–58.

Dittman-Kohl, F. & Baltes, P. B. (1990). Toward a neofunctionalist conception of adult intellectual development: Wisdom as a prototypical case of intellectual growth. In C. Alexander & E. Langer (Eds.), *Higher stages of human development: Perspectives on adult growth*. (pp. 54–78). New York: Oxford University Press.

Dittman-Kohli, F., Lachman, M. E., Kliegl, R., & Baltes, P. B. (1991). Effects of cognitive training and testing on intellectual efficacy beliefs in elderly adults. *Journal of Gerontology: Psychological Sciences, 46*, P162–P164.

Dixon, R. A. & Baltes, P. B. (1988). Toward lifespan research on the functions and pragmatics of intelligence. In R. J. Sternberg & R. K. Wagner |(Eds.), *Practical intelligence: Nature and origins of competence in the everyday world* (pp. 203–235). New York: Cambridge University Press.

Dixon, R. A. & Hultsch, D. F. (1983). Structure and development of metamemory in adulthood. *Journal of Gerontology, 38*, 682–688.

Dixon, R. A., Hultsch, D. F., & Hertzog, C. (1988). The metamemory in adulthood (MIA) questionnaire. *Psychopharmacology Bulletin, 24*, 671–688.

Dobnik, V. (Jan. 22, 2000). Doctor carved his intials on patient. *Charlotte Observer*.

Doering, M., Rhodes, S. R., & Schuster, M. (1983). *The aging worker: Research and recommendations*. Beverly Hills, CA: Sage.

Doty, R. L., Shaman, P., Appelbaum, S. L., Bigerson, R., Sikorski, L., & Rosenberg, L. (1984). Smell identification ability: Changes with age. *Science, 226*, 1441–1443.

Douglas, K. W. & Arenberg, D. (1978). Age changes, cohort differences, and cultural changes on the Guilford-Zimmerman temperment survey. *Journal of Gerontology, 33*, 737–747.

Downes, K. (1995). The youth doctor: How he turned two old women into young beauties. *Sun, 13*, 6–7.

Dresser, R. (1994). Advance directives: Implications for policy. *Hastings Center Report, 24*, 52–55.

Drew, J. C. & Brooke, V. (1999). Changing a legacy: The Eden Alternative nursing home. *The Annals of Long-Term Care, 7*, 115–121.

Duara, R., London, E. D., & Rapoport, S. I. (1985). Changes in structure and energy metabolism of the aging brain.

In C. E. Finch & E. L. Schneider (Eds.), *Handbook of the biology of aging*. New York: Van Nostrand Reinhold, 595–616.

Dubler, N. (1994). Introduction. *Generations, 18*, 2–7.

Dufour, M., Colliver, J., Stinson, F., & Grigson, B. (1988). *Changes in alcohol consumption with age: NHANES I epidemiologic followup*. Paper presented at the annual meeting of the American Public Health Association, Boston.

Dugan, E. & Kivett, V. R. (1994). The importance of emotional and social isolation to loneliness among very old rural adults. *Gerontologist, 34*, 340–346.

Duke, S. (1998). An exploration of anticipatory grief: The lived experience of people during their spouses' terminal illness and in bereavement. *Journal of Advanced Nursing, 28*, 829–839.

Dupree, L. W. & Schonfeld, L. (1996). Substance abuse. In M. Hersen & V. B. Van Hasselt (Eds.), *Psychological treatment of older adults: An introductory text* (pp. 281–297). New York: Plenum Press.

Dustman, R. E., Ruhling, R. O., Russell, E. M., Shearer, D. E., Bonekat, W., Shigeoka, J. W., Woods, J. S., & Bradford, D. C. (1984). Aerobic exercise training and improved neuropsychological function of older adults. *Neurobiology of Aging, 5*, 35–42.

Dwyer, D. S. & Mitchell, O. S. (1999). Health problems as determinants of retirement: Are self-rated measures endogenous? *Journal of Health Economics, 18*, 173–193.

Dwyer, J. W. & Coward, R. T. (1991). A multivariate comparison of the involvement of adult sons versus daughters in the care of impaired parents. *Journal of Gerontology: Social Sciences, 46*, S259–S269.

Dychtwald, K. & Flower, J. (1989). *Age wave*. Los Angeles: Jeremy Tarcher, Inc.

Eberling, J. L., & Jagust, W. J. (1995). Imaging studies of aging, neurodegenerative disease, and alcoholism. *Alcohol World Health & Research, 19*, 279–286.

Eckert, J. K. & Rubinstein, R. L. (1999). Older men's health: Sociocultural and ecological perspectives. *Medical Clinics of North America, 83*, 1151–1172.

Edmonds, S. & Hooker, K. (1992). Perceived changes in life meaning following bereavement. *Omega, 25*, 307–318.

Eglit, H. (1989). Ageism in the work place: An elusive quarry. *Generations, 13*, 31–35.

Egorov, E. E. (1997). Telomerase, aging, and cancer. *Molecular Biology, 31*, 10.

Ekerdt, D. J. (1986). The busy ethic: Moral continuity between work and retirement. *Gerontologist, 26*, 239–244.

Ekerdt, D. J., Kosloski, K., & DeViney, S. (2000). The normative anticipation of retirement by older workers. *Research on Aging, 22*, 3–22.

Emanuel, E. J., Fairclough, D. L., Daniels, E. R., & Clarridge, B. R. (1996). Euthanasia and physician assisted suicide: Attitudes and experiences of oncology patients, oncologists, and the public. *Lancet, 347*, 1805–1810.

Encarta 98 Encyclopedia. (1997). Microsoft Corporation.

Endresen, I. M., Relling, G. B., Tonder, O., Myking, O., Walther, B. T., & Ursin, H. (1991–1992). Brief uncontrollable stress and psychological parameters influence human plasma concentrations of IgM and complement component C3. *Behavioral Medicine, 17*(4), 167–176.

Epstein, R. A. (1989, Spring). Voluntary euthanasia. *The Law School Record*, University of Chicago, 8–13.

Epstein, S. (1993). Bereavement from the perspective of cognitive-experiential self-theory. In M. S. Stroebe, W. Stroebe, & R. O. Hansson (Eds.), *Handbook of bereavement: Theory, research, and intervention* (pp. 112–128). New York: Cambridge University Press.

Erber, J. T. & Danker, D. C. (1995). Forgetting in the workplace: Attributions and recommendations for young and older-employees. *Psychology & Aging, 10*, 565–569.

Ericsson, K. A. & Charness, N. (1994). Expert performance: Its structure and acquisition. *American Psychologist, 49*, 725–747.

Ericsson, K. A., Krampe, R. T., & Tesch-Romer, C. (1993). The role of deliberate practice in the acquisition of expert performance. *Psychological Review, 100*, 363–406.

Erikson, E. H. (1963). *Childhood and society* (2nd ed.). New York: Norton.

Erikson, E. H. (1968). *Identity, youth, and crisis*. New York: Norton.

Erikson, E. H. (1982). *The life cycle completed: A review*. New York: Norton.

Erikson, E. H., Erikson, J. M., & Kivnick, H. Q. (1986). *Vital involvement in old age*. New York: W. W. Norton.

Eriksson, B. G., Hessler, R. M., Sundh, V., & Steen, B. (1999). Cross-cultural analysis of longevity among Swedish and American elders: The role of social networks in the Gothenburg and Missouri longitudinal studies compared. *Archives of Gerontology & Geriatrics, 28*, 131–148.

Erngrund, K., Mäntylä, T., & Nilsson, L. G. (1996). Adult age differences in source recall: A population-based study. *Journal of Gerontology: Psychological Sciences, 51B*, P335–P345.

Escobedo, L. G. & Peddicord, J. P. (1996). Smoking prevalence in US birth cohorts: The influence of gender and education. *American Journal of Public Health*, 231–236.

Faletti, M. V. (1984). Human factors research and functional environments for the aged. In I. Altman, J. Wohlwill, & M.P. Lawton (Eds.). *Human behavior and the environment: Vol. 7. The elderly and the environment*. New York: Plenum Press.

Faletti, M. V. & Clark, M. C. (1984). A capability-demand approach to the aged in technological environments: A case for improved task analysis. In P. K. Robinson, J. Livingston, & J.E. Birren (Eds.). *Aging and technological advances*. New York: Plenum Press.

Faletti, M. V., Gibbs, J. M., Clark, M. C., Pruchno, R. A., & Berman, E. A. (1989). Longitudinal course of bereavement in older adults. In D. A. Lund (Ed.), *Older bereaved spouses: Research with practical applications* (pp. 37–51). New York: Hemisphere Publishing Corp.

Family Caregiver Alliance. (1996). Fact Sheet: Community Care Options. Available from *http://www.caregiver.org/factsheets/community_careC.html*. Accessed on July 21, 2001.

Farberow, N. L., Gallagher-Thompson, D., Gilewski, M., & Thompson, L. (1992). Changes in grief and mental health. *Journal of Gerontology: Psychological Sciences, 47*, P357–P366.

Farrell, M. P. & Rosenberg, S. D. (1981). *Men at midlife.* Boston: Auburn House.

Fastenau, P. S., Denburg, N. L., & Abeles, N. (1996). Age differences in retrieval: Further support for the resource-reduction hypothesis. *Psychology & Aging, 11*, 140–146.

Federal Trade Commission, Division of Consumer Protection. (1994). *Funeral industry practices.* Washington, DC: U. S. Superintendent of Documents.

Feifel, H. & Branscomb, A. B. (1973). Who's afraid of death? *Journal of Abnormal Psychology, 81*, 82–88.

Feifel, H. & Strack, S. (1989). Coping with conflict situations: Middle-aged and elderly men. *Psychology & Aging, 4*, 26–33.

Feig, B. (1998). Fortifying body and soul. *Food & Beverage Marketing, 17*(6), 30–31.

Fein, G., Feinberg, I., Insel, T. R., Antorbus, J. S., Price, L. J., Floyd, T. C., & Nelson, M. A. (1985). Sleep mentation in the elderly. *Psychophysiology, 22*, 218–225.

Fell, N. (1993). *The validation breakthrough: Simple techniques for communicating with people with "Alzheimer's-type dementia".* Baltimore, MD: Health Profession Press.

Ferraro, K. F. (1992). Cohort changes in images of older adults. *Gerontologist, 32*, 296–304.

Ferrini, A. F. & Ferrini, R. (1993). *Health in the later years.* Madison, WI: Brown & Benchmark.

Field, D. (1999). Continuity and change in friendships in advanced age: Findings from the Berkeley Older Generation Study. *International Journal of Aging and Human Development, 48*, 325–346.

Field, D. & Millsap, R. E. (1991). Personality in advanced old age: Continuity or change? *Journal of Gerontology: Psychological Sciences, 46*, P299–P308.

Finch, C. E. (1998). Variations in senescence and longevity include the possibility of negligible senescence. *Journal of Gerontology: Biological Sciences, 53A*, B235–B239.

Finch, C. E. & Tanzi, R. E. (1997). Genetics of aging. *Science, 278*, 407–411.

Fisk, J. E. & Warr, P. (1996). Age and working memory: The role of perceptual speed, the central executive, and the phonological loop. *Psychology & Aging, 11*, 316–323.

Fitzgerald, J. M. & Lawrence, R. (1984). Autobiographical memory across the life span. *Journal of Gerontology, 39*, 692–699.

Fitzpatrick, T. R. (1998). Bereavement events among elderly men: The effects of stress and health. *Journal of Applied Gerontology, 17*, 204–258.

Flaherty, M. G. & Meer, M. D. (1994). How time flies: Age, memory, and temporal compression. *Sociological Quarterly, 35*, 705–721.

Flavell, J. H. (1985). *Cognitive development.* Englewood Cliffs, NJ: Prentice-Hall.

Fleeson, W. & Heckhausen, J. (1997). More or less "me" in past, present, and future: Perceived lifetime personality during adulthood. *Psychology & Aging, 12*, 125–136.

Fleming, K. C., Adams, A. C., & Petersen, R. C. (1995). Dementia: Diagnosis and evaluation. *Connecticut Medicine* (Dec.), 711–725.

Flint, A. J. (1994). Epidemiology and comorbidity of anxiety disorders in the elderly. *American Journal of Psychiatry, 151*(5), 640–649.

Flippen, C. & Tienda, M. (2000). Pathways to retirement: Patterns of labor force participation and labor market exit among the pre-retirement population by race, Hispanic origin, and sex. *Journal of Gerontology: Social Sciences, 55B*, S14–S27.

Floyd, M. & Scogin, F. (1997). Effects of memory training on the subjective memory functioning and mental health of older adults: A meta-analysis. *Psychology & Aging, 12*, 150–161.

Fogel, B. S. (1992). Psychological aspects of staying at home. *Generations, 16*, 15–19.

Fogler, J. & Stern, L. (1994). *Teaching memory improvement to adults.* Baltimore, MD: Johns Hopkins University Press.

Folkman, S., Lazarus, R. S., Pimley, S., & Novacek, J. (1987). Age differences in stress and coping processes. *Psychology & Aging, 2*, 171–184.

Folstein, M. F., Folstein, S. E., & McHugh, P. R. (1975). "Mini-Mental State," a practical method for grading the cognitive state of patients for the clinician. *Journal of Psychiatric Research, 12*, 189–198.

Fonda, S. J., Wallace, R. B., & Herzog, A. R. (2001). Changes in driving patterns and worsening depressive symptoms among older adults. *Journal of Gerontology: Social Sciences, 56B*, S343–S351.

Foos, P. W. (1989a). Adult age differences in working memory. *Psychology & Aging, 4*, 269–275.

Foos, P. W. (1989b). Age differences in memory for two common objects. *Journal of Gerontology: Psychological Sciences, 44*, 178–180.

Foos, P. W. (1997). Effects of memory training on anxiety and performance in older adults. *Educational Gerontology, 23*, 243–252.

Foos, P. W. & Clark, M. C. (April, 1994). *Cross-cultural similarities and differences in images of aging.* Paper presented at the annual meeting of the Southern Gerontolical Society, Charlotte, NC.

Foos, P. W., Clark, M. C., Booth, G. L., Myers, K., & Schmitz, J. (March, 1996). *Adult age and gender differences in memory for brand names.* Paper presented at the annual meeting of the Southeastern Psychological Association, Norfolk, VA.

Foos, P. W. & Dickerson, A. E. (1996). People my age remember these things better. *Educational Gerontology, 22*, 151–160.

Foos, P. W., & Sarno, A. J. (1998). Adult age differences in semantic and episodic memory. *Journal of Genetic Psychology, 159*, 297–312.

Ford, G. R., Haley, W. E., Thrower, S. L., West, C. A. C., & Harrell, L. E. (1996). Utility of Mini-Mental State Exam scores in predicting functional impairment among white and African American dementia patients.

Journal of Gerontology: Medical Sciences, 51A, M185–M188.

Fozard, J. L. (1990). Vision and hearing in aging. In J. E. Birren & K. W. Schaie (Eds.), *Handbook of the psychology of aging* (3rd ed., pp. 150–170). San Diego, CA: Academic Press.

Fozard, J. L., Rietsema, J., Bouma, H., & Graafmans, J. A. M. (2000). Gerontechnology: Creating enabling environments for the challenges and opportunities of aging. *Educational Gerontology, 26,* 331–344.

Fraisse, P. (1984). Perception and estimation of time. *Annual Review of Psychology, 35,* 1–36.

Franks, L. J., Hughes, J. P., Phelps, L. H., & Williams, D. G. (1993). Intergenerational influences on midwest college students by their grandparents and significant elders. *Educational Gerontology, 19,* 265–271.

Frassetto, L. A., Todd, K. M., Morris, C., Jr., & Sebastian, A. (2000). Worldwide incidence of hip fracture in elderly women: Relation to consumption of animal and vegetable foods. *Journal of Gerontology: Medical Sciences, 55A,* M585–M592.

Fredrickson, B. L. & Carstensen, L. L. (1990). Choosing social partners: How old age and anticipated endings make people more selective. *Psychology & Aging, 5,* 335–347.

Freed, C. R., Greene, P. E., Breeze, R. E., Tsai, W-Y., DuMouchel, W., Kao, R., Dillon, S., Winfield, H., Culver, S., Trojanowski, J. Q., Eidelberg, D., & Fahn, S. (2001). Transplantation of embryonic dopamine neurons for severe Parkinson's disease. *The New England Journal of Medicine, 344,* 710–719.

Freidan, B. (1993). *The fountain of age.* New York: Simon & Schuster.

Friedman, H. S. & Schustack, M. W. (1999). *Personality: Classic theories and modern research.* Boston: Allyn & Bacon.

Fries, J. F. (1980). Aging, natural death, and the compression of morbidity. *New England Journal of Medicine, 303,* 130–136.

Fries, J. F. (1999). *Preparing for a long life: Functional capacity.* Presented at the U.S. Administration on Aging Symposium, "Longevity in the new American century" Baltimore, MD, March 29–30. Available from *http://www.aoa.gov/Baltimore99/J.F. Fries-bio.html.*

Fronstin, P. (1999). Retirement patterns and employee benefits: Do benefits matter? *Gerontologist, 39,* 37–47.

Fry, P. S. (1997). Grandparents' reactions to the death of a grandchild: An exploratory factor analytic study. *Omega, 35,* 119–140.

Fujimoto, K. & Takahashi, M. (1997). Telomerase activity in human leukemic cell lines is inhibited by Antisense Pentadecadeoxynucleotides targeted against c-myc mRNA. *Biochemical & Biophysical Research Communications, 241,* 775.

Furstenberg, F. F. (1982). Conjugal succession: Reentering marriage after divorce. In P. B. Baltes & O. G. Brimm Jr. (Eds.), *Life-span development and behavior* (Vol. 4, pp. 107–146). New York: Academic Press.

Furukawa, T., Takeuchi, H., Hirai, T., Fujihara, S., Kitamura, T., & Takahashi, K. (1998). A possible association between paternal longevity and major depression among elderly men. *Psychiatry & Clinical Neuroscience, 52,* 577–579.

Gaesser, G. A. (1999). Thinness and weight loss: Beneficial or detrimental to longevity? *Medicine & Science in Sports & Exercise, 31,* 1118–1128.

Gale, W. G. (1997, Oct.). When baby boomers retire: The coming challenge. *Current* (396), 8–12.

Gall, T. L., Evans, D. R., & Howard, J. (1997). The retirement adjustment process: Changes in the well-being of male retirees across time. *Journal of Gerontology: Psychological Sciences, 52B,* P110–P117.

Gallagher, D., Rose, J., Rivera, P., Lovett, S., & Thompson, L. W. (1989). Prevalence of depression in family caregivers. *The Gerontologist, 29,* 449–456.

Gallagher, W. (1993). Midlife myths. *Atlantic Monthly, 271,* 51–68.

Gallagher-Thompson, D., Arean, P., Rivera, P., & Thompson, L. W. (2001). A psychoeducational intervention to reduce distress in Hispanic family caregivers: Results of a pilot study. *Clinical Gerontologist, 23,* 17–32.

Gallant, M. (1987). *Alcoholism: A guide to diagnosis, intervention, and treatment.* New York: Norton.

Gallo, J. J., Cooper-Patrick, L., & Lesikar, S. (1998). Depressive symptoms of Whites and African Americans aged 60 years and older. *Journal of Gerontology: Psychological Sciences, 53B,* P277–P286.

Gallo, W. T., Bradley, E. H., Siegel, M., & Kasl, S. V. (2000). Health effects of involuntary job loss among older workers: Findings from the Health and Retirement Survey. *Journal of Gerontology: Social Sciences, 55B,* S131–S140.

Gallo, W. T., Bradley, E. H., Siegel, M., & Kasl, S. V. (2001). The impact of involuntary job loss on subsequent alcohol consumption by older workers: Findings from the health and retirement survey. *Journal of Gerontology: Social Sciences, 56B,* S3–S9.

Gambrell, R. D. (1987). Estrogen replacement therapy for the elderly woman. *Medical Aspects of Human Sexuality, 21*(5), 81–93.

Ganzini, L. & Atkinson, R. M. (1996). Substance abuse. In J. Sadavoy, L. W. Lazarus, L. F. Jarvik, & G. T. Grossberg (Eds.), *Comprehensive review of geriatric psychiatry II* (2nd ed., pp. 659–692). Washington, DC: American Psychiatric Press.

Ganzini, L., Nelson, H. D., Schmidt, T. A., Kraemer, D. F., Delorit, M. A., & Lee, M. A. (2000). Physicians' experiences with the Oregon death with dignity act. *The New England Journal of Medicine, 342,* 557–563.

Gardner, A. W. & Poehlman, E. T. (1995). Predictors of the age-related increase in blood pressure in men and women. *Journal of Gerontology: Medical Sciences, 50A,* M1–6.

Garfein, A. J., Schaie, K. W., & Willis, S. L. (1988). Microcomputer proficiency in later-middle-aged and older adults: Teaching old dogs new tricks. *Social Behaviour, 3*, 131–148.

Garfinkel, D. & Zisapel, N. (1998). The use of melatonin for sleep. *Nutrition, 14*, 53.

Garrard, J., Rolnick, S. J., Nitz, N. M., Luepke, L., Jackson, J., Fischer, L. R., Leibson, C., Bland, P. C., Heinrich, R., & Waller, L. A. (1998). Clinical detection of depression among community-based elderly people with self-reported symptoms of depression. *Journal of Gerontology: Medical Sciences, 53A*, M92–M101.

Gatz, M., & Hurwitz, M. (1990). Are old people more depressed? Cross-sectional data on Center for Epidemiological Studies depression scale factors. *Psychology & Aging, 5*, 284–290.

Gatz, M., Pedersen, N. L., Berg, S., Johansson, K., Mortimer, J., Posner, S. F., Viitane, M., Winblad, B., & Anlbom, P. (1997). Heritability for Alzheimer's disease: The study of dementia in aging twins. *Journal of Gerontology: Medical Sciences, 52A*, M117–M125.

Gavrilov, L. A., Gavrilova, N. S., Semenova, V. G., Evdokushkina, G. N., Krut'ko, V. N., Gavrilova, A. L., Evdokushkina, N. N., & Kushnareva, Y. E. (1998). Life-span inheritance in humans: Effects of paternal and maternal longevity on offspring life-span. *Doklady Biological Sciences, 360*, 281–283.

Gavrilova, N. S., Gavrilov, L. A., Evdokushkina, G. N., Semyonova, V. G., Gavrilova, A. L., Evdokushkina, N. N., Kushnareva, Y. E., Kroutko, V. N., & Andreyev, A. Y. (1998). Evolution, mutations, and human longevity: European royal and noble families. *Human Biology, 70*, 799–804.

Gearing, B. (1999). Narratives of identity among former professional footballers in the United Kingdom. *Journal of Aging Studies, 13*, 43–58.

Gendell, M. (1998). Trends in retirement age in four countries, 1965–95. *Monthly Labor Review, 121* (8), 20–30.

Gerbner, G., Gross, L., Signorielli, N., & Morgan, M. (1980). Aging with television: Images on television dramas and conceptions of social reality. *Journal of Communication, 30*, 37–47.

Gerstenblith, G. (1980). Noninvasive assessment of cardiovascular function in the elderly. In M. L. Weisfeldt (Ed.), *Aging*: Vol 12. *The aging heart: It's function and response to stress*. New York: Raven Press.

Giacobini, E. (1998). Aging, Alzheimer's disease, and estrogen therapy. *Experimental Gerontology, 33*, 865–869.

Gibler, K. M., Lumpkin, J. R., & Moschis, G. P. (1998). Making the decision to move to retirement housing. *Journal of Consumer Marketing, 15*, 44–54.

Gibson, R. C. (1991). The subjective retirement of black Americans. *Journal of Gerontology: Social Sciences, 46*, S204–S209.

Gijana, E. W. M., Louw, J., & Manganyi, N. C. (1989). Thoughts about death and dying in an African sample. *Omega, 20*, 245–258.

Gilewski, M. J., Zelinski, E. M., & Schaie, K. W. (1990). The Memory Functioning Questionnaire for assessment of memory complaints in adulthood and old age. *Psychology & Aging, 5*, 482–490.

Giniger, S., Dispenzieri, A., & Eisenberg, J. (1983). Age, experience, and performance in speed and skill jobs in an applied setting. *Journal of Applied Psychology, 68*, 469–475.

Giovino, G. A., Henningfield, J. E., Tomar, S. L., Escobedo, L. G., & Slade, J. (1995). Epidemiology of tobacco use and dependence. *Epidemiological Review, 17*, 48–65.

Gist, M., Rosen, B., & Schwoerer, C. (1988). The influence of training method and trainee age on the acquisition of computer skills. *Personnel Psychology, 41*, 255–265.

Glamser, F. (1980). The impact of preretirement programs on the retirement experience. *Journal of Gerontology, 36*, 244–250.

Glaser, R. (1986). Intelligence as acquired proficiency. In R. J. Sternberg & D. K. Detterman (Eds.), *What is intelligence? Contemporary viewpoints on its nature and definition*. (pp. 77–83). Norwood, NJ: Ablex.

Glasheen, L. K. & Crowley, S. L. (1998, May). A family affair: Hospice eases the way at life's end. *AARP Bulletin, 39*(5), 2, 10–11, 13.

Glass, A. L. & Holyoak, K. J. (1986). *Cognition*. New York: Random House.

Glass, J. C., Jr. & Flynn, D. K. (2000). Retirement needs and preparation of rural middle-aged persons. *Educational Gerontology, 26*, 109–134.

Glass, J. C., Jr. & Kilpatrick, B. B. (1998). Gender comparisons of baby boomers and financial preparation for retirement. *Educational Gerontology, 24*, 719–745.

Glass, J. C., Jr., Mustian, R. D., & Carter, L. R. (1986). Knowledge and attitudes of health-care providers toward sexuality in the institutionalized elderly. *Educational Gerontology, 12*, 465–475.

Glass, T. A., Prigerson, H., Kasl, S. V., & Mendes de Leon, C. F. (1995). The effects of negative life events on alcohol consumption among older men and women. *Journal of Gerontology, 50B*, S205–S216.

Glatzer, R. (1999, May). Longevity from America's healthiest state. *American Health*, 72–78.

Gleitman, H., Fridlund, A. J., & Reisberg, D. (1999). *Psychology*. New York: W. W. Norton.

Glick, P. C. & Ling-Lin, S. (1986). Recent changes in divorce and remarriage. *Journal of Marriage & the Family, 48*, 737–747.

Glynn, R. J., Bouchard, G. R., LoCastro, J. S., & Laird, N. M. (1985). Aging and generational effects on drinking behaviors in men: Results from the Normative Aging Study. *American Journal of Public Health, 75*, 1413–1419.

Gober, F. & Simon, H. A. (1996). The role of recognition processes and look-ahead search in time constrained expert problem-solving: Evidence from grandmaster-level chess. *Psychological Science, 7*, 52–55.

Gold, D. T. (1989). Sibling relationships in old age: A typology. *International Journal of Aging & Human Development, 28*, 37–51.

Gold, D. T. (1990). Late-life sibling relationships: Does race affect typological distribution? *Gerontologist, 30*, 741–748.

Gold, D. T., Woodbury, M. A., & George, L. K. (1990). Relationship classification using grade of membership analysis: A typology of sibling relationships in late life. *Journal of Gerontology: Social Sciences, 45*, S43–S51.

Gold, D., Andres, D., & Schwartzman, A. (1987). Self-perception of personality at midlife in elderly people: Continuity and change. *Experimental Aging Research, 13*, 197–202.

Goldberg, E. L., Comstock, G. W., & Harlow, S. D. (1988). Emotional problems and widowhood: Problems and possibilities. *Journal of Gerontology: Social Sciences, 43*, S206–S208.

Goldstein, I. & Hatzichristou, D. G. (1994). Epidemiology of impotence. In A. H. Bennett (Ed.), *Impotence: Diagnosis and manangement of erectile dysfunction* (pp. 1–17). Philadelphia: W. B. Saunders.

Gose, K. & Levi, G. (1988). *Dealing with memory changes as you grow older.* New York: Bantam Books.

Gould, R. L. (1972). *Transformations: Growth and change in adult life.* New York: Simon & Schuster.

Gould, R. L. (1980). Transformation tasks in adulthood. *In the course of life, Vol. 3: Adulthood and aging processes.* Bethesda, MD: National Institute of Mental Health.

Grant, B. S., Harford, T. C., Dawson, D. A., Chou, P., Dufour, M., & Pickering, R. (1994). Prevalence of *DSM-IV* alcohol abuse and dependency: United States, 1992. *Alcohol, Health, & Research World, 18*, 243–248.

Grayson, P. J. (1997). Technology and home adaptation. In S. Lanspery & J. Hyde (Eds.). *Staying put: Adapting places instead of people* (pp. 55–74). Amityville, New York: Baywood Publishing.

Greenberg, C. & Powers, S. M. (1987), Memory improvement among adult learners. *Educational Gerontology, 12*, 385–394.

Greenblum, J. & Bye, B. (1987). Work values of disabled beneficiaries. *Social Security Bulletin, 50*(4), 67–74.

Greiner, P. A., Snowdon, D. A., & Greiner, L. H. (1996). The relationship of self-rated function and self-rated health to concurrent functional ability, functional decline, and mortality: Findings from the nun study. *Journal of Gerontology: Social Sciences, 51B*, S234–S241.

Greiner, P. A., Snowdon, D. A., & Greiner, L. H. (1999). Self-rated function, self-rated health, and postmortem evidence of brain infarcts: Findings from the nun study. *Journal of Gerontology, 54B*, S219–S222.

Grossman, A. H., D'Augelli, A. R., & Hershberger, S. L. (2000). Social support networks of lesbian, gay, and bisexual adults 60 years of age and older. *Journal of Gerontology: Psychological Sciences, 55B*, P171–P179.

Grote, N. K. & Freize, I. H. (1998). "Remembrance of things past": Perceptions of marital love from its beginnings to the present. *Journal of Social & Personal Relationships, 15*, 91–109.

Guarnaccia, C. A., Hayslip, B., Jr., & Landry, L. P. (1999). Influence of perceived preventability of the death and emotional closeness to the deceased: A test of Bugen's model. *Omega, 39*, 261–276.

Guilford, J. P. (1956). The stucture of intellect. *Psychological Bulletin, 53*, 267–293.

Guilford, J. P. (1967). *The nature of human intelligence.* New York: McGraw-Hill.

Gurland, B. (1996). Epidemiology of psychiatric disorders. In J. Sadavoy, L. W. Lazarus, L. F. Jarvik, & G. T. Grossberg (Eds.), *Comprehensive review of geriatric psychiatry II* (2nd ed., pp. 3–41). Washington, DC: American Psychiatric Press.

Gurland, B., Wilder, D., Cross, P., Phil, M., Lantigua, R., Teresi, J., Barrett, V., Stern, Y., & Mayeux, R. (1995). Relative rates of dementia by multiple case definitions, over two prevalence periods, in three sociocultural groups. *American Journal of Geriatric Psychiatry, 3*, 6–20.

Gurland, B., Wilder, D., Lantigua, R., Mayeux, R., Stern, Y., Chen, J., Cross, P., & Killeffer, E. (1997). Differences in rates of dementia between ethno-racial groups. In L. G. Martin & B. J. Soldo (Eds.), *Racial and ethnic differences in the health of older Americans* (pp. 233–269). Washington, DC: National Academy Press.

Guttman, D. L. (1975). Parenthood, key to the comparative study of the life cycle. In N. Datan & L, Ginsberg (Eds.), *Life-span developmental psychology: Normative life crises* (pp. 167–184). New York: Academic Press.

Guttman, D. L. (1977). The cross-cultural perspective: Notes toward a comparative psychology of aging. In J. Birren & K. W. Schaie (Eds.), *Handbook of the psychology of aging* (pp. 302–326). New York: Van Nostrand Reinhold.

Guttman, D. L. (1987). *Reclaimed powers: Men and women in later life.* Evanston, IL: Northwestern University Press.

Haberlandt, K. (1994). *Cognitive psychology.* Boston, MA: Allyn & Bacon.

Habermas, T. & Bluck, S. (2000). Getting a life: The emergence of the life story in adolescence. *Psychological Bulletin, 126*, 748–769.

Hagberg, B., Samuelsson, G., Lindberg, B., & Dehlin, O. (1991). Stability and change of personality in old age and its relation to survival. *Journal of Gerontology: Psychological Sciences, 46*, P285–P291.

Hagstadius, S. & Risberg, J. (1989). Regional cerebral blood flow characteristics and variations with age in resting normal subjects. *Brain & Cognition, 10*, 28–43.

Haley, W. E., Brown, S. L., & Levine, E. G. (1987). Family caregiver appraisals of patient behavioral disturbance in senile dementia. *Clinical Gerontologist, 6*, 25–34.

Hall, C. S. (1984). A ubiquitous sex difference in dreams revisited. *Journal of Personality & Social Psychology, 46*, 1109–1117.

Hall, G. S. (1922). *Senescence: The last half of life.* New York: Appleton.

Hamilton, J. B. (1948). The role of testicular secretions as indicated by the effects of castration in man and by studies of pathological conditions and short lifespan associated with maleness. *Recent Progress in Hormone Research, 3*, 257–324.

Hamner, T. J. & Turner, P. H. (1996). *Parenting in comtemporary society*. Boston: Allyn & Bacon.

Hannson, R. O., DeKoekkoek, P. D., Neece, W. M., & Patterson, D. W. (1997). Successful aging at work: Annual review, 1992–1996: The older worker and transitions to retirement. *Journal of Vocational Behavior, 51*, 202–233.

Hanrahan, P. & Luchins, D. J. (1995). Access to hospice programs in end-stage dementia: A national survey of hospice programs. *Journal of the American Geriatric Society, 43*, 56–59.

Hanson, B. S., Isacsson, S. O., Janzan, L., & Lindell, S. E. (1989). Social networks and social support influence mortality in elderly men: The prospective population study of "Men born in 1913". *American Journal of Epidemiology, 130*, 100–111.

Hanson, W. (1999). *Older love*. Minneapolis, MN: Waldman House Press.

Hansot, E. (1996). A letter from a patient's daughter. *Analysis of Internal Medicine, 125*, 149–151.

Happé, F. G. E., Winner, E., & Brownell, H. (1998). The getting of wisdom: Theory of mind in old age. *Developmental Psychology, 34*, 358–362.

Harevan, T. K. (2001). Historical perspectives on aging and family relations. In R. H. Binstock & L. K. George (Eds.). *Handbook of aging and the social sciences* (pp. 141–159). San Diego: Academic Press.

Harma, M. I., Hakola, T., & Laitinen, J. (1992). Relation of age of circadian adjustment to night work. *Scandavian Journal of Work, Environment, & Health, 18*, 116–118.

Harper, D. C., & Wadsworth, J. S. (1993). Grief in adults with mental retardation: Preliminary findings. *Research in Developmental Disabilities, 14*, 313–330.

Harris, L. (1976). *The myth and reality of aging in America*. Washington, DC: National Council on Aging.

Harris, S. B. (1996). For better or worse: Spouse abuse grown old. *Journal of Elder Abuse & Neglect, 8*, 1–33.

Harvey, G. & Lawler, J. The rights of elderly people in a nursing home: A little creativity, a lot of respect, a taste for adventure, and an allergy for bureaucracy. In L. F. Heumann, M. E. McCall, & Boldy, D. P. (Eds.). *Empowering frail elderly people: Opportunities and impediments in housing, health, and support service delivery* (pp. 155–173). Westport, CT: Praeger Publishers.

Harwood, J. & Lin, M-C. (2000). Affiliation, pride, exchange, and distance in grandparents' accounts of relationships with their college-aged grandchildren. *Journal of Communication, 50*(3), 31–47.

Hasher, L. & Zacks, R. T. (1979). Automatic and effortful processes in memory. *Journal of Experimental Psychology: General, 108*, 356–388.

Hasher, L. & Zacks, R. T. (1988). Working memory, comprehension, and aging: A review and a new view. In G. H. Bower (Ed.), *The psychology of learning and motivation*. (pp. 193–225). New York: Academic Press.

Haught, P. A., Walls, R. T., Laney, J. D. Leavell, A., & Stuzen, S. (1999). Child and adolescent knowledge and attitudes about older adults across time and states. *Educational Gerontology, 25*, 501–517.

Hauser, M. J. (1987). Special aspects of grief after a suicide. In E. J. Dunn, J. L. McIntosh, & K. Dunne-Maxim (Eds.), *Suicide and its aftermath: Understanding and counseling the survivors* (pp. 57–70). New York: W. W. Norton.

Havighurst, R. J. (1972). *Developmental tasks and education*. New York: McKay.

Haward, L. R. C. (1977). Cognition in dementia presenilis. In W. L. Smith & M. Kinsbourne (Eds.), *Aging and dementia* (pp. 189–202). New York: Spectrum Publications.

Hayashi, T., Ito, I., Kano, H., Endo, H., & Iguchi, A. (2000). Estriol (E3) replacement improves endothelial function and bone mineral density in very elderly women. *Journal of Gerontology: Biological Sciences, 55A*, B183–B190.

Hayflick, L. (1965). The limited in vitro lifetime of human diploid cell strains. *Experimental Cell Research, 37*, 614–636.

Hayflick, L. (1996). *How and why we age*. New York: Ballantine Books.

Hayslip, B. J., Jr. & Panek, P. E. (1993). *Adult development & aging* (2nd ed.). New York: Harper Collins.

Hayslip, B., Jr., Ragow-O'Brien, D., & Guarnaccia, C. A. (1998–1999). The relationship of cause of death to attitudes toward funerals and bereavement adjustment. *Omega, 38*, 297–312.

Hayslip, B., Shore, J., Henderson, C. E., & Lambert, P. L. (1998). Custodial grandparenting and the impact of grandchildren with problems on role satisfaction and role meaning. *Journal of Gerontology: Social Sciences, 53B*, S164–S173.

Hayward, M. D., Friedman, S., & Chen, H. (1998). Career trajectories and older men's retirement. *Journal of Gerontology: Social Sciences, 53B*, S91–S103.

Hayward, M. D., Friedman, S., & Chen, H. (2000). Race inequities in men's retirement. In E. P. Stoller & R. C. Gibson (Eds.), *Worlds of difference: Inequality in the aging experience* (pp. 191–196). Thousand Oaks, CA: Pine Forge Press.

Hazan, H. (1996). *From first principles: An experiment in aging*. Westport, CT: Bergin & Garvey.

Health Care Finance Administration. (2001). National Health Expenditures, 2001. Available from *http://www.hcfa.gov*. Accessed September 8, 2001.

Healy, B. P. (1997). A sage brain, a sturdy skeleton, and a funny bone: A longevity lesson from Madame Calment. *Journal of Women's Health, 6*, 503–504.

Healy, J. (1983). Bereavement issues and anticipatory grief. In *Symposium on death and dying: The role of the family and estate planner*. New York: Foundation of Thanatology.

Heckhausen, J. (1997). Developmental regulation across adulthood: Primary and secondary control of age-related challenges. *Developmental Psychology, 33*, 176–187.

Heglin, H. J. (1956). Problem solving set in different age groups: *Journal of Gerontology, 11*, 310–317.

Heller, K. S. & Wilber, L. A. (1990). Hearing loss, aging, and speech perception in reverberation and noise. *Journal of Speech and Hearing Research, 33*, 149–155.

Heller, T., Factor, A., Sterns, H., & Sutton, E. (1996, Jan./Feb./Mar:). Impact of person-centered later life planning training program for older adults with mental retardation. *Journal of Rehabilitation*, 77–83.

Helsing, K. J., & Szklo, M., & Comstock, G. W. (1981). Factors associated with mortality after widowhood. *American Journal of Public Health, 71*, 802–809.

Helson, R. (1992). Women's difficult times and the rewriting of the life story. *Psychology of Women Quarterly, 16*, 331–347.

Helson, R. (1993). The Mills classes of 1958 and 1960: College in the fifties, young adulthood in the sixties. In K. D. Hulbert & D. T. Schuster (Eds.), *Women's lives through time* (pp. 190–210). San Francisco, CA: Jossey-Bass.

Helson, R. & Moane, G. (1987). Personality change in women from college to midlife. *Journal of Personality & Social Psychology, 53*, 176–186.

Helson, R. & Wink, P. (1992). Personality change in women from the early 40s to the early 50s. *Psychology & Aging, 7*, 46–55.

Helzlsouer, K. J. (1995). Risk of ovarian cancer associated with increased levels of levels of DHEA and DHEAS. *Journal of the American Medical Association, 274*, 1926–1930.

Henderson, P., Williams, C., & Einstein, G. (1996, Nov.). *Paper.* Presented at the annual meeting of the Society for Neuroscience, Orlando, FL.

Henderson, V. W., Watt, L., & Buckwalter, J. G. (1996). Cognitive skills associated with estrogen replacement in women with Alzheimer's disease. *Psychoneuroendocrinology, 21*, 421.

Hendin, H. (1994, December 16). Scared to death of dying. *New York Times*, A19–A20.

Hendrie, H. C. (2001). Exploration of environmental and genetic risk factors for Alzheimer's disease: The value of cross-cultural studies. *Current Directions in Psychological Science, 10*, 98–101.

Hendrie, H. C., Callahan, C. M., Levitt, E. E., Hui, S. L., Musick, B., Austrom, M. G., Nurnberger, J. I. Jr., & Tierney, W. M. (1995). Prevalence rates of major depressive disorders: The effect of varying the diagnostic criteria in an older primary care population. *American Journal of Geriatric Psychiatry, 3*, 119–131.

Hermann, M. (1998, March-April). A call for calcium. *Modern Maturity*, 66–67.

Hertzog, C., Dixon, R. A., & Hultsch, D. F. (1990). Relationships between metamemory, memory predictions, and memory task performance in adults. *Psychology & Aging, 5*, 215–227.

Hertzog, C., Saylor, L. L., Fleece, A. M., & Dixon, R. A. (1994). Metamemory and aging: Relations between predicted, actual, and perceived memory task performance. *Aging & Cognition, 1*, 203–237.

Hess, T. M. (1984). Effects of semantically related and unrelated contexts on recognition memory of different-aged adults. *Journal of Gerontology, 39*, 444–451.

Hetherington, E. M. (1979). Divorce: A child's perspective. *American Psychologist, 34*, 851–858.

Hetherington, E. M., Stanley Hagan, M., & Anderson, E. R. (1989). Marital transitions: A child's perspective. *American Psychologist, 44*, 303–312.

Heumann, J. F. (2001). The role of the built environment in holistic delivery of home and community based care services to frail elderly. In L. F. Heumann, M. E. McCall, & Boldy, D. P. (Eds.). *Empowering frail elderly people: Opportunities and impediments in housing, health, and support service delivery* (pp. 119–136). Westport, CT: Praeger Publishers.

High, D. M. (1993). Advance directives and the elderly: A study of intervention strategies to increase use. *The Gerontologist, 33*, 342–349.

Hilbourne, M. (1999). Living together full time? Middle-class couples approaching retirement. *Aging & Society, 19*, 161–183.

Hill, C. D., Thompson, L. W., & Gallagher, D. (1988). The role of anticipatory bereavement in older women's adjustment to widowhood. *The Gerontologist, 28*, 792–796.

Hill, R., Bäckman, L., Wahlin, A., & Winblad, B. (1995). Visuospatial performance in very old demented persons. *Dementia, 6*, 49–54.

Hilt, M. L. & Lipschultz, J. H. (1996). Broadcast news and elderly people: Attitudes of local television managers. *Educational Gerontology, 22*, 669–682.

Hirano, A., Kurland, L. T., Krooth, R. S., & Lassell, S. (1961). Parkinson dementia complex on Guam, II. Pathologic features. *Brain, 84*, 662–679.

Hoch, C. C., Reynolds III, C. F., Buysse, D. J., Monk, T. H., Nowell, P., Begley, A. E., Hall, F., & Dew, M. A. (2001). Protecting sleep quality in later life: A pilot study of bed restriction and sleep hygiene. *Journal of Gerontology: Psychological Sciences, 56B*, P52–P59.

Hockenbury, D. H. & Hockenbury, S. E. (2000). *Psychology.* New York: Worth.

Hofferberth, B. (1994). The efficacy of Egb 761 in patients with senile dementia of the Alzheimer's type, a double-blind, placebo-controlled study on different levels of investigation. *Human Psychopharmacology Clinical & Experimental, 9*, 215–222.

Hogan, R., Kim, M., & Perrucci, C. C. (1997). Racial inequality in men's employment and retirement earnings. *Sociological Quarterly, 38*, 431–438.

Hollis-Sawyer, L. A. & Sterns, H. L. (1999). A novel goal-oriented approach for training older adult computer novices: Beyond the effects of individual difference factors. *Educational Gerontology, 25*, 661–684.

Hollis-Sawyer, L. A. (2001). Adaptive, growth-oriented, and positive perceptions of mother-daughter elder caregiving relationships: A path-analytic investigation of predictors. *Journal of Women and Aging, 13*, 5–22.

Holloszy, J. O. (1998). Longevity of exercising rats: Effect of an antioxidant supplemented diet. *Mechanisms of Ageing & Development, 100*, 211–219.

Holmes E. R. & Holmes L. D. (1995). *Other cultures, elder years* (2nd ed.). Thousand Oaks, CA: Sage.

Holmes, D. S. (1987). The influence of meditation versus rest on physiological arousal: A second examination. In M. A. West (Ed.), *The psychology of meditation.* New York: Oxford University Press.

Holmes, T. H. & Rahe, R. H. (1976). The social readjustment rating scale. *Journal of Psychosomatic Research, 11,* 213.

Honig, M. (1998). Married women's retirement expectations: Do pensions and Social Security matter? *American Economic Review, 88,* 202–206.

Hooyman, N. R. & Kiyak, H. A. (1996). *Social gerontology: A multidisciplinary perspective* (4th ed.). Boston: Allyn & Bacon.

Horn, J. L. (1982). The theory of fluid and crystallized intelligence in relation to concepts of cognitive psychology and aging in adulthood. In F. I. M. Craik & S. Trehub (Eds.), *Aging and cognitive processes.* New York: Plenum.

Hornblum, J. N. & Overton, W. F. (1976). Area and volume conservation among the elderly: Assessment and training. *Developmental Psychology, 12,* 68–74.

Horner, K. L., Rushton, J. P., & Vernon, P. A. (1986). Relation between aging and research productivity. *Psychology & Aging, 1,* 319–324.

Hortobágyi, T., Zheng, D., Weidner, M., Lambert, N. J., Westbrook, S., & Houmard, J. A. (1995). The influence of aging on muscle strength and muscle fiber characteristics with special reference to eccentric strength. *Journal of Gerontology: Biological Sciences, 50B,* B399–406.

Horton, A. M., & Fogelman, C. J. (1991). Behavioral treatment of aged alcoholics and drug addicts. In P. A. Wisocki (Ed.), *Handbook of clinical behavioral therapy with the elderly client.* NY: Plenum Press, 299–316.

House, J. S., Landis, K. R., & Umberson, D. (1988). Social relationships and health. *Science, 241,* 540–544.

Howarth, G. (1998). "Just live for today", living, caring, ageing, and dying. *Aging & Society, 18,* 673–689.

Howells, J. (1998). The best places to retire in America. *Consumers Digest, 37*(5), 67–70.

Hoyer, W. (1987). Acquisition of knowledge and the decentralization of *g* in adult intellectual development. In C. Schooler & K. W. Schaie (Eds.), *Cognitive functioning and social structure over the life course.* (pp. 120–141). Norwood, NJ: Ablex.

Hoyer, W. J., Rybash, J. M., & Roodin, P. A. (1999). *Adult development and aging.* Boston: McGraw-Hill.

Huang, T-T., Carlson, E. J., Gillespie, A. M., Shi, Y., & Epstein, C. J. (2000). Ubiquitous overexpression of CuZn superoxide dismutase does not extend life span for mice. *Journal of Gerontology: Biological Sciences, 55A,* B5–B9.

Hulicka, I. M. (1982). Memory functioning in late adulthood. In F. I. M. Craik & S. Trehub (Eds.), *Aging and cognitive processes* (pp. 331–351): New York: Plenum.

Hull, R. H. (1980). Talking to the hearing-impaired older adult. *Asha, 22* (Journal of the American Speech, Language, Hearing Association), 427.

Hultsch, D. F., Hertzog, C., Small, B. J., & Dixon, R. A. (1999). Use it or lose it: Engaged lifestyle as a buffer of cognitive decline in aging? *Psychology & Aging, 14,* 245–263.

Humphrey, D. (1991). *The final exit: The practicalities of self-deliverance and assisted suicide for the dying person.* Eugene, OR: Hemlock Society.

Huppert, F. A., Brayne, C., Gill, C., Paykel, E. S., & Beardsall, L. (1995). CAMCOG—A concise neuropsychological test to assist dementia diagnosis: Socio demographic determinants in an elderly population sample. *British Journal of Clinical Psychology, 34,* 529–541.

Huyck, M. H. (1990). Gender differences in aging. In J. E. Birren & K. W. Schaie (Eds.), *Handbook of the psychology of aging* (pp. 124–132). San Diego, CA: Academic Press.

Hyde, J. S., Krajnik, M., & Skuldt-Niederberger, K. (1991). Androgyny across the lifespan: A replication and longitudinal follow-up. *Developmental Psychology, 27,* 516–519.

Iams, H. M. (1986). Characteristics of the longest job for newly disabled workers: Findings from the New Beneficiary Survey. *Social Security Bulletin, 49*(12), 13–18.

Idler, E. L. & Kasl, S. V. (1997a). Religion among disabled and nondisabled persons I: Cross-sectional patterns in health practices, social activities, and well-being. *Journal of Gerontology: Social Sciences, 52B,* S294–S305.

Idler, E. L. & Kasl, S. V. (1997b). Religion among disabled and nondisabled persons II: Attendance at religious services as a predictor of the course of disability. *Journal of Gerontology: Social Sciences, 52B,* S306–S316.

Ilmarinen, J. (1997). Aging and work—Coping with strengths and weaknesses. *Scandavian Journal of Work, Environment, & Health, 23,* 3–5.

Ingram, D. K., Weindruch, R., Spangler, E. L., Freeman, J. R., & Wolford, R. L. (1987). Dietary restriction benefits learning and motor performance of aged mice. *Journal of Gerontology, 42,* 78–81.

Inhelder, B. & Piaget, J. (1958). *The growth of logical thinking from childhood to adolescence* (A. Parsons & S. Milgram, Trans.). New York: Basic Books.

Inouye, S. K., Robison, J. T., Froehlich, T. E., & Richardson, E. D. (1998). The Time and Change Test: A simple screening test for dementia. *Journal of Gerontology: Medical Sciences, 53A,* M281–M286.

Irish, D. P., Lundquist, K. F., & Nelsen, V. J. (1993). *Ethnic variations in dying, death, and grief.* Washington, DC: Taylor & Francis.

Isingrini, M., Fontane, R., Taconnat, L., & Duportal, A. (1995). Aging and encoding in memory: False alarms and decision criteria in a word-pair recognition task. *International Journal of Aging & Human Development, 41,* 79–88.

Israel, E., Dell'Accio, E., Martin, G., & Hugonot, R. (1987). *Psychologic Medicale, 19,* 1431–1439.

Jacobs, E. & Worcester, R. (1990). *We British: Britain under the MORI-scope.* London: Weidenfeld & Nicholson.

Jaffrey, M. (1995). Cremation along the Ganges. In J. O. Reilly & L. Habegger (Eds.), *Traveler's tales: India.* San Francisco, CA: Traveler's Tales Inc.

Jansari, A. & Parkin, A. J. (1996). Things that go bump in your life: Explaining the reminiscence bump in autobiographical memory. *Psychology & Aging, 11*, 85–91.

Jarvik, L. F. & Cohen, D. A. (1973). A biobehavioral approach to intellectual changes with aging. In C. Eisdorfer & M. P. Lawton (Eds.), *The psychology of adult development and aging*. Washington, DC: American Psychological Association.

Jazwinski, S. M. (1999). Longevity, genes, and aging: A view provided by a genetic model system. *Experimental Gerontology, 34*, 1–6.

Jecker, N. S. & Schneiderman, L. J. (1994). Is dying young worse than dying old? *The Gerontologist, 34*, 66–72.

Jerrome, D. & Wenger, G. C. (1999). Stability and change in late-life friendships. *Aging & Society, 19*, 661–676.

Jian-Gang, Z., Yong-Xing, M., Chuan-Fu, W., Pei-Fang, L., Song-Bai, Z., Nui-Fan, G., Guo-Yin, F., & Lin, H. (1998). Apolipoprotein E and longevity among *Han* Chinese population. *Mechanisms of Ageing and Development, 104*, 159–167.

Johansson, B. & Zarit, S. H. (1997). Early cognitive markers of the incidence of dementia and mortality: A longitudinal population-based study of the oldest old. *International Journal of Geriatric Psychiatry, 12*, 53–59.

Johansson, B. G. & Medhus, A. (1974). Increase in plasma alpha-lipoprotein in chronic alcoholics after acute abuse. *Acta Medica Scandanavia, 195*, 273–277.

Johansson, B., Allen-Burge, R., & Zarit, S. H. (1997). Self-reports on memory functioning in a longitudinal study of the oldest old: Relation to current, prospective, and retrospective performance. *Journal of Gerontology: Psychological Sciences, 52B*, P139–P146.

Johansson, B., Zarit, S. H., & Berg, S. (1992). Changes in cognitive functioning of the oldest old. *Journal of Gerontology: Psychological Sciences, 47*, P75–P80.

Johnson, C. & Troll, L. E. (1994). Constraints and facilitators to friendships in late life. *Gerontologist, 34*, 79–87.

Johnson, D. R. & Johnson, J. T. (1982). Managing the older worker. *Journal of Applied Gerontology, 1*, 58–66.

Johnson, E. & Williamson, J. (1987). Retirement in the United States. In K. Markidas & C. Cooper (Eds.), *Retirement in industrialized societies* (pp. 9–41). New York: Wiley & Sons.

Johnson, T. R. (1995). The significance of religion for aging well. *American Behavioral Scientist, 39*, 186–208.

Jones, D. C. & Vaughn, K. (1990). Close friendships among senior adults. *Psychology & Aging, 5*, 451–457.

Jones, H. E. (1959). Intelligence and problem-solving. In J. E. Birren (Ed.), *Handbook of aging and the individual: Psychological and biological aspects*. Chicago, IL: University of Chicago Press.

Joubert, C. E. (1990). Subjective expectations of the acceleration of time with aging. *Perceptual & Motor Skills, 70*, 334.

Joulain, M., Mullet, E., LeComte, C., & Prévost, R. (2000). Perception of appropriate age for retirement among young adults, middle-aged adults, and elderly people. *International Journal of Aging & Human Development, 50*, 73–84.

Kahana, E. & Kahana, B. (1996). Conceptual and empiri-
cal advances in understanding aging well through proactive adaptation. In V. L. Bengston (Ed.). *Adulthood and aging: Research on continuities and discontinuities* (pp. 18–40). New York: Springer.

Kahn, R. L. & Antonucci, T. C. (1980). Convoys over the life course: Attachment, roles, and social support. In P. B. Baltes & O. G. Brim (Eds.), *Life-span development and behavior* (Vol. 3, pp. 254–286). New York: Academic Press.

Kaiser, M. A. (1993, Winter). The productive roles of older people in developing countries. *Generations, 17*, 65–69.

Kamouri, A. L. & Cavanaugh, J. C. (1986). The impact of preretirement education programmes on workers' preretirement socialization. *Journal of Occupational Behaviour, 7*, 245–256.

Kane, R. A. (1991). Personal autonomy for residents in long-term care: Concepts and issues of measurement. In J. E. Birren, & J. E. Lubben (Eds.). *The concept and measurement of quality of life in the frail elderly* (pp. 315–334). San Diego: Academic Press.

Kane, R. A. & Caplan, A. L. (Eds.) (1990). *Everyday ethics: Resolving dilemmas in nursing home life*. New York: Springer.

Kane, R. & Wilson, K. B. (1993). *Assisted living in the United States: A new paradigm for residential care for frail older persons?* Washington, DC: American Association of Retired Persons.

Kannel, W. B. (1996). Cardioprotection and antihypertensive therapy: The key importance of addressing the associated coronary risk factors (The Framingham Experience). *American Journal of Cardiology, 77*, 6B–11B.

Kaplan, G., Barell, V., & Lusky, A. (1988). Subjective state of health and survival among elderly adults. *Journal of Gerontology: Social Sciences, 43*, S114–S120.

Kaplan, R. M. (2000). Two pathways to prevention. *American Psychologist, 55*, 382–396.

Karney, B. R. & Coombs, R. H. (2000). Memory bias in long-term close relationships: Consistency or improvement? *Personality & Social Psychology Bulletin, 26*, 959–970.

Karr, A. (1998, October). Oregon suicide law: A national test case? *AARP Bulletin, 39*, 9–11, 13.

Kastenbaum, R. (1981). *Death, society, & human experience* (2nd ed.). Palo Alto, CA: Mayfield.

Kastenbaum, R. (1992). *The psychology of death* (2nd edition). New York: Springer.

Kastenbaum, R. (1993). Re-constructing death in postmodern society. *Omega, 27*, 75–89.

Kastenbaum, R. (1995). To which self be true? *Contemporary Gerontology, 2*, 34–37.

Kastenbaum, R. (1999). Dying and bereavement. In J. C. Cavanaugh & S. K. Whitbourne (Eds.), *Gerontology: An interdisciplinary perspective* (pp. 155–185), New York: Oxford University Press.

Kaszniak, A. W. (1990). Psychological assessment of the aging individual. In J. E. Birren & K. W. Schaie (Eds.), *Handbook of the psychology of aging* (3rd ed., pp. 427–445). San Diego, CA: Academic Press.

Katan, Y. & Werczberger, E. (1998). Housing for elderly people in Israel. In S. Brink (Ed.). *Housing older people: An international perspective* (pp. 35–48). New Brunswick, NJ: Transaction Publishers.

Katchadourian, H. (1987). *Fifty: Midlife in perspective*. New York: Freeman.

Katzko, M. W., Steverink, N., Dittmann-Kohli, F., & Herrera, R. R. (1998). The self-concept of the elderly: A cross-cultural comparison. *International Journal of Aging & Human Behavior, 46*, 171–187.

Kaufman, A. (1968). Age and performance in oral and written versions of the substitution test. In S. Chown & K. F. Riegel (Eds.), *Psychological functioning in the normal aging and senile aged*. Basel, Switzerland: S. Karger.

Kaufman, G. & Uhlenberg, P. (1998). Effects of life course transitions on the quality of relationships between adult children and their parents. *Journal of Marriage & the Family, 60*, 924–938.

Kaufman, S. R. (1986). *The ageless self: Sources of meaning in late life*. Madison, WI: University of Wisconsin Press.

Kausler, D. H. (1994). *Learning and memory in normal aging*. San Diego, CA: Academic Press.

Kay, D. W., & Bergman, K. (1982). Epidemiology of mental disorders among the aged in the community. In J. E. Birren & R. B. Sloane (Eds.), *Handbook of mental health and aging* (pp. 34–56). Englewood Cliffs, NJ: Prentice-Hall.

Keith, J., Fry, C. L., Glascock, A. P., Ikels, C., Dickerson-Putman, J., Harpending, H. C., & Draper, P. (1994). *The aging experience: Diversity and commonality across cultures*. Thousand Oaks, CA: Sage.

Kelly, C. L., Charness, N., Mottram, M., & Bosman, E. (1994). *The effect of cognitive aging and prior computer experience on learning to use a word processor*. Paper presented at the Cognitive Aging Conference, Atlanta, GA.

Kelman, H. R., Thomas, C., Kennedy, G. J., & Cheng, J. (1994). Cognitive impairment and mortality in older community residents. *American Journal of Public Health, 84*, 1255–1260.

Kennedy, G. E. (1992). Shared activities of grandparents and grandchildren. *Psychological Reports, 70*, 211–227.

Kessler, R. C., McGonagle, K. A., Zhao, S., Nelson, C. B., Hughes, R., Eshleman, S., Wittchen, H., & Kendler, K. S. (1994). Lifetime and 12-month prevalence of *DSM-III R* psychiatric disorders in the United States. *Archives of General Psychiatry, 51*, 8–19.

Khalsa, D. S. (1998). Exelon: A new drug for Alzheimer's disease. *Total Health, 20*(3), 54–56.

Kilner, J. (1990). *Who lives? Who dies?* New Haven, CT: Yale University Press.

Kim, M. (1998). Housing policies for the elderly in Korea. In S. Brink (Ed.). *Housing older people: An international perspective* (pp. 61–72). New Brunswick, NJ: Transaction Publishers.

Kimmel, D. C. (1990). *Adulthood and aging: An interdisciplinary, developmental view*. New York: Wiley & Sons.

Kimmel, D. C. (1992). The families of older gay men and lesbians. *Generations, 16*, 37–38.

Kirschbaum, J. (1988). Effect on human longevity of added dietary chocolate. *Nutrition, 14*, 869.

Kitayama, S., Markus, H., Matsumoto, H., & Norasakkunkit, V. (1997). Individual and collective processes in the construction of the self: Self-enhancement in the United States and self-criticisms in Japan. *Journal of Personality & Social Psychology, 72*, 1245–1267.

Kite, M. E. & Johnson, B. T. (1988). Attitudes toward older and younger adults: A meta-analysis. *Psychology & Aging, 3*, 233–244.

Kitwood, T. (1990). The dialectics of dementia: With particular reference to Alzheimer's disease. *Aging & Society, 10*, 177–196.

Kitwood, T. (1993). Towards a theory of dementia care: The interpersonal process. *Ageing & Society, 13*, 51–67.

Kitwood, T. & Bredin, K. (1992). Towards a theory of dementia care: Personhood and well-being. *Aging & Society, 12*, 269–287.

Kivett, V. (1991). The grandparent-grandchild connection. *Marriage & Family Review, 16*, 267–290.

Kivnick, H. Q. (1982). Grandparenthood: An overview of meaning and mental health. *Gerontologist, 22*, 59–66.

Kivnick, H. Q. & Sinclair, H. M. (1996). Grandparenthood. In J. E. Birren (Ed.), *Encyclopedia of gerontology* (Vol. 1, pp. 611–623). New York: Academic Press.

Klatsky, A. L., Friedman, G. D., & Siegelaub, A. B. (1974). Alcohol consumption before myocardial ifarction. *Annals of Internal Medicine, 81*(3), 294–301.

Kleemeier, R. W. (1962). Intellectual change in the senium. *Proceeding of the Social Statistics Section of the American Statistical Association*, 290–295.

Kleijnen, J. & Knipschild, P. (1992). Gingko biloba for cerebral insufficiency. *British Journal of Pharmacology, 34*, 352–358.

Kligman, A. M., Grove, G. L., & Balin, A. K. (1985). Aging of human skin. In C. E. Finch & E. L. Schneider (Eds.), *Handbook of the biology of aging*. (2nd ed.), New York: Van Nostrand Reinhold, 820–841.

Kline, D. W. & Orme-Rogers, C. (1978). Examination of stimulus persistence as the basis for superior identification performance among older adults. *Journal of Gerontology, 33*, 76–81.

Kline, D. W. & Schieber, F. (1985). Vision and aging. In J. E. Birren & K. W. Schaie (Eds.), *Handbook of the psychology of aging* (2nd ed.). New York: Van Nostrand Reinhold.

Klingman, A. (1985). Responding to a bereaved classmate: Comparison of two strategies for death education in the classroom. *Death Studies, 9*, 449–454.

Knight, B. (1993). A meta-analytic review of interventions for caregiver distress. *The Gerontologist, 32*, 249–257.

Koenig, C. S. & Cunningham, W. R. (2001). Adulthood relocation: Implications for personality, future orientation, and social partner choices. *Experimental Aging Research, 27*, 197–213.

Koenig, H. G. (1995). Religion as a cognitive schema. *International Journal for the Psychology of Religion, 5*, 31–37.

Koenig, H. G. & Blazer, D. G. (1992). Mood disorders and suicide. In J. E. Birren, R. B. Sloane, & G. D. Cohen

(Eds.), *Handbook of mental health and aging* (2nd ed., pp. 379–407). San Diego: Academic Press. •

Koenig, H. G., George, L. K., & Siegler, I. C. (1988). The use of religion and other emotion-regulating coping strategies among older adults. *Gerontologist, 28,* 18–28.

Koenig, H. G., George, L. K., Blazer, D. G., & Pritchett, J. (1993). The relationship between religion and anxiety in a sample of community-dwelling older adults. *Journal of Geriatric Psychiatry, 26,* 65–93.

Koenig, H. G., Hays, J. C., Larson, D. B., George, L. K., Cohen, H. S., McCulloph, M. E., Meador, K. G., & Blazer, D. G. (1999). Does religious attendance prolong survival? *Journal of Gerontology: Medical Sciences, 53A,* M426–M434.

Kogan, N. (1990). Personality and aging. In J. E. Birren & K. W. Schaie (Eds.), *Handbook of the psychology of aging* (3rd ed., pp. 330–346). San Diego, CA: Academic Press.

Kose, S. (1998). Housing elderly people in Japan. In S. Brink (Ed.). *Housing older people: An international perspective* (pp. 125–140). New Brunswick, NJ: Transaction Publishers.

Kosloski, K., Ekerdt, D., & DeViney, S. (2001). The role of job-related rewards in retirement planning. *Journal of Gerontology: Psychological Sciences, 56B,* P160–P169.

Kosslyn, S. M. & Koenig, O. (1995). *Wet mind: The new cognitive neuroscience.* New York: The Free Press.

Kozma, A., Stones, M. J., & Hannah, T. E. (1991). Age, activity, and physical performance: An evaluation of performance models. *Psychology & Aging, 6,* 43–49.

Kraaij, V., Arensman, E., & Spinhoven, P. (2002). Negative life events and depression in elderly persons: A meta-analysis. *Journal of Gerontology: Psychological Sciences, 57B,* P87–P94.

Kramer, D. A. & Woodruff, D. S. (1986). Relativistic and dialectical thought in three adult age groups. *Human Development, 29,* 280–290.

Kramer, M., Kinney, L. & Scharf, M. (1983). Sex differences in dreams. *Psychiatric Journal of the University of Ottawa, 8,* 1–4.

Kranczer, S. (1998). Changes in longevity by State. *Statistical Bulletin, 79*(3), 29–36.

Kranczer, S. (1999). Continued United States longevity increases. *Statistical Bulletin, 80*(4), 20–27.

Krause, N. (1993). Early parental loss and personal control in later life. *Journal of Gerontology: Psychological Sciences, 48,* P100–P108.

Krause, N. (1993). Neighborhood deterioration and social isolation in later life. *International Journal of Aging & Human Development, 36,* 9–38.

Krause, N. (1995a). Religiosity and self-esteem among older adults. *Journal of Gerontology: Psychological Sciences, 50B,* P236–P246.

Krause, N. (1995b). Stress, alcohol use, and depressive symptoms in late life. *Gerontologist, 35,* 296–307.

Krause, N. (1997). Religion, aging, and health: Current status and future prospects. *Journal of Gerontology: Social Sciences, 52B,* S291–S293.

Krause, N. (2001). Social suppot. In *Handbook of aging and the social sciences,* (5th ed., pp. 273–294). New York: Academic Press.

Kressin, N. R., Spiro, A., III, Bosse, R., & Garcia, R. I. (1999). Personality traits and oral self-care behaviors: Longitudinal findings form the normative aging study. *Psychology & Health, 14,* 71–85.

Kübler-Ross, E. (1969). *On death and dying.* New York: Macmillan.

Kübler-Ross, E. (1981). *Living with dying.* New York: Macmillan.

Kukull, W., Larson, E., Teri, L., Bowen, J., McCormick, W., & Pfanschmidt, M. (1994). The Mini-Mental State Examination score and the clinical diagnosis of dementia. *Clinical Epidemiology, 47,* 1061–1067.

Kulik, L. (2001). Marital relationships in late adulthood: Synchronous versus asynchronous couples. *International Journal of Aging & Human Development, 52,* 323–339.

Laboratory Medicine. (1996). No. 9, 567.

La Rue, A., Dessonville, C., & Jarvik, L. F. (1985). Aging and mental disorders. In J. E. Birren & K. W. Schaie (Eds.), *Handbook of the psychology of aging* (2nd ed., pp. 664–702). New York: Van Nostrand Reinhold.

Labouvie-Vief, G. (1985). Intelligence and cognition. In J. E. Birren & K. W. Schaie (Eds.), *Handbook of the psychology of aging* (2nd ed., pp. 500–530). New York: Van Nostrand Reinhold.

Labouvie-Vief, G. (1992). A neo-Piagetian perspective on adult cognitive development. In R. J. Sternberg & C. A. Berg (Eds.), *Intellectual development* (pp. 197–228). New York: Cambridge University Press.

Labouvie-Vief, G., Diehl, M., Tarnowski, A., & Shen, J. (2000). Age differences in adult personality: Findings from the United States and China. *Journal of Gerontology: Psychological Sciences, 55B,* P4–P17.

Lachman, M. E. (1983). Perceptions of intellectual aging: Antecedent or consequnce of intellectual functioning? *Developmental Psychology, 19,* 482–498.

Lachman, M. E. (1985). Personal efficacy in middle and old age: Differential and normative patterns of change. In G. H. Elder, Jr. (Ed.), *Life course dynamics: Trajectories and transitions, 1968–1980.* Ithaca, NY: Cornell University Press.

Lachman, M. E. (1986). Loss of control in aging research: A case for multidimensional and domain-specific assessment. *Psychology & Aging, 1,* 34–40.

Lachs, M. S. & Pillemer, K. (1995). Abuse and neglect of elderly persons. *New England Journal of Medicine, 332*(7), 437–443.

Lack, S. & Buckingham, R. W. (1978). *First American hospice: Three years of home care.* New Haven, CT: Hospice Inc.

Laflamme, L. & Menckel, E. (1995). Aging and occupational accidents: A review of the literature of the last three decades. *Safety Science, 21,* 145–161.

Lakatta, E. G. (1990). Changes in cardiovascular function with aging. *European Heart Journal, 11c,* 22–29.

Lakatta, E. G. (1990). Heart and circulation. In E. L. Schneider & J. W. Rowe (Eds.), *Handbook of the biology of aging* (3rd edition). San Diego, CA: Academic Press, 181–217.

Landman, J., Kotkin, A. M., Shu, W., Droller, M. J., & Liu, B. C-S. (1997). Vitamin D inhibits telomerase activity and tumor cell invasion in human prostrate cancer LNCap cells. *Surgical Forum, 48*, 758.

Landy, F. J. (1994, July–August). Mandatory retirement age: Serving the public welfare? *Psychological Science Agenda: American Psychological Association*, 10–11, 20.

Langer, E. J. & Rodin, J. (1976). The effects of choice and enhanced personal responsibility for the aged: A field experiment in an institutional setting. *Journal of Personality and Social Psychology, 34*, 191–198.

Lanier, J. O., McGinnis, J. M., Sox, H. C., & Weingarten, S. (1999). Confronting the major killers. *Patient Care, 33*(18), 44–64.

Lapp, D. C. (1992). *Maximizing your memory power*. New York: Barron's Educational Series.

Laslett, P. (1985). Societal development and aging. In R. A. Binstock & E. Shanas (Eds.), *Handbook of aging and the social sciences*. (2nd ed.), New York: Van Nostrand Reinhold.

Latimer, E. J. (1992, February). Euthanasia: A physician's reflections. *Ontario Medical Review*, 21–29.

Lattanzi, M., & Hale, M. E. (1984). Giving grief words: Writing during bereavement. *Omega, 15*, 45–52.

Lauer, J. & Lauer, R. (1985). Marriages made to last. *Psychology Today, 19*, 22–26.

Lauer, R. H., Lauer, J. C., & Kerr, S. T. (1990). The long-term marriage: Perceptions of stability and satisfaction. *International Journal of Aging & Human Development, 31*, 189–195.

Lawton, M. P. (1977). The impact of the environment on aging and behavior. In J. E. Birren & K. W. Schaie (Eds.). *Handbook of the psychology of aging* (pp. 276–301), New York: Van Nostrand Reinhold.

Lawton, M. P. (1980). *Environment and aging*. Belmont, CA: Brooks-Cole.

Lawton, M. P. (1982). Competence, environmental press, and adaptation. In P. Lawton, P. G. Windley, & T. O. Byerts (Eds.). *Aging and the environment: Theoretical approaches* (pp. 33–59). New York: Springer.

Lawton, M. P. (2001). The physical environment of the person with Alzheimer's disease. *Aging and Mental Health, 5*, 56–64.

Lawton, M. P., Kleban, M. H., Rajagopal, D., & Dean, J. (1992). Dimensions of affective experience in three age groups. *Psychology & Aging, 7*, 171–184.

Lawton, M. P., Moss, M., Kleban, M. H., Glicksman, A., & Rovine, M. (1991). A two-factor model of caregiving appraisal and psychological well-being. *Journal of Gerontology: Psychological Sciences, 46*, P181–P189.

Lawton, M. P. & Nahemow, L. (1973). Ecology and the aging process. In C. Eisdorfer & P. Lawton (Eds.). *Psychology of adult development and aging* (pp. 464–488). Washington, DC: American Psychological Association.

Lazowski, D-A., Eccleston, N. A., Myers, A. M., Paterson, D. H., Tudor-Locke, C., Fitzgerald, C., Jones, G., Shima, N., & Cunningham, D. A. (1999). A Randomized outcome evaluation of group exercise programs in long-term care institutions. *Journal of Gerontology: Medical Sciences, 54A*, M621–M628.

Leaf, A. (1975). *Youth in old age*. New York: McGraw-Hill.

Lee, G. R., DeMaris, A., Bavin, S., & Sullivan, R. (2001). Gender differences in the depressive effect of widowhood in later life. *Journal of Gerontology: Social Sciences, 56B*, S56–S61.

Lee, I. M., Manson, J. E., Hennekens, C. H., & Paffenbarger, R. S. (1993). Body weight and mortality: A 27-year follow-up of middle-aged men. *Journal of the American Medical Association, 270*, 2823–2828.

Lee, I. M. & Paffenbarger, R. S. (1998). Life is sweet: Candy consumption and longevity. *British Medical Journal, 317*, 1683–1684.

Lee, J. A. (1997). Balancing elder care responsibilities and work: Two empirical studies. *Journal of Occupational Health Psychology, 2*, 220–228.

Lee, J. A. & Clemons, T. (1985). Factors affecting employment decisions about older workers. *Journal of Applied Psychology, 70*, 785–788.

Lee, J. A. (Ed.). (1991). *Gay midlife and maturity*. Binghamton, New York: Harrington Park Press.

Lee, T. R. (1985). Kinship and social support of the elderly: The case of the United States. *Aging & Society, 5*, 19–38.

Lee, T. R., Mancini, J. A., & Maxwell, J. W. (1990). Sibling relationships in adulthood: Contact patterns and motivations. *Journal of Marriage & the Family, 52*, 431–440.

Lefton, L. A. (1997). *Psychology*. Boston: Allyn & Bacon.

Leger, A. S., Cochrane, A. L., & Moore, F. (1979). Factors associated with cardiac mortality in developing countries with particular reference to the consumption of wine. *Lancet, 12*, 1017–1020.

Lehman, H. C. (1953). *Age and achievement*. Princeton, NJ: Princeton University Press.

Lehr, U., Jüchtern, J. C., Schmitt, M., Sperling, U., Fischer, A., Grünendahl, M., & Minnemann, E. (1998). Anticipation and adjustment to retirement. *Aging Clinical & Experimental Research, 10*, 358–367.

Leming, M. R. & Dickinson, G. E. (1990). *Understanding dying, death, and bereavement* (2nd ed.). New York: Holt, Rinehart, & Winston.

Lemlich, R. (1975). Subjective acceleration of time with age. *Perceptual & Motor Skills, 41*, 253–238.

Lerner, R. M. (1986). *Concepts and theories of human development* (2nd ed.). New York: Random House.

Leslie, A. M. (1987). Pretence and representation: The origins of "theory of mind." *Psychological Review, 94*, 412–426.

Levenson, H. (1974). Activism and powerful others: Distinctions within the concept of internal-external control. *Journal of Personality Assessment, 38*, 377–383.

Levenson, R. W., Carstensen, L. L., & Gottman, J. M. (1993). Long-term marriage: Age, gender, and satisfaction. *Psychology & Aging, 8*, 301–313.

Leventhal, H., Rabin, C., Leventhal, E. A., & Burns, E. (2001). Health risk behavior and aging. In J. E. Birren

& K. W. Schaie (Eds.), *Handbook of the psychology of aging* (5th ed., pp. 186–214). San Diego, CA: Academic Press.

Levin, J. S. (1994). Investigating the epidemiological effects of religious experience: Findings, explanations, and barriers. In J. S. Levin (Ed.), *Religion in aging and health* (pp. 3–17). Thousand Oaks, CA: Sage.

Levin, J. S. (1998). Religion, health, and psychological well-being in older adults: Findings from three national surveys. *Journal of Aging & Health, 10,* 504–532.

Levin, J. S., Chatters, L. M., & Taylor, R. J. (1995). Religious effects on health status and life satisfaction among black Americans. *Journal of Gerontology: Social Sciences, 50B,* S154–S163.

Levin, J. S., Markides, K. S., & Ray, L. A. (1996). Religious attendance and psychological well-being in Mexican-Americans: A panel analysis of three generations data. *Gerontologist, 36,* 454–463.

Levine, D. (1995, June). Choosing a nursing home. *American Health,* 82–84.

Levinson, D. J. (1978). *The seasons of a man's life.* New York: Knopf.

Levinson, D. J. (1986). A conception of adult development. *American Psychologist, 41,* 3–13.

Levinson, D. J. (1996). *Seasons of a woman's life.* New York: Alfred Knopf.

Levitt, M. J. (2000). Social relations across the life span: In search of unified models. *International Journal of Aging and Human Development, 51,* 71–84.

Levy, B. & Langer, E. (1994). Aging free from negative stereotypes: Successful memory in China and among the American deaf. *Journal of Personality & Social Psychology, 66,* 989–997.

Levy, B. R. (1999). The inner self of the Japanese elderly: A defense against negative stereotypes of aging. *International Journal of Aging & Human Development, 48,* 131–144.

Lewis, R. (1999, Oct.). Older workers vow to stay on the job. *AARP Bulletin, 40*(9), 4.

Li, G. (1995). The interaction effect of bereavement and sex on the risk of suicide in the elderly: An historical cohort study. *Social Science & Medicine, 40,* 825–828.

Liang, J., Krause, N. M., & Bennet, J. M. (2001). Social exchange and well-being: Is giving better than receiving? *Psychology & Aging, 16,* 511–523.

Lichenstein, P., Gatz, M., & Berg, S. (1998). A twin study of mortality after spousal bereavement. *Psychological Medicine, 28,* 635–643.

Lichstein, K. L., Durrence, H. H., Riedel, B. W., & Bayen, U. J. (2001). Primary versus secondary insomnia in older adults: Subjective sleep and daytime functioning. *Psychology & Aging, 16,* 264–271.

Lichstein, K. L., Riedel, B. W., & Means, M. K. (1998). Psychological treatment of late-life insomnia. In R. Schulz, G. Maddox, & M. P. Lawton (Eds.), *Annual Review of Gerontology & Geriatrics, 18* (74–110). New York: Springer.

Licht, D., Morganti, J. B., Nehrke, M. F., & Heiman, G. (1985). Mediators of estimates of brief time intervals in elderly domiciled males. *International Journal of Aging & Human Development, 21,* 211–225.

Lichtenberg, P. A. (1994). *A guide to psychological practice in geriatric long term care.* Binghamton, New York: Haworth.

Lichtenstein, P., Gatz, M., Pedersen, N. L., Berg, S., & McClearn, G. E. (1996). A co-twin-control study of response to widowhood. *Journal of Gerontology: Psychological Sciences, 51B,* P279–P289.

Lieber, M. D. (1991). Cutting your losses: Death and grieving in a Polynesian community. In D. R. Counts & D. A. Counts (Eds.), *Coping with the final tragedy* (pp. 169–189). Amityville, NY: Baywood.

Lieberman, M. A. (1993). Bereavement self-help groups: A review of conceptual and methodological issues. In M. S. Stroebe, W. Stroebe, & R. O. Hansson (Eds.), *Handbook of bereavement: Theory, research, & intervention* (pp. 411–426). New York: Cambridge University Press.

Lindemann, E. (1944). Symptomatology and management of acute grief. *American Journal of Psychiatry, 101,* 141–148.

Linnehan, M. & Naturale, C. (1998). The joy of learning in retirement. *Journal of Physical Education, Recreation, & Dance, 69,* 32–33.

Litwak, E. & Longino, C. F., Jr. (1987). Migration patterns among the elderly. *Gerontologist, 27,* 266–272.

Livson, N. & Peskin, H. (1980). Perspectives on adolescence from longitudinal research. In J. Adelson (Ed.), *Handbook of adolescent psychology* (pp. 47–98). New York: Wiley-Interscience.

Ljungquist, B., Berg, S., Lanke, J., McClearn, G. E., & Pedersen, N. L. (1998). The effect of genetic factors for longevity: A comparison of identical and fraternal twins in the Swedish Twin Registry. *Journal of Gerontology: Medical Sciences, 53A,* M441–M446.

Loevinger, J. (1976). *Ego development.* San Francisco, CA: Jossey-Bass.

Loewenstein, D. A., Argüelles, S., Bravo, M., Freeman, R. Q., Argüelles, T., Acevedo, A., & Eisdorfer, C. (2001). Caregivers' judgments of the functional abilities of the Alzheimer's disease patient: A comparison of proxy reports and objective measures. *Journal of Gerontology: Psychological Sciences, 56B,* P78–P84.

Loftus, E. F. (1980). *Memory.* Reading, MA: Addison-Wesley.

Lombardi, W. J. & Weingartner, H. (1995). Pharmacological treatment of impaired memory function. In A. D. Baddeley, B. A. Wilson, & F. N. Watts (Eds.), *Handbook of memory disorders* (pp. 577–601). Chichester, England: Wiley.

Long, G. M. & Crambert, R. F. (1990). The nature and basis of age-related changes in dynamic visual acuity. *Psychology & Aging, 5,* 138–143.

Lorber, D. L., & Lagana, D. (1997). Mirror on your health: A guided tour of yourself. *Diabetes Self-Management, 14,* 66–72.

Lortie-Lussier, M., Simond, S., Rinfret, N., & de Konick, J. (1992). Beyond sex differences: Family and occupational roles' impact on women's and men's dreams. *Sex Roles, 26,* 79–96.

Love, D. O. & Torrence, W. D. (1989). The impact of worker age on unemployment and earnings after plant closings. *Journal of Gerontology: Social Sciences, 44,* S190–S195.

Lovelace, E. A. (1990). Basic concepts in cognition and aging. In E. A. Lovelace (Ed.), *Aging and cognition: Mental processes, self-awareness, and interventions* (pp. 1–28). Amsterdam, North Holland: Elsevier.

Lubben, J. E. (1988). Assessing social networks among elderly populations. *Family & Community Health, 11,* 42–52.

Luca, M. D., Pastorino, L., Bianchetti, A., Perez, J., Vignolo, L. A., Lenzi, G. L., Trabucchi, M., Cattabeni, F., & Padovani, A. (1998). Differential levels of platelet amyloid precursor protein isoforms: An early marker for Alzheimer's disease. *Archives of Neurology, 55,* 1195–1200.

Lund, D. A. (1993). Widowhood: The coping response. In R. Kastenbaum (Ed.), *Encyclopedia of adult development* (pp. 537–541), Phoenix, AZ: Onyx Press.

Lund, D. A., Caserta, M. S., Connelly, J. R., Dimond, M. F., Johnson, R. J., & Poulton, J. L. (1985). Identifying elderly with coping problems after two years of bereavement. *Omega, 16,* 212–223.

Lund, D. A., Caserta, M. S., & Dimond, M. F. (1993). The course of spousal bereavement in later life. In M. S. Stroebe, W. Stroebe, & R. Hansson (Eds.), *Handbook of bereavement: Theory, research, and intervention* (pp. 240–254). New York: Cambridge University Press.

Lundin, T. (1984). Morbidity following sudden and unexpected bereavement. *British Journal of Psychiatry, 144,* 84–88.

Luria, A. R. (1968). *The mind of a mnemonist.* New York: Basic Books.

Lyness, J. M., Cox, C., Curry, J., Conwell, Y., King, D. A., & Caine, E. D. (1995). Older age and the underreporting of depressive symptoms. *Journal of the American Geriatrics Society, 43,* 216–221.

Lynn, J. (1991). Dying well. *Generations, 15*(1), 69–72.

Lyubomirsky, S. (2001). Why are some people happier than others? The role of cognitive and motivational processes in well-being. *American Psychologist, 56,* 239–249.

Mace, N. & Rabbins, P. (1991). *The 36-hour day.* Baltimore, MD: Johns Hopkins University Press.

Mace, N. L. & Rabins, P. V. (1999). *The 36 hour day* (3rd ed.). Baltimore, MD: Johns Hopkins University Press.

Mack, R. B. (1997). "Grow dumb along with me": Misuse of DHEA (dehydroepiandrosterone). *North Carolina Medical Journal, 58,* 144–146.

Magai, C. (2001). Emotions over the lifespan. In J. E. Birren & K. W. Schaie (Eds.). *The handbook of the psychology of aging* (5th ed., pp. 399–426). New York: Academic Press.

Magai, C. (2001). Emotions over the lifespan. In J. E. Birren & K. W. Schaie (Eds.) *The handbook of the psychology*

of aging (pp. 399–426). San Diego, CA: Academic Press.

Magai, C., Cohen, C., Milburn, N., Thorpe, B., McPherson, R., & Peralta, D. (2001). Attachment styles in older European American and African American adults. *Journal of Gerontology: Social Sciences, 56B,* S28–S35.

Mahlhorn, R. J. & Cole, G. (1985). The free radical theory of aging: A critical review. *Advances in Free Radical Biology & Medicine, 1,* 165–223.

Mahoney, D. & Restak, R. (1998). *The longevity strategy: How to live to 100 using the brain-body connection.* New York: John Wiley & Sons.

Maier, H., & Smith, J. (1999). Psychological predictors of mortality in old age. *Journal of Gerontology: Psychological Sciences, 54B,* P44–P54.

Malacrida, R., Genoni, M., Maggioni, A. P., Spataro, V., Parish, S., Phil, D., Palmer, A., Collins, R., & Moccetti, T. (1998). A comparison of the early outcome of acute myocardial infarction in women and men. *New England Journal of Medicine, 338,* 8–14.

Malatesta, C. Z. & Kalnok, M. (1984). Emotional experience in younger and older adults. *Journal of Gerontology, 39,* 301–308.

Manchester, J. (1997, Summer). Aging boomers and retirement: Who is at risk? *Generations,* 19–22.

Mancil, G. L. & Owsley, C. (1988). 'Vision through my aging eyes' revisited. *Journal of the American Optometric Association, 59,* 288–294.

Mandelbaum, D. G. (1959). Social uses of funeral rites. In H. Feifel (Ed.), *The meaning of death.* New York: McGraw-Hill.

Mannino, J. D. (1997). *Grieving days, healing days.* Boston: Allyn & Bacon.

Manson, J. E., Willett, W. C., Stampfer, M. J., Colditz, G. A., Hunter, D. J., Hankinson, S. E., Hennekens, C. D., & Speizer, F. E. (1995). Body weight and mortality among women. *New England Journal of Medicine, 333,* 677–685.

Marcellini, F., Sensoli, C., Barbini, N., & Fioravanti, P. (1997). Preparation for retirement: Problems and suggestions of retirees. *Educational Gerontology, 23,* 377–388.

Marcil-Gratton, N. & Légaré, J. (1992). Will reduced fertility lead to greater isolation in old age for tomorrow's elderly? *Canadian Journal on Aging, 11,* 54–71.

Mariske, M., Lang, F. B., Baltes, P. B., & Baltes, M. M. (1995). Selective optimization with compensation: Life-span perspectives on successful human development. In R. A. Dixon & L. Bäckman (Eds.), *Compensating for psychological deficits and declines: Managing loss and promoting gains.* (pp. 35–79). Mahwah, NJ: Erlbaum.

Markey, J. & Parks, W. (1989). Occupational change: Pursuing a different kind of work. *Monthly Labor Review, 112,* 3–13.

Marsden, C. D. (1987). Parkinson's disease in twins. *Journal of Neurology, Neurosurgery, & Psychiatry, 50,* 105–106.

Marsiglio, W. & Donnelly, D. (1991). Sexual relations in later life: A national study of married persons. *Journal of Gerontology: Social Sciences, 46*, S338–S344.

Martin, A., Prior, R., Shukitt-Hale, B., Cao, G., & Joseph, J. A. (2000). Effect of fruits, vegetables, or Vitamin E-rich diet on Vitamins E and C distribution in peripheral and brain tissues: Implication for brain function. *Journal of Gerontology: Biological Sciences, 55A*, B144–B151.

Martin, T. C. & Bumpass, L. L. (1989). Recent trends in marital disruption. *Demography, 26*, 37–51.

Maruta, T., Colligan, R. C., Malinchoc, M., & Offord, K. P. (2000). Optimists vs. pessimists: Survival rate among medical patients over a 30-year period. *Mayo Clinic Proceedings, 75*, 140–143.

Masoro, E. J. (1984). Food restriction in rodents: An evaluation of its role in the study of aging. *Journal of Gerontology: Biological Sciences, 43*, B59–B64.

Masters, W. H. & Johnson, V. E. (1970). *Human sexual inadequacy*. Boston: Little Brown.

Masters, W. H., & Johnson, V. E. (1981). Sex and the aging process. *Journal of the American Geriatrics Society, 29*, 385–390.

Masunaga, H. & Horn, J. (2001). Expertise and age-related changes in components of intelligence. *Psychology & Aging, 16*, 293–311.

Mather, M. & Johnson, M. K. (2000). Choice-supportive source monitoring: Do our decisions seem better to us as we age? *Psychology & Aging, 15*, 596–606.

Matsukura, S., Taminato, T., Kitano, N., Seino, Y., Hamada, H., Uchihashi, M., Nakajima, H., & Hirata, Y. (1984). Effects of environmental tobacco smoke on urinary cotinine excretion in nonsmokers. *New England Journal of Medicine, 311*, 828–832.

Matthews, S. H. (1986). *Friendships through the life course*. Beverly Hills, CA: Sage.

Matthias, R. E., Lubben, J. E., Atchison, K. A., & Schweitzer, S. O. (1997). Sexual activity and satisfaction among very old adults: Results from a community-dwelling Medicare population survey. *Gerontologist, 37*, 6–14.

Mayr, U. & Kliegl, R. (2000). Complex semantic processing in old age: Does it stay or does it go? *Psychology & Aging, 15*, 29–43.

McAdams, D. P. (1994a). *The person: An introduction to personality psychology* (2nd ed.). Fort Worth, TX: Harcourt Brace.

McAdams, D. P. (1994b). A psychology of the stranger. *Psychological Inquiry, 5*, 145–148.

McAdams, D. P. (1994c). Can personality change? Levels of stability and growth in personality across the life span. In T. F. Heatherton & J. L. Weinberger (Eds.), *Can personality change?* (pp. 299–314). Washington, DC: American Psychological Association.

McAdams, D. P. (1995). What do we know when we know a person? *Journal of Personality, 63*, 365–396.

McAdams, D. P. (1998). The role of defense in the life story. *Journal of Personality, 66*, 1125–1146.

McAdams, D. P. & de St. Aubin, E. (1992). A theory of generativity and its assessment through self-report, behavioral acts, and narrative themes in autobiography.

Journal of Personality & Social Psychology, 62, 1003–1015.

McAdams, D. P., de St. Aubin, E., & Logan, R. L. (1993). Generativity among young, midlife, and older adults. *Psychology & Aging, 8*, 221–230.

McAdams, D. P., Diamond, A., de St. Aubin, E., & Mansfield, E. (1997). Stories of committment: The psychosocial construction of generative lives. *Journal of Personality & Social Psychology, 72*, 678–694.

McArdle, W. D., Katch, F. I., & Katch, V. L. (1991). *Exercise physiology: Energy, nutrition, and human performance* (3rd ed.). Philadelphia, PA: Lea & Egbert.

McAuley, E., Blissmer, B., Marquez, D. X., Jerome, G. J., Kramer, A. F., & Katula, J. (2001). Social relations, physical activity, and well-being in older adults. *Preventive Medicine: An International Journal Devoted to Practice and Theory, 31*, 608–617.

McAvoy, L. (1979). The leisure preferences, problems, and needs of the elderly. *Journal of Leisure Research, 11*, 40–47.

McCall, P. L. (1991). Adolescent and elderly white male suicide trends: Evidence of changing well-being? *Journal of Gerontology: Social Sciences, 46*, S43–S51.

McCarthy, M., Ferris, S. H., Clark, E., & Crook, T. (1981). Acquisition of retention of categorized material in normal aging and senile dementia. *Experimental Aging Research, 7*, 127–135.

McCarty, H. J., Roth, D. L., Goode, K. T., Owen, J. E., Harrell, L., Donovan, K., & Haley, W. E. (2000). Longitudinal course of behavior problems during Alzheimer's disease: Linear versus curvilinear patterns of decline. *Journal of Gerontology: Medical Sciences, 55A*, M200–M206.

McCoy, J. L. & Weems, K. (1989). Disabled worker beneficiaries and disabled SSI recipients. *Social Security Bulletin, 52*(5), 15–28.

McCracken, A. L., & Gerdsen, L. (1991, December). Sharing the legacy: Hospice care principles for terminally ill elders. *Journal of Gerontological Nursing, 17*, 4–8.

McCrae, R. R., Arenberg, D., & Costa, P. T. (1987). Declines in divergent thinking with age: Cross-sectional, longitudinal, and cross-sequential analyses. *Psychology & Aging, 2*, 130–137.

McCrae, R. R. & Costa, P. T., Jr. (1984). *Emerging lives, enduring dispositions: Personality in adulthood*. Boston: Little, Brown.

McCrae, R. R. & Costa, P. T., Jr. (1990). *Personality in adulthood*. New York: Guilford Press.

McCrae, R. R., & Costa, P. T., Jr. (1993). Psychological resilience among widowed men and women: A 10-year follow-up of a national sample. In M. S. Stroebe, W. Stroebe, & R. O. Hansson (Eds.), *Handbook of bereavement: Theory, research, and intervention* (pp. 196–207). New York: Cambridge University Press.

McCrae, R. R., Costa, P. T. Jr., de Lima, M. P., Simões, A., Ostendorf, F., Angleitner, A., Marušić, I., Bratko, D., Caprara, G. V., Barbaranelli, C., Chae, J-H., & Piedmont, R. L. (1999). Age differences in personality across the adult life span: Parallels in five cultures. *Developmental Psychology, 35*, 466–477.

McDaniel, J. H., Hunt, A., Hackes, B., & Pope, J. F. (2001). Impact of dining room environment on nutritional intake of Alzheimer's residents: A case study. *American Journal of Alzheimer's Disease, 15*, 29–302.

McDonald-Miszczak, L., Hertzog, C., & Hultsch, D. F. (1995). Stability and accuracy of metamemory in adulthood and aging: A longitudinal analysis. *Psychology & Aging, 10*, 553–564.

McElhoe, J. S. (1999). Images of grandparents in children's literature. *The New Advocate, 12*(3), 249–258.

McElreath, D. D. (1996). What is a grandmother. ddmac@juno.com.

McEvoy, G. M. & Cascio, W. F. (1989). Cumulative evidence of the relationship between employee age and job performance. *Journal of Applied Psychology, 74*, 11–17.

McFadden, S. H. (1999). Religion, personality, and aging: A life span perspective. *Journal of Personality, 67*, 1081–1104.

McGowin, D. F. (1993). *Living in the labyrinth: A personal journey through the maze of Alzheimer's*. New York: Delta (Dell Publishing).

McGue, M., Vaupel, J. W., Holm, N. & Harvald, B. (1993). Longevity is moderately heritable in a sample of Danish twins born 1870–1880. *Journal of Gerontol Biological Science, 51*, 237–244.

McKitrick, L. A., Camp, C. J., & Black, F. W. (1992). Prospective memory intervention in Alzheimer's disease. *Journal of Gerontology, 47*(5), 337–343.

Mead, S. C., & Willemsen, H. W. A. (1995). Crisis of the psyche: Psychotherapeutic considerations on AIDS, loss and hope. In L. Sherr (Ed.), *Grief and AIDS* (pp. 115–127). Chichester, England: John Wiley & Sons.

Meeks, S., Murrell, S. A., & Mehl, R. C. (2000). Longitudinal relationships between depressive symptoms and health in normal older and middle-aged adults. *Psychology & Aging, 15*, 100–109.

Mega, M. S., Cummings, J. L., Fiorello, T., & Gornbein, J. (1996). The spectrum of behavioral changes in Alzheimer's disease. *Neurology, 46*, 130–135.

Mein, G., Higgs, P., Ferrie, J., & Stansfield, S. A. (1998). Paradigms of retirement: The importance of health and ageing in the Whitehall II study. *Social Science & Medicine, 47*, 535–545.

Meinecke, A. & Parker, T. (1997). Women and retirement. *National Educational Secretary, 62*(3), 18.

Menotti, A., Giampaoli, S., & Seccareccia, F. (1998). The relationship of cardiovascular risk factors measured at different ages to prediction of all-cause mortality and longevity. *Archives of Gerontology & Geriatrics, 26*, 99–111.

Merritt, J. M., Stickgold, R., Pace-Schott, E., & Williams, J. (1994). Emotion profiles in the dreams of men and women. *Consciousness & Cognition: An International Journal, 3*, 46–60.

Midanik, L., Sokhikian, K., Ransom, L. J., & Tekawa, I. S. (1995). The effect of retirement on mental health and health behaviors: The Kaiser Permanente Retirement Study. *Journal of Gerontology, 50B*, S59–S61.

Middleton, W., Raphael, B., Burnett, P., & Martinek, N. (1998). A longitudinal study comparing bereavement phenomena in recently bereaved spouses, adult children, and parents. *Australian & New Zealand Journal of Psychiatry, 32*, 235–241.

Miller, P. N., Miller, D. W., McKibbin, E. M., & Pettys, G. L. (1999). *New York Times*, July 3, 1997.

Miller, R. A. (1999). Kleemeier Award Lecture: Are there genes for aging? *Journal of Gerontology: Biological Sciences, 54A*, B297–B307.

Mills, R. B., Vermette, V., & Malley-Morrison, K. (1998). Judgments about elder abuse and college students' relationship with grandparents. *Gerontology & Geriatrics Education, 19*(2), 17–30.

Minaker, K. L., & Rowe, J. W. (1982). Gastrointestinal system. In J. W. Rowe & R. W. Besdine (Eds.), *Health and disease in old age*. Boston, MA: Little, Brown.

Miniter, F. (1999). Mad deer disease: Can venison kill you? *Outdoor Life, 204*, 44–46.

Minkler, M. & Fuller-Thomson, E. (2000). Second time around parenting: Factors predictive of grandparents becoming caregivers for their grandchildren. *International Journal of Aging & Human Development, 50*, 185–200.

Minkler, M., Fuller-Thomson, E., Miller, D., & Driver, D. (1997). Depression in grandparents raising grandchildren: Results of a national longitudinal study. *Archives of Family Medicine, 6*, 445–452.

Mirowsky, J. & Ross, C. E. (1992). Age and depression. *Journal of Health & Social Behavior, 33*, 187–205.

Mishara, B. L. (1999). Synthesis of research and evidence on factors affecting the desire of terminally ill or seriously chronically ill persons to hasten death. *Omega, 39*, 1–70.

Mitchell, J. M. & Kemp, B. J. (2000). Quality of life in assisted living homes: A multidimensional analysis. *Journal of Gerontology: Psychological Sciences, 55B*, P117–P127.

Mitchell, O. S. (1988, July). The relation of age to workplace injuries. *Monthly Labor Review*, Washington, DC: Bureau of Statistics, U. S. Department of Labor.

Mitford, J. A. (1963). *The American way of death*. New York: Simon & Schuster.

Mittleman, M., Ferris, S. H., Shulman, E., Steinberg, G., Ambinder, A., Mackell, J., & Cohen, C. (1995). Efficacy of multicomponent individualized treatment to improve the well-being of Alzheimer's caregivers. In E. Light, G. Niederehe & B. D. Lebowitz (Eds.). *Stress effects on family caregivers of Alzheimer's patients: Research and interventions* (pp. 156–184). New York: Springer.

Modern Maturity. (July–August, 1997). R.

Monk, A. (1994). Retirement and aging: An introduction to the Columbia Retirement Handbook. In A. Monk (Ed.), *The Columbia retirement handbook*, New York: Columbia University Press.

Moon, A. & Williams, O. (1993). Perceptions of elder abuse and help-seeking patterns among African-American, Caucasian-American, and Korean-American elderly women. *Gerontologist, 33*, 386–395.

Morgan, J. D. (1986). Death, dying, and bereavement in China and Japan: A brief glimpse. *Death Studies, 10*, 265–272.

Morgan, L. A. (1984). Changes in family interaction following widowhood. *Journal of Marriage & the Family, 43,* 899–907.

Morgan, M. W. (1988). Vision through my aging eyes. *Journal of the American Optometric Association, 59,* 278–280.

Morrison, R. S. & Meier, D. E. (1994). Physician assisted dying: Fashion public policy with an absence of data. *Generations, 18,* 48–53.

Morrow, D., Leirer, V., Altieri, P., & Fitzsimmons, C. (1994). When expertise reduces age differences in performance. *Psychology & Aging, 9,* 134–148.

Morse, J. M., Prowse, M. D., & Morrow, N. A. (1985). A retrospective analysis of patient falls. *Canadian Journal of Public Health, 76,* 116–118.

Moss, M. S. & Moss, S. Z. (1995). Death and bereavement. In R. Blieszner & V. H. Bedford (Eds.), *Handbook of aging and the family* (pp. 422–439). Westport, CT: Greenwood Press.

Mroczek, D. K. & Kolarz, C. M. (1998). The effect of age on positive and negative affect: A developmental perspective on happiness. *Journal of Personality & Social Psychology, 75,* 1333–1349.

Muggleton-Harris, A., & Hayflick, L. (1976). Cellular aging studied by the reconstruction of replicating cells from nuclei and cytoplasm isolated from normal human diploid cells. *Experimental Cell Research, 103,* 321–330.

Mulder, J. T. (1997, June 29). Death care giant tightens grip on central New York. *Syracuse Herald American,* D4–D9.

Mulligan, T. & Katz, P. G. (1989). Why aged men become impotent. *Archives of Internal Medicine, 149,* 1365–1366.

Mulnard, R. A., Cotman, C. W., Kawas, van Dyck, C. H., C., Sano, M., Doody, R., Koss, E., Pfeiffer, E., Jin, S., Gamst, A., Grundman, M., Thomas, R., & Thal, L. J. (2000). Estrogen replacement therapy for treatment of mild to moderate Alzheimer disease. *Journal of the American Medical Association, 283,* 1007–1015.

Multi-Society Task Force on PVS (1994a). Medical aspects of the persistent vegetative state. *New England Journal of Medicine, 330,* 1499–1508.

Multi-Society Task Force on PVS (1994b). Medical aspects of the persistent vegetative state. *New England Journal of Medicine, 330,* 1572–1579.

Murden, R. A., McRae, T. D., Kaner, S., & Bucknam, M. E. (1991). Mini-Mental State Exam scores vary with education in blacks and whites. *Journal of the American Geriatric Society, 39,*149–155.

Murphy, K. (1998, March 26). Doctor assists Oregon suicide. *The Charlotte Observer,* A10.

Murrell, F. H. (1970). The effect of extensive practice on age differences in reaction time. *Journal of Gerontology, 25,* 268–274.

Musick, M. A., Herzog, A. R., & House, J. S. (1999). Volunteering and mortality among older adults: Findings from a national sample. *Journal of Gerontology: Social Sciences, 54B,* S173–S180.

Mutran, E. J., Reitzes, D. C., & Fernandez, M. E. (1997). Factors that influence attitudes toward retirement. *Research on Aging, 19,* 251–273.

Mynatt, C. R. & Doherty, M. E. (1999). *Understanding human behavior.* Boston: Allyn & Bacon.

Nahemow, L. (1997). The ecological theory of aging: Powell Lawton's legacy. In R. L. Rubenstein, M. Moss, & M. H. Kleban, (Eds.). *The many dimensions of aging* (pp. 22–40). New York: Springer.

Nakra, B. S., Grossberg, G. T., & Peck, B. (1991). Insomnia in the elderly. *American Family Physician, 443,* 477–483.

National Academy on Aging. (1994). *Old age in the 21st century.* Syracuse, New York: Syracuse University, the Maxwell School.

National Alliance for Caregiving & American Association of Retired Persons. (1997). *Family caregiving in the U.S.: Findings from a national survey.* Washington, DC: Authors.

National Center for Health Statistics. (1976). U.S. Public Health Service, Washington, DC.

National Center for Health Statistics. (1990). U.S. Public Health Service, Washington, DC.

National Center for Health Statistics. (1995). *Health: United States, 1994,* Hyattsville, MD: Public Health Service.

National Funeral Directors Association. (1997). *Funeral services and expenses.* Northbrook, IL: Office of Public Affairs.

National Institute on Aging. (1993). *Bound for good health: A collection of Age Pages.* Washington, DC: U. S. Government Printing Office.

National Institutes on Health. (1988). *Why do woman live longer than men?* Bethesda, MD: U. S. Government Printing Office.

Neely, A. S. & Backman, L. (1995). Effects of multifactorial memory training in old age: Generalizability across tasks and individuals. *Journal of Gerontology: Psychological Sciences, 50B,* P134–P140.

Neergaard, L. (March, 1997). Relief from shaking of Parkinson's. *Charlotte Observer.*

Neisser, U. (1967). *Cognitive psychology.* New York: Meredith.

Neugarten, B. L., Moore, J. W., & Lowe, J. C. (1965). Age norms, age constraints, and adult socialization. *American Journal of Sociology, 70,* 710–717.

Neugarten, B. L. & Weinstein, K. K. (1964). The changing American grandparent. *Journal of Marriage & the Family, 26,* 199–204.

Neugarten, B. L., & Neugarten, D. A. (1987, May). The changing meanings of age. *Psychology Today,* 29–33.

Newman, S. C. & Hassan, A. I. (1999). Antidepressant use in the elderly population in Canada: Results from a national survey. *Journal of Gerontology: Medical Sciences, 54A,* M527–M530.

Newman-Hornblum, J., Attig, M., & Kramer, D. A. (1980, August). *The use of sex-relevant Piagetian tasks in assessing cognitive competence among the elderly.* Paper presented at the annual meeting of the American Psychological Association, Toronto.

Newsom, J. T. & Schulz, R. (1996). Social support as a mediator in the relation between functional status and quality of life in older adults. *Psychology & Aging, 11*, 34–44.

Nicholson, T. (2000, May). EEOC sees new trends: Age bias "alive and well". *AARP Bulletin, 41*(5) 3, 6–7.

Nickerson, R. S. & Adams, M. J. (1979). Long-term memory for a common object. *Cognitive Psychology, 11*, 287–307.

Nieboer, A. P., Lindenberg, S. M., & Ormel, J. (1998–1999). Conjugal bereavement and well-being of elderly men and women: A preliminary study. *Omega, 38*, 113–141.

Niederwolfsgruber, E., Schmitt, T. L., Blasko, I., Trieb, K., Steger, M. M., Maczek, Ch., Hager, J., Bobak, K., Steiner, E., & Grubeck-Loebenstein, B. (1998). The production of the Alzheimer amyloid precursor protein (APP) in extraneuronal tissue does not increase in old age. *Journal of Gerontology: Biological Sciences, 53A*, B186–B190.

Nolen-Hoeksema, S. & Ahrens, C. (2002). Age differences and similarities in the correlates of depressive symptoms. *Psychology & Aging, 17*, 116–124.

Norris, F. H. & Murrell, S. A. (1987). Older adult family stress and adaptation before and after bereavement. *Journal of Gerontology, 42*, 606–615.

Nussbaum, P. (1994). Pseudodementia: A slow death. *Neuropsychology Review, 4*, 71–88.

Nyberg, L., Bäckman, L., Erngrund, K., Olofsson, U., & Nilsson, L. G. (1996). Age differences in episodic memory, semantic memory, and priming: Relationships to demographic, intellectual, and biological factors. *Journal of Gerontology; Psychological Sciences, 51B*, P234–P240.

Nye, W. P. (1992–1993). Amazing grace: Religion and identity among elderly black individuals. *International Journal of Aging & Human Development, 36*, 103–114.

Nystrom, E. P. (1974). Activity patterns and leisure concepts among the elderly. *American Journal of Occupational Therapy, 28*, 337–345.

Öberg, P. & Tornstam, L. (1999). Body images among men and women of different ages. *Ageing & Society, 19*, 629–644.

O'Bryant, S. L. (1990–1991). Forewarning of a husband's death: Does it make a difference for older widows? *Omega, 22*, 227–239.

O'Bryant, S. L. & Hansson, R. O. (1995). Widowhood. In R. Blieszner & V. H. Bedford (Eds.), *Handbook of aging and the family* (pp. 440–458). Westport, CT: Greenwood Press.

Ogin, T., Hard, G. C., Schwartz, A. G., & Magee, P. N. (1990). Investigation into the effect of DHEA on renal carcinogenesis induced in the rat by a single dose of DMN. *Nutrition & Cancer, 14*, 57–68.

O'Grady-LeShane, R. (1996). Older women workers. In W. H. Crown (Ed.), *Handbook on employment and the elderly* (pp. 103–109). Westport, CT: Greenwood Press.

O'Rourke, N., & Tuokko, H. (2000). The psychological and physical costs of caregiving: The Canadian Study of Health and Aging. *Journal of Applied Gerontology, 19*, 389–404.

Ohta, K., Kanamaru, T., Morita, Y., Hayashi, Y., Ito, H., & Yamamoto, M. (1997). Telomerase activity in hepatocellular carcinoma as a predictor of postoperative recurrence. *Journal of Gastroenterology, 32*, 791.

Ohtsuka, R. (1997). Aging and efficacy of work: A methodological discussion. *Journal of Human Ergology, 26*, 159–164.

Olshansky, S. J., Carnes, B. A., & Grahn, D. (1998). Confronting the boundaries of human longevity. *American Scientist, 86*, 52–61.

Olshansky, S. J., Carnes, B., & Cassel, C. (1993). The aging of the human species. *Scientific American, 268*, 46–52.

Oman, D. & Reed, D. (1998). Religion and mortality among the community-dwelling elderly. *American Journal of Public Health, 88*, 1469–1475.

Onyx, J. (1998). Issues affecting women's retirement planning. *Australian Journal of Social Issues, 33*, 379–393.

Ordway, G. A. & Wekstein, D. R. (1979). Effects of age on cardiovascular response to static (isometric) exercise. *Proceedings of the Society for Experimental Biology & Medicine, 161*, 189–192.

Ormsbee, T. J. (2001). An age-old story—Forget about layoffs—the problem for IT workers over the age of 40 is just getting an interview. *Infoworld, 23*, 40–42.

O'Rourke, N. & Tuokko, H. (2000). The psychological and physical costs of caregiving: The Canadian study of health and aging. *Journal of Applied Gerontology, 19*, 389–404.

Otten, M. W., Teutsch, S. M., Williamson, D. F., & Marks, J. S. (1990). The effect of known risk factors on the excess mortality of black adults in the United States. *Journal of the American Medical Association, 263*, 845–850.

Oxman, T. E., Freeman, D. H., & Manheimer, E. D. (1995). Lack of social participation or religious strength and comfort as risk factors for death after cardiac surgery in the elderly. *Psychosomatic Medicine, 57*, 5–16.

Oxman, T. E. & Hull, J. G. (2001). Social support and treatment response in older depressed primary care patients. *Journal of Gerontology: Psychological Sciences, 56B*, P35–P45.

Ozawa, M. N. & Law, S. W-O. (1992). Reported reasons for retirement: A study of recently retired workers. *Journal of Aging & Social Policy, 4*(3/4), 35–51.

Pafferbarger, R. S., Hyde, R. T., Wing, A. L., & Hsieh, C. C. (1986). Physical activity, all-cause mortality, and longevity of college alumni. *New England Journal of Medicine, 314*, 605–613.

Paganini-Hill, A. & Henderson, V. W. (1996). Estrogen replacement therapy and risk of Alzheimer disease. *Archives of Internal Medicine, 156*, 2213.

Palmore, E. B. (1971). Attitudes toward aging as shown by humor. *Gerontologist, 11*, 181–186.

Palmore, E. B. (1985). How to live longer and like it. *Journal of Applied Gerontology, 4*, 1–8.

Palmore, E. B. (1986). Attitudes toward aging shown by humor: A review. In L. Nahemow, K. A. McCluskey-

Fawcett, & P. E. McGhee (Eds.), *Humor and aging* (pp. 101–118). San Diego, CA: Academic Press.

Panek, P. E., Barrett, G. V., Sterns, H. L., & Alexander, R. A. (1978). Age differences in perceptual stye, selective attention, and perceptual-motor reaction time. *Experimental Aging Research, 4*, 377–387.

Panzer, A., Lottering, M-L., Bianchi, P., Glencross, D. K., Stark, J. H., & Seegers, J. C. (1998). Melatonin has no effect on the growth, morphology, or cell cycle of human breast cancer (MCF-7), cervical cancer (HeLa), osteosarcoma (MG-63), or lymphoblastoid (TKG). *Cancer Letters, 122*, 17.

Papalia, D. E., Camp, C. J., & Feldman, R. D. (1996). *Adult development and aging*. New York: McGraw-Hill.

Park, D. C., Morrell, R. W., Frieske, D., & Kincaid, D. (1992). Medication adherence behaviors in older adults: Effects of external cognitive supports. *Psychology & Aging, 7*, 252–256.

Park, D. C., Smith, A. D., & Cavanaugh, J. C. (1990). Metamemories of memory researchers. *Memory & Cognition, 18*, 321–327.

Parkes, C. M. (1972). *Bereavement: Studies of grief in adult life*. New York: International University Press.

Parkes, C. M. (1998). Bereavement in adult life. *British Medical Journal, 316*, 856–859.

Parkes, C. M. & Weiss, R. S. (1983). *Recovery from bereavement*. New York: Basic Books.

Parnes, H. S. & Sommers, D. G. (1994). Shunning retirement: Work experience of men in their seventies and early eighties. *Journal of Gerontology: Social Sciences, 49*, S117–S124.

Patterson, C. J. (2000). Family relationships of lesbians and gay men. *Journal of Marriage and the Family, 62*, 1052–1069.

Pearce, J. M. S. (1992). *Parkinson's disease and its management*. New York: Oxford University Press.

Pearlin, L. I., Pioli, M. F., & McLaughlin, A. E. (2001). Caregiving by adult children: Involvement, role disruption, and health. In R. H. Binstock & L. K. George (Eds.). *Handbook of aging and the social sciences* (5th ed., pp. 238–254). San Diego: Academic Press.

Pearls, R. (1931). Studies on human longevity: IV: The inheritance of longevity. *Annals of Human Biology, 3*, 245–269.

Pedri, S. & Hesketh, B. (1993). Time perception: Effects of task speed and delay. *Perceptual & Motor Skills, 76*, 599–608.

Penge, T. & Bear, L. W. (2001). Aging and weighing in the wild. *Journal of Aging Research, 22*, 111–123.

Penninx, B. W. J. H., van Tilburg, T., Kriegsman, D. M. W., Deeg, D. J. H., & van Eijk, J. T. M. (1997). Effects of social support and personal coping resources on mortality in older age: The longitudinal study in Amsterdam. *American Journal of Epidemiology, 146*, 510–519.

Peplau, L. A. (1991). Lesbian and gay relationships. In J. C. Gonsiorek & J. D. Weinruch (Eds.), *Homosexuality: Research implications for public policy*. Newbury Park, CA: Sage.

Perkins, K. (1992). Psychosocial implications of woman and retirement. *Social Work, 37*, 526–527.

Perlmutter, M., Metzger, R., Miller, K., & Nezworski, T. (1980). Memory of historical events. *Exzperimental Aging Research, 6*, 47–60.

Perls, T., Silver, M. H., & Lauerman, J. F. (1999). *Living to 100: Lessons in living to your maximum potential at any age*. New York: Basic.

Peters, A. & Liefbroer, A. C. (1997). Beyond marital status: Partner history and well-being in old age. *Journal of Marriage & the Family, 59*, 687–699.

Peterson, J. & Rosenblatt, R. (1986, March 23). Life past 85: Often sweet but painful. *Los Angeles Times*, I-1,26.

Pfeiffer, E. (1970). Survival in old age: Physical, psychological, and social correlates of longevity. *Journal of the American Geriatrics Society, 18*, 273–285.

Pfeiffer, E., Verwoerdt, A., & Davis, G. C. (1972). Sexual behavior in middle life. *American Journal of Psychiatry, 12B*, 1262–1267.

Phillips, D. P. (1992). The birthday: Lifeline or deadline? *Psychosomatic Medicine, 54*, 532–542.

Phillips, D. P. & King, E. W. (1988, September 24). Death takes a holiday: Mortality surrounding major social occasions. *The Lancet*, 728–732.

Phillips, D. P., & Smith, D. G. (1990). Postponement of death until symbolically meaningful occasions. *Journal of the American Medical Association, 263*, 1947–1951.

Phillips, D. P., Ruth, T. E., & Wagner, L. M. (1993, November 6). Psychology and survival. *The Lancet*, 1142–1145.

Phillips, K. (1996). *White rabbit*. Boston: Houghton Mifflin.

Piaget, J. (1963). *The psychology of intelligence*. New York: International Universities Press.

Piaget, J. (1970). Piaget's theory. In P. H. Mussen (Ed.), *Carmichael's manual of child psychology* (Vol. 1, 3rd ed., pp. 703–732). New York: John, Wiley.

Piaget, J. (1972). Intellectual evolution from adolescence to adulthood. *Human Development, 15*, 1–12.

Pillemer, K. & Finkelhor, D. (1988). The prevalence of elder abuse: A random sample survey. *Gerontologist, 28*, 51–57.

Pillemer, K. & Suitor, J. J. (1991). "Will I ever escape my child's problems?" Effects of adult children's problems on elderly parents. *Journal of Marriage & the Family, 53*, 585–594.

Pinquart, M. & Sorenson, S. (2000). Influences of socioeconomic status, social network, and competence on subjective well-being in later life: A meta-analysis. *Psychology & Aging, 15*, 187–224.

Pletcher, S. D., Khazael, A. A., & Curtsinger, J. W. (2000). Why do life spans differ? Partitioning mean longevity differences in terms of age-specific mortality parameters. *Journal of Gerontology: Biological Sciences, 55A*, B381–B389.

Plett, P. (1990). Training opportunities for older workers. In H. L. Sheppard (Ed.), *The future of older workers* (pp. 87–103). Tampa, FL: International Exchange Center on Gerontology.

Plomin, R., DeFries, J. C., McClearn, G. E., & Rutter, M. (1997). *Behavioral genetics*, New York: Freeman.

Pocs, O., Godrow, A., Tolone, W. L., & Walsh, R. H. (1977, June). Is there sex after 40? *Psychology Today*, xx–xx.

Podnieks, E. (1992). National survey on abuse of the elderly in Canada. *Journal of Elder Abuse & Neglect, 4* (11/2), 5–58.

Ponzetti, J. J. (1992). Bereaved families: A comparison of parents' and grandparents' reactions to the death of a child. *Omega, 25*, 63–71.

Ponzetti, J. J. & Johnson, M. A. (1991). The forgotten grievers: Grandparents' reactions to the death of grandchildren. *Death Studies, 15*, 157–167.

Poon, L. W. (1985). Differences in human memory with aging: Nature, causes, and clinical implications. In J. Birren & K. W. Schaie (Eds.), *Handbook of the psychology of aging* (2nd ed., pp. 427–462). New York: Van Nostrand Reinhold.

Pope, M. (1997). Sexual issues for older lesbians and gays. *Topics in Geriatric Rehabilitation, 12*, 53–60.

Pope, M. & Schulz, R. (1990). Sexual attitudes and behavior in midlife and aging males. *Journal of Homosexuality, 20*, 169–179.

Population Today (1999, December). U.S. children living with their grandparents. Author, 6.

Porter, J. R. & Svec, F. (1996). DHEA diminishes fat food intake in lean and obese Zucker rats. *Annals of the New York Academy of Sciences, 774*, 329–331.

Posner, R. A. (1996). *Aging and old age*. Chicago: University of Chicago Press.

Potts, M. K. (1997). Social support and depression among older adults living alone: The importance of friends within and outside of a retirement community. *Social Work, 42*, 348–362.

Potvin, A. R., Tourtelotte, W. W., Pew, R. W., Albers, J. W., Henderson,. W. G., & Snyder, D. N. (1973). The importance of age effects on performance in the assessment of clinical trials. *Journal of Chronic Disorders, 26*, 699–717.

Price, R. W. (1998). Implications of the AIDS dementia complex viewed as an acquired genetic neurodegenarative disease. In M. F. Folstein (Ed.), *Neurobiology of primary dementia* (pp. 213–234). Washington, DC: American Psychiatric Press.

Prigerson, H. G., Frank, E., Kasl, S., & Reynolds, C. F., III. (1995). Complicated grief and bereavement-related depression as distinct disorders: Preliminary empirical validation in elderly bereaved spouses. *The American Journal of Psychiatry, 152*, 22–36.

Pruchno, R. A. (1997). Caregiving research: Looking backward, looking forward. In R. L. Rubenstein, M. Moss, & M. H. Kleban, (Eds.). *The many dimensions of aging* (pp. 22–40). New York: Springer.

Pynoos, J. & Cohen, E. (1997). *Home safety guide for older people: Check it out/fix it up*. Washington, DC: Serif Press, Inc.

Qualls, S. H. & Abeles, N. (2000). *Psychology and the aging revolution: How we adapt to longer life*.Washington, DC: American Psychological Association.

Quan, J. K. & Whitfird, G. (1992). Adaptation and age-related expectations of older gay and lesbian adults. *The Gerontologist, 32*, 367–374.

Quigley, D. G. & Schatz, M. S. (1999). Men and women and their responses in spousal bereavement. *The Hospice Journal, 14*, 65–78.

Quill, T. E. (1993). Doctor, I want to die. Will you help me? *Journal of the American Medical Association, 270*, 870–873.

Quinn, J. F. (1981). The extent and correlates of partial retirement. *Gerontologist, 21*, 634–643.

Quinn J. F. & Burkhauser, R. V. (1993). Labor market obstacles to aging productively. In S. A. Bass, F. G. Caro, & Y-P Chen (Eds.), *Achieving a productive aging society* (pp. 43–59). Westport, CT: Auburn House.

Quinn, J. F. & Burkhauser, R. V. (1990). Work and retirement. In R. Binstock & L. George (Ed.), *Handbook of aging & the social sciences* (3rd ed., pp. 304–327). San Diego, CA: Academic Press.

Quinn, J. F. & Burkhauser, R. V. (1994). Retirement and labor force behavior of the elderly. In L. G. Martin & S. Preston (Eds.), *Demography of aging* (pp. 50–101). Washington, DC: National Academy Press.

Quinn, J. F. & Smeeding, T. M. (1994, Sept/Oct). Defying the averages: Poverty and well-being among older Americans. *Aging Today*, 9.

Rabinowitz, J. C., Ackerman, B. P., Craik, F. I. M., & Hinchley, J. L. (1982). Aging and metamemory: The roles of relatedness and imagery. *Journal of Gerontology, 37*, 688–695.

Rabinowitz, J. C., Craik, F. I. M., & Ackerman, B. P. (1982). A processing resource account of age differences in recall. *Canadian Journal of Psychology, 36*, 325–344.

Radner, D. B. (1991). Changes in the incomes of age groups: 1984 to 1989. *Social Security Bulletin*, 54.

Rando, T. A. (1991). Parental reaction to the loss of a child. In D. Papadatos & C. Papadatos (Eds.), *Children and death*. New York: Hemisphere Publishers.

Rando, T. A. (1992). The increasing prevalence of complicated mourning: The onslaught is just beginning. *Omega, 26*, 43–59.

Rankin, J. L. & Kausler, D. H. (1979). Adult age differences in false recognitions. *Journal of Gerontology, 34*, 58–65.

Rantanen, T., Harris, T., Leveille, S. G., Visser, M., Foley, D., Masaki, K., & Guralnik, J. M. (2000). Muscle strength and body mass index as long term predictors of mortality in initially healthy men. *Journal of Gerontology: Medical Sciences, 55A*, M168–M173.

Rantanen, T., Harris, T., Leveille, S. G., Visser, M., Foley, D., Masaki, K., & Guralnik, J. M. (2000). Muscle strength and body mass index as long-term predictors of mortality in initially healthy men. *Journal of Gerontology: Medical Sciences, 55A*, M168–M173.

Raphael, B. (1983). *The anatomy of bereavement*. New York: Basic Books.

Ratcliff, R., Spieler, D., & McKoon, G. (2000). Explicitly modeling the effects of aging on response time. *Psychonomic Bulletin & Review, 7*, 1–25.

Ratcliff, R., Thapar, A., & McKoon, G. (2001). The effects of aging on reaction time in a signal detection task. *Psychology & Aging, 16*, 323–341.

Raymond, E., Faivre, S., Dieras, V., & Hoff, D. V. (1997). Inhibition of telomeres and telomerase: Seeking for new anticancer drugs. *Bulletin du Cancer, 84*, 1123.

Rebok, G. W. (1987). *Life-span cognitive development.* New York: Holt, Rinehart, & Winston.

Rees, W. D. & Lutkins, S. G. (1967). The mortality of bereavement. *British Medical Journal, 4,* 13–16.

Regier, D. A., Boyd, J. H., Burke, J. D., Rae, D. S., Myers, J. K., Kramer, M., Robins, L. N., George, L. K., Karno, M., & Locke, B. Z. (1988). One-month prevalence of mental disorders in the United States. *Archives of General Psychiatry, 45,* 977–986.

Reilly, T., Waterhouse, J., & Atkinson, G. (1997). Aging, rhythms of physical performance, and adjustments to changes in the sleep-activity cycle. *Occupational & Environmental Medicine, 54,* 812–816.

Rein D., Paglieroni, T. G., Pearson, D. A., Wun, T., Schmitz, H. H., Gosselin, R., & Keen, C. L. (2000). Cocoa and wine polyphenols modulate platelet activation and function. *The Journal of Nutrition, 130,* 2120S–2126S.

Reisberg, B. (1999). Retrogenesis: Clinical, physiologic, and pathologic mechanisms in brain aging, Alzheimer's, and other dementing processes. *European Archives of Psychiatry in Clinical Neurosciences, 249,* Supplement 3.

Rexroat, C. & Shehan, C. (1987). The family life cycle and spouse's time in housework. *Journal of Marriage & the Family, 49,* 737–750.

Reynolds, D. K. & Nelson, F. L. (1981). Personality, life situation, and life expectancy. *Suicide and Life Threatening Behavior, 11,* 99–110.

Rhodes, S. R. (1983). Age-related differences in work attitudes and behavior: A review and conceptual analysis. *Psychological Bulletin, 93,* 328–367.

Richardson, V. E. (1999). Women and retirement. *Journal of Women & Aging, 11,* 49–66.

Ricklefs, R. E. (1973). Fecundity, mortality, and avian demography. In P. S. Farner (Ed.), *Breeding biology of birds* (pp. 366–435). Washington, DC: National Academy of Sciences.

Riekse, R. J. & Holstege, H. (1996). *Growing older in America.* New York: McGraw-Hill.

Rifat, S. L. (1994). Aluminum hypothesis lives. *Lancet, 343,* 3–4.

Rifat, S. L., Eastwood, M. R., McLachlan, D. R. C., & Corey, P. N. (1990). Effect of exposure of miners to aluminum powder. *Lancet, 336,* 1162–1165.

Rigdon, I. S., Clayton, B. C., & Dimond, M. (1987). Toward a theory of helpfulness for the elderly bereaved: An invitation to a new life. *Advances in Nursing Science, 9*(2), 32–43.

Rinfret, N., Lortie-Lussier, M., & de Konick, J. (1991). The dreams of professional mothers and female students: An exploration of social roles and age impact. *Dreaming: Journal of the Association for the Study of Dreams, 1,* 179–191.

Rissanen, A., Kenkt, P., Heliovaara, M., Aromaa, A., Reunanen, A., & Maatela, J. (1991). Weight and mortality in Finnish women. *Journal of Clinical Epidemiology, 44,* 787–795.

Roadberg, A. (1981). Perceptions of work and leisure among the elderly. *Gerontologist, 21,* 142–145.

Robbins, R. A. (1992). Death competency: A study of hospice volunteers. *Death Studies, 16,* 557–569.

Roberto, K. A. (1997). Qualities of older women's friendships: Stable or volatile? *International Journal of Aging & Human Development, 44,* 1–14.

Roberto, K. A. & Skoglund, R. R. (1996). Interactions with grandparents and great-grandparents: A comparison of activities, influences, and relationships. *International Journal of Aging & Human Development, 43,* 107–117.

Roberto, K. A. & Stroes, J. (1992). Grandchildren and grandparents: Roles, influences, and relationships. *International Journal of Aging & Human Development, 34,* 227–239.

Roberts, S. D. & Zhou, N. (1997). The 50 and older characters in the advertisements of *Modern Maturity:* Growing older, getting better? *Journal of Applied Gerontology, 16,* 208–220.

Robine, J. M. & Allard, M. (1998). The oldest human. *Science, 279,* 1834.

Robinson, B., Kennedy, A. V., & Stevenson, M. J. (2000). Kevorkian sentenced to 10 to 25 years for murder. *Court TV On Line.* <http://www.courttv.com>.

Robinson, J. A. (1976). Sampling autobiographical memory. *Cognitive Psychology, 8,* 578–595.

Robinson, J. D. & Skill, T. (1995). The invisible generation: Portrayals of the elderly on prime-time television. *Communication Reports, 8,* 111–119.

Rockstein, M. & Sussman, M. (1979). *Biology of aging.* Belmont, CA: Saunders.

Rodewald, H-R. (1998). The thymus in the age of retirement. *Nature, 396,* 630–631.

Rogers, R. G. (1995). Marriage, sex, and mortality. *Journal of Marriage & the Family, 57,* 515–526.

Rogers, S. L., Farlow, M. R., Doody, R. S., Mohs, R., Friedhoff, L. T., & the Donepezil Study Group. (1998). A 24-week, double-blind, placebo-controlled trial of donepezil in patients with Alzheimer's disease. *Neurology, 50,* 136–145.

Rosen, B. & Jerdee, T. H. (1976a). The nature of job-related age stereotypes. *Journal of Applied Psychology, 61,* 180–183.

Rosen, B. & Jerdee, T. H. (1976b). The influence of age stereotypes on managerial decisions. *Journal of Applied Psychology, 61,* 428–432

Rosenberg, L., Palmer, J. R., & Shapiro, S. (1990). Decline in the risk of myocardial infarction among women who stop smoking. *New England Journal of Medicine, 322,* 213–217.

Rosenblatt, P. C. (1993). Cross-cultural variation in the experience, expression, and understanding of grief. In D. P. Irish, K. F. Lundquist, & V. J. Nelsen (Eds.), *Ethnic variations in dying, death, and grief: Diversity in universality* (pp. 13–19). Washington, DC: Taylor & Francis.

Rosenblatt, R. A. (1999, Jan. 14). U.S. can afford boomers' retirement, study says. *Charlotte Observer,* 11A.

Rosenbloom, C. A., & Whittington, F. J. (1993). The effects of bereavement on eating behaviors and nutrient intakes in elderly widowed persons. *Journal of Gerontology: Social Sciences, 51B,* S223–S229.

Rosenkoetter, M. M. & Garris, J. M. (1998). Psychosocial

changes following retirement. *Journal of Advanced Nursing, 27*, 966–976.

Roses, A. D. & Pericak-Vance, M. (1995). Alzheimer's disease and other dementias. In E. H. Emery & D. L. Rimoin (Eds.), *Principles and practice of medical genetics* (3rd ed.), Edinburgh: Churchill Livingstone.

Ross, C. E. & Drentea, P. (1998). Consequences of retirement activities for distress and the sense of personal control. *Journal of Health & Social Behavior, 39*, 317–334.

Ross, I. K. (1995). *Aging of cells, humans, and societies.* Dubuque, IA: Wm. C. Brown.

Ross, S. (1991). Subjective acceleration of time with aging. *Perceptual & Motor Skills, 72*, 289–290.

Ross, S. K., Strauss, M. E., Neundorfer, M. M., Smyth, K. A., & Stuckey, J. C. (1997). The relationship of self-restraint and distress to coping among spouses caring for persons with Alzheimer's disease. *Journal of Applied Gerontology, 16*, 91–103.

Roth, M., Huppert, F. A., Tym, E., & Mountjoy, C. Q. (1988). *CAMDEX: The Cambridge Examination for Mental Disorders of the Elderly.* Cambridge: Cambridge University Press.

Rotter, J. B. (1966). Generalized expectancies for internal versus external control of reinforcement. *Psychological Monographs, 80* (1, Whole No. 609).

Roughan, P. A., Kaiser, F. E., & Morley, J. E. (1993). Sexuality and the older woman. *Clinics in Geriatric Medicine, 9*, 87–106.

Rowe, J. W. & Kahn, R. L. (1998). *Successful aging.* New York: Pantheon Books.

Rowland, K. F. (1977). Environmental events predicting death for the elderly. *Psychological Bulletin, 84*, 349–372.

Rubenstein, R. L. & Parmelee, P. A. (1992). Attachment to place and the representation of the life course by the elderly. *Human Behavior and Environment: Advances in Theory and Research, 12*, 139–163.

Rubenstein, R. L., Kilbride, J. C., & Nagy, S. (1992). *Elders living alone: Frailty and the perception of choice.* Hawthorne, NY: Aldine de Gruyter.

Ruberman, W., Weinblatt, E., Goldberg, J. D., & Chaudhary, B. S. (1984). Psychosocial influences on mortality after myocardial infarction. *New England Journal of Medicine, 311*, 552–559.

Rubin (1979). *Women of a certain age.* New York: Harper & Row.

Rudinger, G. & Rietz, C. (2001). Structural equation modeling in longitudinal research on aging. In J. E. Birren & K. W. Schaie (Eds.). *Handbook of the psychology of aging*, (5th ed., pp. 29–52). San Diego, CA: Academic Press.

Rudman, D., Feller, A. G., Nagraj, H. S., Gergans, G. A., Lalitha, P. Y., Goldberg, A. F., Schlenker, R. A., Cohn, L., Rudman, I. W., & Mattson, D. E. (1990). Effects of human growth hormone in men over 60 years old. *New England Journal of Medicine, 323*, 1–6.

Ruhm, C. J. (1990). Career jobs, bridge employment, and retirement. In P. B. Doeringer (Ed.), *Bridges to retirement* (pp. 92–110). Ithaca, New York: ILR Press.

Runyan, W. M. (1980). The life satisfaction chart: Perceptions of the course of subjective experience. *Iternational Journal of Aging & Human Development, 11*, 45–64.

Ruth, J. E. & Birren, J. E. (1985). Creativity in adulthood and old age: Relations to intelligence, sex, and mode of testing. *International Journal of Behavioral Development, 8*, 99–109.

Ryckman, R. M. & Malikioski, M. (1975). Relationship between locus of control and chronological age. *Psychological Reports, 36*, 655–658.

Sachs, G. A. (1994). Improving care of the dying. *Generations, 18*, 19–22.

Sack, R. L., Hughes, R. J., Edgar, D. M., & Lewy, A. J. (1997). Sleep-promoting effects of melatonin: At what dose, in whom, under what conditions, and by what mechanisms? *Sleep, 20*, 908.

Sacks, O. (1985). *The man who mistook his wife for a hat.* New York: Harper Perrennial.

Sacks, O. (1996). *An anthropologist on Mars: Seven paradoxical tales.* Vintage Publishing.

Sacks, O. (1999). *Awakenings.* New York: Vintage Publishing.

Safford, F. (1992). Differential assessment of dementia and depression in elderly people. *Gerontology for Health Professionals*. Washington, DC: National Association of Social Workers Press.

Salthouse, T. A. & Babcock, R. L. (1991). Decomposing adult age differences in working memory. *Developmental Psychology, 27*, 763–776.

Salthouse, T. A. (1984). Effects of age and skill in typing. *Journal of Experimental Psychology: General, 113*, 345–371.

Salthouse, T. A. (1985). Speed of behavior and its implications for cognition. In J. E. Birren & K. W. Schaie (Eds.), *Handbook of the psychology of aging* (2nd ed., pp. 400–426). New York: Van Nostrand Reinhold.

Salthouse, T. A. (1990). Working memory as a processing resource in cognitive aging. *Developmental Review, 10*, 101–124.

Salthouse, T. A. (1991). *Theoretical perspectives on cognitive aging.* Hillsdale, NJ: Erlbaum.

Sanders, C. M. (1982–1983). Effects of sudden vs. chronic illness death on bereavement outcome. *Omega, 13*, 227–241.

Sands, R. G. & Goldberg-Glen, R. S. (2000). Factors associated with stress among grandparents raising their grandchildren. *Family Relations, 49*, 97–105.

Sano, M., Ernesto, C., Thomas, R. G., Klauber, M. R., Schafer, K., Grundman, M., Woodbury, P., Growdon, J., Cotman, C. W., Pfeiffer, E., Schneider, L. S., & Thal, L. J. (1997). A controlled trial of selegiline, alpha-tocopherol or both as treatments for Alzheimer's disease: The Alzheimer's disease cooperative study. *New England Journal of Medicine, 336*, 1216–1222.

Sapolsky, R. M. (1992). Stress and neuroendocrine changes during aging. *Generations, 16*(4), 35–38.

Sasser-Coen, J. R. (1993). Qualitative changes in creativity in the second half of life: A life-span developmental perspective. *Journal of Creative Behavior, 27*, 18–26.

Satariano, W. A., DeLorenze, G. N., Reed, D., & Schneider, E. L. (1996). Imbalance in an older population. *Journal of Aging & Health, 8*, 334–358.

Saunders, C. (1977). Dying to live: St. Christopher's Hospice. In H. Feifel (Ed.), *New meanings of death*. New York: McGraw-Hill.

Sayetta, R. B. (1986). Rates of senile dementia-Alzheimer's type in the Baltimore Longitudinal Study. *Journal of Chronic Diseases, 39*, 271–286.

Scanland, S. & Emershaw, L. (1993). Reality orientation and validation therapy: Dementia, depression, and functional status. *Journal of Gerontological Nursing, 19*, 7–11.

Schächter, F. (1998). Causes, effects, and constraints in the genetics of human longevity. *American Journal of Human Genetics, 62*, 1008–1014.

Schächter, F., Faure-Delanef, L., Guénot, F., Rouger, H., Froguel, P., Lesueur-Ginot, L., & Cohen, D. (1994). Genetic associations with longevity at the APOE and ACE loci. *Nature Genetics, 6*, 29–32.

Schacter, D. L. (1992). Understanding implicit memory: A cognitive neuroscience approach. *American Psychologist, 47*, 559–569.

Schafer, C., Quesenberry, C. P., Jr., & Wi, S. (1995). Mortality following a conjugal bereavement and the effects of a shared environment. *American Journal of Epidemiology, 141*, 1142–1152.

Schaie, K. W. (1965). A general model for the study of developmental change. *Psychological Bulletin, 64*, 92–107.

Schaie, K. W. (1977). Quasi-experimental research designs in the psychology of aging. In J. E. Birren & K. W. Schaie (Eds.), *Handbook of the psychology of aging*. New York: Van Nostrand Reinhold.

Schaie, K. W. (1977/1978). Toward a stage theory of adult cognitive development. *Journal of Aging & Human Development, 8*, 129–138.

Schaie, K. W. (1979). The primary mental abilities in adulthood: An exploration in the development of psychometric intelligence. In P. B. Baltes & O. G. Brim (Eds.), *Life-span development and behavior* (Vol. 2, pp. 67–115). New York: Academic Press.

Schaie, K. W. (1983). The Seattle Longitudinal Study: A twenty-one year investigation of psychometric intelligence. In K. W. Schaie (Ed.), *Longitudinal studies of adult personality development* (pp. 64–155). New York: Guilford Press.

Schaie, K. W. (1989). Individual differences in rate of cognitive change in adulthood. In V. L. Bengston & K. W. Schaie (Eds.), *The course of later life: Research and reflections* (pp. 68–83). New York: Springer Publishing.

Schaie, K. W. (1990). Developmental designs revisited. In H. W. Reese & S. H. Cohen (Eds.), *Life-span developmental psychology: Methodological issues*. Hillsdale, NJ: Erlbaum.

Schaie, K. W. (1990). Intellectual development in adulthood. In J. E. Birren & K. W. Schaie (Eds.), *Handbook of the psychology of aging*. (pp. 291–309). San Diego, CA: Academic Press.

Schaie, K. W. (1994). The course of adult intellectual development. *American Psychologist, 49*, 304–313.

Schaie, K. W. & Hertzog, C. (1983). Fourteen-year cohort sequential studies of adult intelligence. *Developmental Psychology, 19*, 531–543.

Schaie, K. W. & Labouvie-Vief, G. (1974). Generational versus ontogenetic components of change in adult cognitive behavior: A fourteen-year cross-sequential study. *Developmental Psychology, 10*, 305–320.

Schaie, K. W., & Willis, S. L. (1991). *Adult development and aging* (3rd ed.). New York: Harper Collins.

Scharlach, A. E., & Fredriksen, K. I. (1993). Reactions to the death of a parent during midlife. *Omega, 27*, 307–319.

Schatz, R. D. (1997, May). The aging of the work force. *Working Woman*, 64–66.

Scheier, M. F., Matthews, K. A., Owens, J. F., Magovern, G. J., Lefebvre, R. C., Abbott, R. A., & Carver, C. S. (1989). Dispositional optimism and recovery from coronary artery bypass surgery: The beneficial effects on physical and psychological well being. *Journal of Personality & Social Psychology, 57*, 1024–1040.

Schenk, D., Barbour, R., Dunn, W., Gordon, G., Grajeda, H., Guido, T., Hu, K., Huang, J., Johnson-Wood, K., Khan, K., Kholodenko, D., Lee, M., Liao, Z., Lieberberg, I., Motter, R., Mutter, L., Soriano, F., Shopp, G., Vasquez, N., Vandevert, C., Walker, S., Wogulis, M., Yednock, T., Games, D., & Seubert, P. (1999). Immunization with amyloid-b attenuates Alzheimer-disease-like pathology in the PDAPP mouse. *Nature, 400*, 173.

Schmucker, D. L. (1998). Aging and the liver: An update. *Journal of Gerontology: Biological Sciences, 53A*, B315–B320.

Schneider, B. (1997). Psychoacoustics and aging: Implications for everyday listening. *Journal of Speech-Language Pathology and Audiology, 21*, 111–124.

Schneider, D. S., Sledge, P. A., Shuchter, S. R., & Zisook, S. (1996). Dating and remarriage over the first two years of widowhood. *Annals of Clinical Psychiatry, 8*, 51–57.

Schneider, E. L. & Bynum, G. D. (1983). Diseases that feature alterations resembling premature aging. In H. T. Blumenthal (Ed.), *Handbook of diseases of aging*. New York: Van Nostrand.

Schneider, J. S., Pope, A., Simpson, K., Taggart, J., Smith, M. G., & DiStefano, L. (1992). Recovery from experimental Parkinsonism in primates with Gml ganglioside treatment. *Science, 256*, 843–846.

Schonfield, D. & Robertson, B. A. (1966). Memory storage and aging. *Canadian Journal of Psychology, 20*, 228–236.

Schulman, G. L. (1999). Siblings revisited: Old conflicts and new opportunities in later life. *Journal of Marital & Family Therapy, 25*, 517–524.

Schultz, K. S., Morton, K. R., & Weckerle, J. R. (1998). The influence of push and pull factors on voluntary and involuntary early retirees' retirement decision and adjustment. *Journal of Vocational Behavior, 53*, 45–57.

Schulz, J. H. (1995). *The economics of aging* (6th ed.). Westport, CT: Auburn House.

Schulz, R. (1976). Effects of control and predictability on the physical and psychological well-being of the institutionalized aged. *Journal of Personality and Social Psychology, 33*, 563–573.

Schulz, R. (1978). *The psychology of death, dying, and bereavement*. Reading, MA: Addison-Wesley.

Schulz, R. & Heckhausen, J. (1996). A life span model of successful aging. *American Psychologist, 51*, 702–714.

Schulz, R. & O'Brien, A. T. (1994). Alzheimer's disease caregiving: An overview. *Seminars in Speech and Language, 15*, 185–194.

Schulz, R. & Salthouse, T. (1999). *Adult development & aging*. Upper Saddle River, NJ: Prentice Hall.

Schulz, R., & Schlarb, J. (1987–1988). Two decades of research on dying: What do we know about the patient? *Omega, 18*, 299–317.

Schulz, R., Beach, S. R., Lind, B., Martire, L. M., Zdaniuk, B., Hirsch, C., Jackson, S., & Burton, L. (2001). Involvement in caregiving and adjustment to death of a spouse: Findings form the Caregiver Health Effects Study. *Journal of the American Medical Association (JAMA), 285*, 3123–3129.

Schulz, R., Martire, L. M., Beach, S. R., & Scheier, M. F. (2000). Depression and mortality in the elderly. *Current Directions in Psychological Science, 9*, 204–208.

Schulz, R., Musa, D., Staszewski, J., & Siegler, R. S. (1994). The relationship between age and major league baseball performance: Implications for development. *Psychology & Aging, 9*, 274–286.

Schwartz, C. K. & Simmons, J. P. (2001). Contact quality and attitudes toward the elderly. *Educational Gerontology, 27*, 127–137.

Schwartz, M. S. & Schwartz, N. M. (1993). Biofeedback: Using the body's signals. In D. Goleman & J. Gurin (Eds.), *Mind/body medicine: How to use your mind for better health*. Yonkers, NY: Consumer Reports Books.

Scinto, L. F. M., Rentz, D. M., Potter, H., & Daffner, K. R. (1999). Pupil assay and Alzheimer's disease: A critical analysis. *Neurology, 52*, 673–674.

Scogin, F. R., Storandt, M., & Lott, L. (1985). Memory skills training, memory complaints, and depression in older adults. *Journal of Gerontology, 40*, 562–568.

Seale, C. (1991). A comparison of hospice and conventional care. *Social Science Medicine, 32*, 147–152.

Seeman, T., McAvay, G., Merrill, S., Albert, M., & Rodin, J. (1996). Self-efficacy beliefs and change in cognitive performance: MacArthur studies of successful aging. *Psychology & Aging, 11*, 538–551.

Segraves, R. T. & Segraves, K. B. (1995). Human sexuality and aging. *Journal of Sex Education & Therapy, 21*, 88–102.

Sehgal, A., Galbraith, A., Chesney, M., Schonfeld, P., Charles, G., & Lo, B. (1992). How strictly do dialysis patients want their advance directives followed? *Journal of the American Medical Association, 267*, 59–63.

Seidman, S. N. & Rieder, R. O. (1994). A review of sexual behavior in the United States. *American Journal of Psychiatry, 151*, 330–341.

Sekuler, R. & Blake, R. (1994). *Perception* (3rd ed.). New York: McGraw-Hill.

Sell, D. R., Lane, M. A., Johnson, W. A., Masoro, E. J., Mock, O. B., Reiser, K. M., Fogarty, J. F., Cutler, R. G., Ingram, D. K., Roth, G. S., & Monnier, V. M. (1996). Longevity and the genetic determination of collagen glycoxidation kinetics in mammalian senescence. *Proceeding of the National Academy of Science, 93*, 485–490.

Seltzer, M. M., & Karnes, J. (1988). An early retirement incentive program: A case study of Dracula and Pinocchio complexes. *Research on Aging, 10*, 342–357.

Serdula, M. K., Williamson, D. F., Anda, R. F., Levy, A., Heaton, A., & Byers, T. (1994). Weight control practices in adults: Results of a multistate telephone survey. *American Journal of Public Health, 84*, 1821–1824.

Setterstein, R. A., Jr. (1998). Time, age, and the transition to retirement: New evidence on life-course flexibility. *International Journal of Aging & Human Development, 47*, 177–203.

Seuss, Dr. (1986). *You're only old once*. New York: Random House.

Sharpley, C. F. & Layton, R. (1998). Effects of age of retirement, reason for retirement, and pre-retirement training on psychological and physical health during retirement. *Australian Psychologist, 33*, 119–124.

Shea, M. T., Leon, A. C., Mueller, T. I., Solomon, D. A., Warshaw, M. G., & Keller, M. B. (1996). Does major depression result in lasting personality change? *American Journal of Psychiatry, 153*, 1404–1410.

Sheehy, G. (1974). *Passages*. New York: Dutton.

Sheehy, G. (1992). *The silent passage: Menopause*. New York: Random House.

Sheehy, G. (1996). *New passages: Mapping your life across time*. New York: Ballantine.

Sheikh, J. I. (1996). Anxiety disorders. In J. Sadavoy, L. W. Lazarus, L. F. Jarvik, & G. T. Grossberg (Eds.), *Comprehensive review of geriatric psychiatry*, (2nd ed., pp. 615–636) Washington, DC, American Psychiatric Press.

Shenk, D. & Achenbaum, W. A. (1993). Changing perceptions of aging and the aged. *Generations, 17*, 5–8.

Shenk, D. (2001). *The forgetting Alzheimer's: Portrait of an epidemic*. New York: Doubleday.

Shniedman, E. (1992). *Death: Current perspectives* (3rd ed.). Mountain View, CA: Mayfield.

Shumaker, S. A. & Hill, D. R. (1991). Gender differences in social support and physical health. *Health Psychology, 10*, 102–111.

Siddiqui, S. (1997). The impact of health on retirement behaviour: Empirical evidence from West Germany. *Health Economics, 6*, 425–438.

Siebert, D. C., Mutran, E. J., & Reitzes, D. C. (1999). Friendship and social support: The importance of role identity to aging adults. *Social Work, 44*, 522–533.

Siegel, J. M. & Kuykendall, D. H. (1990). Loss, widowhood, and psychological distress among the elderly. *Journal of Consulting & Clinical Psychology, 58*, 519–524.

Siegler, I. C. (1983). Psychological aspects of the Duke longitudinal studies. In K. W. Schaie (Ed.), *Longitudinal studies of adult psychological development*. New York: Guilford Press.

Siegler, I. C. & Brummett, B. H. (2000). Associations among

NEO personality assessments and well-being at midlife: Facet-level analysis. *Psychology & Aging, 15*, 710–714.

Siegler, I. C. & Costa, P. T. (1994). Personality and breat cancer screening behaviors. *Annals of Behavioral Medicine, 16*, 347–351.

Siegler, I. C. & Gatz, M. (1985). Age patterns in locus of control. In E. Palmore, E. Busse, G. Maddox, J. Nowlin, & I. Siegler (Eds.), *Normal aging III*. Durham, NC: Duke University Press.

Siegler, I. C., Dawson, D. V., & Welsh, K. A. (1994). Caregiver ratings of personality change in Alzheimer's disease patients: A replication. *Psychology & Aging, 9*, 464–466.

Siemen, J. R. (1976). Programmed material as a training tool for older persons. *Industrial Gerontology, 3*, 183–190.

Silver, C. B. (1992). Personality structure and aging style. *Journal of Aging Studies, 6*, 333–350.

Silverman, P. R. (1986). *Widow-to-widow*. New York: Springer.

Silverstein, M. & Zablotsky, D. L. (1996). Health and social precursors of later life retirement-community migration. *Journal of Gerontology: Social Sciences, 51B*, S150–S156.

Silverstein, N. M. & Hyde, J. (1997). The importance of consumer perspective in home adaptation of Alzheimer's households. In S. Lanspery & J. Hyder (Eds.). *Staying put: Adapting the places instead of the people* (pp. 91–112). Amityville, New York: Baywood.

Simeone, W. E. (1991). The northern Athabaskan potlatch: The objectification of grief. In D. R. Counts & D. A. Counts (Eds.), *Coping with the final tragedy: Cultural variations in dying and grieving* (pp. 157–167). Amityville, NY: Baywood.

Simoes, E. J., Byers, T., Coates, R. J., Serdula, M. K., Mokdad, A. H., & Heath, G. W. (1995). The association between leisure time physical activity and dietary fat in American adults. *American Journal of Public Health, 85*, 240–244.

Simon, R. (1996). Too damn old. *Money, 25*(7), 88–126.

Simonen, R. L., Videman, T., Battie, M. C., & Gibbons, L. E. (1998). Determinants of psychomotor speed among 61 pairs of adult male monozygotic twins. *Journal of Gerontology: Medical Sciences, 53A*, M228–M234.

Simons, M. (1993, February 10). Dutch parliament approves law permitting euthanasia. *New York Times*, A10.

Simonton, D. K. (1989). The swan song phenomenon: Last works effects for 172 classical composers. *Psychology & Aging, 4*, 42–47.

Simonton, D. K. (1990). Creativity and wisdom in aging. In J. E. Birren & K. W. Schaie (Eds.), *Handbook of the psychology of aging* (3rd ed., pp. 320–329). San Diego, CA: Academic Press.

Simonton, D. K. (1991). Creative productivity through the adult years. *Generations, 15*, 13–16.

Sims, R. V., McGwin, G., Jr., Allman, R. M., Ball, K., & Owsley, C. (2000). Exploratory study of incident vehicle crashes among older drivers. *Journal of Gerontology: Medical Sciences, 55A*, M22–M27.

Singleton, D. (2000, February 13). Obstetrician, carved-up patient settle lawsuit. *Charlotte Observer*, A12.

Sinnott, J. D. (1984). Postformal reasoning: The relativistic stage. In M. L. Commons, F. A. Richards, & C. Armon (Eds.), *Beyond formal operations: Late adolescent and adult cognitive development.* (pp. 298–325). New York: Praeger.

Sinnott, J. D. (1991). What do we do to help John? A case study of postformal problem solving in a family making decisions about an acutely psychotic member. In J. D. Sinnott & J. C. Cavanaugh (Eds.). *Bridging paradigms: Positive development in adulthood and cognitive aging.* (pp. 203–219). New York: Praeger.

Siu, A. (1991). Screening for dementia and investigating its causes. *Internal Medicine, 115*, 122–132.

Skarborn, M. & Nicki, R. (2000). Worry in pre- and post-retirement persons. *International Journal of Aging & Human Development, 50*, 61–71.

Skoog, I., Blennnow, K., & Marcusson, J. (1996). Dementia. In J. E. Birren (Ed.), *Encyclopedia of gerontology: Age, aging, and the aged, 1* (A-K). (pp. 383–403). San Diego, CA: Academic Press.

Slater, P. E. & Scarr, H. A. (1964). Personality in old age. *Genetic Psychological Monographs, 70*, 229–269.

Sliwinski, M. (1997). Aging and counting speed: Evidence for process specific slowing. *Psychology & Aging, 12*, 38–49.

Small, B. J. & Bäckman, L. (1997). Cognitive correlates of mortality: Evidence from a population-based sample of very old adults. *Psychology & Aging, 12*, 309–313.

Small, B. J. & Bäckman, L. (1999). Time to death and cognitive performance. *Current Directions in Psychological Science, 8*, 168–172.

Smith, D. B. & Moen, P. (1998). Spousal influence on retirement: His, her, and their perceptions. *Journal of Marriage & the Family, 60*, 734–744.

Smith, D. W. E. (1993). *Human longevity*. New York: Oxford University Press.

Smith, G. E., Petersen, R. C., Ivnik, R. J., Malec, J. F., & Tangalos, E. G. (1996). Subjective memory complaints, psychological distress, and longitudinal change in objective memory performance. *Psychology & Aging, 11*, 272–279.

Smith, J. & Baltes, P. B. (1990). Wisdom-related knowledge: Age/cohort differences in response to life-planning problems. *Developmental Psychology, 26*, 494–505.

Smith, J., Staudinger, U. M., & Baltes, P. B. (1994). Occupational settings facilitating wisdom-related knowledge: The sample case of clinical psychologists. *Journal of Consulting & Clinical Psychology, 66*, 989–999.

Smith, M. (1979). The portrayal of elders in magazine cartoons. *The Gerontologist, 19*, 408.

Smith, M. E. (1935). Delayed recall of previously memorized material after twenty years. *Journal of Genetic Psychology, 47*, 477–481.

Smith, M. E. (1951). Delayed recall of previously memorized material after forty years. *Journal of Genetic Psychology, 79*, 337–338.

Smith, M. E. (1963). Delayed recall of previously memorized

material after fifty years. *Journal of Genetic Psychology, 102,* 3–4.

Smith, S. D. (1997). The retirement transition and the later life family unit. *Public Health Nursing, 14,* 207–216.

Smoke, S. (1996). *The bill of rights and responsibilities: A book of common sense.* Los Angeles: General Publishing Group.

Snow, C. M., Shaw, J. M., Winters, K. M., & Witzke, K. A. (2000). Long-term exercise using weighted vests prevents hip bone loss in postmenopausal women. *Journal of Gerontology: Medical Sciences, 55A,* M489–M491.

Snowden, L. R. & Cheung, F. K. (1990). Use of inpatient mental health services by members of ethnic minority groups. *American Psychologist, 45,* 347–355.

Snowdon, D. A. (1997). Aging and Alzheimer's disease: Lessons from the Nun Study. *Gerontologist, 37,* 150–156.

Snowdon, D. A., Greiner, L. H., Kemper, S. J., Nanyakkara, N., & Mortimer, J. A. (1999). Linguistic ability in early life and longevity: Findings from the Nun Study. In J. M. Robine, B. Forette, C. Francheschi, & M. Allard (Eds.), *The paradoxes of longevity* (pp. 103–113). Berlin, Germany: Springer-Verlag.

Snowdon, D. A., Gross, M. D., & Butler, S. M. (1996). Antioxidants and reduced functional capacity in the elderly: Findings from the nun study. *Journal of Gerontology: Medical Sciences, 51A,* M10–M16.

Snyder, C. J. & Barrett, G. V. (1988). The Age Discrimination in Employment Act: A review of court decisions. *Experimental Aging Research, 14,* 3–47.

Soeda, A. & Araki, C. (1999). Elder abuse by daughters-in-law in Japan. *Journal of Elder Abuse & Neglect, 11*(1), 47–58.

Sofikitis, N., Miyagawa, I., Dimitriadis, D., Zavos, P., Sikka, S., & Hellstrom, W. (1995). Effects of smoking on testicular function: Semen quality and sperm fertilizing capacity. *Journal of Urology, 154,* 1030–1034.

Sohal, R. S. & Allen, R. G. (1985). Relationship between metabolic rate, free radicals, differentiation, and aging: A united theory. In A. D. Woodhead, A. D. Blackett, & A. Hollaender (Eds.), *Molecular Biology of aging,* New York: Plenum Press, 75–104.

Sokolovsky, J. (1997). *The cultural context of aging.* (2nd ed.). New York: Bergin & Garvey Publishers.

Solomon, J. C. & Marx, J. (1995). "To grandmother's house we go:" Health and school adjustment of children raised solely by grandparents. *Gerontologist, 35,* 386–394.

Solso, R. L. (1998). *Cognitive psychology* (5th ed.). Boston, MA: Allyn & Bacon.

Soper, B., Rosenthal, G., Milford, G. E., & Akers, J. B. (1992). A comparison of self-reported dream themes for traditional and older college students. *College Student Journal, 26,* 20–24.

South, S. J. & Lloyd, K. M. (1995). Spousal alternatives and marital dissolution. *American Sociological Review, 60,* 21–36.

Spencer, G. (1984). U.S. Bureau of the Census, Projections of the population of the United States by age, sex, and race: 1983–2080. *Current Population Reports,* P-25, No. 952.

Spencer, P. S., Nunn, P. B., Hugon, J., Ludolph, A. C., Ross, S. M., Roy, D. N., & Robertson, R. C. (1987). Guam amyotrophic lateral scelorosis—Parkinsonism— dementia linked to a plant excitant neurotoxin. *Science, 237,* 517–522.

Spencer, W. D. & Raz, N. (1995). Differential effects of aging on memory for content and context: A meta-analysis. *Psychology & Aging, 10,* 527–539.

Spirduso, W. W., & Clifford, P. (1978). Replication of age and physical activity effects on reaction and movement time. *Journal of Gerontology, 33,* 26–30.

Spriduso, W. W., & McRae, G. P. (1990). Motor performance and aging. In J. E. Birren and K. W. Schaie (Eds.), *Handbook of the psychology of aging* (3rd ed., pp. 184–200). New York: Academic Press.

Staats, S. (1974). Internal versus external locus of control for three age groups. *International Journal of Aging & Human Development, 5,* 7–10.

Starr, B. D. & Weiner, M. B. (1981). *Sex and sexuality in the mature years.* New York: McGraw-Hill.

Staudinger, U. M., Smith, J., & Baltes, P. B. (1992). Wisdom-related knowledge in a life review task: Age differences and the role of professional specialization. *Psychology & Aging, 7,* 271–281.

Stephenson, J. S. (1985). *Death, grief, and mourning: Individual and social realities.* New York: Free Press.

Stern, Y., Gurland, B., Tatemichi, T. K., Tang, M. X., Wilder, D., & Mayeux, R. (1994). Influence of education and occupation on the incidence of Alzheimer's disease. *Journal of the American Medical Association, 271,* 1004–1010.

Sternberg, R. J. (1990). Wisdom and its relationship to intelligence and creativity. In R. J. Sternberg (Ed.), *Wisdom: Its nature, origin, and development.* (pp. 142–159). Cambridge, England: Cambridge University Press.

Sterns, A. A., Sterns, H. L., & Hollis, L. A. (1996). The productivity and functional limitations of older adult workers. In W. H. Crown (Ed.), *Handbook on employment and the elderly* (pp. 276–303). Westport, CT: Greenwood Press.

Sterns, H. L., Barrett, G. V., & Alexander, R. A. (1985). Accidents and the aging individual. In J. E. Birren & K. W. Schaie (Eds.), *Handbook of the psychology of aging* (2nd ed., pp. 703–724). New York: Van Nostrand Reinhold.

Stevens, J. C., Cain, W. S., & Demarque, A. (1990). Memory and identification of simulated odors in elderly and young persons. *Bulletin of the Psychonomic Society, 28,* 293–296.

Stevens, N. & van Tilburg, T. (2000). Stimulating friendship in later life: A strategy for reducing loneliness among older women. *Educational Gerontology, 26,* 15–35.

Stevens-Long, J. (1990). Adult development: Theories past and future. In R. Nemiroff & C. Colarusso (Eds.), *New dimensions in adult development* (pp. 125–169). New York: Basic Books.

Stewart, A. J. & Ostrove, J. M. (1998). Women's personality in middle age. *American Psychologist, 53,* 1185–1194.

Stewart, A. J. & Vandewater, E. A. (1993). The Radcliffe Class of 1964: Career and family social clock projects in a transitional cohort. In K. D. Hulbert & D. T. Schuster (Eds.), *Women's lives through time* (pp. 235–258). San Francisco, CA: Jossey-Bass.

Stewart, A. J. & Vandewater, E. A. (1998). The course of generativity. In D. P. McAdams & E. De St. Aubin (Eds.), *Generativity and adult development: Psychosocial perspectives on caring for and contributing to the next generation* (pp. 75–100). Washington, DC: American Psychological Association Press.

Stewart, W., Kawas, C., Corrada, M., & Metter, J. (1997). Risk of Alzheimer's disease and duration of NSAID use. *Neurology, 48*, 626–632.

Stillion, J. M. (1996). Survivors of suicide. In K. J. Doka (Ed.), *Living with grief after sudden loss* (pp. 41–71). Bristol, PA: Taylor & Francis.

Stine-Morrow, E. A. L. & Soederberg Miller, L. M. (1999). Basic cognitive processes. In J. C. Cavanaugh & S. K. Whitbourne (Eds.), *Gerontology: An interdisciplinary perspective* (pp. 186–212). New York: Oxford University Press.

Stinnett, N., Knorr, B., DeFrain, J., & Rowe, G. (1981). How strong families cope with crisis. *Family Perspective, 15*, 159–166.

Stoller, E. P. & Gibson, R.C. (2000). *Worlds of difference: Inequality in the aging experience.* Newbury Park: CA: Sage.

Stone, A. (1993). Sleep and aging. *Dialogue: The Emory clinic magazine, 63*, 5–8.

Stone, D. J., Rozovsky, I., Morgan, T. E., Anderson, C. P., & Finch, C. E. (1998). Increased synaptic sprouting in response to estrogen via an Apolipoprotein E-dependent mechanism: Implications for Alzheimer's disease. *The Journal of Neuroscience, 18*, 3180–3185.

Stoner, S. B. & Panek, P. E. (1985). Age and sex differences with the Comfrey Personality Scales. *Journal of Psychology, 119*, 137–142.

Stoner, S. B. & Spencer, W. B. (1986). Age and sex differences on the State-Trait Personality Inventory. *Psychological Reports, 59*, 1315–1319.

Stowe, R., Rosenblatt, R., & Foster, R. D. (1997, Sept.–Oct.). MM reports: Friends. *Modern Maturity, 40W*, 38–45.

Strasser, P. (1997). Retirement activities. *Chemistry in Austrailia, 64*, 42.

Strauss, A. & Glaser, B. (1970). *Anguish: A case history of a dying trajectory.* CA: The Sociology Press.

Strawbridge, W. S., Cohen, R. D., Shema, S. J., & Kaplan, G. A. (1997). Frequent attendance at religious services and mortality over 28 years. *American Journal of Public Health, 87*, 957–961.

Strayer, D. L., Wickens, C. D., & Braune, R. (1987). Adult age differences in the speed and capacity of information processing: 2. An electrophysiological approach. *Psychology & Aging, 2*, 99–110.

Strickland, B. R. & Shaffer, S. (1971). I-E, I-E, and F. *Journal for the Scientific Study of Religion, 10*, 366–369.

Stroebe, M. S. (1998). New directions in bereavement research: Exploration of gender differences. *Palliative Medicine, 12*, 5–12.

Stroebe, M. S., Hansson, R. O., & Stroebe, W. (1993). Contemporary themes and controversies in bereavement research. In M. S. Stroebe, W. Stroebe, & R. O. Hansson (Eds.), *Handbook of bereavement: Theory, research, and intervention* (pp. 457–475). Cambridge, MA: Cambridge University Press.

Stroebe, W. & Stroebe, M. S. (1993). Determinants of adjustment to bereavement in younger widows and widowers. In M. S. Stroebe, W. Stroebe, & R. O. Hansson (Eds.), *Handbook of bereavement: Theory, research, and intervention* (pp. 208–226). New York: Cambridge University Press.

Stroebe, W., & Stroebe, M. S. (1987). *Bereavement and health: The psychological and physical consequences of partner loss.* New York: Cambridge University Press.

Stroebe, W., Stroebe, M. S., & Abakoumkin, G. (1999). Does differential social support cause sex differences in bereavement outcome? *Journal of Community & Applied Social Psychology, 9*, 1–12.

Strom, R., Strom, S., Collinsworth, P., Strom, P., & Griswold, D. (1996). Black grandparents: Curriculum development. *International Journal of Aging & Human Development, 43*, 119–134.

Stuck, A. E., Van Gorp, W. G., Josephson, K. R., & Morgenstern, H. (1992). Multidimensional risk assessment versus age as criterion for retirement of airline pilots. *Journal of the American Geriatrics Society, 40*, 526–532.

Stuck, A. E., Walthert, J. M. Nikolaus, T., Bula, C., Hohmann, C., & Beck, J. C. (1999). Risk factors for functional status decline in community-living elderly people: A systematic literature review. *Social Science and Medicine, 48*, 445–469.

Sullivan, A. D., Hedberg, K., & Fleming, D. W. (2000). Legalized physician-assisted suicide in Oregon—the second year. *New England Journal of Medicine, 342*, 598–604.

Sundén, A. E. & Surette, B. J. (1998). Gender differences in the allocation of assets in retirement savings plans. *American Economic Review, 88*, 207–211.

SUPPORT Principal Investigators. (1995). A controlled study to improve care for seriously ill hospitalized patients: The study to understand prognosis and preferences for outcomes and risks of treatments. *Journal of the American Medical Association, 274*, 1591–1598.

Swayne, L. E. & Greco, A. J. (1986). The portrayal of older Americans in television commercials. *Journal of Advertising, 16*, 47–54.

Sweet, L. (1994, August 27). In memorium: A user's guide on how to behave at funerals of different faiths. *Edmonton Journal, 47*, A10.

Szinovacz, M. E. (1998). Grandparents today: A demographic profile. *Gerontologist, 38*, 37–52.

Szinovacz, M. E. (2000). Changes in housework after retirement: A panel analysis. *Journal of Marriage & the Family, 62*, 78–92.

Szinovacz, M. E. & De Viney, S. (2000). Marital characteristics and retirement decisions. *Research on Aging, 22*, 470–498.

Szinovacz, M. E., De Viney, S., & Davey, A. (2001). Influences of family obligations and relationships on retirement: Variations by gender, race, and marital status. *Journal of Gerontology: Social Sciences, 56B*, S20–S27.

Szinovacz, M. E., DeViney, S., & Atkinson, M. P. (1999). Effects of surrogate parenting on grandparents' well-being. *Journal of Gerontology: Social Sciences, 54B*, S376–S388.

Tamir, L. M. (1989). Modern myths about men at mid-life: An assessment. In S. Hunter & M. Sundel (Eds.), *Midlife myths: Issues, findings, and practical implications* (pp. 157–179). Newbury Park, CA: Sage.

Tang, M., Stern, Y., Marder, K., Bell, K., Gurland, B., Lantigua, R., Andrews, H., Feng, L., Tycko, B., & Mayeux, R. (1998). The APOE-α4 allele and the risk of Alzheimer disease among African Americans, Whites, and Hispanics. *Journal of the American Medical Association, 279*, 751–755.

Tangri, S. & Jenkins, S. (1993). The University of Michigan Class of 1967: The women's life paths study. In K. D. Hulbert & D. T. Schuster (Eds.), *Women's lives through time* (pp. 259–281). San Francisco, CA: Jossey-Bass.

Taylor, G. (1980). Images of the elderly in children's literature. *Reading Teacher, 34*, 344–347.

Taylor, R. J. & Chatters, L. M. (1986). Patterns of informal support to elderly black adults: Family, friends, and church members. *Social Work, 31*, 432–438.

Taylor, S. E. (1995). *Health Psychology* (3rd ed.). New York: McGraw-Hill.

Taylor-Carter, M. A., Cook, K., & Weinberg, C. (1997). Planning and expectations of the retirement experience. *Educational Gerontology, 23*, 273–288.

Teitelman, J. (1990). Sexuality and aging. In I. Parham, L. Poon, & I. Siegler (Eds.), *Aging curriculum content for education in the social-behavioral sciences*. New York: Springer.

The New England Journal of Medicine, 342, 598–604.

Thillet, J., Doucet, C., Chapman, J., Herbeth, B., Cohen, D., & Faure-Delanef, L. (1998). Elevated lipoprotein(a) levels and small apo(a) isoforms are compatible with longevity: Evidence from a large population of French centenarians. *Atherosclerosis, 136*, 389–394.

Thomas, J. L., Sperry, L., & Yarbrough, M. S. (2000). Grandparents as parents: Research findings and policy recommendations. *Child Psychology & Human Development, 31*, 3–22.

Thomas, W. H. (1994). *The Eden Alternative: Nature, hope, and nursing homes*. Sherburne, NY: Eden Alternative Foundation.

Thompson, L. W., Gallagher-Thompson, D., Futterman, A., Gilewski, M., & Peterson, J. (1991). The effects of late-life spousal bereavement over a 30-month interval. *Psychology & Aging, 6*, 434–441.

Thompson, M. G. & Heller, K. (1990). Facets of support related to well-being: Quantitative social isolation and perceived family support in a sample of elderly women. *Psychology & Aging, 5*, 535–544.

Time. (2000, Oct. 16). Nobel prize winners, New York: Author.

Tinetti, M. E. (1989). Instability and falling in elderly patients. *Seminars in Neurology, 9*, 39–45.

Torre, F. La, Silipigni, A. M., Orlando, A., Torre, C, La, & Aragonia, M. (1997). Free radicals, telometers, and telomerase role in aging and cancerogenesis. *Minerva Medica, 88*, 205–214.

Toseland, R. W., Diehl, M., Freeman, K., Manzanares, T., Naleppa, M., & McCallion, P. (1997). The impact of validation group therapy on nursing home residents with dementia. *Journal of Applied Gerontology, 16*, 31–50.

Totman, R., Reed, S. E., & Craig, J. W. (1977). Cognitive dissonance, stress, and induced common colds. *Journal of Psychosomatic Research, 21*, 55–63.

Treas, J. & Chen, J. (2000). Living arrangements, income pooling, and life course in urban Chinese families. *Research on Aging, 22*, 238–261.

Troll, L. E. & Skaff, M. M. (1997). Perceived continuity of self in very old age. *Psychology & Aging, 12*, 162–169.

Tucker, J. S., Friedman, H. S., Tsai, C. M., & Martin, L. R. (1995). Playing with pets and longevity among older people. *Psychology and Aging, 10*, 3–7.

Tucker, J. S., Schwartz, J. E., Clark, K. M., & Friedman, H. S. (1999). Age-related changes in the associations of social network ties with mortality risk. *Psychology and Aging, 14*, 564–571.

Tulving, E. (1985). How many memory systems are there? *American Psychologist, 40*, 385–398.

Tuomi, K., Ilmarinen, J., Seitsamo, J., Huuhtanen, P., Martikainen, R., Nygård, C-H., & Klockars, M. (1997). Summary of the Finnish research project (1981–1992) to promote the health and work ability of aging workers. *Scandanavian Journal of Work & Environmental Health, 23*, 66–71.

U.S. Bureau of the Census. (1979), *Statistical Abstract*, 100th edition, Washington, DC.: U.S. Government Printing Office.

U.S. Bureau of the Census. (1989). Population profile of the United States. *Current Population Reports*. P-23, No. 159, U.S. Department of Commerce.

U.S. Bureau of the Census. (1990), *Statistics*, 111th edition, Washington, DC: U.S. Government Printing Office.

U.S. Bureau of the Census. (1992). *Sixty-five plus in America, Current Population Reports Special Studies*, Washington, DC: U.S. Government Printing Office.

U.S. Bureau of the Census. (1993). Population projections of the U.S. by age, sex, race, and Hispanic origin data: 1993 to 2050. *Current Population Reports*. P-25, No. 1104, U.S. Department of Commerce.

U.S. Bureau of the Census. (1994). *Geographic mobility: March 1992 to March 1993, Current Population Reports*, Washington, DC: U.S. Government Printing Office.

U.S. Bureau of the Census. (1997). *Statistical abstracts of the United States: 1997*. Washington, DC: U.S. Government Printing Office.

U.S. Bureau of the Census. (2000). Population projections of the U.S. by age, sex, race, and Hispanic origin data: 1995 to 2050. *Current Population Reports*. P-25, No. 11304, U.S. Department of Commerce.

U.S. Census Bureau. (1997). Current Housing Reports, Series H150/97, *American housing survey for the United States: 1997.* Washington DC: U.S. Government Printing Office.

U.S. Census Bureau. (1998). Marital status and living arrangements: March 1997 (Update). Washington, DC: United States Department of Commerce News. Available from *http://www.census.gov/population/www/socdemo/ms-la.html.*

U.S. Census Bureau. (2001). Current population survey, March 2000. Washington, DC: Author. Available from *http://www.census.gov/population/www/socdemo/age/pp1-147/tab05.txt.* Accessed September 11, 2001.

U.S. Department of Health & Human Services. (1987). *Smoking and health: A national status report* (DHHS/PHS/Child Development Publication No. 87-8396). Washington, DC: U.S. Government Printing Office.

U.S. Department of Health & Human Services. (1992). *Health, United States, 1991, & prevention profile* (DHHS/PHS Publication No. 92-1232). Washington, DC: U.S. Government Printing Office.

U.S. Department of Health and Human Services. (1995). *Health, United States, 1994* (DHHS Publication No. PHS 95-1232). Washington, DC: U.S. Government Printing Office.

U.S. Senate Special Committee on Aging. (1991). *Developments in Aging: 1990.* Washington, DC: U.S. Government Printing Office.

U.S. Senate Special Committee on Aging. (1992). *Aging America: Trends and projections.* Washington, DC: U.S. Government Printing Office.

Uchino, B. N., Cacioppo, J. T., & Kiecolt-Glaser, J. K. (1996). The relationship between social support and physiological processes: A review with emphasis on underlying mechanisms and implications for health. *Psychological Bulletin, 119,* 488–531.

Uhlenberg, P. L. & Cooney, T. M. (1990). Family size and mother-child relations in later life. *Gerontologist, 30,* 618–625.

Umberson, D., Wortman, C. B., & Kessler, R. C. (1992). Widowhood and depression: Explaining long-term gender differences in vulnerability. *Journal of Health & Social Behavior, 33,* 10–24.

United Nations. (1988). *Demographic yearbook, 1986.* New York: United Nations, Department of International Economics and Social Affairs, Statistical Office.

Vachon, M. L. S., Sheldon, A. R., Lancee, W. J., Lyall, W. A. L., Rogers, J., & Freeman, S. J. J. (1980). A controlled study of self-help intervention for widows. *American Journal of Psychiatry, 137,* 1380–1384.

Vaillant, G. (1993). *The wisdom of the ego.* Cambridge, MA: Harvard University Press.

Vaillant, G. & McArthur, C. (1972). Natural history of male psychologic health. I: The adult life cycle from 18 to 50. *Seminars in Psychiatry, 4,* 415–427.

van Doorn, C. & Kasl, S. V. (1998). Can parental longevity and self-rated life expectancy predict mortality among older persons? Results from an Australian Cohort. *Journal of Gerontology: Social Sciences, 53B,* S28–S34.

Vandenbroucke, J. P. (1998, April 4). Maternal inheritance of longevity. *The Lancet, 351,* 1064.

Van-de-Ven, P. Rodden, P., Crawford, J., & Kippax, S. (1997). Comparative demographic and sexual profile of older homosexually active men. *Journal of Sex Research, 34,* 349–360.

Vasil, L. & Wass, H. (1993). Portrayal of the elderly in the media: A literature review and implications for educational gerontologists. *Educational Gerontology, 19,* 71–85.

Vassar, R., Bennett, B. D., Babu-Khan, S., Kahn, S., Mendiaz, E. A., Denis, P., Teplow, D. B., Ross, S., Amarante, P., Loeloff, R., Luo, Y., Fisher, S., Fuller, J., Edenson, S., Lile, J., Jarosinski, M. A., Biere, A. L., Curran, E., Burgess, T., Louis, J-C., Collins, F., Treanor, J., Rogers, G., & Citron, M. (1999). β-Secretasecleavage of Alzheimer's amyloid precursor protein by the transmembrane aspartic protease BACE. *Science, 286,* 735–741.

Vaupel, J. W. (1998). Demographic analysis of aging and longevity. *American Economic Review, 88,* 242–247.

Vaupel, J. W., Carey, J. R., Christensen, K., Johnson, T. E., Yashin, A. I., Holm, N. V., Iachine, I. A., Kannisto, V., Khazaeli, A. A., Liedo, P., Longo, V. D., Zeng, Y., Manton, K. G., & Curtsinger, J. W. (1998). Biodemographic trajectories of longevity. *Science, 280,* 855–860.

Vena, J. E., Graham, S., Zielezny, M., Swanson, M. K., Barnes, R. E., & Nolan, J. (1985). Lifetime occupational exercise and colon cancer. *American Journal of Epidemiology, 122,* 357–365.

Verghese, J. (1999). Is videopupillography useful in diagnosing Alzheimer's disease? *Neurology, 52,* 674.

Victoroff, J., Mack, W. J., Lyness, S. A., & Chui, H. C. (1995). Multicenter clinicopathological correlations in dementia. *American Journal of Psychiatry, 152,* 1476–1484.

Viney, L. L., & Westbrook, M. (1986–1987). Is there a pattern of psychological reactions to chronic illness which is associated with death? *Omega, 17,* 169–181.

Vinick, B. H. & Ekerdt, D. J. (1989). Retirement and the family. *Generations, 13,* 53–56.

Vining, E. (1978). *Being seventy: The measure of a year:* New York Viking Press.

Wakayama, T., Shinkai, Y., Tamashiro, K., Niida, H., Blanchard, D. C., Blanchard, R. J., Ogura, A., Tanemura, K., Tachibana, M., Perry, A. C. F., Colgan, D. F., Mombaerts, P., & Yanagimachi, R. (2000). Cloning of mice to six generations. *Nature, 407,* 318–319.

Waldman, D. A. & Avolio, B. J. (1986). A meta-analysis of age differences in job performance. *Journal of Applied Psychology, 71,* 33–38.

Walford, R. L. (1969). *The immunologic theory of aging.* Baltimore, MD: Williams & Wilkins.

Walker, A. J., Acock, A. C., Bowman, S. R., & Li, F. (1996). Amount of care given and caregiving satisfaction: A latent growth curve analysis. *Journal of Gerontology: Psychological Sciences, 51B,* P130–P142.

Walker, B. L., Osgood, N. J., Richardson, J. P., & Ephross, P. H. (1998). Staff and elderly knowledge and attitudes toward elderly sexuality. *Educational Gerontology, 24,* 471–489.

Walker, J. T. (1977). Time estimation and total subjective time. *Perceptual & Motor Skills, 44,* 527–532.

Wallerstein, J. S. & Kelly, J. B. (1976). The effects of parental divorce: Experiences of the child in later latency. *American Journal of Orthopsychiatry, 46,* 256–269.

Warr, P. (1994). Age and employment. In H. C. Triandis, M. D. Dunnette, & L. M Hough (Eds.), *Handbook of industrial & organizational psychology, 4,* (pp. 485–550). Palo Alto, CA: Consulting Psychologists Press, Inc.

Warren, C. A. B. (1998). Aging and identity in premodern times. *Research on Aging, 20,* 11–35.

Watson, D. & Clark, L. A. (1984). Negative affectivity: The disposition in experiencing aversive emotional stress. *Psychological Bulletin, 96,* 465–490.

Weale, R. A. (1965). On the eye. In A. T. Welford & J. E. Birren (Eds.), *Behavior, aging, and the nervous system.* Springfield, IL: Charles C. Thomas.

Weggen, S., Eriksen, J. L., Das, P., Sagi, S. A., Wang, R., Pietrzik, C. U., Findlay, K. A., Smith, T. E., Murphy, M. P., Butler, T., Kang, D. E., Marquez-Sterling, N., Golde, T. E., & Koo, E. H. (2001). A subset of NSAIDs lower amyloidogenic Aβ42 independently of cyclooxygenase activity. *Nature, 414,* 212–216.

Wegman, D. H. (1999). Older workers. *Occupational Medicine: State of the Art Reviews, 14,* 537–557.

Weindruch, R. (1996, January). Caloric restriction and aging. *Scientific American,* 46–52.

Weisberg, R. W. (1986). *Creativity.* New York: W. H. Freeman.

Weisburger, J. H. (1991). Carcionigenesis in our food and cancer prevention. *Advances in Experimental Medicine & Biology, 289,* 137–151.

Weishaus, S. & Field, D. (1988). Half a century of marriage: Continuity or change? *Journal of Marriage & the Family, 50,* 763–774.

Weisman, A. D. & Worden, J. W. (1975). Psychological analysis of cancer deaths. *Omega, 6,* 61–75.

Weisman, G. D., Chaudhury, H., & Moore, K. D. (1997). Theory and practice of place: Toward an integrative model. In R. L. Rubenstein, M. Moss, & M. H. Kleban, (Eds.). *The many dimensions of aging* (pp. 3–21). New York: Springer.

Weiss, A. D. (1963). Auditory perception in aging. In J. E. Birren, R. N. Butler, S. W. Greenhouse, L. Sokoloff, & M. R. Yarrow (Eds.), *Human aging: A biological and behavioral study.* P.H.S. Publication No. 986, Washington, DC: U.S. Government Printing Office.

Weiss, R. & Kasmauski, K. (1997). Aging: New answers to old questions. *National Geographic, 192,* 2–31.

Weiss, R. S. & Bass, S. A. (2002). *Challenges of the third age: Meaning and purpose in later life.* London, England: Oxford University Press.

Weiten, W. (2000). *Psychology: Briefer version themes & variations.* Pacific Grove, CA: Wadsworth-Brooks Cole.

Welch, D. C. & West, R. L. (1995). Self-efficacy and mastery: Its application to issues of environmental control, cognition, and aging. *Developmental Review, 15,* 150–171.

Welch, F. (1990). The employment of black men. *Journal of Labor Economics, 8,* S27–S74.

Welford, A. (1984). Psychomotor performance. *Annual Review of Gerontology & Geriatrics, 4,* 237–274.

Wells, Y. D. & Kendig, H. L. (1999). Psychological resources and successful retirement. *Australian Psychologist, 34,* 111–115.

Weng, N., Granger, L., & Hodes, R. J. (1997). Telomere lengthening and telomerase activation during human B cell differentiation. *Proceedings of the National Academy of Sciences of the United States, 94,* 10827.

Weng, N., Palmer, L. D., Levine, B. L., Lane, H. C., June, C. H., & Hodes, R. J. (1997). Tales of tails: Regulation of telomere length and telomerase activity during lymphocyte development, differentiation, activation, and aging. *Immunological Review, 160,* 43.

Wenger, G. C. & Jingming, L. (2000). Family support in Beijing (China) and Liverpool (UK): Differences and similarities. *Hallym International Journal of Aging, 2,* 85–91.

Wenger, G. C., Davies, R., Shahtahmasebi, S., & Scott, A. (1996). Social isolation and loneliness in old age: Review and model refinement. *Aging & Society, 16,* 333–358.

Werber, B. (1998). *Empire of the ants.* New York: Bantam Books.

Werking, K. (1997). *We're just good friends: Woman and men in nonromantic relationships.* New York: Guilford.

West, M. A. (1987). *The psychology of meditation.* New York: Oxford University Press.

Westerholm, P. & Kilbom, Å. (1997). Aging and work: The occupational health services' perspective. *Occupational & Environmental Medicine, 54,* 777–780.

Wheeler, S. (1996, July). Helping families cope with death and dying. *Nursing,* 25–30.

Whitbourne, S. K. (1985). The life-span construct as a model of adaptation in adulthood. In J. E. Birren & K. W. Schaie (Eds.), *Handbook of the psychology of aging* (2nd ed., pp. 594–618). New York: Van Nostrant Reinhold.

Whitbourne, S. K. (1989). Comments on Lachman's "Personality and aging at the crossroads." In K. W. Schaie & C. Schooler (Eds.), *Social structure and aging: Psychological processes* (pp. 191–198). Hillsdale, NJ: Erlbaum.

Whitbourne, S. K. (1996). *The aging individual: Physical and psychological perspectives.* New York: Springer Publishing Co.

Whitbourne, S. K. (2001). *Adult development and aging: Biopsychosocial perspectives.* New York: John Wiley & Sons.

Whitbourne, S. K. & Sherry, M. S. (1991). Subjective perceptions of the life span in chronic mental patients. *International Journal of Aging & Human Development, 33*, 65–73.

Whitbourne, S. K. & Waterman, A. S. (1979). Psychological development during the adult years: Age and cohort comparisons. *Developmental Psychology, 15*, 373–378.

Whitbourne, S. K., Zuschlag, M. K., Elliot, L. B., & Waterman, A. S. (1992). Psychosocial development in adulthood: A 22-year sequential study. *Journal of Personality & Social Psychology, 63*, 260–271.

Whitcomb, J. (1992). The melody lingers on: Music therapy for persons who have Alzheimer's disease. *Open Ear,* 2–6.

White, A. T. & Spector, P. E. (1987). An investigation of age-related factors in the age-job satisfaction relationship. *Psychology & Aging, 2*, 261–265.

White, L. K., Booth, A., & Edwards, J. N. (1986). Children and marital happiness: Why the negative correlation? *Journal of Family Issues, 7*, 131–149.

White, N. & Cunningham, W. R. (1988). Is terminal drop pervasive or specific? *Journal of Gerontology: Psychological Sciences, 44*, P141–P144.

Wilk, C. A. & Kirk, M. A. (1995). Menopause: A developmental stage, not a deficiency disease. *Psychotherapy, 32*, 233–241.

Williams, E. (1988). Health promotion and aging: Alcohol. In Surgeons General's Workshop, *Health promotion and aging.* Washington, DC: U.S. Government Printing Office.

Wilmoth, J. R. (1997). In search of limits. In K. W. Wachter & C. E. Finch, (Eds.), *Between Zeus and the salmon: The biodemography of longevity* (pp. 38–64). Washington, DC: The National Academy Press.

Wilmoth, J. R. (1998). The future of human longevity: A demographer's perspective. *Science, 280*, 395–397.

Wilson, R. S., Gilley, D. W., Bennett, D. A., Beckett, L. A., & Evans, D. A. (2000). Person-specific paths of cognitive decline in Alzheimer's disease and their relation to age. *Psychology & Aging, 15*, 18–28.

Wincor, M. Z. (1999). Gingko biloba for dementia: A reasonable alternative? *Journal of the American Pharmaceutical Association, 39*, 415–416.

Winsborough, H. H., Bumpass, L. L., & Aquilino, W. S. (1991). *The death of parents and the transition to old age.* Paper presented at the annual meetings of the Population Association of America, Washington, DC.

Wisniewski, H. & Klatzo, I. (1965). Experimental production of neurofibrillary degeneration. *Journal of Neuropathology & Experimental Neurology, 27*, 187–199.

Wolf, R. S. (1998). Domestic elder abuse and neglect. In I. H. Nordhus, G. R. VandenBos, S. Berg, & P. Fromholt (Eds.), *Clinical geropsychology* (pp. 161–165). Washington, DC: American Psychological Association.

Wolf, R. S. & Pillemer, K. (1994). What's new in elder abuse programming? Four bright ideas. *Gerontologist, 34*, 126–129.

Wolf, S. & Kurtz, J. (1975). Positive adjustment and involvement during aging and expectancy for internal control.

Journal of Consulting & Clinical Psychology, 43, 173–178.

Wolf, S. L., Barnhart, H. X., Kutner, N. G., McNeely, E., Coogler, C., Xu, T., & the Atlanta FICSIT Group. (1996). Reducing frailty and falls in older persons: An investigation of Tai Chi and computerized balance training. *Journal of the American Geriatrics Society, 44*, 489–497.

Wolfson, L., Whipple, R., Derby, C., Judge, J., King, M., Amerman, P., Schmidt, J., & Smyers, D. (1996). Balance and strength training in older adults: Intervention gains and Tai Chi maintenance. *Journal of the American Geriatrics Society, 44*, 498–506.

Wolinsky, F. D. & Johnson, R. J. (1992). Widowhood, health status, and the use of health services by older adults: A cross-sectional and prospective approach. *Journal of Gerontology, Social Sciences, 47*, S8–S16.

Wong, S. S., Heiby, E. M., Kameoka, V. A., & Dubanoski, J. P. (1999). Perceived control, self-reinforcement, and depression among Asian American and Caucasian American elders. *Journal of Applied Gerontology, 18*, 46–62.

Wood, L. E. & Pratt, J. D. (1987). Pegwood mnemonic as an aid to memory in the elderly: A comparison of four age groups. *Educational Gerontology, 13*, 325–339.

Woodbury, R. G. (1999). Early retirement in the United States. *Statistical Bulletin, 80*(3), 2–7.

Woodruff, D. S. (1985). Arousal, sleep, and aging. In J. E. Birren & K. W. Schaie (Eds.), *Handbook of the psychology of aging* (2nd ed.). New York: Van Nostrand Reinhold, 261–295.

Woodruff-Pak, D. S. (1988). *Aging.* Pacific Grove, CA: Brooks-Cole.

Woodruff-Pak, D. S. (2001). Eyeblink classical conditioning differentiates normal aging from Alzheimer's disease. *Integrative Physiological & Behavioral Science, 36*, 87–108.

Woods, P. & Ashley, J. (1995). Simulated presence therapy: Using selected memories to manage problem behaviors in Alzheimer's disease patients. *Geriatric Nursing, 16*, 9–14.

Worden, J. W. (1982). *Grief counseling and grief therapy: A handbook for the mental health practitioner.* New York: Springer.

Worldwatch Institute. (1994). *Vital signs.* New York: Norton.

Worobey, J. L. & Angel, R. J. (1990). Functional capacity and living arrangements of unmarried elderly persons. *Journal of Gerontology: Social Sciences, 45*, S95–S101.

Wright, P. (1989). Gender differences in adults' same- and cross-gender, friendships. In R. S. Adams & R. Blieszner (Eds.), *Older adult friendship* (pp. 197–221). Newbury Park, CA: Sage.

Wrosch, C. & Heckhausen, J. (1999). Control processes before and after passing a developmental deadline: Activation and deactivation of intimate relationship goals. *Journal of Personality & Social Psychology, 77*, 415–427.

Wrosch, C., Heckhausen, J., & Lachman, M. E. (2000). Primary and secondary control strategies for managing health and financial stress across adulthood. *Psychology & Aging, 15,* 387–399.

Wylde, M. A. (1998). Consumer knowledge of home modifications. *Technology and Disability, 8,* 51–68.

Yalom, I. D. (1989). *Love's executioner and other tales of psychotherapy.* New York: Harper Collins.

Yashin, A. I., DeBenedictis, G., Vaupel, J. W., Tan, Q., Andrew, K. F., Iachine, I. A., Bonafe, M., Valensin, S., DeLuca, M., Carotenuto, L., & Franceschi, C. (2000). Genes and longevity: Lessons from studies of centenarians. *Journal of Gerontology: Biological Sciences, 55A,* B319–B328.

Yatin, S. M., Yatin, M., Aulick, T., Ain, K. B., & Butterfield, D. A. (1999). Alzheimer's amyloid β-peptide associated free radicals increase rat embryonic neuronal polyamine uptake and ornithine decarboxylase activity: Protective effect of Vitamin E. *Neuroscience Letters, 263,* 17–20.

Yeatts, D. E., Folts, W. E., & Knapp, J. (2000). Older workers' adaption to a changing workplace: Employment issues for the 21st century. *Educational Gerontology, 26,* 565–582.

Yee, B. W. K. & Weaver, G. D. (1994). Ethnic minorities and health promotion: Developing a "culturally competent" agenda. *Generations, 18,* 39–44.

Yen, S. S. C., Morales, A. J., & Khorram, O. (1996). Replacement of DHEA in aging men and women. *Annals of the New York Academy of Sciences, 774,* 128–142.

Yerkes, R. M. (Ed.). (1921). Psychological examining in the United States Army. *Memoirs of the National Academy of Sciences, 15,* 1–890.

Yong-Xing, M., Zan-Sun, W., Yue, Z., Shu-Ying, C., Zheng-Yan, Y., Long, Q., Jian-Ying, Y., Shu-Qi, C., Jian-Gang, Z., & Lin, H. (1998). Behavior pattern, arterial partial pressure of oxygen, superoxide dismutase, micro-blood flow state and longevity or aging. *Mechanisms of Aging and Development, 100,* 187–196.

Yoon, C., Hasher, L., Feinberg, F., Rahhal, T. A., & Winocur, G. (2000). Cross-cultural differences in memory: The role of culture-based stereotypes about aging. *Psychology & Aging, 15,* 694–704.

Youngstedt, S. D., Kripke, D. F., Klauber, M. R., Sepulveda, R. S., & Mason, W. J. (1998). Periodic leg movements during sleep and sleep disturbances in elders. *Journal of Gerontology: Medical Sciences, 53A,* M391–M394.

Zacks, R. T., Hasher, L., Doren, B., Hamm, V., & Attig, M. S. (1987). Encoding and memory of explicit and implicit information. *Journal of Gerontology, 42,* 418–422.

Zarit, S. H. & Zarit, J. M. (1983). Cognitive impairment. In P. M. Lewinsohn & L. Teri (Eds.), *Clinical geropsychology.* Elmsford, New York: Pergammon Press, 38–80.

Zarit, S. H., Zarit, J. M., & Rosenberg-Thompson, S. (1990). A special treatment unit for Alzheimer's disease: Medical, behavioral, and environmental features. *Clinical Gerontologist, 9,* 47–63.

Zavos, P. M. (1989). Cigarette smoking and human reproduction: Effects on female and male fecundity. *Infertility, 12,* 35–46.

Zavos, P. M., Correa, J. R., Antypas, S., Zarmakoupis-Zavos, P. N., & Zarmakoupis, C. N. (1998). Effects of seminal plasma from cigarette smokers on sperm viability and longevity. *Fertility & Sterility, 69,* 425–429.

Zick, C. D. & Smith, K. R. (1988). Recent widowhood, remarriage, and changes in economic well-being. *Journal of Marriage & the Family, 50,* 233–244.

Zisook, S. & Shuchter, S. R. (1990). Hovering over the bereaved. *Psychiatric Annal, 20,* 327–333.

Zisook, S. & Shuchter, S. R. (1991). Depression through the first year after the death of a spouse. *American Journal of Psychiatry, 148,* 1346–1352.

Zisook, S. & Shuchter, S. R. (1993). Major depression associated with widowhood. *The American Journal of Geriatric Psychiatry, 1,* 316–326.

Zisook, S., Chentsova-Dutton, Y., & Shuchter, S. R. (1998). PTSD following bereavement. *Annals of Clinical Psychiatry, 10,* 157–163.

Zisook, S., Mulvihill, M., & Shuchter, S. R. (1990). Widowhood and anxiety. *Psychiatric Medicine, 8,* 99–116.

Zisook, S., Paulus, M., Shuchter, S. R., & Judd, L. L. (1997). The many faces of depression following spousal bereavement. *Journal of Affective Disorders, 45,* 85–95.

Zisook, S., Schneider, D., & Shuchter, S. R. (1990). Anxiety and bereavement. *Psychiatric Medicine, 8,* 83–96.

Zisook, S., Shuchter, S. R., & Lyons, L. (1987). Predictors of psychological reactions during the early course of bereavement. *Psychiatric Clinics North America, 10,* 355.

Zisook, S., Shuchter, S. R., & Mulvihill, M. (1990). Alcohol, cigarette, and medication use during the first year of widowhood. *Psychiatric Annals, 20,* 318–326.

Zisook, S., Shuchter, S. R., Irwin, M., Darko, D. F., Sledge, P., & Resovsky, K. (1994). Bereavement, depression, and immune function. *Psychiatry Research, 52,* 1–10.

Zonderman, A. B., Siegler, I. C., Barefoot, J. C., Williams, R. B., & Costa, P. T., Jr. (1993). Age and gender differences in the content scales of the Minnesota Multiphasic Personality Inventory. *Experimental Aging Research, 19,* 241–257.

Zopf, P. E., Jr. (1992). *Mortality patterns and trends in the United States.* Westport, CT: Greenwood Press.

Zubenko, G. S., Moossy, J., Martinez, J., Rao, G., Classen, D., Rosen, J., & Kopp, U. (1991). Neuropathologic and neurochemical correlates of psychosis in primary dementia. *Archives of Neurology, 24,* 233–242.

Zweibel, N. R., & Cassel, C. K. (1989). Treatment choices at the end of life: A comparison of decisions by older patients and their physician selected proxies. *The Gerontologist, 29,* 615–621.

NAME INDEX

SUBJECT INDEX

Photo Credits